Computer–Mediated Communication across Cultures:

International Interactions in Online Environments

Kirk St.Amant
East Carolina University, USA

Sigrid Kelsey
Louisiana State University, USA

Information Science
REFERENCE

Senior Editorial Director:	Kristin Klinger
Director of Book Publications:	Julia Mosemann
Editorial Director:	Lindsay Johnston
Acquisitions Editor:	Erika Carter
Development Editor:	Hannah Abelbeck
Production Editor:	Sean Woznicki
Typesetters:	Keith Glazewski, Natalie Pronio, Milan Vracarich Jr.
Print Coordinator:	Jamie Snavely
Cover Design:	Nick Newcomer

Published in the United States of America by
    Information Science Reference (an imprint of IGI Global)
    701 E. Chocolate Avenue
    Hershey PA 17033
    Tel: 717-533-8845
    Fax: 717-533-8661
    E-mail: cust@igi-global.com
    Web site: http://www.igi-global.com

Library of Congress Cataloging-in-Publication Data

Computer-mediated communication across cultures: international interactions in online environments / Kirk St. Amant and Sigrid Kelsey, editors.
    p. cm.
 Includes bibliographical references and index.
 Summary: "This book provides readers with the foundational knowledge needed to communicate safely and effectively with individuals from other countries and cultures via online media"--Provided by publisher.
 ISBN 978-1-60960-833-0 (hardcover) -- ISBN 978-1-60960-834-7 (ebook) -- ISBN 978-1-60960-835-4 (print & perpetual access) 1. Intercultural communication. 2. Computer networks--Security measures. I. St. Amant, Kirk, 1970- II. Kelsey, Sigrid.
 HM1211.C6546 2011
 303.48'33--dc23
                 2011019907

British Cataloguing in Publication Data
A Cataloguing in Publication record for this book is available from the British Library.

All work contributed to this book is new, previously-unpublished material. The views expressed in this book are those of the authors, but not necessarily of the publisher.

Editorial Advisory Board

Table of Contents

Section 1
The Changing Nature of Relationships: Who is Interacting and How Do They Interact?

Chapter 1

Sejung Marina Choi, University of Texas, USA
Shu-Chuan Chu, DePaul University, USA
Yoojung Kim, University of Texas, USA

Chapter 2

Archana Krishnan, University of Connecticut, USA

Chapter 3

Melinda Jacobs, Level Up Media, The Netherlands

Chapter 4

Bolanle A. Olaniran, Texas Tech University, USA
Natasha Rodriguez, Texas Tech University, USA
Indi M. Williams, Arizona State University, USA

Section 2
The Emerging Trends in Representation: Who May Participate and How Do Individuals
Present Themselves?

Section 3
The New Context for Education: Who are the Students and
How are They Taught?

Detailed Table of Contents

Section 1
The Changing Nature of Relationships: Who is Interacting and How Do They Interact?

Sejung Marina Choi, University of Texas, USA
Shu-Chuan Chu, DePaul University, USA
Yoojung Kim, University of Texas, USA

In today's online environment, social networking sites (SNSs) flourish across the globe as an effective venue for social engagement. The objective of this chapter is to conceptually discuss and empirically demonstrate how social interactions within SNSs are still culturally bound and mirror the users' prevailing cultural orientations. After discussing a conceptual framework for illustrating cultural forces in social relationships within SNSs, the authors present findings from an online survey of SNS users from three cultures: the US, China, and South Korea.

Archana Krishnan, University of Connecticut, USA

Indians use the Internet for a host of applications, and some of these uses are culture-specific, like formalized matrimonial searches. This chapter examines the growth of matrimonial websites in India and explicates how Indians have adopted new Web technologies to preserve the traditional hegemony of arranged marriages. This technology has helped older generations of Indians become a part of the Web revolution and has allowed newer generations to adhere to traditional cultural norms on more progressive terms. Some specific items reviewed in relation to this development are the adaptation of arranged marriages to new technology, the growth of matrimonial websites, the success of such sites in niche groups, and the impact of these sites on Indian cultural norms.

Within the Internet, a range of international and multicultural communities abound, especially within the context of interactive online games known as Massively Multiplayer Online Role-Playing Games (MMORPGs). The clashing of cultures in one particular MMORPG, Omerta, has caused many problems within the related online community. These conflicts have led to online instances of culturalism – discrimination based upon cultural-mindset – within this international online community. This chapter examines the questions: "Do players in international online gaming environments have the right to discriminate based on cultural attitudes and perceptions, or should a player's right to not be discriminated against dominate in such international contexts?" and "How can multiculturalism be successfully managed in international online spaces?"

The Social Information Processing Theory (SIPT) proposes that given time and opportunity to interact, relationships between individuals can form in online environments. The power of the SIPT lies within its ability to foster communication between individuals through communicative behavior that is valued by the other's culture. Therefore, a social information processing approach has the potential to aid the development of trust between virtual team members. It can also facilitate group cohesion and accentuate communication within international work groups.

This chapter focuses on the Internet filtering mechanism the Chinese government adopted to prevent users from accessing foreign online content. Based on the case of Internet filtering in China, the author argues that when citizens are regulated by code rather than by the law, they will experience and perceive such code-based controls as natural. From the Chinese case, it should also be noted that the Internet's effects on politics varies depending upon how its architecture is designed.

Chapter 6

Culture, Online Technology, and Computer-Mediated Technical Documentation:
Marc Hermeking, Ludwig-Maximilians University, Germany

This chapter provides several empirical examples for the influence of culture on the use of online technology and computer-mediated technical documentation. The chapter also examines recent developments and national differences in the global diffusion of mobile phones and the Internet, discussed as examples for culture-specific online communication preferences. In so doing, the author discusses cultural communication preferences and their consequences for the construction and the design of such technologies.

Chapter 7

Tanfer Emin Tunc, Hacettepe University, Turkey
Esin Sultan Oguz, Hacettepe University, Turkey

This chapter examines the current status of Web 2.0 technologies in Turkey and focuses specifically on the use of such technologies by academics. The main focus of the chapter involves presenting the results of two surveys of faculty members at two Turkish universities. The chapter also examines the applicability of Web 2.0 technologies in the Turkish academic setting and the future implications of these technologies both in Turkey and around the world.

Chapter 8

Knowing Through Asynchronous Time and Space: A Phenomenological Study of
Ping Yang, Denison University, USA

This chapter reports the results of a study on cultural differences in computer-mediated communication. An analysis of the dialectic of minimization and amplification manifested in students' online experiences and the significance of contextual variations, power structures, and other features of online interactions allow readers to see the processual, relational, and contradictory nature of cultural differences online. They also provide information that can facilitate more effective intercultural online interactions in the future.

Chapter 9

Cultural Differences in Social Media Usage and Beliefs and Attitudes towards Advertising
Sara Kamal, American University in Dubai, UAE
Shu-Chuan Chu, DePaul University, USA

Social media use is quickly integrating into the daily lives of consumers in the Middle East, where a large number of users represent a variety of cultural milieu. This chapter examines differences between Arab and non-Arab social media users in the United Arab Emirates (UAE), with respect to usage, beliefs, and attitudes towards social media advertising. The chapter also examines managerial and theoretical implications for communication across culturally diverse audiences via online media.

Section 2
The Emerging Trends in Representation: Who May Participate and How Do Individuals Present Themselves?

Chapter 10

Rotimi Taiwo, Obafemi Awolowo University, Nigeria

This chapter examines how online fraudsters explore the language metafunctions of experiential, interpersonal, and textual in the crafting of their emails for global audiences. A critical study of international virtual scam emails over a period of time shows that these scammers tend to improve on how they construct their messages as they rely on experiential knowledge of certain facts they believe will appeal to their audience. This chapter presents and analysis of tactics online scammers use to present themselves to potential victims. It also examines what kinds of online scams seem more effective and why.

Chapter 11

Wengao Gong, Nanyang Technological University, Singapore

In the last 15 years, China has witnessed the world's fastest growth in terms of Internet infrastructure construction and number of Internet users. The Chinese government, however, has maintained a very tight control over the online activities of citizens. In order to avoid or break through the government's regulatory effort, netizens in China have worked out many interesting ways of expressing ideas online. This chapter examines how government monitoring of online media in China is employed to restrict people's freedom of expression and how Chinese netizens are using certain features inherent in their language and culture to exercise their right of free expression in such a context.

Chapter 12

Andrew Mara, North Dakota State University, USA
Miriam Mara, North Dakota State University, USA

This chapter investigates documentation solutions implemented by an Irish Do-It-Yourself (DIY) tour operator. The chapter presents an analysis of how an Irish DIY adventure travel company harnesses user motivations, then applies Appadurai's globalism theories to a particular use of this travel company's documents. The authors also demonstrate how user motivation intrinsic to identity formation can help the technical writer create documentation that effectively assists users in overcoming breakdowns through identity affordances.

Chapter 13

Kathryn Stam, State University of New York Institute of Technology, USA
Indira Guzman, TUI University, USA
Dennis Thoryk, Onondaga Community College, USA

Some websites and Web pages are designed specifically to facilitate online communication across countries and cultures. For this reason, these sites often contain a variety of features for international interaction. Such features include language choices, instant messaging, or use of a translation tool. The purpose of this chapter is to identify current practices and opportunities for online communication between people from different countries or speakers of different languages. To examine this topic, the authors used the Websphere analysis methodology to conduct an analysis of 160 archived international and cross-cultural Web pages in order to identify their communication features.

Chapter 14

Myongho Yi, Texas Woman's University, USA

Effective global information access is more critical now than ever before. The digital world, where users have diverse languages and diverse cultural backgrounds, is increasing more rapidly than at any other time in history. This chapter addresses the cause of ineffective international information access from the standpoint of the user as well as from an information and system perspectives. The chapter also describes the traditional and emerging approaches to enhancing global information access and proposes a system that shows how emerging approaches can minimize cultural differences.

Chapter 15

Reinhard Schäler, University of Limerick, Ireland

Access to information and knowledge in one's native language is a fundamental human right. While individuals often claim these rights for themselves, they do not always afford such rights to others, for there is often a cost involved in the realization of these rights. This chapter highlights how denying this service, particularly as it relates to the translation and the localization of online materials, results in human costs including life threatening information poverty. This situation, in turn, requires urgent and coordinated relief efforts by industry, government, and civil societies on a global scale.

Chapter 16

Jaffer Sheyholislami, Carleton University, Canada

This chapter presents the results of an empirical study of how the Kurds use the Internet. In examining this situation, the author provides suggestions related to the fact that, as much as we need to be concerned with the dominance of a few major languages on the Internet, we also need to map the online presence of linguistic minorities. Such mapping is essential in order to understand the paradoxical nature of a medium that simultaneously homogenizes and fragments linguistic communities and identities.

As health-information websites become more popular, healthcare corporations have worked quickly to create Spanish-language sites to reach the Spanish-speaking population. However, changes have to be made in order to effectively adapt to the Spanish-speaking audience. In order to be successful, site designers must create a sense of community by having interactive elements and by advertising these sites through radio or television with well-known celebrities or known figures in the healthcare realm. This chapter examines how successful health information website can be a strong tool for educating both Spanish and English speakers about preventative care and treatment options that can improve health outcomes.

This chapter presents a discourse analysis of two bulletin board systems (BBS). The analysis was done to identify online language practices within the contextualized parameters of online communities and ongoing sociopolitical development in China. Chinese Internet users employ various discourse strategies to establish community identities, organize online interactions, and defy censorship. These practices demarcate an emergent, public, non-official discourse universe apart from but responsive to the official discourse universe of Chinese political communication.

Section 3
The New Context for Education: Who are the Students and
How are They Taught?

This chapter provides readers with foundational knowledge of how cultural factors mediate online learning and instruction in global education. In this chapter, the authors describe three approaches – social scientific, interpretive, and critical – to theorizing the role of culture in online pedagogy. Next, for each approach, the authors review the existing literature and discuss how each approach applies to online pedagogy. Then, the authors present practical suggestions on how to create effective online materials for students from other countries and cultures.

Chapter 20

Birthe Mousten, Aarhus University, Denmark
John Humbley, Université Paris—Denis Diderot, France
Bruce Maylath, North Dakota State University, USA
Sonia Vandepitte, Hogeschool Gent/University of Ghent, Belgium

This chapter examines the interactive communications of geographically distant virtual classrooms, connected via virtual aids ranging from e-mails to videoconferences. The combination is crucial: through diverse filters, virtual teams mediate a final text for a new language and culture. The authors use linguistic pragmatics as a mechanism to analyze and assess the efficiency and the meaningfulness of such communications. They then use this approach to recommend best practices for educators teaching in cross-cultural virtual environments.

Chapter 21

Madelyn Flammia, University of Central Florida, USA

Global citizens are those individuals who understand the complex and interdependent nature of the world and who take action to address global issues at a local level. Many faculty members recognize the need to prepare students for the demands of global work and citizenship. In this chapter, the author demonstrates how virtual team projects are an ideal means to help students develop global competency. The author also offers suggestions for faculty seeking to structure projects geared to civic engagement in such contexts.

Chapter 22

Angela T. Ragusa, Charles Sturt University, Australia
Emma Steinke, Charles Sturt University, Australia

This chapter uses findings from an online survey of international onshore undergraduate and postgraduate students to critically examine and compare their expectations, experiences, and levels of satisfaction. The results of this study can offer educators important initial insights they can then use to develop online educational materials or online courses for such internationally diverse groups of students. The chapter also provides suggestions on how such factors can and should be addressed when devising online educational materials and environments for such students.

Chapter 23

William Klein, University of Missouri - St. Louis, USA
Bernard E. La Berge, Modern College of Business and Science, UAE

This chapter describes a case of Internet-mediated collaboration between writing classes in the U.S. and in Oman. In the chapter, the authors examine the challenges they experiences including differences in time, culture, academic preparation, language skills, and technological capabilities and literacies. The authors also discuss how such challenges let do their rethinking pedagogical practices and uses of technology and through the structure of institutional affiliation agreements.

Chapter 24

Chun-Min Wang, National Hsinchu University of Education, Taiwan
Jinn-Wei Tsao, University of Georgia, USA
Gretchen Bourdeau Thomas, University of Georgia, USA

The purpose of this chapter is to share a cross-cultural project between Taiwan and the United States for educational practitioners. Taking advantage of Web 2.0 applications as facilitators, the project served as action research to discover better strategies for conducting online cross-cultural collaboration. Specifically, the authors describe the evolution of the instructional design of the project and the difficulties encountered during the cross-cultural collaboration.

Chapter 25

Aimee L. Whiteside, University of Tampa, USA
Amy E. Garrett Dikkers, University of North Carolina at Wilmington, USA

This chapter presents Whiteside's Social Presence Model, course examples, and specific strategies and explains how such factors help facilitators maximize interactions in multicultural, online learning environments. The model provides a framework rooted in socio-cultural learning, linguistic nuances, learning communities, prior experiences, and instructor investment. The chapter also illustrates how the Social Presence Model, coupled with examples from a human rights education case study and research-based strategies, can make significant differences in online interactions.

Chapter 26

Anna M. Harrington, Edison State College, USA

An increasing number of ESL/EFL students are expected to enroll in hybrid (i.e., mixed on-site and online) mainstream courses populated by a majority of native-English-speaking students. However, due to varying language abilities and cultural clashes, the TESOL community has not yet explored the potential online communication problems for ESL/EFL students. This chapter examines issues of differences in language proficiency and cultural norms, identity, community, and muting that can affect computer-based education. The chapter also provides readers with teaching strategies that can be applied in hybrid mainstream courses that include ESL/EFL students.

Chapter 27
International Collaboration and Design Innovation in Virtual Worlds: Lessons
from Second Life
> *Pete Rive, Victoria University of Wellington, New Zealand*
> *Aukje Thomassen, Auckland University of Technology, New Zealand*

Second Life is a popular virtual world that can provide us with valuable lessons about international collaboration and design innovation. This chapter will explore how design practice and design education can assist geographically dispersed design teams working on collaborative designs in a shared virtual space, using real-time 3D constructions and communication tools. We contend that Second Life can provide solutions to collaborative international design and enable knowledge creation and innovation through tacit knowledge exchange.

Chapter 28
Immigration Reform: Re[forming] Theories and Cyber-Designs
> *Barbara Heifferon, Louisiana State University, USA*

This chapter examines the theoretical preparation of students who design online media for other cultural groups. Specifically, the chapter looks at an educational project that involved designing healthcare materials for Spanish-speakers living and working in the United States. In so doing, the chapter articulates the theoretical preparation students need to design online materials for different cultural audiences. The author also discusses local application and pedagogy related to this process.

Foreword

This volume will interest anyone who studies, teaches, or practices cross-cultural computer-mediated communication. The book puts a solid foundation of cross-cultural, linguistic, and rhetorical theory under what, for many of us, is daily work on the Internet. At the same time, alongside a strong theoretical foundation, the chapters in this collection offer a wealth of practical advice. Such a combination of theory and practice, of foundational discussions, and of applicable recommendations for action makes this book appealing to academic researchers and industry practitioners alike.

In reviewing this volume, several key terms stand out. Terms like "social engagement," "culture clash," "cultural exchanges," and others. These terms set the tone for the discussions in the collection. In so doing, they signal what's important in the modern study of computer-mediated cross-cultural communication.

The range of essay topics in this collection is wide and intriguing. Alongside topics that usually get a lot of coverage in academic and professional literature (online education, social networking, and so on) appear discussions on such fascinating subjects as e-matchmaking in India, virtual scams in global contexts, and online game-playing as a multi-cultural practice, to name just a few. This wide range of topics and approaches is another reason why this book is bound to be an important contribution to the conversation about Internet-mediated cross-cultural communication.

21st-century discourse studies have seen a dramatic shift from the study of "text" to the study of context. This shift is evident both in both the academic and in the workplace investigations of how language, media, and culture function. Given such a climate, this collection is a very timely addition to the discussion. It achieves a fine balance between the coverage and analysis of specific discourse instances in cross-cultural computer-mediated communication on the one hand and the coverage of the all-important context of that communication.

Pavel Zemliansky
University of Central Florida, USA

Pavel Zemliansky *is the Director of Writing Across and Curriculum at an associate professor in the Department of Writing and Rhetoric at the University of Central Florida. His research focuses on topics in professional writing, rhetoric, digital media, and intercultural communication. At UCF, Dr. Zemliansky teaches courses in writing, rhetoric, and digital media and consults faculty from various departments on the teaching of writing. He is also the web editor for the Association of Teachers of Technical Writing and a regional editor for the journal IEEE Transactions on Professional Communication.*

Preface

CONSIDERING COMPUTER-MEDIATED COMMUNICATION ACROSS CULTURES

The Global Nature of Cyberspace

At present, almost 2 billion people have access to the Internet (Adair, 2010; Internet usage statistics, 2010). Moreover, with each passing day, the number of individuals gaining online access seems to increase almost exponentially. While the majority of the planet's Internet users do reside in industrialized nations, online access in the developing world has risen rapidly in recent years (Whitney, 2009; High speed Internet access, 2010). The number of citizens with online access in China, for example, has grown from 22.5 million persons to almost 420 million individuals in the last decade (Internet usage in Asia, 2010). And as technologies such as mobile phones increasingly permit inexpensive and easy online access, the number of Internet users worldwide will only continue to expand (Mobile marvels, 2009). These factors beg the question "How is the increasingly international and intercultural nature of the Internet affecting the ways in which individuals act and interact online?"

Answering this question is no easy task, for doing so involves addressing a broad range of factors including culture, language, technology, law, and economics – to name but a few. The complex nature of the question, however, does not mean it should not be asked, nor does it mean that initial initiatives cannot be undertaken to address it. Rather, through a series of small yet focused steps, individuals can begin to unravel to complexities of computer-mediated communication across cultures. The key to taking these first steps is participation and collaboration: By working together across national, cultural, and linguistic lines, individuals can collectively participate in international projects that begin to reflect the scope and scale of online interactions in the modern global age.

The Collaborative Process

This collection represents an international collaborative approach to examining online interactions from different national and cultural perspectives. To explore the topic of computer-mediated communication in global contexts, the editors have assembled the work of over 40 authors from academia, education, and industry. These individuals represent different perspectives related to understanding the continually changing nature of today's global Internet. They also represent perspectives from 15 nations and from different fields of study, educational traditions, and industry sectors. The result is a volume of 28 chapters that focus on a range of aspects affecting how individuals present ideas, exchange information, and discuss topics in international cyberspace.

The development of these chapters, moreover, represents an exercise in international collaboration via online media. For example, several entries are co-authored pieces written by authors who were living in different nations and interacting via Web-based technologies to produce their chapters. The process of developing each chapter, moreover, relied heavily on collaboration involving computer-mediated communication. To begin, all of the initial manuscripts submitted for this collection were read and assessed by reviewers from over a dozen nations. These reviewers provided authors with suggestions and comments for how to develop and organize their chapters within the context of the overall collection. This entire process was driven by online media that were used to share materials, ideas, and opinions across a globally distributed pool of individuals. Finally, the collection's editors used a range of online media – involving both more conventional technologies (e.g., email and Web pages) and newer social media (e.g., Skype and Facebook) to collaborate with authors in the final stages of manuscript development.

Interestingly, all of these interactions transcended time and space – the traditional barriers to collaboration and communication. More importantly, these interactions also involved aspects of culture and language – the newly emerging barriers affecting collaboration in today's online world. Thus, the development of this edited collection represents many of the ideas explored by the contributing authors.

THE OBJECTIVES OF THIS COLLECTION

The primary objective of this text is to provide readers with introductory information, initial insights, and different perspectives on linguistic, cultural, technological, legal, and other factors that affect international online exchanges. The idea is to impart a foundational understanding of computer-mediated communication across cultures. Readers can then use this understanding to make more effective decisions about the applications and the design of online media used in global contexts. Prospective readers might include

- Executives, managers, and other decision makers who need to make informed choices about how their organizations can use online media to address growing global markets
- Marketers, service providers, and support personnel who increasingly use online media to communicate with international clients about products or services
- Researchers (both academic and corporate) studying international or cross-cultural discourse in online environments
- Educators who increasingly find their online courses comprised of students from different cultural and linguistic backgrounds
- Educational administrators who seek to manage the increasing number of international students participating in online programs and who seek to expand their online programs to attract more prospective students located in other nations
- Administrators of international non-profit agencies that increasingly use online media to disseminate information to different nations or to interact with workers and service providers in different nations
- Individuals interested in learning more about this topic area in general

What is important is readers view the overall collection and the individual essays it contains as a foundation for guiding future activities. In this way, this collection should be considered a kind of collaborative text – one that encourages readers to learn more about the topics covered in the various chapters and to use that knowledge to continue the ongoing conversation around such topics.

THE ORGANIZATION OF THIS COLLECTION

To help readers examine these issues and achieve these objectives, the editors have organized the collection into three relatively broad sections. Each section is dedicated to a general theme related to computer-mediated communication across cultures. The chapters in each section then provide different information, ideas, and perspectives associated with that general theme. The organization of the chapters into these three thematic sections does not, however, mean the ideas presented in a chapter only apply to one specific thematic focus. Rather, the purpose of this organization is to help readers better understand the wealth of perspectives and the breadth of topics that can converge around certain contexts created by global cyberspace.

In essence, online media are technologies centered on relationships (Gasner, 1999; Kalawsky, Bee, & Nee, 1999; Olaniran, 2007). That is, these technologies focus on presenting information to others (e.g., Websites), interacting with others (e.g., email), or both (e.g., Facebook). Thus, a study of online media is, in essence, a study of the changing nature of relationships facilitated through such media (St. Amant, 2002b).

The book's first section, "The Changing Nature of Relationships," provides an introduction to cultural, linguistic, technical, and legal factors that can affect how individuals use online media to engage with the greater global community. The entries in this section explore how online media shape the ways in which individuals in different parts of the globe create and maintain relationships. These entries also examine how cultural perspectives on what relationships are and how relationships are created and maintained affects uses of Web-based technologies. Finally, these entries present new perspectives on the notion of community – particularly what constitutes a community and how do individuals become part of different communities created through international online interactions.

Online media also present interesting contexts associated with the notion of representation. That is, the plasticity of online media can allow the users of such media to present themselves in a variety of ways when interacting with others (Hiltz & Turoff, 1993; Turkle, 1995). As a result, online media make it very easy for the lines of truth and fiction to become blurred (St.Amant, 2002b).

The ease with which individuals can access and can use such technologies, however, can allow smaller cultural and linguistic groups to participate on the global stage. Such participation, moreover, would not generally have been possible in the pre-Internet age (Danet & Herring, 2007; Erikson, 2007). Thus, online media can facilitate the representation of different cultural groups in the greater international online discussion of issues. Addressing both aspects of representation requires an understanding of factors affecting one's ability to participate in global online exchanges. The book's second section, "The Emerging Trends in Representation," explores these aspects of presentation and participation in global cyberspace.

Perhaps one of the most interesting and intriguing prospects of global cyberspace involves education. The increasing use of online media in different educational contexts means it is now easier than ever before to have students in different nations collaborate in the same online class (Starke-Meyerring & Wilson, 2008; Starke-Meyerring, 2008; Flammia, Cleary, & Slattery, 2010). Such international collaborative experiences can help students develop the foundational knowledge and skills needed to interact more effectively in international online exchanges (St.Amant, 2002a; St.Amant, 2005).

Effectively taking advantages of this situation is no easy feat. Rather, the more guidance, insights, and cases educators have for addressing such new pedagogical situations, the more effectively they can take advantage of them. The entries in the book's third and final section, entitled "The New Context for Education," provide readers such ideas and information. The chapters here do so by focusing on available technologies, approaches to using such technologies, and the prospective students interacting in such contexts. The entries in this section thus provide readers with practices and perspectives that can facilitate the globalization of online or hybrid classes.

CONCLUSION

Computer-mediated communication across cultures is an inherently complex and nuanced thing. Such aspects should not, however, dissuade individuals from examining interactions in global cyberspace. In fact, an understanding of such interaction can be essential to effective participation in today's global society. By gaining a broad, foundational understanding of factors affecting international online exchanges, individuals can make better and more-informed decisions about how and when to participate in the greater global online community.

The entries in this collection can provide readers with the foundation needed to understand some of the aspects affecting computer-mediated communication across cultures. The collection, however, should not be seen as a comprehensive reference on the topic. Rather, readers should view this collection as a mechanism they can use to make effective and informed decisions related to using online media international contexts. Readers are therefore encouraged to further explore the ideas and perspectives examined in this collection. They are also encouraged to apply the concepts and test the theories, for only through such active collaboration with ideas can we further our understanding of this topic.

Kirk St.Amant
East Carolina University, USA

REFERENCES

Adair, D. (2010, October 19). Internet users to surpass 2 billion. *Indie Pro Pub*. Retrieved October 1, 2010, from http://indiepropub.com/internet-users-to-surpass-2-billion/311248/

Danet, B., & Herring, S. (2007). Multilingualism on the Internet. In Hellinger, M., & Pauwels, A. (Eds.), *Handbook of language and communication: Diversity and change* (pp. 554–585). New York, NY: Mouton de Gruyter.

Erikson, T. H. (2007). Nationalism and the Internet. *Nations and Nationalism, 13*(1), 1–17. doi:10.1111/j.1469-8129.2007.00273.x

Flammia, M., Cleary, Y., & Slattery, D. M. (2010). Leadership roles, socioemotional communication strategies, and technology use of Irish and US students in virtual teams. *IEEE Transactions on Professional Communication, 53*, 89–101. doi:10.1109/TPC.2010.2046088

Gasner, A. (1999). Globalization: The changing face of the workforce. *Business Today, 36*(3), 43–44.

High speed Internet access in Africa takes off. (2010, June 21). *Stratsis Incite*. Retrieved October 1, 2010, from http://stratsisincite.wordpress.com/2010/06/21/high-speed-internet-access-in-africa-takes-off/

Hiltz, S. R., & Turoff, M. (1993). *The network nation: Human communication via computer*. Cambridge, MA: The MIT Press.

Internet usage in Asia. (2010). *Internet World Stats*. Retrieved October 1, 2010, from http://www.internetworldstats.com/stats3.htm

Internet usage statistics: The Internet big picture. (2010). *Internet World Stats*. Retrieved October 1, 2010, from http://www.internetworldstats.com/stats.htm

Kalawsky, R. S., Bee, S. T., & Nee, S. P. (1999). Human factors evaluation techniques to aid understanding of virtual interfaces. *BT Technology Journal, 17*, 128–241. doi:10.1023/A:1009687227736

Mobile marvels. (2009, September 24). *The Economist*. Retrieved November 25, 2010, from http://www.economist.com/node/14483896

Olaniran, B. A. (2007). Challenges to implementing e-learning and lesser developed countries. In A. L. Edmundson (Ed.), *Globalized e-learning cultural challenges* (pp. 18–34). Hershey, PA: Idea Group, Inc.

St.Amant, K. (2005). An online approach to teaching international outsourcing in technical communication classes. *Journal of Technical Writing and Communication, 35*, 191–201. doi:10.2190/H7MP-GJJH-1MHG-KPH6

St.Amant, K. (2002a). Integrating intercultural online learning experiences into the computer classroom. *Technical Communication Quarterly, 11*, 289–315. doi:10.1207/s15427625tcq1103_4

St.Amant, K. (2002b). When cultures and computers collide. *Journal of Business and Technical Communication, 16*, 196–214. doi:10.1177/1050651902016002003

Starke-Meyerring, D., & Wilson, M. (2008). Globally networked learning environments: Shaping visionary futures. In Starke-Meyerring, D., & Wilson, M. (Eds.), *Designing global learning environments: Visionary partnerships, policies, and pedagogies* (pp. 218–230). Rotterdam, The Netherlands: Sense Publishers.

Starke-Meyerring, D. (2008). Genre, knowledge and digital code in Web-based communities: An integrated theoretical framework for shaping digital discursive spaces. *International Journal of Web-based Communities, 4*, 398–417. doi:10.1504/IJWBC.2008.019547

Turkle, S. (1995). *Life on screen: Identity in the age of the Internet*. New York, NY: Touchstone.

Whitney, L. (2009, June 16). Global broadband access on the rise. *cnet News*. Retrieved

September 8, 2010, from http://news.cnet.com/8301-1035_3-10265421-94.html

Acknowledgment

I owe a great deal of thanks and appreciation to my daughters, Lily and Isabelle, who are a source of inspiration in all that I do, and particularly to my wife Dori, whose continued patience and support were essential to this project. I also owe a special thank you to IGI Global's Hannah Abelbeck for all of her patience, understanding, and guidance throughout this process and to Dr. Donna Kain for all of her technical expertise and help.

Kirk St.Amant
East Carolina University, USA

Thank you to my husband, Paul, for his support and patience with my editing, my kids Clare and Paul, who are constant reminders to me of why I am a librarian, and to the members of the Catholic Library Association, who have been tremendously inspiring new colleagues.

Sigrid Kelsey
Louisiana State University, USA

Section 1
The Changing Nature of Relationships:
Who is Interacting and How Do They Interact?

Chapter 1
Culture–Laden Social Engagement:
A Comparative Study of Social Relationships in Social Networking Sites among American, Chinese and Korean Users

Sejung Marina Choi
University of Texas, USA

Shu-Chuan Chu
DePaul University, USA

Yoojung Kim
University of Texas, USA

ABSTRACT

In today's online environment, social networking sites (SNSs) flourish across the globe as an effective venue for social engagement. The objective of this chapter is to conceptually discuss and empirically demonstrate how social interactions within SNSs are still culturally bound and mirror the users' prevailing cultural orientations. After discussing a conceptual framework for illustrating cultural forces in social relationships within SNSs, the authors present findings from an online survey of SNS users from three cultures: the U.S., China, and South Korea.

INTRODUCTION

With the evolution of information and communication technologies, computer-mediated communication among individuals from different cultures continues to increase and transpire in diverse forms. In recent years, social networking

sites (SNSs) have shown exponential growth and currently serve millions of Internet users across the globe as a popular online venue for social engagement (comScore, 2007; Nielsen Online, 2009). A growing roster of SNSs includes diverse platforms that range from MySpace and Facebook to Orkut, LinkedIn, and Cyworld. Although the focus and architecture of SNSs are increasingly

DOI: 10.4018/978-1-60960-833-0.ch001

diversifying as they are designed to fulfill different networking needs (e.g., LinkedIn for business-oriented networking and Flickr for picture sharing and movie-focused Flixter), those sites catering to general audiences such as Facebook and MySpace remain among the most popular and most pervasive (Papacharissi, 2009).

At the heart of SNSs is the practice of using "friends" lists that connect people across space and time as well as using the friend finder and invitation features. Within the realm of SNSs, individuals can build, maintain, and enhance their personal networks by reconnecting with old contacts and making new connections. SNSs also allow users to freely interact with others in their networks through a multitude of communication means such as bulletin boards, emails, and instant messengers. The architecture of SNSs that facilitates and cultivates social navigability and sociality is what makes these sites unique and different from other technologies used for computer-mediated communications.

The objective of this chapter is to conceptually discuss and empirically demonstrate how culture shapes computer-mediated social interaction in the emerging online environment, namely in SNSs. To accomplish this goal, this chapter first presents a review of the distinctive architecture and development of SNSs. Then, the authors provide a thorough review of related constructs and conceptual framework that might explain different norms and approaches in technology-mediated communication across cultures, especially in the SNS environment. Next, the authors use online survey data of college-aged SNS users from three culturally divergent countries (the United States, China, and South Korea) to discuss cross-cultural similarities and differences in the characteristics of social relationships and magnitude of social capital in SNSs. The authors then conclude the chapter with a discussion of the implications of the findings and present directions for future research in the area of intercultural communication in the growing online environment. Given the

mounting popularity and pervasiveness of SNSs on the global scale, this chapter advances our knowledge of cultural impact on social interaction in the technology-mediated environment. It also offers useful insights into how to facilitate online communication across cultures.

BACKGROUND

In theory, SNSs enable users to transcend geographical borders and encourage intercultural communication among them. While SNSs are seemingly ideal for communication among individuals from different cultures, computer-mediated communication does not occur in a cultural vacuum. Thus, such interactions might still be influenced by cultural factors (Halavais, 2000; Orgad, 2006). That is, social interaction within SNSs might operate within the spatial, structural, and cultural perimeters of the societal milieu by which the users are surrounded. Such interactions might also reflect the dominant values and norms of the culture to which participants belong (boyd, 2008). Within this context, an important question to address is

Do cultural forces impact on the nature of social connections in SNSs?

Although the burgeoning body of academic research on SNSs has examined SNSs as a new virtual sphere for identity construction, self-presentation, and social capital generation (e.g., Ellison, Steinfield, & Lampe, 2007; Jung, Youn, & McClung, 2007; Livingstone, 2008), the investigation has largely been limited to users from a single nation and little is known about the applicability of its findings to other cultural contexts. Yet a few recent studies suggest cultural influences on social relations and interaction within SNSs (e.g., Kim & Yun, 2007; Lewis & George, 2008). To begin to understand how such factors affect cross-cultural communication in SNSs, this initial section reviews factors of culture and technology that can affect such exchanges.

Social Networking Sites (SNSs)

A SNS is defined as "an online place where a user can create a profile and build a personal network that connects him or her to other users" (Lenhart & Madden, 2007, p. 1). As body and Ellison (2007) note, SNSs serve three noteworthy functions efficiently: "to (1) construct a public or semi-public profile within a bounded system, (2) articulate a list of other users with whom they share a connection, and (3) view and traverse their list of connections and those made by others within the system" (para. 4). A user's network in SNSs is, in turn, composed of all social ties, both close and remote, that the user identifies as "friends" and interacts with. More specifically, SNSs help the users clearly enunciate their existing contacts such as close friends and family members and converse with them irrespective of physical or temporal constraints.

While the foremost function of SNSs was originally to cement real world relationships/ friendships (boyd & Ellison, 2007; Donath & boyd, 2004), the meaning of "friends" has been relaxed to a great degree in the SNS contexts. In fact, users tend to extend their networks to include mere acquaintances and even strangers they have met only online (Thelwall, 2008). Coupled with the user-friendly features such as the friend finder and suggestions, the loose sense of "friending" in SNSs encourages the users to find and make new connections with other individuals they might have never met except through SNSs (Thelwall, 2008). This "friending" mechanism thus allows users to stretch their networks across space and class and typifies the expanding social media landscape. Moreover, as users can easily observe each other's network, they are in implicit competition with one another for both the number of and types of friends one can meet via SNSs. This factor of competition,

in turn, further fuels the broadening of personal networks among users (Slotnik, 2007).

While there is little doubt that SNSs continue to transform how users create, sustain, and enhance their social relations and fulfill socially oriented goals, academic research in this area is in its early stage. As a result, many questions about SNS usage and its impact on social exchanges remain unanswered. Among them is what characterizes the social relations and benefits users enjoy with regard to their networks in the online social networking environment. Extant literature suggests that individuals in any social network interact and exchange some type of support with one or another (Wellman, 1981). Along this line, the concepts of social capital and social ties should together be useful for illustrating the nature of social relations and benefits in SNSs.

Social Capital and Social Ties in SNSs

Social capital is formally defined as "the sum of the resources, actual or virtual, that accrue to an individual or a group by virtue of possessing a durable network of more or less institutionalized relationships of mutual acquaintance and recognition" (Bourdieu & Wacquant, 1992, p. 14). In Putnam's work (2000), two prominent types of social capital, bridging and bonding, are conceptualized. Closely tied to the two forms of social capital are the classifications of strong versus weak ties in social networks (Granovetter, 1973, 1983). These aspects help expound the nature of the social relationships and resources individuals derive from their communities.

Strong ties refer to close friends and family members, whereas *weak ties* include acquaintances or loose connections (Granovetter, 1973, 1983). *Bonding social capital* is created among strong ties that provide substantive emotional support and a firm sense of belonging for one another. Interestingly, tightly knit networks with strong ties are likely to lack diversity. This situation is related to the fact that, as individuals with similar backgrounds tend to develop strong connections, they foster intimate relationships (Putnam, 2000). Conversely, *bridging social capital* arises when weak ties from diverse social groups offer novel information and new perspectives. Weak ties, which are formed among individuals with different backgrounds, facilitate information mobility across networks. The loosely linked networks with weak ties, however, do not lend substantial support or close relations (Putnam, 2000).

Since the advent of Internet technology, research has applied the notion of social capital, originated in offline contexts, in the online environment. Such research has also examined if the formation of social capital is enhanced or hampered by the use of Internet technology (Wellman, Haase, Witte, & Hampton, 2002). A recent work (Williams, 2007) found that general Internet usage was positively associated with bridging social capital while it also negatively affected bonding. In light of this finding, the computer-mediated environment might be more constructive for expanding social networks by connecting geographically or socially remote individuals rather than for fortifying existing social relations.

Yet SNSs might effectively serve both bridging and bonding functions owing to their unique character and architecture geared towards social connectivity. Specifically, bridging social capital in SNSs might be augmented as a large number of weak ties are easily found and formed across space and class. A recent study of MySpace indeed demonstrated that users' networks on the SNS embrace not only close friends but also acquaintances and even strangers (Thelwall, 2008). Equally, bonding social capital might be enhanced in SNSs because strong ties are articulated and further strengthened by frequent engagement via the myriad of readily available communication modes associated with multimedia (Donath & boyd, 2004; Ellison et al., 2007).

Based on survey data of undergraduate students at Michigan State University, Ellison and colleagues (2007) suggested that college students' use of Facebook, the most popular SNS among that age group, was positively related with both bridging and bonding social capital of their campus community. In their study, Ellison et al. found Facebook to help the college students reconnect with and reinforce their old relationships from high school. Ellison et al.'s findings also indicate SNSs play a facilitatory role in enhancing perceived bridging and bonding social capital among young users of that technology. Similarly, another study examined the relationships between Facebook use and college students' life satisfaction, social trust, civic engagement, and political participation that all promote social capital (Valenzuela, Park, & Kee, 2009). In this study, the researchers suggested that the functions and features of Facebook facilitate the formation and maintenance of both strong and weak ties and thus have positive effects on social capital.

What still remains unclear in these cases is if culture affects the extent and composition of social networks and the resulting creation of social capital in the online social networking landscape. A careful exploration of the nature of the social networks and perceived social capital among SNS users from different cultures should thus shed useful light on the influence culture can have in the growing online environment for social engagement.

Cultural Orientations

Since Hofstede (1980) identified individualism and collectivism as one of the five underlying dimensions of culture, a number of studies have proven its utility for detecting cultural variations. Following Hofstede's original conceptualization (1980, 1984), cross-cultural research has considered individualism and collectivism as the opposing ends of a single dimension and illustrated differences in national cultures along that dimension (Gudykunst & Ting-Toomey, 1988). According to this perspective, archetypal individualistic cultures place emphasis on self-reliance, autonomy, internal attributes, and separateness from others (Triandis, 2001). In contrast, collectivistic cultures are characterized by group harmony, family integrity, connectedness, and in-group membership. Accordingly, individuals from collectivistic cultures tend to regard themselves as interdependent on each other, whereas those from individualistic cultures are likely to be independent of one another (Mills & Clark, 1982).

Recent conceptual developments, however, have proposed that the dichotomous view of individualism and collectivism is too simplistic and that a finer framework is needed to better depict cultural complexity (e.g., Singlis, Triandis, Bhawuk, & Gelfand, 1995). A new typology has answered the call to expand the traditional one-dimensional view of individualism and collectivism into a more sophisticated conceptualization. Creating this more refined approach, in turn, involves adding another dimension: that of horizontal versus vertical (Triandis, 1995, 2001). The idea is that the horizontal and vertical aspect of social relationships further distinguishes individualism and collectivism. The underlying assumption of the horizontal orientation is that everyone sees each other as equal in social relationships. In contrast, the vertical facet of social relationships accepts inequality and emphasizes status and hierarchy. Consequently, four distinctive types of cultures emerge from this more sophisticated perspective:

- Horizontal Individualism (HI)
- Vertical Individualism (VI)
- Horizontal Collectivism (HC)
- Vertical Collectivism (VC)
  (Triandis, 2001; Triandis & Suh, 2002)

According to this conceptualization, HI highlights self-government, individuality, and uniqueness, while VI stresses achievement, eminence and competition. HC is characterized by interdependence, unity, harmony and cooperativeness, whereas VC underscores dutifulness and adherence to social norms and hierarchy.

Previously, East Asian countries such as China and South Korea were uniformly described as collectivistic cultures, while Western countries such as the U.S. and France were characterized as individualistic cultures (Cho, Kwan, Gentry, Jun, & Kropp, 1999; Hofstede, 1984). When examined using this four-way conceptualization, however, all individualistic or collectivistic cultures are not identical (Shavitt, Lalwani, Zhang, & Torelli, 2006; Sivadas, Bruvold, & Nelson, 2008). The U.S., for example, represents a VI culture in which Americans tend to be competitive and strive to "being the best" and achieve goals. Sweden and Denmark, by contrast, are classified as HI cultures as they value equality while focusing on autonomy (Lee & Choi, 2007; Nelson & Shavitt, 2002). Similarly, among collectivistic cultures, China, with its cultural connections to Taoism and Buddhism, is understood as a HC culture wherein people place an emphasis on social bonding and unity and show a strong sense of cooperation (Chen, Meindl, & Hunt, 1997). In comparison, South Korea, where there is a strong history of Confucianism, exemplifies a VC culture that emphasizes social norms and hierarchy and gives priority to group goals over personal goals (Lee & Choi, 2007). As discussed, the four-way typology of cultures illustrates finer qualities of different cultures. Thus, such a classification might serve as a useful framework for comprehending cultural influences on social network and capital development. The question then becomes: How do these factors affect the relationship between culture and social relations?

Culture and Social Relationships

A study investigated the relationship between individualism/collectivism and social capital in the U.S. in comparison with other countries and found that individualism was strongly and positively associated with social capital (Allik & Realo, 2004). That is, when individuals are self-reliant, autonomous, and liberated from interpersonal relationships, they are more likely to rely on the greater society for support and resources. Another study also examined the individualism/collectivism and social capital relationship and observed that family-based and institutional collectivism differentially affected social capital (Realo & Greenfield, 2008). Specifically, familism was negatively associated with social capital, whereas institutional collectivism showed a positive relationship with social capital.

Taking the growing online social exchanges into account, Cardon and colleagues (2009) examined SNS users' social relationships both online and offline in 11 countries and compared the number of social ties between individualistic and collectivistic nations. Contrary to their prediction derived from the literature, Cardon et al. did not find significant differences in the number of online or offline social ties between the two cultures. An interesting finding the study offered, however, was that SNS users from collectivistic countries maintained a greater number of online social relationships never met in person than their counterparts in individualistic nations. Taken together, these findings suggest that culture actually plays a role in the development of social relationships and assets in both online and offline contexts although the pattern of cultural influence is not clear yet. For this reason, a careful examination of cultural forces in socially-oriented activities and perceptions in the growing online environment is timely and necessary.

Given that the aforementioned, four-way cultural classification is founded upon the character of social relationships and SNSs are particularly geared towards social engagement, social relations and interactions in SNSs might closely reflect the prevailing values of the cultures which the users are from. That is, users' cultural orientations might be extended to the online social channel and serve as the guiding principle for social interactions in

SNSs. In this light, American, Chinese, and South Korean users might exhibit differing patterns of social relations in the social networking environment in accordance with the dominant norms and values of their national cultures.

With their VI orientation, American users' networking with others might be goal oriented and often traverse across different groups to find new contacts and obtain new information. Chinese users, with their HC culture, might be open to new relationships and focus on interconnectedness and harmony in social interactions in SNSs. As a result, Chinese users might be more inclusive in their construction of personal networks. In contrast, VC-oriented South Koreans' use of SNSs tends to be exclusive in the formation and maintenance of social relationships and strictly follow social norms and hierarchy (Kim & Yun, 2007). Along this logic, American, Chinese, and South Korean SNS users are expected to exhibit different degrees of perceived bonding and bridging social capital. They are also expected to exhibit differences in the number of strong and weak social ties as to their online social networks. The following sections of this chapter present an empirical study that examined these very issues.

THE STUDY

An online survey of college-aged SNS users from the U.S., China, and South Korea was undertaken to empirically test the postulation of cultural forces in social interactions in SNSs. According to a recent survey, 59%, 70%, and 62% of active Internet users aged 16 to 54 have created a personal profile in a SNS in the U.S., China, and South Korea respectively. These figures, moreover, have been on the rise since 2006 (Power to the people, 2009). While the U.S., China, and South Korea are all among the leading countries and comparable in terms of general Internet usage and SNS development, they represent divergent cultural orientations and thus serve as a suitable cross-cultural context for this examination.

Within the context of international SNS use, college students are largely early adopters and heavy users of the Internet in general and SNSs in particular (Ellison et al., 2007). Although the adoption of SNSs has swiftly expanded to older adults, young people are at the forefront of the social networking phenomenon. College-aged individuals especially comprise the largest segment of the social networking population in the three countries of interest (Blogging increasing in popularity, 2008; 2009 Chinese social networking, 2009; Fallows, 2007; College students' Facebook use, 2009; Lenhart, 2009). Moreover, college students undergo a significant life transition in which their social networks are substantially reconstituted (Putnam, 2000). As the extant literature provides little insight to this age group's use of SNSs in different cultures, the focus on college students in this cross-cultural investigation seems both necessary and appropriate.

Method

Sample: A total of 349 undergraduate students at a large southwestern university participated in the U.S. The South Korean and Chinese samples, in turn, consisted of 240 and 208 undergraduates from a number of universities located in metropolitan areas in their respective countries. American respondents' age ranged from 18 to 24 years, with an average of 20, and 75.1% of them were female. With an even gender ratio, Chinese participants were 21 years old on average, ranging from ages 18 to 33. The South Korean sample ranged in age from 18 to 28 years of age, with an average age of 23, and 45.4% were female. Roughly half of the American participants were juniors (43.7%), followed by seniors (26.3%), freshmen (17.4%), and sophomores (12.3%). Similarly, the Chinese sample was comprised of nearly half of juniors (49.5%), followed by seniors (29.6%), sophomores (19.7%), and freshmen (3.8%). More than

a third of the South Korean respondents were juniors (39.6%), followed by seniors (22.9%), sophomores (20.4%), and freshmen (17.1%). Over 60% of the American participants were Caucasian, followed by Asian-American (13.0%), Hispanic-American (12.9%), and African-American (3.7%), whereas the ethnic make-up of the Chinese and South Korean samples was 100% Chinese and South Korean respectively. Sample characteristics are summarized in Table 1.

Measures: The self-administered online survey contained questions assessing the characteristics of social relations in SNSs. Measures were borrowed from literature and slightly adapted to the context of the present study. The questionnaire was originally developed in English and translated into Chinese and Korean following the standard translation and back-translation procedure by two bilingual graduate students respectively. In the first section of the survey, the usage of SNSs was assessed. Respondents were first

Table 1. Sample Characteristics

	U.S.	China	Korea
N	349	208	240
Gender (%)			
Male	24.9	50.0	54.6
Female	75.1	50.0	45.4
Age			
Range	18-24	18-33	18-28
Mean	20	22	23
School Classification (%)			
Freshman	17.4	3.8	17.1
Sophomore	12.3	19.7	20.4
Junior	43.7	49.5	39.6
Senior	26.3	26.9	22.9
"Friends" on SNSs			
Family	4.18	6.50	3.32
Close friend	48.70	28.38	21.72
Acquaintance	133.37	51.18	14.77
Classmate	182.27	83.02	36.66
Others	23.86	24.48	2.29

asked to indicate a SNS that they used the most on a regular basis.

This initial question was followed by two questions that examined the extent to which respondents used the SNS: (1) amount of daily usage and (2) period of use. Next, the number and types of contacts in the "friends" list (e.g. family, close friends, classmates, and acquaintances) were obtained for the size and composition of personal networks (Boase, 2008). Because some of classmates could be close friends, respondents were instructed to list these contacts under close friends and not include them in the classmate category when both overlapped.

The third section of the questionnaire gauged social capital the respondents derived from their SNS use via the online social capital scale (Williams, 2007) with the endpoints of 1 being "strongly disagree" and 5 being "strongly agree." The specific items and reliabilities of the social capital scale appear in Table 2. In the final section, information on respondents' demographic characteristics such as gender, age, race/ethnicity, and school classification was acquired.

Results

To gain a preliminary understanding of the SNS sphere in the U.S., China, and South Korea, the most mentioned SNSs by respondents as their regular destination were identified in each country. Consistent with findings from previous research

Table 2. Social Capital Measures and Reliability Coefficients

	U.S.	China	Korea
Bridging Social Capital	.91	.87	.86
Interacting with people on the social network site makes me interested in things that happen outside of my town.			
Interacting with people on the social network site makes me want to try new things.			
Interacting with people on the social network site makes me interested in what people unlike me are thinking.			
Talking with people on the social network site makes me curious about other places in the world.			
Interacting with people on the social network site makes me feel like part of a larger community.			
Interacting with people on the social network site makes me feel connected to the bigger picture.			
Interacting with people on the social network site reminds me that everyone in the world is connected.			
I am willing to spend time to support general community activities on the social network site.			
Interacting with people on the social network site gives me new people to talk to.			
I come in contact with new people on the social network site all the time.			
Bonding Social Capital	.89	.77	.86
There are several members of the social network site I trust to help solve my problems.			
There is a member of the social network site I can turn to for advice about making very important decisions.			
There is no one on the social network site that I feel comfortable talking to about intimate personal problems. (R)			
When I feel lonely, there are members of the social network site I can talk to.			
If I needed an emergency loan of $500, I know someone at the social network site I can turn to.			
The people I interact with on the social network site would put their reputation on the line for me.			
The people I interact with on the social network site would be good job references for me.			
The people I interact with on the social network site would share their last dollar with me.			
I do not know members of the social network site well enough to get them to do anything important. (R)			
The people I interact with on the social network site would help me fight an injustice.			

(Nielsen Online, 2009), Facebook enjoyed the most popularity among American participants (83.4%), followed by MySpace (9.7%), YouTube (4.3%), and others (2.6%). Among Chinese respondents, QQ (80.3%) was the most mentioned SNS, followed by Xiaonei (11.5%) and others (5.3%). In South Korea, Cyworld (89.6%) was listed most frequently. Nateon (3.8%) was ranked as second, followed by Daum Planet (3.3%), and others (3.3%). Although the various SNS platforms differed in the specific interface designs, all exhibited the three prominent characteristics of SNSs, 'profiles, friends, and comments' and were considered to be structurally comparable (boyd, 2008, p. 123).

Use of social networking sites: As a first step toward an understanding of SNS usage in the three countries, one-way ANOVAs (analysis of variance) were performed. When the period of SNS usage was examined, Chinese respondents reported having used their favorite SNS for a longer period time, almost three and half years (M = 40.81 months, SD = 28.69), than respondents in South Korea, with over three years (M = 37.29, SD = 19.11), and the U.S. with roughly two and half years (M = 27.82, SD = 13.07), F (2,793) = 31.94, p < .001. With post-hoc Tukey tests, it was confirmed that the mean differences between the groups were statistically significant, p < .01.

Significant differences in the amount of SNS usage were also observed among the countries F (2,795) = 56.37, p < .001. Chinese respondents reported the greatest amount of SNS daily usage (M = 223.61 minutes, SD = 212.10), followed by their South Korean (M = 100.00, SD = 177.89) and American counterparts (M = 89.38, SD = 65.82). Post-hoc Tukey tests confirmed that the mean differences between the groups were all significant, p < .01. To illustrate, Chinese respondents spent over 3.7 hours with their favorite SNS on an average day, while South Korean and American participants used SNSs for less than half of the time reported by Chinese users, about 1.7 hours and 1.5 hours respectively.

Social ties in social networking sites: The nature of social networks and relationships was examined in the following aspects: (1) total number of friends, (2) number of strong ties, (3) number of weak ties, and (4) ratio of strong ties. The total number of friends was obtained by summing up the numbers of contacts in all categories: family, close friend, acquaintance, classmate, and others. Strong ties included contacts in the "family" and "close friends" categories, whereas connections in the "acquaintance" and "classmates" classifications were grouped as weak ties. To understand the network composition, the ratio of strong ties was computed by dividing the number of strong ties by the sum of strong and weak ties.

A series of one-way ANOVAs examined the mean differences by country in the abovementioned measures. First, U.S. respondents had a larger number of friends in their SNS network (M = 412.03, SD = 364.35) than did either Chinese (M = 193.56, SD = 360.20) or

South Korean participants (M = 81.53, SD = 69.48), F (2,794) = 88.53, p < .001. Similarly, American respondents appeared to maintain significantly more strong ties within SNSs (M = 52.73, SD = 81.11) than did either their Chinese (M = 34.88, SD = 51.91) or their South Korean counterparts (M = 25.03, SD = 22.67), F (2,794) = 15.42, p < .001. The number of weak ties in the three countries followed a similar pattern: the average number of weak ties within SNS networks was significantly higher in the U.S. (M = 339.26, SD = 292.00) than in China (M = 134.21, SD = 281.96) or in South Korea (M = 53.72, SD = 50.63), F (2,794) = 108.34, p < .001. A closer look at the ratio of strong ties revealed more interesting results concerning the constitution of networks in SNSs. As predicted, South Korean participants' networks were comprised of a significantly greater portion of strong ties (M = .38, SD = .24) than their Chinese (M = .23, SD = .14) or American counterparts (M = .15, SD = .15), F (2,783) = 110.57, p < .001. Post-hoc Tukey tests confirmed that all of the mean differences between the groups were statistically significant, $p < .01$.

Social capital in social networking sites: Lastly, two one-way ANOVAs examined differences in perceived bridging and bonding social capital across the U.S., China, and South Korea. For bridging social capital, Chinese respondents reported significantly higher ratings ($M = 4.76$, $SD = .90$) than their U.S. ($M = 3.35$, $SD = .86$) or South Korean ($M = 3.11$, $SD = .67$) counterparts, $F (2,796) = 265.29$, $p < .001$. A similar pattern

emerged for bonding social capital as well. The level of bonding social capital among Chinese respondents was significantly higher ($M = 4.07$, $SD = .90$) than that in the U.S. ($M = 3.27$, $SD = .85$) or South Korea ($M = 3.25$, $SD = .70$), $F (2,796) = 74.49$, $p < .001$. Post-hoc Tukey tests demonstrated that the observed mean differences between the countries were statistically significant, $p < .01$. The mean scores and ANOVA results for all measures are reported in Table 3.

Table 3. Social Networking Site (SNS) Usage, Social Ties, and Social Capital by Country

	Grand Mean (*SD*)	**Country**	**N**	**Mean (*SD*)***
Usage				
SNS usage period	34.06 (*20.76*)	U.S.	348	27.82 (*13.07*)
(Months)		China	208	40.81 (*28.69*)
		Korea	238	37.29 (*19.11*)
SNS usage amount	127.64 (*162.37*)	U.S.	349	89.38 (*65.82*)
(Minutes per day)		China	208	223.61 (*212.10*)
		Korea	239	100.00 (*177.89*)
Social Ties				
Total number of friends	255.51 (*337.85*)	US.	348	412.03 (*364.35*)
		China	208	193.56 (*360.20*)
		Korea	239	81.53 (*69.48*)
Number of strong ties	39.73 (*62.27*)	US.	348	52.73 (*81.11*)
		China	208	34.88 (*51.91*)
		Korea	239	25.03 (*22.67*)
Number of weak ties	199.77 (*273.55*)	US.	348	339.26 (*292.00*)
		China	208	134.21 (*281.96*)
		Korea	239	53.72 (*50.63*)
Ratio of strong ties	.24 (*.20*)	US.	342	.15 (*.15*)
		China	205	.23 (*.14*)
		Korea	237	.38 (*.24*)
Social Capital				
Bridging social capital	3.64 (*1.06*)	US.	349	3.35 (*.86*)
		China	208	4.76 (*.90*)
		Korea	240	3.11 (*.67*)
Bonding social capital	3.47 (*.89*)	US.	349	3.27 (*.85*)
		China	208	4.07 (*.90*)
		Korea	240	3.25 (*.70*)

* ANOVA and post-hoc Tukey test results indicate that all mean differences are significant at p=.001.

SUMMARY AND DISCUSSION

With the continuing advances of information and communication technology, social interactions are no longer bounded to geographical perimeters. Rather, people from different parts of the world can easily communicate with one another. Within this context, SNSs have recently gained mounting popularity on the global scale and have emerged as the most common and viable venue for social exchange and relationship building in the online environment. Ideally, SNSs can further facilitate communication among physically dispersed individuals. The resulting increase in border-crossing communication could contribute to the lessening of cultural gaps and enhanced cultural convergence around the world.

The social relations and networks that users construct and sustain might, however, echo the focal individuals' social and cultural orientations (boyd, 2008; Papacharissi, 2009; Zhao & Elesh, 2008). Although adapted to fit the modality of communication in the online setting, social engagement within SNSs might still be under the significant influence of accepted norms and dominant values in the specific cultural, social surroundings in which the users are set. Along this line, social interaction within SNSs is culturally loaded and closely associated with the cultural system to which the users belong. As noted by Hutchby (2001), "technologies can be understood as artifacts which may be both shaped by and shaping of the practices humans use in interaction with, around and through them" (p. 44). In order to unravel the related interplay between the modality of computer-mediated communication and cultural forces in practice, a thoughtful examination of SNSs in differing cultural environments is warranted.

The goal of this chapter was to cross-culturally investigate the nature of social relationships formed and maintained via the emerging medium of social interaction. In particular, this chapter examined bridging and bonding characteristics of networks and ensuing social benefits perceived by the users. By using empirical data from college-aged SNS users from three countries, the authors found cultural differences in the mediated social interaction within SNSs. Overall, the findings of the study presented here confirm the general pattern of predictions derived from the four-way cultural classification comprised of Horizontal and Vertical Individualism and Collectivism (HVIC) (Triandis, 1995, 2001).

As predicted, these findings suggest that U.S. college students tend to focus on the spreading out of relationships in SNSs and expand their social networks to a greater degree by including a large number of remote connections than do their Chinese or South Korean counterparts. Consequently, U.S. college students' networks are much larger but looser with a far greater portion of weak ties as compared to those of Chinese and South Korean college students that are relatively smaller and tighter with a substantial fraction of strong ties.

Of significant note is that the social networks among all respondents from the three countries contained more weak ties than strong ties. This finding of commonality among the three countries indicates that, regardless of culture, the foremost function of SNSs is to promote and facilitate bridging among the users across space and class. Their social navigability features, coupled with the borderless nature of the Internet-based interface, enable the users to traverse across different networks and easily find and form new, often loose, connections.

Another interesting finding is that Chinese college students derive both bridging and bonding social capital from their networks in SNSs significantly more than do their U.S. or South Korean counterparts. Perhaps the greatest amount of daily usage of SNSs among Chinese users accounts for the heavy reliance on SNS-based networks for generating both types of social capital. Younger Chinese generations are described as heavy Internet users who increasingly rely on the Internet for social engagement. Because most of these individuals are from single-child families, they tend to gratify their social and relational needs online. Also, Chinese users tend to be more enthusiastic and open in social engagement in an online environment while being more passive and quiet in face-to-face communication. This behavior might, in turn, lead to active engagement in online social interactions. Indeed, a study found that Facebook users who were more introverted offline tended to be more active and seek for popularity online (Zywica & Danowski, 2008). In this light, for Chinese users, SNSs might be a primary and unique social place wherein they bond together as well as develop new online companionships with different self-presentation and social interaction strategies.

Perhaps the most important insight revealed through this study comes from the comparison between Chinese and South Korean SNS users. Earlier literature assumed that China and South Korea represent similar cultures with strong collectivistic values. Yet the findings related to this research suggest that Chinese collectivism is different from collectivism in South Korea. Although both cultures are rooted in the belief that individuals are interdependent, Chinese people stress equality and harmony whereas social hierarchy and responsibility guide South Koreans' social relationships.

In fact, the authors' findings lend empirical support for such cultural influences. Chinese users' networks were more extensive compared to their South Korean counterparts and held more contacts in all categories (i.e., total number of contacts, strong ties, and weak ties). In addition, South Korean users maintained a greater portion of strong ties within networks than did their Chinese counterparts. Further, bonding social capital was greater than bridging only in South Korea. Collectively, these findings suggest that South Koreans' SNS usage is more strongly geared towards bonding with strong ties even when compared to that of Chinese users that share collectivistic backgrounds. Chinese individuals appear to be more open to and accepting of relationships with out-group members and see little trouble in networking with strangers as they regard everyone as equal (Meng & Zuo, 2008). Conversely, South Koreans often seem to adhere to rigid social hierarchy, conform to social norms and be more exclusive in social engagement since they focus on bonding with close ties.

Taken together, the findings presented in this chapter point to the importance of culture in understanding the nature of computer-mediated communications. In general, the nature of social relationships and interaction in SNSs is not uniform across cultures, yet some behaviors do appear to be shared or be common patterns across the three cultural groups. Social interactions in SNSs, to some extent, reproduce the dominant cultural orientations of the users. Along this logic, the affordances of SNSs as a means of social exchange can partly shape the social practices, but the determining role of technology is also subject to cultural contextuality. In the light of the findings presented here, it would seem that while intercultural communication is theoretically effortless in the online environment, social engagement mediated via SNSs is still culturally loaded and requires careful attention to cultural meaning, norms and nuances.

Given these factors, SNS interface design and development should take into consideration the culturally divergent needs and norms with regard to social interactions therein. For instance, Cyworld in South Korea is said to respond to and reinforce the locals' exclusive relationship orientation and limit the network formation and articulation strictly to mutual agreement. Also, its specification of different groups depending on intimacy satisfies the users' strong privacy and public presentation concerns and allows their vigilant decisions as to the degree of openness and interaction. On the other hand, while recently adopting more privacy and control features, Facebook, originated from the U.S., has been generally liberal and accepting of loose relationship formation.

CONCLUSION

In comprehending the cultural forces examined in this chapter, the HVIC typology proved useful for capturing finer differences across cultures. Future research in the area of computer-mediated intercultural communication should also benefit from the cultural classification and should examine more groups representing different cultures. Another promising avenue for future research lies in the potentially varied effectiveness of diverse social networking platforms for intercultural communication. Moreover, different social networking applications are designed to serve different audiences with specific relational needs. Thus, an empirical assessment their architecture and interface in their ability to facilitate interaction among individuals from diverse cultures would be illuminating.

Another issue for future studies to address is generational gaps in computer-mediated communication. While the study reported in this chapter surveyed college students only, different age groups might use SNSs for different purposes and show dissimilar patterns of social engagement. Future research in this area should thus offer additional insight into intercultural communications via SNSs among the users of different ages. Continued research efforts in this area should also help decipher cultural nuances and disentangle the intricacy of cultural forces and confluence in computer-mediated interactions among individuals around the globe.

REFERENCES

Allik, J., & Realo, A. (2004). Individualism-collectivism and social capital. *Journal of Cross-Cultural Psychology*, *35*, 29–49. doi:10.1177/0022022103260381

Anderson Analytics. (2008). *Blogging increasing in popularity among generation Y*. Retrieved November 20, 2010, from http://www.anderson-analytics.com/index.php?mact=News,cntnt01,detail,0&cntnt01articleid=56&cntnt01origid=47&cntnt01detailtemplate=newsdetail.tpl&cntnt01dateformat=%25m.%25d.%25Y&cntnt01returnid=46

Boase, J. (2008). Personal networks and the personal communication system: Using multiple media to connect. *Information Communication and Society*, *11*, 490–508. doi:10.1080/13691180801999001

Bourdieu, P., & Wacquant, L. (1992). *An invitation to reflexive sociology*. Chicago, IL: University of Chicago Press.

Boyd, D. (2008). Why youth (heart) social network sites: The role of networked publics in teenage social life. In Buckingham, D. (Ed.), *Youth, identity, and digital media* (pp. 119–142). Cambridge, MA: MIT Press.

Boyd, D., & Ellison, N. B. (2007). Social network sites: Definition, history, and scholarship. *Journal of Computer-Mediated Communication*, *13*(1), article 11. Retrieved November 20, 2010, from http://jcmc.indiana.edu/vol13/issue1/boyd.ellison.html

Cardon, P. W., Marshall, B., Norris, D. T., Cho, J., Choi, J., & Cui, L. (2009). Online and offline social ties of social network website users: An exploratory study in eleven societies. *Journal of Computer Information Systems*, *50*, 54–64.

Chen, C. C., Meindl, J. R., & Hunt, R. G. (1997). Testing the effects of vertical and horizontal collectivism: A study of reward allocation preferences in China. *Journal of Cross-Cultural Psychology*, *28*, 44–70. doi:10.1177/0022022197281003

Cho, B., Kwan, U., Gentry, J. W., Jun, S., & Kropp, F. (1999). Cultural values reflected in theme and execution: A comparative study of U.S. and Korean television commercials. *Journal of Advertising*, *28*, 59–73.

CNNIC. (2009). *2009 Chinese social networking service research report*. Retrieved November 20, 2010, from http://www.cnnic.cn/html/Dir/2009/11/11/5721.htm

Donath, J., & Boyd, D. (2004). Public displays of connection. *BT Technology Journal, 22*, 71–82. doi:10.1023/B:BTTJ.0000047585.06264.cc

Ellison, N. B., Steinfield, C., & Lampe, C. (2007). The benefits of Facebook "friends": Social capital and college students' use of online social network sites. *Journal of Computer-Mediated Communication, 12*(4), article 1. Retrieved November 20, 2010, from http://jcmc.indiana.edu/vol12/issue4/ellison.html

Granovetter, M. S. (1973). Strength of weak ties. *American Journal of Sociology, 78*, 1360–1380. doi:10.1086/225469

Granovetter, M. S. (1983). The strength of weak ties: A network theory revisited. *Sociological Theory, 1*, 201–233. doi:10.2307/202051

Gudykunst, W. B., & Ting-Toomey, S. (1988). *Culture and interpersonal communication*. Newbury Park, CA: Sage.

Halavais, A. (2000). National borders on the World Wide Web. *New Media & Society, 1*, 7–28. doi:10.1177/14614440022225689

Hofstede, G. (1980). *Culture's consequences*. Beverly Hills, CA: Sage.

Hofstede, G. (1984). *Culture's consequences: International differences in work-related values*. Beverly Hills, CA: Sage.

Hutchby, I. (2001). Technologies, texts and affordances. *Sociology, 35*, 441–456.

Inside Facebook. (2009). *College students' Facebook use easing up over the summer, while parents logging on in record numbers*. Retrieved November 20, 2010 from http://www.insidefacebook.com/ 2009/07/06/college-students -facebook-use-easing-up-over -the-summer-while-parents-logging -on-in-record-numbers/

Jung, T., Youn, H., & McClung, S. (2007). Motivations and self-presentation strategies on Korean-based "Cyworld" weblog format personal homepages. *Cyberpsychology & Behavior, 10*, 24–31. doi:10.1089/cpb.2006.9996

Kim, K. H., & Yun, H. (2007). Cying for me, cying for us: Relational dialectics in a Korean social network site. *Journal of Computer-Mediated Communication, 13*(1), article 15. Retrieved November 20, 2010, from http://jcmc.indiana.edu/vol13 /issue1/kim.yun.html

Lee, W.-N., & Choi, S. M. (2007). Classifying web users: A cultural value based approach. In St. Amant, K. (Ed.), *Linguistic and cultural online communication issues in the global age* (pp. 45–62). Hershey, PA: Idea Group, Inc. doi:10.4018/978-1-59904-213-8.ch004

Lenhart, A. (2009). Adults and social network websites. *Pew Internet & American Life Project*. Retrieved November 20, 2010, from http://www.pewinternet.org/PPF /r/272/report_display.asp

Lenhart, A., & Madden, M. (2007). *Social networking websites and teens: An overview*. Pew Internet & American Life Project. Retrieved November 20, 2010, from http://www.pewinternet.org

Lewis, C. C., & George, J. F. (2008). Cross-cultural deception in social networking sites and face-to-face communication. *Computers in Human Behavior, 24*, 2945–2964. doi:10.1016/j.chb.2008.05.002

Livingstone, S. (2008). Taking risky opportunities in youth content creation: Teenagers' use of social networking sites for intimacy, privacy and self-expression. *New Media & Society, 10*, 393–411. doi:10.1177/1461444808089415

Meng, Z., & Zuo, M. (2008). Why MSN lost to QQ in China market? Different privacy protection design. *International Journal of Security and Its Applications, 2*, 81–87.

Mills, J., & Clark, M. S. (1982). Exchange and communal relationships. *Review of Personality and Social Psychology, 6*, 91–127.

Nelson, M. R., & Shavitt, S. (2002). Horizontal and vertical individualism and achievement values: A multimethod examination of Denmark and the United States. *Journal of Cross-Cultural Psychology, 33*, 439–458. doi:10.1177/0022022102033005001

Nielsen Online. (2009*). Global faces* and networked *places. A Nielsen report on social networking's new global footprint*. Retrieved November 20, 2010, from http://blog.nielsen.com/nielsenwire /wp-content/uploads/2009/03/nielsen_globalfaces_mar09.pdf

Orgad, S. (2006). The cultural dimensions of online communication: A study of breast cancer patients' Internet spaces. *New Media & Society, 8*, 877–899. doi:10.1177/1461444806069643

Papacharissi, Z. (2009). The virtual geographies of social networks: A comparative analysis of Facebook, LinkedIn and ASmallWorld. *New Media & Society, 11*, 199–220. doi:10.1177/1461444808099577

Putnam, R. D. (2000). *Bowling alone: The collapse and revival of American community*. New York, NY: Simon & Schuster.

Realo, A. J. A., & Greenfield, B. (2008). Radius of trust: Social capital in relation to familism and institutional collectivism. *Journal of Cross-Cultural Psychology, 39*, 447–462. doi:10.1177/0022022108318096

Shavitt, S., Lalwani, A., Zhang, J., & Torelli, C. J. (2006). The horizontal/vertical distinction in cross-cultural consumer research. *Journal of Consumer Psychology, 16*, 325–342. doi:10.1207/s15327663jcp1604_3

Singlis, T. M., Triandis, H. C., Bhawuk, D., & Gelfand, M. J. (1995). Horizontal and vertical dimensions of individualism and collectivism: A theoretical and measurement refinement. *Cross-Cultural Research, 29*, 240–275. doi:10.1177/106939719502900302

Sivadas, E., Bruvold, N. T., & Nelson, M. R. (2008). A reduced version of the horizontal and vertical individualism and collectivism scale: A four-country assessment. *Journal of Business Research, 61*, 201–210. doi:10.1016/j.jbusres.2007.06.016

Slotnik, D. E. (2007, February 26). Too few friends? A website lets you buy some (and they're hot). *New York Times*. Retrieved November 19, 2010, from http://www.nytimes.com/2007/02/26/technology/26fake.html

Thelwall, M. (2008). Social networks, gender, and friending: An analysis of MySpace member profiles. *Journal of the American Society for Information Science and Technology, 59*, 1321–1330. doi:10.1002/asi.20835

Triandis, H. C. (1995). *Individualism and collectivism*. Boulder, CO: Westview.

Triandis, H. C. (2001). Individualism-collectivism and personality. *Journal of Personality, 69*, 907–924. doi:10.1111/1467-6494.696169

Triandis, H. C., & Gelfand, M. J. (1998). Converging measurements of horizontal and vertical individualism and collectivism. *Journal of Personality and Social Psychology, 74*, 118–128. doi:10.1037/0022-3514.74.1.118

Triandis, H. C., & Suh, E. M. (2002). Cultural influences on personality. *Annual Review of Psychology, 53*, 133–160. doi:10.1146/annurev.psych.53.100901.135200

Universal McCann. (2009). *Power to the people: social media tracker wave 4*. Retrieved November 20, 2010, from http://universalmccann.bitecp.com/wave4/Wave4.pdf

Valenzuela, S., Park, N., & Kee, K. F. (2009). Is there social capital in a social network site? Facebook use and college students' life satisfaction, trust, and participation. *Journal of Computer-Mediated Communication, 14*, 875–901. doi:10.1111/j.1083-6101.2009.01474.x

Wellman, B. (1981). Applying network analysis to the study of support. In Gottlieb, B. H. (Ed.), *Social networks and social support* (pp. 171–200). London, UK: Sage.

Wellman, B., Haase, A. Q., Witte, J., & Hampton, K. (2001). Does the Internet increase, decrease, or supplement social capital? Social networks, participation, and community commitment. *The American Behavioral Scientist, 45*, 436–455. doi:10.1177/00027640121957286

Williams, D. (2007). The impact of time online: Social capital and cyberbalkanization. *Cyberpsychology & Behavior, 10*, 398–406. doi:10.1089/cpb.2006.9939

Zhao, S., & Elesh, D. (2008). Copresence as "being with": Social contact in online public domains. *Information Communication and Society, 11*, 565–583. doi:10.1080/13691180801998995

Zywica, J., & Danowski, J. (2008). The faces of Facebookers: Investigating social enhancement and social compensation hypotheses: Predicting Facebook™ and offline popularity from sociability and self-esteem, and mapping the meanings of popularity with semantic networks. *Journal of Computer-Mediated Communication, 14*, 1–34. doi:10.1111/j.1083-6101.2008.01429.x

KEY TERMS AND DEFINITIONS

Bonding Social Capital: Social capital derived from the links between close connections or like-minded people.

Bridging Social Capital: Social capital obtained from the building of loose connections between heterogeneous groups.

Horizontal Collectivism: A cultural orientation characterized by interdependence, unity, group harmony and cooperativeness.

Horizontal Individualism: A cultural orientation that highlights self-government, individuality, and uniqueness.

Social Capital: The sum of the resources, actual or virtual, which result from possessing a durable social network.

Social Network: A social structure of individuals that are connected by various mutual relationships.

Social Networking Site: An online place where a user creates a profile and builds a personal network with other users.

Social Tie: Information and/or emotion-carrying connection between people.

Strong Tie: Close relationships such as friends and families.

Vertical Individualism: A cultural orientation that stresses personal achievement, eminence and competition.

Vertical Collectivism: A cultural orientation that underscores dutifulness and adherence to social norms and hierarchy.

Weak Tie: Loose relationships such as mere acquaintances.

Chapter 2

e–Matchmaker, e–Matchmaker, Make Me a Match:
Indian Matrimonial Services in the Internet Age

Archana Krishnan
University of Connecticut, USA

ABSTRACT

Indians use the Internet for a host of applications, and some of these uses are culture-specific, like formalized matrimonial searches. This chapter examines the growth of matrimonial websites in India and explicates how Indians have adopted new Web technologies to preserve the traditional hegemony of arranged marriages. This technology has helped older generations of Indians become a part of the Web revolution and has allowed newer generations to adhere to traditional cultural norms on more progressive terms. Some specific items reviewed in relation to this development are the adaptation of arranged marriages to new technology, the growth of matrimonial websites, the success of such sites in niche groups, and the impact of these sites on Indian cultural norms.

INTRODUCTION

The proliferation of the Internet has been meteoric even by conservative standards. Several developing nations are taking advantage of new communication technologies to propel themselves into the center of this global revolution. One country that is successfully riding the Internet wave is India. Its adoption of the Internet has been slow but steady, and the number of Internet users in India has grown from less than 2 million users

in 1998 to over 80 million users (and growing) today – this factor translates to a whopping 1,500% penetration rate in the last decade (Internet World Stats, 2009). Today, Indians use the Internet for a host of common applications including email and instant messaging, job searches, online banking, shopping etc. They also use the Internet for certain culture-specific applications such as formalized online matrimonial searches (Internet & Mobile Association of India, 2008).

Within the cultural context of India, online matrimonial searches are conducted through matrimonial websites that are really a variation

DOI: 10.4018/978-1-60960-833-0.ch002

of dating sites. The main difference is that these matrimonial websites focus on marriage rather than dating. Users of these sites upload their information, pictures, and partner preferences onto a searchable database maintained by the Website's owner, and individuals can then search this database via customized criteria like nationality, age, gender, religion, caste, and geographic location. These online "life-partner portals" are the new wave of an age-old Indian tradition of arranged marriages – marriages where alliances are initiated by family members and bound by cultural, social, and ethnic conventions.

India has a long and continuing history of traditions, some of which have transcended centuries of cultural evolution; the practice of "arranging" marriages is one such tradition. With the innovation of technology, the spread of globalization, and the breakdown of large joint family systems, Indians are now part of the global village – a world where pizzas, burgers, denim, and rock music are as integral a part of the landscape as they are for Americans, Europeans, and other Asians. Today's Indians, thus, are in the midst of what can really be described as a homogenization of culture. It should be noted, however, that this "e-technologization" of age-old traditional systems has been more drastic for urban, educated Indians and that a large majority of the Indian population still continues to live a thread-bare existence with irregular access to nutritious food, clean drinking water, electricity, and other basic amenities (Guha, 2007). Despite these disparities, the need to conform to traditional marital practices is a trait that that can be found in most Indian communities.

In this chapter, the author examines how new communication technologies have had a profound effect on the culture of arranged marriages. To do so, the author has divided the chapter into five distinct sections. The first section provides a review of the history of arranged marriages in India and is followed by a discussion on the evolution of the matrimonial matchmaker in Indian society.

The second section examines the growth of the online matrimonial industry. The purpose of these sections is to introduce the reader to the cultural significance and proliferation of arranged marriages in India and help the reader comprehend the importance of India's online matrimonial industry. The third section presents a dialectical perspective concerning online matrimonial services. The fourth section, in turn, discusses the popularity of Indian matrimonial websites in niche groups, especially diasporic Indians and the social effects of matrimonial websites. The fifth and final section then examines two different theoretical perspectives in order to explain the adoption of Indian online matrimonial services.

Overall, the purpose of the chapter is to provide readers with a thorough understanding of the use of new media technology in preserving the tradition of arranged marriages in India. The chapter also offers various theoretical explanations for the effects of technology on culture and society. On a more abstract level, the chapter will allow readers to comprehend the dialectical relationship of social and technological determinism – the twin arguments of whether humans shape technology or are shaped by it. By exploring this facet of cyberspace, individuals can gain a deeper understanding of cultural processes at work and the role of technology in maintaining cultural norms.

BACKGROUND

History of Arranged Marriage in India

In India, marriage is seen not just as a social and physical bond, but also as a religious, familial and, most importantly, a spiritual bond. The Hindu scriptures written between 200 B.C. and 900 A.D. put forth four religious ways of acquiring a wife (Gupta, 1979) – and these practices have scarcely changed over centuries. Socially, marriage alliances helped forge kinship ties between families within castes and sub-castes, and thus allowed class systems to evolve (Gupta, 1979; Ross, 1961; Uberoi, 2005). It is often said that marriage in India is a joining of two families; India has a joint family system that stresses the importance of combining two families instead of focusing on a nuclear family between spouses (Rao & Rao, 1982).

The religious importance of marriage in Indian society can be seen by Bhat and Hali's (1999) observation that kanyadaan, or the giving of one's daughter in marriage, was considered the greatest sacrifice a man could make. Also, because people in ancient times married very young, it made sense for the parents to make the decision to choose their children's life partner. The decisions of the elders also were considered significant because of the newly-wed couple's lack of physical or psychological resources (Bhagat, 2002). With the interplay of so many dimensions, it is easy to see why the decision to marry in India is not taken lightly and is thus "arranged" through the participation of family elders. According to Prakasa and Rao (1979), arranged marriages have the following effects:

- They help maintain the social stratification system
- They give parents control over family members
- They enhance the chance to preserve the ancestral line
- They allow for the consolidation and extension of family property

Within this context, it is not uncommon for friends and business partners to strengthen their relationships by arranging marriages between their respective children.

Although arranged marriages were not uncommon in Roman, Greek, and other early civilizations, the trend eventually faded as industrialization and urbanization took over. In India, however, this ancient practice has prevailed over centuries of cultural invasions by the Muslims, French, Portuguese, and eventually the British (Guha, 2007). Interestingly, despite imbibing several customs from the invading cultures, the custom of arranged marriages were virtually untouched. In fact, in Muslim, Parsi, and Anglo-Indian communities today, it is not unusual to see the the prevalence of arranged marriages.

Indians in the 21st century, regardless of caste, religion and social class, still have a somewhat conservative attitude towards marriage compared to most Western societies which have encouraged "experimentation towards domestic arrangements" (Uberoi, 1993, p. 438). By contrast, the only experimentation in India has been to expand the typology of arranged marriages. Apart from the traditional arranged marriage in which parents or family elders make key decisions, today, most urban Indians prefer an arranged marriage that gives them more control in the selection process. In some cases, courtship is also allowed, although this usually means a shorter engagement period (to avoid chances of rejection during the courtship period).

Another entry to the marriage typology is the phenomenon known as "love marriage" or "free-choice marriage." The subject of countless Indian books and movies, love marriages are the equivalent of Western-style courtship and marriage, where the marital partners initiate the relationship. Long considered taboo, love and free-choice marriages are fast becoming a part of mainstream culture, especially in educated and highly urbanized families. Despite the rise of such marriages, Amar (2008) contends that love marriages still account for an insignificant minority of marriages in India. (The next section of this chapter will examine how matrimonial websites bridge the gap between proponents of arranged marriages and advocates of love marriages.)

Several studies have examined the mate and marriage preferences of Indians across the decades

(Kurian, 1961; Prakasa & Rao, 1979; Ross, 1961; Zaidi & Shuraydi, 2002). The results of these studies suggest more young Indians would like to have their say in choosing their partner – albeit with the approval of the parents. This trend has become more apparent in the past decade and is especially the case among educated families in urban areas (Zaidi & Shuraydi, 2002). Thus, it seems that although the expectations associated with the process have gradually become more open (i.e., most people insist on interacting, meeting or even courting before marriage), the one thing that is constant is the need for parental approval and parental involvement in the entire process (Prakasa & Rao, 1979). There are, however, some variables that seem to be better predictors of attitudes to freedom of choice in marital partner choice, such as level of education and urban residency (Gore, 1969; Zaidi & Shuraydi, 2002).

Due to rapid urbanization in India and a growing emphasis for higher education, it is possible to see marked changes even across subsequent generations of Indians. The author can offer a personal familial example to illustrate this concept. The author's grandparents' alliance was arranged solely by the family patriarchs. The marriage of the author's parents, in turn, was initiated by the family elders, but was approved by both of the author's parents. The author and her husband, by contrast, initiated their relationship themselves and later received approval from both sets of parents. In all of these cases, and regardless of the manner of the alliance, one role that has remained constant in the process over time is that of the matchmaker.

The Evolution of the Matchmaker

One cannot discuss the topic of arranged marriages in India without discussing the quintessential role of the "matchmaker" in the process. In traditional arranged marriages, once the son or the daughter attains marriageable age, parents – along with family elders, friends, and kinspersons – scout for potential partners for the child. Because of

religious conventions dictating specific caste, sub-caste, and class preferences (Inden, 1976), most marriage alliances required the support of a wide social network. This network consisted of aunts, uncles, family friends, neighbors etc. As geographical distances grew, this practice eventually gave way to the rise of marriage brokers – professional matchmakers who arranged alliances for a fee and went door-to-door with bunches of customer profiles (Pepper, 2007). What was once "an interpersonal and word-of-mouth activity" (Chatterjee, 2007, p. 1) soon became a successful moneymaking operation. Individual matchmakers gave way to marriage bureaus that cropped up all over India; these bureaus were brick and mortar places with physical databases of prospective brides and grooms. Marriage bureaus offered parents customized attention, and they acted as consultants who advised prospective suitors on profile enhancement, selection criteria, and other marriage matters (Kamat, 2005).

The evolution of the matchmaker continued with the advent of the print media, which introduced the concept of matrimonial advertisements. These advertisements, in turn, broadened the scope of prospective alliances to a larger geographical area (Jana, 2000). Soon, several newspapers and magazines had thick classified sections that focused exclusively on prospective brides and grooms. Today, a typical matrimonial advertisement tries to use a select few words to capture the complex preferences for an Indian alliance and to do so without sounding fastidious. As Kalyanam (2004) notes, "the wording of the matrimonial ads tends to be sober and direct" (p. 34), and these ads tend to list a number of attributes including age, education, salary, physical characteristics (height, weight, complexion), religion, community, personality attributes, and interests. It is also not uncommon to see parents placing advertisements on behalf of their children. Figure 1 shows examples of typical print advertisements that might appear in a leading daily newspaper.

Figure 1. Examples of typical print matrimonial advertisements. (These items are examples, and the name and contact information provided here are fictional.)

> MADHWA GHANDI KAMTHAN 1978/165 M.Sc M.Phil B.Ed school teacher, seeks employed / unemployed any Brahmin bride. Box No.HB-123, XYZ.
>
> HINDI SPEAKING UP Dhobi Parents Seek Suit Groom well Emp from Decent Family for Girl BE, MBA, 26y/165 Wheat Brown Complexion Prof Emp. Ph.: 000-555-12312. Correspond XXXX, FFF, FFF, Ch – 99

With the hastening of technological innovation, the matchmaker has finally transitioned to the Internet (Hein, 2004; Tickoo, 2006). Web-based matrimonial services, in fact, came at a fitting time for India's new generation, and they coincided with two major events that set the stage for the success of matrimonial websites. First, both cable television and several international companies entered India as a result of India's globalization policies in the 1990s (Kulkarni, 2005), and these media brought about a stark change in people's attitudes and behaviors. Second, because of Indian software engineers' role in the Information Technology revolution and Silicon Valley, the Internet was readily adopted by both diasporic Indians living overseas and those living back in India (Sharma, 2006). Although many urban Indians were now independent and successful, their customs, traditions and core values were still salient to them. Matrimonial websites arrived at an opportune time to address these factors. These sites allowed young Indians and their parents to play an equal part in choosing marriage partners while keeping each other's sensibilities at heart. As Sharma (2006) explains, within this context, the Internet can be viewed as being juxtaposed with parental/communal choosing as a way to meet a spouse. The traditional arrangement of marriage by the bride/groom's parents has, in turn, evolved considerably. Today, parents and social circles are being replaced by formal communication channels. Thus, the growth of media outlets (especially the World Wide Web) has forever changed the notion of the matchmaker as a single entity.

THE GROWTH OF ONLINE MATRIMONIAL WEBSITES

Today, the success of Indian matrimonial websites is staggering even by conservative standards. The online matrimony business in India is currently worth approximately 1 billion rupees (the equivalent of $21 million USD) with 7 million active users who subscribe to matrimonial Websites (Internet & Mobile Association of India, 2008). Additionally, every month, some 150,000 new users register with these sites (Philip, 2005). The matrimonial Websites now number in the hundreds, but the two most prolific are Shaadi. com with 9 million users and Bharathmatrimony. com with 7.5 million users (Goel, 2006). Other than these two, there are other successful sites like JeevanSaathi.com, Allindiamatrimony.com, A1im.com, and Indianmarriages.com, Rediffmatchmaker.com, and each of these sites is trying to grab a piece of India's growing matrimonial services market with several daily newspapers already having their own online versions of matrimonial advertisements (Philip, 2005). As Vivek Khare, business head of Jeevansaathi.com observes, "Nearly 20 million Indians get married every year and if we get even 2% of this market, it's a profitable business" (Ramalingam & Nair, 2005). Recognizing the success of online matrimonial services, Yahoo, Inc. is investing millions in Bharathmatrimony.com (Tickoo, 2006). In fact, it is hard to miss the advertisements for Bharathmatrimony.com on Yahoomail.com and other Yahoo sister sites.

Figure 2. Homepage of a leading matrimonial Website. (© bharatmatrimony.com. Used with permission.)

The popularity of matrimonial websites can be linked to savings in time and cost along with the factor of convenience. With the word-of-mouth matchmaking process and print advertisements, the entire process of narrowing a partner might take anywhere from several months to a couple of years (Philip, 2005). Registering on a matrimonial website is usually free with basic membership, and comprehensive memberships come with extra benefits such as email alerts and horoscope matching along with a high degree of interactivity. The search engines on these websites are intricate, and searching for a prospective partner can be as simple or as elaborate as the user wants. Most sites also have sub-sites that cater to different ethnic segments within India. For example, Bharatmatrimony.com has fifteen separate tabs labeled "Tamil," "Urdu," "Assamese," "Bengali," etc. (different communities). Thus, users can directly choose a tab and search. In fact, Bharath-matrimony.com is actually an umbrella site of the fifteen regional sites like Tamilmatrimony.com, Telugumatrimony.com, Bengalimatrimony.com, etc. (See Figure 2.)

The search criteria on these sites are quite complex, and alliances might be forged on the basis of matching horoscopes, preference for certain physical attributes, and even dietary constraints. But, for the true followers of India's pervasive caste system, there is the "Advanced Search" option that allows users to specify a particular community, caste, sub-caste, and lineage in order to find the ideal candidate. The intricacies of such search engines, however, do not end here. Rather, searches can also be done by typing a set of words into a text box to create personalized search criteria. But Bharatmatrimony.com's latest (and quite possibly most superficial) search tool is the facial tool. This item allows individuals to search for a prospective partner by specifying a facial type. To aid in this search, a set of face (based on the face structures of popular Indian movie stars) types is provided.

As is the case with most matrimonial websites, basic memberships in Bharatmatrimony. com and its fiercest competitor, Shaadi.com, are free. However, the lure of the premium packages that can run up to $50 for one year is strong, for such packages can offer personalized matchmaking and horoscope matching services along with profile highlights and top placement guarantees. Additionally, most of these Websites include "success stories" showcasing customers, who have been successfully matched through the site. In fact, one leading matrimonial website boasts of nearly 500,000 such success stories (Philip, 2005). Some Websites, such as Shaadi.com, also offer customers the "Shaadi Seal" to indicate that personal information listed on the site has been authenticated by the company.

Competition in this market is fierce as companies try to outbid each other in order to gain a sizeable share in the market. Shaadi.com, for example, boasts of an ISO 9001:2000 certification, whereas Bharatmatrimony.com touts its Limca Record for having facilitated the largest number marriages online. More recently, these websites have begun to foray into the same brick and mortar shops they once replaced. This new initiative started by the leading Indian matrimonial websites has been envisioned as a network of physical centers across India, and such centers would offer services ranging from matchmaking to wedding planning (Pepper, 2007; Ramalingam & Nair, 2005). In a way, Indians are seeing the rebirth of traditional matchmaking aided by the power of new technologies. Moreover, a trend that started with India's educated and urban elite is now trickling down to the masses. Today, Indians who have never used a computer can go to these matrimony franchises and access the vast databases of prospective alliances.

PRESERVING CULTURAL NORMS VERSUS CULTURAL LIBERALIZATION

The success of matrimonial websites in India can be measured by their expeditious growth. In just over a decade, the online matchmaking market has garnered over 10% of the $400 million matchmaking service industry in India (Amar, 2008). This increase has primarily been due to the myriad of advantages matrimonial websites offer. They are fast, convenient, and offer greater access to potential partners across various geographical regions when compared to old-fashioned marriage brokers or offline social networks.

Moreover, they allow for new a degree of inter-generational connectedness related to the marriage process. For the first time, both parents and children are, on a relatively large scale, taking part in the marriage process together. Although parents usually take the initiative of creating profiles for their children, everybody in the family has access to the account. Joint decisions are made while short-listing and contacting interested candidates. Emails may be exchanged and phone calls and enquiries made. Within this system, only when everything checks out and both parties show interest is face-to-face contact even entertained. Because screening in the online process happens on multiple levels and contact is usually restricted to CMC (Computer-mediated Communication), the trauma of being rejected is not as intense as it often is in face-to-face situations (Philip, 2005). Similarly, it is less taxing to browse through several online profiles than to physically accept or reject alliances offline. Thus, despite the drastic change in medium, Indians have been able to hang on to the cultural norms that dictate marriages in India.

Individuals can also view matrimonial websites through the lens of cultural hegemony, especially because of the overt presence of reinforcing messages about caste preferences and physical attributes. In an interesting study by Jha and Adelman (2009), the authors' content analysis of profiles posted on matrimonial websites revealed that men were more likely than women to specify physical attributes such as skin color, and when men did specify this attribute, they generally seemed to prefer prospective brides who were lighter-complexioned than they were. Furthermore, the "success stories" profiled on the websites show couples who are often predominantly light-skinned. According to Jha and Adelman (2009), the websites' prevalent use of light-skinned brides in "successful" marriages reinforces the invalidation of women with darker skin. Thus, the websites do not seem to challenge the dominion of Indian mentalities about culture and tradition. Rather, they appear to fortify them by implementing search criteria that include every possible trait. Ironically, the advantage of having millions of profiles a click away has resulted in the illusion of an infinite number of mate choices, thereby allowing people to place undue importance on superficial qualities.

The other side of the dialectical argument is the view that matrimonial websites have become a tool of liberalization. Firstly, they are popular with those who wish to have a "love-marriage" or choose their partners without any interference from the family (Goel, 2006). Before online matrimonial services, these individuals would have had limited choices for marriage partners. Since love-marriages were infrequent in the past (and in some places still are), it was difficult to find a partner who also was willing to engage in such an alliance (Amar, 2008). The advent of matrimonial websites has, however, opened up options for proponents of love-marriages. In sum, by liberating the marriage space, matrimonial websites have garnered acceptance from Indians with disparate views on partner-selection. Thus, while matchmaking has survived centuries of evolution and while the medium has altered, the objective has not. As a result, today's matrimonial websites can be seen both as a tool for preserving cultural norms while also adding a degree of freedom to the process, for parents' roles in the

arranged marriage process have not been compromised. Rather, the children's role has been amplified. Despite the conflicting arguments over norm-preservation and cultural liberalization, the one aspect of matrimonial websites that cannot be ignored is their role in expanding the marriage space for niche groups.

NICHE GROUPS

The broad base offered by a web-mediated marriage portal not only entails access by all groups, big and small, but also offers significant advantage to niche groups such as NRIs (Non-Resident Indians) or diasporic Indians (Indians who have migrated to other countries), divorcees, and widows/widowers. Interestingly, matrimonial websites were initially targeted to the NRI community, and only after its success there, did the focus of these sites start to shift to the mainstream community in India (Kapoor, 2003; Philip, 2005). NRIs are a select group of people who make up a significant majority (approximately 35%) of matrimonial service users (Ramalingam & Nair, 2005). This statistic is hardly surprising since diasporic Indians have been shown to be active users of the Internet (Jana, 2000). Matrimonial websites are useful to NRIs because of their ability to bridge geographical distances – it is possible for these diasporic Indians to seek marriage alliances with the constant involvement of their families throughout the process.

Matrimonial websites seem to strike a compromise between ancient Indian social traditions and the contemporary attitudes of many NRIs. In an age where social networks are not as localized as they used to be, the Internet has become a useful tool to arrange marriages in the absence of relatives or paid matchmakers. This situation is especially true of NRIs who operate outside the normal social network, but who still want to avail themselves of a traditional arranged marriage (Kapoor, 2003).

According to Sharma (2006), disaporic Indians have always used new ways of connecting with potential marriage partners, and matrimonial websites just happen to be the latest tool. Some of the earliest matrimonial websites were, in fact, started by enterprising NRIs who understood the need for professional matchmaking services. There are now hundreds of websites that focus only on the NRI community, such as Internetmatrimonials.com, Imilap.com, Indianmarriages.com and Suitablematch.com. Matrimonial Websites are also a way for diasporic Indians to maintain their identity (Sharma, 2006). For NRIs who may have always referred to themselves as "Indian" or "South Asian," matrimonial Websites are a medium to establish their identity as per their regional, ethnic, and linguistic uniqueness. So they may refer to themselves as "Punjabi," "Palakkad Brahmin," etc. in their profiles in order to establish a sense of cultural identity. As Sharma eloquently states, these NRI men and women use matrimonial Websites "to produce Indian identities, create diasporic communities, and reach home 'virtually'" (p. 248).

Matrimonial websites can also be seen as liberators for other niche groups, some of which are not as glamorous as the NRI community. For people who have been divorced or widowed and are looking to marry again, matrimonial websites offer the privacy and choice that regular socially-based alternatives cannot. With the changing Indian demographic, divorce and remarriage are on the rise, and there is a vacuum for sites catering to these groups (Philip, 2005). Although a few exclusive websites exist for this community (e.g., Garamchai.com/BridesForDivorcees.htm and Garamchai.com/BridegroomsForDivorcees.htm), most matrimonial websites have customized searches that make it easier for members to find divorced or widowed singles if they are looking for them (Babu, 2005).

Another group that has benefited from the opening up of matchmaking in cyberspace is the Indian gay and lesbian community. With the de-criminalization of Section 377 of the Indian Penal Code (legislation that declared homosexuality to be a criminal offense) in 2009, the Indian gay and lesbian community has moved a small but significant step closer to social acceptance. The annulment of Section 377 has granted India's gay and lesbian community the freedom to actively and publicly search for potential partners through matrimonial sites. Currently, there is one website – Gaydate.in – that offers gay Indians the option and the privacy to search for partners. For these different niche communities, such progress means that people who feel like social outcasts can privately look for suitable partners without having the involvement of their communities or families. At the same time, the inclusion of these previously invisible groups into traditional cyberspace can help them become more included in mainstream society.

THEORETICAL PERSPECTIVES

It is essential to view the use of online matrimonial websites from a theoretical perspective instead of just viewing it as a phenomenon. Theory allows us to explain and predict social phenomenon with an eye to extend the theory, thus creating a cyclical process. The two theories discussed in this section come from primarily the field of media studies, and here they are used in conjunction with the examination of social media (i.e., online matrimonial services).

Uses and Gratifications Approach

The uses and gratification theory (also known as U&G theory) seeks to explain media use and the satisfactions derived from them in terms of the motives and self-perceived needs of audience members. This perspective has been suggested as an effective method for studying various media motives including the examination of what motivates consumers to shop online (Charney &

Greenberg, 2003; Lin, 1998). The assumptions outlined in uses and gratification theory are that

- The audience is active, and there is a logical explanation for audience behavior and formation
- The audience member initiates the process of selection and use of the media
- The media compete with other forms of communication for uses and needs such as interpersonal interaction
- People are self-aware and logical enough to be able to report their interests and motives (Katz, Blumler, Gurevitch, 1974)

These factors mean that the uses and gratifications approach can serve as an appropriate mechanism for explaining Internet use as it does not focus on one particular type of media, but rather on which media fulfills the needs of an individual (Katz et al., 1974).

According to the assumptions of the uses and gratifications theory, available media compete with each other to satisfy individual needs. This concept suggests that the Internet not only competes with other media for audience gratification, but it also plays host to internal rivalry, with different options within the Internet vying for user attention. This situation is true when discussing matrimonial websites, for there are alternative matchmaking services that vie for users' attention. Parents and marriageable Indians, for example, actively seek information about prospective alliances online. (This behavior also ties in with the assumptions of the uses and gratifications approach.)

Studies examining the gratifications associated with Internet use have found that need for information, socialization, entertainment, communication, and social escapism are also important motivating factors for using the Internet (Korgaonkar & Wolin, 1999; Charney & Greenberg, 2003). The author knows of no academic studies to date that

have been published on a uses and gratifications approach to using matrimonial websites, but one may hypothesize that need for information and social adherence may predict use of these websites. Demographic variables such as age, gender, and education have also been found to be significantly associated with Internet use (Korgaonkar and Wolin, 1999). So, because level of education and urban dwelling have already been shown to be significant predictors of freedom of choice in the marital partner selection process (Zaidi & Shuraydi, 2002), it can be hypothesized that these variables will also be related to the use of matrimonial Websites.

Diffusion of Innovation

The Diffusion of Innovations theory is another approach for looking at the characteristics and process in which the use of online matrimonial services operate. According to this approach, "diffusion" can be defined as the *"process by which (1) an innovation (2) is communicated through certain channels (3) over time (4) among the member of a social system"* (Rogers, 2003, p. 11). When discussing matrimonial websites in India, the innovation is not just the website/technology, but the practice of online matchmaking as well. Communication channels are the means by which information about an innovation is passed to potential adopters. In general, two forms of channels – interpersonal and mass media – are seen as important to the diffusion of an innovation. In the case of matrimonial websites, the positive experience of users added to the media attention can be shown as having aided diffusion (Goel, 2006). The third element, as noted in the preceding quotation, is time – a concept that refers to the time between knowledge of an innovation and its adoption. The diffusion of an innovation is also dependent on the structure of a social system (item four in the previous quoatoin) and the people in it because they can either help or hinder the diffusion process. Matrimonial websites can be viewed as successful because of their quick diffusion based on widespread acceptance by Indians (both within and outside of India) as a whole (Amar, 2008; Philip, 2005).

Adoption of an innovation largely depends on the innovation's attributes – relative advantage, compatibility, complexity (the degree to which an innovation is easy to understand and use), trialability (the degree to which an innovation can be adopted on a small scale and limited basis), and observability (the degree to which the results of an innovation are visible to others in the social system). With regard to matrimonial websites, we can summarize its success in terms of adoption according to the above attributes. To begin, matrimonial websites have been shown to be faster and more convenient to use (have a relative advantage) as compared to traditional matchmaking services (Kapoor, 2003). It can also be argued that educated people might be able to better grasp the complexities of an innovation, and this argument is supported by that fact that matrimonial websites were popular with educated and urbanized users first before diffusing into mainstream society (Ramalingam & Nair, 2005). Moreover, matrimonial websites were designed such that basic memberships were free and thus allowed one to evaluate and observe the results (trialability and observability). Also since marriages are a vociferous part of Indian society, initial successes through word-of-mouth and positive reviews (again, trialability and observability) helped diffuse the technology (Chatterjee, 2007).

The diffusion model takes into consideration both the rate of adoption and the effect of adoption. The diffusion of any innovation or technology follows an S-shaped curve when plotted on a cumulative basis with regard to time. The curve depends on the rate at which individuals accept the innovation. Rogers (2003) categorizes adopters into five groups based on the time it takes them to adopt an innovation – innovators,

early adopters, early majority, late majority and laggards. Research has shown that there is a positive relationship between early adoption and income, level of education, and high status in a society (Atkin, 1993; Atkin & LaRose, 1994; Rogers, 2003; Lin, 1998). Because the adoption of an innovation requires high cost and receptivity to change, it is no surprise that in the case of matrimonial Websites, innovators tended to be urbanized, educated, young Indians (especially NRIs) who were more aware of the technology and more receptive to change.

CONCLUSION

The success of matrimonial websites in India represents an amalgamation of Indian cultural norms and web technology. This situation also illustrates the way in which the Internet has shaped and reshaped traditional forms of finding marriage partners. In a way, the Internet is not only allowing this part of Indian culture to evolve, but is also sustaining and strengthening it. As Sharma (2006) points out, this dialectical perspective is different from one that shows Internet use to be influenced by the Westernized world. Matrimonial websites have shown to be successful even among older patrons (like parents and family elders) because they respect the process of arranging marriages while at the same time accommodating the needs of the younger generations (Pepper, 2007). While there has been a marked change in attitudes towards more autonomous decisions in partner-selection, the family's influence is undeniable for most Indians (Chatterjee, 2007). The Internet has thus helped restructure the approach of finding a marital partner and still keeping the core purpose unchanged. Rather than being based on familiarity and family relationships, the web-based portal opens a plethora of options for the bride and groom-to be.

A point of comparison for matrimonial websites are Western-style dating/matchmaking websites that are worth somewhere in the range of a half a billion dollars (Hein, 2004). Some of the major players like eHarmony.com and Match.com seem to be success stories because these websites focus on individuals looking for serious long-term relationships instead of focusing on a generic audience (Smith, 2005). By taking a serious approach to matchmaking, these Western dating websites can ironically be seen as their version of matrimonial websites (it should be noted, however, that in these websites, success is measured by obtaining a match and not necessarily a marriage proposal). In terms of niche groups, matrimonial websites can be seen as attempting to integrate them into mainstream society. They have liberated this space for NRIs who have had to endure lengthy cross-continental matrimonial searches (Jana, 2000). With the growing legal and social acceptance of the gay and lesbian fraternity in India, it will be interesting to see how matrimonial websites which are exclusively heterosexual in their coupling, adapt to this new social trend.

The literature on the social effects of CMC in the Indian context is limited. Indeed, the current research on Indian matrimonial websites is lacking. The objective of this chapter was to shed light on this recent phenomenon with a view to encourage inquiry. The contentions made in here are critical in nature; however, a quantitative model must be applied in order to explicate the phenomenon of the effects of matrimonial websites on society and peoples' attitudes towards marriage. The importance of online matrimonial services for urbanized and diasporic Indians cannot be underestimated. They are seen as being at a providential juncture – they are compatible with the traditional notion of partner selection, but they are equally compatible with more contemporary notions with the individuals taking an active role (Chatterjee, 2007). Indeed, these Websites are a unifying platform for individuals with both individualistic and collectivistic ideologies.

REFERENCES

Amar, S. (2008, June 29). *India's Internet matchmakers see potential boom.* Retrieved July 6, 2010, from www.internetevolution.com/ author. asp?section _id=687&doc_id=160162

Atkin, D. (1993). Adoption of cable amidst a multimedia environment. *Telematics and Informatics, 10*, 51–58. doi:10.1016/0736-5853(93)90017-X

Atkin, D., & Larose, R. (1994). Profiling call-in poll users. *Journal of Broadcasting & Electronic Media, 38*, 217–227.

Babu, M. (2005). *The business of online matchmaking.* Retrieved March 10, 2007, from http://www.garamchai.com/ mohan/ITP05Apr04.htm

Bhagat, R. B. (2002). *Early marriages in India: A socio-geographical study.* New Delhi, India: Rajat Publications.

Bhat, P. N. M., & Halli, S. S. (1999). Demography of brideprice and dowry: Causes and consequences of the Indian marriage squeeze. *Population Studies, 53*(2), 129–148. doi:10.1080/00324720308079

Blumler, J. G., & Katz, E. (1974). *The uses of mass communications: Current perspectives on gratifications research.* Beverly Hills, CA: Sage.

Charney, T., & Greenberg, B. S. (2003). Uses and gratifications of the Internet. In Lin, C. A., & Atkin, D. J. (Eds.), *Communication technology and society: Audience adoptions and uses* (pp. 379–409). New Jersey: Hampton Press, Inc.

Chatterjee, J. S. (2007). *The Internet as matchmaker: A study of why young Indians are seeking marriage alliances online.* Paper presented at the annual meeting of the International Communication Association, San Francisco, CA.

Goel. (2006, November 2). Online marriages are a runaway success. *Knight Rider Tribune Business News,* 1.

Gore, M. S. (1969). *Urbanization and family change*. Bombay, India: Popular Prakash.

Guha, R. (2007). *India after Gandhi: The history of the world's largest democracy*. New York, NY: Ecco.

Gupta, G. R. (1979). Love, arranged marriage and the Indian social structure. In Kurian, G. (Ed.), *Cross-cultural perspectives of mate-selection and marriage* (pp. 11–32). Connecticut: Greenwood Press.

Hein, K. (2004, November 29). Matchmaker e-Harmony makes note of successes. *Brandweek New York, 45*(43), 13.

Inden, R. B. (1976). *Marriage and rank in Bengali culture: A history of caste and clan in middle period Bengal*. Berkeley, CA: University of California Press.

Internet & Mobile Association of India. (2008). *Website*. Retrieved November 23, 2009, from http://www.iamai.in/

Internet World Stats. (2009). *Top 20*. Retrieved November 25, 2009, from http://www.internet-worldstats.com /top20.html

Jana, R. (2000, August 17). Arranged marriages, minus the parents [Electronic version]. *New York Times*. Retrieved September 1, 2009, from http://tech2.nytimes.com/mem /technology/techreview. html? res=940CE7DA163EF934 A2575B-C0A9669C8B63

Jha, S., & Adelman, M. (2009). Looking for love in all the white places: A study of skin color preferences on Indian matrimonial and mate-seeking websites. *Studies in South Asian Film and Media, 1*(1), 65–83. doi:10.1386/safm.1.1.65_1

Kalyanam, C. (2004). *Seeking an alliance: A psychiatrist's guide to the Indian matrimonial process in America*. Bloomington, IN: iUniverse.

Kamat, V. (2005). *India's arranged marriages*. Retrieved from http://www.kamat.com/indica/culture/sub-cultures/ arranged_marriage.htm

Kapoor, G. (2003). *Partners online*. Retrieved from http://www.rediff.com/netguide /2003/apr/17nri.htm

Katz, E., Blumler, J. G., & Gurevitch, M. (1974). Ulilization of mass communication by the individual. In Blumler, J. G., & Katz, E. (Eds.), *The uses of mass communications: Current perspectives on gratifications research* (pp. 19–32). Beverly Hills, CA: Sage.

Korgaonkar, P. K., & Wolin, L. D. (1999). A multivariate analysis of Web usage. *Journal of Advertising Research, 39*(2), 53–68.

Kulkarni, K. G. (2005). *Effect of globalization on India's economic growth*. Paper presented in the Oxford Roundtable Conference. Oxford University, UK.

Kurian, G. (1961). *The Indian family in transition: A case study of Kerala Syrian Christians*. The Hague, the Netherlands: Mouton and Company.

Lin, C. A. (1998). Exploring personal computer adoption dynamics. *Journal of Broadcasting & Electronic Media, 42*, 95–112.

Pepper, D. (2007, March). Matchmaking Indian-style. *Fortune, 155*(5), 14.

Philip, A. (2005, October 17). *Getting married the snappy, global way*. Indian Express. Retrieved October 18, 2005, from http://www.expressindia.com/ fullstory.php?newsid= 56735&pn=0

Prakasa, V. V., & Rao, V. N. (1979). Arranged marriages: An assessment of the attitudes of the college students in India. In Kurian, G. (Ed.), *Cross-cultural perspectives of mate-selection and marriage* (pp. 11–32). Connecticut: Greenwood Press.

Ramalingam, A., & Nair, S. (2005). Swayamvar in mouse mode: Matrimonials get an e-twist [Electronic version]. *The Financial Express*. Retrieved September 1, 2005, from http://www.financialexpress.com/ fe_full_story.php?content_id=82474

Rao, V. V. P., & Rao, V. N. (1982). *Marriage, the family, and women in India*. Columbia, MO: South Asia Books.

Rogers, E. M. (2003). *Diffusion of innovations* (5th ed.). New York, NY: Free Press.

Ross, A. D. (1961). *The Hindu family in its urban setting*. Toronto, Canada: University of Toronto Press.

Sharma, A. (2006). *Girl seeks suitable boy: Indian marriage dot com*. Ph.D. dissertation, University of Toronto, Canada. Retrieved January 22, 2010, from Dissertations & Theses: Full Text.

Smith, A. D. (2005). Exploring online dating and customer relationship management. *Online Information Review, 29*(1), 18-33. Emerald Group Publishing Limited. Retrieved September 18, 2005, from http://www.emeraldinsight.com/ Insight/viewContentItem.do? contentType=Article&contentId =1464923

Tickoo, U. (2006, August). *Yahoo! Inc. invests in Indian marriage portal*. Retrieved March 17, 2007, from http://www.thebizofcoding.com/ 2006/08/yahoo-inc-invests-in-indian-ma/

Uberoi, P. (Ed.). (2005). *Family, kinship and marriage in India*. Oxford University Press.

Zaidi, A. U., & Shuraydi, M. (2002). Perceptions of arranged marriages by young Pakistani Muslim women living in a western society. *Journal of Comparative Family Studies, 33*(4), 495–514.

KEY TERMS AND DEFINITIONS

Caste System: The stratification of Indian society generally identified with Hinduism but also practiced by some groups of Muslims and Christians in India. There are five categories in the caste system – Brahmins (priests, educators), Kshatriyas (rulers, warriors), Vaishyas (merchants), Shudras (artisans, agriculturalists) and finally the Harijans who are considered to be outside the caste system (previously referred to as "untouchables"). Although the Indian Constitution has outlawed caste-based discrimination, it continues to exist and dictate hierarchical rules for most Indians in terms of birth, marriage and death.

Cultural Hegemony: The philosophical concept developed by Marxist philosopher Antonio Gramsci that suggests that a culturally-diverse society is ruled by one of the social classes, i.e., the dominance of one social group over another. The theory claims that the ideas of the ruling class come to be seen as universal ideologies and are perceived to benefit everyone while actually only benefitting the ruling class.

Cultural Norms: These refer to guidelines that limit and direct individuals' behaviors in a cultural group. Norms are useful for group affiliation and membership and may either be implicit or explicit.

Indian Penal Code (IPC): An exhaustive document or code that applies to any offence committed by an Indian Citizen anywhere and on any Indian registered ship or aircraft. The IPC was enacted in 1861 under British rule by Thomas Babington Macaulay and is regularly amended to reflect changes in criminal law in India.

Matrimonial Portals/Websites: Portals or Websites which are designed for the sole purpose of finding a marriage partner. These Websites are modeled after dating Websites with users uploading their profiles onto a database and using various search criteria to find potential partners.

Silicon Valley: This term was coined by Ralph Vaerst, a Californian entrepreneur to refer to the presence of silicon-chip innovators and manufacturers in the southern part of the San Francisco Bay Area in California. The term 'Silicon Valley' eventually became a reference to all the high-tech businesses in the area and the U.S.A. in general.

Social /Technological Determinism: Social and technological determinism are contradictory hypotheses that argue the relationship between societal and technological change. Social determinists perceive technology as a result of the society in which it was developed whereas technological determinists believe the characteristics of a given technology determine the way it is used by the society in which it was developed.

Chapter 3
Playing "Nice":
What Online Gaming Can Teach Us about Multiculturalism

Melinda Jacobs
Level Up Media, The Netherlands

ABSTRACT

Within the Internet, a range of international and multicultural communities abound, especially within the context of interactive online games known as Massively Multiplayer Online Role-Playing Games (MMORPGs). The clashing of cultures in one particular MMORPG, Omerta, has caused many problems within the related online community. These conflicts have led to online instances of culturalism – discrimination based upon cultural-mindset – within this international online community (Jacobs, 2009). This chapter examines the following questions: Do players in international online gaming environments have the right to discriminate based on cultural attitudes and perceptions, or should a player's right to not be discriminated against dominate in such international contexts? And how can multiculturalism be successfully managed in international online spaces?

INTRODUCTION

Every new electronic communicative technology brings with it the means to change communication, often taking it to a new level.. Thus, from the telegraph to the telephone to the television and beyond, as our engineering skills advance, modern technology has shaped both our ways of communicating, and expanded our abilities to communicate with others. With the advent of the Internet, communicative technology advanced once again, and it did so in a way that was completely unexpected to many individuals. The connective power of the Internet, in combination with its ever increasing availability, is constantly changing the dynamics of our communicative landscape, and these changes are causing us to rethink and re-explore our methods and approaches for interactions.

Arguably one of the biggest changes the Internet has brought about is the opportunity for people from all over the world to interact and com-

DOI: 10.4018/978-1-60960-833-0.ch003

municate with one another in an instant fashion. In this way, the Internet has changed the scope of our own personal lives by moving the nature of our everyday interactions from the local to a global stage. With this global access come the natural collisions of cultures within the Internet, and such collisions often create new forms of collaborations that were not previously feasible. These developments have led to the formation of many multicultural online communities (i.e., online groups comprised of individuals from multiple cultures). This development, in turn, brings with it a need to further explore the ideas and the principles of multiculturalism and cultural cooperation in cyberspace.

This chapter examines the constraints of multicultural Internet communities and considers how to approach the discriminatory problems surrounding them. In doing such an examination, the chapter also explores aspects of discrimination (the right to discriminate and the right to not be discriminated against) within the context of digital multiculturalism. The chapter will also address the ramifications of discrimination, and of not allowing discrimination, for the reader to consider when encountering multiculturalism within their own online interactions. It should be noted that the objective of this chapter is not to consider if discrimination is fair or unfair, or good or bad. Rather, the purpose of the chapter is to address and quantify the issue in as neutral an academic discussion as possible; the goal is to explore and not to pass moral judgment.

CULTURE AND CONFLICT

The general idea behind multiculturalism is that several independently different cultures should be able to coexist on peaceful and equal terms within a single territory. This concept thus exists in opposition to the idea of having a need for a solitary national culture (i.e., nationalism) in order to achieve the same results. In theory

multiculturalism seems to be the best approach to humanity's quest for equality, as its dogma is grounded in the principal belief that no culture is superior to another culture (Parekh, 2000). In practice, however, this objective appears to be not as feasible as the strength of multicultural communities often wavers and might eventually tip to the point of total collapse.

Two recent examples of this kind of collapse can be seen in cultural conflicts within the Netherlands and within Cyprus. In both of these instances, different cultural affiliations have been thrown together within a single country while the members of each group are still encouraged to keep their cultural identity strong. The negative results of such situations have ranged from the development of further distinction between the cultures to violence and even legal chaos.

Within the Netherlands, the Dutch legal system is struggling to keep a hold on the Moroccan and Turkish communities that have immigrated to the Netherlands and have refused to adapt to the Dutch law when it conflicts with the Moroccan and Turkish cultural values (Phalet & Schönpflug, 2001). This situation has led to violence, including the assassination of a Dutch political figure, as well as further distance between the Dutch, Turkish, and Moroccan cultures. Such cultural differences have led many Dutch citizens and politicians to develop a defensive attitude about culture, and this stance has led many of them to become more nationalistic than they were previously (at the beginning of the immigrations). In the case of Cyprus, after the Turkish invasions in 1974, instead of the two cultures (Greek and Turkish) mixing together within the independent state to form a new nation, both cultures divided the island into sections, occupied by either the Turkish Cypriots or the Greek Cypriots. Initially a wall was even built between the two sections of the island, and this structure represented the division between the two cultures (Kurop, 1998). Although the wall has since gone down (in 2008), both communities continue to experience functional divisions.

To stop at these two examples of failed multiculturalism would be to err, for an important aspect of both cases can be easily overlooked. In both situations, and most other situations similar to those, the space in which multiculturalism is attempting to succeed is not a neutral space. Rather, it is a biased space already owned by one culture and is a context where the laws of that space reflect the cultural beliefs of that culture. This lack of neutrality makes it difficult, if not impossible, for cultures that strongly differ from one another to coexist peacefully in a shared physical space. Thus, for multiculturalism to treat all cultures as equal, all cultures must have the opportunity to *be* equal, thus requiring a neutral territory in which they can co-exist and interact. Although truly neutral territory is rarely found in modern times in the physical sense, such a neutral territory has, in fact, come into existence through the third-space – that of the Internet. Unlike all other physical territories, excepting perhaps Antarctica, the Internet is not claimed or owned by any country. This lack of national ownership thus makes online spaces purely neutral territories that can be accessed by people from a range of cultures and nations.

THE NEUTRAL 'NET

In essence, the Internet is a nationalistically neutral space in which, although additional communities and collaborations[1] might be created within it, all users enter and exit with an already existent and stable national identity. In this context, the term "neutral" refers not to the fact the Internet has no specific national or cultural affiliation. Rather, it is connected to the idea that the Internet offers users a space that exists beyond traditional rules, and thus beyond traditional nationalities. Within online spaces, cultures are forced to coexist with each other in a context where no culture has a default bias within the space.

What separates the Internet from its physical counterparts (e.g., the Netherlands or Cyprus) is the fact that it is a neutral space that contains multiple cultures as opposed to a biased physical space that attempts to allow multiple cultures to co-exist. Therefore, the Internet allows for a new aspect of multiculturalism that was not previously possible, and this unique aspect must be considered when addressing communication between cultures. This multiculturalistic aspect offers increased benefits, such as ease in increasing awareness and understanding of cultures beyond one's own culture. This same aspect also brings more problematic issues to light, such as issues of discrimination and dominance within online spaces. Problems that might have been more easily be solved in an environment with only one set of culturally-influenced laws, become much larger issues in a nation-free cyberspace. This lack of control in the latter, moreover, has the potential to result in more discriminatory and radical responses.

Such situations are especially visible within the context of online gaming communities, specifically Massively Multiplayer Online Role-Playing Games (MMORPGs). In the online communities created around such games, new cultures are developed, new identities are created, and new cooperative groups and alliances are constantly being formed (Taylor, 2006; Mortensen, 2009). Interestingly it is within these MMORPGs that the effects of multiculturalism seem to be most common. In the online environments associated with these games, many cultures *are* often able to work together in the neutral space to create a "new territory" within a game. It is a territory full of people with many different individual cultures collaborating to achieve a common goal.

Some cultures, however, appear not to be immersing within these multicultural contexts. As a result, cultural ghettos are forming in games, and these ghettos appear outside of the other groups of individuals who have successfully immersed themselves in the game. This situation gives rise to several questions: Do these digital ghettos represent a success for multiculturalism, or a failure? What does the formation of such structures say for the equality of cultures when placed in a neutral space and given the ability to regroup and reorganize? Is what is occurring within the game unfair discrimination or natural, sometimes self-selected, discrimination? Can this discrimination be avoided? Should this discrimination be avoided? How should we respond to such discrimination? And of course, what does this then say about its physical world counterparts? If the discrimination in these games is seemingly healthy and natural, is it wise for nations to become more nationalistic than multiculturalistic? To begin to understand such situations, we must first consider how online communities are formed, and how such formations affect interactions and perceptions.

COMMUNITIES AND CONSTRAINTS

Although the Internet is full of communities (such as television communities, digital gaming communities, sporting communities, shopping communities, etc.), for the purpose of this paper, I will focus specifically upon one form of community: that of digital gaming. I will focus on this community specifically because it is the type of community that most frequently requires internal cooperation as "more forms of advancement in MMORPGs require increasing cooperation or dependency on other users" (Yee, 2006, p. 189). Because most online communities are composed of an international audience, an important aspect to explore within multiculturalism is successful interactions and communications within *mutual* environments in which the goal of the interaction is to successfully solve a problem to achieve a common goal.

Naturally, it is important to explore the places in which any interactions between different cultures are positive and in which individuals from different cultures are able to discuss and socially engage each other successfully. However, a temporary interaction that requires little compromise only scratches the surface of multiculturalism and fails to dig as deeply as is necessary to fully explore this topic. A social conversation, even if continued throughout a number of years, only ever requires both parties to listen to each other, but such interactions often never require actual compromise or the need to find a common ground. While both parties involved in the conversation can have strong cultural opinions on how to handle a situation, if they do not need to address a situation together, they are never required to find a middle ground in which both feel their culture has been represented and not undermined or ignored. Therefore, success in social discussion is more readily achieved than is success in discussion upon a common agreeable solution that appeases both sides. The best environments to examine thus are those that provide situations that force individuals to engage with each other to solve shared problems and allow for the real issues and conflicts that arise from the interactions of many people from many different, strong, and independent cultures to come to the surface. Online gaming communities provide such an environment for studying these behaviors.

In a MMORPG context, if two players in the same player group were to have a disagreement over how a policy of the group, or an event that occurred, should be handled, the discussion usually begins with statements of personal opinion (e.g., "I think this" or. "I think that"). In the end, however, the players cannot walk away leaving the situation at "we disagree." Rather, they must, for the sake of the unity of the group (if it is to stay united), come to a decision on how to address the situation. Thus, we can see more clearly not only *where* and on *what* the cultures disagree, but *whether or not, given these disagreements the cultures can continue to co-exist*. Because successful or unsuccessful conflict resolution (or in other worlds successful cooperation and co-existence) is the pivotal point of discussion concerning multiculturalism, related research needs to consider environments in which conflict resolution and necessity of cooperation are high. I believe that MMORPGs provide this model.

UNDERSTANDING MMORPGs

In order for teamwork and cooperation to be necessary within an environment, everyone has to be able to access the same environment. All participants must also be able to influence the same environment. Persistent world MMORPGs are games in which the gameworld environment is always existent, even when the player is not accessing it (Taylor, 2006; Mortensen, 2009). In a typical game environment, once the player has exited the environment, the environment stays in stasis until the player accesses the environment again. The environment and game only change when the player changes it. A persistent world, however, is accessible by numerous players and is accessible constantly. Therefore, when a player logs out and then logs back in again, the world might be *completely different*. Thus, naturally, persistent world MMORPGs are most similar to earth environments as, like the persistent worlds, the earth is always accessible and always changing as we all access it on a daily basis.

With environments that are both persistent and full of independently operating players, persistent world MMORPGs offer the most similarities to complex "real-world" societies with their political, cultural, and social aspects (Jacobs, 2009; McGonigal, 2007). Such online environments are thus perfect for studying multiculturalism, for while online territory begins as neutral, it is then harvested and claimed by groups of players, and new working territories are formed. In international games, these territories are often formed by groups of players from different national cultures. Therefore, such contexts represent

the basic definition of multiculturalism: people with strong cultural backgrounds are placed in a common environment and must work together and find common ground while not infringing on anyone's cultural background and beliefs. This environment either results in success as defined as cooperation (resulting in multi-national groups of players) or failure as defined as further segregation by nationality and/or culture with no common ground established.

Among MMORPGs, there are two basic formats: graphic-based and text-based. Graphic-based games have a game interface that relies heavily on graphic-based interactions with the environment and other players. An example of this is *World of Warcraft*, a middle-earth themed MMORPG. Gameplay is, in general, based on the manipulation of a character (avatar) within a visible world environment. Quests and tasks are completed through visual challenges (such as killing a monster or running through a forest) and players can interact visually. Textual communication is necessary for some aspects of visual-based games; however, more often it is not inherently necessary. It may make the experience more enjoyable, but the games are often solo-based, relying on interactions between the player and the environment. Many players, in fact, enjoy the solo aspect of the game while still being surrounded by others, in other words being "alone together" (Ducheneaut et al. 2006, p. 415).

Text-based games have a game interface that relies heavily, if not solely, on text-based interactions with the environment and with other players. An example of this is *Omerta*, a mafia-themed MMORPG. Gameplay generally consists of choosing a crime from a selection of text-described events and clicking a button that results in the player receiving a final textual message stating whether or not he or she completed the crime. For the most part gameplay requires little skill, and a character's strength is based only upon the frequency of successful crimes. However, as the game is text-based, and there are no visuals, the game is mostly played through channels of communication. In the case of *Omerta*, this is through Internet Relay Chat (IRC) – a chat server where players can create different channels where they can communicate with one another about the happenings of the game. The majority of the game is then based around communication, negotiation, and establishing boundaries. Thus, more players are forced to join chats and interact with other players, as that is where the real action takes place (Kollock & Smith, 1999).

THE DYNAMICS OF THE MMORPG OMERTA

To examine dimensions of multiculturalism in online environments, this paper focuses on one specific MMORPG community: that of *Omerta*. The reason I choose to use *Omerta* as a point of reference is due to the overwhelming presence of multicultural conflict and the heavy effect this conflict has on the functioning of the community.

To begin playing *Omerta*, players must first create a character by choosing a character name and gender. Once a character is created, the objective of the game is then to "rank" –complete activities that, upon successful completion, give "rank points" which are added to a player's character's total score. Players can earn points by carrying out a variety of activities, such as committing petty crimes, trafficking drugs and alcohol, and participating in multi-player organized crimes. Through the completion of these various activities, users advance their character through 14 set ranks, starting at Empty Suit and ending at Bruglione. Where earning enough points to complete the rank of Empty Suit might take less than an hour, completing the rank of Bruglione might take over one month, and that is assuming the player is "only" playing 10 or more hours a day.[2]

Once a player reaches the rank of Pickpocket or Thief (the fourth and fifth ranks), that player usually attempts to join a "family,"[3] which is a group of players that all agree to work together and play together under the same faction. Families are the core aspect of the game, and it is the dynamics between families that create the political, social, and strategic environment of the game. Within this context, it requires very little skill to rank, but it requires a lot of skill to succeed and rise up in the ranks in a family.

As families are the center of *Omerta*, most of the game is actually played through discussion within a multi-user chat (Internet Relay Chat, IRC) – a computer program that allows users to communicate in chat rooms by connection to a common server hosted by the game administration. Most families have a public channel where any player in the game can join to contact a member of the family. They also have a private channel where only players that are already members of the family can join to contact other members of the family. It is within these IRC channels that negotiations between families are held and wars among families are organized.

Although there is a strong in-game aspect when families fight each other in wars (finding a target, purchasing bullets, and clicking the "kill" button when a player's target is found), the majority of these wars are organized on IRC and involve activities such as assigning players to targets, strategizing the best form of attack, negotiating terms of war with the opposing family, etc.. As in-game rank does not determine one's ability on IRC, it is common for low-ranked in-game characters to be in high status positions within a family. This is because IRC "status" is more important in these instances than in-game rank status. In fact, players who are in charge of a family might stay low-ranked for extended periods of time because the time necessary to put into negotiations on IRC cuts into the time necessary to focus on in-game ranking.

With the majority of the focus being on the complex relationships between players on IRC, the entire structure of the game is based upon teamwork, compromise, and negotiation. It is impossible to be successful in the game without approaching issues of communication and becoming successful at it. Therefore, international games such as *Omerta* are effective places to observe multiculturalism at work. Once again, as the Internet is legally a nationalistically neutral ground, *Omerta* is not directly controlled by a pre-existing country. Rather, the game controls itself in the form of a new, neutral country, *Omerta*, where there are no pre-existing residents until individuals from pre-existing countries immigrate to it. This factor is important, for it means that *all participants in the community are non-natives and all participants must partially adapt to the new culture and new laws, while still keeping their cultural and national identity*. This situation is thus the precise definition of multiculturalism: a community where everyone agrees to abide by a set of rules and no one is forced to integrate their culture into one mass. Therefore, when communities are formed within *Omerta*, even if the communities themselves are not all multicultural in nature, the world of *Omerta* is still multicultural. Moreover, as the families must interact to be successful, some form of multicultural communication is necessary.

On the surface, *Omerta* may seem to be a failed attempt at multiculturalism (Jacobs, 2009). What started off as an integrated community has, over the course of several years, deteriorated into a separated community comprised of two families. One family is composed of members from Western Europe, the U.S., and Canada. The other is composed of members from Eastern Europe (specifically Turkey). This division has formed cultural ghettos in the game – situations where Turkish players are not frequently recruited by families composed of mainly Western cultures. This behavior, in turn, results from the common Westerner's perception that players from Turkey are unreliable and a danger to the family. This perception is due to the frequency with which Turkish players place their nationality (of being Turkish) over allegiance within the game (of being a member of a family). Through such behaviors, the

Turkish players effectively exiled themselves to "Turkish families" – families mainly composed of individuals from Turkey. And, in many instances, these Turkish families refuse to cooperate with the "Western families" operating in the game. A study of these dynamics within *Omerta* can thus offer a lesson in how to better understand and approach multiculturalism in both computer and non-computer mediated communications.

OMERTA: EXAMINING DISCRIMINATION IN ONLINE GAMING

Although many cultures within *Omerta* have learned to address differences and work together, there is one clashing of cultures that has caused many problems within the community. These clashes, moreover, have led to multiple forms of discrimination within the international group of individuals playing the game. In essence, players who are of Turkish nationality are often refused admission into families due to broader community perceptions that the Turkish player's primary loyalties are to other members of their own real-life nationality (i.e., other Turks) rather than to the members of their current internationally diverse in-game family.

The dynamics tend to work as follows: When joining an in-game family, the expectation is that the player will follow the rules of the family. Players who fail to follow these rules will be kicked out or "killed," for they become a liability to the family and its ability to achieve objectives within the game. These rules are put in place by the higher-ranking members of a family, and the objective of these rules is to protect the players in the family. For example, one common rule states "Do not shoot another player in another family without permission." In this case, the rule prevents random attacks that could result in a war among families, and such wars can easily result in everyone losing the hard-earned capital they have put into their current user accounts (i.e., time, ingame money, strength, etc.). Even if such an action does not result in war, breaking this rule will almost always result in one family having to pay the other family compensation money and shoot their own player in an eye for an eye, tooth for a tooth fashion.

This particular rule of not randomly shooting members of other families is one many players consider particularly problematic in relation to Turkish players within the game. That is, in many instances, families might hesitate to recruit Turkish players, for there is a perception, based on previous experiences within the game, that Turkish players are more likely to shoot and kill players in other families for any reason the Turkish player deems appropriate – even when the Turkish player is forbidden to do so by his or her in-game family. The comments of some Omerta players seem to link this behavior to the high value the Turkish culture places on personal and family honor (Sev'er & Yurdakul, 2001). Non-Turkish Omerta players have, for example, stated that: "Turks, for example, are a proud people, but many go off and shoot you for taking something the wrong way in chat, most of their English is not good so they assume insult and shoot" (Male, Australian, 2007).

In this case, it can be argued that such perceptions indicate not racism or nationalism but culturalism, which is discrimination based upon a particular cultural-mindset (Jacobs, 2009). Given this interpretation, it is then possible to move beyond the question of "What is occurring?" to the questions of: "Do these players have the right to discriminate, or do the Turkish players have the right not to be discriminated against?" Answering this question is not easy, but such answers can be important to understanding how to address a range of behaviors in international cyberspace. The question then becomes "What existing models or practices can we use to examine these situations in order to better understand and address them?"

EXCLUSIONARY PRACTICES IN OMERTA

To see how the concepts of selection and discrimination apply to Omerta, we need to view the families within the game as a business. According to this perspective, family member are employees. Even though there is no applicable law in this neutral space, the basic principles of selection based upon ability to perform required job tasks provide an interesting framework for understanding the dynamics taking place in the game. If recruitment of a player would be detrimental to the performance of the family, should the family then retain some right to discriminate/not allow that player to become a member of that family? If it is mandatory that English be used in all online family interactions, is it acceptable for a family to refuse to admit a player who cannot speak English with relative proficiency (i.e., the proficiency needed to correctly understand what others are saying and to be understood by others)? Likewise, if a family mandates a player must be online a certain number of hours or during a certain period of time, is it reasonable for a family to exclude individuals who cannot meet those time requirements (e.g., for many U.S.-based players, the six-to-seven-hour time difference can make it difficult to participate in a community of gamers based in Europe)?

Within this context, what is the argument for culture? If an employer is set up in such a way that an employee's cultural mindset might render that employee unable to effectively perform a job, can the employer decide not to hire/work with that player? In the case of *Omerta,* not all Turkish players shirk rules such as the "don't kill without the approval of your family" rule, but it is difficult to say which players would or would not follow this rule based on previous experiences in the game (Sev'er & Yurdakul, 2001; Jacobs, 2009). In such cases, if there is a risk many players associate with recruiting members from a particular cultural group, should the family be forced to take it? The question international online groups need to consider in this case is: "Can free-access online groups be allowed to refuse to include certain individuals in their groups?" Or, from the specific perspective of gaming: "Can and should the families in *Omerta* refuse to include certain players based upon what the members of that group consider to be 'business' related reasoning?"

WHAT DOES IT ALL IMPLY?

From this discussion, it would not be unreasonable to expect an answer to a seemingly critical question: How can discrimination in online communities be prevented? The answer is simple: It is neither possible to prevent discrimination, nor to avoid it. Although this perspective might seem like a pessimistic end to what appeared to be an optimistic discussion; this is not the case. Instead, I request a redirection of the original concern in the form of a new question, which this paper has been addressing all along: How can discrimination be managed in international online contexts?

In looking at the evidence presented in this chapter, an argument can be made for approaching discrimination, multiculturalism, and communication between cultures on the Internet in the following way:

- First, *the environment should be accessible and non-discriminatory based on an extension of the model of the basic principles of hiring qualified employees to include the issue of culture*. In terms of the online gaming industry, discrimination against a player based on their culture by the game administration, concerning access to a game environment, can be argued to be inapplicable here. The environment itself is protected by the End User License Agreement to which all players (regardless of culture) have to agree before entering the environment. If the player does not abide by these rules as agreed to in the EULA, that player is legally liable to be punished by the game administration. In fact, a player can even be banned from the environment in some instances. However, with great power comes great responsibility. This being said, there are a few things the EULA should or should not do. The EULA should not contain rules of which the aim is to prevent the entrance of a player of a specific culture into the game.

- Second, *the communities within the environment should not be required to be accessible and non-discriminatory*. In terms of the online gaming industry, discrimination against a player based on their culture by players, concerning access to an internal community within the game environment, can be argued to be applicable here as the community has to take a risk of loss of capital for those they include in the community. Although the environment itself is protected by the EULA, the community's space within the environment is not protected by a set of rules punishable by the administration of the community. If a member of the community breaks a rule, there are consequences for the player (but not as efficient as the EULA), but there are also consequences for the community. Whether this is ethical or not is another issue, and one I will not address. Realistically and legally, however, this form of discrimination cannot be controlled. To draw a comparison to the hiring in a business, such a situation is similar to forcing an organization to hire an employee that the employer believes cannot complete the job.

Before anyone assumes I am insinuating that cultural discrimination is acceptable, they should first consider a further observation. In over six years of observing the online communities of *Omerta,* I have not witnessed one instance in which any family has enacted a policy that has completely refused entrance to anyone of a certain nationality. I have seen many policies that hold bias to avoid recruiting from a specific nationality, and I have seen families whose majority of members share one specific nationality or culture, but I have also seen many successful integrations of multiculturalism within families in the game. I have also seen players from all cultures interact successfully enough to play a text-based game (which, as discussed earlier, requires an extraordinarily high amount of communication and cooperation) which requires negotiation, interaction, and management internally within a family and externally between families. These observations all indicate that *it is possible to have successful multicultural cooperation in online spaces*. However, it also provides an argument for letting the community sort itself out.

Interestingly, multiculturalism was more successful when the game administrators were not trying to alter the game or the structure of the game to accommodate a culture they felt was being unfairly discriminated against. The action of the administration within the communities immediately removed the possibility for an equal multicultural community because one culture was being favored. Even if that culture was being favored in the attempt to make a peaceful community, it was still favored, and thus is being unwillingly enforced on the other cultures. There may be enough issues between various cultures that the players might not be able to get along enough to play the game from within the same faction, but if the freedom to choose how to play within the environment were taken away it could be argued that *no* culture would be allowed to be a strong, unique, individual culture. For this reason, multiculturalism is more successful when the potential for discrimination is there, but the members of an online group choose not to use it.

To take this discussion back outside of the online gaming community and into the broader field of computer-mediated communication between

cultures, a lesson is apparent – discrimination cannot be prevented; it can only be managed. In order for discrimination to be managed to provide for a potential environment for successful multicultural integration, management must create an environment for all to inhabit, but allow for natural conflict between cultures to occur. This is not to say that all conflicts should be left unattended. Rather, there are instances where the administration needs to step in and put an end to the discrimination. This approach can be seen in the occurrence in *Omerta* where a large group of Dutch players joined the newly opened German version with the intentions to kill off any German player who joined (which they did). The administration eventually banned the players doing so from that specific version. However, discrimination that is a part of negotiating how to work together must be tolerated. Any interaction of the management within that negotiation of cultural status will be seen as favoritism and will only result in further conflict.

It must be accepted that, in some instances, multiculturalism will not work if both cultures interacting online do not wish for it to work. Even if one side wishes for it to work, if the other does not, then true multiculturalism will not be possible. This is why, although it does not appear to be effective to force multiculturalism, it is perhaps effective to encourage multiculturalism through reward. According to this approach, if there are rewards for working together, then the community will be much more likely to work together than not.

This awards-based approach could be seen indirectly in *Omerta* in an incident where the administration placed a ban on IRC for the word "Fingon," a player-run newspaper that the game administration does not approve of. Most players strongly opposed the ban and all players, regardless of nationality, worked together to attempt to fight it. Although protesting was ultimately unsuccessful, the reward of having the word unbanned was motivation enough to put aside nationality in order to fight it. This is the same reaction as when

Omerta administration placed a ban on all languages besides English in the RIP forums (created when an account "dies" for that player's friends to memorialize their "death"). In that case, the community once again came together as a whole and revolted – including community members who were native English speakers. The common theme in these instances, although masked by the instances themselves, is that *the players all had a motivation to work together to get what they want.* Thus, to increase multiculturalism, instead of punishing players who don't wish to work together, the administration should instead consider increasing the benefits associated with players working together. This approach is one that can then be used in almost any international online situation: rather than forcing cooperation between cultures, it is better to encourage cooperation between cultures.

CONCLUSION

As the Internet is, in theory, a neutral space, it provides an interesting model for exploring multiculturalism as well as a unique environment for learning the limitations and advantages it provides. Multiculturalism is, arguably, a somewhat natural occurrence in the instance of the Internet. Within a neutral and void gamespace, users of all cultures are thrown together; they must then collaborate in order to establish a system where communication and strategy succeed. Even within the Internet, one can find instances that mirror the physical world, and these instances raise key questions: What is public space and what is private space, and, within that, what is an acceptable risk and what is an unacceptable risk? Arguably, the intolerance of cultural disagreement, and then the imposed change forcing the cultures to accept each other, *is where the failure of multiculturalism occurs.* In addition, it can be argued that multiculturalism can succeed on one level, while not succeeding on another. As the *Omerta* example referenced in this chapter indicates, all the cultures can agree to the general overall structure of the online community (i.e., the game) while they might not all agree on the best way to play it. For this reason, we are left with both a success and a failure. In this instance, however, the responsibility for this situation lies with the game administration to keep the environment open for all while also being tolerant of what the players do with that responsibility. By keeping out of the internal cultural conflicts (but providing a space for them to attempt to work in), the game allows multiculturalism to function, ironically, by not trying to impose the by-the-letter definition of multiculturalism.

REFERENCES

Ducheneaut, N., Yee, N., Nickell, E., & Moore, R. (2006). "Alone together?" Exploring the social dynamics of massively multiplayer online games. In *Proceedings of the CHI 2006, ACM* (pp. 407-416). New York, NY: Association for Computing Machinery.

Jacobs, M. (2008). Multiculturalism and cultural issues in online gaming communities. *Journal for Cultural Research, 12*(4), 317–334. doi:10.1080/14797580802561182

Kollock, P., & Smith, M. A. (1999). Communities in cyberspace. In Smith, M. A., & Kollock, P. (Eds.), *Communities in cyberspace* (pp. 1–26). New York, NY: Routledge.

Kurop, M. C. (1998). Greece and Turkey: Can they mend fences? *Foreign Affairs (Council on Foreign Relations), 77*(1), 7–12. doi:10.2307/20048357

McGonigal, J. (2007). The puppet master problem: Design for real-world, mission-based gaming. In Harrigan, P., & Wardrip-Fruin, N. (Eds.), *Second person: Role-playing and story in games and playable media* (pp. 251–264). Cambridge, MA: The MIT Press.

Mortensen, T. E. (2009). *Perceiving play: The art and study of computer games*. New York, NY: Peter Lang.

Parekh, B. (2000). *Rethinking multiculturalism: Cultural diversity and political theory*. Cambridge, MA: Harvard University Press.

Phalet, K., & Schönpflug, U. (2001). Intergenerational transmission of collectivism and achievement values in two acculturation contexts: The case of Turkish families in Germany and Turkish and Moroccan families in the Netherlands. *Journal of Cross-Cultural Psychology*, *3*(2), 186–201. doi:10.1177/0022022101032002006

Sev'er, A., & Yurdakul, G. (2001). Culture of honor, culture of change: A feminist analysis of honor killings in rural Turkey. *Violence Against Women*, *7*(9), 964–998. doi:10.1177/10778010122182866

Taylor, T. L. (2006). *Play between worlds: Exploring online game culture*. Cambridge, MA: The MIT Press.

Yee, N. (2006). The demographics, motivations, and derived experiences of users of massively multi-user online graphical environments. *Presence (Cambridge, Mass.)*, *15*(3), 309–329. doi:10.1162/pres.15.3.309

KEY TERMS AND DEFINITIONS

Culture: Culture is the behavioral characteristics of a particular demographic (such as nationality, age, or social constructions).

Discrimination: Discrimination is the favorable or unfavorable treatment of a person based on the person's general identification or categorization (such as religion, nationality, gender, or race) rather than on individual merit.

IRC: IRC, short for Internet relay chat, is an international network of Internet servers through which participants can converse in real-time online.

MMORPG: An MMORPG, short for massively multiplayer online role-playing game, is a game where a large amount of players can play together in a persistent virtual world (connected together through the Internet).

Multiculturalism: Multiculturalism is a theory arguing that people from multiple unique cultures (as opposed to one national culture) can coexist harmoniously and equitably in a single country.

Nationalism: Nationalism occurs when people have a strong devotion or attachment to the interests and culture of a common nation.

ENDNOTES

[1]   For example, the world of Azeroth in the popular Massively Multiplayer Online Role-Playing Game (MMORPG) *World of Warcraft* is a neutral space, while the guilds, (a formal collection of players working together within the game to complete game achievements), that form within the game are a collaboration within the neutral space. They provide a new identity within the space, but do not necessarily replace the players personal nationalistic identity.

[2]   Although a player may technically rank 24 hours a day 7 days a week, there are two ways in which rank speed is controlled and limited; through time limits imposed on frequency of actions and a general rank limit to prevent unrealistic ranking.

[3]   Within families there are five main forms of positions of responsibilities: Capo, an object holder, Sottocapo, Consiglieri, and Don. Sottocapo, Consiglieri, and Don are the three positions with the most power. These "top three" are the ones that run the family. Below that there is the Capo, several players that are in charge of maintaining and managing smaller sections of people within a family. Finally objects holders are

the ones that hold objects, either casinos featuring roulette or blackjack which other players may play and generates (or in some cases loses) money for the family, or benefit granting spots. Although object holders are not directly involved with the running of the family, they must be trusted to run and protect the object, therefore, making an object holder a position of power.

Chapter 4
Social Information Processing Theory (SIPT):
A Cultural Perspective for International Online Communication Environments

Bolanle A. Olaniran
Texas Tech University, USA

Natasha Rodriguez
Texas Tech University, USA

Indi M. Williams
Arizona State University, USA

ABSTRACT

The Social Information Processing Theory (SIPT) proposes that given time and opportunity to interact, relationships between individuals can form in online environments. Although not an overt assumption of the SIPT, it is essential to understand how cultural factors are important components of any CMC interaction. The power of the SIPT lies within its ability to foster communication between individuals through communicative behavior that is valued by the other's culture. Therefore, Social Information Processing has the potential to aid the development of trust between virtual team members, establishing group cohesion, and accentuating cross-communication within international work groups.

INTRODUCTION

The use of computer-mediated communication (CMC) has grown exponentially in the last decade. Among the reasons for this expansion is an increase in international online access. However, increased access brings with it a variety of new challenges and concerns that affect international communication and interactions in online environments. In fact, many of these interactions entail communication expectations based upon cultural differences in interpretation, particularly in the face of diverse languages and cultural norms. Other issues, to name a few, include: the actual media of choice, technological compatibility in the global arena, a variety of laws governing interactions,

DOI: 10.4018/978-1-60960-833-0.ch004

and differing hardware and software standards. All of these factors contribute to international online interactions, the usefulness of communication technologies, and the effectiveness of these technologies in international contexts. This chapter proposes using the social information processing theory to understand such international online interactions.

The Social Information Processing (SIPT) moves beyond social influence and relational models of interaction by arguing that meanings in communication activities are not mediated only by past interactions and time (Walther, 1992; Walther & Burgoon, 1992); rather, meanings are also bound by culture. In addition, SIPT accepts that social presence and media richness, or the ability of a medium to support or carry multiple cues, influences media perception. In turn, this perception of the medium becomes embedded and reinforced by culture. Social presence, media richness, and media appropriateness, then, are important issues because they emphasize media attributes that vary by context and are influenced by individual differences (Rice, 1993). Simultaneously, individual differences and experiences are rooted in culture, which influences perceptions and interpretations made about media attributes.

If one accepts the idea that meanings are influenced by—and entrenched in—culture, then according to SIPT, perceptions of CMC media attributes and social interaction would reflect the nuances of cultural differences of norms and beliefs in multinational (intercultural) and multi-domestic (cross-cultural) organizations. In other words, messages can be transmitted among people, but not meanings. For instance, CMC media are conduits and transmitters of symbols, which in turn influence meaning (Sitkin, Sutcliffe, & Barrios-Choplin, 1992). As a result, it is paramount that the culture from which meaning evolves is taken into consideration when studying online communication technologies (Hiemstra, 1982; Mesdag, 2000).

Because interaction in most globalized organizations involves relationships between people from diverse cultures, such interactions can be classified as intercultural. SIPT, in turn, appears to take this factor into consideration. For instance, CMC offers paralinguistic codes, or signs and symbols, that express emotion and meaning in written text through icon manipulation, capitalization, parenthetical notes (Spears & Lea, 1992), and recently, emoticons. Caution, however, must be exercised with paralinguistic cues in CMC, for they have localized meanings (Spitzer, 1986; Turkle & Papert, 1990). Thus, they can never convey a fixed meaning to all groups (Barthes, 1977; Olaniran, 2001). For these reasons, SIPT is a valuable tool in understanding specific issues and challenges facing encounters in international online communication environments.

While the effects of technology are certainly important in this debate, the goal of this chapter is to shed light on 1) how we come to understand international online interactions, and 2) the role that a good theoretical perspective plays in such a discussion. Hence, this chapter explores (SIPT) as an indispensable tool for understanding specific issues and challenges facing encounters in international online communication environments. The chapter also explores the value and contribution a SIPT approach can make to the current CMC literature—in particular, in the area of interpersonal communication.

THEORETICAL FRAMEWORK

SIPT Core Assumptions

In its initial formation and in the earlier organizational literature, Fulk, Schmitz, and Steinfield (1990) use the term "social information processing" to illustrate a model of media choice, where socially constructed and subjective assessments of media and their features determine channel selection. For example, Walther (1992) uses SIPT to explain how individuals process social information, and based on that information, communicate their relationships. Similarly, Olaniran (1994) alludes to the role of context and specifically, the anticipation of future interaction (AFI) as crucial to positive relational mechanism. In other words, the degree to which individuals expect to engage in future interaction influences, or facilitates, positive interactions and warm relational messages (see also, Walther, 1994).

SIPT takes into account a variation of relational aspects of CMC. Walther (1995), in an alternative explanation, proposes that the significant difference between CMC and Face-to-Face (FtF) communication is due to the rate of transmission of information, rather than the capability of the media to transmit the information. Among the factors affecting such transmissions are varying "linguistic and typographic manipulations which may reveal social and relational information in CMC" (Walther, 1995, p. 190; also see, Olaniran, 1995; Spears & Lea, 1992). Another factor, relational tone, is considered to change as a function of time in CMC. SIPT integrates these factors and "refers to the way by which communicator's process social identity and relational cues (i.e., social information) using different media" (Walther, 1995, p. 190). SIPT attempts to explain, as well as predict, an individual's interpersonal adjustment through the use of CMC and FtF.

Issues in Previous SIPT Research: CMC vs. FtF

Due to limited bandwidth, CMC is often thought to offer less total information per exchange when compared to FtF interactions (Spears & Lea, 1992; Walther, 1995). For instance, individuals such as Branon and Essex (2001), Spears and Lea (1992), Tanis and Postems (2003), Walther (1995), and Yum and Hara (2005) believe relational development is delayed due to reduced social cues by participants. It is assumed that "equal time intervals" might create unintended

effects and alter the experimental manipulation of media (Spears & Lea, 1992). This perception is because CMC systems require more messages to communicate the same amount of information and more time to exchange the same amount of messages when compared to FtF interactions. In other words, asynchronous exchanges further slow the transmission of messages.

Therefore, it stands to reason that relational development amongst participants exchanging information via CMC should progress more slowly than in FtF exchanges. This proposed reduction is attributed to the bandwidth limitations of some participants and limitations in the amount of information given per exchange. Walther (1992) suggests that if given ample, "time and message exchanges for interpersonal impression formation and relational development to accrue, and all other things being equal, relational [communication] in later periods of CMC and face-to-face communication will be the same" (p. 69). Therefore, despite the rate and frequency of messages between participants, relationships can develop through CMC. Though there has been an increased use of synchronous CMC (e.g., audio chat, IMs, and video conferencing), most significant online communication remains relegated to the asynchronous mode and corresponding media formats. This situation is especially true for international and cross-cultural online communication exchanges (Olaniran, 2004).

The cross-cultural significance of CMC exchanges is mainly attributed to the globalization process, which increases the likelihood people from different ethnic and national cultures will collaborate in groups and organizations that constantly communicate through online interactions (Gasner, 1999; Kalawsky, Bee, & Nee, 1999; Olaniran, 2007a). The lack of strong research support for the original information processing theory indicates that the theory, as presented in the social influence model, is insufficient (Rice & Aydin, 1991; Rice, Grant, Schmitz, & Torobin, 1990; Schmitz & Fulk, 1991). A reason for this situation might be that perception is culturally based, and perception differs even for individuals in similar job positions. Furthermore, when one adds the intercultural complexity of international online collaboration (IOC), there is a divergence in perception of one's role even in the same organizational context and similar positions. While information processing theory acknowledges differences across groups in the same cultural context, it fails to take the wider societal cultures into account as a source of the varying perceptions of a group. In other words, SIPT, in its original formation, is not presented to account for culture. However, its assumptions are germane to understanding cross-cultural communication encounters in CMC and other online environments.

Overall, SIPT is specifically influenced by cultural factors (e.g., perception, social influence, norms, expectation, meaning negotiation, etc.), as well as three major factors affecting message construction. First, communication is viewed contextually, indicating that the environment and our perceptions of the environment influence our communication behaviors. Second, culture is considered an essential component of the environment, which influences perceptions and shapes behaviors. Third, meanings represent the core values and shared understandings that are created during communication that define social interaction. As a result, the meaning attached to encoded messages is a function, not only of the message, but of the individual's encoding and decoding of the message (i.e., cognitive patterns), and the cultural context of messages as well (Gudykunst & Kim, 1992). Therefore, the employment of SIPT to CMC allows for the integration of a cultural perception and understanding of the media used—a situation that increases the chances of successful cross-cultural communicative exchanges.

Values of SIPT

Postmes et al. (1998) found that the opportunity to be liberated via communication technology does not always lead to the choice, or preference, for such liberation from social influence. Therefore, SIPT embraces perception as a key issue in understanding culture. Similarly, culture remains an essential component to understanding CMC perception and technology usage. Faulk et al. (1990) describe perception as attitudes, statements, and behaviors about a given object. For instance, information processing, as presented in the social influence model of media use, gives the impression that job positions and communication networks determine appropriate media. Rice (1993) explains that occupants of similar jobs have similar perceptions of acceptable media and the use of such media. In contrast, when job positions vary, this variation subsequently results in differing media opinions (Rice, 1993). Therefore, cultural perceptions and assumptions influence individual and/or group media preferences. Likewise, SIPT assumes that wider cultural norms also influence shared attitudes and behaviors.

Differences between groups are also expected to result in differing perceptions of a medium's appropriateness within that society. This is especially true in situations of varying task demands, work socialization and general value preferences at large. For example, a CMC system's capacity to function like a traditional, and/or any other communication medium, is related to its ease of accessibility, lower cost, and autonomy to engage in interactions regardless of the national, ethnic, religious, or status restrictions of the individuals involved. This functionality is also known to offer users greater freedom and self-sufficiency (Dubrovsky, Kiesler, & Sethna, 1991; Kiesler, Siegel, & McGuire, 1984; Postmes Spears, & Lea, 1998). Nevertheless, the increased freedom and lack of strict controls have the potential to increase antisocial behaviors in CMC and to decrease the regulatory function of social norms (e.g., Lea, 0' Shea, Fling, & Spears, 1992; Postmes et al., 1998; Walther, 1997; Walther, Anderson, & Park, 1994).

CHALLENGES IN ONLINE VIRTUAL GROUP COLLABORATIONS

There are numerous problems and challenges in international online collaboration (IOC) with information technology (IT). Among these problems are culture, trust, and IT compatibility and proficiency (i.e., Technology) (Dube & Pare, 2001; Olaniran, 2004). These challenges not only influence the usage of ITs but also impact the effectiveness of communication and interaction in IOC as a whole (see, Dube & Pare, 2001; Munkvold, 2005; Olaniran, 2004).

While the motivation to use CMC systems is often economically driven (i.e., cost cutting, increasing speed, and improving efficiency), there are key challenges that hinder their effectiveness and even their selection. Armstrong and Cole (2002) point out that while collaborative groups sometimes become integrated over time, these groups also experience problems due to distance (Crampton, 2002; Olaniran, 1996; 2001; Solomon, 2001; Walther, 2002). Some of these problems in virtual teams include frequent misunderstandings and confusion from fragmented communication between group members. Armstrong and Cole (2002) also found that national cultures and different locations create a dimension of distance that extends beyond miles and time zones, even within integrated groups. Furthermore, Armstrong and Cole argue that when organizational problems arise, these same problems possess the potential to magnify the differences between participants. If this is the case, SIPT can function as a way to understand the magnitude and depth of individual differences by exploring how and why those differences exist. Along this line, Crampton (2002) contends that working across dispersed locations often reduces the situational information that collaborators have about each other. These challenges can include how information is processed and how deadlines are established, increasing the chances of in-groups vs. out-group development based on location alone.

Research has identified that different languages, communication style preferences, expectations about behaviors, and information processing create additional complexities in multinational teams (e.g., James & Ward, 2002; Olaniran, 2007a; Roebuck & Britt, 2002). Even through the choice of online collaboration, participants can create the perception that certain cultures or geographical regions are not valued. Moreover, perceptions can create an environment where communicators perceive the need, or obligation, to use the selected media. Much has been written about the fact that a majority of online content is offered in the English language—to the detriment of end users who are non-native English speakers (e.g., Olaniran, 2007a; Roebuck & Britt, 2002; Ya'u, 2004).

At the same time, differences in perception and communication can be traced or linked to culture, motivation, and personality factors that influence attribution processes (Armstrong & Cole, 2002; Olaniran, 2001). Consequently, it is assumed that attribution, or the manner in which an individual determines who or what is responsible for an event or action, biases or alters the perception of others' behaviors (Choi, Nisbett, & Norenzayan, 1999). For example, the attribution of behaviors leans toward dispositional tendencies (i.e., habitual, ingrained beliefs for the cause of an action), rather than situational ones (i.e., perceptions that are based upon the situational factors surrounding the occurrence of an event or action) (Branzei, Vertinsky & Camp II, 2007a).

SIPT presents a framework from which participants can understand that differences do exist, and that many times these differences are a result of underlying cultural beliefs and values. Overall, the key to SIPT in international CMC and online collaboration is Olaniran's (2004) argument that intra-cultural communicative competence may not translate to cross-cultural competence. This premise is based on the fact that the dimensions of communication competence involve two factors: effectiveness and appropriateness. *Effective-*

ness focuses on the ability to accomplish goals, while *appropriateness* emphasizes the contextual suitability of behaviors (Roy, 2001; Spitzberg & Cupach, 1989). However, success is seldom accomplished in both dimensions. Individuals from different cultures have varying beliefs, values, and norms as the foundation of their perception and interpretation of other members' actions (Vroman & Kovacich, 2002). When this is the case, *appropriateness* becomes a difficult dimension to master in cross-cultural settings that are transferred to virtual group communication interactions (Olaniran, 2004; Olaniran & Edgell, 2008). Therefore, the development of meaningful communication exchanges, or collaborations, call for a greater communication competence. This competence must address and overcomes distance challenges and cultural boundaries, especially in IOC, fostering greater understandings between participants.

Culture and Technology

Given the increased use of online communication and virtual group collaboration in the global economy, there is a greater need for organizations to assist their employees in adapting their communicative behaviors in virtual communication environments (Economides, 2008; Lee, 2002; Olaniran, Burley, & Chang, 2009) Moreover, this adaptation is particularly important for the facilitation of cross-cultural exchanges than for co-located, or nearby, settings. For instance, the social structure in East Asian cultures shows cultural differences resulting in the resistance or refusal to use email in online communication (Lee, 2002). The Dutch, on the other hand, were found to prefer a more significant level of structure in communication encounters than their U.S. counterparts (Gezo, Oliverson, & Zick, 2000; Kiser, 1999). For example, in a cross-border project between individuals from Taiwan and the U.S., Teng (2007) noted the U.S. students were more comfortable interacting online by virtue of the number of messages they posted and responded to as compared to Taiwanese participants (see also Economides, 2008). Additionally, collaboration between Europeans and Latin Americans indicate misunderstandings and confusion due to cultural differences in perception, which impede communication and relegate interaction to strict task orientation (Qureshi & Zigurs, 2001).

These examples point to the difficulty with *appropriateness* in cross-cultural online communication contexts. National and organizational cultures affect how people interact and behave in a given context. In IOC, cultural and communicative preferences often clash. For example, people from different cultures may have different ideas about what constitutes good performance. Furthermore, notions of accountability can vary according to whether a culture is more collectivistic or individualistic (Dube & Pare, 2001).

Studies have shown that online interactions involving participants from the U.S., Japan, and Europe, demonstrated significant cultural differences in perceptions of communication task-technology fit (Massey, Montoya-Weiss, Hung, & Ramesh, 2001). The study indicates that participants from the U.S. perceived less difficulty conveying their opinions than participants from Asian and European origin. The collaborative technology was seen as conducive to a sender-oriented communication style inherent in individualistic, low-context cultures (e.g., the U.S.) that exhibit greater tendencies to express and accept communications at face value. In contrast, participants from Asia perceived technology to be a better medium for explaining themselves (Economides, 2008; Olaniran, 2007). Individuals from high-context cultures (e.g., Asia) need to know whether others understand them, and whether they can understand others, within the same communication circumstances. Thus, participants from Asia view the asynchronous groupware media as allowing enough time to compose messages and explain information in depth.

Culture and Silence

Silence is perceived differently in communication encounters, which affects participation in IOC. For instance, failure to post, or respond, to online messages in a timely manner when members are geographically distant is a major complaint in online collaboration (Roebuck & Britt, 2002). Massey et al. (2001) found Asian and European participants perceived ITs to be a better fit for convergence-oriented communication than their U.S. counterparts. For example, when participants encountered conflict, U.S. members viewed such conflicts as an impasse and attributed the situation to difficulty in reaching an agreement. On the other hand, Asians—who are normally regarded as collectivist, high-context, and higher uncertainty avoidance cultures (e.g., Chinese and Koreans)—often prefer to reach decisions through indirect communication. This communication is understood to include some degree of vagueness used in order to avoid direct conflict and confrontation. Thus, Asians tend to lean toward media that serve their purposes.

Such reliance, or comfort, with vagueness, however, contrasts with U.S. participants from an individualist, low-context, and lower uncertainty avoidance culture. In contrast, U.S. participants—who prefer direct communication, value confrontation, and enjoy intellectual debate—find it rather difficult to incorporate these communication values within the confines of asynchronous media exchanges. Consequently, ITs enable certain culturally driven communication behaviors while simultaneously hindering others. Therefore, participants from different cultures adapt ITs in order to fit within various perceived local norms and customs (Davidson & Vreede, 2001).

Furthermore, Lee (2002) found that, in many Asian cultures, the value of showing respect is more important than simply getting things done. Ultimately, this factor influences the communication within organizational environments. For example, this perspective might explain why Korean and Japanese employees shy away from email use, for they consider email sent directly to supervisors to be rude. Therefore, many Asians will often use alternative communication media deemed to be more respectful (Lee, 2002). However, Western cultures do not share similar perceptions of respect and, do not perceive the use of email with supervisors as rude (Lee, 2002; Olaniran, 2007a). In essence, the role of culture and the complexity it adds among international online communications, or collaborative projects, is crucial as individuals exchange messages. Consequently, culture is required to negotiate meanings that are sometimes based upon different perceptions and/or norms (Olaniran, 2009a).

Relationship building in online interactions also relies on different ways of interpreting silence. The idea of silence can be interpreted in various ways by different cultures, and such factors can alter perceptions in international exchanges. Silence, in reaction to a request or business proposal, for example, would be perceived negatively among Americans, Europeans, and Arab businesspersons. By contrast, silence is cherished among listening cultures (e.g., Chinese, Korea, and Nigeria) where it is considered a natural part of social interaction and not a failure to communicate (Lewis, 2000; Olaniran & Edgell, 2008).

Silence might be intensified in asynchronous online exchanges as participants from listening cultures either choose not to use a particular medium (e.g., email), or in order to show respect, wait until requested information is collected before formulating a response (Olaniran, 2004). In general, with asynchronous media, the time lag between messages, when unknown, can result in other participants' attributing non-communication to a lack of manners (Crampton, 2002; Pauleen & Young, 2001). A perception of a lack of manners cannot only damage relationships (Crampton, 2002; Pauleen & Yoong, 2001), but it can also greatly hinder willingness to communicate in the future. Similarly, certain cultures inhibit individuals from revealing their lack of understanding.

Therefore, when an individual considers requests for clarification to be impolite (Lewis, 2000), that person's performance and participation in asynchronous CMC collaboration can be drastically diminished. Such communication behaviors can, in turn, greatly affect the performance of the entire virtual team.

In general, online communication technology is believed to decrease sociability, group solidarity, and trust, yet all of these aspects are necessary and essential for members to communicate openly (Bal & Foster, 2000; Carleta, Anderson, & McEwan, 2002; Tanis & Postmes, 2005). It stands to reason that culture and a lack of close proximity (e.g., distance) inevitably interferes with international online interactions. Furthermore, individuals in co-located virtual groups that are geographically located in the same area have greater access to multiple communication media and have the benefit of arranging FtF meetings with ease. These local groups can use multiple channels, which, in turn, allow for a broader range of messages and cues, and at times, permit the immediate response to inquiries and/or unresolved issues. However, participants in IOC are relatively limited in their choice of online communication media. For instance, physical time differences restrict the use of synchronous online media such as videoconferencing, audio, and teleconferencing technologies in certain contexts (Olaniran, 2004). Armstrong and Cole's (2002) findings reinforce these effects of proximity in team conflict. The researchers discovered managers and facilitators in virtual groups felt there was as much conflict between sites that were 15km away as those that were 800km away.

Technology Selection

The issue of technology usage in virtual groups revolves around the choice of media. Additionally, issues of hardware and software compatibility are also germane to the discussion of factors affecting interactions in IOC. The selection of a technology medium itself represents a means by which globally adopted identities are imposed by the home office, or headquarters. Subsequently, these choices regarding media influence socially constructed identities sustained by individuals (Gimenez, 2002).

The issue of technology usage in virtual groups revolves around the choice of media. At the same time, issues of the hardware and software compatibility are also germane to the discussion of factors affecting IOC. Whether or not a particular IT medium is selected, and/or implemented, directly relates to affordability, and/or the accessibility, of that medium. Specifically, it is important to note that access to a particular IT infrastructure is not evenly distributed across the globe. This situation is frequently referred to as a *global digital divide*. Just as inroads and growth in Internet access have been made around the world, especially among less economically developed countries, significant portions of the globe still have no online access (Oyelaran-Oyeyinka & Lal, 2005). This fact makes Internet technology adoption difficult, if not impossible, within certain regions.

Adding to this problem are issues of software and hardware compatibility, and different technology platforms that are readily available (Olaniran, 2007a; 2009a). Furthermore, bandwidth is again germane to the technological infrastructure, for it has the ability to restrict, and/or limit, the choice, or the use, of a particular medium (Ya'u, 2004). For instance, while videoconferencing offers a high degree of social cues, it requires a significant amount of bandwidth, and faster connections to make it a reality. Consequently, videoconferencing might not be a viable option in certain regions where access, and/or high bandwidth connections are not available. Although heralded as a solution, Internet access on affordable mobile devices is still in infancy (Olaniran, 2007a; Olaniran, 2009b). Therefore, the lack of Internet accessibility, acceptable bandwidth and current and updated technology greatly affect the successful adoption and implementation of online media. Collectively, all of these factors influence communication interactions in IOC.

Moreover, the choice of a particular technology has different implications in different cultural contexts. Technology can convey a culture's core values and assumptions, and thus attain the status of a symbol apart from the message being communicated (Sitkin, et al., 1992). Therefore, when one considers the symbol carrying capacity of communication technology (see Olaniran, 2009b for further discussion), it is well documented that unequal distribution of IT media (i.e., cost affordability and the innovation process etc.), especially during the adoption of technology, allows certain users a given status within a society (Sitkin, et al., 1992).

This status difference comes with its own challenges. For instance, those who wield status rarely want to relinquish it, and thus, attempt to protect it at all cost. This is the case in some power distance cultures located within less economically developed countries, in particular, countries with governments that are slow in funding the adoption of online media (see Ess, 2002; Olaniran, 2007a). Therefore, the selection of a technology medium itself represents a means by which globally adopted identities are imposed by the home office, or headquarters. In this regard, both the adoption and the use of media are social (Contractor & Eisenberg, 1990). Subsequently, it is these choices related to media that influence the socially constructed identities sustained by individuals (Gimenez, 2002).

Much attention has been devoted to the issue of media selection, and its implications for communication interaction in online environments. Different theoretical perspectives have been proposed to gain a better understanding of the role of technology media. In one particular camp are those thinkers who focus on media richness. Such a perspective implies the mechanical and physical characteristics of technology are the primary determinants of communication outcomes (e.g., Daft & Lengel, 1986; Daft, Lengel, & Trevino, 1987; Dennis & Kinney, 1998; Rice, 1992). Another camp focuses on the social influence perspective, which argues that the social contexts in which technology media is used contributes to the communication outcomes by influencing users' overall perception of that media (e.g., Desanctis & Poole, 1994; Fulk, Schmitz, & Steinfield, 1990; Olaniran, 1995, 1996; Walther, 1995). SIPT, while aligning more with the latter, is truly a blend of the two models.

In one way, SIPT assumes media features influence perceptions drawn about them. At the same time, SIPT accommodates the notion of communication contexts. Advocates of SIPT note that both the technology media and the social factors involved in an exchange are important and should be taken into consideration when using technology within a virtual interaction (Olaniran, 2004; Yoo & Alavi, 2001). Similarly, different media are able to convey different levels of cues through bandwidth. These factors mean that more or less information can be communicated depending on the medium employed. For instance, communication technology media such as videoconferencing increase the amount social cues within a communication context. Consequently, this provides virtual teams with the opportunity to see one another within the context of the group, experience verbal and nonverbal cues, and gain immediate feedback. Such factors, in turn, provide users with a basis for understanding—a basis that takes into account cultural differences and language variety (Kasper-Fuehrer & Ashkanasy, 2001; Olaniran, 2007b).

Trust and Relationship Building

Trust is another major challenge facing international online communication. Trust is essential to facilitate technology-mediated meanings in support of accurate attribution especially with message intent. Perception of *intent* within ITs is often faced with skepticism, especially when a prior relationship has not been established. One need not forget that potential IT users tend to resist the adoption of technology when they associate it with negative implications such as loss of job security (Olaniran, 2004; Munkvold, 2005).

The concept of trust in virtual teams has been explored in detail by Olaniran (2004, 2009b). For instance, he argues that participants in international online collaborations are frequently concerned with the temporary and short common history of many geographically dispersed teams. Similarly, this lack of familiarity affects not only the attribution drawn on a medium, but also the participants' experiences within the collaboration process. In other words, team members who have not built trust for one another cannot draw on experience with each other in making attribution, thereby affecting the working environment as a whole (Olaniran, 2001; Crampton, 2002). It seems that when mediated members in dispersed groups have limited time, they often fail to seek adequate social and contextual information to support their attributions (Olaniran, 1994; Crampton, 2002; Walther, 2002). This situation causes difficulties for participants in maintaining relationships, or cohesion, during interaction because casual attributions made based upon incomplete information are often erroneous. Therefore, when things go wrong in IOCs, members tend to blame one another instead of focusing on assessments of possible situational factors.

Past studies on online interactions focus on outcomes associated with the lack of nonverbal cues that rendered mediated communication as impersonal. Some of these studies conclude that IOCs need time to adjust to communication technologies and to one another. Differences between FtF and virtual groups reduce with time, and more time together allows the development of trust among participants (e.g., Olaniran, 1994, 1995; Walther, 1994). This factor speaks to the SIPT proposition that relational development over time influences and shapes the evaluation of technologies, not to mention the roles that others play in reaching negative or positive conclusions about the experience.

Moreover, Vroman and Kovacich (2002) note that deadlines are often liberally interpreted in virtual groups. Similarly, Olaniran (2004) argues that people in international online collaborations emphasize critical incidents; thus, actual time lines are seldom the focus. This case is especially true in circumstances where asynchronous interactions and different time zones are the norm. Notwithstanding, different interpretations of project deadlines influence the level of participation, which, in turn, affects trust. For example, Cogburn and Levinson (2003) found that the lack of trust between U.S. and South African virtual group collaborations was due to the perception of an uneven distribution of work, infrequent communication among group members, and failure by team members to respond to other team members' initiatives. Ultimately, all of these cross-cultural differences in communication led to challenges in the virtual work environment.

In virtual group collaborative situations, national culture creates challenges for trust and is many times responsible for communication problems. These problems naturally result in different attitudes toward group behavior that are viewed as either acceptable or unacceptable within virtual group interactions (Rutkowski, Vogel, Genuchten, Bemelmans, & Favier, 2002). Additionally, Rutkowski et al. (2002) found that while group support systems provided structure during group activities, the perception of that structure was viewed by some as enabling, while others had seen the structure as a hindrance. This situation is especially true when multiple cultures (e.g., Asian, Dutch, and French) are represented in the group.

When participants appeared to keep an open mind and change their own perceptions, they were less likely to change their perceptions about their co-participants. Moreover, participant perceptions were discovered to be inaccurate when compared to other team members' self-perceptions of their actions (Rutkowski, et al., 2002). However, when virtual team participants from different cultures share a similar professional culture, they still perceived each other differently.

Attention has been given to the social effects of CMC technologies (e.g., Hampton & Wellman, 2001; Hiltz, Johnson, & Turoff, 1986; Sproull & Kiesler, 1986; Tanis & Postmes, 2005) and the capacity to support social cues that serve as a foundation for creating and maintaining relationships. This phenomenon is otherwise known as media richness (Daft & Lengel, 1986; Daft et al., 1987; Kishi, 2008; Robert & Dennis, 2005).

The literature is rife with the opinion that different IT media vary by the bandwidth, or numbers of cues, they can support. Consequently, FtF medium is considered as the richest medium given its ability to support nonverbal cues, personalization, and language variety (Conolly, Jessup, & Valacich, 1990; Hiltz, Johnson, & Turoff, 1986; Rockmann & Northcraft, 2008). Online media, on the other hand, are considered to be less friendly, less emotional, and/or more task-oriented (Garton & Wellman, 1995; Rice & Love, 1987; Tanis & Postmes, 2007). Hence, global virtual teams are challenged with a trust issue, which is compounded by cultural differences. Furthermore, trust in international online collaboration and global virtual teams is believed to be fragile and temporal (Holton, 2001; Jarvenpaa & Leidner, 1999; Kasper-Fuehrer & Ashkanasky, 2001; Olaniran, 2007b).

By implication, the perceived lack of multiple *cue-carrying capacity* of online media hinders trust and leads users to question their suitability for virtual teamwork and group processes that require a certain degree of cohesion through personal and socio-emotional factors. Thus, using the SIPT framework, not only do perceived communication tasks affect media use behavior, but they also affect the attitudes, and/or cultural context surrounding the media in general (Gu & Higa, 2009). Therefore, should a culture place more value upon FtF interaction than CMC interactions, it stands to reason that development of trust between interactants will also be reduced.

Within virtual team building, it is thus imperative that these matters be of the foremost importance and cultural understanding facilitated and ultimately integrated within the media to be used. This approach is the only way to assure successful collaborations and increase productivity in virtual intercultural teams.

APPLICATION OF IDEAS TO INTERNATIONAL INTERACTIONS

Individuals can adopt the following strategies in order to operate more effectively in the increasingly complex area of international online communication:

Strategy 1: Increase the Time for Collaborative Teams to Interact and Communicate

It stands to reason that because FtF is the most cue-rich communication environment, it should also be the most effective means by which virtual group members can establish trust (Kasper-Fuehrer & Ashkanasy, 2001). Consequently, decisions made in FtF work groups have a tendency to be more effective than decisions made through CMC virtual groups (Kasper-Fuehrer & Ashkanasy, 2001). Because international virtual groups FtF meeting is not feasible, it is important to increase the length of communicative encounters, and to integrate facial displays (e.g., emoticons, photographs, voice clips, and video) whenever possible. In other words, the creation of an actual virtual workplace where accidental communication can occur is essential to team success.

This accidental or informal communication can be initiated when individuals log into the common space. Here, they can see pictures of other members who are also present in the virtual workspace. They can also have the option to read profiles of other participants and/or begin informal chat session when desired (Kasper-Fuehrer

& Ashkanasy, 2001). These interactions, in turn, extend the time that teams communicate and allow for relationships and trust to develop between group members.

Strategy 2: Technology Selection Should Be in Accordance With Available IT Infrastructure

As discussed previously, many of the less economically developed countries possess limitations in IT infrastructure and bandwidth (Olaniran, 2004, 2007a). Although virtual groups are often part of a multinational corporation with technology resources that span the globe, this situation is not always the case. Media selection can only be made after a careful analysis of the cost of communication and regionally established IT infrastructure that is available to all participants. If the infrastructure is found to be unevenly distributed, then a mixture of asynchronous and synchronous media must be used so all participants can participate equally. This approach will create transparency, or a clear and accessible communication network, such that all group members can understand the procedures and monitor project progress (Moenaert et al., 2000).

Strategy 3: Consider Cultural Competency Development

The most effective way in which to address cross-cultural differences is to increase the cultural competency of all participants who work together within virtual groups. This cultural understanding must be two fold: 1) individual and 2) organizational. As discussed previously, individual participants are often culturally diverse in international online interactions. Thus, cultural perceptions (e.g., language, beliefs, and values) might lead to casual attributions of the other participants involved (Choi, Nisbett, & Norenzayan, 1999). However, an organization's culture, although often times solidified, can easily

be misinterpreted through the cultural lens of the individual. Therefore, virtual groups must first have clear understanding of the organizational culture and project objectives (i.e., purpose for the establishment of the virtual group) and then establish specific communication guidelines with which to accomplish project tasks (Moenaert, Caeldries, Lievens & Wauters, 2000). Within this framework, participants must adopt a four-fold culturally sensitive approach that entails:

- Knowing the task, consideration of the participants
- Understanding of other's cultural limitations
- Respecting all values and beliefs
- Tailoring of behaviors to foster a strong and vibrant work environment. (Foronda, 2008; Williams, Warren, & Olaniran, 2009)

Strategy 4: Media Selection Must Coincide With Cultural Values

Media selection that conflict with cultural values reduces productivity and increases the chances of misunderstandings and non-participation by individual virtual team members. Thus, media must be implemented with cultural understanding, so that it provides interactants with the ability to communicate in a manner that is not in conflict with their beliefs and values. Conversely, the adoption of culturally appropriate media will reduce the occurrences of negative casual attributions (Olaniran, 2001; Armstrong & Cole, 2002). Many times, these attributions are simply a misunderstanding of team members' actions as unwillingness to participate within collaborative exchanges. When in actuality, these members' are just culturally opposed to the technology being employed. This situation can easily be resolved through a reselection of media such that all participants are comfortable.

Strategy 5: Remember Language Learning

One of the greatest challenges to cross cultural communication is language barriers. A second challenge to international virtual groups is the fact that most of the content offered to end-users is presented in the English language (see Roebuck & Britt, 2002; Ya'u, 2004; Olaniran, 2007a). In order to bridge the cross-cultural divide, it is important for all participants to have the ability to communicate in one another's language. This situation will not only help increase the development of cultural competency (as discussed previously), but it will also aid in the creation of multilingual IOC content and project development. Subsequently, this approach will foster greater understanding for all participants involved.

IMPLICATIONS

This chapter has discussed the core assumptions, values, and the role of SIPT with the goal of shedding light upon how we come to understand international interactions via the Internet. Moving beyond social influence and relational models, SIPT argues that meanings derived from communication activities are not only mediated by past interactions and time (Walther, 1992), but are culture-bound as well. Given the globalization process, it is crucial to emphasize the cultural aspects of communication. This situation becomes more pertinent as more individuals from various ethnic groups increasingly interact in online environments and as they strive to work together in organizations. Thus, the SIPT assumptions are critical for understanding the use of CMC, the perceptions of CMC interactions, and cross-cultural communication encounters in online environments.

According to SIPT, meanings are influenced by culture, thus perceptions of CMC attributes/ features, and social interactions, should reflect cultural differences in intercultural and cross-cultural organizations. This perspective implies that when dealing with CMC and other technologies, it is critical to consider the culture from which meanings, interpretations, and perceptions evolve. Cultural differences and dispersed geographic locations cause differences among mediated group members. Such factors can be problematic by creating organizational issues that ultimately increase differences among individuals. SIPT can be used as a function for minimizing cultural differences by exploring and understanding the depth and magnitude as well as how and why differences are the way they are.

The development of meaningful collaboration calls for greater competence to alleviate distance challenges and cultural boundaries that exist in IOC, where SIPT plays a critical role. The key issue discussed in SIPT literature is the argument that intra-cultural communicative competence (e.g., effectiveness and appropriateness) might not translate to cross-cultural competence in international CMC and online collaboration (Olaniran, 2004). Due to cultural differences (e.g., beliefs, values, and norms), an individual's perception and interpretation of other members' actions may be different from the original intent. Furthermore, different languages, communication styles, and behaviors can result in variation in work group composition. These factors coupled with differences in information processing styles create complexities in multinational organizations and teams that can create challenges to collaboration (Roebuck & Britt, 2002; James & Ward, 2002; Olaniran, 2007a).

SIPT discusses the reduction of interpersonal uncertainty through long-term communication, the formation of relationships, and ultimately trust between individuals. Although this situation has not always been evident, SIPT continues to be a dominating theory and guiding principal in explaining how to structure both local and cross-cultural CMC interactions. This factor remains true despite the fact that researchers such as Garton and Wellman (1995) and Rice and Love (1987) among others discuss how online media appear less friendly, less emotionally driven, and more task focused when compared to FtF interactions.

The truth is that many cultures do not perceive the sharing of information with the same value as is seen in many Western nations. Castells (2009) explains that the power in a network, or globalized, society lies in the construction of meaning as evidence in what he terms mass (media) self-communication. This type of communication possesses the potential to reach a global audience (e.g., YouTube, Facebook, etc.), and is composed of content that is self-directed by the creator and self-selected by the user. Although Massey et al. (2001) found that many Asian participants view asynchronous communication as allowing time to explain information in-depth, the core assumption for this usage was to foster understanding. For within these actions lie the collectivist, high context, and higher uncertainty avoidance value preferences in which clear meanings, not just the dissemination of information for information sake, is the end goal. Thus, Castells' (2009) definition of a global culture built upon the power of information creation and sharing is not always valued by all involved. In this case, SIPT alone cannot and does not always accomplish the goals of increasing understanding between cultures, and/or increasing trust between cultural groups. This is because the cultural foundation upon which the group is founded is not similar for all individuals involved in the interaction.

CONCLUSION

The power of the SIPT lies within its ability to foster communication between individuals through communicative behavior that is valued by the other's culture. Whether this communication is organizational, or occurs between individuals during a personal exchange, the proper encoding, decoding, and cultural context of the message is es-

sential for success. Although not an overt assumption of the SIPT, it is essential to understand how cultural factors (e.g., perception, social influence, norms, expectations, meaning negotiations, etc.) are important components of any CMC interaction. When specifically addressing intercultural CMC interactions, SIPT requires an understanding of the cross-cultural value of information in addition to the corresponding cross-cultural conveyance of knowledge. Therefore, this information must be encoded in such a way that the contextual meaning is clearly expressed between individuals of different backgrounds. This situation is especially the case within an organizational environment. So, if it is true that communication is contextual and based upon environmental factors, then it stands to reason that the core cultural values shared between individuals during communication defines the social interaction.

Yet, this social interaction continues to present challenges to groups who view and interpret CMC cues differently, particularly if these differences are culturally motivated. Consequently, all of these factors affect the trust levels that developed between individuals interacting through CMC. By using cultural sensitivity perspectives such as SIPT, CMC interactions can, and will, be successful. This situation is particularly true when diverse groups allow more time for interpersonal adjustmen,t and begin to develop trust in working and/or personal relationships.

However, adjustment to CMC technologies also remains contingent upon the communicator's adaptation to various cultural values, norms, and perspectives. There remains significant need for organizations to assist their employees in adapting their communicative behaviors in IOC especially when teams are addressing cross-cultural issues. SIPT assumes IT features influence the perception that is drawn about them, while accommodating for the communication context. This aspect further implies that the technology medium and social factors are critical and should be considered when using technology in virtual interactions

(Olaniran, 2004). Finally, the issue of trust is a challenge for IOC, where participants tend to be concerned with the temporary, or short common history, of geographically dispersed teams, attribution drawn about a particular medium and participant's experience during collaboration. In order to have accurate attribution, specifically with message intent, trust is essential to technology-mediated meaning.

The implication deriving from SIPT is that relational development over time influences and shapes the evaluation of technologies and the role that others play in the evaluation, positive and/ or negative. Therefore, if given ample time to interact and ample time to develop a relationship, mediated group members might be less likely to question their suitability for virtual teamwork. This approach will aid in the establishment of trust between members and the establishment of group cohesion within the virtual team. The Social Information Processing theory (SIPT) is a valuable perspective for exploring and understanding diversity in the context of cultural differences and international communication via CMC. For it is within this theoretical context that differences can be recognized and understood in order to develop a strategic plan for managing challenges and issues faced by IOC.

REFERENCES

Armstrong, D. J., & Cole, P. (2002). Managing distances and differences in geographically distributed work groups. In Hinds, P., & Kiesler, S. (Eds.), *Distributed work* (pp. 167–186). Cambridge, MA: The MIT Press.

Bal, J., & Foster, P. (2000). Managing the virtual team and controlling effectiveness. *International Journal of Production Research, 38*(17), 4019–4032. doi:10.1080/00207540050204885

Barthes, R. (1977). The death of the author. In Heath, S. (Ed.), *Image, music, text* (pp. 101–105). New York, NY: Hill & Wang.

Branon, R. F., & Essex, C. (2001). Synchronous and asynchronous communication tools in distance education: A survey of instructors. *TechTrends, 45*, 36–42. doi:10.1007/BF02763377

Branzei, O., Vertinsky, I., & Camp, R. D. II. (2007). Culture-contingent signs of trust in emergent relationships. *Organizational Behavior and Human Decision Processes, 104*(1), 61–82. doi:10.1016/j.obhdp.2006.11.002

Carleta, J., Anderson, A., & McEwan, R. (2000). The effects of multimedia communication technology on non-collocated teams: A case study. *Ergonomics, 43*(8), 1237–1251. doi:10.1080/00140130050084969

Castells, M. (2009). *Communication power*. Oxford, England: Oxford University Press.

Choi, R. E., Nisbett, R., & Norenzayan, A. (1999). Causal attribution across cultures: Variation and universality. *Psychological Bulletin, 125*, 47–63. doi:10.1037/0033-2909.125.1.47

Cogburn, D. L., & Levinson, N. (2003). U.S.-Africa virtual collaboration in globalization studies: Success factors for complex cross-national learning teams. *International Studies Perspectives, 4*, 34–52. doi:10.1111/1528-3577.04103

Connolly, T., Jessup, L. M., & Valacich, J. S. (1990). Effects of anonymity and evaluative tone on idea generation in computer-mediated groups. *Management Science, 36*, 97–120. doi:10.1287/mnsc.36.6.689

Contractor, N. S., & Eisenberg, E. M. (1990). Communication networks and new media in organizations. In Fulk, J., & Steinfield, C. W. (Eds.), *Organizations and communication technology* (pp. 143–172). Newbury Park, CA: Sage.

Crampton, C. D. (2002). Attribution in distributed work groups. In Hinds, P., & Kiesler, S. (Eds.), *Distributed work* (pp. 191–212). Cambridge, MA: The MIT Press.

Daft, R. L., & Lengel, R. H. (1986). Organizational information requirements, media richness and structural design. *Management Science, 32*, 554–571. doi:10.1287/mnsc.32.5.554

Daft, R. L., Lengel, R. H., & Trevino, L. K. (1987). Message equivocality, media selection, and manager performance: Implications for information systems. *Management Information Systems Quarterly, 11*, 355–366. doi:10.2307/248682

Davidson, R., & Vreede, G. (2001). The global application of collaborative technologies. *Communications of the ACM, 44*(12), 69–70.

Dennis, A. R., & Kinney, S. T. (1998). Testing media richness theory in the new media: The effects of cues, feedback, and task equivocality. *Information Systems Research, 9*(3), 256–274. doi:10.1287/isre.9.3.256

Desanctis, G., & Poole, M. S. (1994). Capturing the complexity in advanced technology use: Adapative structuration theory. *Organization Science, 5*(2), 121–147. doi:10.1287/orsc.5.2.121

Dube, L., & Pare, G. (2001). Global virtual teams. *Communications of the ACM, 44*(12), 71–73. doi:10.1145/501317.501349

Dubrovsky, V. J., Kiesler, S., & Sethna, B. N. (1991). The equalization phenomenon: Status effects in computer-mediated and face-to-face decision-making groups. *Human-Computer Interaction, 6*, 119–146. doi:10.1207/s15327051hci0602_2

Economides, A. A. (2008). Culture-aware collaborative learning. *Multicultural Education & Technology Journal, 2*(4), 243–267. doi:10.1108/17504970810911052

Ess, C. (2002). Cultures in collision philosophical lessons from computer-mediated communication. *Metaphilosophy, 33*(1-2), 229–253. doi:10.1111/1467-9973.00226

Foronda, C. L. (2008). A concept analysis of cultural sensitivity. *Journal of Transcultural Nursing, 19*(3), 207–212. doi:10.1177/1043659608317093

Fulk, J., Schmitz, J., & Steinfield, C. W. (1990). A social influence model of technology use. In Fulk, J., & Steinfield, C. W. (Eds.), *Organization and communication technology* (pp. 117–140). Newbury Park, CA: Sage.

Garton, L., & Wellman, B. (1995). Social impacts of electronic mail in organizations: A review of the research literature. In Burleson, B. R. (Ed.), *Communication yearbook, 18* (pp. 434–453). Thousand Oaks, CA: Sage.

Gasner, A. (1999). Globalization: The changing face of the workforce. *Business Today, 36*(3), 43–44.

Gezo, T., Oliverson, M., & Zick, M. (2000). Managing global projects with virtual teams. *Hydrocarbon Processing, 79*, 112c–112i.

Gimenez, J. (2002). New media and conflicting realities in multinational corporate communication: A case study. *IRAL, 40*, 323–343. doi:10.1515/iral.2002.016

Gu, R., & Higa, K. (2009). A study on communication media selection in IT and service work groups. *International Journal of Services Sciences, 2*(3-4), 381–397. doi:10.1504/IJSSCI.2009.026548

Gudykunst, W. B., & Kim, Y. Y. (1992). *Communicating with strangers: An approach to intercultural communication* (2nd ed.). New York, NY: McGraw Hill.

Hampton, K., & Wellman, B. (2001). Long distance community in the network society: Contact and support beyond Netville. *The American Behavioral Scientist, 45*(3), 476–495. doi:10.1177/00027640121957303

Hiemstra, G. (1982). Teleconferencing, concern for face, and organizational culture. In Burgoon, M. (Ed.), *Communication yearbook* (*Vol. 6*, pp. 874–904). Beverly Hills, CA: Sage.

Hiltz, S. R., Johnson, K., & Turoff, M. (1986). Experiment in group decision making communication process and outcome in face to face vs. computerized conference. *Human Communication Research, 13*, 225–252. doi:10.1111/j.1468-2958.1986.tb00104.x

Holton, J. A. (2001). Building trust and collaboration in a virtual team. *Team Performance Management, 7*(3/4), 36–47. doi:10.1108/13527590110395621

James, M., & Ward, K. (2001). Leading a multinational team of change agents of Glaxo Welcome. *Journal of Change Management, 2*(2), 148–159. doi:10.1080/714042500

Jarvenpaa, S. L., & Leidner, D. E. (1999). Communication and trust in global virtual teams. *Organization Science, 10*, 791–815. doi:10.1287/orsc.10.6.791

Kalawsky, R. S., Bee, S. T., & Nee, S. P. (1999). Human factors evaluation techniques to aid understanding of virtual interfaces. *BT Technology Journal, 17*, 128–241. doi:10.1023/A:1009687227736

Kasper-Fuehrer, E. C., & Ashkanasy, N. M. (2001). Communicating trustworthiness and building trust in interorganizational virtual organizations. *Journal of Management, 27*, 235–254.

Kiesler, S., Siegel, J., & McGuire, T. W. (1984). Social psychological aspects of computer-mediated communication. *The American Psychologist, 39*, 1123–1134. doi:10.1037/0003-066X.39.10.1123

Kiser, K. (1999, March). Working on world time. *Training (New York, N.Y.), 36*(3), 28–34.

Kishi, M. (2008). Perceptions and use of electronic media: Testing the relationship between organizational interpretation differences and media richness. *Information & Management, 45*(5), 281–287. doi:10.1016/j.im.2008.02.008

Kock, N. (1998). Can communication medium limitations foster better group outcomes? An action research study. *Information & Management, 34*(5), 295–305. doi:10.1016/S0378-7206(98)00066-4

Lea, M., O'Shea, T., Fung, P., & Spears, R. (1992). "Flaming" in computer-mediated communication: Observations, explanations, implications. In M. Lea (Ed.), *Context of computer-mediated communication* (pp. 89-112). London, England: Harvester- Wheatsheaf.

Lee, O. (2002). Cultural differences in email use of virtual teams a critical social theory perspective. *Cyberpsychology & Behavior, 5*(3), 227–232. doi:10.1089/109493102760147222

Lewis, R. D. (2000). *When cultures collide: Managing successfully across cultures.* London, England: Nicholas Brealy Publishing.

Massey, A. P., Montoya-Weiss, M., Hung, C., & Ramesh, V. (2001). Cultural perceptions of task-technology fit. *Communications of the ACM, 44*(12), 83–84. doi:10.1145/501317.501353

Mesdag, M. V. (2000). Culture-sensitive adaptation or global standardization-the duration of usage hypothesis. *International Marketing Review, 17*, 74–84. doi:10.1108/02651330010314722

Moenaert, R. K., Caeldries, F., Lievens, A., & Wauters, E. (2000). Communication flows in international product innovation teams. *Journal of Product Innovation Management, 17*, 360–377. doi:10.1016/S0737-6782(00)00048-5

Munkvold, E. (2005). Experiences from global e-collaboration: Contextual influences on technology adoption and use. *IEEE Transactions on Professional Communication, 48*(1), 78–86. doi:10.1109/TPC.2005.843300

Olaniran, B. A. (1994). Group performance and computer-mediated communication. *Management Communication Quarterly, 7*, 256–281. doi:10.1177/0893318994007003002

Olaniran, B. A. (1995). Perceived communication outcomes in computer-mediated communication: An analysis of three systems among new users. *Information Processing & Management, 31,* 525–541. doi:10.1016/0306-4573(95)00006-3

Olaniran, B. A. (1996). A model of satisfaction in computer-mediated and face-to-face communication. *Behaviour & Information Technology, 15,* 24–36. doi:10.1080/014492996120373

Olaniran, B. A. (2001). The effects of computer-mediated communication on transculturalism. In Milhouse, V., Asante, M., & Nwosu, P. (Eds.), *Transcultural realities* (pp. 83–105). Thousand Oaks, CA: Sage.

Olaniran, B. A. (2004). Computer-mediated communication in cross-cultural virtual groups. In Chen, G. M., & Starosta, W. J. (Eds.), *Dialogue among diversities* (pp. 142–166). Washington, DC: National Communication Association.

Olaniran, B. A. (2007a). Challenges to implementing e-learning and lesser developed countries. In Edmundson, A. L. (Ed.), *Globalized e-learning cultural challenges* (pp. 18–34). Hershey, PA: Idea Group, Inc.

Olaniran, B. A. (2007b). Culture and communication challenges in virtual workspaces. In St. Amant, K. (Ed.), *Linguistic and cultural online communication issues in the global age* (pp. 79–92). Hershey, PA: Idea Group, Inc.doi:10.4018/978-1-59904-213-8.ch006

Olaniran, B. A. (2009a). Culture, learning styles, and Web 2.0. *Interactive Learning Environment: International Journal, 17*(4), 261–271. doi:10.1080/10494820903195124

Olaniran, B. A. (2009b). A proposition for developing trust and relational synergy in international e-collaborative groups. In Salmons, J., & Wilson, L. (Eds.), *Handbook of research on electronic collaboration and organizational synergy* (pp. 472–486). Hershey, PA: IGI-Global.

Olaniran, B. A. (2009c). Discerning culture in e-learning and in the global workplaces. *Knowledge Management & E-Learning: An International Journal, 1*(3), 180–195.

Olaniran, B. A., & Edgell, D. (2008). Cultural implications of collaborative information technologies (CITs) in international online collaborations and global virtual teams. In Zemliansky, P., & St. Amant, K. (Eds.), *Handbook of global virtual workspaces* (pp. 118–133). Hershey, PA: IGI Global.

Oyelaran-Oyeyinka, B., & Lal, K. (2005). Internet diffusion in sub-Saharan Africa: A cross-country analysis. *Telecommunications Policy, 29,* 507–527. doi:10.1016/j.telpol.2005.05.002

Pauleen, D., & Yoong, P. (2001). Facilitating virtual team relationships via Internet and conventional communication channels. *Journal of Internet Research: Electronic Networking Applications and Policy, 11*(3), 190–202. doi:10.1108/10662240110396450

Postmes, T., Spears, R., & Lea, M. (1998). Breaching or building the social boundaries? SIDE-Effects of computer-mediated communication. *Communication Research, 25,* 689–715. doi:10.1177/009365098025006006

Qureshi, S., & Zigurs, I. (2001). Paradoxes and prerogatives in global virtual collaboration. *Communications of the ACM, 44*(12), 85–88. doi:10.1145/501317.501354

Rice, R. (1992). Task analyzability, use of new media, and effectiveness: A multi-site exploration of media richness. *Organization Science, 3*(4), 475–500. doi:10.1287/orsc.3.4.475

Rice, R. E. (1993). Media appropriateness: Using social presence theory to compare traditional and new organizational media. *Human Communication Research, 19,* 451–484. doi:10.1111/j.1468-2958.1993.tb00309.x

Rice, R. E., & Aydin, C. (1991). Attitudes toward new organizational technology: Network proximity as a mechanism for social information processing. *Administrative Science Quarterly, 36,* 219–244. doi:10.2307/2393354

Rice, R. E., Grant, A., Schmitz, J., & Torobin, J. (1990). Individual and network influences on the adoption and perceived outcomes of electronic messaging. *Social Networks, 12,* 27–55. doi:10.1016/0378-8733(90)90021-Z

Rice, R. E., & Love, G. (1987). Electronic emotion: Socioemotional content in a computer-mediated network. *Communication Research, 14,* 85–108. doi:10.1177/009365087014001005

Robert, L. P., & Dennis, A. R. (2005). Paradox of richness: A cognitive model of media choice. *IEEE Transactions on Professional Communication, 48*(1), 10–21. doi:10.1109/TPC.2004.843292

Rockmann, K. W., & Northcraft, G. B. (2008). To be or not to be trusted: The influence of media richness on defection and deception. *Organizational Behavior and Human Decision Processes, 107*(2), 106–122. doi:10.1016/j.obhdp.2008.02.002

Roebuck, D. B., & Britt, A. C. (2002). Virtual teaming has come to stay: Guidelines and strategies for success. *Southern Business Review, 28,* 29–39.

Roy, M. H. (2001). Small group communication and performance: Do cognitive flexibility and context matter? *Management Decision, 39*(4), 323–330. doi:10.1108/00251740110391501

Rutkowski, A. F., Vogel, D. R., Genuchten, M. V., Bemelmans, T. M., & Favier, M. (2002). E-collaboration: The reality of virtuality. *IEEE Transactions on Professional Communication, 45*(4), 219–229. doi:10.1109/TPC.2002.805147

Schmitz, J., & Fulk, J. (1991). Organizational colleagues, information richness, and electronic mail: A test of the social influence model of technology use. *Communication Research, 18,* 487–523. doi:10.1177/009365091018004003

Sitkin, S. B., Sutcliffe, K. M., & Barrios-Choplin, J. R. (1992). A dual capacity model of communication media choice in organizations. *Human Communication Research, 18,* 563–598. doi:10.1111/j.1468-2958.1992.tb00572.x

Solomon, C. M. (2001). Managing virtual teams. *Workforce, 80*(6), 60–65.

Spears, R., & Lea, M. (1992). Social influence and the influence of the "social" in computer-mediated communication. In M. Lea (Ed.), *Contexts of computer-mediated communication* (p. 30-65). Hemel Hempstead, UK: Harvester-Wheatsheaf.

Spitzberg, B. H., & Cupach, W. R. (1989). *Handbook of interpersonal competence research.* New York, NY: Springer-Verlag.

Spitzer, M. (1986). Writing styles in computer conferences. *IEEE Transactions on Professional Communication, 29,* 19–22.

Sproull, L., & Kiesler, S. (1986). Reducing social context cues: Electronic mail in organizational communication. *Management Science, 32,* 1492–1512. doi:10.1287/mnsc.32.11.1492

Tanis, M., & Postmes, T. (2003). Social cues and impression formation in CMC. *The Journal of Communication, 53*(4), 676–693. doi:10.1111/j.1460-2466.2003.tb02917.x

Tanis, M., & Postmes, T. (2005). Short communication. A social identity approach to trust: Interpersonal perception, group membership and trusting behaviour. *European Journal of Social Psychology, 35,* 423–424. doi:10.1002/ejsp.256

Tanis, M., & Postmes, T. (2007). Two faces of anonymity: Paradoxical effects of cues to identity in CMC. *Computers in Human Behavior, 23*(2), 955–970. doi:10.1016/j.chb.2005.08.004

Turkle, S., & Papert, S. (1990). Epistemological pluralism: Styles and voices within the computer culture. *Signs, 16*, 128–157. doi:10.1086/494648

Vroman, K., & Kovacich, J. (2002). Computer-mediated interdisciplinary teams: Theory and reality. *Journal of Interprofessional Care, 16*, 161–170. doi:10.1080/13561820220124175

Walther, J. B. (1992). Interpersonal effects in computer-mediated interaction: A relational perspective. *Communication Research, 19*, 52–90. doi:10.1177/009365092019001003

Walther, J. B. (1994). Anticipated ongoing interaction versus channel effects on relational communication in computer-mediated interaction. *Human Communication Research, 20*, 473–501. doi:10.1111/j.1468-2958.1994.tb00332.x

Walther, J. B. (1995). Relational aspects of computer-mediated communication: Experimental observations over time. *Organization Science, 6*(2), 186–203. doi:10.1287/orsc.6.2.186

Walther, J. B. (1997). Group and interpersonal effects in international computer-mediated collaboration. *Human Communication Research, 23*, 342–369. doi:10.1111/j.1468-2958.1997.tb00400.x

Walther, J. B. (2002). Time effects in computer-mediated groups: Past, present, and future. In Hinds, P., & Kiesler, S. (Eds.), *Distributed work* (pp. 235–257). Cambridge, MA: The MIT Press.

Walther, J. B., Anderson, J. E., & Park, D. (1994). Interpersonal effects in computer-mediated interaction: A meta analysis of social and antisocial communication. *Communication Research, 23*, 3–42. doi:10.1177/009365096023001001

Walther, J. B., & Burgoon, J. K. (1992). Relational communication in computer-mediated interaction. *Human Communication Research, 19*, 50–88. doi:10.1111/j.1468-2958.1992.tb00295.x

Williams, I. M., Warren, H. N., & Olaniran, B. A. (2009). Achieving cultural acquiescence through foreign language e-learning. In Chang, M., & Kuo, C. (Eds.), *Handbook of research on learning culture and language via ICTs: Methods for enhanced instruction*. Hershey, PA: IGI Global.

Ya'u, Y. Z. (2004). The new imperialism & Africa in the global electronic village. *Review of African Political Economy, 99*, 11–29. doi:10.1080/0305624042000258397

Yoo, Y., & Alavi, M. (2001). Media and group cohesion: Relative influences on social presence, task participation, and group consensus. *Management Information Systems Quarterly, 25*(3), 371–390. doi:10.2307/3250922

Yum, Y. O., & Hara, K. (2005). Computer-mediated relationship development: A cross-cultural comparison. *Journal of Computer-Mediated Communication, 11*(1), article 7. Retrieved April 25, 2010, from http://jcmc.indiana.edu/ vol11/ issue1/yum.html

KEY TERMS AND DEFINITIONS

Anticipation of Future Interaction (AFI): The degree to which individuals expect to engage in future relations with others.

Culture: A set attitudes, beliefs, values, preferences, goals, and practices shared by a group of individuals.

Information Processing Theory: A systemic approach to how the human mind processes information through rules and strategies.

Media Richness Theory: The ability of a medium to carry multiple cues that affect communication between individuals.

Paralinguistic Codes: Codes and symbols used in communication.

Social Information Processing Theory (SIPT): States that, given enough time and frequency of interactions, online relationships can develop between individuals or groups.

Social Presence Theory: Examines the degree of awareness of another individual's presence during a communicative interaction.

Chapter 5
Filtering Online Content in China

Jyh-An Lee
National Chengchi University, Taiwan

ABSTRACT

This chapter focuses on the Internet filtering mechanism the Chinese government adopted in order to prevent individual users from accessing foreign online content. Based on the case of Internet filtering in China, the author argues that when citizens are regulated by code rather than by the law, they will experience and perceive such code-based controls as natural. From the Chinese case, it should also be noted that the Internet's effects on politics varies depending upon how its architecture is designed.

INTRODUCTION

Increasingly, commentators claim that the Internet enables free flow of information and contributes to the creation of a freer and more open society (Deibert, 2002; Stevenson, 2007). This situation might be true in many of the world's countries today, but in some nations, such as China, the diffusion of Internet access and use has not led to increased freedom for Internet users (Stevenson, 2007; Farrell, 2007). Rather, in the People's Republic of China (i.e., mainland China), the national government has built probably the world's most sophisticated Internet filtering system. It is

a system designed to block a number of foreign Websites that the national government views as a threat to the Chinese state. Interestingly, these blocked Websites include those pages containing information associated with Tibetan Independence, Taiwanese Independence, human right, Falun Gong, and other movements the ruling Communist Party sees as a threat or a challenge to its control (Stevenson, 2007; Faris & Villeneuve, 2008). The government, moreover, argues that such widespread and common filtering is desirable, for it can prevent the Western world from "dumping" information on China. In sum, it is online protectionism based upon real-world nationalism.

DOI: 10.4018/978-1-60960-833-0.ch005

During the early days of Internet access in China, some individuals optimistically believed access to and use of the Internet would make that medium a librating force that could help democratize China by opening new venues for political debate and discussion. On the contrary, the Chinese government has actually used online networking technologies to control the dissemination of information within the nation's borders. The government has adeptly used the Internet as a medium for advocating its own ideologies and perspectives while actively blocking any expressions of dissent. Thus, digital technologies have become the government's tool to tamp down political threats (Yang, 2009). For example, the Chinese government has ordered Chinese Internet carriers, like China Telecom, to deploy Cisco's equipment to block unwanted materials from entering China. This practice has, in turn, significantly changed the open nature of the Internet.

While the government can choose to use the law to regulate people's online behavior, controlling access to online information via technical architecture seems to be a much more effective approach. In fact, the Chinese government has been attempting to control online content via several different targets, including Internet content providers, individual consumers, and content on foreign Websites (Wacker, 2003; Yang, 2009). An investigation of the complex dynamics involved in this process could fill an entire library. For this reason, understanding the nature of government control of the Internet in China often requires one to examine the overall puzzle one piece – or component – at a time. This chapter, therefore, focuses on the topic of filtering mechanism used to prevent individuals in China from accessing foreign online content.

In examining this topic, this chapter will use Lawrence Lessig's (2006) pronouncement "code is law" as a mechanism for examining and understanding the Internet filtering system used by China's government. According to Lessig's ideas, technology can often fulfill a regulatory function or can be used in a way that has the same effects as regulation. The essential characteristic of code-as-regulator, for example, is that "[a] rule is defined, not through a statute, but through the code that governs" (Lessig, 2006, p.24). Through the application of Lessig's theory to online filtering practices in China (i.e., the "great firewall of China"), the author illustrates the implications this approach has for a government's ability to regulate online information sharing. The aim of the chapter is not to criticize the Chinese Internet filtering system, but rather to illustrate how a government can regulate and shape human behavior via architecture. Such an examination can provide important insights that can be used to examine how other governments or agencies use similar approaches to control online information dissemination in other contexts.

INTERNET FILTERING IN CHINA

The use of information and communications technologies (ICTs), including the Internet, in China has grown rapidly over the last decade due, in large part, to strong support from the Chinese government (Wacker, 2003). The Internet infrastructure in China has, as a result, experienced extraordinary growth in terms of scale, scope, and quality (Wu, 1996; Zhu & Wang, 2005). At the same time, the Chinese government has endeavored to control the dissemination of online information via various approaches, such as regulations and the use of certain filtering and monitoring technologies.

Within this context, the term "filter" generally refers to programming a router in such a way as to block data from entering or leaving a network (Human Rights Watch, 2006). The original objective of such programming is to give Internet service providers (ISPs) the means to control malicious or destructive programs such as viruses, worms, and spam (Human Rights Watch, 2006). Governments, however, can use the same technologies to selectively block certain kinds of online information from being transmitted or received (Human Rights Watch, 2006). Such organized and coordinated blocking efforts by a government becomes "Internet filtering," which represents a technical approach to preventing Internet users from accessing specific Internet Protocol ("IP") addresses, Websites, or Web pages (Nawyn, 2007, p.505, 510). The reason for such filtering (i.e., blocking the access citizens have to certain online information) is, in most cases, because such blocked information is deemed too sensitive or too inflammatory by a particular government or agency (Zittrain & Palfrey, 2008).

In recent years, a number of countries have developed their own Internet filtering systems in response to a variety of political, moral, or security concerns (Zittrain & Palfrey, 2008; Faris & Villeneuve, 2008). In most of these cases, one of two types of Internet filtering techniques is used: the inclusion filter and/or the exclusion filter (Nawyn, 2007). The inclusion filter typically uses a "white list" to indentify Websites a government has deemed acceptable for its citizens to access online. An exclusion filter, by contrast, employs a "blacklist," which specifies Websites a government deems as "suspect" and thus uses technology to prohibit its citizens from accessing sites containing that information (Nawyn, 2007). In the case of exclusion filtering, the governments wishing to block online access to certain Websites usually request or require Internet service providers (ISPs) to implement the filtering task, for this approach is often the cheapest method to filter online information (Faris & Villeneuve, 2008).

The Chinese government has adopted the exclusion filter approach and has enacted this approach by requesting carriers/ISPs such as China Telecom to install Cisco's apparatus, which can drop information from at least three hundred IP addresses (Goldsmith &Wu, 2006; Faris & Villeneuve, 2008). Under this system, the Chinese government provided the carriers with a list of forbidden Websites and the addresses of those sites. The government then orders the ISP to use Cisco's equipment to block or prevent Chinese citizens from being able to access those sites (Goldsmith & Wu, 2006). These blocked sites include those for Amnesty International's (www.amnesty.org), Reporters without Borders (www.rsf.org), the BBC (news.bbc.co.uk), the Economist (http://www.economist.com), and the New York Times (http://www.nytimes.com) (Deibert, 2002; Farrell, 2007). Through this approach, certain online information gets dropped/cut off and can never reach end users located in the People's Republic of China.

From the government's perspective, the fact that new Websites are continuously and rapidly emerging means inclusion filters are seen as including/blocking too few Websites, while exclusion might block/exclude too few sites (Nawyn, 2007). In order to avoid potential over-blocking or under-blocking related to filtering, governments have started to employ the "content-analysis" technique as a new tool for Internet filtering (Nawyn, 2007, p.511). The content-analysis approach prevents users from accessing any Website or any URL path that contains or uses certain keywords the government has designated as suspicious or problematic (Nawyn, 2007; Faris & Villeneuve, 2008). One advantage to this content-analysis approach is that it does not require a government to incessantly update the white list or the blacklist used to filter online content. In China, for example, keywords for content analysis might include politically "hot button" issues such as Tibetan Independence, Taiwanese Independence, discussions of human rights violations, comments on the treatment of Falun Gong practitioners, etc. (Goldsmith &Wu, 2006).

In order to filter online information, the Chinese government has been continually installing a complicated technical system into the Internet ever since the initial days of online access in China (Nawyn, 2007; Stevenson, 2007). In 2002, Jonathan Zittrain and Ben Eldman (2003) worked with an end user in China to produce a list of foreign Websites blocked by the Chinese government.

The resulting list covered a range of organizations and topics the Chinese government blocked based on the perspective these subjects were a threat to the Chinese state. Of course, China is not the only country that filters away politically sensitive content. A number of other nations use this same approach, and these nations include Bahrain, Ethiopia, Libya, Iran, Myanmar, Thailand, Pakistan, Saudi Arabia, Syria, Tunisia, Uzbekistan, and Vietnam (Faris & Villeneuve, 2008).

But how can the Chinese government, or any government, control the online flow of information into the country? The answer is that the government of China worked with the U.S. hardware vendor Cisco to create a great firewall between Chinese citizens and online information (Goldsmith & Wu, 2006; Stevenson, 2007). This firewall, in turn, has altered Internet access in China in such a way as to convert it into, essentially, a huge intranet within the nation's borders (Deibert, 2002; Stevenson, 2007). It is estimated that this conversion process earns Cisco some USD$500 million each year in China (Stevenson, 2007, p.542). But Cisco is not alone. Other companies that provide filtering software to China include the U.S.-based companies Sun Microsystems (acquired by Oracle in 2009), Websense, and Bay Networksboth (Stevenson, 2007; Deibert, 2002). Through working with these organizations, the Chinese government has created a filter that is constructed on different layers of China's Internet. The central backbone/foundation of this system, however, is the physical infrastructure that links the domestic Internet in China to global networks that exist outside of its borders (Farrell, 2007; Nawyn, 2007).

Different from the firewalls established to protect enterprises' information security, the Chinese great firewall is set around the whole country (Goldsmith & Wu, 2006). The country's Ministry of Information Industry (MII) alone is authorized to build the network used to connect China to the global Internet. This arrangement, thus, ensures government control over the network and thus what individuals can use that network to

access or distribute (Farrell, 2007; Human Rights Watch, 2006). Because this approach means online information can only enter the country through a limited number of points, the Chinese government is able to control the information via controlling these points (Goldsmith & Wu, 2006). Under this system, government control over information flow is coordinated via several Internet access providers (IAPs), "each of which has at least one connection to a foreign Internet backbone" (Internet filtering in China, 2007; Faris & Villeneuve, 2008, p.14). In this system, IAPs peer at three Internet exchange points (IXPs) run by the Chinese government, and these IAPs "grant regional Internet service providers (ISPs) access to backbone connections" (Goldsmith & Wu, 2006, p.93). Put differently, individual Chinese end users purchase Internet access from several thousand ISPs, and those ISPs are, in effect, retail sellers of Internet access purchased wholesale from the few IAPs in the country. Thus, by effective managing the IAPs and IXPs, the Chinese government is able to control information flowing from abroad and to do so in a relatively manageable way.

CODE-IS-LAW IN THE CONTEXT OF INTERNET FILTERING

This section applies the code-is-law theory to Internet filtering practices in China. This application reveals how strategic uses of programming, or code, can achieve a regulatory function akin to focused legal oversight or legal intervention. It also reveals how architecture shapes human behavior.

Code-is-Law Theory

As Lawrence Lessig (2006) has argued, code — be it related to software or hardware — can be designed to perform a regulatory function. As a result, governments can use code in strategic ways to create many of the same effects as legal regulation (Lessig, 2006; Faris & Villeneuve, 2008).

According to Lessig, the "code"/programming that controls the Internet effectively creates the Internet's architecture and thus its "laws" (Lessig, 2006, p.5-6). Therefore, if and how the Internet is regulated depends upon the architecture or the design of code. In Lessig's words, "[a] rule is defined, not through a statute, but through the code that governs the space" (Lessig, 2006, p.24). He goes on to explain that

The software and hardware that make cyberspace what it is constitute a set of constraints on how you can behave…The code or software or architecture or protocols set [certain] features, which are selected by code writers. They constrain some behavior by making other behavior possible or impossible. The code embeds certain values or makes certain values impossible. In this sense, it too is regulation. (Lessig, 2006, pp.124-125)

In commenting on this situation, Lessig observes "We can build, or architect, or code cyberspace to protect values that we believe are fundamental, or we can build, or architect, or code cyberspace to allow those values to disappear" (Lessig, 2006, p.6). From a policy perspective, Lessig reminds legislators and regulators that they need to carefully consider what law and architecture, or code, can best advance their goals (Lessig, 2006). Although Lessig explicitly recognizes the fundamental differences between the law (regulation via statute) and the code (regulation via programming/design) (Lessig, 2006), some commentators criticize his theory as a disingenuous representation of the role of technologies in regulation (Wagner, 2005).

Theory Application

By building one of the most complicated Internet filtering architecture in use today, the Chinese government has crafted a new Internet architecture according to its own nationalist ideology (MacKinnon, 2008). This architecture differs markedly from its counterpart in the Western world where Internet architecture has been characterized as open and free (Stevenson, 2007; MacKinnon, 2008). Comparing the differences between the Internet architectures of China and of the West, it is not difficult for the average observer to understand Lessig's argument that "some architectures enable better control than others" (Lessig, 2006, p.24).

Law vs. Code as Regulation

The code-is-law theory raises interesting questions regarding the role and the use of code or architecture as an alternative to law-based regulation. When policymakers have regulatory options of code or law, they often consider the effectiveness of each approach and evaluate the costs and benefits associated with each method (Kesan & Shah, 2005). In many cases, the deciding factor becomes a matter of breadth (the scope of the activities that can be regulated) and depth (the degree to which certain activities can be regulated).

In the case of China, the government has employed several mechanisms to regulate the amount and the kind of online information available to citizens. Such mechanisms include a mix of law and code. This mixed approach involves legislation (i.e., law) (Deibert, 2002; Farrell, 2007; Nawyn, 2007; Stevenson, 2007; Yang, 2009) and legal enforcement activities – based on existing statutes (i.e., law) – that force search engines to remove inappropriate content (Lessig, 2006; Stevenson, 2007). They also include a heavy focus on using technologies (i.e., code) that filter online content (Stevenson, 2007).

In comparison to being regulated exclusively by law, regulation by code – or by a mix of law and code –usually makes it more difficult for citizens to determine when they are being regulated and when their access to content is being actively blocked or controlled. When, for example, a Chinese Internet user is unable to open a forbidden/blocked Website, the message that appears on the computer screen does not read or note that the "Website has been blocked by the Government" (Goldsmith & Wu, 2006, p.94). Rather, that individual receive the same "site not found" message they would encounter if the related site was no longer online, if an incorrect URL had been used, or if a technical problem had arisen (Goldsmith & Wu, 2006). This kind of ambiguity means Chinese Internet users can never be sure when their failure to access certain sites represents a conscious attempt by the government to filter online content vs. some form of error or problem on the part of the user or the Website's sponsor/sponsoring organization.

A variety of code-based options exist for creating such ambiguous messages when engaging in active blocking of online content. Countries such as Tunisia, for example, use U.S.-developed SmartFilter software as a proxy filter. This software (i.e., code) uses "a blockpage that looks like the… browser's default error page" (Faris & Villeneuve, 2008, p.15). Uzbekistan's Internet filtering practices similarly hide the government's blocking actions by redirecting users to Microsoft's search engine www.live.com (Faris & Villeneuve, 2008). The software/code-based approach used by China is similar to the SmartFilter and the Microsoft strategies, but the Chinese government relies on a software/code developed in China by Chinese programmers (Human Rights Watch, 2006, p.10; Internet filtering in Tunisia, 2005). In all of these cases, the software (code) involved helps conceal the fact that a government or government agency is actively attempting to block citizens' access to certain sites and specific online information. It is thus quite difficult for Internet users in these nations to know if the problems they experience when accessing certain Websites is a matter of government intervention and regulation or involve an actual technical problem (Goldsmith & Wu, 2006).

This difficulty proves that Lessig's (2006) concern over code-based regulation is not over-stated. Lessig has long warned us that because regulating by code is not as transparent as regulating by the law, the former may weaken the democratic values of a society. Or, more simply stated, when

citizens are regulated by code rather than by the law, they will "experience these controls as nature" (Lessig, 2006, p.138). This situation is what is now happening in China. When citizens are more accustomed to the fact that a great number of Websites cannot be viewed via their computers, they will be more likely to take such intervention and control for granted.

Of course, governments implementing filtering system can choose not to disguise the fact that they are blocking a Website. The government of Saudi Arabia, for example, uses SmartFilter and has decided to provide citizens with a blockpage that notifies them when the online content they have requested has been blocked by the government (Faris & Villeneuve, 2008). Theses blockpages also inform users of how to lift the block on a particular site (Faris & Villeneuve, 2008). However, Saudi Arabia is just one of the few countries willing to disclose such blocking information and to provide users with a method for addressing that block (Faris & Villeneuve, 2008). Therefore, when regulating by code, a government has the option of whether to disclose its intent in constraining behavior or to leave that factor ambiguous.

Using law or code to regulate might bring about different costs to a society. Law regulates behavior through an *ex post* approach. That is, a law will not be enforced until a violation takes place (Lessig, 2006). Although law enforcement might threaten potential punitive actions in the future, doing so might incur significant costs for the regulator. From the perspective of the Chinese government, for example, jailing violators who use the Internet to disseminate prohibited content could draw considerable international attention and create negative public impression of China on the global stage. Such factors might even counteract China's relatively recent attempts to re-brand itself as an enticing location for foreign investors. Thus, the costs associated with direct legal action are extraordinarily high.

In contrast, regulating by code is an *ex ant* approach. That is, although the adoption of infrastructure-based Internet filtering might lead to certain criticisms regarding citizens' rights to information, such practices create a relatively low cost for the government (i.e., domestic complaints by citizens – and complaints that are easy to dismiss as "technical errors") as opposed to regulating by law and addressing international concerns expressed over public trials or public arrests. This cost-benefit balance might explain why the Chinese government prefers to rely on the code-based approach to Internet control (Faris & Villeneuve, 2008).

Fulfilling Policy Goals via Architecture Design

As a number of commentators have noted, the Internet has historically represented freedom and openness (Lessig, 2006). The original architecture of the Internet was designed as a distributed network that had no central control. Thus, by its very design, the Internet is quite difficult to control. The values underlying the original design of the Internet, moreover, included interconnectivity, openness, flexibility, and the lack of a pervasive centralized authority (Naughton, 2000). Nonetheless, such attributes do not exist in full within the architecture of today's Internet in China as the Chinese government is weaving nationalist ideology into the design of the Internet itself.

In truth, the Chinese government has dominated the design of the Internet in that nation, and had controlled the development and dissemination of the Internet there since its inception (Nawyn, 2007). As a result, the Chinese government was able to create an Internet architecture that mapped its preferences onto that technology – an approach that made the Chinese Internet significantly different from its counterpart in the Western world. China, however, is not alone in creating such a system. The government of Saudi Arabia, for example, has also created its own unique network that governs how Internet traffic flows through three "choke points" overseen by its Communications

and Internet Technology Commission (Internet and Saudi Arabia, 2010). Both China and Saudi Arabia have designed centralized control points in the international gateway of their Internet architecture, and these points were built in mid 1990. Therefore, the filtering systems used by these nations have been implemented at the international gateway level regardless the cooperation from ISPs (Faris & Villeneuve, 2008). This approach might partly explain why these filtering systems work so well in both nations.

In understanding this code-based approach to filtering, it can be helpful to balance the restrictive nature of China's Internet with that of filtering attempts tried by nations where Internet infrastructure developed in a different way. Australia can, in turn, provide a good contrastive example to the approach taken in China. The Australian government has attempted to build a filtering system into its existing Internet architecture (Bambauer, 2009). However, because the country's Internet is as decentralized as its counterpart in other Western countries, the government can hardly find a controlling point to use for deploying an effective filtering system (Bambauer, 2009). The case of Australia helps explain how the cost and difficulty of implementing an Internet filtering system are quite high if a government did not take such system into consideration when structuring the Internet architecture from the very beginning.

The difference between the Australian and the Chinese Internet filtering systems also illustrates how a government can decide to regulate the subject architecture and how an open architecture can constrain government's power. As Lessig (2006) points out

[W]hether [the Net] can be regulated depends on its architecture. Some architectures would be regulable, others would not. I have then argue that government could take a role in deciding an architecture would be regulable or not. (pp. 151-52)

Therefore, if the Internet architecture in a nation has been crafted as an open and decentralized one since its inception, a government's power to regulate the network is greatly reduced. In other words, an open architecture represents a constraint on the power or a government. This situation echoes Lessig's suggestion that the architecture of the Internet often checks government control over the Internet and the ideas carried on it (or the values embedded in it)(Lessig, 2006).

Despite these factors, the Chinese government is also attempting to create an Internet with positive externalities in relation to business and economic development, education, and information exchange (Deibert, 2002; MacKinnon, 2008). Although such an intention and the open nature of the Internet are somehow conflicting with state's control over the network in these cases, the Chinese government has managed to carefully maintain the balance of openness and control associated with its Internet policy. One commentator cited a 2005 edition of *People's Daily* explains this approach as follows:

As long as we use more ways of properly looking at the Internet, we can make use of the best parts, we go for the good and stay away from the bad and we use it for our purposes, and we can turn it around on them...we won't be defeated in the huge Internet wars by the various intranational and international reactionary ideological trends in various areas. (MacKinnon, 2008, p.33)

Interestingly, according to the Chinese government, the purpose of filtering online information is to block "spiritual pollution" from the country (Deibert, 2002). In sum, the Chinese government encourages taking advantage of digital technologies, but such usage cannot be done to undermine the state's control.

Architecture's Impact on Human Behavior

Although sophisticated users can always circumvent Internet filtering technologies and reach the blocked foreign sites, it is perhaps the case that the filtering system employed by the Chinese government has effectively prevented most Chinese users from accessing foreign Websites deemed "inappropriate" by the authorities (Nawyn, 2007). This situation is just one aspect of how architecture (i.e., code) regulates online behavior. However, the most profound consequence of this architecture is not that it immediately stops citizens' access to sensitive foreign content. Rather, the major factor to consider is how such uses of code are gradually shaping human behavior in cyberspace.

Together with other regulations and monitoring techniques imposed by the government, the Chinese are using the Internet in the way that has been prescribed by the nation's government. According to a 2005 study conducted by the Chinese Academy of Social Science, most Chinese Internet users look for entertainment services and information rather than try to find political discussions when online (MacKinnon, 2008; Yang, 2009). Influenced by the filtering architecture and perhaps other factors, not many Chinese Internet users seem interested in seeking out political information online.[1] Even university students, users who are often aware of technologies such as proxy servers that can circumvention of Internet filtering, appear not to be widely interested in taking advantage of existing technologies to reach blocked foreign Websites (MacKinnon, 2008). For those technologically savvy Chinese youth who do access blocked Websites, such actions are just a game that often lacks much (if any) political interest (Wacker, 2003). This phenomenon also echoes Lessig's (2006) argument that we cannot conclude that effective control of code is not possible only because complete control or perfect control does not exist.

By shaping citizens' online behavior via Internet architecture, the Chinese government has slowed the Internet's impact as a tool for political change (MacKinnon, 2008). In so doing, the government of China has reinforced its political authority. Obviously, in the short run, the Internet's role in enabling a public discourse around political and policy debates in China will be limited because of governmental control. Nevertheless, it is difficult to assess if and how circumvention of Chinese Internet filtering will make a difference in the long run.

Regulating the Intermediaries

As mentioned, Chinese Internet filtering is primarily implemented at international gateways an on the level of IAPs, IXPs, and ISPs. This practice provides a good example of how governments can regulate the decentralized architecture of the Internet. Because of the open and decentralized nature of the Internet, it is extremely difficult and costly to directly regulate each Internet user's behavior. Therefore, as Lessig (2006) has argued, it is more difficult to regulate scattered individuals than to regulate a few large firms. In the case of online content control in China, it would be more effective for the government to indirectly regulate users by directly regulating intermediaries like IAPs or IXPs. A possible explanation for such indirect regulation is that intermediaries, such as IAPs or IXPS, are far more susceptible to pressures from the government than are individual Internet users. As Jack Goldsmith and Tim Wu (2006) argue, "[W]hen government practices control through code, it is practicing a commonplace form of intermediary control" (p.72). In sum, it would be much less effective to control individual Internet users' access to foreign Website than to directly mandating Internet filtering implemented by IAPs or IXPs.

CONCLUSION

The Internet might have the power to eliminate sovereign boundaries in certain scenario, but this potential does not mean the Internet exists in a social and political vacuum. Conventional wisdom states that the Internet provides almost anyone with near-perfect access to information. However, this belief turns out to be not true in many countries that implement Internet filtering systems. Like many other countries around the world, China filters Internet content that the government has deemed "too sensitive for ordinary citizens." And it has done so with precision and effectiveness for a number of years.

In the case of China, we learn that Internet's impact on politics varies depending upon how its architecture is designed. As China has changed the original nature of the Internet, it has become obsolete for commentators to claim that the Internet will democratize the country. This chapter claims that the Internet filtering technology in China verifies Lessig's (2006) code-is-law theory. When a person fails to open a prohibited Website in China, he or she might view this factor as a technique problem rather than consider it government intervention of some sort. In this way, a code-based regulation is not as transparent as law-based regulation. Moreover, from the government's perspective, regulating by code might occasionally lead to much less cost than regulating by law. This belief is seems to be especially true in the context of the Chinese government regulating online flows of information.

The history of the Chinese Internet has made it unique and effective in filtering online information. Like Saudi Arabia, the government of China designed the nation's Internet architecture from the very beginning and did so with the aim of controlling and blocking information flow from abroad. Therefore, the Chinese government is able to filter or block information much more effectively and efficiently than other countries with a traditional open and decentralized network. Together, with other surveillance mechanisms, Internet filtering has to a certain degree shaped the online behavior of Chinese citizens and has done so according to the government's preferences.

REFERENCES

Bambauer, D. E. (2009). Filtering in Oz: Australia's foray into Internet censorship. *The University of Pennsylvania Journal of International Law, 31*, 493–513.

Deibert, R. J. (2002). Dark guests and great firewalls: The Internet and Chinese security policy. *The Journal of Social Issues, 58*, 143–159. doi:10.1111/1540-4560.00253

Faris, R., & Villeneuve, N. (2008). Measuring global Internet filtering. In Deibert, R. (Eds.), *Access denied: The practice and policy of global Internet filtering* (pp. 5–27). Cambridge, MA: The MIT Press.

Farrell, K. (2007). The big mamas are watching: China's censorship of the Internet and the strain on freedom of expression. *Michigan State Journal of International Law, 15*, 577–603.

Goldsmith, J., & Wu, T. (2006). *Who controls the internet: Illusions of a borderless world. New York*. NY: Oxford University Press.

Human Rights Watch. (2006). *Race to the bottom: Corporate complicity in Chinese Internet Censorship*. New York, NY: Human Rights Watch.

Internet.gov.sa. (2010). *Internet in Saudi Arabia*. Retrieved November 15, 2010, from http://www. internet.gov.sa/ learn-the-web/guides/ internet-in-saudi-arabia

Kesan, J. P., & Shah, R. C. (2005). Shaping code. *Harvard Journal of Law & Technology, 18*, 319–399.

Lessig, L. (2006). *Code and other laws of cyberspace version*. New York, NY: Basic Books.

MacKinnon, R. (2008). Flattered world and thicker walls? Blogs, censorship, and civil discourse in China. *Public Choice, 134*, 31–46. doi:10.1007/s11127-007-9199-0

Naughton, J. (2000). *A brief history of the future*. Woodstock, NY: The Overlook Press.

Nawyn, M. D. (2007). *Code red: Responding to the moral hazards facing U. S. Information.*

October 10, 2010, from http://www.opennetinitiative.net/ studies/tunisia/ONI_Tunisia_ Country_Study.pdf.

OpenNet Initiative. (2005). *Internet filtering in Tunisia in 2005: A country study*. Retrieved

OpenNet Initiative. (2007). *Internet filtering in China: 2006-2007*. Retrieved March 26, 2010, from http://opennet.net/studies/china2007

Stevenson, C. (2007). Breaching the great firewall: China's Internet censorship and the quest for freedom of expression in a connected world. *Boston College International and Comparative Law Review, 30*, 531–558.

Technology companies in China. *Columbia Business Law Review, 2007*, 505-564.

Wacker, G. (2003). The Internet and censorship in China. In Hughes, C. R., & Wacker, G. (Eds.), *China and the Internet: Politics of the digital leap forward* (pp. 58–82). New York, NY: Routledge.

Wagner, R. P. (2005). On software regulation. *Southern California Law Review, 78*, 457–516.

Wu, W. (1996). Great leap or long march: Some policy issues of the development of the Internet in China. *Telecommunications Policy, 20*, 699–711. doi:10.1016/S0308-5961(96)00050-X

Yang, G. (2009). *The power of the internet in China. New York*. NY: Columbia University Press.

Zhu, J. J. H., & Wang, E. (2005). Diffusion, use, and effect of the Internet in China. *Communications of the ACM, 48*, 49–53. doi:10.1145/1053291.1053317

Zittrain, J., & Edelman, B. (2003). Internet filtering in China. *IEEE Internet Computing, 7*, 70–77. doi:10.1109/MIC.2003.1189191

Zittrain, J., & Palfrey, J. (2008). Internet filtering: The politics and mechanisms of control. In Deibert, R. (Eds.), *Access denied: The practice and policy of global Internet filtering* (pp. 29–56). Cambridge, MA: The MIT Press.

KEY TERMS AND DEFINITIONS

Content-Analysis Filter: An Internet filtering approach preventing users from accessing any Website or any URL path that contains or uses certain keywords the government has designated as suspicious or problematic.

Exclusion Filter: An Internet filtering approach employing a "blacklist," which specifies Websites a government deems as "suspect" and thus uses technology to prohibit its citizens from accessing sites containing that information.

Internet Exchange Point (IXP): A physical infrastructure through which Internet service providers (ISPs) exchange Internet traffic between their networks.

Internet Filtering: A technical approach to preventing Internet users from accessing specific Internet Protocol ("IP") addresses, Websites, or Web pages.

Internet Service Provider (ISP): An entity that provide its customers with access to the Internet.

Inclusion Filter: An Internet filtering approach using a "white list" to indentify Websites a government has deemed acceptable for its citizens to access online.

Router: A device that connects two or more computer networks, and selectively interchanges packets of data between them.

ENDNOTE

[1]   In making this argument, I do not mean that Chinese citizens in the People's Republic of China are not interested in engaging in online political discussions. I only wish to point out that many of them might lose interested in finding sensitive political information online.

Chapter 6

Culture, Online Technology, and Computer–Mediated Technical Documentation:
Contributions from the Field of Intercultural Communication

Marc Hermeking
Ludwig-Maximilians University, Germany

ABSTRACT

The global diffusion of technology is increasingly accompanied by both computer-mediated and online communication. Several empirical examples for the influence of culture on the usage of online technology and computer-mediated technical documentation are illustrated with relevant theories from the field of intercultural communication (e.g., Edward T. Hall's model of low-/high-context in particular). Recent developments and national differences in the global diffusion of mobile phones and the Internet are discussed as examples for culture-specific online communication preferences. Similar cultural influences on computer-mediated technical documentation and operational instructions are demonstrated by online manuals from Southeast Asia and by an aviation control system. Beyond the understanding of cultural communication preferences, consequences for construction and design of such technologies are also discussed.

DOI: 10.4018/978-1-60960-833-0.ch006

INTRODUCTION

As a precondition and as a result of the era of globalization, the world-wide diffusion of technology – both traditional, mechanical, offline technology and modern, computerized online technology – tends to increase enormously. This phenomenon interconnects people and cultures from all over the world, and, at first sight, this situation seems to indicate a culture-free character of technology. Most of all, this culture-free global image seems to hold true for information and communication technology (ICT) and all related forms of computer-mediated communication (CMC), both wired and wireless/mobile.

The latter, especially, gains an increasing share in nearly all kinds of technical products beyond formerly typical ICT products: Examples for such additional elements of our online environments are cars, trains, ships, airplanes, and even household appliances of the near future – the usage of which tends to be more and more accompanied by computer-mediated instructions and online technical documentation. Consequently, a lot of offline documentation, such as printed operation manuals, has already disappeared and continue to be substituted by human-machine interaction (human-computer interaction) in online environments around the world.

An increasing number of empirical studies, however, confirm the manifold and sometimes subtle, but nevertheless very critical influences of culture on technology in general (Hermeking, 2001; Hermeking, 2010) and on CMC (e.g., the Internet, websites) in particular (Hermeking, 2005; Singh, Zhao, & Hu, 2005; Hermeking 2007; An, 2007; Li & Zhao, 2009; Gevorgyan & Manucharova, 2009; Hauser, 2010). Such cultural influences on technology might not only apply to the perceived design and the visual surface of technical products. Rather, they might also apply to the different contexts and ways of using technologies –as well as the ways of communicating with and about technology. Cultural communication styles exert many, and sometimes utmost critical, impacts on such human-machine interactions.

This chapter provides some empirical examples for the influence of culture on the usage of online technology and on computer-mediated technical documentation. These connections will, in turn, be illustrated by examining relevant theories and models from the field of intercultural communication.

INTERCULTURAL COMMUNICATION

Culture, Communication, and Technology

The implications of cultural diversity and the interactions between members from different cultures are central issues of the academic and the practical field of intercultural communication – a field based on various academic disciplines including cultural anthropology/ethnology, cross-cultural psychology, and translation studies/linguistics. Though personal face-to-face interaction is its traditional focus, intercultural communication is related by many ways to material culture in general (Roth, 2001) as well as to technology and its cross-cultural transfer in particular (Hermeking, 2001; Jansen & Riemer, 2003). The pioneer work of anthropologist Edward T. Hall of the 1950s is commonly regarded as the starting point of this discipline. Since then, it has found broad acceptance and additional theoretical development by many others.

Like many renowned ethnographers of his time, Hall was influenced by anthropological theories of functionalism. According to this perspective, culture comprises material and immaterial products as instruments to cope with problems to which all human beings are exposed during their existence. These problems are identical worldwide, but what instrument out of a variety of possible choices is preferred depends on the specific priorities or values that people in social units, groups, or cultures, collectively share. Consequently, different groups or cultures are characterized by different sets of values that guide their existence. Technical products, or instruments, are clearly – though not explicitly – included in that conception of culture.

Hall's work focused on the interdependence of culture and communication, which is also expressed in his most central statement "culture is communication" (Hall, 1959, p. 94). In accordance with that perspective, Hall introduced 10 universal cultural categories as "primary message systems" (Hall, 1959), of which three categories – the orientation towards "temporality" (time) as well as "territoriality" (space), and "interaction" (context, message flow) – were elaborated by Hall in more detail and consequently gained larger popularity in the later years (Hall & Hall, 1990). Being similar to other popular categories like Hofstede's (1991; 2001) cultural dimensions or project GLOBE's core dimensions of culture (House, Quigley, & Sully de Luque, 2010), Hall's model is based on macro-cultural entities like lingual communities, regional populations, or nations. Such a focus has been noted as having both advantages and disadvantages (Hermeking, 2005).

Though Hall's cultural categories of time, space, and context were originally not related to technology or technical documentation explicitly, they can well be applied to those areas. This adaptability results from the fact that CMC is increasingly central to both the use of technology and the creation of associated technical documentation. Consequently, distinctions between the use of technology in general, of ICT in particular, and their related technical documentations are fading. By contrast, cross-cultural aspects of online communication, of human-machine interaction, and of digital user interfaces are growing in importance.

Mono-/Polychronic Time, Space, and Low/High Context

According to Hall, cultures can be differentiated into "monochronic" and "polychronic" with respect to their conceptions of time. In monochronic cultures, time is linear, passing ('time is money'), handled precisely, and divided in an orderly fashion. Thus, action chains generally are compartmentalized and sequential – one thing is completed after the other. Classic examples for monochronic cultures are Britons, Germans, Swiss, Scandinavians, and Anglo-Americans. In polychronic cultures, by contrast, time is generally regarded as circular and repeating, subject to social relationships or needs, and therefore handled in a flexible, imprecise way. Action chains in such systems are structured in a less detailed way and are interrupted more often because many things are done simultaneously. Classic examples for polychronic cultures are Latin-Americans, Arabs, Mediterranean peoples, and many others.

Resulting from a stronger compartmentalization, most members of monochronic cultures divide their environmental space strictly into private and public spheres. Conversely, members of polychronic cultures, who are more open to interruptions and social commitments, more often are mixing these spheres.

Resulting from their different degree of involvement with people, most monochronic cultures also are "low-context" cultures, whereas most polychronic cultures are "high-context" cultures. This distinction characterizes their different message flows and communication preferences. Members of low-context cultures, for example, have less personal contact with each other. As a result, communication must be very detailed and very explicit. A great amount of formal information is communicated in a direct way, often by way of written texts ("high content"). In contrast, members of high-context cultures have closer and more familiar contacts with each other. A great deal of information is already shared among the members of high-context cultures. For this reason, the members of such cultures prefer modes of communication that are more informal, indirect, and often based merely on symbols or pictures ("low content"). Members of high-context cultures are, for example, the French, Spaniards, Arabs, and the Japanese (Hall, 1976; Hall & Hall, 1990). Such strong generalizations, however, have yet to be empirically validated (Cardon, 2008).

CONVERGENCE AND DIVERGENCE IN ONLINE ENVIRONMENTS

Mobile Phones: Voice vs. Text/Data Messages

A prominent example for the global spread of online technology is the mobile phone (also known as the smart phone), which, among other CMC features, also provides Internet services. After its commercial introduction in 1983, it took many years until mobile communication found intensive global popularity. Today, however, the number of mobile-phones surpasses by far the number of fixed telephone lines. In fact, according to an estimation of the International Telecommunication Union, nearly 5 billion mobile-phone subscriptions currently exist worldwide, but fewer than 1.5 billion fixed lines exist globally (Fryer, 2009).

In the beginning, the diffusion of mobile phones had followed culture-specific patterns of openness towards innovations in countries known as "low uncertainty avoidance" cultures (specifically in the U.S., U.K., and Scandinavia as early adopters) (Hofstede, 1991; de Mooij, 2004). Though national differences still exist – for example, penetration rates in northern European countries were much larger (in 2008, over 120%) than in most Mediterranean countries (TNS-infratest, 2009) – the enormous global diffusion of mobile phones during the last five years might be regarded as the beginning of a final cultural convergence towards a globally homogeneous mobile-phone culture.

With respect to the various ways, contexts, and contents of mobile communication, lots of culture-specific differences, however, exist. Italians, for example, are notoriously known for frequent mobile phone usage, whereas people from Ireland are not known for making much use of mobile phones. Interestingly, usage frequency data (e.g., minutes/user/year) indicate an equally high usage of mobile phones in Ireland. Based on their culturally different conception of space, Italians tend to use their mobile phones much more in the public than the Irish, who prefer to use their mobile phones in a more private (and therefore less visible) sphere. A similar difference in the usage of mobile phones had been observed between (more polychronic) Parisians or Madrileniens, who felt freer to talk aloud in crowded public, and (monochronic) Londoners, who tended to withdraw to certain, less disturbing and more discrete zones (Fryer, 2009).

With respect to voice versus text-messaging, for a while, cultural differences seemed to be reflected by a stronger preference for the latter in low-context cultures. Recently, however, text-messaging and other mobile data services have gained enormous popularity in high-context cultures like Japan. Silence is often an important virtue in such cultures – talking aloud on the phone in public is a taboo and even strictly forbidden in commuter trains in Japan – and smaller living areas offer very little privacy, especially for young people (Kohima, 2005; Tee, 2005). Consequently, writing short-text-messages (SMSs), emails or web-logs (blogs), and reading comics (*Manga*) or even online novels are the most popular contents – in addition to online games and music – of Japan's frequent mobile phone usage, whereas voice messages (in 2009, 133 minutes/user/month, compared to 788 in the U.S.) equal only half the world average and still continue to decrease (Fryer, 2009; Coulmas, 2008).

The more indirect and maybe more polite way of using text instead of direct voice messages might be regarded as a culture-specific preference. Another reason for such text-heavy CMC in high-context Southeast-Asia is its somewhat more picture-like and less abstract writing system (Usunier & Lee 2009), which may be more compatible to communicating by way of visuals and symbols. In addition to that factor, technical development during the last decade has changed the low-context style text-messaging systems towards some more high-context style. In emails, for example, former ASCII-based informal symbols, also known as emoticons, have been replaced by elaborated icons (e.g., smileys). Likewise, instant-messaging systems have been increasingly enriched by full-color icons (e.g., flowers) and additional visual elements (e.g., animations, videos, and games). Thus, increased usage of written CMC by members from high-context cultures was accompanied – even if not invoked – by an increased share of visual contents.

Another example for text-heavy mobile communication in a high-context culture is Indonesia. In that nation, ethnographers have observed a high popularity of sophisticated mobile phones with Global Positioning System (GPS) technology. This popularity is less based on innovativeness, but first of all based on religious interest to locate the direction of Mecca (Erard, 2004).

The Internet: Recent Developments

Global Diffusion Patterns

Another prominent example for the global diffusion of online technology is the Internet and its most popular user interface – the World Wide Web (WWW). In the last two decades, various global Internet access quotas have shown remarkable national differences – relative penetration rates in particular have revealed a clear continuum of descent from high Internet usage in the (western) "North" to low usage in the (non-western) "South"

(Hermeking, 2005). In 2005, for example, the percentage of the population using the Internet as "active web users" was

*   Sweden–53%,
*   United States–48%
*   Australia–46%
*   U.K.–38%
*   Germany–36%,
*   France–26%
*   Japan–29%
*   Spain–22%

By contrast, Brazil, for that same period of time, had an Internet penetration rate of only 6%. In 2007, this percentage was

*   Sweden–57%
*   Australia–50%
*   United States–49%
*   U.K.–41%
*   Germany–40%
*   France–34%
*   Spain–33%
*   Japan–30%

Again, Brazil showed relatively smaller gains with an Internet penetration rate of only 9% for that same period (Nielsen Netratings, n.d.).

Though these figures reveal a continuous increase in global Internet diffusion, their national differences also indicated an important influence of culture beyond economic, political, technical, and other hard factors, for these numbers reveal correlations with several cultural value categories and communication preferences (Hermeking, 2005; Hermeking, 2007). Accordingly, the diffusion of the Internet from its country of origin (the U.S.) to other countries during nearly two decades obviously depended – among other factors – on cultural similarities to the U.S. Such similarity seems particularly connected to two value categories of Hofstede's (2001) model of cultural dimensions – those of strong "individualism" and low "uncertainty avoidance." The latter (uncertainty avoidance) represents cultural openness to adopt innovations like this new medium. The former (individualism) corresponds to a relatively impersonal medium of communication between individuals, and is strongly related to Hall's context model. Moreover, in general, the Internet seems to be preferred more in low-context cultures than in high-context cultures.

These obvious cultural communication preferences showed analogies with the global consumption pattern of traditional media such as newspapers and TV. In general, the former, based on explicit written text, are more popular in low-context cultures. The latter, strongly based on pictures and sounds, is more popular in high-context cultures. This difference indicates that the nature of the Internet during the first two decades was more similar to print media (i.e. based mainly on a text-heavy, explicit and informational communication style), which was consequently accepted most of all in low-context cultures like large parts of the U.S., where the Internet (as the Arpanet of 1969) originally was developed for sharing explicit scientific information (Hermeking, 2007).

Recently, however, as a result of more efficient data transfer and possibilities of mobile usage in particular, the Internet has gained much popularity in highly developed high-context cultures (e.g., Japan). At first sight, this factor simply seems to support the modernization thesis of a diffusion of low-context communication practices on global scale (Hofstede, 2001; Cardon, 2008). But the newer Internet (Web 2.0) offers users more options in terms of pictures, videos (e.g. YouTube), and sounds – even TV programming is increasingly provided online (e.g., IPTV). All of these developments indicate a gradual change of that originally strong low-context style medium towards more high-context style – a shift also reflected in the global acceptance and diffusion of the Internet. In addition to such gradual but essential change from print to TV style, the development of mobile

Internet might meet both polychronic habits of doing many things at a time and spatial habits of frequently mixing private and public spheres.

Accordingly, the general increase in referred "active web usage" rates between 2007 and 2009 is characterized by an over-proportional increase in high-context France, Spain, and Japan – with France recently surpassing low-context Germany in web usage rates. High-context India, Brazil, and China – traditionally characterized by very moderate usage (e.g. in 2008, penetration rates of 8% in India, and 22% in China) – recently showed a marked increase in their usage rates. China in particular had experienced a unique increase rate of nearly 50% in 2008, of nearly 30% in 2009, and it might undergo an estimated additional increase of 30% in 2010 (TNS-infratest, 2009; Anonymous, 2010).

Different Usage Patterns

Like mobile phone diffusion, the rate of increase in global Internet penetration rates is no indicator of cultural convergence. Rather, numerous differences in ways of using the Internet remain. With respect to the locus of Internet access, users from polychronic, high-context cultures tend to be more open toward mobile as well as public access to the Internet. In Japan, for example, such access is often done via mobile phones, and in China, most individuals prefer to access the Internet either by visiting one of the country's approximately 200,000 Internet-cafés, or by mobile phones (Riegner, 2008).

In contrast, users from monochronic, low-context cultures tend to prefer Internet access at home – in northern European countries, for example, home access quotas in 2008 were nearly all largely exceeding the U.K.'s 75%, compared to the Mediterranean countries' quotas of less than France's 53% (TNS-infratest, 2009). Similarly, U.S. broadband users spent 72% of their total online time at home and only 17% of their Internet access was done at work (Riegner, 2008). These behaviors might also reflect cultural orientations towards private vs. public space.

With respect to the preferred online contents and services, remarkable differences in the usage of information resources, e-commerce, entertainment, and social networks exist worldwide. In most high-context cultures, especially in Southeast-Asia, accessing entertainment is the most preferred function of the Internet. In China, for example, an average 48% of time spent online in 2009 was used for playing games, followed by watching videos, and social networking (Anonymous, 2010). In contrast, in many low-context cultures, especially in Europe, information resources and e-commerce tend to be preferred to entertainment when it comes to being online. E-commerce, for example, had a penetration rate of an average 65% among users from northern European countries in 2008, compared to less than 40% in Mediterranean countries during that same time (TNS-infratest, 2009).

While social networks (e.g., chats, blogs, tweets, etc.) show different but increasing popularity worldwide, cross-cultural comparisons might unveil qualitative differences related to the uses of these media (Hauser, 2010). In France, for example, web-logs/blogs are much more popular than in Germany, and these French blogs also deal with more explicit political content than what is found in German blogs (Schönberger, 2007). Among several possible reasons for this higher popularity of specific, written CMC in a high-context culture, different orientations towards space – in particular, the Germans' stronger differentiation between the public (i.e. the Internet) and the private sphere (i.e. personal political attitudes) – may be relevant, too.

In general, (national) culture-specific Internet usage patterns correspond with (national) culture-specific online supplies, including websites in particular. The latter are characterized by a higher degree of variability of its communication style than traditional media, and elements of print media, TV, radio, or telephone, can be combined

here. Accordingly, cross-cultural comparisons of commercial websites reveal many (national) differences and adaptations of their design/style. Such differences, in turn, show remarkable analogies to culture-specific advertising styles and creative strategies in the traditional media (e.g., TV and newspapers). In general, indirect and transformational messages creating emotions through pictures and entertainment are more favoured in high-context cultures, whereas direct and rational messages providing information above all play a more important role in low-context cultures. This general tendency also holds true for the design or communication style of websites along several structural design criteria (e.g., content appeal, layout, multimedia presentation, structure of content, and degree of navigation support). This relationship also corresponds to mono-/polychronic orientations towards time spent online (Hermeking, 2005; Hermeking, 2007; Kim, Coyle & Gould, 2009).

Both Internet use (wired or wireless/mobile) and the design of websites as elements of its most important user interface are prominent examples for the close interconnections between technology, communication, and culture. Another aspect of that interconnection is the Internet's central role as a new medium of technical documentation – namely information about technical products and instructions for their usage are increasingly distributed via the WWW as digital documents for download or for presentation on screen. As a specific form of CMC, such technical documentation via online technology also reveals considerable influences of culture.

TECHNICAL DOCUMENTATION

Traditional Documentation via the WWW

As a specific form of communication, technical documentation reflects both cultural communication styles and culture-specific attitudes towards technology and its usage. Traditional documentation with instructions describing technical operation and maintenance is strongly affected by cultural influences when in printed version or digital presentation on screen via the WWW. This factor can be demonstrated with the following research results in which several technical product manuals from highly developed Southeast Asian countries were compared to ones created for a German audience (Hermeking, 2008).

High-Context vs. Low-Context Documentation

Comparisons of technical documentation of nearly all kinds of products (e.g., cars, household appliances, and ICT) reveal a much higher ratio of pictures and visuals to text in Southeast Asian countries (e.g., Japan, China, or South-Korea) than in western countries like Germany, where text-heavy contents also correspond to a stronger division into separate chapters. However, the culture-specific visual style of the documentation from the Southeast Asian countries is even more significant. Unlike in western countries, most technical products are not represented directly by real photographs or precise technical drawings. Rather, these items are presented more indirectly through the use of comic-like illustrations. Such visuals include little "living" characters in a cartoon. In most cases, technical products are represented as cartoon drawings with eyes, a mouth, hand, and feet. Such features, in turn, allow these products to gesticulate by way of non-verbal communication or express themselves verbally with text bubbles. In addition, such documentation is also characterized by many natural motifs (e.g., flowers, birds, butterflies, and the like). From a western perspective, such depictions might seem more "childish" than as "technical" content designed for adults.

Again, the communication preferences of high-context vs. low-context cultures are represented in the visual- vs. text-heavy layout of

documentations. This trait also holds true for the stronger divisions or compartmentalizations of the detailed written contents in western countries like Germany, where information is presented in a more orderly structure or in a monochronic (step-by-step) way. Even the more indirect representation of technical products by playful illustrations or quite imprecise drawings in contrast to real photographs refers to high-context preferences in technical documents from Southeast Asia.

Western vs. Southeast Asian Styles

The significant visual style of illustrating technical objects like friendly little creatures, combined with many natural motifs, is related to culture-specific attitudes towards technology. Within technical documents, western "either-or" logic in presenting information, is replaced by a specific Southeast Asian "both-and" logic. Such a "both-and" approach has been described by Galtung (1981), Imamichi (1998), Nisbett (2003), and others (Hermeking, 2008).

According to the "both-and" style of thinking, there is a lot of harmonic co-existence of entities that, from a western point of view, seem to be contradictory and excluding each other. Such entities include multiplex religious adherences, and traditionalism (e.g., Feng Shui) as well as modernity (e.g., high-tech usage) in everyday life. They also encompass both centralized and market economies (in China) and ambivalence in verbal communication (both yes and no). In online contexts, this "both-and" perspective can be seen in the written text and visual-heavy layouts of websites or advertisements created by Southeast Asians. Such a concept of "both-and" harmony is also represented in the Taoist symbol of the opposing elements Yin-Yang (shadow-sunlight).

Within this "both-and" context, even technology and nature are by no way contradictions. Rather, they are interdependent entities that are to be combined in harmony – nature is made perfect by technology and technology is made perfect by nature. Consequently, technical products are illustrated like natural, living, and even friendly little creatures. Such technology creatures are, in turn, depicted as in harmony with other surrounding elements of nature.

Another aspect related to that is a significant enthusiasm towards robots, artificial intelligence, and virtual technology in highly developed Southeast Asian countries. Such technical products can be seen in androids (e.g., Kitech's female EveR-1), artificial pets (e.g., Sony's Aibo dog), and virtual mates for children (e.g., Japanese tamagotchis) or for adult Internet users (e.g., avatars). Obviously, like such preferences for hardware technologies that simulate intelligent and autonomous living creatures, vivid elements in online communication and CMC with lots of visuals, animations and real multimedia elements are likewise preferred by the members of these cultures. These culture-based attitudes toward technology, in turn, have interesting implications for the creation and design of the documentation related to such products.

Online Instructions and Human-Machine Interaction

The use of technology products is increasingly characterized by online instructions and information distributed with these products or via digital interfaces of a related product website. The advantages to this approach might, in turn, include additional comfort and more safety for the users of these products. Problems, however, might result from different communication styles associated with the culture of the users and the creators of a technology product. Such cultural differences might lead to poor usability, misunderstandings, and even fatal mistakes in the interaction between the user and the technology. According to a survey from the early 1990s, about 98% of at least 100 lethal accidents involving the use of computerized technology were caused by misunderstandings in communication and mistakes in human-computer-interaction (MacKenzie, 1996).

In a cross-cultural context, differences in cultural communication styles can make these problems even worse, as evidenced by the tragic airplane collision over Ueberlingen, Germany and the related problems with CMC that contributed to this event (Hermeking, 2008)

The Example of Ueberlingen

In July of 2002, two airplanes collided above Ueberlingen, Germany. Both airplanes – a Russian machine on its way from Moscow to Barcelona and a German machine on its way from Bergamo, Italy, to Brussels – were flying at an identical height of 36,000 ft. (11.000 m). In accordance with international aviation standards, both airplanes were equipped with the traffic alert and collision avoidance system (TCAS), which calculates the movements of the individual airplane and other airplans in its surrounding in order to warn or to give system-coordinated, short acoustic flight instructions to the related pilots.

In the Ueberlingen case, TCAS reacted as expected, and it instructed both the German pilots flying to Brussels to decrease their altitude ("Descend!") and the Russian pilots flying to Barcelona to increase height ("Climb!"). At the same time, however, a skyguide (a person who monitors air traffic) in Zurich instructed one machine to descend, but this message was erroneously sent to the Russian plane, which should have been instructed to "Climb."

While the German pilots followed TCAS instructions and were descending, the Russian pilots were confronted with two contradictory sets of instructions. They decided to follow the skyguide's instructions so they descended too. As a result of these actions, both planes maintained an identical altitude – in direct contrast to TCAS instructions. A few seconds after the German pilots finally contacted the skyguide, the two planes collided.

The critical behavior of the Russian pilots can be characterized with their preference for the skyguide (human source of information) instead of the CMC system (technology source of information). The critical behavior of the German pilots, by contrast, can be characterized with their preference for the CMC system instead of the skyguide (who otherwise could have been contacted earlier). Ignoring any individual behavioral tendencies, this preference pattern obviously seems to correspond with a culture-specific attitude towards technology, which in a former study on technology usage in Russia (and other countries) as well as Germany has been summed up as "people are preferred to technology" in Russian culture while "technology is equal to people" in the German culture (Hermeking, 2001, p. 199; author's translation) – where, like in this case, technology sometimes is even preferred to people.

Using Hofstede's (1991 & 2001) model of cultural dimensions, this tendency is also related to a stronger orientation towards objective tasks in more individualistic cultures like Germany, in contrast to a stronger orientation towards persons and social relationships in less individualistic (more collectivistic) cultures like Russia. In addition, Hofstede's reference to the correlation of individualism/low-context communication and collectivism/high-context communication unveils another aspect: Computers can be characterized as low-context devices in general (Batteau, 2004). Similarly, Hall (1976) described explicit, direct low-context messages as a kind of "digital", and more informal, indirect high-context messages as a kind of "analogic" communication. Although these terms originally were used as metaphors only, in the case of the Ueberlingen collision, they seem to be quite precise descriptions of the cultural preferences for instructions given by human beings vs. by CMC systems.

From such an intercultural perspective, the pilots of both the Russian and the German planes reacted in a plausible way (i.e. in accordance with their culturally different preferences of communication and technology usage). These differences conflicted in an unconscious way with each other via interactive technology. Like the Internet and CMC in general, such technology is not culturally neutral. Rather, it tends to represent the cultural values and the communication preferences of the country or the culture in which it was created – in the case of the Ueberlingen collision, the CMC reflected the low-context style of the western aviation industry.

Lessons Learned and Lessons Still to Learn

As a consequence of the Ueberlingen collision, international aviation standards now prescribe an absolute priority of CMC over humans (i.e. TCAS instructions are to be followed, no matter what a human skyguide might communicate). With respect to the many unconscious cultural tendencies of behavior, it is doubtful if such a superficially imposed universal standard of interactive technology usage is the ultimate solution. According to Hofstede (1991), cultural practices (e.g., rituals) as conscious behavior can be learned and modified, but unconscious behavior like cultural values and communication preferences is more difficult to change, and this takes much time. Hall (1959) was even more sceptical about humans' abilities to change their culture-based behaviors.

With respect to culturally different communication preferences, an internationalization procedure in the sense of technical adaptation of the TCAS digital user interface and its more or less low-context style towards some more high-context communication style seems to be desirable as well. The computer animated visual reconstructions of the two airplanes approaching each other might provide a good example for that. Would the Russian pilots in their cockpit have ignored such kind of visual-heavy information on screen, too?

According to sociologists Bijker and Law (1992), there is no "pure" technology with respect to its construction. Thus, there are also no culture-free technical products. Therefore, not only in the aftermaths of examinations and reflections of such "moments of catastrophic failure" (Bijker & Law, 1992), the development and construction of technology as well as its communication and interface design can be, and should be, inspired by contributions from the field of intercultural communication and its related disciplines. Because technical development in the near future will be increasingly characterized by online communication during human-machine interaction, these contributions and their consideration will become more and more important.

CONCLUSION

The increased computerization of the world means aspects of culture are inextricably intertwined with global CMC use. Consequently, the culture-specific usage of technology, technical documentation, and interactive operational instructions can be described to a large part by culture-specific communication styles and preferences. Yet, while online technology is spreading across cultures all over the world, cultural differences within global online environments remain and need to be examined and addressed if possible.

New technologies shape cultural forms and practices, but culture also shapes new technologies and the ways individuals use these technologies (Bell & Kennedy, 2007). Understanding culture-specific preferences and the ways the members of different cultures use technologies like those described in this chapter can improve cross-cultural interactions in online exchanges by helping to avoid misunderstandings and mistakes in communication. The objective is also of high importance for the construction and design of interactive technical systems.

In the given examples for such culture-specific usage of technology, Hall's low-/high-context model proved to be very useful. Though this model was non-rigorously developed and lacks empirical validation (Cardon, 2008), it is one of the most popular theoretical frameworks in the field of intercultural business and technical communication. It is also compatible with other relevant macro-cultural models from the field of intercultural communication. Such models, which by definition always are simplifications of a very complex reality, do not provide any concise analysis or thick description of a given culture. They do, however, offer initial insights into, and a larger sensitivity for, the general influence of culture on various phenomena of everyday life – both offline and online.

Contributions from intercultural communication can markedly improve the mutual understanding of and the interaction between members from different (national) cultures. They can also mediate between the often culturally insensitive disciplines or occupations of technical engineering and the often technologically insensitive cultural sciences in order to motivate and qualify members from these different knowledge cultures for a prosperous cooperation.

Such cooperation is already happening. During the last few years, several renowned industrial producers of ICT (e.g., Intel, Microsoft, Xerox, Philips) have started to hire cultural anthropologists in order to gain deeper insights into the culture-specific demands and contexts of usage of their technical products (Squires & Byrne, 2002; Jordan, 2003; Erard, 2004). Through the use of ethnographic methods, these researchers have begun to unveil essential micro-cultural details in specific situations. In addition to improving hardware design and constructions for successful global usage, continued exploration into culture and CMC will help humans better connect and interact across a range of media and personal and professional contexts.

REFERENCES

An, D. (2007). Advertising visuals in global brand's local websites: A six-country comparison. *International Journal of Advertising, 26*(3), 303–332.

Anonymous. (2010, March 10). Moneymaker: Internet – Zocken, Shoppen, Daddeln. *Focus Money,* 10-12.

Batteau, A. W. (2004). Anthropology and HCI. In Sims Bainbridge, W. (Ed.), *Berkshire encyclopedia of human-computer interaction* (*Vol. I,* pp. 17–25). Great Barrington, MA: Berkshire.

Bell, D., & Kennedy, B. M. (2007). *The cybercultures reader* (2nd ed.). New York, NY: Routledge.

Bijker, W. E., & Law, J. (1992). General introduction. In Bijker, W. E., & Law, J. (Eds.), *Shaping technology – building society. Studies in sociotechnical change* (pp. 1–16). Cambridge, MA: The MIT Press.

Cardon, P. W. (2008). A critique of Hall's contexting model: A meta-analysis of literature on intercultural business and technical communication. *Journal of Business and Technical Communication, 22*(4), 399–428. doi:10.1177/1050651908320361

Coulmas, F. (2008, May 15). Mobiles Internet: Handy verrückt. *Zeit Online.*

de Mooij, M. (2004). *Consumer behavior and culture. Consequences for global marketing and advertising.* Thousand Oaks, CA: Sage.

Erard, M. (2004, May 17). When technology ignores the East-West divide. *The New York Times,* p. 4.

Fryer, J. (2009, December 30). Mobile-phone culture: The Aparatgeist calls. *The Economist.* Retrieved January 2, 2010, from http://www.economist.com/ displaystory.cfm?story_id=15172850

Galtung, J. (1981). Structure, culture and intellectual style: An essay comparing Saxonic, Teutonic, Gallic and Nipponic approaches. *Social Sciences Information. Information Sur les Sciences Sociales, 20*(6), 817–856. doi:10.1177/053901848102000601

Gevorgyan, G., & Manucharova, N. (2009). Does culturally adapted online communication work? A study of American and Chinese Internet users' attitudes and preferences toward culturally customized Web design elements. *Journal of Computer Mediated Communication, 14*(2), 393-413. Retrieved January 10, 2011 from http://onlinelibrary.wiley.com /doi/10.1111/j.1083-6101.2009.01446.x/full

Hall, E. T. (1959). *The silent language.* Garden City, NY: Anchor Press/Doubleday.

Hall, E. T. (1976). *Beyond culture.* Garden City, NY: Anchor Press/Doubleday.

Hall, E. T., & Hall, M. R. (1990). *Understanding cultural differences: Keys to success in West Germany, France and the United States.* Yarmouth, ME: Intercultural Press.

Hauser, R. (2010). *Technisierte Kultur oder kultivierte Technik: Das Internet in Deutschland und Russland. Cultural diversity and new media* (*Vol. 14*). Berlin, Germany: Trafo.

Hermeking, M. (2001). *Kulturen und Technik: Techniktransfer als Arbeitsfeld der interkulturellen Kommunikation. Beispiele aus der arabischen, russischen und lateinamerikanischen Region.* Münster/München, Germany: Waxmann.

Hermeking, M. (2005). Culture and Internet consumption: Contributions from cross-cultural marketing and advertising research. *Journal of Computer Mediated Communication, 11*(1). Retrieved January 15, 2010, from http://jcmc.indiana.edu/vol11 /issue1/hermeking.html

Hermeking, M. (2007). Global Internet usage, website design, and cultural communication preferences: Contributions from cross-cultural marketing and advertising research. In St.Amant, K. (Ed.), *Linguistic and cultural online communication issues in the global age* (pp. 160–176). Hershey, PA: Information Science Reference. doi:10.4018/978-1-59904-213-8.ch011

Hermeking, M. (2008). Kulturelle Kommunikationsstile in der Mensch-Maschine-Interaktion: Einflüsse auf technische Bedienungsanleitungen und Internet-Webseiten. In Rösch, O. (Ed.), *Technik und Kultur* (pp. 163–185). Berlin, Germany: News&Media.

Hermeking, M. (2010). Kultur und Technik: Schnittstellen für die Interkulturelle Kommunikation. In Banse, G., & Grunwald, A. (Eds.), *Technik und Kultur: Bedingungs- und Beeinflussungsverhältnisse* (pp. 163–178). Karlsruhe: KIT Scientific Publishing.

Hofstede, G. (1991). *Cultures and organisations: Software of the mind*. London, UK: McGraw-Hill.

Hofstede, G. (2001). *Cultures consequences, 2ⁿᵈ edition: Comparing values, behaviors, institutions, and organizations across nations*. Thousand Oaks, CA: Sage.

House, R. J., Quigley, N. R., & Sully de Luque, M. (2010). Insights from project GLOBE: Extending global advertising research through a contemporary framework. *International Journal of Advertising, 29*(1), 111–139. doi:10.2501/S0265048709201051

Imamichi, T. (1998). The character of Japanese thought. In Imamichi, T., Wang, M., & Liu, F. (Eds.), *The humanization of technology and Chinese culture* (pp. 279–296). Washington, DC/Tokyo, Japan: Kluwer.

Jansen, D. E., & Riemer, M. J. (2003). Interkulturelle Kommunikation für den globalen Ingenieur. *Global Journal of Engineering Education, 7*(3), 303–310.

Jordan, A. (2003). *Business anthropology*. Long Grove, IL: Waveland Press.

Kim, H., Coyle, J. R., & Gould, S. J. (2009). Collectivist and individualist influences on website design in South Korea and the U.S.: A cross-cultural content analysis. *Journal of Computer Mediated Communication, 14(3), 581-601*. Retrieved January 10, 2011 from http://onlinelibrary.wiley.com/doi/10.1111/j.1083-6101.2009.01454.x/full

Kohima, K. (2005). A decade in the development of mobile communication in Japan (1993-2002). In Ito, M., Okabe, D., & Matsuda, M. (Eds.), *Personal, portable, pedestrian: Mobile phones in Japanese life* (pp. 61–75). Cambridge, MA: The MIT Press.

Li, H., Li, A., & Zhao, S. (2009). Internet advertising strategy of multinationals in China: A cross-cultural analysis. *International Journal of Advertising, 28*(1), 125–146. doi:10.2501/S0265048709090441

MacKenzie, D. A. (1996). *Knowing machines: Essays on technical change*. Cambridge, MA: The MIT Press.

Nielsen NetRatings. (n.d.). *Active digital media universe: Home panel*. Retrieved January 12, 2010, from http://www.nielsennetratings.com /news.jsp?section=dat_to

Nisbett, R. E. (2003). *The geography of thought: How Asians and Westerners think differently... and why*. New York, NY: The Free Press.

Retrieved January 3, 2010, from http://www.zeit.de/2008/21/ III-Gesellschaft-Japanhandys

Riegner, C. (2008). Wired China: The power of the world's largest Internet population. *Journal of Advertising Research, 48*(4), 496–505. doi:10.2501/S0021849908080574

Roth, K. (2001). Material culture and intercultural communication. *International Journal of Intercultural Relations, 25*(5), 563–580. doi:10.1016/S0147-1767(01)00023-2

Schönberger, K. (2007). Technik als Querschnitt-sdimension. Kulturwissenschaftliche Tech-nikforschung am Beispiel von Weblog-Nutzung in Frankreich und Deutschland. *Zeitschrift fur Volkskunde, 103*(2), 197–221.

Singh, N., Zhao, H., & Hu, X. (2005). Analyzing the cultural content of websites: A cross-national comparison of China, India, Japan, and US. *International Marketing Review, 22*(2), 129–146. doi:10.1108/02651330510593241

Squires, S., & Byrne, B. (Eds.). (2002). *Creating breakthrough ideas: The collaboration of anthropologists and designers in the product development industry.* Westport, CT/London, UK: Bergin & Garvey.

Tee, R. (2005). Different directions in the mobile Internet: Analysing mobile Internet services in Japan and Europe. In Lasen, A., & Hamill, L. (Eds.), *Mobile world: Past, present and future (computer supported cooperative work)* (pp. 143–160). New York, NY: Springer.

TNS-infratest. (2009). *Monitoring-Report Deutschland Digital.* Retrieved January 10, 2010, from http://www.tns-infratest.com/ monitoring-deutschland-digital

Usunier, J. C., & Lee, J. A. (2009). *Marketing across cultures* (5th ed.). London, UK, New York, NY, Boston, MA: Prentice Hall.

KEY TERMS AND DEFINITIONS

High-Context: The cultural mode of communication characterized by a high share of formal, written, explicit, or direct information.

Low-Context: The cultural mode of communication characterized by a high share of informal, visual, metaphorical, or indirect information.

Monochronic Time: The cultural concept of time being linear, passing, calculated precisely, and divided orderly ("one thing after the other").

Polychronic Time: The cultural concept of time being circular, repeating, subject to personal relationships and handled in an imprecise or flexible way.

Individualism: The cultural concept of individuals being autonomous and independent, less group-oriented *and* interdependent ("collectivism").

Chapter 7
Communicating in the Age of Web 2.0:
Social Networking Use among Academics in Turkey

Tanfer Emin Tunc
Hacettepe University, Turkey

Esin Sultan Oguz
Hacettepe University, Turkey

ABSTRACT

This qualitative study examines the current status of Web 2.0 technologies in Turkey and focuses specifically on the use of such technologies by academics. The main focus of the chapter involves presenting the results of two surveys (using samples of convenience) conducted on faculty members at Hacettepe University (a public research-oriented institution located in Ankara) and Bilkent University (a private research-oriented institution, also located in Ankara). In both universities, the majority of instruction is done in English, and English is the native language or second language of most faculty members. The chapter also examines the applicability of Web 2.0 technologies in the Turkish academic setting and the future implications of these technologies both in Turkey and around the world.

INTRODUCTION

The Internet has radically altered not only the way we communicate with each other, but also the way that research, especially in the academic

DOI: 10.4018/978-1-60960-833-0.ch007

setting, is conducted. We are now able to send messages transnationally in a matter of seconds and collaborate with colleagues that we most likely would have never met in the "paper and pencil" age. Accessing research materials such as online journal articles and e-books has also catalyzed the production of new knowledge and has led to the spreading of ideas almost instantaneously in a global "information explosion."

As a secular Muslim "nation that eludes categorization—part of Europe and Asia, but somehow beyond the socially constructed label 'Eurasian'; bordered by the Mediterranean Sea, but somehow not 'Mediterranean'; contiguous with the Middle East, but not 'Middle East-ern'"—Turkey embodies the changing nature of communication in online environments in a global age (Tunc, 2009, pp. 131-132). The globalization of the Internet, and its parent language English, has facilitated the infiltration of communication technologies into Turkey, where only ten years ago fewer than 10% of Turks owned personal computers. In today's Turkey, computer-mediated communication (CMC) has become a part of daily life, and it involves both men and women and includes members of different social classes. A tourist, for example, can readily observe peasants living in self-constructed homes with coal burning stoves communicating with relatives in Europe, North America, or even Australia using 3G cell phones, or through laptops with Internet access (via portals such as Skype), all while listening to Michael Jackson on their iPods.

Like most developed and developing countries, Turkey has become a nation of technological convergence (i.e., a nation where technologies intertwine). The same cell phone that is used for phone calls is also used to access the Internet, take pictures, listen to music, and even locate one's global position through GPS tracking. Turks also use their computers in multiple ways—to communicate, to entertain, and to archive their lives. Thus, it is not surprising that their use of social networking applications also converge in a similar fashion. Facebook, YouTube, MySpace, LinkedIn, Twitter, and other Web 2.0 social net-working sites (SNS) have become important com-ponents of Turkish life in the same way they have infiltrated the communications market globally. These media are employed for personal reasons (i.e., to contact friends and family members be-

yond national borders, access information about hobbies and interests, and self-expression) and are increasingly being used for professional and educational reasons, even though many of these technologies were never intended for the latter. The simplicity of these technologies, and their ability to be personalized at little or no cost, make them attractive, user-generated, modes of communica-tion. Moreover, they also facilitate the building of social capital, especially among academics and students who have fast-paced lifestyles.

The Web 2.0 social networking of academics in Turkey has, to date, eluded in-depth consider-ation.[1] Examining the use of CMC technologies within this group is particularly important due to the increasing number of college and university students in Turkey. Moreover, being computer literate enough to navigate one's way through a social network with electronic resources, and to be able to interact with colleagues and virtual librar-ians, will be essential skills in the future, especially in developing nations that do not have rich paper resources (like books and professional journals). In this context, social networking could concur-rently function as a leisure activity that occupies free time or allows one to "keep in touch" with family and friends, as well as an academic tool used to access new information and network cross-culturally with colleagues in foreign countries.

The qualitative study presented in this chap-ter examines these issues, as well as the current status of Web 2.0 technologies in Turkey. The particular focus of this research is on the use of such technologies by academics. It will report the results of two surveys (using samples of convenience), conducted on faculty members at two different universities in Turkey. The first university, Hacettepe University, is a *public* research-oriented institution located in Ankara. The second institution, Bilkent University, is a *private* research-oriented university that is also located in Ankara. At both of these universities, the majority of the instruction is done in English. Moreover, English is either the native language or second language of most faculty members. This study will predominantly assess the use (i.e., reasons and frequency) of social networking by faculty members at these two Turkish institutions, and will consider factors such as professional field, age, gender, and Internet familiarity as well as language barriers and cultural influences. The authors will also examine the applicability of Web 2.0 technologies to the Turkish academic setting, where CMC might facilitate the building of social capital, trust, and increased cross-cultural flows of knowledge among academics.

BACKGROUND

Before the advent of CMC, intricate social networks existed in Turkey; however, these structures connected interdependent nodes (individuals or organizations) sharing friendship/kinship bonds, similar interests, or backgrounds, mostly through physical means ranging from intense face-to-face contact, to casual acquaintance through a third party. The Internet has removed the physicality of social networking and has created an intangible layer of electronic communication that can even exist among individuals who have never met and who will never meet in person. Web 1.0 technologies, such as email, listservs, computer conferencing, instant messaging, chat rooms, and Skype, enabled the initial creation of this electronic social map. Over the last 5 years, Web 2.0 technologies have redefined communication and the meaning of electronic social networks and have created a three-dimensionality in CMC—a kind of networking that had not previously existed.

Web 2.0 technologies include user-generated, community-building, collaborative, and interactive technologies such as weblogs, wikis, newscasts (Digg), social bookmarking (del.icio.us), tagging folksonomies, podcasts, RSS feeds, searchable document repositories (Slideshare, Scribd), electronic journals, mashups, virtual reality environments such as Second Life and The

Sims, music/photograph/video sharing (iTunes, Last.fm, YouTube, Google Video, Picasa, Flickr), and social networks such as Facebook, MySpace, LinkedIn, Enterprise 2.0, Twitter, and Academia. edu—all of which allow users to register, generate personal profiles, and use that profile to communicate with others. As conveyed by Gray, et al. (2008), SNS are used not only to convey personal characteristics and interests, but also to create instant kinship networks by connecting subscribers through virtual communities, user rankings, and interactive "read/write" functions.

More importantly, these social webs are multifunctional. They are used for socializing and marketing as well as for educational and professional networking. Cohen (2007) suggests that Web 2.0 technologies, and social networks in particular, will have a significant impact on academia and that the next generation of intellectuals will be "social scholars," or individuals who will feel just as comfortable with non-traditional electronic media as with traditional books and paper journals. While these digital scholars will certainly suffer from new concerns such as "information overload" (Hardesty & Sugarman, 2007; Young, 2005) and "technostress" (Sahin & Coklar, 2009), they will also be the first to adapt to the twenty-first century academic computer-mediated research environment, which is increasingly relying on electronic sources as e-journals, e-books, and online social networking forums.

As Pearson predicted in 1999, CMC, or electronic "shared spaces," have provided a unique opportunity for academics, both in terms of their research and pedagogy. These spaces have served as transnational vehicles for expertise and knowledge-sharing; dialogue on new concepts and techniques; and collaboration—all without time-restrictions, interruptions, the tedium involved in face-to-face meetings, and the competition to have one's voice heard over more aggressive colleagues. Even though CMC is accompanied by undeniable inhibiting factors such as the "lack of physical cues (facial expressions, voice intonations, gestures), nuances of speech (humor, irony), [and] the 'vulnerability' of contributing ideas" without the ability to gauge audience reaction (Pearson, 1999, p. 226), the use of social networking in the past 5 years has become an indelible part of the academic setting. This situation is mainly due to the fact that such media support the active, rather than passive, consumption of information and involve communication that transgresses socially-constructed boundaries.

According to Mason and Rennie (2007), the increasing popularity of social networking sites for educational purposes is due to three major factors:

1. Personalization through modifiable, user-generated profiles;
2. The existence of traversable, shared community spaces, which not only connect users to friends, family and colleagues, but also permit access to sites maintained by unknown users (i.e., teamwork and self-organizing mass collaboration, as opposed to isolation);
3. "Semi-persistent," refreshable, "readable/writeable" interactive forums for public comments that by-pass competing "experts," and rely on the self-construction of experience/knowledge.

All of these "exciting" factors clearly have the potential to contribute to professors' motivations to research and teach, and students' enthusiasm to learn.

According to Alexander (2008), "higher education faculty have been quietly blogging for some time, and in various formats. Professors 'web up' course syllabi, blog about their research interests, advocate for their field in the public sphere (as public intellectuals), require students to blog, and hold professional seminars in distributed inter-blog conversations" (p. 199). Thus, the transition to the "social scholar" is well underway, especially in developed nations such as the United States, Canada, Australia, and those in Western Europe.

Interestingly, as research conducted by Herring (2001) suggests, the adoption of new CMC technologies varies based on academic discipline. While most academics (studies report numbers around 80%) agree that the Internet is useful as a "foraging tool" for information, younger/lower-ranking academics, as well as those faculty in science and engineering fields, actually use it more often than older/higher-ranking faculty members in the humanities and social sciences. Moreover, frequent users are also more likely to venture beyond foraging, employing the Internet to enhance communication with colleagues both domestically and internationally, to access databases, to locate updates and conference alerts, and to communicate with students. More recent research by Pfeil, et al. (2009) also corroborates the existence of an inter-generational "digital divide," especially between students, their parents, and their grandparents. This divide is significant in the educational context because university professors are often one or two generations removed from their students. This data suggests that there may be a large (and perhaps even widening) gap between students and older instructors, especially as today's academics are retiring at a later age than in previous generations. Additionally, those faculty who are over 60, who are often also "unfamiliar/vaguely familiar" with computers, are reluctant to explore CMC beyond basic email.

According to studies by Crane (1972), Stoan (1991), and Sonnenwald and Liewrouw (1997), social networking, particularly in computer-mediated environments, represents the future of academia. In the twenty-first century, faculty members who have the most social ties, influence, and e-visibility will almost certainly be the most productive in terms of publications, conference papers, transnational collaboration, and cross-cultural projects. Thus assessing, evaluating, understanding, and encouraging the CMC—and specifically the Web 2.0—usage of faculty members will, in coming years, prove to be crucial to the success of universities, especially in their implementation of web-based research and pedagogical tools.

Knowing the global status of Web 2.0 technologies will also be of importance because it will influence the extent to which communication will occur across cultures. Some US universities, such as the University of Iowa, the University of Michigan, and Rice University, already maintain official blogs and Facebook pages, which augment public relations by encouraging the spread of information about these universities to the outside world. However, such efforts will be useless on the global scale unless there are international users on the receiving end.

The scientific literature is replete with Web 2.0 studies concerning the developed world, yet the research on Turkey—which possesses the world's seventeenth largest economy and is poised to serve as the bridge between East and West during the twenty-first century—is scarce. With the notable exception of Arikan (2009), who deals with the social networking use of prospective English language teachers, to our knowledge, no major study has been conducted (as of this writing) on the use of Web 2.0 technologies by academics working in the Turkish university setting, despite the obvious global reach of this form of CMC. With its more than 400 million active users, the most popular Web 2.0 SNS at the moment is Facebook. Fifty percent of active Facebook users log onto this particular SMS any given day, and more than 25 billion pieces of content (web links, news stories, blog posts, notes, photo albums, etc.) are shared via Facebook each month. Moreover, about 70% of Facebook users are outside the United States, and, in terms of members, Turkey ranks fourth in Facebook usage globally (Facebook, 2010; Burcher, 2010). Turkey has the seventh largest online population in Europe (in terms of numbers of users, which is not that surprising since it has one of the largest populations in Europe) and, on average, Turks spend more than one hour a day online. These factors make Turks among

the five most engaged online populations in the world (ComScore, 2009). After Google and Microsoft sites, Facebook is the third most accessed web property in Turkey, is the most used social network, and is accessed by 81% of the Turkish online population.

Moreover, the rate of growth of Turkish SNS users is exploding. In April 2009, social networking represented 9% of total time spent online in Turkey. Only six months later (September 2009), social networking represented 15% of all time spent online, underscoring the rapid emergence of social networking in the country. With 16.1 million visitors, in September 2009, Facebook ranked as the most popular SNS site among Turks, accounting for 92% of the total time spent on SNS during the month (ComScore, 2009). Other Web 2.0 sites such as MySpace and Twitter are also becoming increasingly popular with Turks, especially as more and more homes acquire personal computers and Internet access.

Social networking is particularly popular with young adults (according to ComScore, 2009, 70% of Internet users in Turkey are 34 years old or younger), and it is not uncommon for Turkish faculty members to hear about the latest Web 2.0 developments from students. The fact that Western supersites dominate in Turkey, and the reality that the nation is attaining an increasingly-large share in the global Internet market, suggest that Turkey—with its young, educated, Internet-using population—might be a key player in academic social networking in the twenty-first century. Moreover, as recent research is now revealing (Herrington, et al., 2009; Virkus, 2008; Ajjan & Hartshorne, 2008; Mason & Rennie, 2007), Web 2.0 technologies are poised to revolutionize education. Therefore, studies such as this one are crucial not only for what they reveal about specific academic populations and their research/ pedagogical habits, but also because they evaluate the potential of CMC and SNS as a means of scholarly collaboration across cultures.

METHODOLOGY

The data for this study was collected using an anonymous questionnaire developed by the authors. The questionnaire was distributed in the fall of 2009 via an online survey tool, and the authors used a convenience sampling method to survey subjects at two urban universities (Hacettepe and Bilkent Universities) located in Ankara, Turkey.

Hacettepe University, a public state university, was established in 1967 and is comprised of 13 Faculties, 13 Institutes, 35 Research Centers, a Music Conservatory, 3 Applied Schools, and 6 Vocational Schools. It is known throughout the country and the world for its medical school and its strong arts and sciences program (the Faculty of Letters is the largest faculty in the university). As of fall 2009, 26,800 students are enrolled at the university. They are taught by 4,594 faculty members, 60% of whom are female, and 40% of whom are male (this number includes full, associate, and assistant professors, instructors, tutors, specialists, and research assistants).

Bilkent University is a private university (the first of its kind in Turkey) that was established in 1984. Around 12,000 students are currently enrolled in its 9 Faculties, 2 Applied Schools, and 3 Vocational Schools. There are 1,033 faculty members at Bilkent University (53% of whom are female, and 47% of whom are male). International academics from approximately 40 countries comprise roughly 30% of its faculty (in contrast to Hacettepe University, which employs around 20 foreign faculty members who make up roughly 0.5% of its faculty population).

The instrument used to examine these populations consisted of a series of 12 survey-style questions and a final empty box for comments (Question #13). The first 10 questions were multiple choice and sought to gain information about respondents' gender, age group, academic rank/faculty, years of computer usage, social networking usage (frequency/time spent/sites), and reasons for (non)usage. Questions 11 and 12 consisted of a series of items using a five point Likert-scale ("Completely Disagree" to "Completely Agree"; "Completely Unnecessary" to "Extremely Necessary"), and were used to assess the importance and overall role of SNS in the respondents' personal and professional lives. The respondents were allowed to select the language of the survey (Turkish or English) based on personal comfort.

RESULTS

Hacettepe University

The Hacettepe University survey was completed by 270 individuals, 57.4% of whom were female and 42.6% of whom were male, thus reflecting the overall gender-composition of the institution's faculty. In terms of age breakdown, 19.6% of respondents were women between the ages of 23 and 29, and 20.4% were women between the ages of 30 and 39. Women between the ages of 40 and 49 comprised 11.1% of responses, while women over 50 only 6.3%. On the other hand, men between the ages of 23 and 29 represented 12.6% of the surveys completed, while those between 30 and 39 years of age accounted for 17.4% of the total number of respondents. As with the female respondents, the percentages for those over 40 were considerably smaller (8.9% of respondents were men between 40 and 49, while 3.7% were men over 50). When the respondents are analyzed for age alone, we observe that 32.2% of the surveys were completed by faculty members between the ages of 20 and 29, and 37.8% by those between 30 and 39. Thus, 70% of survey respondents were under the age of 40, and 60.9% of those respondents were women.

As for academic ranking, almost half (45.1%) of respondents were research assistants, 7.1% were specialists, 7.5% were tutors, and 13.4% were instructors (73% in total), which corresponds to the overwhelmingly young respondent pool. On the other hand, 6.3%, 6.3%, and 14.2% were assistant, associate, and full professors, respectively. Most of the respondents were employed in the Faculty of Letters (18.2%), the School of Medicine (17.0%), the Education Faculty (12.1%), and the Faculty of Science (11.4%), which correlates to both Hacettepe University's faculty distribution and its areas of academic concentration.

These results also provide us with a broad pool of respondents whose answers span the range of academic specialties. 73.5% of the respondents surveyed use SNS, and of these 86.8% have been using computers for 10 years or more. This finding illustrates an extremely strong correlation between age, gender, computer use, and social networking (younger female respondents, who have been using computers for 10 years or more, are more likely to use SNS). 44.1% of those who use social networking spent 10-29 minutes per day on these sites, compared to 27.2% who use them for 30-59 minutes, 19.5% for more than 1 hour, and 9.2% who are on these sites the entire day.

When asked why they use these sites, the majority of respondents (59.3%) indicated "to communicate with family and friends." Other popular replies included "to communicate with colleagues" (45.4%), "to seek information about topics of personal interest" (35.0%), "to share photos and videos" (32.9%), "because colleagues and friends use social networking sites" (30.0%), "to access research resources" (29.6%), and "because SNS are more convenient than email or telephone" (18.6%). Those who use SNS at Hacettepe University are less likely to use these sites to publicize or share research, communicate with students outside the classroom setting, to share knowledge with others, or as a substitute for email.

The most popular social networking websites are (in descending order) Facebook (58.9%), Twitter (10.4%), and Windows Live (which includes MSN Messenger, a "people network" and photo-sharing capabilities) (10.0%). This breakdown does not exactly correspond to the findings in the literature regarding Turkey, suggesting that

SNS usage among academics may function differently compared to the general public. Other social networking activities such as blogging, the use of wikis, and RSS are also relatively popular (10.7%, 13.2% and 21.8% of respondents use these functions, respectively).

Despite recent findings suggesting their popularity among Turks (ComScore, 2009), only 5.7% of respondents frequent MySpace; 8.9% use Slideshare; 6.4% use Flickr; 6.4% use del.icio.us; 6.4% use Lastfm; and 6.8% use podcasts. Similarly, only 2.9% respondents admit to using YouTube actively as contributors. However, this finding might be due to the previous ban on the website in Turkey.[2] Those sites associated with academic networking, such as LinkedIn (4.3%), Academia.edu (0.7%), Blackboard (0.7%), Epernicus (0.7%), and Pubmed (0.7%) had the lowest number of users. These results clearly correlate to faculty members' disinterest in using social networking for academic purposes beyond casual contact and foraging.

The 26.5% of the respondents who do not use SNS do so for predictable reasons such as "I don't have time" (10.7% of the total respondent population), "I don't trust social networking sites" (6.8%), and "social networking sites are unimportant" (5.4%). A few respondents also noted that the fear of identity theft prevents them from using SNS, while only 0.7% of the respondents conveyed the idea that they are too difficult to use. These responses suggest that, at least with this highly-educated population, ease of use is not a factor.

When asked about the importance of SNS in their personal and professional lives, 39.8% agreed that they are important in their *personal* lives, while 29.1% agreed that they are important in their *professional* lives. The same number of respondents (29.1%), however, conveyed that SNS are unimportant to their *professional* lives, compared to 23% who stated that they are unimportant in their *personal* lives. Thus, this group of respondents is equally torn as to the importance of SNS in their personal and professional lives.

A series of more detailed, Likert-type questions, revealed similar findings: 58.4% of respondents conveyed that SNS are necessary to share videos and pictures; 57.5% to communicate with family and friends; 49.0% for entertainments purposes; and 39.8% in order to remain current with social and cultural developments. 40-50% of respondents indicated that SNS are necessary in sharing academic knowledge/sources, communicating with students, and sharing publications/calls for papers. However, these same individuals are reluctant to actually use SNS for these purposes, indicating a gap between perception and reality. Clearly, mitigating factors such as time restrictions and trust issues could be influencing the use of SNS for academic purposes beyond casual contact and foraging—even among those computer-literate scholars who are willing to use these sites for personal reasons.

Some respondents provided additional insight into these discrepancies in the free-response section of the survey. While one respondent admitted using SNS to "spy on her children," and wished that she had learned how to use these sites earlier, another respondent conveyed that SNS "consume too much time…make users lazy and are not social at all." Moreover, SNS are only "as successful as those who are using them." In other words, output is a function of user-generated input, which, of course, is a function of time and ability.

Other respondents commented that SNS communication is superficial, unsatisfying, and oriented towards useless information, and that they would much rather use the time spent on SNS to communicate, more effectively, on an in-depth and face-to-face basis. As one respondent commented, "no one should care where we are, and what we're doing every minute of the day…we should spend more time doing research and less time discussing it." One respondent even warned about our increasing overreliance on technology, stating that "every new communication technol-

ogy comes with its own problems…on one hand, they accelerate the exchange of knowledge, but on the other, they can lead to addiction." Another respondent provided further insight into why s/he did not use SNS for academic purposes—"how can we trust anything or anyone on these sites?"—thus suggesting that academic integrity might actually be comprised by SNS.

Bilkent University

The Bilkent University survey was completed by 145 individuals, 65.5% of whom were female and 34.5% of whom were male (just like Hacettepe University, more women responded to the survey than men). In terms of age breakdown, 13.1% of respondents were women between the ages of 23 and 29, and 24.8% were women between the ages of 30 and 39. Women between the ages of 40 and 49 comprised 17.2% of responses, while women over 50 only 10.3%. On the other hand, men between 23 and 29 represented 6.2% of the surveys completed, while those between 30 and 39 accounted for 4.8% of the total. Unlike the female respondent pool, the percentages for men over 40 were considerably larger (13.1% of respondents were men between 40 and 49, while 10.3% were men over 50).

When the Bilkent University respondents are analyzed for age alone, we observe that 19.3% of surveys were completed by faculty members between the ages of 20 and 29, 29.7% by those between 30 and 39, 30.3% by those between 40 and 49, and 20.7% by those over 50. Unlike Hacettepe University, which consisted of a young sample, 51% of Bilkent respondents were over 40. This finding might be due to the fact that Bilkent University is a private institution that attracts retired Turkish and older foreign faculty members who are usually hired, and remain, on the instructor level.[3] Bilkent University's smaller graduate programs and fewer students might also account for the difference in age distribution, although this factor might change in the future along with user demographics.

As for academic ranking, more than half (67.6%) of respondents were instructors, 17.2% were assistant professors, 4.8% were research assistants, 4.1% were associate professors, 3.4% were full professors, and 2.8% were tutors. This breakdown, in turn, corresponds to the faculty hiring practices at Bilkent University. An overwhelming one-third (30.3%) of those surveyed were employed in Bilkent University's English Language School; this factor again correlates to the relatively high number of foreign, English-speaking faculty members at the University. Faculty members from the School of Engineering comprised 11.3% of respondents, while 10.6% were from the Faculty of Education. Ironically, faculty members from Bilkent University's School of Computer Technology and Office Management displayed very little interest in our survey (their replies only comprised 1.4% of the surveys).

71.7% of Bilkent respondents use SNS (which corresponds to the numbers obtained through the Hacettepe survey), and of these individuals, 89.4% have been using a computer for 10 years or more. With the Bilkent pool, women over 40 who have been using computers for 10 years or more are more likely to use SNS than other respondents. 42.3% of those individuals who use social networking media spent 10-29 minutes per day on these sites, compared to 26.9% of the respondents who use these media for 30-59 minutes per day, 25.0% for more than 1 hour per day, and 3.8% who are on these sites the entire day. Thus, as with the Hacettepe respondents, close to 70% of SNS users spend less than an hour on these sites per day.

When asked why they use these sites, the majority of Bilkent University respondents (59.2%) indicated "to communicate with family and friends." Other popular replies included "to communicate with colleagues" (27.9%) (markedly lower than the Hacettepe respondents), "to seek information about topics of personal interest" (25.2%), "to share photos and videos" (46.9%) (markedly

higher than Hacettepe respondents), "because colleagues and friends use social networking sites" (34.7%), "to access research resources" (15.6%) (markedly lower than Hacettepe University), and "because SNS are more convenient than email or telephone" (29.9%) (markedly higher than Hacettepe University). Those who use these sites at Bilkent are, unlike Hacettepe faculty members, more likely to use SNS to communicate with students (17%), and as a substitute for email and telephone (29.9%).

For the Bilkent respondents, the most popular social networking websites are, in descending order, Facebook (59.2%), Twitter (15.6%), and LinkedIn (13.6%). CMC such as blogs and chats are also relatively popular (10.2% and 23.1% of respondents use these functions, respectively), which contrasts with Hacettepe, where research-oriented Web 2.0 services such as wikis and RSS feeds were more popular (only 7.5% and 1.4% of Bilkent faculty members used these products, respectively). MySpace was also unpopular (2.7% of Bilkent respondents used this SNS), while del.icio.us (10.9%) and Acedemia.edu (10.9%) were more popular when compared to the Hacettepe respondents. Strikingly, 25.2% of respondents actively use YouTube, which correlates to our theory about the legality and accessibility of YouTube in Turkey, and the idea that state employees might have been reluctant to use a banned service while on campus.

Also interesting to note is the Bilkent interest in Moodle (8.9% of Bilkent respondents use this course management system) and Skype (2.0%). Bilkent's foreign faculty population undoubtedly contributes to the pool's interest in using SNS for teaching purposes (perhaps adapting techniques used in their home countries; Moodle, for example, is popular in the U.K.) and communicating/sharing photos and videos with family and friends (many of whom are probably located outside of Turkey). Thus, while the percentage of SNS usage and the number of years of computer use are similar for both universities, the age of users and the reasons for SNS usage are noticeably different. Such factors are most likely linked to the public/private nature of the institution, as well as to faculty characteristics.

The 28.3% of Bilkent respondents who do not use SNS do so for predictable reasons such as "I don't have time" (34.9% of those who do not use SNS), "social networking sites are unimportant" (15.9%), and "I don't trust social networking sites" (12.7%). When asked about the importance of SNS in their personal and professional lives, 30.0% agreed that they are important in their *personal* lives, while only 16.9% agreed that they are important in their *professional* lives. A similar number of respondents (25.4%), however, conveyed that SNS are unimportant in their *personal* lives, compared to 33.8% who stated that they are unimportant in their *professional* lives (22.5% stated that they were marginally important, while 21.8% were neutral). Thus, this group of respondents perceives the personal use of SNS to be more important than professional, academic use. A series of more detailed, Likert-type questions revealed similar findings: 38.7% of respondents conveyed that SNS are necessary to share videos and pictures, 45.1% to communicate with family and friends, 45.1% for entertainments purposes, and 47.9% in order to remain current with social and cultural developments. The latter category seems to be more important to Bilkent faculty members, most likely because many of them are expatriates living thousands of miles away from home.

The Bilkent respondents were, again, much more concerned with the use of SNS for teaching and long-distance communication. As one faculty member noted, "I use Flickr to share photos with friends in other countries and Facebook to read about what my nieces are doing occasionally...I really prefer the personal touch of voices on a phone...or video and voices with close friends on Skype." Another respondent commented that his "main professional use of social networking is [the course management system] Moodle,

which...is on the cusp of social networking and content provision." Moodle contrasts with other SNS which, to the respondent, seem to be "used to develop a network of connections that are not real friends or contacts of any academic value, encourage people to exchange pointless information (your favorite movies, etc.), and in some cases to live in a kind of fantasy world with all the friends they've never met!"

DISCUSSION

Although this study contains obvious limitations (e.g., it includes respondents from only two large, research-oriented universities, both of which are located in Ankara, Turkey; those who answered the survey are self-selecting in that they are more inclined to use the Internet, check email and complete online surveys and thus more comfortable with CMC; and the existence of obvious language barriers that may prevent those with weak or non-existent English skills from participating in SNS), it reveals a great deal about Web 2.0 and social networking usage among academics in Turkey. Web 2.0 is still relatively new to Turkish academia, and increased professional and educational use is expected over time, especially given global trends. (According to Perez, 2008, over the next three years, Forrester Research has predicted a compound annual increase of 43% in the use of Enterprise 2.0 in the U.S. and U.K. alone.) Nevertheless, the current situation in Turkey is important because it supports the most recent literature with respect to the growing number of female SNS users. This research maintains that participation in social networks has increased exponentially since 2006, and that such participation has been dominated by women (Mo, et al., 2009; Jackson, et al., 2008).

Over the past few years, numerous studies have shown that the fastest growing demographic for social networks is women over the age of fifty, and this growth is largely attributed to early saturation by a younger market (Ibid.). The study presented here conveys the reality that academic women in Turkey use computers, the Internet, and Web 2.0 services just as much as their male counterparts do, and this finding supports the observations of Cummings and Kraut (2002), Ono and Zavodny (2003), and Wasserman and Richmond-Abbott (2005) who have all elucidated that the gender gap in computer usage and CMC closed between 2000 and 2005 as women began using computers and Internet services in unprecedented numbers.

Interestingly, Mo et al. (2009) and Jackson et al. (2008), express that the increasing popularity of the Internet, and specifically Web 2.0 technologies, among women might be due to the fact that these forums allow them to adopt active (and in some cases aggressive) roles that, because of male/female gender conditioning and double standards, are still not accepted in polite society. This claim, of course, would make sense in a patriarchal society such as Turkey, where women's voices—even those of academics—are either stifled by over-bearing male colleagues, or ignored as unimportant. As this study suggests, the Internet, and specifically CMC and SNS, are empowering especially to women who, because of social and personal restrictions, might find the World Wide Web both a convenient and effective means of advancing their professional careers.

As Thelwall (2008) has discovered, there seems to be a class divide (at least in the United States) among college-educated Facebook users and non-college-educated MySpace users. After all, the former was originally established as a SNS for Harvard University students in 2004, and thus is not so surprisingly preferred by college-educated users. This divide seems to be the case with academics in Turkey as well. Our sample population exhibited an overwhelming preference for Facebook over MySpace. However, this preference might be a reflection of Turks overall who, for the most part, do not use MySpace, despite the existence of a large number of non-

college-educated computer users, many of whom are under the age of 18.

While the significant number of male and female SNS users at both universities implies that Web 2.0 technologies are transcending gender, the use of SNS is still inextricably linked to age, especially at the state university level. Although the qualitative approach used in this study could have been assisted by unstructured interviews that might have revealed the reasons for such divides, the divergence between admitted practice and reality would clearly limit closer subject analysis. This aspect, as Guimaraes (2005) notes, is one of the many problems that emerge when cyber-ethnography and in-depth qualitative analysis are used to assess computer, Internet, Web 2.0, and CMC usage.

According to Ajjan and Hartshorne (2008), pre-existing attitudes regarding computer technologies—specifically their perceived usefulness (*the degree to which the individual believes that a technology will improve his/her job performance*), perceived ease of use (*the degree to which an innovation is easy to understand and operate*), and compatibility (*the degree to which technology fits with the existing values and experiences*)—are important factors in faculty members' adoption of Web 2.0 technologies. As Ajjan and Hartshorne (2008) elucidate, faculty members who perceive Web 2.0 technologies favorably are also more likely to use these technologies in the classroom. This correlation is clearly the case for academics working in Turkey. Most of them (over 75% in both studies) use SNS, predominantly for personal/social reasons. Some (though not many) also use these media for varying educational and academic purposes such as the distribution of syllabi, reading materials, exam review sheets, student participation (through blogs and posting forums) as well as staying current with research topics, colleagues, and professional feedback. However, non-users convey major, significant reservations (such as efficiency, safety, and the possibility for anti-social behavior) that collectively serve as roadblocks to their adoption of SNS in personal and professional settings. Once these unfavorable associations are mitigated, there will undoubtedly be a surge in the use of Web 2.0 services in Turkey.

Although the use of SNS in the Turkish academic settings is still in its developmental phase, CMC such as user-generated content (i.e., the "read/write" aspect of Web 2.0) and self-organizing mass collaboration through on-line communities such as Wikipedia (Tapscott & Williams, 2008), Flickr, YouTube, and Second Life clearly have the potential to assist in building social capital, trust, knowledge (what Bruns, 2008 calls "produsage"), and increased informational flow between peers and students (what Biocca, 2003 calls "transparency"). Given the popularity of SNS with students, these sites might also have the ability, in the foreseeable future, to expand the borders of the classroom and facilitate the offering of online courses, which are not very popular or very wide-spread in Turkey as of 2010.

Such technologies could also have a positive impact on cross-cultural/international communication. Although our study reveals that such communication is occurring on the *personal* level, especially among foreign faculty members teaching in Turkey, and younger, more computer-literate academic users, the amount and content of such communication on the *professional* level was difficult to quantify given the limited amount of SNS usage for academic purposes. These findings thus indicate another area of future research. Important factors to be examined could include the effectiveness of such cross-cultural professional communication and potential disparities between Turkish and foreign citizens in such interactions (as well as the reasons for these disparities).

Clearly, differences between private versus public universities and faculty profiles (including country of origin, the number of years spent living and/or studying abroad, and the respondents' knowledge of English) are all significant factors deserving further study. For example, the predominance of international academics at Bilkent University could have affected the adoption of certain types of social media due to previous usage in their home country (e.g., Moodle tends to be more popular in U.K. institutions). More research also needs to be conducted on the different ways in which "fun" social networking tools, such as Facebook and MySpace, are being used for academic purposes as compared to more collaborative, learning-based tools such as Moodle. There is little sense of how academics in Turkey are using Facebook, except to communicate with friends and family, and one cannot assume that "fun" social media cannot play a role in the acquisition of professional social capital, especially transnationally. Thus, the increase in social networking among academics in Turkey is interesting, but further correlations need to be drawn between professional practice, user-generated content, the read/write web, and personal pastimes. In the Turkish context, it might be that Web 2.0 technologies, such as Facebook, MySpace and even YouTube, are necessary precursors to the adoption of more complicated professional CMC technologies, such as Enterprise 2.0, Moodle, and Wikis, which have proven to be important building blocks of social capital between academics, and vehicles for the free exchange of knowledge between East and West.

CONCLUSION

The results of this study have multiple applications, not only in terms of improving communication, especially across cultures, but also in terms of updating Turkish pedagogy in the twenty-first century to include Web 2.0 technologies. In order for research within Turkey, and communication between scholars working in Turkey, to function effectively, academics must take full advantage of the Internet and begin the process of developing a transnational network of both colleagues and research resources. Unfortunately, many Turkish academics are still very provincial in their outlook with respect to such technologies. While this behavior might have been acceptable 20 or even 10 years ago, it is no longer feasible in the current information age. However, as this study suggests, the more recent adoption of Web 2.0 technologies might signal the beginning of changing attitudes and approaches, especially as older academics are replaced by the younger generation. Other countries in the West are now engaging in personal *and* professional cross-cultural communications as a result of using Web 2.0 network technologies for a number of years. Turkey, and its academics in particular, could follow this international trend if the current interest in CMC and SNS continues. After all, there are early signs of interaction through user-generated content such as Moodle, and growing interest in Enterprise 2.0 as a content management or knowledge-creation tool, even though the shift from "friends and family" social networking to professional collaboration has not yet occurred.

Many Turkish institutions, especially those on the forefront of the educational system like Hacettepe and Bilkent Universities, have already taken steps to usher their faculty members into the world of Web 2.0. Hacettepe University, for example, has recently implemented a program to encourage the usage of SNS, such as Moodle, in teaching, and it has also initiated a campaign to familiarize faculty members with its new Blackboard system. Bilkent University, on the other hand, has established online discussion boards in order to connect its faculty members to each other, and it also offers numerous electronic services to academics (such services range from providing basic email, webpage creation, and computer conferencing to the development of online courses and access to remote teaching technologies). Our study reveals that while most academics in Turkey perceive SNS as being potentially useful to their teaching and research careers, many are still reluctant to engage with CMC in this way. Instead, they limit their behavior to "passive" activities (e.g., directing students to SNS) and not "active"

engagement (such as creating user-generated content for classes on SNS). This behavior is perhaps due to what Biocca (2003) has called the "psychological" barrier of participating in virtual and augmented spaces. Bridging the gap between SNS perception and reality will not only increase the use of SNS for professional purposes, but it will also undoubtedly facilitate the introduction of virtual workplaces to Turkish academia—an idea that is just as foreign today as email was in the Turkish university setting ten years ago (Zemliansky & St.Amant, 2008).

Academics in Turkey must also make the effort to communicate transnationally through CMC and SNS, especially because the "social scholar" seems to be the trend of the future (Cohen, 2007). While the "friends and family" applicability of Web 2.0 technologies are evident, more emphasis needs to be placed on their applicability towards scholarly collaboration and communication with other cultures. One way to accomplish this objective could be for Turkish universities to stress the ways in which the personal interests of academics can overlap with professional practice through Web 2.0 technologies. Turkish academic libraries, for example, could follow the lead of the aforementioned U.S. universities and establish their own searchable archival/manuscript databases, digital collections, Facebook pages, blogs, or at least listservs. This strategy could serve as an effective way of introducing scholars in Turkey to the entire range of resources available internationally—e-books, e-journals, and major information databases (such as JStor, Project Muse, Medline, ISI Web of Knowledge and EBSCO)—as well as to the non-Turkish academics contributing to such information networks. Such an approach (of adopting academic Web 1.0 technologies as a precursor to adopting academic Web 2.0 technologies) could increase the social and academic capital of SNS and CMC in Turkey, and could improve the flow of knowledge between peers and across cultures.

CMC and SNS have the potential to enhance the quality of university teaching as well as the sharing of cross-cultural information. Not only can these technologies increase communication between faculty members both inside and outside Turkey, faculty members and students at Turkish universities, and faculty members and university administrations, but they can also do a great deal to augment the quality, accessibility and cost-effectiveness of university teaching (Chickering & Ehrmann, 1997). In the age of Web 2.0, this approach can take the form of using Facebook, Twitter, or even blogging as a way to facilitate joint problem-solving and shared learning across borders. Interactive teaching can clearly revolutionize learning, encouraging educators to examine closely the ways in which information is transmitted, received and absorbed, and reassess the processes through which effective communication can occur. In the Turkish setting, this approach can lead to the de-emphasization of rote learning and memorization (which has dominated the academic system since its inception) and the promotion of creative thinking and critical analytic skills. Web 2.0 technologies can also encourage collaboration between teachers and students across both physical and psychological boundaries and extend the provision of knowledge far beyond classroom walls, restrictive course hours, and national borders (i.e., the idea of a "global curriculum" as explored by Tiffin & Rajasingham, 2003). Dual-directional feedback, as accessed through Web 2.0, can clearly provide instructors with the information needed to make appropriate adjustments to content, allowing them to tailor their courses to relevant social, cultural, and international developments as well as to personal needs, student input, academic ability levels, and professional interests.

ACKNOWLEDGMENT

We would like to thank David E. Thornton and Ebru Kaya for their assistance with the administration of our survey to Bilkent University faculty members.

REFERENCES

Ajjan, H., & Hartshorne, R. (2008). Investigating faculty decisions to adopt Web 2.0 technologies: theory and empirical tests. *The Internet and Higher Education*, *11*, 71–80. doi:10.1016/j.iheduc.2008.05.002

Alexander, B. (2008). Social networking in higher education. In Katz, R. N. (Ed.), *The tower and the cloud: Higher education in the age of cloud computing* (pp. 197–201). Boulder, CO: Educause E-Books.

Arikan, A. (2009). *A closer look into prospective English language teachers' social-networking activities*. Paper presented at the Second International Online Language Conference, 25-26 June 2009.

Biocca, F. (2003). Preface. In *Being there: Concepts, effects and measurements of user presence in synthetic environments*, Retrieved April 28, 2010, from http://www.emergingcommunication.com /volume5.html

Bruns, A. (2008). *Blogs, Wikipedia, Second Life, and beyond: From production to produsage*. New York, NY: Peter Lang.

Burcher, N. (2010). *Facebook usage statistics: March 2010*. Retrieved April 23, 2010, from http://www.nickburcher.com/2010/ 03/facebook-usage-statistics -march-2010.html

Chickering, A. W., & Ehrmann, S. C. (1997). *Implementing the seven principles: Technology as lever*. Retrieved May 1, 2010, from http://www.aahe.org/technology/ehrmann.htm

Cohen, L. I. (2007, April 5). *Social scholarship on the rise*. Retrieved December 3, 2010, from http://liblogs.albany.edu/library20 /2007/04/social_scholarship _on_the_rise.html

Colley, A., & Maltby, J. (2008). Impact of the Internet on our lives: Male and female personal perspectives. *Computers in Human Behavior*, *24*, 2005–2013. doi:10.1016/j.chb.2007.09.002

ComScore. (2009). *93 percent of Internet users in Turkey visited Google sites in September 2009: Facebook popularity highlights rapid emergence of social networking*. Retrieved April 28, 2010, from http://www.comscore.com/Press_ Events/ Press_Releases/2009/11/9 3_Percent_of_Internet_Users_in_Turkey_Visited_Google_Sites_in _September_2009/(language)/eng-US

Crane, D. (1972). *Invisible colleges: Diffusion of knowledge in scientific communities*. Chicago, IL: University of Chicago Press.

Cummings, J. N., & Kraut, R. (2002). Domesticating computers and the Internet. *The Information Society, 18*, 221–231. doi:10.1080/01972240290074977

Facebook. (2010). *Facebook statistics*. Retrieved May 11, 2010, from http://www.facebook.com/press /info.php?statistics

Gray, K., Thompson, C. R., Sheard, J., & Hamilton, M. (2008). Web 2.0 authorship: Issues of referencing and citation for academic integrity. *The Internet and Higher Education, 11*, 112–118. doi:10.1016/j.iheduc.2008.03.001

Guimaraes, M. (2005). Doing anthropology in cyberspace: fieldwork boundaries and social environments. In Hine, C. (Ed.), *Virtual methods: Issues in social research on the Internet* (pp. 141–156). New York, NY: Berg.

Hardesty, S., & Sugarman, T. (2007). Academic librarians, professional literature, and new technologies: A survey. *University Library Faculty Publications, Paper 3*. Retrieved May 17, 2010 from http://digitalarchive.gsu.edu /univ_lib_fac-pub/3

Herring, S. D. (2001). Using the World Wide Web for research: Are faculty satisfied? *Journal of Academic Librarianship, 27*(3), 213–219. doi:10.1016/S0099-1333(01)00183-5

Herrington, J., Herrington, A., Mantei, J., Olney, I., & Ferry, B. (Eds.). (2009). *New technologies, new pedagogies: Mobile learning in higher education*. Wollongong, Australia: University of Wollongong.

Jackson, L. A., Ervin, K. S., Gardner, P. D., & Schmitt, N. (2008). Gender and the Internet: Women communicating and men searching. *Sex Roles, 44*, 363–380. doi:10.1023/A:1010937901821

Mason, R., & Rennie, F. (2007). Using Web 2.0 for learning in the community. *The Internet and Higher Education, 10*, 196–203. doi:10.1016/j.iheduc.2007.06.003

Mo, P., Malik, S., & Coulson, N. (2009). Gender differences in computer-mediated communication: a systematic literature review of online health-related support groups. *Patient Education and Counseling, 75*(1), 16–24. doi:10.1016/j.pec.2008.08.029

Ono, H., & Zavodny, M. (2003). Gender and the Internet. *Social Science Quarterly, 84*, 111–121. doi:10.1111/1540-6237.t01-1-8401007

Pearson, J. (1999). Electronic networking in initial teacher education: Is a virtual faculty of education possible? *Computers & Education, 32*, 221–238. doi:10.1016/S0360-1315(99)00005-6

Perez, S. (2008). *Enterprise 2.0 to become a $4.6 billion industry by 2013*. Retrieved April 23, 2010, from www.readwriteweb.com/archives/ enterprise_20_to_become_a_46_billion_industry.php

Pfeil, U., Arjan, R., & Zaphiris, P. (2009). Age differences in online social networking: a study of user profiles and the social capital divide among teenagers and older users in MySpace. *Computers in Human Behavior, 25*, 643–654. doi:10.1016/j.chb.2008.08.015

Sahin, Y. L., & Coklar, A. N. (2009). Social networking users' views on technology and the determination of technostress levels. *Procedia-Social and Behavioral Sciences, 1*, 1437–1442. doi:10.1016/j.sbspro.2009.01.253

Sonnenwald, D. H., & Liewrouw, L. A. (1997). Collaboration during the design process: A case study of communication, information behavior, and project performance. In Vakkari, P., Savolainen, R., & Dervin, B. (Eds.), *Information seeking in context: Proceedings of an international conference on research in information needs, seeking and use in different contexts* (pp. 179–204). London, UK: Taylor Graham.

Stoan, S. K. (1991). Research and information retrieval among academic researchers: Implications for library instruction. *Library Trends*, *39*(3), 238–257.

Tapscott, D., & Williams, A. D. (2008). *Wikinomics: How mass collaboration changes everything*. New York, NY: Portfolio.

Thelwall, M. (2008). Social networks, gender and friending: An analysis of MySpace member profiles. *Journal of the American Society for Information Science and Technology*, *59*(8), 1321–1330. doi:10.1002/asi.20835

Tiffin, J., & Rajasingham, L. (2003). *The global virtual university*. New York, NY: Routledge-Falmer. doi:10.4324/9780203464670

Tunc, T. E. (2009). Technologies of consumption: The social semiotics of Turkish shopping malls. In Vannini, P. (Ed.), *Material culture and technology in everyday life: Ethnographic approaches* (pp. 131–143). New York, NY: Peter Lang.

Virkus, S. (2008). Use of Web 2.0 technologies in LIS education: Experiences at Tallinn University, Estonia. *Program: Electronic Library and Information Systems*, *42*(3), 262–274. doi:10.1108/00330330810892677

Wasserman, I. M., & Richmond-Abbott, M. (2005). Gender and the Internet: Causes of variation in access, level, and scope of use. *Social Science Quarterly*, *86*, 252–270. doi:10.1111/j.0038-4941.2005.00301.x

Young, J. R. (2005). Knowing when to log off. *The Chronicle of Higher Education*, A34.

Zemliansky, P., & St.Amant, K. (2008). Preface. In Zemliansky, P., & St.Amant, K. (Eds.), *Handbook of research on virtual workplaces and the new nature of business practices* (pp. xxvii–xxxii). Hershey, PA: Information Science Reference. doi:10.4018/978-1-59904-893-2

KEY TERMS AND DEFINITIONS

Social Networking: The practice of expanding one's business and/or social contacts by making connections through other individuals.

Web 2.0: This term is commonly associated with web applications that facilitate interactive information sharing, interoperability, user-centered design, and collaboration on the World Wide Web.

Educational Networking: The use of social networking technologies for educational purposes.

Professional Networking: The use of social networking technologies for professional purposes.

Social Scholar: Those scholars whose academic practices incorporate Web 2.0 social tools.

Facebook: A social networking website launched in February 2004 that is operated and privately owned by Facebook, Inc., with more than 500 million active users in July 2010, or one out of every fourteen people in the world.

ENDNOTES

[1] In this chapter, "academics in Turkey" will be defined as those scholars residing and teaching in Turkey, regardless of their national origin or citizenship (i.e., both Turkish and foreign academics).

[2] Countries such as the People's Republic of China, Morocco, and Thailand have blocked access to YouTube due to the presence

of what they deem "offensive material." YouTube was blocked in Turkey between 2008 and 2010 after controversy over video postings insulting Mustafa Kemal Ataturk, the founder of the Republic of Turkey and its first President. Despite this censorship, Turkish Prime Minister Recep Tayyip Erdogan admitted to accessing YouTube through an open proxy. Nevertheless, these proxies were frequently disabled, and illegal software, such as "YouTube Jacker" failed more often than they succeeded. Thus, an individual working at a state university may have been relectant to attempt to use YouTube, especially while on campus. For more information, see: Doğan News Agency. "Ban on YouTube Proves Virtual." *Hürriyet*, Nov. 26, 2008: http://arama.hurriyet.com.tr/arsivnews.aspx?id=10441126. Last accessed May 10, 2011.

[3] It was, and still is, common to find retired Turkish faculty members in their 40s. In the Turkish academic system, research assistants are considered to be employees first, and students second. Thus, many Turkish academics begin their working careers not after receiving a PhD, but as Masters students at the age of 22 or 23. Until quite recently, Turkish law mandated citizens to complete 20 years of full-time employment prior to retiring, without fulfulling any sort of pre-set minimum retirement age requirement. Mandatory full-time employment has subsequently been increased to 30 years, but this situatoin only applies to individuals who began full-time employment after the legal change. Thus, for many years, it was routine practice for faculty members at state institutions to complete their 20 years of service, retire in their early to mid-40s, receive a lump-sum retirement package and retirement checks for the rest of their lives, and find positions at private institutions as instructors, which provided them with a second income.

Chapter 8

Knowing Through Asynchronous Time and Space:
A Phenomenological Study of Cultural Differences in Online Interaction

Ping Yang
Denison University, USA

ABSTRACT

This chapter reports the results of a study that employed phenomenological and dialectical perspectives to explore cultural differences in computer-mediated communication. An analysis of the dialectic of minimization and amplification manifested in students' online experiences and the significance of contextual variations, power structures, and other features of online interactions allow us to see the processual, relational, and contradictory nature of cultural differences online. They also provide information that can facilitate more effective intercultural online interactions in the future.

INTRODUCTION

We are all global villagers. Since McLuhan (1962) coined the term "global village" over 40 years ago, residents of the world are becoming increasingly connected via communication technologies – particularly online communication

technologies. Intercultural interaction through computer-mediated communication (CMC) is no longer the privilege of some. Rather, it is now a necessity for all. Increasing worldwide access to cyberspace has introduced a favorable online environment for the frequent occurrence of communication across cultures. The internationalization and interdependence of people from every part of the world, moreover, makes cultural

DOI: 10.4018/978-1-60960-833-0.ch008

differences in online interaction a fascinating research area for scholars of communication and many other disciplines to investigate. Within this context, understanding cultural differences in computer-mediated communication might play a significant role in increasing cultural sensitivity and communication effectiveness in international interactions.

Originated in the 1950s, the Internet has become a mass medium and created a new dimension for global communication (Barnes, 2003; McPhail, 2006). Statistics, furthermore, indicate a rapid increase in international online access. For example, as of September 2009, Internet users have reached approximately 1.8 billion worldwide (Internet World Stats, 2009). The growth of the worldwide online environment has, in turn, influenced people's communication experiences in a variety of fields including the professional and private, the economic and political, and the academic and educational. In today's fast-developing and highly competitive world, studies on intercultural communication in cyberspace have great potential for helping individuals across all of these spheres interact more effectively with each other.

Many studies investigating computer-mediated communication in relation to culture focus on cross-cultural comparisons and identifying variations in communication behaviors (Kim & Papacharissi, 2003; Smith, Coldwell, Smith, & Murphy, 2005; Vishwanath & Chen, 2008). While these studies have contributed to our understanding of online communication and cross-cultural differences, a growing number of scholars have challenged the practice of essentializing cultural differences through uncritical acceptance of dualisms and logical positivism. These individuals have recognized the importance of engaging context and power in studying culture and communication (Chuang, 2003; Martin & Nakayama, 1999; Collier, 2005; Martinez, 2008; Halualani, Mendoza, & Drzewiecka, 2009). Characteristics of computer-mediated communication such as

the common lack of nonverbal cues, ambiguity, anonymity, and pseudo-anonymity present new scholarly challenges (St.Amant, 2002; Shim, Kim, & Martin, 2008).

To adequately describe the complex realities of online interactions, the study presented in this chapter uses phenomenological and dialectical perspectives to explore the dynamic and dialectical nature of cultural differences as they are experienced online. In so doing, the study draws upon the dialectical approach previously used by Martin and Nakayama (1999; 2011). The chapter reports the results of a study on college students' consciousness and pre-consciousness in experiencing cultural differences online within the framework of phenomenology and the dialectical approach. Such scholarly work on cultural differences helps provide suggestions to increase communication effectiveness and develop a sense of knowing through asynchronous time and space.

CULTURAL DIFFERENCES AND COMPUTER-MEDIATED COMMUNICATION

Two sets of research are related to the study on cultural differences in intercultural online interactions presented in this chapter. These sets of research are studies on cultural variability and studies on computer-mediated communication. These two strands of previous research provide the theoretical foundation for the research examined here.

Many existing studies focus on communication between people from different cultures and attempt to describe or explain intercultural communication behaviors (Gudykunst & Lee, 2002; Martin & Nakayama, 1999). Several of them are based on the assumption that cultural values influence these communication differences. As a result, the related researchers employ traditional social science quantitative methodologies to examine such situations (Martin & Nakayama, 1999). For example, Hofstede (1980, 1997) has identified five dimensions of value and cultural variability. These dimensions are

- Individualism-collectivism
- Low-high uncertainty avoidance
- Low-high power distance
- Masculinity-femininity
- Short-long orientation to life

Many studies, in turn, use Hofstede's five dimensions to examine cross-cultural differences in communication – be it face to face or online. Ting-Toomey and Oetzel (2002), for example, explored how three variables – individualism, power distance, and self construals – influence cross-cultural differences in face concerns, facework, and conflict behaviors. Their research findings note clear patterns of differences between cultures in relation to these concepts. For example, individualism and independent self-construals lead to self-face concerns, and these concerns result in dominating and competing conflict styles. Collectivism and dependent self-construals, by contrast, lead to other and mutual-face concerns and often result in avoiding, obliging, and integrating conflict styles. In addressing similar kinds of cross-cultural differences, other scholars examined how language (Lim, 2002), nonverbal communication (Park & Guan, 2009), and gender-role ideology (Marshall, 2008) vary across cultures and affect interactions.

Other research studies investigate the relationship between social identities of race, ethnicity, gender, class, and age and their cultural components of shared values, norms, and history, which all contribute to intercultural communication variations. Ellis (1999), for example, studied how ethnicity and social class affected discourse processes. His work explores how social categories of class and ethnicity were linked to concreted communicative events and reflected in language and communication. More recently, Mo, Malik, and Coulson (2009) conducted a review of studies that examined gender differences in communica-

tion within online health communities. The study results reveal that there were obvious differences between male and female discussion boards on health-related issues. There were also a range of situational and contextual factors that might affect how men and women used online health support groups. A number of intercultural communication research, in turn, focuses on communication differences across groups of different ethnic, racial, gender, and age groups (Philipsen, 1990; Williams and Nussbaum, 2001; Houston, 2004).

Many of these studies on computer-mediated communication have identified cultural variations in people's online behaviors – behaviors such as differences in self-presentations between interactants from South Korea and the U.S. (Kim & Papacharissi, 2003). Such research applies the concept of independent and interdependent self-construals to online context. In so doing, the related researchers have found cultural differences relate to manifestations of individualism and collectivism. U.S. home pages, for example, tend to present information in a direct and personal manner whereas Web pages created by South Koreans tend to provide interlinks to special interest.

More recently, Vishwanath and Chen (2008) conducted a cross-cultural comparison of people's associations with communication technologies across U.S., Germany, and Singapore. They have investigated the psychological distance between technologies and the individual self, revealing the importance of technologies to the individuals. Technologies nearer to the self would be considered more important and closer self reflections/extensions of the self. The opposite is true with technologies further from the self. The results of their research indicate that technologies close to the self were similar in these three countries. In the United States, however, Instant Messenger was furthest from the self whereas in Germany blogs were seen as being furthest from the self, and in Singapore, it was home pages that were seen as furthest from the self. These variations suggest a strong influence of cultural norms on personal technology choice.

The new time and space relations created via CMC provide a changing environment for communicators to express their cultural selves. In the world of virtual communities, the lines between identities are blurring, and identity itself becomes ambiguous. St.Amant (2002), for example, has noted how cyberspace creates interesting situations associated with culture, the creation of identity, and establishing ethos. These factors, in turn, create points of contention associated with potential problems in intercultural online exchanges. St.Amant's research also points out the faceless and anonymous dimension of online identity and notes how the fluid and changing identity in CMC might cause problems for cultures that require a fixed, unchanging, and discernible identity in communication (St.Amant, 2002). Donath (1999) calls additional attention to issues of ambiguity, identity, and possibilities of identity deception in the virtual community. Thus, credibility is one of the most significant issues to consider in the international mediated environment.

Power is another significant issue in studying culture in online communication. Interactions online tend to replay many social tensions and problems in offline realities (Gajjala, 1998). Meanings and stereotypes associated with cultural selves in realities might still exist behind the computer screen. A related set of studies examine causes and consequences of the digital divide – the gap in media access and use of computer and the Internet – and consider the relations between technological disparities and social/economic factors in global cyberspace (van Dijk, 2004; Mehra, Merkel, and Bishop, 2004).

In sum, the rapidly growing number of Internet users requires more scholarly work on intercultural online communication to meet the challenges of the electronic age. As a result, there need to be more interpretive descriptions and interpretations of the complex and unique process related to cultural

variability and online interactions – particularly in relation to power dynamics.

The research project presented in this chapter aims to further examine these issues by employing phenomenology in exploring how students experience cultural differences online with integration of the intersections between culture, communication, and technology. By using a phenomenological framework, this study examines cultural variability in online communication by explicating the relational, processual, and contradictory nature of intercultural interactions emphasized in the dialectical perspective. To examine cultural variability in the new context of online communication, the research presented here attempts to address the primary research question:

What are the students' experiences of recognizing and confronting cultural differences during intercultural online communication? How do students' consciousness and pre-consciousness of cultural differences manifest in their discourses?

METHODOLOGY

This study employs phenomenology to explore how students from diverse cultural backgrounds experience cultural differences online. Phenomenology, as a theory and a methodology, investigates human conscious experience – the relationship between a person and the lived world that he or she lives in (Martinez, 2006). Phenomenology is the name for a historical movement born in Germany, sustained in France, and complemented by a group of American scholars in the human sciences (Lanigan, 1988). This movement focuses on lived experience and the inherent interrelatedness of human conscious experience with the fact that a person is always situated in time, place, and culture (Martinez, 2006). The phenomenological method consists of three steps: description, reduction, and interpretation. This methodology is synergistic in nature as each step is a part of a whole, and the continuous practice of these steps contributes new parts to the total (Lanigan, 1988). Phenomenology provides researchers with an important approach for investigating the fundamental meanings of human communication.

To understand the meaning of lived experience and the intricacies in intercultural online interactions, this study takes a dialectical approach. The dialectical approach, introduced by Martin and Nakayama (1999), provides a conceptual framework for understanding intercultural communication practice. Instead of seeing the world in single ways, the dialectical approach opens up a new perspective in studying culture and communication in multiple ways (Martin & Nakayama, 1999, 2011). Martin and Nakayama (1999) identified six dialectics characterizing intercultural interactions: cultural – individual, personal – contextual, differences – similarities, privilege – disadvantage, static – dynamic, and history/past – present/future. These six dialectics provide a framework for studying intercultural communication (Chen, 2002; Cools, 2006; Brown, 2004; Orbe, 2008) and for teaching intercultural communication (Fong & Chuang, 2004; Schmidt, Conaway, Easton & Wardrope, 2007; Rimmington & Alagic, 2008).

Phenomenology is congruent with the combination of paradigms emphasized in the dialectical approach as it helps provide descriptions of the lived experience of participants while placing this experience within particular contexts. Martinez's (2000) phenomenological research, for example, examines her cultural identity development by challenging the dominant cultural structures. In so doing, it demonstrates how one can combine the interpretive and critical perspectives in providing a more in-depth understanding of the research phenomenon. Phenomenology, thus, is well suited to the current project, for it enables the researcher/author to examine the complex realities of students' online experiences as they exist in social, cultural, and historical time and space.

This current research project took place in an intercultural communication course at a large

Southwestern university. Personal descriptions, online discussions, and in-depth interviews were collected as research artifacts for review. That is, the researcher received individual consent from 21 students to use their written assignments on their intercultural online experiences, and this consent was provided after these students had completed the related course.

For this particular assignment, students were paired with another student from a different cultural background and were required to use only online media to investigate each other's cultural identities. Students then wrote an individual paper, called Experience of Intercultural Online Interactions, about their personal experiences of intercultural online interactions. A second group of capta was collected from a total of 86 discussion postings on Blackboard (an online course management system). In this case, students were encouraged to discuss their online intercultural experiences and to post their responses to each other's experiences. What is more, research capta were also collected from interviews with eight of the students who participated in these projects. Interview respondents, in turn, varied in terms of majors, years at college, and cultural backgrounds. Each interview consisted of 25 semi-structured open-ended questions and lasted for 60 minutes. The research methods for this study were approved by the Human Subjects Board of the researcher's/author's university. Participation in this research was entirely voluntary, and information provided by subjects/students was completely confidential.

The rich and complicated capta generated though personal descriptions, online discussions, and interviews serve as a resource for developing a deeper understanding of cultural differences online. The researcher/author used the phenomenological methodology of description, reduction, and interpretation to examine the capta, and the resulting analysis provides richly nuanced descriptions of students' lived experiences. Moreover, capta were read and analyzed many times in order to identify patterns and note trends. The following set of themes emerged from phenomenological analysis, and these themes speak directly to the essential structures of online experiences of cultural variability.

MINIMIZATION AND AMPLIFICATION OF CULTURAL DIFFERENCES ONLINE

Phenomenologists obtain people's experiences and reflections on their experiences in order to come to a deeper understanding of the meanings and significance of human experience (van Manen, 2003). In order to grasp the meanings of the students' lived experience, the researcher reflects phenomenologically on student participants' online experiences of cultural variability and analyzes the thematic aspects of the experiences. The research phenomenon is examined in the text as approachable in terms of themes, or meaning units. Phenomenology and the dialectical approach allow the researcher to describe and analyze the themes identified in the research capta and uncover the essential structures as they appear in students' pre-consciousness and consciousness in experiencing cultural differences online. The resulting theme shows how a phenomenological framework reinforces and extends the dialectical perspective – in that cultural differences are both minimized and amplified in online intercultural interactions.

Cultural Differences are Minimized in Online Communication

The study capta showed how online communication technologies allow people from different cultural backgrounds to interact with each other more conveniently and quickly than face-to-face communication. People encounter each other directly regardless of distance and time. A few scholars have emphasized the facelessness of computer-mediated communication (Bargh &

McKenna, 2004; Merryfield, 2003; St.Amant, 2002). As Bargh and McKenna (2004) note, one of the critical differences between online communication and face-to-face communication is "the absence of nonverbal features of communication such as tone of voice, facial expressions, and potential influential interpersonal features such as physical attractiveness, skin color, gender, and so on" (p. 577). This section discusses how cultural differences become minimized in online interactions due to the absence of nonverbal cues, reduction of stereotypes, degradation of language barriers, and employment of increasingly advanced technologies.

Students' online experiences reinforce the notion that the lack of physical presence makes differences less prominent between ages, race, ethnicity, class, gender, and nationality, if communicators are speaking the same language. As most of the students point out, online communication allows them to easily encounter people of diverse cultural backgrounds with increasing frequency and convenience. The Internet becomes a multicultural space for people from cultures around the world to engage in intercultural interactions and establish or maintain intercultural relationships. Dana, for example, shares her experience communicating with intercultural friends around the globe:

My intercultural communication experience started off when I went to an overnight camp and met so many people from Australia, New Zealand, and South Africa. We would all e-mail back and forth for a while after the camp because we became so close....Now with Facebook, it has become a common tool for communication among internationals. It is a great tool that is used to let us look at pictures, email friends, and write quick responses to one another's comments.

Modern technologies provide numerous opportunities to meet the cultural "other," explore common interests, and have fun with individuals from different cultures.

At the same time, these technologies provide opportunities to native and non-native speakers to alter their communication styles and vocabulary when communicating with others from different linguistic and cultural backgrounds. The student participants in this research, for example, constantly expressed the ease of typing in conversations and editing what they write online. Language, thus, becomes less of a barrier in intercultural online interactions because people from different language backgrounds are able to compose messages more carefully and even edit/revise what they have already posted. This feature is especially helpful when students who are non-native English speakers use online translation tools and spelling check devices to communicate with more ease and confidence in a language that is not their native tongue.

In relation to the research done by the author, Patricia is an exchange student from Prague, the Czech Republic. In her descriptive account, she describes her enjoyment of the convenience that online communication brings to her regardless of language differences. On Facebook, one of the most popular social networking websites, for example, English is the language used most often between Patricia and her friends from the Czech Republic, the U.S., Britain, France, and Germany. Although there are numerous differences in using English, no one cares about the grammar, words, or spelling, as long as everyone understands what has been written. Language differences are minimized on Facebook because Patricia and her friends use it mainly for maintaining their friendships and exchanging information. Language differences are thus no longer barriers in intercultural interactions. As a matter of fact, Patricia enjoys her intercultural experiences on the Facebook even more than meeting her international friends in person because, as Patricia says, "I can joke there; I can think about it; I can write witty and humor-

ous replies…I don't feel dumb; people cannot hear my accent and I feel more confident there."

The use of advanced communication technologies assists people in choosing what they wish to express regarding their cultural selves online. Emails, text message, video chat, and social networking sites have provided multiple ways of identity construction. On Facebook, as students' experiences reveal, people have the liberty to determine what and which part of themselves they want others to see. Facebook users have the freedom to choose profile pictures that are either meaningful or attractive, and they can even post videos about themselves for others to view. This freedom in expressing one's cultural self online blurs social and cultural boundaries in intercultural communication. According to the students who participated in this research project, online communication frees people from holding stereotypes against each other based on ethnicity or physical looking, as shown in Robert's experience online.

Robert is a student of Hispanic origin. He provides an example of how he finds it easier to avoid being judged because of his cultural background on the Internet. According to Robert, online communication provides a context that allows people to avoid bias and stereotypes associated with physical features – features that, in face-to-face communication cannot be avoided as easily. Robert narrates his experience of eliminating cultural differences online in his discussion of choosing to disclose less information online and taking the color out of online pictures of himself:

[In online context] I don't disclose information about my age, ethnicity, race, or religion. I chose to do things this way so that there will be little biases and stereotypes when looking at my pages or talking to me. I also take the color out of my pictures to make it more difficult to judge me because of the color of my skin. Normally, I present myself as a human being that is overall not different from anyone.

Robert enjoys online interactions because they allow him to connect with people based on factors other than race/ethnicity or physical features. Because people do not know what the persons they are talking to online look like, it is possible to reduce prejudgment and eliminates the chances of prejudice and discrimination. However, it should also be noted that this freedom of self presentation might also lead to concerns related to authenticity and trust, especially when online identity construction is largely reduced to words.

Students' reflections showed how online communication can link people of diverse backgrounds and bridge the gap between groups of different race, ethnicity, age, socio-economic class, and language backgrounds. Cultural differences become less prominent when communicators cannot see the physical appearance of other online interactants. Similarly, language differences are minimized through the use of online devices and technologies that provide users with more time and freedom to edit and revise what they say. Online communicators thus enjoy a greater freedom in choosing what they want to present and describe, and they often choose to present themselves in a way that minimizes differences across cultural and social groups.

To investigate cultural differences from diverse perspectives, the following section uses the dialectical approach to examine how cultural differences are not only minimized in online interactions. Rather, they might be amplified in certain cases.

Cultural Differences are Amplified in Online Communication

Consonant with the dialectical perspective, the capta also show that cultural differences are amplified in online communication. The invisibility of physical presence blurs the differences among social and cultural identities. However, because human interaction online is largely reduced to words (St.Amant, 2002), many cultural differences in verbal communication are amplified in online contexts.

Communication style is one of the major factors that intensify cultural differences in online interactions. Communication style is defined as the meta-message that contextualizes how people express and interpret verbal messages (Martin & Nakayama, 2009). The two dimensions of direct – indirect, elaborate – understated styles in communication both play a significant role revealing cultural variability, which sometimes leads to misunderstandings in online interactions. A number of students' descriptive accounts narrate their own experiences of cultural shock when they encountered communication styles that were different from their own.

Nancy from Turkey, for example, shares her experience of how different communication styles between the U.S. and Turkey lead to misunderstandings in doing business and how she and her colleagues have eventually found a common ground in writing business emails. According to Nancy, in business letters in Turkey, people usually write something about themselves, the weather, or anything – to create a more conversational interaction before getting into the business part of the communiqué. For this reason, Nancy would often write at least a few conversational sentences at the beginning of her emails. These sentences included items such as "thank you for your email," "thank you for your prompt response," "how are you," "here we are really busy," or "it has begun to rain." When Nancy received emails from her colleague in Los Angeles, however, she was surprised to find that he skipped the greeting part and got directly to the point. As Nancy puts it, "His style was very direct and right to the point. It felt a little patronizing when someone just says, 'Nancy, do this and that'. I was like, 'Ok, but first of all, what did I do wrong?' It was very uncomfortable in that sense." Due to these differences in online communication styles, Nancy felt her colleague's email was "short" and "cold." He never greeted her; instead, Nancy perceived him as being "condescending" and "critical." Fortunately, Nancy and her colleague were able to reach a cultural understanding of communication style differences through their continuous contact and the use of jokes, and humor. Over time, they adapted to each other's communication styles, and their relationship became closer.

In addition to communication style, self-disclosure also makes cultural differences prominent in online interactions. Different cultural groups, for example, might have different levels of self-disclosure, which includes different perceptions of what kinds of information they feel comfortable sharing with others. In online communication, this difference related to disclosure makes interaction less effective and frustrating at times. People from low-context cultures, for example, might disclose more information about their identities, while people from high-context cultures might not reveal as much information in online contexts.

The students who participated in this study noted experiencing different levels of self-disclosure when using Facebook in international contexts. According to them, an American Facebook page, for example, might be bursting with information about the individual and her/his identity. The Facebook pages of individuals located in Ecuador and Chile, by contrast, tend to have less information about the individual but provide more updated news about the person's family. And a similar page in Germany would be used more for receiving information than socializing with others or engaging in small talk.

The reduction of human interaction online to words and symbols means cultural differences play a more important role in affecting our intercultural understandings. As Nancy's experience shows, a business letter considered to be professional in one culture might not be regarded as appropriate in another. Due to the lack of nonverbal cues, people from cultures other than the U.S. might have greater difficulty interpreting the meanings and the tones of online messages.

Patricia, from the Czech Republic, experienced misunderstandings when exchanging emails during the process of applying to a university in the U.S. When Patricia started a letter with details inquiring if someone would offer her choices related to where she could live in relation to the campus, the reply she received was only a link, "no explanation," "no hello," and "no signature." In online exchanges, Patricia thought the sender did not like her; however, when she met that person (the department secretary) in person, she found it to be a misunderstanding. Patricia realized it was a matter of different approaches to writing emails – most Czechs prefer details in writing, whereas in the U.S., most individuals expect the sender of a message to get to the point right away.

A similar kind of situation was also true for Robert's experience of cracking jokes with his friends from different cultural backgrounds. Robert, who was of Hispanic origin, would often find it offensive when his classmates made jokes about their family members. Thus, it is important to remember that a remark one individual finds humorous might not be viewed the same way due to different cultural interpretations. The dynamism of each every culture amplifies cultural differences by the use of different communication styles, self-disclosure levels, abbreviations, slang, jokes, as well as increasingly emerging new terms. This ever changing communication pattern enlarges the gap for effective communication between insiders of a cultural group and outsiders.

RECOMMENDATIONS FOR COMMUNICATING EFFECTIVELY ACROSS CULTURES ONLINE

The findings of this study revealed the unique feature of intercultural online communication in that cultural differences are both minimized and amplified by online media. Based on these findings, the author suggests the following recommendations or strategies as mechanisms that can facilitate more effective online interactions with individuals from different cultures.

Pay Attention to Communication Contexts

Cultural differences are minimized or amplified in online communication depending on the contexts of the encounters. Numerous factors, including participants, purposes of communication, and the time and space of specific web tools can all affect the interaction. For this reason, it is important that individuals remember contexts play a significant role in intercultural online interactions.

As shown in Patricia's personal narrative, when she communicated with friends on Facebook, language differences are minimized because she can spend more time revising what she writes, and people tend to be more tolerant of grammatical errors online. However, cultural differences can be maximized in more formal contexts such as in business transactions and educational settings as illustrated in Nancy's and Patricia's experiences. When communication contexts change from informal to formal, from private to public, from casual conversations to heated arguments, or from a friend to a professor, people need to adjust their communication in order to achieve the most effectiveness. Online communication is complicated by the existence of many fluid, tenuous, and temporal spaces created by asynchronicity. Individuals therefore need to pay particular attention to the specific context in which they are interacting when they move in and out of these spaces.

Be Aware of Power Structures

Cultural differences are also minimized or maximized depending on the power and privilege of communicators in online interactions. Just as an individual takes a position and status in offline world, that individual often takes on a similar kind of role in cyberspace. Thus, power structures are present in every facet of online communication.

As noted earlier, modern technologies such as email and Facebook link the world closely by making it easy to access individuals from other cultures. However, these technologies might also enlarge the gaps among people from diverse social and cultural backgrounds. On the Internet, communicators have the power to give out as much or little information as they want. Privilege and disadvantages in offline interactions may be reduced, as shown in Robert's decision to remove color from his photos to avoid prejudgment. On the other hand, some students have experienced more cultural or racial biases because of their names, expressions of religions, or being a member of dominant/marginalized groups. Therefore, people need to be aware of hierarchical structures when online communication is largely reduced to verbal interactions.

Develop Sensitivity in Verbal Exchanges

Language is a huge issue in intercultural online communication because a large amount of information is exchanged through the use of text-based messages. The students who participated in this project noted their experiences of culture shock when interacting with individuals from different backgrounds via text-based interactions. Nancy from Turkey, for example, felt patronized when she received emails from her colleague in Los Angeles who told her "do this and that" directly. Patricia from the Czech Republic thought the department secretary did not like her when her email reply was only a link. For people of different linguistic and cultural backgrounds, it is hard to understand slang, abbreviations, and jokes. Robert, for example, felt uncomfortable hearing jokes making fun of one's family. To Robert, "people who are blood, in Hispanic culture, are sacred." Thus, intercultural online communication requires great sensitivity in verbal exchanges.

Know Complexities of Cultural Identity

The minimization and amplification of cultural differences reflect the complexities of developing cultural identity online. Online, individuals enjoy the freedom to present their cultural selves as they wish. Concerns with ambiguity, authenticity, stability, and trust, however, often linger in people's minds whenever they interact via computer networks.

Students' experiences reveal cross-cultural differences in identity development. Take self-disclosure as an example; an American Facebook page seems to be relatively low context because people disclose more information about their identities. However, a similar page in Germany tends to contain more factual descriptions. If one feels excluded or does not share similar cultural backgrounds with others, one might choose to disclose less information about cultural identities via online media such as Facebook. Such was the case for Robert, who noted how he did not disclose information about his age, ethnicity, race, and religion online. However, students of majority cultural group (Anglo Americans, for example) also appreciate the important tactful expression of cultural selves online. It is hard to express pride in one's own cultures with individuals who have a different ethnic or racial identity. This situation is especially the case in online contexts. Because CMC provides opportunities to construct, reconstruct, and experiment with cultural identities, it is important to note complexities of the issue in intercultural online interactions.

Understand the Dynamic Nature of Culture

The dialectic of minimization and amplification of cultural differences online has revealed that online communication increases the dynamism and flexibility of culture in computer-mediated communication. No matter how culture is defined – as nation-state, learned systems of codes, shared contextual symbolic meanings, or contested site of struggles – culture is always preeminent and dynamic in intercultural communication studies (Shutter, 2008).

Online communication technologies such as the Internet create new time and space for expressing cultural differences. Such situations often result in increasing fluidity and flexibility of culture. The virtual spaces created by asynchronicity are multiple, temporal, and tenuous. As a result, cultural differences might be minimized or amplified in relation to contextual variations, power structures, verbal interactions, and identity development. All of these significant issues are manifest in students' lived experiences of cultural variability online. The dialectic of minimization and amplification of cultural differences as noted by this study highlights the increasing dynamic nature of culture – particularly in online contexts. Understanding the new meanings and changing nature of culture online is vital to communicators and scholars in intercultural online communication.

CONCLUSION

In this chapter, the employment of phenomenological framework with dialectical perspective was used to explore students' experiences of cultural differences. The results reveal the underlying modality of consciousness upon which these experiences are manifested. Seeing how cultures are similar or different from each other in online communication, how cultural differences are present or absent, and how they are minimized or amplified during interactions helps individuals experience the "other's" modality as our own. In so doing, it increases our ability to understand the complexities of intercultural online communication.

With this phenomenological inquiry, readers are able to live through the students' lived experiences of cultural differences online. The phenomenological analysis of students' experiences as presented here has extended and supported the dialectical framework in that cultural differences are both minimized and amplified in online communication. The dialectic of minimization and amplification of cultural differences that emerged from students' experiences as noted here reinforces Martin and Nakayama's (1999; 2011) dialectical perspective in understanding culture and communication. Future research might identify additional dialectics that are unique to intercultural online interactions. These dialectics will continue to support and extend the dialectical framework and make contribution to the study of intercultural communication.

In addition, the minimization – amplification dialectic reveals the importance of contextual variations, power structures, verbal interactions, identity development, as well as the dynamic nature of culture in online communication. These are significant issues that require high levels of intercultural sensitivity in dealing with cultural differences in computer-mediated communication. The dialectic demonstrated from students' lived experiences reveals an increasing dynamism and flexibility of culture online. It is a dynamic with unique features created by the changing time and space associated with computer-mediated communication. By exploring such dynamics further, we can gain a better understanding of cultural differences and develop practices that can facilitate more meaningful online contacts in international cyberspace.

REFERENCES

Bargh, J. A., & McKenna, K. Y. A. (2004). The Internet and social life. *Annual Review of Psychology, 55*, 573–590. doi:10.1146/annurev.psych.55.090902.141922

Barnes, S. B. (2003). *Computer-mediated communication: Human-to-human communication across the internet*. Boston, MA: Allyn and Bacon.

Brown, T. J. (2004). Deconstructing the dialectical tensions in *The Horse Whisperer*: How myths represent competing cultural values. *Journal of Popular Culture, 38*(2), 274–295. doi:10.1111/j.0022-3840.2004.00112.x

Chen, G. (2002). Communication in intercultural relationships. In Gudykunst, W. B., & Mody, B. (Eds.), *Handbook of international and intercultural communication* (2nd ed., pp. 241–258). Thousand Oaks, CA: Sage.

Chuang, R. (2003). Postmodern critique of cross-cultural and intercultural communication. In W. J. Storosta & G. M. Chen (Eds.), *Ferment in the intercultural field* (International and Intercultural Communication Annual, Vol 26) (pp. 24-53). Thousand Oaks, CA: Sage.

Collier, M. J. (2005). Theorizing cultural identifications: Critical updates and continuing evolution. In Gudykunst, W. (Ed.), *Theorizing about intercultural communication* (pp. 235–256). Thousand Oaks, CA: Sage.

Cools, C. A. (2006). Relational communication in intercultural couples. *Language and Intercultural Communication, 6*(3&4), 262–274. doi:10.2167/laic253.0

Donath, J. S. (1999). Identity and deception in the virtual community. In Smith, M., & Kollock, P. (Eds.), *Communities in cyberspace* (pp. 27–58). London, UK: Routledge.

Ellis, D. G. (1999). *Crafting society: Ethnicity, class, and communication theory*. Mahwah, NJ: Lawrence Erlbaum.

Fong, M., & Chuang, R. (2004). *Communicating ethnic and cultural identity*. Lanham, MD: Rowman & Littlefield.

Gajjala, R. (1998). *The sawnet refusal: An interrupted cyberethnography*. Dissertation Abstracts International, (pp. 99-131).

Gudykunst, W. B., & Lee, C. (2002). Cross-cultural communication theories. In Gudykunst, W. B., & Mody, B. (Eds.), *Handbook of international and intercultural communication* (pp. 19–24). Thousand Oaks, CA: Sage.

Halualani, R. T., Mendoza, S. L., & Drze-wiecka, J. A. (2009). "Critical" junctures in intercultural communication studies: A review. *Review of Communication, 9,* 17–35. doi:10.1080/15358590802169504

Hofstede, G. (1980). *Culture's consequences: International differences in work-related values.* Beverly Hills, CA: Sage.

Hofstede, G. (1997). *Cultures and organizations, software of the mind: Intercultural cooperation and its importance for survival* (Rev. ed.). New York, NY: McGraw-Hill.

Houston, M. (2004). When black women talk with white women: Why the dialogues are difficult. In Gonzales, A., Houston, M., & Chen, V. (Eds.), *Our voices* (pp. 119–125). Los Angeles, CA: Roxbury Publishing Company.

Kim, H., & Papacharissi, Z. (2003). Cross-cultural differences in online self-presentation: A content analysis of personal Korean and US home pages. *Asian Journal of Communication, 13*(1), 100–119. doi:10.1080/01292980309364833

Lanigan, R. L. (1988). *Phenomenology of communication: Merleau-Ponty's thematics in communicology and semiology.* Pittsburgh, PA: Duquesne University Press.

Lim, T. (2002). Language and verbal communication across cultures. In Gudykunst, W., & Mody, B. (Eds.), *Handbook of international and intercultural communication* (pp. 69–87). Thousand Oaks, CA: Sage.

Marshall, T. C. (2008). Cultural differences in intimacy: The influence of gender-role ideology and individualism-collectivism. *Journal of Social and Personal Relationships, 25*(1), 143–168. doi:10.1177/0265407507086810

Martin, J. N., & Nakayama, T. K. (1999). Thinking dialectically about culture and communication. *Communication Theory, 9,* 1–25. doi:10.1111/j.1468-2885.1999.tb00160.x

Martin, J. N., & Nakayama, T. K. (2009). *Intercultural communication in contexts* (5th ed.). Boston, MA: McGraw Hill.

Martin, J. N., & Nakayama, T. K. (2011). Intercultural communication dialectics revisited. In Halualani, R. T., & Nakayama, T. K. (Eds.), *The handbook of critical intercultural communication* (pp. 59–83). Malden, MA: Blackwell.

Martinez, J. (2000). *Phenomenology of Chicana experience and identity.* Lanham, MD: Rowman & Littlefield.

Martinez, J. (2006). Semiotic phenomenology and intercultural communication scholarship: Meeting the challenge of racial, ethnic, and cultural difference. *Western Journal of Communication, 70*(4), 292–310. doi:10.1080/10570310600992103

Martinez, J. (2008). Semiotic phenomenology and the dialectical approach to intercultural communication: Paradigm crisis and the actualities of research practice. *Semiotica, 169,* 135–153. doi:10.1515/SEM.2008.028

McLuhan, M. (1962). *The Gutenberg galaxy: The making of typographic man.* Toronto, Canada: University of Toronto Press.

McPhail, T. L. (2006). *Global communication: Theories, stakeholders and trends* (2nd ed.). Malden, MA: Wiley-Blackwell.

Mehra, B., Merkel, C., & Bishop, A. P. (2004). The Internet for empowerment of minority and marginalized users. *New Media & Society, 6,* 781–802. doi:10.1177/146144804047513

Merryfield, M. (2003). Like a veil: Cross-cultural experiential learning online. *Contemporary Issues in Technology & Teacher Education, 3,* 146–171.

Mo, P. K., Malik, S. H., & Coulson, N. S. (2009). Gender differences in computer-mediated communication: A systematic literature review of online health-related support groups. *Patient Education and Counseling, 75*(1), 16–24. doi:10.1016/j.pec.2008.08.029

Orbe, M. P. (2008). Theorizing multidimensional identity negotiation: Reflections on the lived experiences of first-generation college students. In Azmitia, M., Syed, M., & Radmacher, K. (Eds.), *The intersections of personal and social identities. New directions for child and adolescent development* (pp. 81–95). New York, NY: Jossey-Bass.

Park, H. S., & Guan, X. (2009). Cross-cultural comparison of verbal and nonverbal strategies of apologizing. *Journal of International & Intercultural Communication, 2*(1), 66–87. doi:10.1080/17513050802603471

Philipsen, G. (1990). Speaking "like a man" in Teamsterville. In D. Carbaugh (Ed.), *Cultural communication and intercultural contact* (pp. 11-26). Hillsdale, NJ: Lawrence Erlbaum.

Rimmington, G. M., & Alagic, M. (2008). *Third place learning: Reflective inquiry into intercultural and global cage painting.* Charlotte, NC: Information Age Publishing.

Schmidt, W. V., Conaway, R. N., Easton, S. S., & Wardrope, W. J. (2007). *Communicating globally: Intercultural communication and international business.* Thousand Oaks, CA: Sage.

Shim, T. Y., Kim, M. S., & Martin, J. N. (2008). (Eds.). *Changing Korea: Understanding culture and communication.* New York, NY: Peter Lang.

Shutter, R. (2008). The centrality of culture. In Asante, M. K., Miike, Y., & Yin, J. (Eds.), *The global intercultural communication reader* (pp. 11–26). New York, NY: Routledge.

Smith, P. J., Coldwell, J., Smith, S. N., & Murphy, K. L. (2005). Learning through computer-mediated communication: A comparison of Australian and Chinese heritage students. *Innovations in Education and Teaching International, 42*(2), 12–134. doi:10.1080/14703290500062441

St. Amant, K. (2002). When cultures and computers collide: Rethinking computer-mediated communication according to international and intercultural communication expectations. *Journal of Business and Technical Communication, 16*(2), 196–214. doi:10.1177/1050651902016002003

Stats, I. W. Usage and Population Statistics. (2009). *Home page.* Retrieved June 25, 2010, from: http://www.internetworldstats.com

Ting-Toomey, S., & Oetzel, J. G. (2002). Cross-cultural face concerns and conflict styles: Current status and future directions. In Gudykunst, W., & Mody, B. (Eds.), *Handbook of international and intercultural communication* (pp. 143–163). Thousand Oaks, CA: Sage.

van Dijk, J. (2004). Divides in succession: Possession, skills, and use of new media for societal participation. In Bucy, E. P., & Newhagen, J. E. (Eds.), *Media access: Social and psychological dimensions of new technology use* (pp. 233–254). Mahwah, NJ: Lawrence Erlbaum.

van Manen, M. (2003). *Researching lived experience: Human science for an action sensitive pedagogy* (2nd ed.). Ontario, Canada: The Althouse Press.

Vishwanath, A., & Chen, H. (2008, May). *Personal communication technologies as an extension of the self: A cross-cultural comparison of people's associations with technology and their symbolic proximity with others*. Paper presented at the annual meeting of the International Communication Association, Montreal, QC, Canada.

Williams, A., & Nussbaum, J. F. (2001). *Intergenerational communication across the lifespan*. Hillsdale, NJ: Lawrence Erlbaum.

KEY TERMS AND DEFINITIONS

Asynchronicity: The state of occurring at different times and frequency.

Communication Contexts: The physical, social, political, and historical aspects of the situation in which communication occurs.

Dialectic: The complex relationship between opposite qualities/entities and a method of logic based on that.

Dialectical Approach: A conceptual framework for understanding the processual, relational, and contradictory nature of intercultural communication practice.

Identity: The concept of who we are or who a person is.

Intercultural Communication: The interaction between people of different cultural backgrounds.

Phenomenology: A theory and methodology that investigates the fundamental meanings of human conscious experience.

Phenomenological Methodology: The synergistic research procedures that consist of the steps of description, reduction, and interpretation.

Chapter 9
Cultural Differences in Social Media Usage and Beliefs and Attitudes Towards Advertising on Social Media:
Findings from Dubai, United Arab Emirates

Sara Kamal
American University in Dubai, UAE

Shu-Chuan Chu
DePaul University, USA

ABSTRACT

Social media use is quickly integrating into the daily lives of consumers in the Middle East, where a large number of users represent a variety of cultural milieu. This chapter examines differences between Arab and non-Arab social media users in the United Arab Emirates (UAE), with respect to usage, beliefs, and attitudes towards social media advertising. The chapter also examines managerial and theoretical implications for communication across culturally diverse audiences via online media.

INTRODUCTION

Social media have become one of the foremost online communication venues, attracting millions of global Internet users (Global faces, 2009). Given the huge potential of social media

for intercultural communication in the global marketplace, marketers attempt to use this new mode of online communication to augment brand awareness, create brand loyalty, and establish long-term relationships with global consumers. According to eMarketer (2008), advertising spending on social networking sites (SNSs), one

DOI: 10.4018/978-1-60960-833-0.ch009

of the major applications of social media, will reach $2.6 billion worldwide by 2012. Despite the global prevalence of social media and its impact on marketing communications practices, little investigation has been done on how individuals beyond the United States perceive and use social media (boyd & Ellison, 2007). Prior research on new communication technologies suggests individuals' usage pattern and outcomes vary from culture to culture. Indeed, a few studies have suggested that communication online is culturally contingent (Pfeil, Zaphiris, & Ang, 2007; MacKinnon, 2008). Individuals' cultural backgrounds play a crucial role in determining online usage patterns and preferences toward culturally customized web designs (Gevorgyan & Manucharova, 2009). As social media is becoming prevalent on a global scale, an investigation of if social media usage reflects distinctions in cultural values should shed deeper light on computer-mediated communication (CMC) across cultures and advertising practices within the emerging media.

The growth of social media across geographic and cultural milieu, coupled with increased marketing messages within social media, raises questions as to beliefs and attitudes towards advertising on social media among culturally diverse users. Undoubtedly, these beliefs and attitudes mediate the effectiveness of any promotional attempts within social media, making it imperative to understand cultural differences in beliefs and attitudes towards marketing messages within this vehicle of communication. Thus, the objective of this chapter is to examine usage, beliefs and attitudes of consumers towards advertising on social media among Arab and non-Arab consumers. Using an online survey, two primary research questions are proposed for a fuller understanding of the roles of the online social medium in the particular cultural setting: 1) what are the differences in overall social media usage, beliefs, and attitudes toward advertising in social media between Arab versus non-Arab social media users in Dubai? 2) Do non-Arab social media users exhibit higher

levels of independent self-construal values than their Arab counterparts? Do Arab users exhibit higher levels of interdependent self-construal values than their non-Arab counterparts? Results of this study could help marketers develop promising communication strategies and target diverse cultural groups effectively.

CONSIDERING CULTURE AND MEDIA

A cultural dimension that distinguishes people from different cultures is Markus and Kitayama's (1991) *independent* and *interdependent* self-construal. Markus and Kitayama (1991) defined self-construal as "the relationship between the self and others and, especially, the degree to which they [people] see themselves as separate from others or as connected with others" (p. 226). Two prominent aspects of self-construal are independence and interdependence. The distinction of self-construals corresponds to Hofstede's (1980) dimensions of individualism and collectivism. Individuals with an independent orientation, view themselves as unique from others, are more likely to be observed in Western cultures. Whereas interdependent individuals consider themselves as part of an interconnected social relationship, are more prevalent in Eastern cultures (Markus & Kitayama, 1991; Singelis, 1994). Kim and Yun (2007) noted that self-construals have a mediating role in the influence of culture on users' behavior and communication patterns. Accordingly, the current study incorporates self-construals into our analysis.

Due to the potential influence of culture on social media usage, the study presented here examines social media usage among a culturally diverse group of participants in Dubai, an Emirate of the United Arab Emirates (UAE). Given the growing popularity of social media in UAE, rapid growth of regional Internet users, and increased spending power of UAE consumers (Dubai economy,

2009), empirical research in this area is needed. Internet users in the Middle Eastern region have also increased markedly—from over nine million in 2005 to approximately 26.3 million users today. Within the region, the UAE is the leader in terms of Internet usage and penetration rates (United Arab Emirates: Internet usage, 2009). Over three decades, Dubai has transformed into a global city, with approximately 80 percent of the population comprised of expatriates from across the globe (United Arab Emirates: Internet usage, 2009). Thus, Dubai provides an ideal context to study differences in social media usage and beliefs and attitudes toward advertising within social media, where a myriad of cultural backgrounds are represented: Arabs and non-Arabs (e.g. Asians, Western, and Africans).

SOCIAL MEDIA USE IN THE UAE: THE CASE OF DUBAI

In recent years, there has been a surge in online marketing for The Middle East and North Africa (MENA), particularly in terms of global social media usage. Meddah (2009) estimates that approximately 8.3 percent of active global Facebook users are MENA-based. Another study concluded that the MENA region has the world's fastest growth rate in terms of new users for social media (ComScore, 2008). Given the increasing pervasiveness of social media in the regional mediascape, the importance of social media as an advertising medium in the Middle East will continue to grow as users interact with brand related communications and attitudes (Esra'a, 2008). For example, a recent study on Twitter use in the MENA region found 70 percent of respondents indicated Twitter had a major role to play in developing positive and negative attitudes towards brands (Middle East & North Africa, 2009). This finding underscores the need for more research to better understand the beliefs and attitudes of consumers from this region with respect to advertising on social media.

Such information could, in turn, help marketers comminute effectively in the computer-mediated environment across cultures.

The UAE has, in turn, contributed significantly to the development of and the economic boom within the Middle East (United Arab Emirates: Country overview, 2009) where it has acted as a major trading hub for the region (Doing business 2010, 2009). With respect to Internet usage, the UAE's 18.3 million Internet users make it an important market within the MENA region (United Arab Emirates: Internet usage, 2009). More importantly, the UAE accounts for over 40 percent of all social media users in the Middle East and makes it the region's leading user of such media (Middle East & North Africa, 2009). In fact, Synovate (Global survey, 2008) found that the UAE Internet users have the second highest rate of participation in social media globally. Additionally, a recent survey of social media users in the UAE revealed the majority of these users believe social media is a vital form of interaction that is quickly replacing personal contact (Menon, 2008). Taken collectively, this evidence suggests the sense of importance and salience social media has with its users in the UAE. Given the expansion of this mode of computer-mediated communication, it is important for researchers to examine if cultural factors affect related attitudes, beliefs and behaviors associated with social media.

CULTURAL GROUPS IN THE UAE: ARABS AND NON-ARABS

Arab Consumers

The Arab world consists of twelve countries in the Middle East region. These nations are Bahrain, Iraq, Jordan, Kuwait, Lebanon, Oman, Palestine (the Gaza Strip and West Bank), Qatar, Saudi Arabia, Syria, United Arab Emirates, and Yemen. The Arab world also includes the African countries of Algeria, Egypt, Eritrea, Djibouti, Libya, Mauritania, Morocco, Somalia, Sudan, and Tunisia. It is approximated that the combined population of these nations - and thus the Arab world - numbers approximately 260 million people. The members of this population share similar cultural norms, values, and beliefs (Karande, Almurshidee, & Al-Olayan, 2006) often attributed to a shared language and religion, as well as close geographic proximity (Beeston, 1974; Cleveland, 1964).

In terms of the cultural values, the members of Arab cultures tend to be highly collectivists in nature (Hofstede, 1980; Kalliny & Gentry, 2007). Most Arab societies, like that of the UAE, are based on a strong group culture (Piecarge, 2003). Buda and Elsayed-Elkhouly (1998), for instance, found that Arabs are significantly more collectivistic than Americans. Arab individuals tend to place a strong emphasis on collectivism and are emotionally connected to the members of their culture by their shared institutions and organizations (Buda & Elsayed-Elkhouly, 1998). In particular, Barakat (1993) noted that family is an important factor in the structure of Arab society, where it emphasizes more interdependent values. In addition, Kalliny and Gentry's (2007) research on Arab and American television advertising found advertising in UAE depicts interdependent cultural values more than in the U.S. Even though all Arabs are not Muslim, Islamic values tend to dominate the socio-cultural landscape, as many countries within the region were historically under the rule of various Islamic caliphates, such as Omayyads, Abbasids, and Ottomans (Karande et al., 2006), and this shared history is connected to a relatively high degree of homogeneity within the region.

Non-Arab Consumers

In the past 50 years, the population of the Middle Eastern Gulf countries has increased to over eight times its original size and the highest population growth rate globally (Kapiszewski, 2006). This rapid population increase has not been caused by

a natural growth of indigenous population. Rather it was driven by an influx of foreign workers who relocated to the region due to the competitive salaries and tax-free incentives available there. In fact, most expiates belong to religious and ethnic backgrounds that have little connection with Arab culture or with Islam (Barkho, 2007).

The UAE in particular is a country that consists largely of expatriates including Arabs from across the region and non-Arab immigrants (United Arab Emirates Country overview, 2009). With respect to the ethnic breakdown of the population in the UAE, it is estimated that Emiratis constitute 19 percent of the total population, while other Arabs represent 23 percent (Kapiszewski, 2006). Thus, over 58 percent of the UAE's population consists of non-Arabs from various ethnic backgrounds including Western and Eastern Europe, North America, and the Asia Pacific region. Previous studies have shown that individuals who have migrated to other countries tend to be more individualistic in orientation than those persons who stay in their home countries (e.g., Realo & Allik, 1999; Triandis, Bontempo, Villareal, Asai, & Lucca, 1988; Triandis, McCusker, & Hui, 1990). Given that many non-Arabs in the UAE are immigrants, it is expected that non-Arab consumers might be more individualistic and independent than are Arab consumers, who focus on social systems and the institutions to which they belong.

CONCEPTUAL FRAMEWORK

Social media such as social networking sites (SNSs) enable users not only to articulate their offline connections, but also to develop new relationships with members outside of their immediate network (boyd & Ellison, 2007; Ellison, Steinfield, & Lampe, 2007). Due to the dynamic nature of social media, Internet users can easily disseminate consumer experiences and make peer recommendations, which can create a transformational change in online communication. As a result, advertising through social media has become an important strategic component of marketing communications in computer-mediated environments on a worldwide basis.

Within this context, we propose that a consumer's attitudes and beliefs toward advertising on social media might relate to an individual's usage behavior related to media. To examine this relationship, we applied Pollay and Mittal's (1993) advertising model in order to determine if cultural values, such as independent and interdependent self-construal, are reflected in the attitudes Arabs and non-Arabs in the UAE have toward social media used for advertising. In this section, we discuss independent and interdependent self-construal and then overview Pollay and Mittal's (1993) advertising attitude and belief model as related to these ideas.

Cultural Orientations: Independent and Interdependent Self-Construal

One of the cultural dimensions that distinguishes people from different cultures is Markus and Kitayama's (1991) independent and interdependent self-construal. Individuals who uphold an *independent* self-construal view the self as separate and autonomous from the group and perceive their behaviors as primarily contingent on their internal repertoire of thoughts, feelings, and actions, rather than dependent on external and social influences (Markus & Kitayama, 1991). In contrast, individuals with an *interdependent* self-construal see the self as part of connected social relationships and perceive their behavior as largely determined by the thoughts, feelings, and actions of others in the relationship (Markus & Kitayama, 1991). Several studies note that the independent self-construal is dominated in individualistic cultures such as North America, whereas the interdependent self-construal is common to collectivistic cultures such as East Asian, Latin

American, and Arab countries (Triandis, 1989; Markus & Kitayama, 1991; Singelis, 1994; Buda & Elsayed-Elkhouly, 1998). The relative degree of independence and interdependence of the self provides an ideal framework for detecting how an individual feels connected to others and is useful in examining CMC cross-culturally. Accordingly, Markus and Kitayama's (1991) framework of independent and interdependent self-construals highlight the distinctions that pervade Arab and non-Arab cultures.

From a theoretical perspective, it is reasonable to suspect that perceptions about the self and relations with others would differ among Arab and non-Arab social media users. Indeed, Kim and Yun (2007) suggest that social media users may be affected by the dominant cultural dimension of independent and interdependent self-construal. Kim and Yun (2007) examined social media through cultural lenses and argue that self-construal plays a mediating role in the influence of culture on users' behavior and communication patterns, and thus lead to differences in self-presentational styles across cultures. Along the same logic, it is expected that non-Arab respondents will have a dominant independent self, and these users might therefore embrace social media to create a positive sense of self and to define the self in terms of internal attitudes, traits, and opinions. In contrast, Arab social media users, with a dominant interdependent self, tend to focus on group membership (Piecowye, 2003), collectivistic goals (Hofstede, 1980), and maintaining harmonious relationships with close contacts (Barakat, 1993). Thus, it is imperative to understand whether distinctions between independent and interdependent self-construals are embedded in social media users from Arab and non-Arab cultures. Such knowledge could add to a further understanding of the effect of culture on consumer responses to advertising as well as culturally dependent CMC within online social media.

Beliefs Towards Advertising on Social Media

Pollay and Mittal (1993) provide a comprehensive model of advertising attitude and belief factors. Specifically, their model represents seven factors that model which test four socio-economic factors (Good for Economy, Falsity/No Sense, Materialism and Value Corruption) and three personal-utility factors (Product Information, Hednoic/Pleasure, and Social Role and Image). In fact, Pollay and Mittal's (1993) model has been widely used in research examining consumer's attitudes and beliefs related to advertising across various media (Alwitt & Prabhaker, 1994; Shavitt, Lowry, & Haefner, 1998; Wolin, Korgaonkar, & Lund, 2002; Karson, McCloy, & Bonner, 2006). Given that social media are a new form of online media for social interaction and communication, an empirical investigation using Pollay and Mittal's (1993) scale is timely and necessary to explore the major antecedents of attitudes and beliefs towards advertising via social media. The following section provides an overview of these belief factors.

The *Product Information* factor examines the personal use of advertising as source of information (Ju-Pak, 1999). Past studies such as Ducoffe (1996) found a significant and positive correlation between consumers' value of advertising on the web and the informativeness of that advertising. Indeed, social media provides users with both the marketer-dominated sources of information (e.g., marketer-generated brand pages) and other consumer-dominated sources of information (e.g., brand comments from friends). In terms of the *Hedonic/Pleasure* belief factor, Watson, Akselsen, and Pitt (1998) note that web advertising provides content that consumes see as humorous, entertaining, and motivating. Due to the highly interactive nature of social media, it is posited that social media allow for a lively exchange between users, thus providing enjoyment.

Another belief factor is *Social Role and Image*. Mass media advertising advances social

and lifestyle messages to consumers (Pollay & Mittal, 1993); certainly social media advertising is then no exception. Users of social media are interlinked by a variety of personal contacts that provide portrayals relevant to brand and social image. Given the pervasive nature this medium, advertising messages transmitted via social media possess the ability to convey frequent messages that pertain to the social role and image of its users.

Good for Economy is another factor identified in Pollay and Mittal's (1993) model. E-commerce has emerged as a source of global economic growth. No doubt advertising on social media will be a natural progression with the advancement of regional and national e-commerce. The Internet provides consumers with purchase related information without the restriction of time or location. Thus, the economic motivation to seek out information within this medium might be high for consumers. Another form of economic motivation relevant to social media is the opportunity for users to receive sales promotions such as discounts or give-aways.

Next, the *Materialism* factor deals with consumer beliefs and attitudes toward the importance and role of consumption. Materialism has been defined as the belief that goods and money constitute the central path to happiness and social progress (Belk, 2000; Belk, Devinney, & Eckhardt, 2005). Social media users are constantly exposed consumption related experiences and message. These online promotions of commercial content may result in higher materialism among users (Wolin et al., 2002).

Another factor that is related to social media is *Falsity/No Sense*. The issue of falsity in advertising is an important concern for consumers (Ross, 1998). Consistent with other forms of advertising, scholars maintain that web-related advertising might promote deceptive claims, false or exaggerated information, and commercial promises that fall short of consumer experiences (Wolin et al., 2002). Lastly, similar to advertising on other mediums, the potential that advertising on social media has the ability to mould users values, exists. Thus, the *Value Corruption* factor might be associated with users' responses to advertising within the medium. In the MENA region, with over 60 percent of respondents visiting and updating their profile more than once per day (Middle East & North Africa, 2009), commercial messages within social media might be frequently encountered by users and help change users' values.

Attitudes Towards Advertising on Social Media

A majority of marketing research shows consumers follow a hierarchal sequence in their behaviors. Classical models such as Palda (1966) and Lavidge and Steiner (1961) advocate that consumer responses follow a hierarchy of effects sequence, stating that that consumer behavior falls into three broad categories: 1) cogitative; 2) affective and 3) behavior. Specifically, consumers first go through the cognitive phase of responses in which they develop awareness and knowledge of a product. Next, consumers gain affective responses, where they develop liking, preference and conviction in relation to products. Therefore, it is posited that the beliefs about advertising on social media mentioned noted in the earlier section of this chapter will be a precursor to attitudes towards advertising on the media. The study presented here examines the potential differences in overall social media usage, beliefs, and attitudes toward advertising in social media between Arab versus non-Arab social media users in Dubai. This study also explores whether non-Arab social media users are more independent and whether Arab users are more interdependent.

METHOD

This study involved an online survey of college students recruited at a major university located in metropolitan area of Dubai, UAE, where nearly

half of Internet users are members of social media (Menon, 2008). Past research shows that college students constitute the largest segment of social media users (Ellison et al., 2007) and they are more likely than any other group to actively engage in higher levels of social media use. Furthermore, many CMC researchers have indicated the importance of studying college-age social media users (e.g., Ellison et al., 2007; Pelling & White, 2009; Valenzuela, Park, Kee, 2009). Thus, the use of a college student sample seems representative and appropriate for examining this situation. It is crucial to study this young generation to gain a preliminary understanding of how social media is used across Arab and non-Arab groups within the UAE.

Sample

Six hundred and thirty-seven undergraduate students from a major university in Dubai, UAE participated in the study. Five hundred and seventy-three useful responses were included for data analysis. Students were recruited from two introductory business classes and were offered extra credit for their participation in the project. Out of the 573 respondents, 54.5% were Arabs, and 45.5% were non-Arabs. Arab respondents consisted of 59.0% males and 41.0% females, and non-Arab respondents consisted of 60.2% males and 39.8% females. In both cultural groups, more than 99% of participants were under age 30 years. Both Arab and non-Arab respondents reported similar general levels of household income and personal income. These demographic results suggested that the two groups were relatively comparable, and Table 1 presents demographic characteristics of the sample subjects.

Measures

The self-administered survey investigated social media usage (Bush & Gilbert, 2002; Ellison et al., 2007), beliefs and attitudes towards adver-

Table 1. Sample Characteristics

Characteristics	Arabs (%)	Non-Arabs (%)
Cultural Groups	54.5 (312)	45.5 (261)
Gender		
Male	59.0	60.2
Female	41.0	39.8
Age		
Under 20 years	46.8	51.7
20-30 years	52.6	47.5
31-40 years	0.3	0.8
41-50 years	0.3	0.0
Household Income		
Less than $20,000	6.4	8.0
$20,001 - $40,000	7.7	12.3
$40,001 - $60,000	10.9	12.6
$60,001 - $80,000	18.9	14.2
$80,001 - $100,000	14.4	15.3
More than $100,000	41.7	37.5
Personal Income		
Less than $200	6.4	6.4
$201 - $400	11.9	11.9
$401 - $600	13.5	13.5
$601 - $800	8.3	8.3
$801 - $1000	16.7	16.7
$1001 - $1200	11.5	11.5
$1201 - $1400	5.4	5.4
$1401 - $1600	3.5	3.5
More than $1600	22.8	22.8

Total n = 573

tising on social media (Wolin et al., 2002), and independent and interdependent self-construal (Singelis, 1994). All measures were adopted from prior research and were modified when necessary to fit the context of this study.

Social media usage. Social media usage was measured by accessing respondents' absorption of social media activity and social media intensity. For this project, an absorption of social media activity scale was adopted from Bush and Gilbert (2002) and is an effective measure to conceptualize Internet usage behavior. This scale used four-item, five-point, Likert scale, with anchors of "unlikely" and "likely" to assess levels of social media activity. Social media intensity was measured by adopting items from previous research by Ellison et al. (2007) who developed the Facebook intensity scale to measure Facebook usage that goes beyond frequency or duration indices. (Ellison et al.'s measure focused on users' active engagement in Facebook activities, emotional connection with Facebook, and the integration of Facebook into their daily activities.) We adopted Ellison et al.'s measure to examine distinct social media platforms, including SNSs (e.g., Facebook, MySpace, and LinkedIn), microblogging sites (e.g., Twitter), photosharing sites (e.g., Flickr and Snapfish), video sharing sites (e.g., YouTube), and Wikis sites (e.g., Wikipedia).

The first two items gauged the number of friends the respondents have on their specific social media platform and the time respondents spent using that platform each day. The rest five items were measured by using a five-point, Likert scale (1 = strongly disagree and 5 = strongly agree).

Beliefs and Attitudes towards Advertising on Social Media. A social media advertising beliefs scale was adopted from Wolin et al. (2002), and a total of 23 items were used to capture seven underlying advertising beliefs dimensions, including product information, hedonic/pleasure, social role and image, good for the economy, materialism, falsity/no sense, and value corruption. Each item was measured on a five-point scale (1 = strongly disagree and 5 = strongly agree). To assess respondents' attitudes toward advertising on social media, four attitudinal items adopted from Wolin et al. (2002) were used. These items were originally chosen from past studies by Mittal (1994) and Ducoffe (1996). These items were also measured on a five-point scale where 1 = strongly disagree and 5 = strongly agree.

Independent and Interdependent Self-Construal. To measure respondents' cultural orientation, an established scale developed by Singelis (1994) was used. Twelve items were used for each to access independent and interdependent self-construal. As a result, a twenty-four, five-point, Likert scale

assessed Arabian and non-Arabian respondents' cultural orientations (1 = strongly disagree and 5 = strongly agree).

RESULTS

Recent studies have found that gender serves as a predictor of social media usage patterns (Hoy & Milne, 2010; Thelwall, 2008). Thus, before answering research questions, independent sample t-tests were conducted to examine if there appear to be gender differences with regard to Arab and non-Arab respondents' social media usage, beliefs, and attitudes toward advertising on social media. The results indicated no substantial gender differences in terms of social media advertising beliefs and attitudes. When examining usage within Arab respondents, female respondents ($M = 3.26$) were found to have a higher level of absorption with social media activity than do male participants ($M = 3.00$) ($t(1,310) = -2.53$, $p < .05$). On the other hand, male respondents exhibited a higher level of usage than do female participants in the use of microblogging sites ($M_{male} = 2.57$; $M_{female} = 2.24$, $t(1,310) = 2.62$, $p < .01$), photosharing sites ($M_{male} = 2.64$; $M_{female} = 2.17$, $t(1,310) = 3.52$, $p < .001$), and Wikis sites ($M_{male} = 2.73$; $M_{female} = 2.51$, $t(1,310) = 2.06$, $p < .05$). In terms of non-Arab participants, female respondents ($M = 3.83$) demonstrated a higher level of SNS usage than do male participants ($M = 3.51$) ($t(1,259) = -2.70$, $p < .01$). Overall, these results were consistent with findings from past research, suggesting that some gender differences exist in the use of social media (Hoy & Milne, 2010; Thelwall, 2008).

Usage of Social Media

First, we examined if Arab and non-Arab social media users reveal different usage patterns. We also performed descriptive analyses to examine specific social media applications prevalent among the two groups in Dubai, UAE. The results showed

Table 2. Social Media Usage

Measurement Items	Arabs		Non-Arabs		*t*
	M	S.D.	*M*	S.D.	
Absorption with Social Media Activity Scale (Arabs α = .84; non-Arabs α = .84)	3.10	.90	3.07	.93	.41
How likely are you to genuinely enjoy the time you spend on the social media?	3.20	1.15	3.16	1.12	
How likely are you to feel that social media helps you forget about daily problems?	3.06	1.12	3.07	1.14	
How likely are you to feel totally absorbed while you are on the social media?	3.19	1.00	3.13	1.11	
How likely are you to get so involved while on the social media that you forget everything else?	2.96	1.11	2.93	1.16	
Social Media Intensity					
SNSs (e.g., Facebook, MySpace, and LinkedIn) (Arabs α = .87; non-Arabs α = .82)	3.56	1.05	3.64	.93	-.91
Microblogging sites (e.g., Twitter) (Arabs α = .92; non-Arabs α = .94)	2.44	1.11	2.44	1.20	-.01
Photosharing sites (e.g., Flickr and Snapfish) (Arabs α = .92; non-Arabs α = .95)	2.45	1.16	2.25	1.23	1.90
Video sharing sites (e.g., YouTube) (Arabs α = .89; non-Arabs α = .91)	3.01	.97	2.81	1.02	2.42*
Wikis sites (e.g., Wikipedia) (Arabs α = .90; non-Arabs α = .91)	2.64	.94	2.61	1.00	.42

*Significant at .05;

that SNSs (Arab: $M = 3.56$, $S = 1.05$; non-Arab: $M = 3.64$, $S = .93$), video sharing sites (Arab: $M = 3.01$, $S = .97$; non-Arab: $M = 2.81$, $S = 1.02$), and Wikis sites (Arab: $M = 2.64$, $S = .94$; non-Arab: $M = 2.61$, $S = 1.00$) were the top three popular platforms among both groups. We then conducted a series of independent samples t-tests to examine any differences in absorption with social media activity and social media usage intensity across two cultural groups. However, a non-significant difference was found in the extent of absorption with social media activity ($M_{arab}=3.10$; $M_{non-arab}=3.07$, $t(1,571)=.41$, $p=.68$). When specific social media applications were examined, the results showed that Arab users were more likely to use video sharing sites ($M_{arab}=3.01$; $M_{non-arab}=2.81$, $t(1,571)=2.42$, $p<.05$) and photosharing sites ($M_{arab}=2.45$; $M_{non-arab}=2.25$, $t(1,571)=1.90$, $p=.06$) than their non-Arab counterpart. Note that the difference for photosharing sites was marginally significant. These results suggest no cross-cultural differences in absorption

with social media activity, whereas differences were found in video sharing and photosharing site usage intensity between the two groups. Table 2 presents a summary of these results.

Beliefs Towards Advertising on Social Networking Sites

Next, we explored if differences exist in beliefs toward advertising in social media between Arab versus non-Arab social media users in Dubai, UAE. First, the mean scores for the seven advertising beliefs dimensions were averaged to gain an overall score of beliefs toward advertising on social media. To answer this question, we performed another independent samples t-test with the Arab and non-Arab data, respectively. We found these results did not produce a significant difference in respondents' beliefs toward advertising on social media ($M_{arab}=3.25$; $M_{non-arab}=3.20$, $t(1,571)=1.42$, $p=.16$). The results suggest that

Table 3. Beliefs Towards Advertising on Social Media

Measurement Items	Arabs		Non-Arabs		*t*
	M	S.D.	*M*	S.D.	
Beliefs toward Advertising on Social Media (Arabs α = .64; Non-Arabs α = .66)	3.25	.44	3.20	.47	1.42
Product information (Prodinfo) Social media advertising is a very valuable source of information about sales Social media advertising tells me which brands have the features I am looking for Social media advertising helps me keep up to date about products available in the marketplace	3.40	.79	3.27	.85	
Hedonic/pleasure (Hedonic) Sometimes I take pleasure in thinking about what I saw or heard in social media advertisements Sometimes social media advertising is even more enjoyable than websites Some social media advertisements make me feel good	3.30	.82	3.22	.86	
Social role and image (Socrole) From social media advertising I learn what is in fashion and what I should buy for keeping a good social image Social media advertisements tell me what people like myself are buying and using Social media advertising helps me know which products will or will not reflect the sort of person I am	3.19	.76	3.19	.83	
Good for the economy (Goodecon) Social media advertising improves people's standard of living We need social media advertising to support the web There have been times when I have bought something because of a social media advertisement	3.23	.74	3.15	.81	
Materialism (Material) Social media ads make you buy things you don't really need Social media advertising increases dissatisfaction among consumers by showing products which some consumers can't afford Social media advertising is making us a materialistic society - interested in buying and owning things Social media advertising makes people buy unaffordable products just to show off	3.32	.75	3.23	.77	
Falsity/no sense (Falsity) One can put more trust in products advertised on social media than in those not advertised on social media (R) Certain products play an important role in my life; social media advertisements reassure me that I am doing the right thing in using these products (R) Social media advertising helps the consumer buy the best brand for the price (R)	2.91	.79	2.89	.82	
Value corruption (Valcorrup) Social media advertising sometimes makes people live in a world of fantasy Social media advertising takes undue advantage of children Social media advertising leads children to make unreasonable purchase demands on their parents There is too much sex in social media advertising today	3.41	.76	3.45	.74	

Table 4. Attitudes Towards Advertising on Social Media

Measurement Items	Arabs		Non-Arabs		*t*
	M	S.D.	*M*	S.D.	
Attitude toward Advertising on Social Media **(Arabs α = .86; Non-Arabs α = .88)** Overall, do you consider social media advertising a good or bad thing? (1= bad and 5= good) Overall, do you like or dislike social media advertising? (1= dislike and 5= like) I consider social media advertising…(1= unimportant and 5= important) To me, social media advertising is…(1= unimportant and 5= important)	3.29	.81	3.16	.80	2.06*

*Significant at .05; **Significant at .01; ***Significant at .001

Arab and non-Arab social media users' social media advertising beliefs did not differ. The t-test results are presented in Table 3.

Attitudes toward Advertising on Social Networking Sites

We next needed to examine if Arab versus non-Arab social media users maintain different levels of attitudes toward advertising in social media. To do so, we used another independent samples t-test to compare attitudes toward advertising in social media between the two cultural groups in Dubai. As shown in Table 4, we found a significant difference in attitudes toward social media advertising. Arab users (M = 3.29) indicated a more favorable attitudes toward advertising in social media than did their non-Arab counterparts (M = 3.16) (t (1,571) = 2.06, p<.05). The t-test results indicate that Arab respondents have more positive attitudes toward advertising in social media than did non-Arab participants.

Cultural Orientations

Finally, we examined:

1. If non-Arab social media users exhibit higher levels of independent self-construal values than their Arab counterparts

2. If Arab social media users exhibit higher levels of interdependent self-construal values than their non-Arab counterparts.

To examine these factors, we used two independent samples t-tests were performed to determine the degree of independent and interdependent self-construal between Arab versus non-Arab participants. Interestingly, we found a significant difference with regard to interdependent self-construal. Non-Arab users (M = 3.57) exhibit higher levels of interdependent self-construal values than did their Arab counterparts (M = 3.46) (t (1,571) = -2.34, p<.05). However, we found no significant difference in independent self-construal between the two groups (M_{arab}=3.52; $M_{non-arab}$=3.54, t(1,571)=-.43, p=.67). The results indicate that non-Arab social media users tend to focus on collectivistic relationships with close contacts than Arab users. The t-test results are summarized in Table 5.

DISCUSSION AND IMPLICATIONS

We found no significant difference in social media usage and absorption rates among the Arab and non-Arab users who participated in this study. This finding suggests culture might not mediate the intensity and level of absorption of social media among UAE users. These findings are not surprising given that others such as Loch, Straub, and

Table 5. Cultural Orientations of Social Media Users

Measurement Items	Arabs		Non-Arabs		*t*
	M	S.D.	*M*	S.D.	
Interdependent Self-Construal **(Arabs α = .81; Non-Arabs α = .86)** I have respect for the authority figures with whom I interact. It is important for me to maintain harmony within my group. My happiness depends on the happiness of those around me. I would offer my seat in a bus to my professor. I respect people who are modest about themselves. I will sacrifice my self-interest for the benefit of the group I am in. I often have the feeling that my relationships with others are more important than my own accomplishments. I should take into consideration my parents' advice when making education/career plans. It is important to me to respect decisions made by the group. I will stay in a group if they need me, even when I'm not happy with the group. If my brother or sister fails, I feel responsible. Even when I strongly disagree with group members, I avoid an argument.	3.46	.56	3.57	.61	-2.34*
Independent Self-Construal **(Arabs α = .81; Non-Arabs α = .85)** I'd rather say "No" directly, than risk being misunderstood. Speaking up during a class is not a problem for me. Having a lively imagination is important to me. I am comfortable with being singled out for praise or rewards. I am the same person at home that I am at school. Being able to take care of myself is a primary concern for me. I act the same way no matter who I am with. I feel comfortable using someone's first name soon after I meet them, even when they are much older than I am. I prefer to be direct and forthright when dealing with people I've just met. I enjoy being unique and different from others in many respects. My personal identity independent of others, it very important to me. I value being in good health above everything.	3.52	.56	3.54	.61	-.43

*Significant at .05; **Significant at .01; ***Significant at .001

Kamel (2003) reported technological acculturation tends to overcome cultural inhibitors. Specifically, users often adopt new technologies despite cultural differences because these technologies are beneficial to their lives. We found no significant difference in beliefs towards advertising on social media between both groups. Perhaps this finding suggests that globalization of beliefs is often a function of unifying technologies, specifically the increased flow of computer-mediated communications such as social media (Mattelart, 1995).

Interestingly, when gender differences were explored, results indicated that Arab females reported a higher absorption level of social media than Arab males, even though Arab males ranked higher in terms of social media usage. Therefore, despite the fact that female Arab respondents use social media less frequently than their male counterparts do, the intensity and level of absorption of social media is still higher among females. In light of this finding, it might be suitable for practitioners to target female consumers with social media initiatives that demand higher levels of involvement (e.g., contests, games, personalization, etc.). Due to higher levels of involvement, female Arab users might also be more likely to share links and information with their peers than male users. Such practices imply that, for advertising practitioners, these group of users help disseminate promotional messages.

On the other hand, the results also indicate that, overall, Arab users have a more positive attitude towards advertising on social media, as compared to their non-Arab counterparts. Al-Olayan and Karande (2000) have previously noted that Arab consumers place a lot of importance on getting product information through social sources such as peers, family, and friends. Thus, applying this preference on a virtual scale, social media act as a platform for social exchange and interaction among users. This factor might be one of the reasons why Arab consumers studied here showed a more positive attitude towards social media advertising than their non-Arab counterparts. Because the nature of social media allows for promotional messages to be embedded within the social context of peer and family sharing, such media are likely to be favorable for advertisers of new brand and product advertising targeting Arab consumers. Thus, this finding provides important managerial implications, for it indicates that advertisers should use this medium to target Arab consumers, given the existing positive attitudes of Arab users towards it.

It should be noted that the UAE has witnessed a boom in e-commerce in recent years. Industry experts estimate that e-commerce in the UAE will reach $36 billion in 2010, while current estimates for e-commerce earnings in the Gulf region within the Middle East are approximately $100 billion (Elsidafy, 2009). Additionally, the UAE developed a free trade zone, Dubai Internet City (DIC), specifically for e-commerce (E-commerce, 2010). The establishment of the DIC, the first of its kind in the Middle East, signals both the increasing importance of e-commerce for the UAE economy and the growing importance of the UAE as a leader in Internet technologies in the Middle East. As a newly developed nation, the economic significance of ecommerce in the UAE might also

contribute to the positive attitudes towards social media advertising among Arab users in the region.

Interestingly, when cultural orientations were examined between groups, a significant difference was found. Specifically, non-Arab users exhibited a higher level of interdependent self-construal than did Arab users. Individuals who have an interdependent self-construal define the self in the context of fundamental relationships within a larger social system (Triandis, 1989; Markus & Kitayama, 1991). One explanation for this finding could be that, as foreigners in a predominately Arab culture, non-Arab users rely on social media as means of keeping in touch with and maintain links to their cultural roots. Thus, these individuals might use social media to preserve cultural and group links in a predominately Arab culture. Another possible explanation is that Non-Arab users comprise people from a variety of ethnic backgrounds such as Europe (e.g., Germany and French) and Asia (e.g., China and Japan). According to Hofstede's (1980) classification, these countries scored higher on collectivism than individualism. Thus, the fact that a higher level of interdependent value was observed among non-Arab users seems plausible. Conversely, Arab users whose culture is classically defined as collectivistic displayed less interdependent values. One reason behind this finding might be that Arab users employ social media to express their sense of self and explore aspects of individualism in society where group dominated culture is advocated (Piecowye, 2003).

CONCLUSION

This chapter examined social media usage and attitudes and beliefs towards social media advertising. The context of our study, Dubai, UAE, is a region experiencing accelerated growth in online technologies. As a result, it provides an important context for examine cultural factors that might affect attitudes, beliefs, and behaviors related to online media. By examining users in the UAE, a nation with the world's highest per capita GDP and growing consumer spending, this chapter provides important insights into current and future consumers that are of interest to practitioners in a number of fields. Additionally, this chapter addresses the lack of general research with respect to consumers in the Middle East, as noted by Karande et al. (2006) and Barkho (2007). Furthermore, this chapter extends Pollay and Mittal's (1993) advertising beliefs and attitudes model by applying its ideas to a new form of computer-mediated communications — namely social media. This application, in turn, has both important theoretical and practical implications.

Global interconnections facilitated by social media remind us of what distinguishes one group of users from another. The findings of this study show that while Arab and non-Arab users in the UAE do not differ in terms of their social media usage and beliefs towards advertising on social media, they do differ in terms of their overall attitude towards advertising on social media and their social media use to express their self construal. Given Arab and non-Arab users have different social and cultural backgrounds that might moderate the effects of social media on communications in computer-mediated environments, then marketers should put emphasis on the cultural differences between the two groups when using social media as part of their global communications strategies.

In conclusion, Arab and non-Arab social media users provide for an interesting comparative study as they share close geographical proximity, yet have different cultural backgrounds. However, this study is not without its limitations. Namely it might be oversimplified to view non-Arab users as a monolithic cultural group. Despite the fact that prior research suggests that migrants in general are more likely to be individualistic (Realo & Allik, 1999), the mixed ethnic backgrounds of non-Arabs may display cultural differences while sharing some core values. Continued research should take this factor into consideration and explore the underlying cultural variations within

the non-Arab communities. Another venue for future research is to examine social media users of different age groups. This study focused on social media use and responses to social media advertising among college students, who are perhaps the largest and most active population using social media. As an increasing number of older groups connect and interact with others via the growing mediated-communication channel (Global faces, 2009), research examining how older generations use such media is needed. Moreover, it would be illuminating for future research to examine cross-cultural similarities and differences between American and Arab social media users.

REFERENCES

Al-Olayan, F. S., & Karande, K. (2000). A content analysis of magazine advertisements from the United States and the Arab world. *Journal of Advertising, 29*, 69–82.

Alwitt, L. F., & Prabhaker, P. R. (1994). Identifying who dislikes television advertising: Not by demographics alone. *Journal of Advertising Research, 34*(5), 17–29.

Barakat, H. (1993). *The Arab world: Society, culture, and state*. Berkeley, CA: University of California Press.

Barkho, L. (2007). Advertising resources in oil rich Arab Gulf states – Implications for international marketers. *International Journal of Business Studies, 19*(2), 1–24.

Beeston, A. (1974). *The Arab language today*. London, UK: Hutchinson & Co Ltd.

Belk, R. W. (2000). Are we what we own? In A. L. Benson (Ed.), *I shop, therefore I am: Compulsive buying and the search for self* (pp. 27-53). Northvale, NJ: Jason Aronson Inc. boyd, d., & Ellison, N. B. (2007). Social network sites: Definition, history, and scholarship. *Journal of Computer-Mediated Communication, 13*(1), 210-230.

Belk, R. W., Devinney, T. M., & Eckhardt, G. (2005). Consumer ethics across cultures. *Consumption . Markets and Culture, 8*(3), 275–289. doi:10.1080/10253860500160411

Buda, R., & Elsayed-Elkhouly, S. (1998). Cultural differences between Arabs and Americans: Individualism-collectivism revisited. *Journal of Cross-Cultural Psychology, 29*(3), 487–492. doi:10.1177/0022022198293006

Bush, V. D., & Gilbert, F. W. (2002). The Web as a medium: An explanatory comparison of Internet users versus newspaper readers. *Journal of Marketing Theory & Practice, 10*, 1–10.

Cleveland, W. L. (1964). *A history of the modern Middle East*. Boulder, CO: Westview Press.

ComScore. (2008). *Social networking explodes worldwide as sites increase their focus on cultural relevance*. Retrieved November 20, 2010, from http://www.comscore.com/ Press_Events/ Press_Releases/ 2008/08/Social_Networking_ World_Wide

Doing Business. (2009). *Doing Business 2010: Reforming through difficult times- International Finance Corporation*. Retrieved December 10, 2010, from http://www.doingbusiness.org/ Documents/CountryProfiles/ ARE.pdf

Dubai eGovernment. (2009). *Dubai economy*. Retrieved December 4, 2010, from http://www.dubai. ae/en.portal? topic,Article_000239,0,&_nfpb =true&_pageLabel=home

Ducoffe, R. H. (1996). Advertising value and advertising on the Web. *Journal of Advertising Research, 36*(5), 21–35.

Ellison, N. B., Steinfield, C., & Lampe, C. (2007). The benefits of Facebook friends: Social capital and college students' use of online social network sites. *Journal of Computer-Mediated Communication, 12*(4), 1143–1168. doi:10.1111/j.1083-6101.2007.00367.x

Elsidafy, M. (2009). E-commerce in UAE to hit $36bn by 2010. *Emirates Business 24-7*. Retrieved December 3, 2010, from http://www.business24-7. ae/Articles/2009/7/ Pages/04072009/07052009_ b30f3ffaa4d94a639dc703 fcdcf5264b.aspx

eMarketer. (2008). Social network marketing: Ad spending update. Retrieved December 3, 2010, from http://www.emarketer.com

Encyclopedia of Nations. (2009). *United Arab Emirates: Country overview*. Retrieved December 3, 2010, from http://www.nationsencyclopedia. com /economies/Asia-and-the-Pacific/ United-Arab-Emirates.html

Esra'a. (2008). Online social networking: The strength of weak ties. *Mideast Youth*. Retrieved December 10, 2010, from http://www.mideasty-outh.com/ 2008/11/15/online-social-networking-the-strength-of-weak-ties/

Gevorgyan, G., & Manucharova, N. (2009). Does culturally adapted online communication work? A study of American and Chinese Internet users' attitudes and preferences toward culturally customized Web design elements. *Journal of Computer-Mediated Communication, 14*(2), 393–413. doi:10.1111/j.1083-6101.2009.01446.x

Hofstede, G. (1980). *Culture's consequences: International differences in work-related values*. Beverly Hills, CA: Sage.

Hoy, M. G., & Milne, G. (2010). Gender differences in privacy-related measures for young adult Facebook users. *Journal of Interactive Advertising, 10*(2), 28–45.

Internetworldstats.com. (2009). *United Arab Emirates: Internet usage and marketing report*. Retrieved December 10, 2010, from http://www. internetworldstats.com /me/ae.htm

Ju-Pak, K.-H. (1999). Content dimensions of Web advertising: A cross-national comparison. *International Journal of Advertising, 18*(2), 207–231.

Kalliny, M., & Gentry, L. (2007). Cultural values reflected in Arab and American television advertising. *Journal of Current Issues and Research in Advertising, 29*(1), 15–32.

Kapiszewski, A. (2006). *Arab versus Asian migrant workers in the GCC countries, United Nations expert group meeting on international migration and development in the Arab region.* New York, NY: Department of Economic and Social Affairs, United Nations Secretariat.

Karande, K., Almurshide, K. A., & Al-Olayan, F. (2006). Advertising standardisation in culturally similar markets: Can we standardise all components? *International Journal of Advertising, 25*(4), 489–511.

Karson, E. J., McCloy, S., & Bonner, P. G. (2006). An examination of consumer' attitudes and beliefs towards website advertising. *Journal of Current Issues & Research in Advertising, 28*(2), 77–91.

Kim, K.-H., & Yun, H. (2007). Cying for me, Cying for us: Relational dialectics in a Korea social network site. *Journal of Computer-Mediated Communication, 13*(1), 298–318. doi:10.1111/j.1083-6101.2007.00397.x

Lavidge, R. J., & Steiner, G. A. (1961). A model for predictive measurements of advertising effectiveness. *Journal of Marketing, 25*, 59–62. doi:10.2307/1248516

Loch, K. D., Straub, D. W., & Kamel, S. (2003). Diffusing the Internet in the Arab World: The role of social norms and technological acculturation. *IEEE Transactions on Engineering Management, 50*(1), 45–63. doi:10.1109/TEM.2002.808257

MacKinnon, R. (2008). Blogs and China correspondence: Lessons about global information flows. *Chinese Journal of Communication, 1*(2), 242–257. doi:10.1080/17544750802288081

Markus, H. R., & Kitayama, S. (1991). Culture and the self: Implications for cognition, emotion, and motivation. *Psychological Review, 98*(2), 224–253. doi:10.1037/0033-295X.98.2.224

Mattelart, A. (1995). Unequal voices. *The Unesco Courier, 48*(2), 11.

Meddah, M. M. (2009). *Active Facebook users in Middle East & North Africa.* Retrieved December 10, 2010, from http://www.startuparabia.com/2009/08/active-facebook -users-in-middle-east-north-africa/

Menon, V. (2008). *UAE second in world list for online social networking.* Retrieved December 10, 2010, from http://www.arabianbusiness.com /532785-uae-second-in- world-list-for-online-social-networking?ln=en.

Mittal, B. (1994). Public assessment of TV advertising: Faint praise and harsh criticism. *Journal of Advertising Research, 34*(1), 35–53.

Nielsen Online. (2009). *Global faces and networked places. A Nielsen report on social networking's new global footprint.* Retrieved December 10, 2010, from http://blog.nielsen.com/nielsenwire /wp-content/uploads/2009/03 / nielsen_globalfaces_mar09.pdf

Palda, K. S. (1966). The hypothesis of a hierarchy of effects: A partial evaluation. *JMR, Journal of Marketing Research, 3*, 13–24. doi:10.2307/3149430

Pelling, E. L., & White, K. M. (2009). The theory of planned behavior applied to young people's use of social networking websites. *Cyberpsychology & Behavior, 12*(6), 755–759. doi:10.1089/cpb.2009.0109

Pfeil, U., Zaphiris, P., & Ang, C. S. (2006). Cultural differences in collaborative authoring of Wikipedia. *Journal of Computer-Mediated Communication, 12*(1), 88–113. doi:10.1111/j.1083-6101.2006.00316.x

Piecowye, J. (2003). Habitus in transition? CMC use and impacts among young women in the United Arab Emirates. *Journal of Computer-Mediated Communication, 8*(2). Retrieved December 10, 2010, from http://jcmc.indiana.edu/vol8/issue2/piecowye.html

Pollay, R., & Mittal, B. (1993). Here's the beef: Factors, determinants, and segments in consumer criticism of advertising. *Journal of Marketing, 57*(3), 99–114. doi:10.2307/1251857

Realo, A., & Allik, J. (1999). A cross-cultural study of collectivism: A comparison of American, Estonian, and Russian students. *The Journal of Social Psychology, 139*(2), 133–142. doi:10.1080/00224549909598367

Ross, P. D. (1998). Interactive marketing and the law: The future rise of unfairness. *Journal of Interactive Marketing, 12*(3), 21–31. doi:10.1002/(SICI)1520-6653(199822)12:3<21::AID-DIR3>3.0.CO;2-4

Shavitt, S., Lowrey, P., & Haefner, J. (1998). Public attitudes toward advertising: More favorable than you might think. *Journal of Advertising Research, 38*(4), 7–22.

Singelis, T. M. (1994). The measurement of independent and interdependent self-construals. *Personality and Social Psychology Bulletin, 20*(5), 580–591. doi:10.1177/0146167294205014

Singelis, T. M., & Brown, W. J. (1995). Culture, self, and collectivist communication: Linking culture to individual behavior. *Human Communication Research, 21*(3), 354–389. doi:10.1111/j.1468-2958.1995.tb00351.x

SpotOnPR. (2009). *Middle East & North Africa Twitter demograhpics & user habits survey.* Retrieved December 10, 2010, from http://interactiveme.com/wp-content/uploads/2009/09/twitter_survey_report_interactiveME.pdf

Synovate. (2008). *Global survey.* Retrieved December 10, 2010, from http://www.synovate.com/news/article/2008/09/global-survey-shows-58-of-people-don-t-know-what-social-networking-is-plus-over-one-third-of-social-networkers-are-losing-interest.html

Thelwall, M. (2008). Social networks, gender, and friending: An analysis of MySpace member profiles. *Journal of the American Society for Information Science and Technology, 59*, 1321–1330. doi:10.1002/asi.20835

Triandis, H. C. (1989). The self and social behavior in differing cultural contexts. *Psychological Review, 96*, 506–520. doi:10.1037/0033-295X.96.3.506

Triandis, H. C., Bontempo, R., Villareal, M. J., Asai, M., & Lucca, N. (1988). Individualism and collectivism: Cross-cultural perspectives on self-ingroup relationships. *Journal of Personality and Social Psychology, 54*, 323–338. doi:10.1037/0022-3514.54.2.323

Triandis, H. C., McCusker, C., & Hui, C. H. (1990). Multimethod probes of individualism and collectivism. *Journal of Personality and Social Psychology, 59*, 1006–1020. doi:10.1037/0022-3514.59.5.1006

UAE Federal Government Portal. (2010). *E-commerce: Fact & figures.* Retrieved December 10, 2010, from http://www.government.ae/gov/en/biz/ecommerce/facts.jsp

(2009). *United Arab Emirates business forecast report.* London, UK: Business Monitor International.

Valenzuela, S., Park, N., & Kee, K. F. (2009). Is there social capital in a social network site? Facebook use and college students' life satisfaction, trust, and participation. *Journal of Computer-Mediated Communication, 14*(4), 875–901. doi:10.1111/j.1083-6101.2009.01474.x

Watson, R. T., Akselsen, S., & Pitt, L. (1998). Attractors: Building mountains in the flat landscape of the World Wide Web. *California Management Review, 40*(2), 36–56.

Wolin, L., Korgaonkar, P., & Lund, D. (2002). Beliefs, attitudes and behavior towards Web advertising. *International Journal of Advertising, 21*(1), 87–113.

KEY TERMS AND DEFINITIONS

Advertising Attitudes and Behaviors: An individual's liking/disliking and behavioral responses toward advertising.

Cross-Cultural Consumer Behavior: Consumer decision-making process of two or more cultures.

Social Media Advertising: An ad on social media such as Facebook and Twitter that incorporates customization, targeting, and social interaction components.

Section 2
The Emerging Trends in Representation:
Who May Participate and How Do Individuals Present Themselves?

Chapter 10
Discursive Manipulation Strategies in Virtual Scams in Global Contexts

Rotimi Taiwo
Obafemi Awolowo University, Nigeria

ABSTRACT

This chapter examines how online fraudsters explore the experiential, interpersonal, and textual language metafunctions in the crafting of their emails for global audiences. A critical study of international virtual scam emails over a period of time shows that these scammers tend to improve on how they construct their messages as they rely on experiential knowledge of what they believe will appeal to their audience. Recent scam emails use fewer pressure tactics, and writers present their identity as that of a non-confident, naïve, vulnerable, and ignorant persons, thereby increasing the discursive power of their addressees in the interaction. Scammers also use different forms of politeness strategies to bait their victims.

INTRODUCTION

The arrival of the Internet has had a great impact on language to the extent that the medium has led to the evolution of new genres that appear to be suitable only in the context of online discourse. Linguists in particular have focused different aspects of the features of language used in computer-

mediated communication (CMC) – basically, the orthographic and discourse features (Herring, 1999; Thurlow, 2003; Park, 2007; Holmer, 2008). Apart from identifying the unique orthography and structure (Crystal, 2006), the issue of identity has been a major focus of internet researchers (Huffaker & Calvert, 2005; Harrison & Thomas, 2009).

Due to the relative anonymity of interlocutors in online interactions, the Internet has encouraged all sorts of uninhibited discourse behavior.

DOI: 10.4018/978-1-60960-833-0.ch010

These behaviors include uninhibited verbal and sexual behavior, trolling, flaming, identity theft, internet fraud, and so forth. In social psychology, the concept of online disinhibition explains that, in online communication, there is a loosening of social restrictions and inhibitions that are typically observed in offline communication contexts. This loss of inhibition brings alive the concepts of dissociative anonymity and invisibility; that is, users can operate without any indication of identity (Suler, 2004). As online access spreads across the globe, these behaviors increasingly made their way into international online exchanges, perhaps the most notorious of which involved Internet crimes perpetrated in global contexts.

Since the early 1990s, large number of scam messages are sent around the world every day. Despite the fact that many of the recipients of these emails ignore them, a few individuals do respond to these messages and get baited by the scammers. In the process, they lose their money or get their identity stolen. As online media allow scammers to target victims anywhere there is computer access, the scope of these scams has become global in nature. And as more parts of the globe gain online access – be it through computer terminals or mobile phones, the international field for such crimes will only increase. Perhaps the most common of the global-reaching online scams is "Advance fee fraud," also known as "419," and this scam is named after a statute of the Nigerian criminal code.

This chapter is explores how online scammers use Halliday's (1973, 1985) metafunctions of language (experiential, interpersonal, and textual functions) in their mails and the discursive strategies used by these online fraudsters to make their communication relevant across cultures. To examine this phenomenon, the author analyzed two hundred scam mails sent over a period of four years (2005-2009) and focused in particular on language metafunctions in scam mails. In this chapter, the author presents the results of that research while also providing an overview of certain uninhibited behaviors common in online communication in general and found in virtual scamming in particular. The author also briefly discusses future research directions in virtual behavior.

UNINHIBITED ONLINE BEHAVIOR

Online communication encourages the inflicting of malicious behavior through different channels of digital media including email, instant messaging, and text messaging. Some behaviors are typically associated with the online culture. Such behaviors are said to be encouraged by the context of online communication, which makes users feel insulated and anonymous. Such feelings of isolation and anonymity, in turn, can cultivate what social psychologists generally refer to as *deindividuation*. Deindividuation means the loss of the sense of individual identity. This loss, which is also associated with a loosening of normal inhibitions, often promotes behavior that violates social standards (Joinson, 1998). Several uninhibited online behaviors have been identified over time, but for the purpose of this chapter, we shall discuss four of them: cyberbullying, flaming, spamming, and scamming.

Cyberbullying, or online bullying, involves the dissemination of harmful or cruel speech or engaging in other forms of social cruelty using the Internet or other information communication technologies (Willard, 2007; Hinduija & Patchin, 2008). Patchin and Huinduja, (2006) also define cyberbullying as willful and repeated harm inflicted through the medium of electronic text. According to Ramirez, et al. (2010: 731), cyberbullying often includes everything from voice, text, picture, or video information exchanged via cellular phones to e-mail, instant messaging, Websites, or online chat rooms. It also entails the act of the repeated and deliberated threatening or harming of others through the cyberspace.

Another undesirable online behavior is flaming, which refers to any uninhibited expression of hostility that often manifests as an aggressive style of writing in which language is overly provocative, incendiary and/or vulgar (Kaynay, 1998; Abrams, 2003). Flaming, according to O'Sullivan & Flanagin (2003) is "a concept that emerged from popular discourse surrounding the online community to describe aggressive, hostile, profanity-laced interactions" (p. 70). Flaming occurs in synchronous modes of CMC (e.g., Internet Relay Chats and Multiple User Dungeons) as well as in asynchronous modes (e.g., email messages, postings to electronic discussion groups, newsgroups, and bulletin boards). Danet (2004) relates the prominence of flaming in CMC modes to the absence of important non-verbal cues that often indicate the intention behind a message. Such cues would include intonation, body language, the age, sex, and demeanor of the writer/sender of an online message. In addition, physical features of the setting in which the message is composed are thought to lead recipients to misinterpret text-based online messages.

Spamming, which is another negative use of the Internet, refers to the act of spreading several copies of the same message via online media. Typically, spamming involves the mass distribution of unsolicited commercial or bulk emails, with a view to distributing the message to people who would not otherwise choose to receive it. There is also some kind of profit motive behind spamming.

Finally, scamming, which is our focus in this chapter, is somewhat related to spamming. Scamming generally refers to fraudulent or deceptive business proposals that are usually sent to victims by scammers using fake identities, addresses, template letters, and documents. Scam letters also come in the form of spam mails. Internet fraudsters use various tricks to extract a surfer's email address from a Web browser and send the same mail to several people at the same time (spam-

style distribution). These professional scammers are also sometimes referred to as "confidence tricksters" or "con men," and they are generally known to exploit certain human characteristics, such as greed, dishonesty, and naivety.

PERSPECTIVES ON INTERNET SCAMS

Several scholarly research efforts on social computing have examined how persistent access to interactive technologies in the context of CMC encourages lack of inhibition. Chawki (2009), for example, did a general survey of what he calls the "Nigerian 419 scam," which is a popular form of international cyber crime. He identifies that such crimes include advancing sums of money to participate in business proposals, romance, lottery and charity scams. Within this context, linguists have also begun to examine how online writers use aspects of language to manipulate their targets and convince them to believe in fraudulent proposals.

One of such use of language is noted in Bloomaert and Omoniyi (2006). These two scholars reviewed a corpus of email messages known as "419 scams," which they describe as typical instance of "globalized" communication. They identify such activities as global because they are electronically-mediated, produced in the margins of the world, written in varieties of "world languages" (mostly English), and targeted at a wide, international audience.

According to Bloomaert and Omoniyi, such emails reveal a blend of at least three different forms of communicative competence. These competencies are

- **Technological competence:** Knowledge of communicative opportunities offered by global email systems
- **Cultural competence:** Awareness of genres and genre expectations among their

addressees in order to stand a chance of success

- **Linguistic competence:** The capacity to actually produce linguistic messages that are congruent with the projected identities and relationships in the transaction

Bloomaert and Omoniyi also found that scammers were able to develop the first two forms of competence. However, they also found that the third form did not appear to be well-developed, thereby making the texts scammers produced relatively easy to identify as fraudulent.

Because deception is the goal of cyberspace scammers, several authors have focused on the discursive arts of deception in scam emails. Using Herring's (2004) Computer-Mediated Discourse Analysis (CMDA), Chiluwa (2009) studied discourse structure and functions of deceptive online messages. He identified the use of specific discourse/pragmatic strategies like socio-cultural greeting formulas, confidence building, self-identification, and other interest-sustaining strategies by the writers of scam emails. In a related study, Druyd (2005) examined over 100 electronic mails and identified the various persuasive techniques used by the writers to make their bid successful. Druyd describes how the scammers, who garner substantial but unethical reward from their targets, appeal to the religious sentiments of their targets to fleece them. Some of the persuasive techniques Druyd identified in his research include appeals to pity, trust, and greed.

Smith (2009) also identified reasons why scammers keep finding a wide, global audience. He observed that scams are adept at exploiting common presuppositions in British and American culture regarding Africa and the relationships that are assumed to exist between the U.K. and the U.S. and those nations in the global south. In addition to Smith's findings, other researchers have noted that scam emails appear to reveal the processes by which wealth is created and distributed in the global economy. Holts and Graves's (2007) investigation of fraudulent emails, for example, notes how the emails they studied demonstrate multiple writing techniques designed to generate responses from the targets. Holts and Graves also found that scammers use deceptively simple messages, and in an attempt to identify and victimize their targets, scammers also link their messages to current events by using religious and emotional language.

Several other studies that have focused more generally on fraud and corruption, and Nigeria prominently features in these studies because most of the major international online fraud scams are traced to that country (Buchanan & Grant, 2001; Smith, 2007). Zook (2007) also observes that virtual scammers' activities have strong historic ties to Nigeria, where similar frauds were operated via physical letters and faxes during the 1970s and 1980s. However, as noted by Ofulue (2010: 298), much emphasis has been given to Nigeria as the origin of Advanced Fee Fraud (AFF) perpetrators while foreigners are identified as the victims of such scams. At this point, it is important to note that Nigerians are equally victims of such scams, thus giving the crime both a local and an international face (Tive, 2006; Adomi, 2008). Indeed, Tanfa (2006) observed the fact that scam emailing has developed into an international phenomena implies that the scammers are no longer Nigerians, only but are also of "different nationalities from around the globe" (p. 41).

Some authors have also shown that there is a consistent pattern in hoax emails – a finding that points to the fact that the fraudsters might be employing scripts or templates to rapidly generate messages (Edelson, 2003; Holts and Graves, 2007). Edelson (2003) identified and discussed some common themes used by online scammers, and these include claiming to want to use the addressee as a front for transferring illegally obtained money by claiming that the sender is the next of kin to a deceased customer of a bank,

KINDS OF VIRTUAL SCAMS

Online scammers hide behind the Internet to draw on real world perceptions and to invent fictional identities. These scammers propose different kinds of deceptive business – a type of activity usually subsumed under one name – Advanced Fee Fraud (AFF). Some of the commonly identified ones are identified and discussed here.

Next-of-Kin Inheritance

This approach represents a very common fraudulent tactic. Targets are contacted through email in which the sender claims to be an official of a bank or the spouse or child of a deceased person. If the sender claims to be a bank official, the related email often presents a bogus story of how one of their fellow countrypersons has recently passed on. Often, the senders of such fraudulent messages share news stories of tragic accidents or natural disasters that were widely reported by the international news media. The sender, in turn, claims to be the "bill and exchange manager" or "accountant" of huge sums of money left behind by the deceased who has no in-country next-of-kin to inherit the money currently in the bank. When conveying this information, the related email presents a tone of urgency – the money is about to be frozen or forwarded to an inaccessible account. The intended victim is thus advised to come forward immediately and claim rights to the non-existent inheritance. In essence, the fraudster asks the victims to be a partner in perpetuating fraud. The fraudster also requests the recipient/victim first provide some sort of vital information that can be used to establish identity (and thus, ownership), and the fraudster promises to share

the inheritance in a particular ratio once the funds have been freed.

Spoof

This kind of scam involves emails that appear to be sent by a representative of a well-known company. Such scam mails are distributed in the hopes of enticing or just tricking the naïve into releasing some sensitive personal information to some fake websites that have been designed to resemble that of a legitimate financial institution or other commercial entity. Although such scams can be difficult to spot, they generally ask the addressee to click a link back to a spoof website and provide, update, or confirm sensitive personal information. To bait the target, the fraudster might allude to an urgent or threatening condition concerning the recipient's bank account or other kind of personal account. The criminal usually aims at securing the target's password or pin, credit card validation code, ATM/debit or credit card number, bank account details, or social or national identification numbers with the goal of using them to perpetuate identity theft later.

Lottery Scam

Lottery scammers send emails announcing that the recipient of the message has won some lottery. The email generally quotes a bogus winning ticket number and a huge sum of money as payout. "Winners" are usually expected to come forward in a matter of weeks to collect their entitlements or forfeit their winnings. Often, as in other lottery scams, the lottery scammers con people into providing personal details and bank account information.

Charity Scam

The goal of this scam is to make money out of the generosity of others who are trying to alleviate suffering and misery in the world. Charity scammers present themselves as representatives of non-existent charity organization and ask prospective victims to donate money and material for orphanages, poor villagers, prisoners, or for victims of war and those of natural disasters (e.g., earthquakes, floods, etc.). Again, the objective is to convince the victim to reveal some sort of personal information related to his or her bank account, credit card details, or other personal information.

Government Debt Payments

This is an email-based scam in which the sender of a message falsely represents him- or herself as "the manager," "the chairman," "the authorized attorney," "the director," etc. of an overseas bank. The sender of the message also often faxes counterfit financial paperwork to the victim, and such documents usually note something like the Federal Government of Nigeria has been empowered by "the Presidency," "the Secretary to the Federal Government," "an Economic Advisor," etc to repay the government's past debts. Often, scammers use fake bank letterhead for these faxes, which subsequently provide fake mailing addresses, emails, and telephone numbers. In some cases, the solicitors even use the names of actual staff members working in a particular overseas administration to strengthen the "credibility" of their solicitation.

Job Offer Scam

This kind of scam targets foreign employment seekers and prospective immigrants. The email presents victims with attractive job offers in any number of industrialized nations, usually nations in Western Europe and North America. The scammer then asks the recipient to pay an initial fee for travel expenses and work visa.

DISCURSIVE MANIPULATION AND REALIZATION OF LANGUAGE METAFUCTIONS IN GLOBAL ONLINE SCAMS

Michael Halliday (1973) describes how language users produce different modes of meaning in clauses when those individuals are engaged in any form of discourse. Halliday identifies three broad functions he refers to as *metafunctions*. These are

- Ideational or Experiential
- Interpersonal
- Textual

According to Halliday, the *ideational* metafunction represents what is going on in the world – that is, the representation of experience of the world that lies in the imagination and around the language user (Halliday, 1985). The *interpersonal* metafunction represents the relationship between language users in the social world – the language users' role in the communicative situation and their personal commitments, while interacting with others (Melrose, 1991). The *textual* function, in turn, represents the verbal world - the organization of information in clauses as messages in discourse. Online scamming behavior involves these concepts in a number of ways.

First, scamming is not a new phenomenon in human social relations. Deception is part of human nature. However, online communication has further helped scammers manipulate others successfully by means of texts as they are able to present different identities that are not easily verifiable. Virtual scammers' deceptive emails play on their victims' experiential knowledge of the real world. Scam emails are thus crafted in such a way that they are made to appeal to their addressee's sentiment through the use of explicit information. As Chiluwa (2009) notes, narrativity is one of the discourse strategies used by scammers to strengthen their proposals.

The narration used by scammers is usually based on certain facts that most global citizens are able to experientially identify with regardless of their background. Such narratives make allusions to well-known natural disasters like the earthquake in Haiti, plane crashes (with links to some real websites), wars (in Iraq, Sierra Leone, or Liberia), bomb blast in Iraq and Lebanon, etc. In addition, the scammers use fictitious names that can easily be identified with some parts of the world presented in the related email.

To achieve their objectives, virtual scammers combine three interrelated strategies of deception, persuasion, and manipulation. The goal of this three-fold approach is to affect a target/victim in such a way that the target's subsequent behavior or actions become an instrument for attaining the scammer's goal (Galasinki, 2000). In this context, deception is a type of linguistic manipulation, the ultimate goal of which is to persuade the addressee/recipient to identify with the purposes of the deceiver. In identifying experientially with their addressees, virtual scammers present their targets with the option of rejecting the offer. For example,

- VS 1: Please if my offer if of no appeal to you, delete this message and forget. I am not a criminal
- VS 2: I have a proposal for you, this is however not mandatory nor will I in any manner compel u you to honor it against your will

Expressions like these present the scammer as a non-desperate person and probably someone who is just honestly trying to help. However, this wording represents a subtle way of gaining the confidence of the target without demonstrating any form of desperation or putting pressure on that target. One of the ways people easily identify scam mails is the pressure the emailer put on the addressees/victim. It is therefore a possibility that some people might fall victims of virtual scammers

when those individuals fail to notice the kind of pressure that typically accompanies scam emails.

Similarity in the generic structure of most scam emails has led some scholars to conclude that these messages employ templates in order to rapidly generate correspondences. A more critical look at these emails reveals that fraudsters improve their strategies seemingly every day. Changes appear to be based on the fraudsters' experiential knowledge of certain facts that they believe will appeal to their audience – things such as using lower-pressure tactics as illustrated in the previous examples of VS 1 and 2. Additionally, claims of naivety, feigning ignorance, and expressing some form of regrets also appear to be key strategies as demonstrated in the following examples:

- VS 3: Honestly, I don't really know which area to invest in because I am still schooling and I have never invested before and don't have an idea of investment issues this is why I need you to be my partner, guardian/adviser.
- VS 4: If you have an idea of what should be done to carry the money out of Africa, please tell me. I need your advice seriously and I have the impression that you are a nice gentle person.
- VS 5: I have not particularly lived my life so well, as I have never really cared for anyone. Though I am very rich, I was never generous. I was always hostile to people and only focus on myself as that was the only thing I cared for. But now, I regret all this as I now know that there is more to life than just wanting to have or make all the money in the world. I believe god gives me a second chance to come to this world. I would live my life a different way from how I lived it. Now that I know my time is near I have been touched by God to donate what I have inherited form my late husband for the good work of God, rather

than allow my relatives to use my husband hard earned funds ungodly.

Unlike the typical scam email that employs reassurance and confidence-building discourse strategies (Chiluwa, 2009), virtual fraudsters in these example emails portray themselves as non-confident, naïve, vulnerable, and ignorant persons. This strategy increases the discursive power of the addressees and gives them a kind of privilege to assume the position of the primary knower (K1), or the person who already knows the information. This strategy seems to place the recipient in a more powerful position in the interaction as his/her contribution confers a kind a stamp of authority in the discourse (Berry, 1987).

Scammers require the addressee to assume this role, while the scammers themselves assume the role of the secondary knower (K2), someone to whom the information is imparted. Being placed in K2 role in a discourse has been described as being in a less powerful position (Poynton, 1985; Togher, McDonald, & Code, 1999). This approach is contrary to what happens in many of the earlier scam emails where the writer posed as a more confident person who possessed more power in the discourse than the addressee. These shifts to a seemingly more passive role are clearly part of the baiting strategies of email scammers.

The VS 5 example is a charity scam, which appeals to addressees' religious sentiments. The sender/scammer is feigning regrets about how she lived her life. In so doing, she presents an identity of a one-time hard-hearted now penitent but dying woman who has been donating to charity organizations and would like to donate her fortune to widows, the motherless, and other "less privileged." Perhaps not surprisingly, previous studies have identified how appeals to religious sentiments are one of the strategies used in deceptive emails (Holts & Graves, 2007; Chiluwa, 2009). Using popular phrases in Islam and Christianity, presenting the sender as a missionary, a born again Christian, or a devoted Muslim, and quoting

profusely from the Bible or another religious text are some of the strategies used in these kinds of emails. Some extracts from the emails studied are

- VS 6: In the Name of Allah, the most Beneficient, The Most Merciful.
- VS 7: Greetings to you in the name of our Lord
- VS 8: I want you and the church to always pray for me because the Lord is my shepherd. My happiness is that I lived a life of a worthy Christian and whoever that wants to serve the Lord must serve him in spirit and Truth

Expressions in these extracts represent discursive ways of identifying with those individuals who practice the two major religions in the world: Islam and Christianity. The diction used, in turn, clearly represents what people in these religions would identify with.

Signals of interpersonal function are typically reflected in greetings and the first paragraphs of scam emails – a point at which the writers introduce him- or herself and also demonstrates some level of politeness and experiential knowledge of the ethics of interpersonal relationships – especially in respect to persons they have never met. Though these emails vary on how the writers express politeness by apologizing, the goal is essentially the same – for the scammer to take on the identity of a seemingly "decent personality." Consider the following examples of such linguistic behavior:

- VS 9: Do accept my sincere apologies if my mail does not meet your personal ethics, I am Mr SULEMAN MUHAMMED
- VS 10: I did not mean to embarrass you with my business proposal, but seriously, I need your assistance
- VS 11: I crave your indulgence for the unsolicited nature of this letter. I am The Director of audit and accounts with the ECOWAS region office.

- VS 12: It is understandable that you might be a little bit apprehensive because you do not know me. Please forgive this unusual manner to contact you.
- VS 13: This mail might come to you as a surprise and the temptation to ignore it as unserious could come into your mind, but please consider it a divine wish and accept it with a deep sense of humility.
- VS 14: I am quite sure that this mail will come to you as a surprise since I have not been having previous correspondence with you.

Apart from these scammers expressing politeness by apologizing for sending unsolicited emails, some of the messages also attempt to explain how the sender came about the addressee's email. In addition, online fraudsters pre-empt the likely reactions of their addressees, which is the tendency to ignore or delete such mails. They accomplish this objective by feigning being polite in an attempt to persuade their audience to read and possibly react appropriately to scam emails.

Scam mailers have also mastered most of the terms used in standard official and business correspondences. As a result, they often try to make their emails reflect the standard business correspondence format as much as possible. Interestingly, identity theft is one of the strategies many scammers use to create the right context. According to this approach, the names of some prominent people as well as letter head from known multinational organizations are used to lend credence to the claims of scammers.

Additionally, writer of scam emails often claim to be highly placed officials in a variety of multinational organizations. Most scam emails are not always totally official in nature, as tone of the message sometimes reflects some note of familiarity with the addresses – a strategy used to gain the confidence of the recipient. It is not uncommon to see expressions, such as the following in scam mails:

- VS 15: Dear friend, how are you doing?
- VS 16: Dearest love

These are clear strategies used to gain the confidence of the unsuspecting targets.

As Blommaert and Omoniyi, (2006) and Ofulue (2010) have noted, there is no doubt about scammers' awareness of genre expectations, and their emails are carefully crafted to reflect these textual expectations. However, scam emails are typically full of learners' errors, which do not project the expectations one has of the kinds of texts that would come from the claimed sources. As observed by Blommaert and Omoniyi (2006), "many of the authors of the messages struggle with basic literacy skills and have an incomplete control over standard varieties of English" (p.589). This factor probably would be one of the reasons people would generally associate these emails with non-native English varieties, such as, English as Second Language (ESL) or English as a Foreign Language (EFL) contexts typically found in countries in West Africa – mainly Nigeria, Ghana, Sierra Leone, Cote d'Ivoire, Burkina Faso, Cameroon, and so forth.

CONCLUSION

This chapter has examined discursive manipulation strategies used by virtual scammers. It corroborates the findings of some previous scholars that virtual scammers appeal to their addressees' religious sentiments, trust, and greed to perpetuate some form of global fraud. In addition, scammers use greeting formulas, confidence building, and self-identification strategies to gain trust in international online contexts. However, a critical study of scam emails over the years reveals that the strategies scammers use keep changing to reflect the growing experiential knowledge of the targets of such scams. Unlike their practice in earlier emails, scammers now pretend to yield discursive power to their targets, and they often present themselves as an ignorant, non-desperate, vulnerable, and naïve person. These scammers often also pretend to demonstrate more than before their experiential knowledge of the ethics of interpersonal relationship. These strategies sometimes work as these fraudsters are able to manipulate English, the global language, to reach people across different cultures. Scammers' knowledge of what an international audience expects in online official and business communication has given them more confidence to continue to use seemingly authentic and persuasive messages that transcend borders despite the general outcry against international cybercrime.

FUTURE RESEARCH DIRECTIONS

Several studies have been carried out on virtual scams, and these studies have used different approaches. Studies on virtual scams have been dominated by social psychologists and linguists. These studies have generally focused on the historical backgrounds of email fraud, strategies used by the fraudsters, the perpetrators and the criminal networks involved, the victims and the law enforcement personnel, and judicial approaches to the problem (Dillion, 2008; Chawki, 2009). Very few research efforts have focused on the discursive features of the virtual scams. More importantly, studies have not essentially addressed how these emails vary in terms of their style and diction over time. As knowledge spreads on the nefarious activities of Internet scammers, fewer people fall victim to their schemes. However, it is obvious from the findings of this study that as these scammers achieve less successful results, they are inventing newer communication styles to exploit new aspects of online communication. A broader study of a larger amount of scam emails than examined in this chapter will possibly yield more interesting results.

REFERENCES

Abrams, Z. I. (2003). Flaming in CMC: Prometheus' fire or Inferno's. *CALICO Journal, 20*(2), 245–260.

Adomi, E. (2008). Combating cybercrime in Nigeria. *The Electronic Library, 26*(5), 716–725. doi:10.1108/02640470810910738

Berry, M. (1987). What is theme? – A(nother) personal view. In Halliday, M. A. K., & Fawcett, R. P. (Eds.), *New developments in systemic linguistics* (pp. 1–64). London, UK: Pinter.

Blommaert, J., & Omoniyi, T. (2006). Email fraud: Language, technology, and the indexicals of globalization. *Social Semiotics, 16*(4), 573–605. doi:10.1080/10350330601019942

Chiluwa, I. (2009). The discourse of digital deceptions and email "419" solicitations. *Discourse Studies, 11*(6), 1–26. doi:10.1177/1461445609347229

Crystal, D. (2006). *Language and the Internet* (2nd ed.). Cambridge, UK: Cambridge University Press. doi:10.1017/CBO9780511487002

Danet, B. (2004). Flaming. In V. P. Bouisaac (Ed.), *The Garland encyclopaedia of semiotics*. New York, NY: Garland. Retrieved June 12, 2009, from http://pluto.mscc.huji.ac.il/~msdanet/flame.html

Dillon, E. (2008). *The fraudsters: How con artists steal your money*. London, UK: Merlin Publishing.

Druyd, M. A. (2005). "I brought you a good news": An analysis of Nigerian 419 letters. *Proceedings of the 2005 Association of Business Communication Annual Convention*, 1-11.

Edelson, E. (2003). The 419 scam: Information warfare on the spam front and a proposal for local filtering. *Computers & Security, 22*(5), 392–401. doi:10.1016/S0167-4048(03)00505-4

Galasinki, D. (2000). *The language of deception: A discourse analytic study*. London, UK: Sage.

Grabowsky, P., Smith, R. G., & Dempsy, G. (2001). *Electronic theft: Unlawful acquisition in cyberspace*. Cambridge, UK: Cambridge University Press.

Halliday, M.A.K. (1973). *Explorations in the functions of language*. London, UK: Edward Arnold.

Halliday, M. A. K. (1985). *An introduction to functional grammar*. London, UK: Longman.

Harrison, R., & Thomas, M. (2009). Identity in online communities: Social networking sites and language learning. *International Journal of Emerging Technologies and Society*, 7(2), 109–124.

Herring, S. C. (1999). Interactional coherence in CMC. *Journal of Computer Mediated Communication, 4*(4). Retrieved December 23, 2008, from http://jcmc.indiana.edu/vol4/ issue4/herring.html

Herring, S. C. (2004). Computer-mediated discourse analysis: An approach to researching online communities. In Barab, S. A., Kling, R., & Gray, J. H. (Eds.), *Designing for virtual communities in the service of learning* (pp. 338–376). New York, NY: Cambridge University Press.

Hinduja, S., & Patchin, J. W. (2008). Cyberbullying: An exploratory analysis of factors related to offending and victimization. *Deviant Behavior, 29*(2), 1–29. doi:10.1080/01639620701457816

Holmer, T. (2008). Discourse structure analysis of chat communication. *Language@Internet*. Retrieved March 29, 2009 from: http://www.languageatinternet.de /articles/2008/1633

Holts, T. J., & Graves, D. C. (2007). A qualitative analysis of advance free fraud email schemes. *International Journal of Cyber Criminology, 1*(1), 137–154.

Huffaker, D. A., & Calvert, S. L. (2005). Gender, identity, and language use in teenage blogs. *Journal of Computer-Mediated Communication, 10*(2), article 1. Retrieved from http://jcmc.indiana.edu/vol10 /issue2/huffaker.html

Joinson, A. (1998). Causes and implications of disinhibited behavior on the internet. In Gackenbach, J. (Ed.), *Psychology and the Internet: Intrapersonal, interpersonal and transpersonal implications* (pp. 43–60). San Diego, CA: Academic Press.

Kaynay, J. (1998). Contexts of uninhibited online behavior: Flaming in social newsgroups on usenet. *Journal of the American Society for Information Science American Society for Information Science, 49*, 1135–1141. doi:10.1002/(SICI)1097-4571(1998)49:12<1135::AID-ASI8>3.0.CO;2-W

Melrose, R. (1991). *The communicative syllabus: A systemic functional approach to language teaching*. London, UK: Pinter.

O'Sullivan, P., & Flanagan, A. (2003). Reconceptualizing "flaming" and other problematic messages. *New Media & Society, 5*(1), 69–94. doi:10.1177/1461444803005001908

Ofulue, I. C. (2010). A digital forensic analysis of advance fee fraud (419). In Taiwo, R. (Ed.), *Handbook of research on discourse behavior and digital communication: Language structures and social interaction* (pp. 296–317). Hershey, PA: IGI Global. doi:10.4018/978-1-61520-773-2.ch019

Park, J. R. (2007). Interpersonal and affective communication in synchronous online discourse. *The Library Quarterly, 77*(2), 133–155. doi:10.1086/517841

Patchin, J. W., & Hinduja, S. (2006). Bullies move beyond the schoolyard: A preliminary look at cyberbullying. *Youth Violence and Juvenile Justice, 4*, 148–169. doi:10.1177/1541204006286288

Ramirez, A., Palazolo, K. E., Savage, M. W., & Deiss, D. M. (2000). New directions in understanding cyberbullying. In Taiwo, R. (Ed.), *Handbook of research on discourse behavior and digital communication: Language structures and social interaction* (pp. 729–744). Hershey, PA: IGI Global.

Schoenmakers, Y. M. M., de Vries, R., & van Wijk, E. A. (2009). *Mountains of gold: An exploratory research on Nigerian 419-fraud*. Amsterdam, The Netherlands: SWP Publishing.

Smith, A. (2009). Nigerian scam emails and the charms of capital. *Cultural Studies*, *23*(1), 27–47. doi:10.1080/09502380802016162

Smtih, D. J. (2007). *A culture of corruption: Everyday deception and popular discontent in Nigeria*. Princeton, NJ: Princeton University Press.

Suler, J. (2004). The online disinhibition effect. *Cyberpsychology & Behavior*, *7*(3), 321–326. doi:10.1089/1094931041291295

Tanfa, D. Y. (2006). *Advance fee fraud*. Unpublished doctoral dissertation, University of South Africa, Pretoria.

Thurlow, C. (2003). Generatn txt? The sociolinguistics of young people's text-messaging. *Discourse Analysis Online*. Retrieved October 2, 2004, from http://extra.shu.ac.uk.daol/articles/vl/a3/thurlow2002003-paper.html

Tive, C. (2006) *419 scam: Exploits of the Nigerian con man*. Bloomington, IN: iUniverse.

Togher, L., McDonald, S., & Code, C. (1999). Communication problems following traumatic brain injury. In McDonald, S., Togher, L., & Code, C. (Eds.), *Communication disorder following traumatic brain injury* (pp. 1–18). Hove, UK: Psychology Press Ltd.

Wall, D. S. (2001). Cybercrimes and the Internet. In Wall, D. S. (Ed.), *Crime and the Internet* (pp. 1–17). New York, NY: Routledge.

Willard, N. E. (2005). *Cyberbullying and cyberthreats*. Paper presented at the U.S. Department of Education Office of Safe and Drug-free Schools National Conference, Washington, D.C.

Zook, M. (2007). Your urgent assistance is requested: The intersection of 419 spam and new networks of imagination. *Ethics Place and Environment*, *10*(1), 65–88. doi:10.1080/13668790601153713

KEY TERMS AND DEFINITIONS

Computer-Mediated Communication: Any communicative situation which occurs through the use of connected computer networks.

Deindividuation: This refers to the absence of a person's sense of individuality, especially in online communication. Deinvidiation encourages fraudulent practices online.

Metafunctions: These are the functions language users explore when producing meaning in any instance of language use every day. They are Experiential, Interpersonal and Textual in nature.

Scam: The act of obtaining money from others by means of deception using fake personalities, letter-head headed, non-existent address, and fake documents.

Spamming: The abusive use of the electronic media to send unsolicited messages into the mail box of internet users. The overall goal of spamming is to force the message on people who would not otherwise choose to receive it. Such messages include commercial advertising, often for dubious products, get-rich-quick schemes, and so forth.

Virtual Scam: Unsolicited letters sent to people's email with the aim of defrauding them of their money and other valuables.

Chapter 11
Government Monitoring of Online Media and Its Influence on Netizens' Language Use in China

Wengao Gong
Nanyang Technological University, Singapore

ABSTRACT

In the last 15 years, China has witnessed the world's fastest growth in terms of Internet infrastructure construction and number of Internet users. In order to realize its ambition in maximizing the economic value of the Internet while minimizing its destabilizing and disruptive potential, the Chinese government has adopted a policy that encourages the technological development of the Chinese Internet. The government, however, also maintains a very tight control over the Chinese people's online activities. In order to avoid or break through the government's regulatory effort, netizens in China have worked out many interesting ways of expressing ideas online. Among the various linguistic strategies adopted by Chinese netizens, five are particularly prominent and arguably more effective. They are using homophony, dismantling Chinese characters, using sarcasm, extending the semantic sense of words, and using English or Pinyin initials. This chapter examines how government monitoring of online media in China is employed to restrict people's freedom of expression and how Chinese netizens are using certain features inherent in their language and culture to exercise their right of free expression in such a context.

DOI: 10.4018/978-1-60960-833-0.ch011

INTRODUCTION

China is often criticized by Western powers for its close control over its people's freedom of expression. However, with the increasing penetration of the Internet into Chinese people's daily lives, it is getting increasingly difficult for the Chinese government to maintain the kind of control it exercised during the pre-Internet years. The anonymous nature of online communication (especially blogs and forums) and the fast speed of information dissemination have gradually turned China's online media into an invisible "battlefield" between the Chinese government and the Chinese netizens (i.e. individuals communicating online) –especially when it comes to sensitive political issues or cultural taboos. At present, the government of the People's Republic of China is trying every means possible to monitor the flow of information in Chinese society whereas Chinese citizens are simultaneously trying to find any and every means possible for expressing their own opinions.

As text is still the major means of opinion expression in online context in China, and as the government's general approach to content censorship involves key-word filtering/blockage, the game between the Chinese government and Chinese netizens has been largely turned into a linguistic one. In order to avoid or circumvent the government's content censorship, netizens in China have devised many innovative ways of expressing ideas online. By examining linguistic phenomenon in online communication in the People's Republic of China, the author explores the socio-political conflicts incurred by the popularity of online media in China and examines how these conflicts are verbalized in Chinese discourse via online media.

THE INTERNET, FREEDOM OF EXPRESSION, AND MONITORING

When the Internet was first invented, its primary function was to facilitate information sharing free from the constraints of time and geographic location. Many people believe that "cyberspace has no territorially based boundaries" (Johnson & Post, 1997, p. 6). This seemingly borderless nature of the cyberspace created by the Internet and the World Wide Web has fired many people's imaginations about what changes this new technology would bring. Terms like "free access of information," "freedom of speech," and "democratization of information" soon became buzzwords in news media and academic writings alike. Many scholars (e.g., Friedman, 2000) and politicians hailed the Internet as an ideal tool for promoting democracy and free access of information, especially in countries often labeled as "authoritarian" or "totalitarian" regimes. Within this context, Friedman (2000, p. 62) describes the Internet as "the pinnacle of the democratization of information" because it is totally decentralized, it is owned by no one, and it cannot be turned off.

This Web-based democratization of information, according to Friedman (2000), could render repressive regimes powerless, and the trend to test this claim is often irresistible. Friedman argues that authoritarian regimes could not afford to refuse Internet technology; otherwise they would fall economically behind the nations that adopted it. Once authoritarian states embrace such technology, however, they will not be able to control information as they had previously because it is virtually impossible to control what people are doing online.

Wacker (2003) expresses similar sentiments about the power of the Internet in confronting government regulation and control. According to him,

the global nature of the Internet, the wide geographic distribution of its users, and the diverse character of its contents lead many policy-makers to believe that activity in cyberspace is beyond the regulation and control of any single state (2003, p. 58).

It is true to say that cyberspace is more difficult to regulate than real-world/physical space, but does it follow that the online environment is really a borderless and anarchic space as preached by some scholars? Should the Internet be regulated? A review of literature shows that there is no consensus as to the answers to these questions, especially when it comes to the issue of Internet regulation.

Necessity of Internet Regulation

The necessity of regulating the Internet has become a non-issue nowadays. Cyberspace might appear to be borderless, but the people who congregate in this invisible realm are still living in a physical world divided by things like differences in language, belief, culture, and ideology (Goldsmith & Wu, 2006). Due to the global nature of the Internet, "publication anywhere means publication everywhere" (Kahin & Nesson, 1997, p. ix). Thus, information considered legal or even harmless in one country might well be considered illegal or harmful in another. The capability of the Internet to penetrating physical borders almost effortlessly has made the legal-illegal issue even more complicated. These factors become even more nuanced when one considers the threats of cyber crime, cultural invasion, and information warfare (Kahin & Nesson, 1997). In other words, like the real world, the virtual world also needs to be regulated.

Opponents of Internet regulation believe government control or oversight of the Internet might infringe on people's freedom of speech. The problem is freedom of speech is never something absolute, be it in real/physical space or cyberspace. The reason seems to be obvious: "one person's right to freedom of speech or expression can infringe on another's rights, and can clash with other goods" (Weckert, 2000, p. 106). As a result, "there will be no nation that has no speech that it wishes to regulate on the Internet" (Lessig, 2006, p. 297). If we take a look at what governments from different parts of the world are actually doing, we will soon find that national restrictions on online freedom of speech are commonplace around the globe. According to Mayer-Schönberger & Foster,

individual nations, each intent upon preserving what they perceive to be within the perimeters of their national interests, seek to regulate certain forms of speech because of content that is considered reprehensible or offensive to national well-being or civic virtue. (1997, p. 235)

They have also pointed out that certain things will incur regulation in the majority of the world's governments – items such as libel, pornography (obscenity and related areas), subversive information and subversive advocacy (information advocating anti-government violence), hate speech, and privacy-related issues. If we look at this list more closely, we will soon find that certain things (e.g., subversive information) are more vulnerable to government-imposed interpretations than others (e.g., pornography). Perhaps that is one of the main reasons for opponents of Internet regulation to be concerned about the risk of infringement on people's freedom of expression. This concern makes plenty of sense, especially when it comes to countries where conceptualizations of democracy, freedom, and human rights are not the same as that of industrialized Western countries. China would be a good case in point for this issue, as we will see later in this chapter.

Feasibility of Internet Regulation and Monitoring

Some scholars (e.g., Johnson & Post, 1997) hold that it might not be possible for any government to meaningfully control the Internet, even if one wanted to. Unfortunately, recent developments seem to be contradicting this wisdom. According to Lessig (2006), pushed by governments and driven by commercial interests and profits, the Internet has been converted into "an architecture that will perfect control and make highly efficient regulation possible", because the "technologies that make commerce more efficient are also technologies that make regulation simpler" (p. 61). To cite an example, Google, like all the other search engines, keeps a copy of every search it is asked to perform and it "links that search to a specific IP address, and, if possible, to a Google user's account" (Lessig, 2006, p. 204).

The existence of such mechanisms makes it possible for governments to monitor and control people's online activities. In fact, governments can achieve a large degree of control by regulating the intermediaries of online exchanges. Such intermediaries include Internet Service Providers (ISPs), content providers, search engines, browsers, the physical network, and financial intermediaries. By controlling the most important ISPs that service the vast majority of Internet users in a nation, governments can effectively monitor people's online activities (Goldsmith & Wu, 2006; Zittrain & Palfrey, 2008).

In addition to technological control, governments can take legislative and administrative measures to achieve similar results. These measures can create an atmosphere of self-regulation and self-censorship. It is a context in which individuals monitor what they say online (i.e. censor themselves) out of a fear of being detected and punished by their government. By using a combination of these strategies, a government can regulate and monitor a wide range of people's online activities if that government chooses to do so.

THE INTERNET AND CHINA

The Development of the Internet in China

Ever since its official connection to the Internet in the early 1990s, China has experienced the world's fastest growth in the development of Internet infrastructure (e.g., Hughes & Wacker, 2003; Kluver, 2005; Lum, 2006; MacKinnon, 2008; Rayburn & Conrad, 2004; Tai, 2006; Tsui, 2003; Yang, 2003, 2009; Zheng, 2008; Zhou, 2006; Zittrain & Edelman, 2003). According to the latest statistics released by the China Internet Network Information Center[1], Internet users in China had reached 420 million by June 30, 2010. Moreover, broadband users accounted for 364 million of these 420 million individuals.

Without the full support of the Chinese government, this growth would simply not have been possible. Despite the rapid expansion of its Internet infrastructure, China - the most powerful "Communist regime" in the eyes of the Western world- is often the target of attack in terms of government endeavors involving Internet regulation. The Google Incident[2] once again, put the Chinese government and its tight control over the Internet in the international spotlight. The Incident was even elevated to the level of a diplomatic jigsaw between the Obama Administration and the Chinese government. The row between Google and the Chinese government resulted in Google shutting down its search service in mainland China and re-launching an uncensored Chinese language service in Hong Kong. Google claimed that it made such a move in order to defend its core principle of "doing no evil" (which refers to cooperating with the Chinese government in internet censorship in this particular context).

Depending on one's perspectives, different people could see different things in the booming of China's Internet development. Just like many people could never figure out why their prophecies about the collapse of "Communist China" have never been fulfilled, it is equally difficult for them to understand why China can sustain a higher Internet penetration rate while simultaneously maintain rather stringent Internet regulation according to Western standards. China is also (arguably) the only country in the world that has embraced the latest waves of the information age while developing "a sophisticated control mechanism with a combination of technical and policy initiatives to harness the destabilizing and disruptive potential of information technologies" (Tai, 2006, p. 81). Perhaps Kluver's (2005) remarks might give us a clue about how to understand what is actually happening in China when it comes to the Internet:

Chinese policy toward the Internet, as an extension of its other media policies, moved toward more long-range and nuanced political goals. Although it was clear that the Internet was going to introduce some political and social tensions, the government saw that it could be both a tool for economic development as well as a means of enhancing the legitimacy of the Party and helping China to gain greater cultural power, or soft power. (Kluver, 2005, p. 307)

If we try to look at the process of China's Internet development over the past 15 years from a perspective that accounts for the responsibilities a government assumes in improving its people's welfare (economic and social life alike) and the historic, cultural, and political traditions, we can see more of the dynamics of the interactions among the Chinese government, the Internet, Chinese netizens, and China's economic and social developments. In fact, as Yang (2009) notes, the process of China's Internet development is full of contentions:

Of all the aspects of Chinese Internet culture, the most important and yet least understood is its contentious nature. Media stories and survey reports have perpetuated two misleading images of the Chinese Internet: one of control and the

other of entertainment. These two images create the misconception that because of government control, Chinese Internet users do nothing but play. The real struggles of the Chinese people are thus ignored, and the radical nature of Chinese Internet culture is dismissed. Yet, not only is Internet entertainment not apolitical, but political control itself is an area of struggle. Contention about all other domains of Chinese life fills the Chinese cyberspace and surges out of it. (Yang, 2009, p. 1)

It is these contentions that have shaped Chinese Internet culture and some aspects of the social realities of current Chinese society. Many of these contentions have found their expressions in a variety of linguistic phenomena that often originated from and were copied to and spread through the Internet. Some of these phenomena have even penetrated the print media and ordinary people's daily speech patterns (including many non-Internet users).

To a certain extent, the contention between the Chinese government and Chinese netizens has evolved into a linguistic game. In order to understand the nature of this game better, we need a basic knowledge of how the Chinese Internet is regulated and monitored and to what extent the Chinese government tolerates expression of personal opinions in Chinese cyberspace. We can not understand the relationship between government internet regulation and certain linguistic behaviors of Chinese netizens until we place this relationship within the broader context of an important transitional period of China's economic, social, and political development.

Internet Regulation and Monitoring in China

According to Hachigian (2001), the Chinese government has adopted a three-part Internet strategy: "providing economic growth and some personal freedoms, managing the Internet's risks, and harnessing its potential" (p. 118). Government intervention has become more and more proactive with the explosive growth of the Internet over the past decade. Like other governments in the world, the Chinese government's Internet regulation is mainly enforced by technological, legislative, and administrative means. Technically speaking, the architecture of the Chinese Internet lends itself for the government to block the websites they rendered harmful because Internet data enter or leave China at a limited number of points (or gateways). As a result, the Internet backbone and gateway routers can be configured to deny access to government-forbidden foreign websites.

It is hard to say whether the system was deliberately designed this way. Considering the high-cost of Internet connection at the initial stages of its development in China, having a limited number of backbone connection points may well be a temporary solution which was later found to be of administrative advantage by the Chinese government. Guarding its national gateways of Internet connection is of great importance to the Chinese government, but it is not the most important form of Internet control in China (2006). The reason is that ordinary Chinese netizens' interest in foreign websites is not very high – partly because foreign sites do not focus on China. Even if they do, this focus is mostly negative. Moreover, these sites are usually not written in Chinese. As a result, "the real centerpiece of China's system of information control is its internal controls" (Goldsmith & Wu, 2006, p. 95).

One very common way to create internal controls is the installation of content filtering software developed by domestic firms in China and then approved for use by China's Ministry of Public Security. This kind of software blocks access to a wide variety of websites that contain pornographic, violent, and other "objectionable" content including politically sensitive topics (Deibert & Villeneuve, 2005).

A second commonly adopted way is promoting self-regulation and self-censorship through leg-

islative and administrative regulatory measures. The Chinese government has implemented a very powerful directive specifying that "every individual and company is responsible for what is published on its part of the network, thereby effectively creating a situation where everybody is his own self-censor" (Tsui, 2003, p. 70). As a result of these measures, Chinese Internet users and ISPs have generally taken censorship as part of the necessary tradeoff for online speech and Internet-based business.

Different ISPs have adopted different approaches to dealing with online content that contains sensitive information. Some service providers, for example, choose to filter sensitive phrases by regularly updating their list of sensitive words or phrases. Other service providers choose to replace the offending phrases by using an asterisk (*) in place of each character in the banned phrase (MacKinnon, 2008).

Within this context, it is not true that the Chinese government is trying to control everything on the Internet; however, the bottom line is clear: "you can talk about what you want, but no direct threats to Government" (Goldsmith & Wu, 2006, p. 89). Content that goes beyond the tolerance level of the government in terms of such threats is often deleted within a very short time after it is posted. Yet individuals can often view such deleted contents via the cache function of the search engines they use. Still, there are cases of websites being shut down either temporarily or permanently due to publishing of disallowed contents, but they are not the norm.

Contentions between the Government and Netizens

While the Chinese government is continually trying to monitor and censor those destabilizing, dangerous or "unhealthy" aspects of activity (as defined by the government) in cyberspace, Chinese netizens are simultaneously trying various ways to circumvent or break through the government's regulation or censorship. There are, moreover, a number of ways for the Chinese Internet users to circumvent the blocking of websites. They can, for instance, use proxy servers or peer-to-peer technology. They can also use innovative ways of saying things to avoid being detected by government monitoring.

Proxy servers are mainly used for gaining access to foreign websites the Chinese government has blocked for "national security" reasons. As using proxy servers requires the user to have some information technology skills, and this method of circumvention is often used by college students. Because the IP addresses of proxy servers need to be provided and often have foreign connections, using proxy servers is generally not very effective and is prone to being blocked. Foreign governments' involvement in helping Chinese Internet users to circumvent such blocks generally increases the determination of the Chinese government to crack down on such attempts and thus further reduces people's interests in using such technologies (Lum, 2006). Perhaps as a result, MacKinnon's (2008) findings show that the number of Internet users who are willing to use technologies like proxy servers to circumvent Internet censorship seems to be dropping despite the rapid growth of the Internet population in China. Besides, since most Chinese netizens have problems reading English content, relatively few are interested in Western news media. As a consequence, whether Western news websites are blocked or not has actually become a sort of non-issue in China (MacKinnon, 2008).

Chinese netizens' decreasing interest in browsing English-mediated foreign websites does not stop them from trying to express their opinions about domestic affairs that are more relevant to their daily lives. In fact, the Chinese government has realized that the Internet has a role to play in maintaining its ruling status. By allowing enough room for the online discussion of a sufficiently wide range of subjects (e.g., letting off steam about government corruption or incompetence), the Chinese government is actually using the Internet as a safety valve so as to keep the ever-increasing number of mass incidents under control (MacKinnon, 2008). According to this perspective, offering people a channel to vent their anger is much better than forcing them to take their complaints to the streets. However, when it comes to political taboos and topics or issues which have great potential for putting the government in negative light, the Chinese government will tighten its control over online speech, and the normal practice is to block or filter sensitive contents.

Blocking or deleting undesirable information from the Internet in China is very annoying to Chinese netizens. It is also an effective way for the government to stop certain information from disseminating rapidly and on a large scale while at the same time avoid taking too many unnecessary legal actions against those people who have tried to "cross the red line" in posting such information. Otherwise, the government will be putting itself totally on the opposite side of its own people, which is a position the Chinese government wants to avoid.

Because the content filtering or censorship technology is mainly based on key words or phrases, this battle of censoring and counter-censoring has been largely turned into a linguistic one. In order to outsmart the filtering software or the cyber police, Chinese netizens have created many innovative ways of saying things online. Many of these linguistic endeavors have something to do with certain features of the Chinese language or with particular aspects of traditional Chinese culture. One thing that deserves a particular mention here is despite a situation that looks rather "dire and oppressive" from the perspective of people who live in Western democracies, Chinese netizens do not view themselves as a group of "oppressed victims who are waiting to be liberated." Rather, it is a story of tenacious optimists, slowly and patiently pushing back the boundaries, and believing that – in the end – history is on their side (MacKinnon, 2008).

THE LINGUISTIC GAME

As mentioned, the normal practice for the Chinese government to implement internal Internet control is through content filtering systems embedded in the Chinese Internet. Content filtering has a great deal to do with linguistics. The effectiveness of content filtering relies heavily on the exhaustiveness of the list of banned words or phrases used to screen content. In fact, even if the list is exhaustive, it cannot be effective all the time.

To be effective, content filtering software should also be able to differentiate "desirable" collocates from "undesirable" ones. The term "collocates" refers to the words that co-occur with a particular word or phrase. For instance, the phrase "共产党" (*gong4chan3dang3*, meaning *the Communist Party*) might well develop a strong negative connotation if the Chinese netizens frequently discuss the mistakes the Party has made or has been making. In order to screen the negative comments associated with this phrase, the government will have to put these three characters in the banned wordlist so that the filtering software can screen these words when necessary.

That action will, in turn, cause another problem for the government in relation to state-controlled media. That is, the state-controlled media might also run the risk of being filtered or screened if they are just normally performing their duties of disseminating propaganda for China's Communist Party. Furthermore, if the government decides to screen any word which has developed a politically negative connotation, very soon the Chinese people will find they will have no words left to use online. (Of course, there are other ways to allow the use of these words, for instance, by indentifying the source of information. If a certain post or piece of news comes from state-controlled media, the filtering system can be set not to respond to this particular posting.)

Situations such as these are why the Chinese government needs to develop a more sophisticated system of content filtering that can detect the "undesirable" collocates. Addressing this collates issue is thus a major challenge for Chinese censors, for collates remain a popular way Chinese netizens use to communicate around government control. Of course, that is not to say there are no other linguistic strategies at the netizens' disposal. In fact, among the various other linguistic strategies adopted by Chinese netizens in confronting the government's Internet regulation, five are more prominent and arguably more effective. These five strategies are

1. Using homophony
2. Dismantling Chinese characters
3. Using sarcasm
4. Extending the semantic sense of words
5. Using English or Pinyin initials

The author will discuss each of these strategies in the remaining sections of this chapter.

The Power of Homophony

The biggest challenge for the Chinese government's attempts to implement content filtering based on keyword identification technology is that the Chinese language contains numerous homophones (words having the same or very similar pronunciations but different in meaning; e.g., the English words *bear* and *bare* are homophones). When compared to the English language, the Chinese language can be seen as having an almost endless number of these homophones.

According to Su and colleagues (1996, pp. 117-118), there are 127 Chinese characters which share the same syllable *yi* in *Xinhua Dictionary* (the most popular Chinese dictionary in China). Even if we categorize these characters by tones (there are four tones in Mandarin Chinese), we will still get 18 characters for *yi1 (e.g.* 衣, meaning *clothes;* 医, meaning *doctor*); 28 for *yi2 (e.g.* 移, meaning *move*; 疑, meaning *doubt*); 15 for *yi3 (e.g.* 已, meaning *already*; 椅, meaning *chair*); and 66 for *yi4 (e.g.* 易, meaning *easy* or *change*;

异, meaning *different*). In other words, there are at least 18 Chinese characters which share the same pronunciation of *yi1* (e.g., 一meaning *one* and 医 meaning *doctor*). The total number of Chinese characters expressed by the syllable *yi* can amount to 272 if we consult another dictionary *Cihai* (which can be literally translated into *Sea of Words*), with 25 for *yi1*, 62 for *yi2*, 36 for *yi3*, and 148 for *yi4*. Even in the standard Chinese character library there are still 110 characters for the syllable *yi*, and this library is what Chinese netizens use when keying in Chinese characters.

Another example of such a diverse homophone is the syllable *ji*, which is also used to express 110 characters. In both the examples of *yi* and *ji*, the variations caused by the Chinese dialects are not counted. The same Chinese characters can be pronounced in many different ways, depending on which regional variety of Chinese the speaker is adopting. As a result, the number of homophones will increase considerably if such variants are also counted. This diversity of homophones is truly a huge challenge for individuals who attempt to compile lists of banned words. Depending on the number of homophones a Chinese character could have, the list of banned words can become too long to be of any practical use.

Worse still, using homophony for pragmatic functions is a very important part of Chinese people's cultural tradition. Yu and Li (2007) have presented a good review about the relationship between the Chinese homophony and the Chinese culture. To a certain extent, we can say that homophony-related culture is a part of Chinese people's cultural gene. Two salient features of this kind of culture include:

1. The use of homophony
2. The association of the sound with certain concrete things (animals, plants, flowers, or objects)

To illustrate the importance of homophony in the Chinese culture (especially folk culture),

the author cites two examples here. One is about birthday celebration, and the other is related to Chinese wedding ceremonies. Chinese has a special phrase for people who are above seventy years old (actually 70-80): 耄耋 (*mao4die2*). In ancient times, people (rich people) would send a vase engraved with the picture of a cat chasing a butterfly (or cats chasing butterflies) to celebrate birthday for someone who was over 70 years old. The reason cats and butterflies were chosen is that 猫 (*mao1*, meaning *cat*) and 蝶 (*die2*, meaning *butterfly*), when combined, sound quite similar to 耄耋 (*mao4die2*) – or the expression used to indicate one is over 70 years of age.

The second example is related to weddings. In many places in China, people will place dates and peanuts on the bed of the newly-wed couple in a gesture that wishes the newlyweds to *have children soon*. *Date* (a kind of fruit) is called 枣 (*zao3*) in Chinese, which is a homophone of another Chinese character 早 (*zao3*, meaning *early* or *soon*). *Give birth to* in Chinese is 生 (*sheng1*), which is part of the word 花生 (*hua1sheng1*, meaning *peanuts*). Due to the phonetic similarities, the dates and peanuts have acquired symbolic meanings which are associated with marriage and reproduction.

There are other cultural factors at play in this case. For instance, peanuts are also associated with the concept of abundance, and being able to have many children is taken as a great blessing in traditional Chinese culture. It is, however, beyond the scope of this chapter to offer detailed explanation about the formation of Chinese folk culture. What the author is trying to convey through these examples is homophony is a very common linguistic phenomenon in Chinese culture, and part of Chinese culture is deeply rooted in this phenomenon. Because of this relationship, it is almost instinctive for Chinese people to find cultural or political information that has been hidden or embedded through the use of homophonies.

The popularization of the Internet in China and the subsequent flourishing of Internet-based communication have contributed to the emergence of a new subculture which is also characterized by the frequent use of such homophony-triggered linguistic features. As a result, Chinese netizens generally have little problem understanding the intended meaning imbedded in seemingly non-sensical combination of characters online. This feature of the Chinese language has become an important weapon for Chinese netizens to use in fighting against the government's attempts at censorship. Of course, the use of homophones has also added a playful or humorous flavor (sometimes it may well be black humor) to the linguistic battle (maybe game is a more accurate word) between the Chinese netizens and the Chinese government. The following are just a few rather recent examples of the homophony-related phenomenon.

It is widely acknowledged that talking about issues like democracy, dictatorship, or other politically sensitive topics is rather difficult because the Chinese equivalents of these concepts often fall into the list of banned words or phrases, which will normally be censored once spotted by the filtering system. Nevertheless, netizens have found ways to outsmart the content filtering system by taking advantage of Chinese homophony. As mentioned, a feature of homophony-related culture is that the homophonies are often associated with animals, plants, or objects. This association is probably why all the examples the author is going to cite here have something to do with animals, though not all of which are real animals.

One well-known example of such homophony is that netizens often use 河蟹 (*he2xie4*, meaning *river crab*) to replace 和谐 (*he2xie2*, meaning *harmony*) when they are mocking at the government policy of trying to create a harmonious society out of censorship (by suppressing people's freedom of speech). More recent examples include what the Chinese netizens call "中华四/十大神兽" (*zhong1hua2si4/shi2da4shen2shou4*), meaning *the four/ten mythical Chinese creatures*.

There are several different lists of the creatures and the number varies from four to twelve. Among these creatures, some are so famous that

almost every Chinese netizen knows them. Here are some of the more frequently mentioned creatures: 草泥马 (*cao2ni2ma3*, meaning *the grass-mud horse*), 毒豺 (du2cai2, meaning *poisonous jackal*, a homophone of 独裁 *du2cai2*, meaning *dictator/dictatorship*), 鸣猪 (min2zhu4, meaning *talking pig*, a homophone of 民主 *min2zhu3*, meaning *democracy*), 鹳狸猿 (*guan3li3yuan2*, meaning *the stork-fox-ape*, a homophone of 管理员 *guan3li3yuan2*, meaning *system operator*), 绿霸 (lü4ba4, meaning *the green tyrant*, a homophone of 绿坝 *lü4ba4*, meaning *the Green Dam*, a Chinese filtering software), and 亚克蜥 (*ya4ke4xi1*, a lizard-like animal, a homophone of 亚克西 *ya4ke4xi1*, a literal Chinese translation of a Uyghur word meaning *good*). The author is not going to explain the origin of all these terms, but will instead focus on four typical examples to illustrate how Chinese netizens are using their linguistic wisdom to challenge the government's attempt to restrict its people's freedom of expression.

Among the various mythical creatures which only exist in the Chinese netizens' discourse, one is now world-famous. It is a creature called "the grass-mud horse" in English. This species is so uniquely Chinese that it is hardly possible to find mention of it in places outside of China. Nobody outside China knew much about this unique animal before Michael Wines introduced this "animal" to the Western world in his *New York Times* article published on March 12, 2009.

The official Chinese name for this "horse" is 草泥马 (*cao3ni2ma3*). It is not a horse, nor is it even an animal. It is a near-homophone of a notorious Chinese profanity 操你妈 (*cao1ni2ma1*, meaning *f**k your mother*). People may wonder why a phrase whose original meaning was "an especially vile obscenity" was hailed by the Chinese netizens and the Western media as a hero. The emergence of this mythical creature is said to have something to do with the Chinese government's initiative of curbing the rampage of obscene and vulgar online content. Launched in early 2009, the policy is probably due to the use of content filtering regulatory method and "the national cursing" is also one of the banned phrases. As a consequence, each time netizens use a profanity in online chat or forums, a message will pop up and say something like "Sorry, your post consists of unhealthy content, please post it after revision." This message is very annoying, of course. When enough people found such messages totally unbearable, they devised a way of using homophones to replace the original words in order to break through the censorship.

The government is obviously the loser in this round of contention concerning low-taste and vulgar content. What has caught people's attention is the political significance brought about by a homophone of a vulgar phrase. (It is rather ironic that it is the homophone of a vulgar phrase which has defeated the government.) According to Wines (2009b), "the grass-mud horse is an example of something that, in China's authoritarian system, passes as subversive behavior. Conceived as an impish protest against censorship, the foul-named little horse has not merely made government censors look ridiculous, although it has surely done that" (para. 3).

Another mythical creature, which is less well-known than the grass-mud horse, is something called "poisonous jackal" in English. In Chinese, this creature is called 毒豺 (*du2cai2*), which is a near-homophone of 独裁 (*du2cai2*), meaning *dictator* or *dictatorship*. In this case, the netizens using this term are not rebelling against the government's initiatives of curbing the spread of pornographic content through the internet and the mobile phones. Rather, the netizens are directly challenging the politically taboos, as the translation of a blog entry (written by an anonymous blogger[3]) published in Baidu portal reveals:

毒豺原产于中国,其历史悠久,已不可考,曾经遍布全世界,如今仍活跃在中国,古巴,苏丹,朝鲜等地。本世纪40年代,毒豺繁殖迅速,险些造成其他物种的整体灭绝。其危害性,可见

一斑。*(Translation: The poisonous jackal was a native species in China. No one really knows for how long this creature has been living in this country. It used to spread all over the world, but now they are only active in China, Cuba, and North Korea. In the 1940s, the number of poisonous jackals increased so rapidly that other species of animals were almost close to extinction. From this we can see how dangerous this animal is.)*

If Chinese netizens use the normal phrase "独裁", or "dictator," they will definitely not survive the content filtering system.

The third homophone-based creature used by Chinese netizens is called 绿霸 (*lü4ba4*), meaning *the Green Tyrant*. This is the Chinese netizens' way of referring to 绿坝花季护航 (*lü4ba4hua-1ji4hu4hang2*), meaning *the Green Dam Youth Escort*. 绿坝 (also pronounced *lü4ba4*) is the short form. This item is an anti-virus kind of software with the purported intent of filtering out harmful online text and image content in order to prevent the effects this information could have on Chinese youth and promote a healthy and harmonious Internet environment.

On May 19, 2009, the Chinese Ministry of Industry and Information Technology announced a policy which requires all new PCs sold in China after July 1, 2009 to have this filtering software pre-installed. The China Ministry of Education also requires all the primary and second schools to install this software in their PCs. Other governments in the world have taken similar measures to keep children from pornographic and other harmful information. For instance, the United Stated passed the Children's Internet Protection Act that requires schools in the United States to have content filtering and blocking technology installed (Cabe, 2002; Deibert & Villeneuve, 2005). The Australian government has also taken similar initiatives to protect children from accessing pornography and other indecent Internet content.

The Chinese government's decision to have the Green Dam installed in each and every PC sold in

China has triggered such great complaints among computer users (especially home computer users) that the government had to postpone the implementation of this initiative. In order to show the netizens' resentment of this government initiative, many people began to call the Green Dam "the Green Tyrant." They listed this software as one of the mythical creatures and jokingly depicted as a new species of biological weapon. The following translation of a blog entry[4] tells something about Chinese netizens' attitude towards the Green Dam:

绿霸: 杀伤力极强的终极神兽, 据说是政府耗费巨资, 由国家生化武器研究所的顶尖专家融合了河蟹, 鹳狸猿等中国特色物种的优秀基因杂交出的无?生物,传说可以不费吹灰之力可以杀死其他所有神兽。政府号?此生物能保证人们免受各种有害生物侵袭,因此将让中国境内每家每户?制领?。 *(Translation: The Green Tyrant is the most potent Chinese mythical creature with a horribly strong power to kill. Rumor has it that the government has invested huge amount of money on creating such a beast. The project was led by top scientists from the national institute of biochemical weaponry. This matchless creature is a hybrid of several uniquely Chinese species such as the River Crab and the Stork-Fox-Ape. Legend has it that it can effortlessly kill all other mythical creatures. The government claims that this creature can protect people from the attack of various kinds of harmful organisms and forces all the families in the Chinese soil to adopt one.)*

What we can sense from this post is the netizens' resentment against Internet censorship. Again, the blogger intentionally ignored the potential function of installing the Green Dam in protecting children from accessing harmful information.

One latest species on the list of mythical creatures is an animal called 亚克蜥 (*ya4ke1xi1*), which sounds like a species of lizard. According to the report of Hong Kong-based *Mingpao*, on February 19, 2010, Chinese netizens created this new creature to mock at one of the programs

performed on the China Central Television 2010 Spring Festival Gala Evening entitled "党的政策亚克西" (meaning *the Party's Policy Is Good*). *Yakexi* is a Uygur word, meaning *good*. Many Chinese netizens disliked this program because it praised the Chinese Communist Party.

What we can learn from the four examples noted in this section is that Chinese netizens are using homophony, a salient feature of the Chinese language, together with their own imagination and humor, to circumvent the government's regulation and censorship endeavor or to mock the government's Internet censorship policy.

Dismantling Chinese Characters

Apart from using homophony, Chinese netizens have also tried other linguistic means for breaking through the government's censorship. Again, they are taking full advantage of another feature of the Chinese language: The dismantleability of the Chinese characters. Many Chinese characters can be dismantled into parts or radicals. In other words, one Chinese character can be dismantled into two or more characters. People can easily understand the meaning of the dismantled characters simply by putting them together. This dismantling is a very common practice when people who come to know each other for the first time introducing themselves.

Part of the reason for this dismantling is that the Chinese language contains too many homophones – even when it comes to the characters related to people's family names. For instance, somebody with the family name 章, instead of 张will probably introduce himself or herself by saying something like "我姓章,立早章",meaning "my family name is Zhang (章), which consists of the characters 立*li4* (meaning *stand*) and 早 *zao3* (meaning *early*). If the family name is another Zhang (张), that person is very likely to say something like "我姓张, 弓长张", meaning "my family name is Zhang" (张), which consists of the characters 弓 *gong1* (meaning *bow*) and 长 *chang2* (meaning *long*).

This feature of the Chinese characters can also help Chinese netizens break through or outsmart the government's Internet censorship. Normally this strategy is employed when certain people's names become politically taboo and are included on the government's list of banned words or phrases. For instance, there is an AIDS patient human right activist called Hu Jia (胡佳, *hu2jia1*), and his name was among the blacklist of banned phrases for quite a while. It was once very difficult to talk about him or finding information about him due to the content filtering system in place. Later, some netizens started to use 古月人圭 (*gu3yue4ren2gui1*) to circumvent the censorship. Netizens will often immediately understand to whom this 古月人圭 refers if they have some knowledge about the context in which those characters appear. A similar strategy has been used in the case of 刘晓波 (Liu Xiaobo), a political dissent in China. Instead of using his original name, which will definitely be blocked or filtered, netizens use 刘日尧波 (*liu2ri4yao2bo1*) or 刘曰尧波 (*liu2yue4yao2bo1*) to talk about him. Other examples include 言覃作人 (*yan2tan2zuo4ren2*), referring to 谭作人 (Tan Zuoren), and 黄王奇 (*huang2wang2qi2*), referring to 黄琦 (Huang Qi). These are some of the names that the government does not want its people to talk about for one reason or another. Of course, this strategy is less effective than using homophony, due to the constraints of the Chinese characters. After all, not all Chinese characters lend themselves to dismantling.

Sarcastic Ways of Saying Things

There are other linguistic strategies which can be used to express opinions, yet allow the speaker to do so with less risk of being censored. One commonly practiced approach is the use of sarcasm online. The advantage of using sarcasm is that netizens can talk about certain issues without using potentially sensitive words or phrases that would be noted by Chinese censors. Here is one interesting example. A blogger wrote the following words in one of his blog entries:

有网友总结说:*Facebook*的原罪是它能让人认? 想认?的人,*Twitter*的原罪是它能让人说出想说的话,*Google*的原罪是它能让人知道想知道的东西,*YouTube*的原罪是它能让人证明需要证明的现实。所以它们都被干掉了。这些我用得少,*twitter*刚用了不到一周,就在伟大的甲子前夕被干掉了。*(Translation: A net friend has figured out why Internet tools such as Facebook, Twitter, Google, and YouTube are all disallowed in China: they all have original sins. The original sin of Facebook is that it allows people to get to know whom they want to know. The original sin of Twitter is that it allows people to speak what they want to say. The original sin of Google is that it allows people to know what they want to know. The original sin of YouTube is that it allows people to prove things which need to be proved in reality. I do not use these tools very often. I used Twitter for less than a week and it was banned on the eve of the Glorious 60 Years) (Han, 2010).*

When the blogger used the phrase "伟大的甲子前夕" (meaning *on the eve of the Glorious 60 Years*), he was using a sarcastic way of saying the 60th anniversary of the founding of People's Republic of China. For expressions like this, the content filtering system could not identify them and thus would not filter them out unless human intervention is implemented. Content filtering systems are computer programs that can only mechanically carry out their developers' orders, but they do not have the intelligence to really understand human language, at least for the time being.

Apart from sarcastic ways like the one cited above, Chinese netizens have already invented many other innovative ways of saying things in sarcastic manner, yet without using any sensitive words. They have found one magic word that is simple and ordinary, yet is also expressive and

Table 1. Bei4-phrases in Chinese

Chinese Phrase	English Translation	Chinese Phrase	English Translation
被代表(*bei4dai4biao2*)	Be involuntarily represented	被小康 (*bei4xiao3kang1*)	Be counted as "being better-off"
被就业 (*bei4jiu4ye4*)	Be counted as one of the employed	被自愿 (*bei4zi4yuan4*)	Be volunteered
被自杀 (*bei4zi4sha1*)	Be forced to have committed suicide	被捐款 (*bei4juan1kuan3*)	Be forced to donate
被和谐 (*bei4he2xie2*)	Be harmonized	被艾滋 (*bei4ai4zi1*)	Become an aids patient through blood transfusion/selling
被开心 (*bei4kai1xin1*)	Be referred to as being happy	被赞成 (*bei4zan4cheng2*)	Be counted as saying "agree"
被增长 (*bei4zeng1zhang3*)	Be counted as "have increased"	被痊愈 (*bei4quan2yu4*)	Be pronounced "cured" (but actually not cured)

innovative. This word is 被 (*bei4*). Originally, it is a functional word often used to form passive voice in the Chinese language. Prior to the Internet, however, few individuals likely realized that this word could be so powerful when it co-occurs with phrases which are not normally passivized. Huang (2010) makes a rather comprehensive list of these *bei4*-phrases. Many netizens even claim that China has entered a *bei4*-Era. The author has no intention to offer a theoretical linguistic explanation about why this seemingly abnormal pattern of language use is linguistically possible, as that is beyond the scope of this chapter. What is more relevant here is the pragmatic function of this innovative way of saying things.

The idea being this approach works as follows: When two self-contradictory concepts are combined into one phrase, it will trigger the readers to make a logical inference out of something seemingly illogical. The inherent meaning of the word 被 (bei4) (that is, the involuntariness) naturally becomes the most important clue for people to make sense out of the new phrase. As Huang (2010) remarks, when netizens deliberately use a covert way of saying things, they are actually conveying a crystal-clear message: "You all know exactly whom I'm talking about" (para. 34). The emergence of so many *bei4*-phrases is a signal to show that the people could not be fooled any

longer. They are actually urging the government to stop fooling its people. Table 1 contains some examples of these *bei4*-phrases. For some of them, the author finds it very difficult to translate the concept conveyed by the original Chinese expression into English. Thus, the English translation presented here might be merely a close approximation to the real meaning intended.

Extending Semantic Senses of Words

Some words or phrases have become such a political taboo that even state-owned media dare not use them: For instance, 游行示威 (*you2xing2shi-4wei1*, meaning *demonstration*) is considered a taboo phrase. Interestingly, demonstration is a right the Chinese people are supposed to exercise if they find it necessary, and it is a right that still appears in the current Constitution of People's Republic of China. Unfortunately, after the 1989 Political Incident, "legal" demonstrations have become an extremely rare scene except when China faces great challenges from foreign governments and the Chinese government finds nationalist sentiments favorable to rallying its people's support.

The strange thing is that this phrase seems to be applicable only to when the Chinese state-controlled media report on demonstrations happening in foreign countries. When they have no choice but to report similar cases in China, the same media will normally describe such events as 群体事件 (*qun2ti3shi4jian4*), meaning *mass incidents*, violent or otherwise. Chinese netizens, on the other hand, will not always take such things so seriously or so negatively. They often rather use the phrase 散步 (*san4bu4*, meaning *take a walk or stroll*) to express their intention to demonstrate on the street. The government might not approve a people's demonstration application for such an event, but the government also has no reasons to forbid people from taking a walk or stroll. Moreover, no Chinese law has ever specified that people need to apply for permission before they decide to take a walk. Taking a walk also shows a strong intention of being peaceful. For phrases like *taking a walk*, the government would find it very difficult to put it on the list of banned words. Doing so simply does not make sense.

As a result of these factors, this phrase – "taking a walk" – has been used by netizens to mobilize people in order to show their anger about human rights abuse in China. One example is when netizens called for "taking a walk" on the day when the verdict in the case of Deng Yujiao, a 21-year-old waitress who fatally stabbed a Communist Party official as he tried to rape her, was going to be read. Due to huge pressure from organized Chinese netizens (individuals who used phrases such as "taking a walk" to coordinate their efforts), the court ruled that Deng had acted in self-defense and thus freed her without criminal penalties (Wines, 2009a).

Using English/Pinyin Initials

Influenced by the English language and emergence of Internet Chinese Language, netizens in China have also started to use English initials or Chinese Pinyin initials. (Pinyin is a written form of Chinese that uses Roman letters instead of characters to form words.) Some initials are transparent in meaning, while others might be quite

opaque. Since initials are relatively more opaque than Chinese characters, Chinese netizens can use these initials strategically to circumvent Internet censorship. For instance, netizens often use the initials TG to refer to the Chinese Communist Party. TG is the initials of the Chinese phrase 土共(*tu3gong4*)which used to be a term used by the Kuomingtang government in the early 1930s to refer to the then Chinese Communist Party. Chinese netizens revived this term by just using the first two letters (TG) of the two constituent words. Among Chinese netizens, the connotation of this abbreviation is obviously negative.

Another example would be ZF, which are actually the initials of the Chinese words 政府 (*zheng4fu3*, meaning *the government*). Most probably because of its opaqueness or because of the harmlessness, initials like this are normally not censored. Not all initials are so lucky, of course. For instance, initials such as FLG – which represent the religious sect Falungong, will normally be censored. The author is not going to make more detailed description about the use of initials. As a linguistic strategy to break through or outsmart the censorship system, it is proved to be useful sometimes.

Summary

As has been shown in the previous sections, Chinese netizens have employed various linguistic strategies to challenge the Chinese government's Internet regulation and censorship endeavors. Innovative as some of the strategies appear to be, they are still very vulnerable to censorship. These strategies might help Chinese netizens circumvent the government's filtering system, but such strategies might not survive a manual check, especially when certain innovative expressions become well-known. In fact, all the methods noted in this chapter could eventually end up in being blocked or deleted, but the government can only act in a passive manner. Within this context, some Chinese netizens compare the government's filtering effort to shadow-chasing that will eventually prove to be in vain. As one Chinese blogger says, in the Internet-age, as long as something is published, it does not really matter that much even if it is later blocked or deleted, because the message has already been sent out (Han, 2010).

CONCLUSION

The advent of the Internet has raised many issues that would have never existed in the pre-Internet ages (e.g., whether governments should regulate or monitor people's activities on the Internet and how). From what has been presented in this chapter, we can see how government regulation measures could influence people's lives and even their daily linguistic expression. Within this context, the contention between the Chinese government and Chinese netizens in terms of Internet control and counter-control might well be an extreme case.

The linguistic instruments that the Chinese netizens have employed in circumventing or outsmarting government censorship might well be language- or even culture-specific. However interesting the language game between the Chinese government and the Chinese netizens might appear to be, it is abnormal. Language changes with the development of the society, but language change should never be the result of having to avoid the normal way of saying things. Hopefully, this situation is something that can only be observed at this moment in history when China is experiencing unprecedented transformation, economically, socially, and politically. In fact, it is unfair to say that all the initiatives of the Chinese government in regulating Internet development in China are absolutely politically motivated, although no one can deny the existence of the political calculations behind many of them. There are many things in this world which need to be controlled, for instance, pornographic information. There are always evil things in the world which

need to be contained. Nevertheless, it is not wise for any government to try to achieve politically selfish purposes under whatever glorious names. How to hold a balance between the protection of people's freedom of expression and filtering out the truly harmful information on the Internet is an issue all governments in this world will have to address properly.

There are no simple solutions to this issue, but what the Chinese government is currently doing is definitely not in the right direction. The world would be better if government policy makers regulated speech "in a structured, principled, and internationally acceptable manner" (Mayer-Schönberger & Foster, 1997, p. 236). Chinese netizens' linguistic innovation can be viewed as a kind of compromise between their awareness of their human rights and the realities as represented by a cyberspace monitored by the government.

REFERENCES

Cabe, T. (2002). Regulation of speech on the Internet: Fourth time's the charm? *Media Law and Policy, 11*(1), 50–61.

Deibert, R. J., & Villeneuve, N. (2005). Firewalls and power: An overview of global state censorship of the Internet . In Klang, M., & Murray, A. (Eds.), *Human rights in the digital age* (pp. 111–124). London, UK: The GlassHouse Press.

Friedman, T. L. (2000). *The Lexus and the olive tree: Understanding globalization*. New York, NY: Anchor Books.

Goldsmith, J., & Wu, T. (2006). *Who controls the Internet? Illusions of borderless world*. New York, NY: Oxford University Press.

Hachigian, N. (2001). China's cyber-strategy. *Foreign Affairs (Council on Foreign Relations), 80*(2), 118–133. doi:10.2307/20050069

Han, Y. (2010). Wangyou pinglun liangze yu wangjin (Two pieces of comments from net friends and Internet censorship). Retrieved February 18, 2010, from http://www.hanyimin.com/post/1173.html

Huang, J. (2010, February 11). 2009 liuxing yuwen yipian: toukecai songgei 2010 (A glimpse of the buzz words in 2009: Stealing a vegetable and present it to 2010 as a gift). *Nanfang Zhoumo (Southern Weekly)*. Retrieved February 18, 2010, from http://nf.nfdaily.cn/nfzm/content /2010-02/11/ content_9188181.htm

Hughes, C. R., & Wacker, G. (Eds.). (2003). *China and the Internet: Politics of the digital leap forward*. London, UK & New York, NY: Routledge Curzon.

Johnson, D. R., & Post, D. G. (1997). The rise of law on the global network . In Kahin, B., & Nesson, C. (Eds.), *Borders in cyberspace information policy and the global information infrastructure* (pp. 3–47). Cambridge, MA: The MIT Press.

Kahin, B., & Nesson, C. (Eds.). (1997). *Borders in cyberspace: Information policy and the global information infrastructure*. Cambridge, MA: The MIT Press.

Kluver, R. (2005). US and Chinese policy expectations of the Internet. *China Information, 19*(2), 299–324. doi:10.1177/0920203X05054685

Lessig, L. (2006). *Code: And other laws of cyberspace, version 2.0*. New York, NY: Basic Books.

Lum, T. (2006). Internet development and information control in the People's Republic of China.

MacKinnon, R. (2008). Flatter world and thicker walls? Blogs, censorship and civic discourse in China. *Public Choice, 134*(1/2), 31–46.

Mayer-Schönberger, V., & Foster, T. E. (1997). A regulatory Web: Free speech and the global information infrastructure . In Kahin, B., & Nesson, C. (Eds.), *Borders in cyberspace: Information policy and the global information infrastructure* (pp. 235–254). Cambridge, MA: The MIT Press.

Rayburn, J. M., & Conrad, C. (2004). China's Internet structure: Problems and control measures. *International Journal of Management, 21*(4), 471–480.

Su, X., Cao, N., Yang, Q., & Cui, J. (1996). *Hanziwenhua yinlun (An introduction to the culture of Chinese characters)*. Nanning, China: Guangxi Education Press.

Tai, Z. (2006). *The Internet in China: Cyberspace and civil society*. New York, NY & London, UK: Routledge.

Tsui, L. (2003). The panopticon as the antithesis of a space of freedom: Control and regulation of the Internet in China. *China Information, 17*(2), 65–82. doi:10.1177/0920203X0301700203

Wacker, G. (2003). The Internet and censorship in China . In Hughes, C. R., & Wacker, G. (Eds.), *China and the Internet: Politics of the digital leap forward* (pp. 58–82). London, UK & New York, NY: Routledge Curzon.

Weckert, J. (2000). What is so bad about Internet content regulation? *Ethics and Information Technology, 2*(2), 105–111. doi:10.1023/A:1010077520614

Wines, M. (2009a, June 17). Civic-minded Chinese find a voice online. *The New York Times*. Retrieved February 18, 2009, from http://www.nytimes.com/2009 /06/17/world/asia/17china.html

Wines, M. (2009b, March 12). A dirty pun tweaks China's online censors. *The New York Times*. Retrieved February 18, 2009, from http://www.nytimes.com/2009 /03/12/world/asia/12beast.html?_r=1

Yang, G. (2003). The Internet and the rise of a transnational Chinese cultural sphere. *Media Culture & Society, 25*(4), 469–490. doi:10.1177/01634437030254003

Yang, G. (2009). *The power of the Internet in China: Citizen activism online*. New York, NY: Columbia University Press.

Yu, Q., & Li, X. (2007). Hanzixieyin yu hanwenhua yanjiu zonglun (A review of studies concerning Chinese homophony and Chinese culture). [Philosophy and Social Sciences]. *Journal of Bohai University, 6*, 125–129.

Zheng, Y. (2008). *Technological empowerment: The Internet, state, and society in China*. Stanford, CA: Stanford University Press.

Zhou, Y. (2006). *Historicizing online politics: Telegraphy, the Internet, and political participation in China*. Stanford, CA: Stanford University Press.

Zittrain, J., & Edelman, B. (2003). Internet filtering in China. *IEEE Internet Computing*, 70–77. doi:10.1109/MIC.2003.1189191

Zittrain, J., & Palfrey, J. (2008). Reluctant gatekeepers: Corporate ethics on a filtered Internet . In Deibert, R., Palfrey, J., Rohozinski, R., & Zittrain, J. (Eds.), *Access denied: The practice and policy of global Internet filtering* (pp. 103–122). Cambridge, MA: The MIT Press.

KEY TERMS AND DEFINITIONS

Content Filtering Software/System: Software or system designed for blocking access to websites that contain "objectionable content" as defined by the society and/or government.

Homophone: A word that is pronounced the same as another word but differs in meaning.

Internet Censorship: Control or suppression of the publishing or accessing of information on the Internet.

ENDNOTES

[1]   Source: http://www.cnnic.net.cn/

[2]   In January 2010, Google claimed that it is going to end business operation in China due to its intolerance of the Chinese government's practice of asking Google to content filter its search results and hand over information of political dissents in China. This incident has worsened the already tensioned political and diplomatic relations between China and the United States.

[3]   The author of this blog entry cannot be traced.

[4]   Source: http://bbs.canghai.org/thread-199787-1-1.html

Chapter 12
Irish Identification as Exigence:
A Self-Service Case Study for Producing User Documentation in Online Contexts

Andrew Mara
North Dakota State University, USA

Miriam Mara
North Dakota State University, USA

ABSTRACT

To address some of the technical writing pressures concomitant with globalization, this chapter investigates documentation solutions implemented by an Irish Do-It-Yourself tour operator. The same identity-dependent approaches that these DIY tourism companies use to fulfill tourist expectations can provide technical writers with additional tools for analyzing user motivation. This chapter first analyzes how an Irish DIY Adventure travel company harnesses user motivations, then applies Appadurai's (1996) globalism theories (especially his use of ethnoscapes, technoscapes, and mediascapes) to a particular use of this travel company's documents, and finally demonstrates how user motivation intrinsic to identity formation can help the technical writer create documentation that effectively assists users in overcoming breakdowns through identity affordances.

INTRODUCTION

The sharing of expertise, which is an easily understood and frequently practiced form of human discourse, has become an archetypal task *of online engagement and interaction.* - Stuart Selber (2010, p. 99)

In order to address some of the technical communication pressures concomitant with globalization—just two of which are de-professionalization and intensification of documentation practices—many scholars have sought alternatives to the

DOI: 10.4018/978-1-60960-833-0.ch012

purely instrumental technical writing paradigms that typically prevail in technical communication practice. Technical communicators are professionals who create documents that allow people to accomplish tasks. Within this context, user documentation usually refers to instructions for end users of a (often technical) product rather than persons within an organization, although that definition does not always suffice. David Dobrin, in his landmark article "What's Technical about Technical Writing" (1983), defines technical communication (then more commonly known as "technical writing") as "writing that accommodates technology to the user," (p. 118) admitting that at each point in a document's life "the reader is a user" (p. 121). Documentation, in this sense, then consists of the artifacts where this writing inheres.

In his 2003 article "Rearticulating Civic Engagement Through Cultural Studies and Service-Learning," J. Blake Scott asserts cultural studies and civic engagement can solve what he calls the "hyperpragmatist" orientation of technical writing (p. 289). Other technical communication scholars believe that paying attention to identity within communities can simultaneously preserve the status of the writer and improve the practice of technical writing (Faber, 2002).

As with previous research such as Faber (2002) and Spinuzzi (2003), we have found that some of the best solutions to globalist pressures in technical documentation are already being practiced in other industries in ad hoc and unofficial ways. The solutions we found when studying an Irish Do-It-Yourself (DYI) tour operator reflect the same kind of wiliness and ad hoc improvisation that not only helps solve the wide range of problems that Spinuzzi and Faber identify in organizational, community, and regional settings, but also addresses problems that cross national boundaries. The same identity-dependent approaches that these DIY tourism companies use to fulfill postmodern tourist expectations (Reichel et. al, 2008) can help technical communicators begin to address some

of the crushing pressures endemic to increasingly global trade and travel. This chapter will analyze an Irish DIY adventure travel company in its economic context. In so doing, we will demonstrate how technical communicators can apply Arjun Appadurai's (1996) globalism theories to create identity affordances that effectively assist users in overcoming breakdowns.

AN OVERVIEW OF TOURISM IN IRELAND

From 1994 to the 2008, Ireland globalised and grew rapidly to become the economic power many called the Celtic Tiger. Within that growth and change, lingering tensions between the traditional and the new re-emerged. New technology industries like software programming transplanted a host of new business and corporate practices, including documentation processes, into what had been an economically depressed island. One traditional Irish industry, tourism, integrated the new wealth and growth. However, unlike the newly imported fields of pharmaceuticals and software production, tourism had a stake in pre-Tiger Ireland. While Ireland has learned much from recent global corporate in-migration, there is much that documentation experts could learn from adaptations that the service industry made during this period to accommodate new global flows without destroying already-existing methods of cultivating and satisfying audience desire. The tourism trade, one of Ireland's oldest global industries, demonstrates how user identification with an assumed ethnic and/or national group can enlist the user to both the co-create and maintain user documentation and other language-based affordances.

The Irish tourist industry depends on constructing national landscape and experiences in the midst of a global, transnational economic reality. Current tourism companies faintly resemble early ascendency landlords (British and Scottish transplants to Ireland) who gained land through conflict or fiat, and were seen as usurpers of local landowners by indigenous Irish. Williams (2008) suggests that these landlords "literally organized the ground for tourists" (p. 9). Tourism outfits similarly facilitate tourist experiences that fulfill tourist expectations about landscapes in terms of the nation of Ireland. Ireland's current transnational tourism success depends upon tourist expectations of rustic retreats, "trad" music and unimpinged vistas of the ocean and emerald hills, which can all be contrasted with a more modern everyday lived experience. This desire for the distinctly postmodern combination of postnational conveniences of universal affordances (e.g., translated and climate-controlled exploration of Irish landmarks and access to products like Starbucks coffee and Hilton hotels) and the highly-individuated "Irish" signifiers of rustic Irish wildness and fabled Celtic hospitality offer both challenges and opportunities for the service industry. The service industry, in turn, both covers the dissonant modernity and enlists tourists to resolve the dissonance between the signifiers of postnationalism/postmodernity and an imagined pre-modern Ireland.

One Irish tourism company's methods for resolving this dissonance provides a case study from which other technical communicators might benefit. Put most simply, the case study presented here provides a key insight that a technical communicators might implement to tap user desire for a consistent and consubstantial experience with an imagined ethnos of a national group. By inviting users to imagine their common identity with other users (e.g., people of Irish descent identifying with an imagined past in a wild West Ireland), the technical communicator can distribute some of the work associated with translating and individuating user documentation to the end user of those materials.

CURRENT TECHNICAL COMMUNICATION MODELS FOR USER MOTIVATION

Current technical communication practices for determining why individuals use instructions typically consists of either rhetorical analysis, user observation and testing, or assuming universal cognitive models. The first two approaches involve gathering data particular to the user and use of a document or set of instructions. As a result, these approaches cannot inform technical communicators of larger arrays of motivations that might help the documenter select an instruction strategy that enlists user assistance in task completion in a wide range of instructional tasks. Universalized cognitive modeling, however, provides a more robust framework for understanding when users might be enlisted in filling in the details on more complex tasks or subroutines that might prevent a breakdown.

In exploring the *why* of user motivation to guide technical documentation in general, and minimal manual design in particular, van der Meij (2007) notes how most documentation approaches aim to optimize "goal-related management and control of attention, time, and effort" (p. 295). Minimalist technical documentation, like tourism, adheres to a just-in-time information approach in order to help users actively engage in goal accomplishment. The primary reason for the lack-of-information approach is to help users keep their attention focused on the task at hand. Although other documentation approaches attempt to create more cognitive scaffolding prior to task engagement, most of them share the aim of optimizing user efforts in order to accomplish goals in an efficient manner. While van der Meij is quite consistent in locating user motivation, the instrumental approaches to user documentation he describes do little to account for differing user motivations, other than to characterize motivations as situated and rhetorical (Farkas 1999). As a result, the models for rhetorical documentation approaches truncate along a generally Aristotelian universalism and a universalized cognitive parsing (i.e., cognitive, emotional, and perceptual) (Van der Meij 2007, p. 299). The affective documentation approaches that van der Meij discusses focus upon a universal set of emotions and subsume affect to the larger goal of accomplishing objectives. These approaches attempt to describe a stable and complete set of categories that describe what moves people emotionally. These universal models, located internally and acontextually, do not account for individual motivations that might map more usefully using external and contextual descriptors.

Because universal emotional motivation models do not easily explain why tourists choose to overcome breakdowns—after all, most tourists don't travel because they are grappling with hunger, fear, or other universalized needs—an online documentation expert might do well to consider alternative user motivation theories. In our examination of tourism documentation, we found that globalism theory provided more robust explanations for how users interacted with online documentation to chart their course and use offline documentation to overcome numerous breakdowns and create ad-hoc solutions to unanticipated problems. The globalist documentation approach of the Irish tourism company used for this case study challenges and extends universalized motivation models in two ways. First, this globalist approach provides specific contexts against which more different international models of user types can be measured. Second, this approach can help account for user motivation in the face of what might be considered sub-optimal environments. Specifically, using Appadurai's (1996) variety of "scapes" to discuss how users construct continuous and coherent meaning across a dizzying variety of cultures, media, and affordances can help the documenter enlist specific user motivations to overcome breakdowns and disruptions in goal achievement. Rather than foregrounding ideal emotions or states of mind

that users seek to achieve (i.e., the *why* of motivation), Appadurai's various "scapes" highlight both *why* and *how* users construct coherence, even in fragmented, contextually-specific, and poorly-documented tasks.

In their article "The Kindness of Strangers: The Usefulness of Electronic Weak Ties for Technical Advice" David Constant, Lee Sproull, and Sara Kiesler (1996) investigate the limits of identity as motivation for proffering technical help among employees of a global computer manufacturer. While they were not addressing end-users, their study identifies multivalent motivations for addressing technical challenges in documentation and beyond, some of which connect to identity. In the article, Constant, Sproull, and Kiesler detail how "people are not only pragmatic but also expressive of feelings, values, and self-identities" (1996, p.121). They go on to explain "If technical expertise is important in self-identity, experts can gain personal benefits from helping strangers on a computer network with technical problems" (Constant, Sproull, & Kiesler, 1996, p. 121). Specifically, the study indicates that strong connective ties between individuals need do not have to be present in order to motivate users. The same motivational appeals might be extrapolated from these employees to end-users.

GLOBALISM CHANGES MOTIVATION

Arjun Appadurai's globalism theory (1996) provides a method for analyzing how Ireland's contemporary tourist industry navigates (and sometimes obfuscates) globalisation in postnational Ireland. Appadurai traces the contours of a post-national globalism using his five scapes: mediascapes, ethnoscapes, technoscapes, ideoscapes, and financescapes. For the purposes of this chapter we are only going to focus upon the first four, as they are the ones that the technical communicator must consider in mapping user motivation. Financescapes are also useful, but an economic analysis of the situation goes well beyond documentation in the strict sense, and it involves both finance and accounting dimensions of business.

The most obvious place to start in explaining how these scapes can facilitate communication practices would be with ethnoscapes, for Appadurai includes tourists in his definition of ethnoscapes. Appadurai defines ethnoscapes as "the landscape of persons who constitute the shifting world in which we live: tourists, immigrants, refugees, exiles, guest workers, and other moving groups and individuals constitute an essential feature of the world" (p. 33). Despite having less of a stated and direct connection to tourism, the three other scapes can also prove useful in describing user motivation beyond utilitarian or universalized survival or homeostatic goals. These three additional "scapes"—technoscapes, mediascapes, and ideoscapes—describe the difference between contemporary travel practices in Ireland and earlier 20th-century diasporic returns.

Appaduri's second "scape," the technoscape, connects diverse and seemingly disconnected forms of technology that create ever-faster networks to convey people, supplies, and currency over borders: "By technoscape, we mean the global configuration, also ever fluid, of technology and the fact that technology, both high and low, both mechanical and informational, now moves at high speeds across various kinds of previously impervious boundaries" (1996, p. 34). It is this configuration of material, economic, and labor networks that creates the first parallel between technical communication and global tourism. Both industries rely upon an array of networks, often misaligned or in conflict, in order to complete transactions. The technical communicator creating materials for both the DIY tourism company and the technology company must anticipate how these materials will traverse a range of unknowable contexts in order to address an incredibly complex range of needs. In *NetWork* (2009), Spinuzzi describes some of these self-organizing networks as a

process of "splicing" rather than the industrial and nationalist "weaving" that depends upon groups adhering to differing interests according to their work-specific or location-precise identity. This weaving, in turn, is a way "to impart 'institutional anatomy' to continually interconnecting actors" (Spinuzzi, 2009, p. 46). In Ireland's post-national tourist industry, the work of resolving cognitive dissonance is now left to the tourist rather than assigned to a Disney Imagineer or a service-industry worker.

The final two scapes, mediascapes and ideoscapes, are ways of creating narrative coherency in landscape through seemingly-disconnected media practices and political ideas: "Mediascapes refer both to the distribution of the electronic capabilities to produce and disseminate information... and to the images of the world created by these media" (Appadurai, 1996, p. 35). Mediascapes connect different meditational technologies through the circulation of identifying images and signs through the landscape. Ideoscapes, by comparison, provide the main ideas for these connections as this concept centers on signification that demarcates particular political or national identifiers: "[i]deoscapes are also concatenations of images, but they are often directly political and frequently have to do with the ideologies of states" (Appadurai, 1996, p. 35). In a space like Ireland, ideoscapes formed about place predetermine how tourists read what they encounter, and the repetition of signifiers – like the shamrock, the harp, and the tri-color (Irish flag) – create layered meanings about the Republic of Ireland as an independent, democratic, European state with a history of colonization and tragedy as well as being a place associated with mysticism and magic.

Although signifiers can be easily arranged and categorized as pertaining to a particular identity, they can also be powerfully deployed as affordances. Affordances, which psychologist James Gibson (1997) first characterized as qualities in objects that enable action, also help define virtual environments and documents by providing users with recognizable ways to interact with and manipulate an environment, a document, or an ecology that interconnects the two. Although affordances are typically described as either being universal (e.g., like cognitive models) or situationally specific, there is precedent for seeing them as culturally motivating. Scacci's (2010) definition of an affordance as referring "to situated, interactional properties between objects and actors that facilitate certain kinds of social interactions in a complex environment" (pp. 2-3) helps locate entire documents or even document genres as possible affordances. Scacci further claims that online Freeware/Open Source Software Design project digests function as a type of affordance that traces values, imparts motivation, and aligns users as producers, albeit salaryless ones (pp. 7-8). This powerful example of de-centralized and uncompensated software development disrupts models of user motivation that prize universalized notions of why people act. Specifically, the use of online documentation to motivate and guide uncompensated yet dedicated problem solvers further illustrates how a tourism company and, by analogy, a technical communicator might use documentation to encourage user identification to overcome technical difficulties.

Online documentation participates in the creation of mediascapes and provides identity affordances that underpin the ideoscapes that are disseminated through particular mediascapes. For Irish tourism companies, online images of green fields and ocean views invite users to imagine themselves in spaces that serve as symbolic motivation. In our case study, the online description of the self-guided walking tour includes thumbnail narrative portraits of the towns and villages that walkers might encounter. These portraits both provide information to help plan the trip and reinforce the ideoscape that circulates a particular form of Irish identity through a larger mediacape. Although the wild Western Irish ideoscape is almost ubiquitous enough to obscure its own

constructedness to most U.S. tourists, alternative and disruptive ideoscapes circulate online as well.

For example, the parent company, Killary Tours, has a web page titled "Irish Stags & Hens," and this page included photographs of Irish people engaging in outdoor and decidedly ahistoric activities. The background of green found on both the Killary Tours and the SouthWest Walks Ireland sites for tourists disappears to display oranges, reds, and yellows. The ideoscape of the ancient, wild, mystical countryside is nowhere to be found. Instead, the company markets the same rugged landscape as a place where young European men and women participate in paintball, kayaking, cliff jumping, and adventure sports before getting married. This alternative identity affordance, a menu of adventure tours divorced from any diasporic history, shows how online documentation depends upon much larger cultural narratives to compel users through a complex set of steps and possible disruptions.

THE KERRY WAY CASE STUDY

Our case-study focuses upon an Irish destination that has long been touted as a touchstone of Irish culture—The Kerry Way—because this walking path on the Iveragh Peninsula parallels one of the busiest tourist destinations for diasporic returners—the Ring of Kerry. The Ring of Kerry is an approximately 170 kilometer tourist-frequented road that encircles the Iveragh Penisula in County Kerry. As Marion Casey remarked at her plenary session at the 2008 Midwest American Conference on Irish Studies, County Kerry is an area that has been sold to Americans for decades. The ring course starts from Killarney, and circumnavigates the Iveragh Peninsula through Black Valley, Killorglin, Cahersiveen, Waterville, Sneem, and Kenmare. Attractions around the peninsula include the Skelligs, Derrynane House (the home of "The Liberator," Daniel O'Connell), Muckross House, Staigue stone fort, and Killarney National Park.

Traversing "The Ring" is a very popular day trip, and many bus companies offer their versions of circumnavigating this peninsula during the summer months. However, a well-signposted walking path named The Kerry Way parallels the more heavily traveled roads. Because the small roads of the Ring of Kerry quickly become choked with buses during high season, the Kerry Way provides an attractive option for people wishing to avoid the larger crowds and the motorized means of accessing this pathway.

The Kerry Way roughly follows the scenic driving route of the Ring of Kerry, but it includes more rugged walking routes over small mountain passes and through agricultural land as well. It is also is made up of multiple kinds of paths (some obviously visible, some not). From the more bucolic and frequently touted butter roads, to the cobblestone paths, to muddy slogs across farms, the thing that unites the Kerry Way is the sense that this is one path. The century-long marketing of Killarney (and it's even-more-famous and easily rhymed Blarney Castle) as emerald hills, empty landscapes, and old-world values sets up expectations of a coherent walk back through time. It is this ideoscape that provides the audience expectations for SouthWest Walks Ireland and its partner, Killary Tours, which markets this hike as one of their own before it gets outsourced.

When taking one of these walks, the DIY tour operator (i.e., the tourist doing the walking) does not have to create a coherent experience that actually matches the audience expectations of shamrock-lined butter roads and sweeping views that guide hikers from village to village. Instead, instructions ask the hiker to connect wildly different looking pathways into one journey. Additionally, a cell phone is mailed to the hikers as an intrusive, but reassuring, technoscape intervention just in case the imagined and interpreted ideoscapes cannot turn a thousand steps into an actual journey. Still, hiker/user desires for a hike of significance helps the small company produce documentation without having to engineer a per-

fectly seamless experience OR provide perfectly coherent documentation.

Although the first contact is often through the Website, the primary interface between the hiker and the countryside is the aforementioned set of instructions that guide the user/tourist through a week of hiking. These instructions include day-by-day directions for traversing the spaces instructions, and they can be as granular as "About 400m after the gates, you will arrive at a T-Junction. Turn left. Ignore the sign pointing right," or more basic information about various eating and entertainment establishments in the nearby villages or towns. Detailed documentation like these directions makes walking through bogs, farming and grazing land, and forests possible for suburban and exurban travelers who might be unfamiliar with such terrain. The walking directions also include information about historical contexts and archeological sites of importance. Through such documentation, SouthWest Walks Ireland manages complex interactions between people, landscape, animals, organizations, transportation systems, and technology. By creating a number of detailed instructions and supplemental documents, they smooth the way for travelers to navigate new spaces and people (ethnoscapes and mediascapes).

While the Ring of Kerry provides the kinds of tourist accommodation one would expect from full-service bus tours, the hiking trails require more extensive planning as there are few restrooms and no food, accommodations, healthcare, or public safety infrastructure outside of the destination cities. Tour companies like SouthWest Walks Ireland offer information and organization to plan hiking and biking trips from a great distance. Using online media tools and Internet-based international systems, they package the Irish countryside for easy access. Despite crossing the roads and seeing the huge buses full of other tourists, the Kerry Way trail allows hikers and walkers to feel removed from global technology. In what appears to be access to wildness those walking tours create the tourist experience of moving outside of time.

The ideoscape that is initially created in the recurring online marketing gains traction when the interested tourist (and future documentation user) makes an initial inquiry – via online media – about setting up a tour. On SouthWest Walk Ireland's Website, for example, a tempted tourist can find a description of the Kerry self-guided walking tour. As noted on the company's Website, "This trip takes us on a circular route from Killarney, unveiling some of the most beautiful scenery in the region, exploring both the southern and northern coastlines of the Iveragh peninsula. … The daily stages take you cross-country, and the landscape can be quite hilly at times. During the week you'll experience dramatic, almost wild, scenery, along with picturesque coastal villages" (SouthWest Walk Ireland, 2008, para. 4). This inviting description is surrounded by several online images that provide an idealized online representation of the walking experience. With no travel agent or company representative actually present, the viewer of this Web page must decide to take the next step and book the tour. Within this context, the appeal of such online images as representing what the prospective hiker will "actually" experience is a key motivator in making travel related decisions.

DOCUMENTATION FACILITATES NARRATIVE TO OVERCOME BREAKDOWNS

Tourism in Ireland confronts Appadurai's (1996) global ethnoscapes both through tourists, who travel large distances to visit, and through workers, who migrate for tourism and other service jobs. Pauline Cullen (2009) suggests that of the "15% of the population now of non-Irish descent" most are from Poland, Latvia, Lithuania, Romania, and the Philippines (p. 106). She further explains that "most migrants are young, well educated, and concentrated in the service industries and agriculture" (p. 106). Because these migrants work in the service industries, they are likely to interact with tourists. The global ethnoscapes created by such interactions might confound tourist ideals even as they make tourism in Ireland possible. Thus companies like SouthWest Walks Ireland must somehow adjust or shape tourist expectations or their interactions. To do so, they use online materials that display and draw attention to the famous hospitality and friendliness of native-born Irish people, while the company concurrently desire (and need) to recruit hospitality service workers from abroad. While on-site ethnoscapes in Ireland reflect the global realities, the tourist industry has yet to integrate that into its online marketing and promotional material. For example, the bed and breakfast establishments in the villages of Sneem and Caherciveen are mature businesses with long-time owners, suggesting tourist ethnoscapes that package native Irish in the same way that they package landscape. Conversations with longtime Bed and Breakfast hosts allow walkers to insulate themselves from the influx of new Irish who staff most service industry jobs, even in remote villages in Ireland. The legendary hospitality of the Irish becomes part of the experience even as the ability to interact with native-born Irish people diminishes. After decades of immigration, in-migration transforms segments of the tourist trade by substituting the new Irish for native-born Irish or the ethnically Irish, if such a thing exists.

In addition to the conflicting model of local versus global ethnoscapes, the tourist industry projects another online incompatibility. It depends on the ability to use online media to display varied landscapes including natural, untouched scenery that tourists' wish to see, in opposition to the push to create vacation homes, other facilities, and conveniences for tourists in those very untouched spaces. This second contradiction in Irish tourism, that of real-world land use to bring tourists vs. online depictions of land use that tourists subject to the gaze proves a tricky one, as no nation can afford to disguise its entire production infrastructure. Because Ireland is progressing in much the same cultural logic that saturates much of late capitalism, this infrastructure threatens to implode all distinctions. Just a few steps away from international tourist destinations are big box retailers, outlet malls, and suburban and exurban development. While the landscape fills with unmistakable globalism, the Irish tourist industry continues to use online media to weave increasingly just-in-time technoscapes to fulfill the expectations of the postmodern tourist.

One way that Irish tourism fills the gap between national expectations and global realities is to create tours that emphasize natural landscapes while limiting actual interactions with local people, including migrant workers. Of course, highlighting wild landscapes via initial online displays and follow-up on-site tours is hardly a ploy to keep tourists from noticing the influx of immigrants. It does, however, constrain the amount of time spent inhabiting spaces of global alterations while also extending the time in what some tourists may think of as "real Ireland." Thus, the merger of online and on-site landscape enters into global tourism both as a replacement for people and as a space where authenticity gets virtually constructed and perhaps later undercut by real-world experiences. However, in addition to the conflicting model of local versus global ethnoscapes, the tourist industry projects another incompatibility via online media. They depend on the ability to use online media to display varied landscapes including natural, untouched scenery that tourists' wish to see, in opposition to the push to create vacation homes, hotels, and other facilities and conveniences for tourists in the midst of those very untouched spaces.

The preliminary information about the Kerry Way self-guided walk that is available from the SouthWest Walks Ireland Website explains that "KERRY gives you a taste of everything—mountains, bogs, coastline, beaches—you name it, we have it" (SouthWest Walk Ireland, 2008, para.

1). Of course, this listing of different types of landscape omits any mention of people or industry (the ways that people earn money to stay alive). The website touts the familiar formula of empty, beautiful landscapes describing the land as

Impossibly green pastures stretch as far as the eye can see, completely empty save for small herds of sheep or goats, and at almost every turn there are spectacular views of mist-covered mountains and wild stretches of uninhabitable coastline where deep fissures have been carved, over the eons, by the pounding waves of the Atlantic Ocean. Here and there along the coast, pretty fishing villages, such as Caherdaniel and Portmagee, have successfully withstood the elements and offer a picturesque contrast to the verdant hills that surround them. (SouthWest Walk Ireland, 2008, para. 1)

SouthWest Walks wants to sell a tourist experience, but the language used on the related Websites models the colonial enterprise of entering an empty space as if the viewer (in this case the tourist) controlled that space. In the walk, one might see backpackers from the continent through hiking, other day hikers, or even locals walking on the boreens, but some days you might walk all day without encountering other humans. Websites marketing tourist holidays in the West and Southwest of Ireland thus present the empty landscape.

Such virtual displays of "emptiness" might both eschew interactions with people and construct a colonial encounter, but it also avoids representations of global capitalism. Because tourism is formulated as the opposite of work (i.e., as leisure, even when it involves strenuous activity), tourism Websites are preserved to avoid reminding tourists of work via imagery that might be associated with work or working. As Barbara O'Connor (1993) explains, "a break from the mundanity of everyday life, particularly a break from work, is a primary rationale for tourists travel"

(p. 71). For these reasons, tourist Websites and online plans carefully construct spaces and routes that do not involve spaces of industry or of other work venues like office parks, downtown buildings, factories, etc. In order to elide any vision of work life, isolation becomes a key component of the tourist landscapes presented online. The pre-modern desires of modern subjects reach to natural vistas to escape images of production and commerce, which, in-turn helps reinforce notions of modernity and superiority.

Online representations of tours like South West Walks' self-guided walk through the Kerry Way push tourists to return to landscapes, the origin of Appadurai's (1996) scapes, while taking advantage of global ethnoscapes, ideoscapes, and mediascapes at the same time. While this online push back to the landscape seems to escape globalism's reach, it cannot. O'Connor (1993) explains that "While Ireland has always enjoyed a 'green' image in terms of the colour and freshness of the landscape it has acquired an additional inflection in the recent past as an unpolluted land" (p. 74). Even in the wild, seemingly natural areas of the Kerry Way hiking tour, the effects of global economic progress are displayed in some online images. An image of a clearcut forest between Sneem and Caherdaniel displays a shocking space of resource management in the midst of the unspoiled scenery the tour must tout, while the image of suburban housing developments that crop up in the midst of sheep farms suggested to us that the housing obsession and bubble that moved from Japan to the US, made its way to Ireland as well. While the tour mainly displays the green landscape, these moments of interruption in that landscape created a gap between our tourist expectations and global reality, a gap that our tour company filled with our desire for narrative. While it was true that cognitive, emotional, and task goals play a role in driving through the landscape, it is the desire to merge online information with real-world experiences into a coherent story that keeps tourists slogging through muddy fields, tripping past new developments, and struggling on an exposed ridge that skirted an open mine.

HIDING IDEOSCAPE DISRUPTIONS WITH TECHNOSCAPE SPLICING

Distinct tourism practices bridge different elements of culture, narrative, and serendipity into individualized routes through landscapes via ethnoscapes and mediascapes. The wayfinding connections between landmarks, ethnomarks, and mediamarks in online media and on-site experiences involve a wide range of communicative practices—from some of the more traditional narrative foregrounding in travel writing and guidebooks, to more contemporary practices of webpage advertisement, technical documentation, multi-medic tourist attractions, and remote cellphone communication. Technical communication and new media seal the seams between a contemporary, more globalized tourist experience of the Celtic Tiger and an ancient peripatetic transection of the Iveragh Peninsula. Writing mediates the relationship between transnational media practices and the reproduction of ethos/credibility through tourist border crossing via do-it-yourself postnational tourism facilitated through online media. Technoscape and ideoscape assemblages attest to different narratives besides a famine-cleared rustic landscape and the postmodern and global tourist trade. Railroad ties that once undergirded the rails of the now-defunct branch-line services in Kerry have been repurposed as dry paths through mushy glens. Beaches that once provided the final scene for the masses who left in famine ships now provide the backdrop for tourists exiting the Daniel O'Connell Derrynane House multimedia presentation as well as landings for fishing boats and sports craft. Online images of repurposed elements of the landscape and the once-lonely beaches now filled with pleasure craft and tourists present the cultural tourist with possible disruptions.

DOCUMENTATION BEST PRACTICES LEAN ON IDENTITY

The documentation that guides tourists across the Irish landscape are produced cheaply and maintained online through the kind of collaborative effort that would be the envy of open-source communities. Walking directions must alter as the landscape changes. One particularly noteworthy breakdown in the documentation the authors experienced personally involved encountering a segment of trees that had been clear-cut and cordoned off with a fence warning people away from entering the newly shorn space. While the large directions did not indicate that this event had happened or that the fence stood between us and our route, we were able to find our way by climbing over the gate and progressing through the maze of tree stumps (there were temporary plastic signs affixed to a few tree stumps to urge hikers forward, despite the lack of any visible directions at the fence).

This experience represented a difficult moment in the walking tour – and exemplified the challenges of balancing the virtual and the real Ireland – for a number of reasons. To begin, the razed trees erased the greenness and freshness of the landscapes we had seen online and reminded us of the technological prowess required to clear cut a large area quickly and cleanly, leaving brown stubbly trunks. The obvious industrial uses for trees like construction of new homes overshadows more traditional forms of husbandry to the land and led to an emotional rejection of what we were seeing. Our experience of the ideoscape as presented to us in the pre-trip online media we reviewed conflicted with our wishes for the real-world ideoscape we were experiencing. We wanted a pre-modern experience of Irish green hills—the online representation that had attracted us here—and not a contemporary walk through a working tree farm. Additionally, at this point, the documentation breaks down, revealing the weaknesses in what had otherwise been a nearly

flawless description of the space as had been presented online. While the online documents can be updated to indicate the way through this altered landscape, they might not be able to overcome the shock of interpolating contemporary technological adjustment into natural spaces. It was only the combination of user desire to overcome the cognitive dissonance between the virtual and the real and the knowledge that we were contributing to a larger effort that propelled us through the difficulties.

Through this examination of the tourism industry in Ireland, we have seen how appeals to user identity apply to documentation for Irish tourism in the global context, but those appeals could be used in other fields. To return to Constant, Sproull, and Kiesler's (1996) work, industries like computer manufacturing could take up these lessons in user motivation to improve their online documentation. Examining local, national, and global identities for spaces of desire, specifically spaces for connecting to others and completing tasks (goals that tourism and computer manufacturers share), documentation authors can create more effective online materials. With documents that integrate users' identities with their tasks, individuals conveying information globally online can provide individuals with motivation for both using the online information to complete tasks and for helping others with similar tasks.

Using an open methodology might be a way to convince individuals to use online documentation as desired by the creators of those materials. In other words, a two-way relationship, where users can talk back to online documents and possibly effect change related to improving such materials builds in an incentive for users to pay close attention to online information and instructions. Looking forward, this case study provides online global businesses with alternatives to help users work through breakdowns. Based on these ideas, individuals can adopt the following strategies to apply these ideas when interacting with other cultures via online media:

- Design online documentation to appeal to local, national, and global identity. The same kinds of motivations that inspire tourists to endure hardship across breakdowns can provide inspiration for documentation users to identify, attend to, and overcome technical breakdowns.
- Provide users with opportunities to provide feedback on how they used or needed to augment existing online instructions or information. Identity consists not in just satisfying ever-occurring cognitive needs, but in movement across online spaces in order to achieve individual and group-driven goals.
- Create a way to record breakdowns (i.e., problems created by incomplete or dated online documentation) when they occur and to provide feedback through multiple channels. In the case of the tourism company, this option to supply feedback consisted of both phone comments made during the hike and written comments given to the company after the hike was completed. Online documenters should avail themselves of similarly diverse methods of recording and reporting breakdowns.
- Provide users of online documents with multiple ways for verifying and modifying online instructions and other online information. The tourism company cited in this chapter provided individuals with not only methods for recording breakdowns, but also for navigating technoscapes, ethnoscapes, and ideoscapes through instruction customization.
- Use open design features to ensure buy-in from users from different cultures. Although more closed forms of documentation (i.e., localization and other self-contained pre-composed instructions, for example) can provide satisfying and complete user experiences, more open methods for revising and contributing to

online document development can address different user experiences related to cultural differences. Successful global tourism companies create documentation that acknowledges this diversity through open methodology.

Giving individuals a chance to modify online documentation based on their experiences using it invites a range of persons to provide alternative ways of progressing through what may seem instrumental steps (but what ultimately can be a malleable and culturally-specific logic of progression through tasks). Finally, documentation experts should appeal to identity as a motivating factor to convince users to take steps that engage with open models for creating online materials. Providing users with the chance to participate in such processes can lead to the creation of more effective online materials that address the needs and expectations of a wide range of international audiences.

REFERENCES

Appadurai, A. (1996). *Modernity at large: Cultural dimensions of globalization*. Minneapolis, MN: University of Minnesota Press.

Burke, K. (1950). *A rhetoric of motives*. Berkeley, CA: University of California Press.

Constant, D., Spoull, L., & Kiesler, S. (1996). The kindness of strangers: The usefulness of electronic weak ties for technical advice. *Organization Science*, 7(2), 119–135. doi:10.1287/orsc.7.2.119

Cullen, P. P. (2009). Irish pro-migrant nongovernmental organizations and the politics of immigration. *Voluntas*, *20*, 99–128. doi:10.1007/s11266-009-9084-1

Dobrin, D. N. (1983). What's technical about technical writing? In Johnson-Eilola, J., & Selber, S. (Eds.), *Central works in technical communication* (pp. 108–123). Oxford, UK: Oxford University Press.

Faber, B. (2002). *Community action and organizational change: Image, narrative, identity.* Carbondale, IL: Southern Illinois University Press.

Farkas, D. K. (1999). The logical and rhetorical construction of procedural discourse. *Technical Communication, 46*(1), 42–54.

Gibson, J. J. (1977). The theory of affordances. In Shaw, R. E., & Bransford, J. (Eds.), *Perceiving, acting, and knowing* (pp. 67–82). Hillsdale, NJ: Erlbaum.

O'Connor, B. (1993). Myths and mirrors: Tourist images and national identity. In B. O'Connor & M. Cronin (Eds.), *Tourism in Ireland: A critical analysis* (pp/ 68-85). Cork, Ireland: Cork University Press.

Reichel, A., Uriely, N., & Shani, A. (2008). Ecotourism and simulated attractions: Tourists' attitudes towards integrated sites in a desert area. *Journal of Sustainable Tourism, 16*(1), 23–41. doi:10.2167/jost711.0

Scacci, W. (2010). Collaboration practices and affordances in free/open source software development. In Mistrik, I. (Eds.), *Collaborative software engineering* (pp. 307–328). Berlin, Germany: Springer-Verlag. doi:10.1007/978-3-642-10294-3_15

Scott, J. B. (2003). *Risky rhetoric: AIDS and the cultural practices of HIV testing.* Carbondale, IL: Southern Illinois University Press.

Selber, S. A. (2010). A rhetoric of electronic instruction sets. *Technical Communication Quarterly, 19*(2), 95–117. doi:10.1080/10572250903559340

SouthWest Walks. (2008, August 16). *Kerry Way self-guided 8-day holiday programme.* Retrieved November 1, 2010, from http://www.southwestwalks ireland.com/walking-holiday-ireland-kerry-peninsula/ self-guided-walks.html

Spinuzzi, C. (2003). *Tracing genres through organizations: A sociocultural approach to information design.* Cambridge, MA: The MIT Press.

Spinuzzi, C. (2008). *Network: Theorizing knowledge work in telecommunications.* New York, NY: Cambridge University Press. doi:10.1017/CBO9780511509605

Van der Meij, H. (2007). Goal-orientation, goal-setting, and goal-driven behavior in minimalist user instructions. *IEEE Transactions on Professional Communication, 50*(4), 295–305. doi:10.1109/TPC.2007.908728

Williams, W. (2008). *Tourism, landscape, and the Irish character: British travel writers in pre-famine Ireland.* Madison, WI: University of Wisconsin Press.

KEY TERMS AND DEFINITIONS

Affect: An individual's lived emotional state considered apart from physical or intellectual explanations.

Affordances: Properties or qualities of systems that help users achieve goals or execute actions (i.e., a menu button).

Do-It-Yourself (DIY): Any task that depends upon and foregrounds the intrinsic motivation of the client/customer to complete a set of tasks beyond purchase and consumption of a prefabricated good or experience.

Documentation: Genres of writing created for support in the use of various technologies and/or processes.

Ethnoscapes: The landscape of people demarcated by group identification markings and practices that transcend and cross national boundaries.

Identity: A narrative or persona whereby people integrate details and experiences into a coherent story about themselves.

Ideoscapes: Series of linked images with political meaning, sometimes in the service of nation-states.

Motivation: Desire to begin, continue, extend, or improve activity, especially interaction with technologies or documents.

Postnational: Systems, entities, situations that disregard or supercede national borders, especially non-governmental organizations or global capital flows.

Self-Service: Any service that depends upon and foregrounds the intrinsic motivation of the client/customer to complete a set of tasks beyond purchase and consumption of a prefabricated good or experience.

Tourism: Traveling for leisure purposes, often involving sightseeing.

Technoscapes: An array of connected technologies that move stories quickly across boundaries in global flows.

Chapter 13

Studying Online Communication Features on International and Cross-Cultural Web Pages Using Websphere Analysis Methodology

Kathryn Stam
State University of New York Institute of Technology, USA

Indira Guzman
TUI University, USA

Dennis Thoryk
Onondaga Community College, USA

ABSTRACT

Some websites, and the specific Web pages within them, are designed specifically to facilitate online communication across countries and cultures. For this reason, these sites often contain a variety of features for international interaction. Such features include language choices, instant messaging, or use of a translation tool. The purpose of this chapter is to identify current practices and opportunities for online communication between people from different countries or speakers of different languages. To examine this topic, the authors used the Websphere analysis methodology (Schneider & Foot, 2004) to conduct an analysis of 160 archived international and cross-cultural Web pages in order to identify their communication features.

INTRODUCTION

Communication across cultures and languages is essential for certain kinds of international work, commerce, and education, as well as other reasons. Examples of this work include Web page design, the development of Web pages for study abroad programs, creating online travel sites, and developing international online dating services. Web pages designed specifically for these purposes can facilitate online communication or hinder it due, in large part, to the features a Web designer

DOI: 10.4018/978-1-60960-833-0.ch013

includes on such pages. Some of these features for communication or further interaction might include contacting the owner of the Web page, signing up for a newsletter, becoming a member, using a translation tool, or following hyperlinks to related resources.

The purpose of this chapter is to identify and evaluate current practices and opportunities for online communication between people from different countries and languages as identified within a set of archived Web pages. For the purpose of this study, the terms "international" and "cross-cultural" are used interchangeably to refer to Websites designed to help people from different nations and cultural groups access or share information online. The main goal of this research project was to identify a large number of possible features that corresponded to particular actions a user might be able to locate or to perform on a given page. The main collection of Web pages examines sites that were hosted in a variety of countries but that also targeted audiences from a variety of cultures or nations (i.e., sites designed for international vs. domestic audiences).

The approach the authors/researchers used to collect and review data for this study involved Schneider and Foot's (2004) Websphere analysis methodology. The authors/researchers selected this approach because they felt it was an appropriate mechanism based upon its focus on defining a topic of interest, creating a collection of relevant Web pages, and saving these pages as a "Websphere" for closer study and analysis later. In the study discussed in this chapter, the authors identified and archived 160 Websites of interest, and these sites were selected based on their anticipated international audience vs. a specific domestic/national one. The researchers then used Zotero (a powerful online research tool) to archive Web pages of interest. The authors wish to note that this study focused on the features and contents of the archived Web pages identified for review and not on the particulars of the cultures of any of the countries in which these Websites were created or located.

BACKGROUND

The context of the work presented here is situated within current research on the relationship between culture and the design and the use of Web pages. In this section, the authors present a small selection of related materials that served as a foundation that guided the research they did on this topic area.

To begin, it is important to note that the role of communication styles and other cultural features on the Internet has long been accepted as important by researchers from a range of fields. For example, Hermeking's (2004) work found that customers from "Uncertainty Avoidance" cultures, where predictability is important overall, also tended to be less innovative in their Internet use. Similar work (de Mooij, 2004) focuses on the role of individualism as a cultural characteristic, as well as high-context vs. low-context communication styles online (Wurtz, 2004). According to this concept, people from high-context cultures (e.g., individuals from Japan or Latin America) are considered as tending to have close and familiar communication with each other and were comfortable with informal and indirect styles of conveying information. By contrast, individuals from low-context cultures (e.g., individuals from the German-speaking part of Switzerland or from Germany) tend to focus on detailed and explicit methods for conveying information.

Other studies further reflect the idea that research subjects in experiments usually prefer Web content that reflects information related to their particular cultural group (Baack & Singh, 2007). This factor relates to the study presented here because there is much to be learned about how different cultures attempt to facilitate cultural communication online. The challenge then becomes determining what role and how great a role cultural factors play in online interactions. The analysis presented in this chapter aims to reveal the current state of Web designers' efforts to bridge cultural gaps in creating online materials for international audiences comprised of members of many different cultures.

Previous cross-cultural comparison of corporate Websites found that U.S. Websites studied emphasized online marketing and social responsibility while Chinese Websites studied seemed to focus more on consumer-consumer interactions (Cho & Hongsik, 2005; Pan & Xu, 2009). These findings support the thought that Website communications follow traditional cultural communication styles. International tourism Websites have similarly been studied in terms of how cultural differences explain design and content variations in sites created by individuals from different cultures (Kang & Mastin, 2008). In other instances, cultural cognition theory has been used to emphasize how cultural cognitive processes might shape Web design. Such research claims users find information more quickly when using sites designed by people from their (the users') same culture (Faiola & Matei, 2005). The conclusion often drawn from these studies is that corporate marketers would benefit more from locally customizing (i.e., localizing) their Websites rather than using a standard for global marketing to create sites for broad, international audiences.

Differences in how cultures use Websites and adjustments that should be made for different cultural groups are the subject of Seidenspinner and Theuner's (2007) work that compares vastly different language groups (e.g., Mandarin, Egyptian, and German) in their uses of online materials. Seidenspinner and Theuner found that culture might affect preferences related to navigation tools, the quality or aesthetics of Web designs, and the processing of online information available on a given site. It follows that users from different cultures would also interact with communication features in different ways that tended to be bound by culture. For these reasons, individuals such as Al-Badi and Naqvi (2009) recommend that Web designers take into account the variety of serious and unexpected differences - everything from date formats to phone number formats - that suggest

knowing the target customer's culture and making accommodations to localize online materials for the members of specific cultures.

A major development in the concept of applying cultural factors into Web development is the theoretical cross-cultural Web design model (Hsieh et. al., 2009, p. 718). The emphasis of this model is to suggest improved Web design that is localized and takes into account the many factors that enhance cultural appropriateness. This model is generally seen as thorough, and it requires individuals (i.e., Web designers or Web localizers) to synthesize a wide array of literature to develop a model for creating a culture-specific Website.

The authors of this chapter approach the problem of culture and Web design from a different angle. Although the theoretical cross-cultural Web design model is quite relevant to the work of the authors, the authors are trying to understand a smaller piece of Web communication in order to study the phenomenon empirically and to survey and describe current practice. For this reason, the authors take a slightly different approach to examining how factors of culture and communication affect Website design in international contexts.

Companies and other organizations that have international Websites have realized that local cultural perspectives can be a major determining factor for how useful the members of a particular culture consider a Website to be. One consideration in relation to this topic area is the use of cultural attractors (Smith et al., 2004) in the design of a Website. Cultural attractors are the elements that comprise the look and feel of a Website. These elements include the color combinations, language cues, formats for elements such as dates and currency, and other visual and navigation elements that users from a specific culture might expect to find on the average Website they use. Interestingly, early studies of e-commerce Websites – such as the study conducted by World Trade (2000) – determined that Websites tailored to local cultures should be more successful than Websites designed for "generic" international audiences. Thus, cultural attractors are a major factor to consider in designing online materials for individuals from different cultures.

The idea of cultural attractors is based on semiotics, or the study of signs and their meanings. This notion can also be applied to computer-based signs. That is, cultural and social influences play a part determining the meaning users assign to computer-based signs (Smith et al., 2004). This kind of association relates to the research done by the authors because the elements examined in the authors' feature analysis could be considered cultural attractors according to this semiotics-based definition. The aim of the authors, however, is not to verify the actual significance of cultural dimensions. Rather, the authors wish to focus on examining existing Web features that seem to facilitate cross-cultural communication in online settings.

DESCRIPTION OF THE WEBSPHERE

The vision behind the data set examined by the authors came from the Websphere concept (Schneider & Foot, 2004). This concept involves the identification and archiving of a collection Web pages based on the theme of cross-cultural or international communication. A Websphere, in turn, is defined as "a hyperlinked set of dynamically defined digital resources spanning multiple Websites deemed relevant or related to a central theme" (Schneider & Foot, 2005; Foot & Schneider, 2002, p. 226). This is a mixed method approach, and it involves content and feature analysis to categorize the main attributes and important communication possibilities of Web pages. Note that the term, "Web page" is used to describe the specific pages that were archived, while the term "Website" refers to the original sites viewed.

The sample of Web pages the authors visited for their analysis and that were then used to comprise the Websphere for this study came from 120 general Websites selected because they represented/ were the communication product of organization or companies that operated globally and thus sought to share information online with a wide, international audience. Many of the Websites selected for analysis were hosted in the U.S., but the sites that were reviewed also include multinational sites hosted in other nations. An additional set of sites that were reviewed contained 40 Web pages focused on Thai and Brazilian topics. These sites were added to the study in order to maximize the variety of features the authors would be able to find. Although the authors often viewed more than one page within a site, they archived the homepage, or the first page of a site, where cross-cultural or international communication features were present. The archived Web pages were organized by type of Web page, the communication features contained on ancillary pages individuals could access from the splash page via a single click, and by the country that created and housed the site.

METHODS

The focus of the study presented in this chapter is the different cross-cultural communication features that exist within Web pages and the type of communication these features facilitate. In this study, communication refers to the different information exchange options between the user and the Website administration. These options include features that allow a user to contact the Website owner, search the Website, or just view the information posted on the Website in order to understand the message the Website is trying to convey to the user. Cross-cultural communication features can include graphical icons, text only, other tools or applications, or some combination of all of these items. In the view of the authors, communication could be facilitated through the use of the variety of features already on certain types of Websites or popular in some geographical areas.

The method for data collection involved determining what Websites should be included in the sample set. The Website of a company or an organization that had a global presence or organizational Websites that seemed targeted toward international audiences/users from different countries were used as the theme for the Websphere. No particular key words were used to search for such sites. Rather, the authors'/researchres' experiences drove the identification process. Once a Web page for analysis was located, the related site was archived using Zotero (www.zotero.org). Zotero, in turn, is a free Firefox research tool that helps with the management of bibliographic resources and allows the storage of Web pages in a manner that allows these pages to be shared with other members of a research team.

The Websphere analysis method often has a temporal aspect, and this aspect has been previously used by other researchers to examine topics such as political elections. In the case of this research project, the authors chose to use this Websphere to capture an archive of current practices at one point in time. The Web pages selected for analysis were not particularly time sensitive. Additionally, all 160 pages were archived within about two weeks of each other.

The authors/researchers performed the data analysis process as a team of four, and they used a spreadsheet with rows to delineate each Web page studied and columns used to log the availability of each communication feature found on a given Web page. The Web pages were then visited to determine if and what cross-cultural or cross-language communication features were present. Each site was, in turn, crosschecked by another team member to establish inter-rater reliability associated with the identification of a particular design feature.

The cross-cultural communication features were then identified and marked on a master spreadsheet. In performing this process, the authors/researchers viewed the splash page for each site. In reviewing these pages, however, the authors/researchers either stayed on the main/splash page for each site or only followed links one level down (i.e., only viewed pages one could access via a single click from the splash page). The authors used this approach because they were interested in opportunities users could find quickly and without much time or effort. It should be noted that the feature categories reviewed during this research were not determined ahead of time. Rather, these categories emerged intuitively as the authors progressed in this review process. The aim of this approach (and of the overall project) was inclusion, so the authors tried to find and to count as many features as possible that might be used for communication, be it direct or indirect communication. The researchers then collected country-specific Websites/pages separately and they analyzed these sites separately as well.

RESULTS

This section contains a list of the communication features the authors found in their review of the entire Websphere comprised of the 160 Web pages they reviewed. This listing of features also presents a summary of the features' frequency across the various Websites that were reviewed. The authors have also provided a comparison of the general group of Web pages reviewed and provide country-specific information in order to try to identify culture-specific features or differences on and across different sites.

The authors found that there are many current Website features that can facilitate communication. Through a review of these sites, the authors were able to identify a set of international and/or cross-cultural Websites and archived the relevant pages from these sites. The authors found similar, or in some cases identical, sites/pages when they searched the Websphere they had compiled. Additionally, the communication features were identifiable. That is, different authors/researchers found identical communication features across different Web pages and identified them as communication features.

In terms of the research tools used, Zotero and Excel worked well for archiving, sharing, and analyzing data. Zotero was reliable and easy to learn. Additionally, its data sharing, annotations, and archive functions worked well for purposes of this study. Through using these tools, the researchers found that many Web designers appear not to be using the full potential of the various communication features available to them. It is unclear what the reason for this factor is. It would, however, be interesting to find out if such restricted use is due to lack of awareness, preferences on the part of the related organization, cultural differences, or some other explanation. In the remainder of this section, the authors describe these results in more detail.

Categories of Websites/Pages

The first result the authors found was that the process of identifying a large number of international and cross-cultural Websites was a rather straightforward one. The authors began the process by purposefully choosing search actions based on their personal experiences, and they then expanded them to find similar Websites. The collection of sites was separated into categories for convenience and to explore the possibility that there were differences between the features found across these sites. Examples of categories identified were:

- Language and Interpreting
- Travel, Religion
- Multinational Food and Beverage Companies
- Gaming and Entertainment,
- Museums
- Humanitarian
- Media
- Banks

There are some miscellaneous Websites that did not naturally fit into one of these larger categories. The list of categories and one example Website for each category are listed in Table 1.

Communication Features Found in the Websphere

Next, the authors found it was possible to identify a large number of communication features for each site, and these features were identified and described consistently by different individuals within the research team. The list of the top ten communication features identified by the researchers as being present across the various sites in the Websphere are shown in Table 2. Some of these features are not specifically cross-cultural or cross-language in nature, but the researchers interpreted them as possible routes by which a user could learn more about or communicate with a person from another culture. (Such interaction could start with the contacting of representatives of an organization as noted on its Website.)

The most popular features the researchers found were

- Contact Options
- Search Capability
- Language Options
- Option to Join or Become a Member

Following these features in popularity were options for

- Country Choice
- Signing Up for Twitter Updates
- Cultural Descriptions
- Signing up for RSS Feed Updates
- Participation in Facebook

Less frequently found features included

- E-newsletters
- Information Maps

Table 1. List of Categories and Examples of Web Pages in Each Category

Category	Title or Brief Description of one example within the category	URL of Example
Language and Interpreting	Rosetta Stone	http://www.rosettastone.com
Travel	Travelocity	http://www.travelocity.com
Religion	The Daily Lama Official Site (Tibetan Buddhism)	http://www.dalailama.com
Multinational Food and Beverage companies	Starbucks Coffee Company	http://www.starbucks.com
Gaming and Entertainment	Nintendo	http://www.nintendo.com
Telecommunications	Skype	http://www.skype.com
Museums	Van Gogh Museum, Netherlands	http://www.vangoghmuseum.nl
Humanitarian	World Health Organization	http://www.who.int/en
Media	BBC World Service	http://www.bbc.co.uk/worldservice
Banks	World Bank	http://www.worldbank.org
Major International Corporations	Proctor & Gamble	http://www.pg.com

- Options to Download Fact Sheets
- Blogs
- "Remember Me" Icons
- Donate or Sponsor Options
- Email
- Forums
- Translation Box
- Testimonials

Features that trailed the others, with less than 5% frequency in the Websphere were

- Podcasts
- Mobile Devices Support
- YouTube Videos
- Picture Gallery
- Money Converter
- Live Chat
- Mailing List
- Online Audio
- Widgets
- Online Publications
- Image Sharing (Flickr)
- Time Conversion Application
- Language Snippet
- Wiki
- Event Announcements

Given all of the possibilities, the authors found it surprising that the Web designers did not take advantage of more of the features. For example, the range in the number of features on a page was from 1-11 out of 35 possibilities that the authors identified. Although certain features might not be appropriate for specific pages, it is likely that adding additional features could enhance the effectiveness of the pages in terms of achieving greater cultural awareness or facilitating further cross-cultural communication.

Frequency of Features of Note in Each Category

The Websphere can be described as containing a diverse set of Websites/pages, as they might have different purposes from commerce to education or awareness about a specific religious tradition. In general, it appeared that a global audience was targeted by most pages in the Websphere.

The most common features appeared throughout the entire list. However, the researchers noticed that certain features were more common in some categories than in others. For example, museum Web pages tended to use cultural descriptions, while language-related Web pages used text

Table 2. Frequency and Description of Communication Features in the Websphere

	Feature	Description of what the feature allows user to do	Facilitates this type of communication:	Frequency (%)
1	Contact Options Org -> User User -> Org	User can contact Webmaster or organizational representative	Direct communication of user with Webmaster or organizational representative	81
2	Search Capability Org -> User Web -> User	User can search the site or an external search engine without going beyond the main page	Info search by user within page/site or externally but not beyond main page	73
3	Language Options Org -> User	A drop box or icon giving choices of the user's preferred language	Info reception by the user in the user's preferred language (2 choices or many)	69
4	Join or Become a Member User -> Org	Option to join the organization or become a member	Formal involvement (commitment) of the user with the organization	48
5	Country Choices Org -> User	A selection of countries where the organization operates is listed in a drop box	User access to Websites specific to geographical location(s) where the organization operates	29
6	Sign up for Twitter Updates User -> Org Org -> User	User can choose to receive Twitter updates (popular social media)	Broadcasting to users using social media	23
7	Cultural Description Org -> User	Some text is provided that explains some cultural points of interest	User's reception of info about cultural points of interest	19
8	RSS Feed Org -> User	User can sign up for updates using an RSS feed, a summary of Web content that shows updates since last visit	User's reception of updated info of Web content since the last visit	16
9	Facebook User -> Social Network	Option to visit Facebook (social media) page or broadcast info about organization or related event using organizational logo designed for Facebook	User's broadcasting of info of his/her interest to a social network through Facebook (social media)	15
10	E-Newsletter Org -> User	Availability of an electronic-newsletter	User access to info on organizational news (updates)	10
11	Information Maps Org -> User	Color-coded maps with information about the organization or about the areas in which the organization operates	Info access for the user in a graphical format (i.e. color-coded maps, areas of which organization operates)	10
12	Download Fact Sheets Org -> User	Availability of downloadable files in a variety of formats, giving organizational information	nfo access for the user to factual information about the organization in easy to use formats	9
13	Blogs Org -> User User -> Org User -> Web Org -> Web	Option to go to a blog (Weblog) with more information or commentary about organizational activities	Exchange of info. (i.e. opinions, answers and questions) between the user, the organization of other Web visitors	9
14	Remember Me User -> Org	Option to have browser recognize site and login information for easier access to Web page	Instant site recognition of the user's preferences as saved on user's browser	7
15	Donate or Sponsor User -> Org	Option to donate money or sponsor an activity using a credit card or other service; leads to registration form or instructions	Formal involvement of the user with the organization's activities through registration and donation	6
16	Email Org -> User User -> Org	Option to send email to Webmaster or organizational representative	Direct communication of the user with the Webmaster or organizational representative.	6
17	Discussion Forums Org -> User User -> Org User -> Web Org -> Web	User can participate in chat group or discussion forums about organizational activities; can pose questions or get help from community or organization	Exchange of information (i.e. opinions, answers and questions) between the user, the organization and other Web visitors	6

continues on the following page

Table 2. continued

	Feature	Description of what the feature allows user to do	Facilitates this type of communication:	Frequency (%)
18	Translation Box Org -> User	User can insert text in one language and get an instant translation in another, or user can submit URL and get translation of entire Web page (Note: quality is unpredictable)	Information reception by user in user's preferred language	6
19	Testimonials Web -> User Org -> User	User can access testimonials by members, consumers, or other interested parties	Exchange of info (i.e. opinions, answers and questions) between previous visitors and user. This could be info selected by the org.	5
20	Podcasts Org -> User	User can sign up for downloadable or streamed audio podcasts from org. reps. or about org. activities	Access for the user to info on organizational news (updates) in audio format	5
21	Mobile Devices Support Org -> User	User can have updates about the organization or their account, etc., sent to their mobile phone or other device	User's reception of updated information to their mobile phone or similar device	6
22	YouTube Org -> User	Link to YouTube video or embedded player available for showing video about organizational activities	User access to information on organizational news (updates) in video format	5
23	Photo or Image Gallery Org -> User	Photos or other images are displayed on a gallery page or main page	User access to information on organizational news (updates) in visual format	6
24	Currency converter Org -> User	User can use converter to find out up-to-date currency conversion rates for the relevant countries	Financial information reception by the user in the user's preferred currency	5
25	Live Chat User -> Org Org -> User	Option to talk with a live person using a chat window	Direct live communication of user with Webmaster or organizational representative	3
26	Mailing List User -> Org Org -> User	User can sign up for a mailing list that will send information physically or by email to the address they provide	Direct reception of updates through email or regular mail to user. User provides personal address	2
	Online Audio Org -> User	User can listen to audio related to organizational activities	User access to info on organizational news (updates) in audio format	2
27	Widgets Web -> User	A convenient tool, such as a weather forecast or calendar that is only one keystroke away	Engagement in process of using tool to access additional information	2
28	Online version of publications Org -> User	User can access digital copies of articles, white papers, or books	User access to info on organizational news (updates, articles, reports, books, etc.)	2
29	Photo Sharing (Flickr) User -> Social Network	Connection to an image sharing site (For ex., Flickr), is facilitated from the page	User's broadcasting of visual information of his/her interest to a social network through Facebook (social media)	1
30	Time Conversion Applications Web -> User	Option to open an application or widget that tells what time it is in the other countries relevant to Web page activities	User access to information about local time and reduces misunderstandings	1
31	Language snippets Org -> User	User can listen to audio or view samples of a language of choice	User access to info about the organization in audio and video formats	1
32	Wiki Org -> User User -> Web User -> Org	Option to visit online wiki, a Website that allows community creation and/or editing	Exchange of information (i.e. opinions, answers and questions) between the user, the organization and other Web visitors	1
33	Events Org -> User	Information about organization or related events is offered on the page	User access to info on organizational updated events	1

translation boxes. Banking pages and multinational companies tended to offer country options. Downloadable fact sheets were more common in the Brazilian Web pages studied. Offers for sponsorship or donation options were common in the humanitarian Web pages. Multinational companies tended to have country options, while most of the other Web pages did not contain this feature. (Or at least did not have it on either the site's splash page or any of the pages located one level down on an overall site's architecture.)

Comparison of General Group of Web Pages vs. Country-Specific Web Pages

Note that this comparison is used to give a very rough sense of current practices. The Web pages were not chosen randomly, do not reflect parallel types of sites for each country, and there is a relatively low number of Web pages in each set.

This comparison revealed that there were a similar number of communication features per set of country Web pages (86 for Brazil vs. 91 for Thailand), which would also yield a similar average because there were 20 pages in each set. In general, other features were remarkably similar, for example "language options" for Brazil (16) vs. Thai (13), "money conversion tools" (3) for both, "Twitter" option (3 for each), and neither had any "live chat" options. However, there were some minor differences in features that were popular for each country-specific set. The "search option" feature was more common in the Brazilian set (17) vs. the Thai set (9). Downloadable fact sheets were found in the Brazilian set (9) vs. Thai (0). On the other hand, the feature "information map" was more common in the Thai set (8) vs. Brazil (2) and "picture gallery" was present in the Thai set (5) and not in the Brazilian set.

These findings do not suggest major differences in Web page design across cultures, in part because identifying such distinctions was not the aim of this research project. These findings do suggest,

however, that there are some differences in the popularity/use of specific communication features. This study shows how one might go about studying this topic with larger numbers of Web pages, a wider range of countries, more deliberate choice of Web pages, and deeper analysis included.

DISCUSSION

This study expands the literature on communicative features on Websites because the authors were able to identify and categorize some of the main features, as well as less common features, currently being used by Web designers. The features provide a myriad opportunity to promote cultural exchange, including the use of different languages, location images, updated information, sound, and videos that – if used correctly – can facilitate interaction, involvement, and awareness among people from different cultures. In addition, the communication features identified through this research also provide opportunities to facilitate formal involvement of the users through registration, membership, and donations. Finally, these features facilitate the broadcast of information from an organization to a user and possibly to the various social networks in which that user participates. If users appreciate the information they receive, they can contribute to this information by including their own opinions and experiences (e.g., by using blogs, discussion forums, and testimonials) as well as use online media to share that information with others.

The Thailand and Brazil-related Websites were quite different from the main set of international sites reviewed, and this factor made comparison across sites difficult. Although these Brazilian and Thai sites were important for identifying a larger number of features, the authors think it would be important to choose a larger number parallel sites if they were to use such sites for comparison. On the other hand, it is quite possible that a large group of parallel Websites might not exist for different countries or cultures precisely because of their cultural and linguistic differences. Overall, the authors found it interesting that certain features appeared more commonly in the Thailand-related vs. the Brazil-related Websites.

The author's efforts to reveal the current state of international Web designers' activities did not, however, explain much about how the actual Web designers are attempting to bridge cultural gaps with their work. It was evident that designers seem to put features on Websites to facilitate communication, but more information is needed to understand the actual intentions of the Web designer in making design choices. These Web features are very powerful for disseminating cultural characteristics, and it is unfortunate that Web developers do not seem to use them more. At the same time, it is not clear that adding such features would align with the objectives of the other Websites.

CONCLUSION AND FUTURE RESEARCH

This study shows it is possible to identify a group of international Websites, archive the main pages of each site as a data set, and then analyze these sites and data sets as a group. There are, of course, a variety of features in current use that can facilitate communication between people from different cultures. The authors were able to identify a set of international and/or cross-cultural Websites and then archive the main pages from these Websites. The search by four different team members reveals similar results, and the communication features were also identifiable. Different team members found identical communication features across Web pages and identified them as communication features.

The authors think the combination of the Web-sphere analysis method and archiving with Zotero is promising. The method, used for one time unit rather than the more typical temporal method,

was still useful for helping a group of researchers identify and analyze features found on Websites/pages. Accordingly, the authors' assessment of Web designers' use of these features was that the designers did not appear to be using the full potential of the various communication features available to them. What factors are prompting this lack of use of these features remains unclear, but it would be interesting to find out if this lack of use is due to lack of awareness, preferences on the part of the organizations, cultural differences, or some other explanation. It would also be interesting to review the collected Web pages through the lens of Hsieh et al.'s (2009) model or identify and test areas in which the Web design could be enhanced through localization and attention to the many measures of cultural appropriateness. Along the same lines, further investigation of the potential to encourage more widespread adoption of communication features that are not currently used in a certain category or country would be intriguing as well.

Another area for further study would be how these online design features could be presented in culturally specific ways in order to make it easier for someone from another culture to recognize and use them. One could imagine combining the archiving method used for this research project with expertise from the field of human-computer interaction (perhaps with a focus on usability). The authors hope that the research results presented in this chapter have provided readers with a better sense of what features and content are helpful for creating and improving international Web pages in order to enhance cross-cultural communication online.

REFERENCES

Al-Badi, A., & Naqvi, S. (2009). A conceptual framework for designing localized business websites. *Journal of Management & Marketing Research, 2*, 113–120.

Baack, D. W., & Singh, N. (2006). Culture and Web communications. *Journal of Business Research, 60*(3), 181–188. doi:10.1016/j.jbusres.2006.11.002

Blake, B. F., & Neuendorf, K. (2004). Cross-national differences in website appeal: A framework for assessment. *Journal of Computer-Mediated Communication, 9*(4). Retrieved October 10, 2010, from http://jcmc.indiana.edu/vol9/ issue4/ blake_neuendorf.html

Cho, C. H., & Hongsik, J. C. (2005). Cross-cultural comparisons of interactivity on corporate websites: The United States, the United Kingdom, Japan, and South Korea. *Journal of Advertising, 34*(2), 99–115.

Faiola, A., & Matei, S. A. (2005). Cultural cognitive style and Web design: Beyond a behavioral inquiry into computer-mediated communication. *Journal of Computer-Mediated Communication, 11*(1). Retrieved October 10, 2020, from http:// jcmc.indiana.edu/vol11 /issue1/faiola.html

Foot, K. A., & Schneider, S. M. (2002). Online action in campaign 2001: An exploratory analysis of the US political Web sphere. *Journal of Broadcasting & Electronic Media, 42*(2), 222–244. doi:10.1207/s15506878jobem4602_4

Hermeking, M. (2005). Culture and Internet consumption: Contributions from cross-cultural marketing and advertising research. *Journal of Computer-Mediated Communication, 11*(1). Retrieved October 10, 2010, from http://jcmc. indiana.edu/vol11/ issue1/hermeking.html

Hsieh, C. H., Holland, R., & Young, M. (2009). A theoretical model for cross-cultural Web design. *Human-Computer Interaction, 10*, 712–721.

Kang, D., & Mastin, T. (2008). How cultural difference affects international tourism public relations websites: A comparative analysis using Hofstede's cultural dimensions. *Public Relations Review, 34*(1), 54–56. doi:10.1016/j.pubrev.2007.11.002

Luna, D., Peracchio, L. A., & de Juan, M. D. (2002). Cross-cultural and cognitive aspects of website navigation. *Journal of the Academy of Marketing Science, 30*(4), 397–410. doi:10.1177/009207002236913

Mooij, M. (1998). *Global marketing and advertising: Understanding cultural paradoxes*. Thousand Oaks, CA.

Nelson, M., & Otnes, C. C. (2005). Exploring cross-cultural ambivalence: A netnography of intercultural wedding message boards. *Journal of Business Research, 58*(1), 89–95. doi:10.1016/ S0148-2963(02)00477-0

Pan, P., & Xu, J. (2009). Online strategic communication: A cross-cultural analysis of U.S. and Chinese corporate websites. *Public Relations Review, 35*(3), 251–253. doi:10.1016/j.pubrev.2009.04.002

Schneider, S. M., & Foot, K. A. (2005). Web sphere analysis: An approach to studying online action . In Hine, C. (Ed.), *Virtual methods: Issues in social research on the Internet*. Basingstoke, UK: Berg Publishers.

Seidenspinner, M., & Theuner, G. (2007). Intercultural aspects of online communication: A comparison of Mandarin-speaking, U.S., Egyptian, and German user preferences. *Journal of Business Economics & Management, 8*(2), 101–109.

Simon, S. J. (2001). The impact of culture and gender on websites: An empirical study. *The Data Base for Advances in Information Systems, 32*(1), 18–37.

Singh, N., & Baack, D. (2004). Web site adaptation: A cross-cultural comparison of U.S. and Mexican websites. *Journal of Computer-Mediated Communication, 4*. Retrieved October 10, 2010, from http://jcmc.indiana.edu/vol9/ issue4/ singh_baack.html

Smith, A., Dunckley, L., French, T., Minoch, S., & Chang, Y. (2004). A process model for developing usable cross-cultural websites. *Interacting with Computers, 16*(1), 63–91. doi:10.1016/j. intcom.2003.11.005

Würtz, E. (2005). A cross-cultural analysis of websites from high-context cultures and low-context cultures. *Journal of Computer-Mediated Communication, 11*(1). Retrieved October 10, 2010, from http://jcmc.indiana.edu/vol11/ issue1/ wuertz.html

KEY TERMS AND DEFINITIONS

Communication Features: These are features for a user and a Web page host to facilitate communication in some way, and that a researcher can identify on a Web page (For example, contact options, language options, opportunities to sign up for information).

Country-Specific Web Pages: Web pages originating from a certain country, or intended to be used by people of a certain country.

Cross-Cultural/International: (used interchangeably) refers to Websites designed to help people from different nations or cultural groups access information online.

Websphere: a group of Websites around a specific theme (for example, an event such as an election or a disaster) connected by hyperlinks and spanning multiple Websites. A Websphere may or may not include a temporal focus.

Zotero: An online research tool that helps the researcher archive, organize, and analyze Webpages and Websites.

Chapter 14
Minimizing Cultural Differences Using Ontology–Based Information Retrieval System

Myongho Yi
Texas Woman's University, USA

ABSTRACT

Effective global information access is more critical now than ever before. The digital world where users have diverse languages and diverse cultural backgrounds is increasing more rapidly than at any other time in history. This chapter addresses the cause of ineffective international information access from the standpoint of the user as well as from an information and system perspectives. The chapter also describes the traditional and emerging approaches to enhancing global information access and proposes a system that shows how emerging approaches can minimize cultural differences.

INTRODUCTION

According to the Ethnologue organization, there are 6,809 distinct languages in the world (Anderson, 2004). Although many Internet users speak English as a native or as their second language, a recent study shows that only 27.6% of individuals use English when online (Internet World Stats, 2009). This factor is significant. Not only do lan-

guage differences inhibit the ability to search, but individual differences can also make information searching ineffective and inefficient.

When it comes to searching for information, everyone uses different words (or, at least different symbols). Each individual, moreover, has a unique conceptualization of ideas and uses different terms when he or she searches for information. Therefore, everyone searches and interprets information differently. Kelly (1955) asserts that each individual constructs his or her own con-

DOI: 10.4018/978-1-60960-833-0.ch014

cepts – a process Kelly calls Personal Construct Theory. The central idea is that everyone has different concepts that are created by variations associated with each person's particular culture (Taylor, 2004). Park's (2004) study supports this idea as he demonstrates cultural differences affect learners' searching for, analysis of, and use of information – particularly in a technology-based learning environment. Park's study shows that East Asians' information retrieval is based on relationships such as associative relationships, while European Westerners' information retrieval is based on categories such as classification.

A number of more recent studies have been conducted on similar aspects of online information seeking behavior. In particular, some studies on understanding individual differences (Maureen E, Detlor, Toms, & Trifts, 2009; Nancy M. Salbach, Sara J.T. Guilcher, Jaglal, & Davis, 2009) have received much attention. Related studies, such as Zhao's (2009) work on Internet users associated with social and economic conditions are also interesting in terms of understanding the importance of different approaches to Internet use.

Perhaps the overarching aspect of these studies is that most information retrieval systems are dependent on users entering terms and initiating a search. However, these terms might or might not match the informational frameworks used by those system. Within this context, minimizing language and individual differences in information retrieval is a vital issue because diverse cultures are brought close together through technologies – particularly online communication technologies. While research establishes the usage of Council on Library and Information Resources (CLIR) may minimize language differences, substantive empirical work remains to be done in identifying how individual users perform a multicultural information searches using an ontology-based information retrieval system.

The purpose of this chapter is to describe the limitations of traditional information organization approaches and introduce the emerging informa-

tion organization approaches with the proposed system. This chapter examines this issue by introducing the cause of ineffective global information access from a user, an information, and a system perspectives. The chapter also describes traditional and emerging approaches to enhancing global information access. It then presents a system that demonstrates how emerging approaches in ontology can minimize cultural differences associated with online searching by using an ontology-based information retrieval system.

To address these aspects, the chapter is organized as follows: The first section addresses three causes of ineffective global information access. The second section then presents traditional and emerging approaches to enhancing global information access. The chapter's third section describes a system that allows users to access information with enhanced global information access. The chapter then concludes with a section that examines the future direction of research in the context of global information access.

USER, INFORMATION, AND SYSTEM DIFFERENCES

Seeking information is a common and an essential human behavior. Every day, we engage in the use of networked information systems and the Internet to search for information. But often, searching for information is neither effective nor efficient. Users are frequently required to review a lengthy list of irrelevant results in order to find relevant information, and such situations often result in information anxiety (Wurman, 1989) and cognitive overload (Conklin, 1987). In recent years, numerous studies have attempted to find and to explore the causes of ineffective and inefficient searching.

From the perspective of the user, most search systems rely on users to enter terms in order to begin a search. These terms, however, might not match those in the system the individual is using.

Moreover, each individual has a unique conceptualization process. Therefore, he or she often uses different terms when searching for information. In other words, everyone has different concepts that are created by variations in culture, and as a result, everyone can use different terms to try to search for the same thing. This variation means everyone searches for and interprets information differently. This problematic factor is supported by the research. For example, in a study on vocabulary problems in human-system communication, Furnas, Landauer, Gomez, and Dumais (1987) show the probability of two people favoring the same term in a given situation is less than 0.20. These researchers go on to argue that many alternative access terms are necessary for users to determine relevant information. Furthermore, research also indicates users do not use lengthy expressions to search for information. A study by Jansen, Spink, and Saracevic (2000), for example, found that users used an average of 2.21 terms in each search.

From the perspective of the information content, significant progress has been made in terms of information creation. We now possess the network infrastructure and the bandwidth – as well as large volumes of information – need for available and easy to access to information. However, the Giga Information Group asserts that unstructured data accounts for nearly 80% of all corporate data on record (Moore, 2002). This figure encompasses all data types including e-mail and voice messages, presentations, videos, attachments, paper documents, and other forms of information (Moore, 2002). Further complicating this situation is the rapid growth of intranets and the Internet – tools individuals can use to create, archive, and retrieve this data.

From the perspective of the system, keyword-based information retrieval processes have been used to find information and to provide access to large amounts of data. For example, information retrieval systems accept keywords as input and return as output a list of links to documents containing those keywords. However, keyword-based information retrieval systems have some fundamental drawbacks. They do not, for example, "understand" the words the user types into them. Similarly, keyword-based information retrieval systems cannot cope with the fact that the same subject might be referred to by multiple names (the "synonym problem"), nor that the same name may refer to multiple subjects (the "homonym problem"). Therefore, when individuals try to search for information via keywords, the systems might come up with an enormous number of false hits (Pepper, 2002; Younger, 1997). A large part of this problem is that huge amounts of unstructured information are contained within each system, and many of the current systems offer only finding objectives but lack collocation objectives (Svenonius, 2000). As Svenonius (2000) explains, some users know what to search for, but other users do not know or are unable to express the object of their search, and yet they are able to know it immediately when they find it. Such users expect some guidance from an information retrieval system. And while hyperlinking is one way to support the navigation objective, it is not sufficient in all cases. Ontology might also play a role in supporting the navigation objective.

In sum, individual differences, unstructured information, and keyword-based searches are possible causes for ineffective and inefficient searching (see Figure 1).

In order to minimize individual differences such as culture and language, new approaches from either the information or system categories must be studied, and the next section of this chapter reviews traditional and emerging approaches to examining these concepts.

TRADITIONAL AND EMERGING INFORMATION ORGANIZATION METHODS

We organize items because we need to retrieve them later. In the field of library and information

Figure 1. Three causes of ineffective global information access

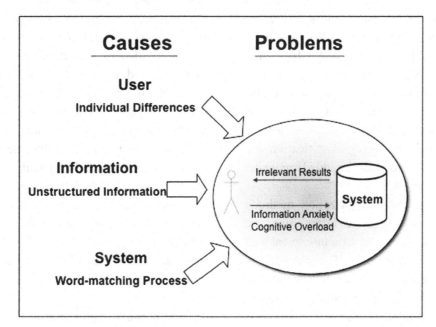

studies, authority files have provided control of terms and their relationships to other terms (Taylor, 2004). In the digital world, ontologies – or methods for thinking about and categorizing items – are being constructed to formally define relationships among terms, usually terms in a particular field. The section summarizes traditional and emerging information organization approaches.

In recent years, numerous studies have explored the areas of users, information, and systems. In all three areas, organization is one of the key components associated with information retrieval (Norton, 2000). Efforts for information organization can be summarized into three major categories of methods: term lists, classification/categorization, and relationship groups (Zeng, 2005). The term lists, which contain lists of words, phrases or definitions, give emphasis to lists of terms – especially controlled terms. (Examples of such terms lists are authority files and dictionaries.) The term lists approach, however, does not provide sufficient structure, and thus does not make information searching any easier.

There are many possible organizing principles for documents such as by author, by time period, etc., and keywords are a primitive form of subject-based classification. The simplest form of controlled vocabulary is a list of terms. In the library and information systems (LIS) field, terms are words or phrases and concepts are what the terms refer to (L. Garshol, 2005).

Hodge (2000) defines authority files as a series of headings utilized to index different names for the domain values in a certain field. Non-preferred terms may be linked to the preferred terms. This type of knowledge organization approach generally does not provide a detailed organization or complex structure. An alphabetical or classification scheme is used to present terms (Hodge, 2000). Authority files may apply a limited hierarchy applied for simple browsing, and examples of authority files include the Library of Congress Name Authority File and the Getty Geographic Authority File.

An index, by contrast, is a list of subjects, names, titles, etc. that helps users to find information (Tenofsky, 2004). The main constituents of this and any index include an (alphabetical) list of names of topics and page numbers (locators for occurrences) (Pepper, 2002). While systems can locate indexed terms, they cannot distinguish among them, and they also cannot recognize higher-level terms or determine synonyms. Within this context, lists of terms do not provide much structure, which makes searching for specific information difficult. Using classification and categorization, structure may be added to enhance information retrieval.

Classification and categorization methods, which classify or categorize information into groups of similar units, add structure to enhance information retrieval processes. Examples of classification and categorization approaches include faceted classification. As was defined more than a century ago, a catalog fulfills three major objectives associated with these ideas of information organization and retrieval (Cutter, 1875). First, it enables a person to find a book – finding objective. Second, it helps show what a library has in its collection – collocating objective. Third and finally, a catalog assists individuals in the choice of the book to select – choice objective. This catalog framework can be used to understand current models of searching for and retrieving information. That is, most of the current search engines or information retrieval systems, which base their search functions on keywords and thus return lengthy and irrelevant result sets, serve very well on the first objective (finding objective). The second objective (collocating objective), however, is not served very well. That is, information is better classified, yet the relationships among information units are not well supported.

Faceted classification is the most commonly-used form of classification in thesaurus construction (Aitchison, Gilchrist, & Bawden, 2000). A faceted classification has a structure similar to a thesaurus, and there are three benefits to using faceted classification in thesaurus construction (Aitchison, Gilchrist, & Bawden, 2000). First, faceted classification provides a mechanism for the

analysis of terms or concepts and for determining the relationships between concepts. Second, the results of faceted classification may be used for systematic display in a thesaurus. Third, facets may be added to terms in existing vocabularies. Bliss' classification (Bliss Classification Association, 1998). Dewey decimal classification (Miksa, 1998) and colon classification (Ranganathan, 1987) are common faceted classifications. Originally invented by S. R. Ranganathan in the 1930s, faceted classification defines a number of facets or dimensions and defines a set of terms within each facet. Sometimes these terms are arranged in a taxonomy (L. Garshol, 2005). Ranganathan's original faceted classification system consisted of five facets:

1. Personality (the main subject of the document)
2. Matter (the material or substance with which the document deals)
3. Energy (the processes or activities described)
4. Space (the location described)
5. Time (the time period described).

These five facets have sometimes been referred to as "PMEST."

Taxonomy is a subject-based classification that organizes the terms in the controlled vocabulary into a hierarchy. The advantage of taxonomy is that it allows related terms to be grouped together and categorized in ways that make it easier to find the correct term to use whether searching for or describing an object (L. M. Garshol, 2004). Even though a taxonomy provides relationships among terms, it can only represent limited relationships, namely hierarchical relationships. More precisely, taxonomy only represents generic relationships among the four hierarchical relationships (generic relationships, whole-part relationships, instance relationships, and polyhierarchical relationships).

Ontology

The term *ontology* has been applied in many different ways, but the core meaning is a model for describing the world that consists of a set of types, properties, and relationship types (L. M. Garshol, 2004). In the context of knowledge sharing, Gruber (1993a) uses the term ontology to mean a specification of a conceptualization. Gruber (1993b) describes conceptualization as the act of defining an abstract idea in order for it to be applicable in other instances. Every knowledge management system is committed to some conceptualization, explicitly or implicitly (Gruber, 1993b). Ontology can define relationships among resources and find related resources. For example, a "lives at" link or "works for" link in ontology is used to track these types of relationships and their corresponding values for listed individuals. It is important to emphasize that there are multiple relationships between specific words and concepts. This factor means that, in practice, different words may refer to the same concept, and a single word may refer to several concepts.

Welty and Guarino (2001) suggest four different types of ontologies. These include:

1. Top-level ontology: very general concepts like space, time, and events, which are independent of particular problems or domains.
2. Domain ontology: the vocabulary related to a generic domain by specializing the concepts introduced in the top-level ontology.
3. Task ontology: the vocabulary related to a generic task or activity in the top-level ontologies.
4. Application ontology: the most specific of ontologies. Concepts in application ontologies often correspond to roles played by domain entities while performing a certain activity.

Traditional approaches, such as taxonomy and thesaurus building, have some characteristics of ontology. Although a taxonomy and thesaurus enhance the semantics of terms in a vocabulary, ontology includes richer relationships among terms (Smith, n.d.). Ontology possesses a set of well-defined constructs that can be leveraged to build structured knowledge. In practice thesauri are not considered to be ontology because their descriptive power is far too weak (L. M. Garshol, 2004). Mizoguchi (2003) mentioned that ontology is not just a set of terms and not a simple hierarchy of concepts. A simple taxonomy of a vehicle has a simple classification of vehicles that includes ground vehicles, cars, motor bikes, air craft, etc., but this hierarchy is not good enough to build a vehicle ontology (Mizoguchi, 2003).

Humans require words (or at least symbols) to communicate efficiently, and the mapping of words into things is only indirectly possible (Genesereth & Nilsson, 1987; Pepper & Schwab, 2003). The relationship between symbols and things has been described in the form of the meaning triangle shown in Figure 2 (Ogden & Richards, 1923).

As shown in Figure 2, when a user searches for a information about a "jaguar," the system cannot clarify whether the term refers to the animal "jaguar" or a "Jaguar" automobile. The symbol, jaguar, differs from user to user because humans understand that one can only interpret language in a social context (sometimes termed the semiosphere). Semiotics is the study of how meaning is transmitted and understood, and it is very useful for understanding symbols that are part of ontology construction. Term clarification is less problematic in human-to-human communication because humans can infer what the sender or receiver means from the context. However, communication between humans and systems demands an intermediary to clarify the term (Maedche & Staab, 2001).

Ontology description can serve this role, and it is critical for effective and efficient communication between humans and systems. Namely, ontology provides a formalized and shared description of a domain (Stojanovic, Stojanovic, & Handschuh,

Figure 2. Triangular relationship among concept, symbol, and thing (Ogden & Richards, 1923)

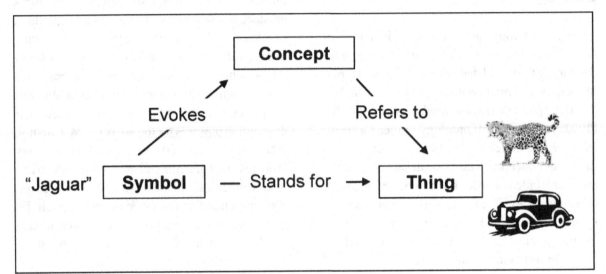

2002) between humans and systems. Therefore, both humans and systems can have a set of agreements for used terms. Assisting effective and efficient communication between humans and systems is another potential for ontology.

Ohlms (2002) asserts that ontology is the key to the next generation of information retrieval systems and knowledge management applications because ontology provides meaning (representation) and structure (relationship) to data, thus making valuable knowledge accessible. Enhancing the representation and relationship of information through ontology is a promising emerging approach for knowledge organization, and this improved knowledge organization is vital for effective and efficient searching. While many researchers address the potential of ontology (Allemang, Coyne, & Hodgson, 2003; Li, Hsieh, & Sun, 2003; Ohlms, 2002; Ras & Dardzinska, 2004), there are few studies that examine differences in user performance between traditional (thesaurus) and emerging (ontology) information organization approaches.

Semantic Web Architecture and Ontology

The main components required for Semantic Web Framework include URIs, XML, RDF, and ontologies. URIs provides a way to find every resource. XML allows creators of resources to create their own tags to explain sections of contents.

The relationships among XML, XML Schema, RDF/OWL, and ontologies are the following: XML itself does not provide any meaning. XML is a subset of SGML. In the last 15 years, the Web has grown very rapidly and the demand for various services via Web has increased. However, HTML has been criticized because it is too basic to provide for many required applications (Taylor, 2004). A full SGML was suggested to meet the demand but it is too complicated. Many plug-ins are provided to meet the needs. However, the user has to download. Java also considered as an alternative but the user has to know how to program.

The solution is XML. XML is as easy to use on the Web as HTML but at the same time being as strong as SGML (Taylor, 2004). XML schema is necessary to provide an XML vocabulary for expressing data's business rules. Even though

XML contains some data, search agents do not know the meaning or relationships to user's request. For example, when a user looking for "swine flu," a system does not understand the user's request because a system only has information about "H1N1 Flu" even though "Swine Flu" and "H1N1 Flu" have the same meaning. In order for a search agent to consider the two terms the same, ontology is needed. The examples of source code on RDF/OWL are shown in Figure 3.

This interoperability was achieved by using the OWL H1N1 Ontology and this approach can minimize the cultural and linguistic differences.

ONTOLOGY-BASED MEDICAL INFORMATION RETRIEVAL (OMIR) SYSTEM

To enhance global information access, many studies have been conducted. Word to world translation among languages is not sufficient to accommodate cultural differences. Cross language information retrieval has several difficulties such as translation ambiguity (Ballesteros & Croft, 1998) and vocabulary mismatch (Gao, et al., 2001). Rich semantic relationships among resources can help to minimize cultural differences. A system must provide popular terms over scientific terms. A system must show different languages and relationships among resources. The ontology-based Medical Information Retrieval system meets all the requirements for effective and efficient global information access. For this study, medical areas have been chosen because medical terms are not familiar to users.

Ontology Development

The proposed ontology-based medical information retrieval system constitutes ontology development by list terms, classify/categorize, add semantic relationships, normalize ontology and implement ontology. The first step is to list terms by ontology engineers and domain experts. By reusing the back of the book index or existing index terms, this step can be done very easily. Automatic indexing solutions are available to index if index terms are not available. The second step is to classify and categorize the resources. The system does not require detail classification or categorization. For example, disease, medicine, vaccine, symptom, side effects are an example of classification for OMIR system. The third step is adding semantic relationships.

This process can be done automatically; however, semantic relationships are added manually for experiment purpose. Equivalent, hierarchical, and associative relationships are added. Preferred terms, popular terms, different languages are added to enrich and to provide multiple access points for global users. The fourth step is to normalize the ontology. Examination of any missing resources or isolated resources from the semantic relationships is very critical because all the information must be semantically connected. Lastly, implementation of this design is left. There are two ontology languages; RDF and Topic Maps.

Figure 3. OWL source code

```
<owl: DatatypeProperty rdf:="H1N1 Flu">

    <owl:equivalentProperty rdf:resource="#Swine Flu"/>

<owl: DatatypeProperty>
```

As shown in Figure 4, five steps involved for Ontology development.

Ontology Languages: RDF and Topic Maps

Topic Maps and RDF are two available data models in the Semantic Web. Topic Maps and RDF are different from user and information perspectives. From the users' perspectives, Topic Maps searches and browses based on explicitly shown semantic relationships. On the other hand, RDF searches based on implicit semantic relationships. The relationships are hidden from users. From the information perspectives, Topic Maps can express multiple relationships using associations but RDF has limitations on expressing the multiple relationships using subject, predicate, and object.

However, the World Wide Web Consortium (W3C) and ISO have set up a task force to make these two standards interoperable. The Semantic Web Best Practices and Deployment (SWBPD) Working Group supports the RDF/Topic Map Interoperability Task Force (RDFTM) to help users who want to combine data from W3C RDF/OWL and ISO topic maps. In the future, interoperability between RDF and topic maps will not be an issue.

Both Topic Maps and RDF use URI as an identifier. When systems use the same URI to refer to different resources, it creates confusion. For example, system A uses http://www.unt.edu/ research to refer to UNT's home page, while system B uses the same URI to refer to UNT. When these two systems try to exchange data, they cannot because of their different usages of the same URI. While RDF does not have a mechanism to cope with this confusion, Topic Maps provides a subject identifier and subject indicator to resolve this confusion. We cannot rely on names because of synonym, homonym, and multiple language problems.

To resolve these issues, we need to use identifiers that are clear both to humans and machines. A subject identifier is an URI used by a machine to identify a subject and a subject indicator is information used by humans to identify a subject. The topic "apple" can be identified by a machine using http://psi.fruit.org/#apple. A subject indicator about "apple" can be used for a human to identify it. Both subject identifier and indicator refer to the same subject in the real world.

Topic Maps provides rich representations on a topic by using three different kinds of topic characteristics: topics, associations and occurrences. RDF has only one way to make assertions about things: triple (subject, predicate, object), and triplet notation is not expressive enough. Topic Maps is an ISO standard and it is a great way to connect semantically for any types of resources. Topics, associations, and occurrence are the three components to connect resources. Topics classify the resources into certain categories. For example,

Figure 4. Ontology development process

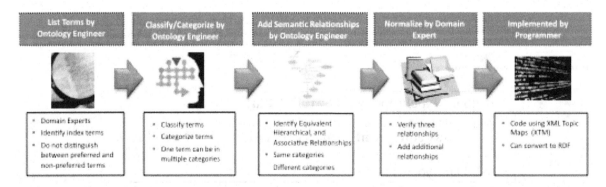

Alfuria, Flumist, Fluvirin, and Fluzone are classified as a vaccine to treat swine flu. Association shows an explicit relationship to other resources. For example, treat relationship between vaccine and swine flu links between two resources. Occurrences show both internal occurrence and external occurrences. Internal occurrences links internal resources that an organization or person owns. External occurrences link external resources such as websites, blogs, and wikis. Topic Maps provides seamless resources browsing and searching.

A CROSS-CULTURAL EXAMPLE OF ONTOLOGY-BASED SYSTEMS

H1N1 is not a local epidemic but a global epidemic. It is the most highly spread virus in the 21st century. According to the World Health Organization (WHO), H1N1 is a level six type of disease and they anticipated that 1/3 of people on earth will be contaminated by 2015. Therefore, people from all over the world have inquired about this disease. There are three issues when trying to access this information. First, most information is unstructured or semi-structured as the current Web is. According to a study, 80% of information is unstructured. Second, most users have limited medical knowledge. Medical terms are not popular terms to the most people. Lastly, most medical information is written in English, and this factor is highly problematic from a global perspective.

A 2009 study published by Internet World Stats indicates only 27.6% of Internet users communicate in English when online. Thus, there is a demand for various languages-supported systems – particularly when it comes to sharing important information about public health and the spread of infectious diseases. Within this context, a key aspect becomes how to create systems that allows users from different cultural and linguistic backgrounds to effectively search and browse medical resources using ontology-based medical information retrieval system in order to find the

information they need to address public health crises. The need to develop such a system is significant as users' quest for relevant and timely information is becoming increasingly complicated by the ever-growing amount and complexity of resources. Building meaningful and rich semantic relationships among resources holds the promise of allowing researchers to find cultural information effectively and efficiently.

As shown in Figure 5, search and retrieval systems can be designed with features that minimize the cultural differences of users seeking information. First, this system shows the types of information one can retrieve from this particular database. In the case of this example system, users with limited medical knowledge know what swine flu is by looking at the type of information available on the interface (i.e., swine flu is a disease). All the resources displayed for the user are semantically connected. Therefore, users can browse the same type of information to find possible semantic relationships.

This example system also displays the same information in different languages. For the purpose of this chapter, this sample system displays information in English, Korean, and Chinese. This trilingual feature allows users from different cultural and linguistic backgrounds to find and to browse information in their native languages. In this example system, users can do searches using their native or primary language and the system will match the search results with entries both in the native language of the user and in other languages used by that database. For example, if a user searches for the Korean term "돼지독감", the system returns "swine flu."

This kind of ontology-driven system also shows users relationships among resources that are accessible in that system. Even for global users who have no prior knowledge of a given medial topic or who might have a language barrier related to accessing certain information within the system, the system shows explicit relationships among resources. For example, a user will learn how

Figure 5. Screenshot of ontology-based medical information retrieval system

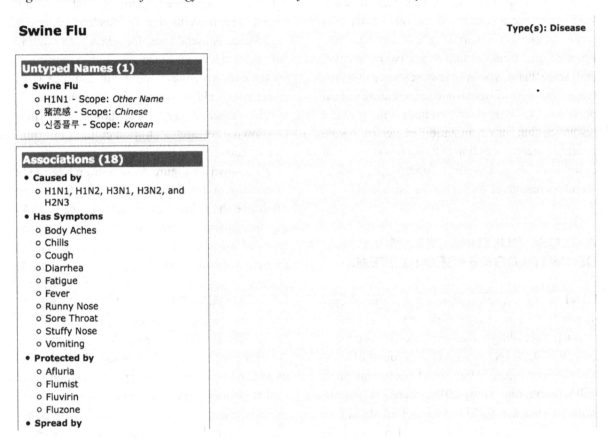

the swine flu is treated, the causes of swine flu, the symptoms of swine flu, and the vaccine for swine flu. The system shows that swine flu can be treated with four types of medicine: Alfuria, Flumist, Fluvirin, and Fluzone.

The three ontology-based features of this example database system allow international users with different language backgrounds, limited medical knowledge, and different cultural perspectives to effectively and efficiently search for health-related information and browse medical resources. Figure 6 provides a visual model of how this ontology-based system allows users from different cultural and linguistic backgrounds to use the system to find specific kinds of health-related information. The graphic also allows users to see the whole relationships among resources.

CONCLUSION AND FUTURE WORK

This chapter describes three causes for ineffective information searching. To enhance global information access, three information organization approaches are introduced. The Topic Maps based medical information retrieval system provides many features that traditional information organization approaches can't support such as this system shows semantic relationships among resources. Even users without prior knowledge, the system shows explicit relationships among resources. A proposed system shows how emerging information organization approach, ontology, can minimize individual and cultural differences.

The ontology-based approach and system proposed in this chapter aims to bridge the traditional approaches and emerging approaches.

Figure 6. Graphic representation of the H1N1 ontology

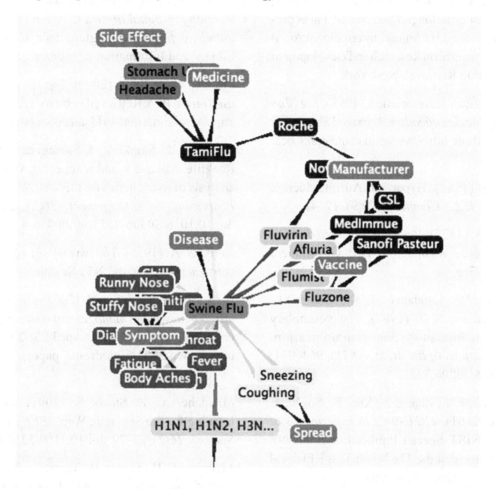

In an initial study, this ontology-based medical information retrieval system was developed that included a few samples. For future study, many ontologies have been created, but the research on integration or sharing ontology has received little attention. More research on ontology integration is needed to encourage and to promote significant ontology penetration in existing database systems. Further testing is needed with larger samples of medical resources and more relationships in order to determine how to proceed with development of this new challenge. Large numbers of ontologized medical resources, however can allow users or medical professionals to find medical information more effectively in international contexts.

REFERENCES

Aitchison, J., Gilchrist, A., & Bawden, D. (2000). *Thesaurus construction and use: A practical manual* (4th ed.). Chicago, IL: Fitzroy Dearborn.

Allemang, D., Coyne, R., & Hodgson, R. (2003). *Solution envisioning for ontology-based applications.* Paper presented at the Technology Appreciation Webinar, Beaver Falls, PA.

Anderson, S. R. (2004). *How many languages are there in the world?* Washington, DC: Linguistic Society of America.

Ballesteros, L., & Croft, W. B. (1998). *Resolving ambiguity for crosslanguage retrieval.* Paper presented at the the 21st Annual International ACM SIGIR Conference on Research and Development in Information Retrieval, New York.

Bliss Classification Association. (1998). *The Bliss bibliographic classification.* Retrieved September 15, 2005, from http://www.sid.cam.ac.uk/ bca/ bchist.htm

Conklin, J. (1987). Hypertext: An introduction and survey. *IEEE Computer, 20*(9), 17–41.

Cutter, C. A. (1875). *Rules for a printed dictionary catalogue.* Washington, DC: Government Printing Office.

Furnas, G. W., Landauer, T. K., Gomez, L. M., & Dumais, S. T. (1987). The vocabulary problem in human-system communication. *Communications of the ACM, 30*(11), 964–971. doi:10.1145/32206.32212

Gao, J., Nie, J. Y., Zhang, J., Xun, E., Su, Y., & Zhou, M. (2001). *TREC-9 CLIR experiments at MSRCN.* (NIST Special Publication 500–249). Paper presented at the The Ninth Text REtrieval Conference, Gaithersburg, MD.

Garshol, L. (2005). *Topic maps and information design.* Majorstuen, Norway: Ontopia.

Garshol, L. M. (2004). Metadata? Thesauri? Taxonomies? Topic maps! Making sense of it all. *Journal of Information Science, 30*(4), 378–391. doi:10.1177/0165551504045856

Genesereth, M. R., & Nilsson, N. J. (1987). *Logical foundations of artificial intelligence.* San Mateo, CA: Morgan Kaufmann Publishers.

Gruber, T. (1993a). *A translation approach to portable ontology specifications.* Stanford, CA: Stanford University Press.

Gruber, T. (1993b). *What is an ontology?* Retrieved December 12, 2004, from http://www-ksl. stanford.edu/kst /what-is-an-ontology.html

Hodge, G. (2000). *Systems of knowledge organization for digital libraries: Beyond traditional authority files.* Washington, DC: Council on Library and Information Resources.

Internet World Stats. (2009). *Top ten languages used on the Web.* Retrieved Febuary 1, 2010, from http://www.internetworldstats.com /stats7.htm

Jansen, B. J., Spink, A., & Saracevic, T. (2000). Real life, real users, and real needs: A study and analysis of user queries on the Web. *Information Processing & Management, 36*(2), 207–227. doi:10.1016/S0306-4573(99)00056-4

Kelly, G. A. (1955). *The psychology of personal constructs.* New York, NY: Norton.

Li, S., Hsieh, H., & Sun, I. (2003). *An ontology-based knowledge management system for the metal industry.* Retrieved April 23, 2004, from http://www2003.org/cdrom/ papers/alternate/ P620 /p620-li.html

Maedche, A., & Staab, S. (2001). Ontology learning for the Semantic Web. *IEEE Intelligent Systems, 16*(2), 72–79. doi:10.1109/5254.920602

Maureen, E. H., Detlor, B., Toms, E., & Trifts, V. (2009). *Online information seeking: Understanding individual differences and search contexts.* Paper presented at the The annual Americas' Conference on Information Systems (AMCIS) 2009, San Francisco, California.

Miksa, F. L. (1998). *The DDC, the universe of knowledge and the post-modern library.* Albany, NY: OCLC Forest Press.

Mizoguchi, R. (2003). Tutorial on ontological engineering. *New Generation Computing, 21*(4), 365–384. doi:10.1007/BF03037311

Moore, C. (2002). Diving into data. *InfoWorld.* Retrieved November 14, 2004, from http://www. infoworld.com/ article/02/10/25/021028 feundata_1.html

Norton, M. J. (2000). *Introductory concepts in information science*. Medford, NJ: Information Today, Inc.

Ogden, C. K., & Richards, I. A. (1923). *The meaning of meaning*. New York, NY: Harvest Books.

Ohlms, C. (2002). *The business potential of ontology-based knowledge management*. New York, NY: McKinsey & Company.

Park, Y. (2004). *Cultural difference and cognitive style affecting information search behaviors: A proposal for a new study*. Paper presented at the World Conference on Educational Multimedia, Hypermedia and Telecommunications 2004, Chesapeake, VA.

Pepper, S. (2002). *The TAO of topic maps*. Retrieved January 12, 2006, from http://www.ontopia.net/topicmaps /materials/tao.html

Pepper, S., & Schwab, S. (2003). *Curing the Web's identity crisis*. Retrieved November 23, 2004, from http://www.ontopia.net/topicmaps / materials/identitycrisis.html #Pepper2003

Ranganathan, S. R. (1987). *The colon classification* (7th ed.). Bangalore, India: Sarada Ranganathan Endowment for Library Science.

Ras, Z. W., & Dardzinska, A. (2004). Ontology-based distributed autonomous knowledge systems. *Information Systems*, *29*(1), 47–58. doi:10.1016/S0306-4379(03)00033-4

Salbach, N. M., Guilcher, S. J. T., Jaglal, S. B., & Davis, D. A. (2009). Factors influencing information seeking by physical therapists providing stroke management. *Physical Therapy*, *89*(10), 1039–1050. doi:10.2522/ptj.20090081

Smith, H. (n.d.). *What is an ontology?* Retrieved December 16, 2004, from http://www.ontology.org/main /papers/faq.html

Stojanovic, L., Stojanovic, N., & Handschuh, S. (2002). Evolution of the metadata in the ontology-based knowledge management systems. *Proceedings of the 1st German Workshop on on Experience Management: Sharing Experiences about the Sharing of Experience* (pp. 65-77). New York, NY: Association for Computing Machinery.

Svenonius, E. (2000). *The intellectual foundation of information organization*. Cambridge, MA: The MIT Press.

Taylor, A. (2004). *The organization of information* (2nd ed.). Westport, CT: Libraries Unlimited.

Tenofsky, D. (2004). *Glossary of library terms*. Retrieved April 2, 2006, from http://www.lib.umich.edu/science /instruction/glossary.html

Welty, C., & Guarino, N. (2001). Supporting ontological analysis of taxonomic relationships. *Data & Knowledge Engineering*, *39*, 51–74. doi:10.1016/S0169-023X(01)00030-1

Wurman, R. S. (1989). *Information anxiety*. New York, NY: Doubleday.

Younger, J. (1997). Resources description in the digital age. *Library Trends*, *45*(3).

Zeng, M. L. (2005, August). Using software to teach thesaurus development and indexing in graduate programs of LIS and IAKM. *Bulletin of the American Society for Information Science and Technology*, (pp. 11-13).

KEY TERMS AND DEFINITIONS

Cultural Differences: The differences between cultures in a specific region, or in the world as a whole.

Global Information Access: Information access by global users whose native language is not English.

Information Retrieval: The science of searching for information.

Ontology: Formal and consensual specifications of conceptualizations.

Semantic Web: An extension of the current Web in which information is given well-defined meanings, better enabling computers and people to work in cooperation.

Thesaural Relationships: Relationships among resources. Three types of thesaural relationships include equivalent, hierarchical, and associative relationships.

Topic Maps: An ISO standard (ISO/IEC 13250:2003) for the representation and interchange of knowledge.

Chapter 15
Information Sharing Across Languages

Reinhard Schäler
University of Limerick, Ireland

ABSTRACT

Access to information and knowledge in one's native language is a fundamental human right. It is a right deeply rooted in the legal systems of many Western nations where it is considered to be as important as access to healthcare or to other potentially life-saving services. While individuals often claim these rights for themselves, they do not always afford such rights to others, for there is often a cost involved in the realization of this right. This chapter highlights how denying this service, particularly as it relates to the translation and the localization of online materials, results in human costs including life threatening information poverty. This situation, in turn, requires urgent and coordinated relief efforts by industry, government, and civil societies on a global scale.

Bridging the know-do gap is the foremost challenge and opportunity for public health in the 21ˢᵗ century. -Ariel Pablos Mendez, Rockefeller Foundation

Change will not come if we wait for some other person or some other time. We are the ones we've been waiting for. We are the change that we seek. -Barack Obama

INTRODUCTION

Digital content publishers – including the producers of software applications, educational and game developers, and Web publishers – strive to sell their products in new markets in order to increase the return on their investment (ROI) in the development of the original electronic content. In essence, these publishers make a localization decision based upon the promise of almost immediate financial returns in the short-term (e.g., a business quarter). In the process, these digital content publishers are growing and maintaining a translation services industry that will be worth

DOI: 10.4018/978-1-60960-833-0.ch015

almost US$25 billion by 2013 (Beninatto & Kelly, 2009). This sum represents a considerable amount of money, but it also represents a fraction of the value that the localization industry has created in financial returns for some of the world's largest digital publishers. (Interestingly, many of these publishers now generate more than 60% of their revenues from international markets.)

Localization, in essence, is the linguistic and cultural adaptation of digital (e.g., online) content to the requirements and the *locale* of a foreign market. Localization practices, in turn, include the provision of services and technologies for the management of multilingualism across the digital global information flow. Thus, mainstream localization becomes an instrument of and the prerequisite for economic globalization – the strategic pursuit of successful digital publishers to push their products and services (particularly their online products and services) into new international markets. If there are no viable markets in any given region or country for any given content or language, then mainstream localization services are not made available. As a result, access to information and knowledge via online and other digital media are severely curtailed in the poorer regions of the world. This factor is important, for while mainstream localization can *contribute* to the international sharing of electronic information it can also *prevent* information sharing across languages – particularly via online media.

The objective of this chapter is to highlight the background creating the current unacceptable situation and to describe and analyze some of the more promising attempts to rectify this problem. In the chapter, the author will report on initiatives by both large multinational corporations (e.g., Google and Microsoft) and by social entrepreneurs and charities (e.g., The Rosetta Foundation, the International Development Research Centre, and the World Wide Web Foundation) to bring individuals in poorer nations into the digital world from which they have previously been excluded because they are not consumers with sufficient

spending power. The eradication of information poverty and diffusion of online global information sharing has been described as one of the key challenges of our century. It has potential long term social, political, cultural, and economic effects on a scale that has not been recognized by many of the key stakeholders, and now is the time to examine and address this situation.

A GROWING DIVIDE

The effect of this denial of service in certain languages is the so-called *language barrier*. In reality, there has never been a *language* barrier. Rather, there is an *access* barrier (i.e., access to translation and localization services). This access barrier is lowered for people living in affluent, commercially attractive target markets because companies wish to access such markets in order to sell products and services in them. For this reason, organizations are willing to undertake the cost of localization (which generally includes the associated costs of translation), for such localization provides access to these affluent markets. While Norway, for example, has only 4 million inhabitants, most multinational organizations undertake the cost of localizing for Norwegian audiences. Such costs are considered acceptable, for the related cultural audience has a relatively high income and can purchase a range of products.

For those individuals living in poor or deprived and thus commercially unattractive target markets, however, the language barrier remains high. This situation persists because companies do not think it is worth their efforts to localize content for the relatively small numbers of potential consumers in these regions – and thus make their information accessible to those consumers. Madagascar, for example, has 15 million inhabitants (almost 4 times the population of Norway), but the average citizen has a very low income. For this reason, most multinationals do not see it as cost effective to translate online or other electronic content into

Malagasy or to localize content for a Madagascarian audience.

There are further examples for the unequal treatment of people and their languages when it comes to the provision of online access to knowledge and information. Consider the cases of Iceland (population just over 300,000 and a 2009 GDP per capita of US$39,000), and Ethiopia (population 88 million with a 2009 GDP per capita of roughly US$900). While there are large volumes of online and other electronic content available in Icelandic, there are relatively negligible amounts of online content available in Amharic (or Amarigna), the official language of Ethiopia. Similar inequities exist between the large amounts of digital content available in Romantsch, one the official languages spoken by just 0.5% of the population of Switzerland (population of 7.6 million speakers and a 2009 GDP per capita of US$41,400), or Irish (Gaelic or Gaeilge), which is spoken by less than 10% of the population of Ireland (4.6 million people with a 2009 GDP per capita of US$41,000) and which is one of the official languages of the European Union on one hand, and the negligible amount of digital content available in the languages of Uganda (population 33 million and a 2009 GDP per capita of US$1,200) such as Ganda or Luganda. The same is the case with the languages of Nepal (population of 29 million and a 2009 GPD per capita of US$1,200) such as Nepali, Maithali, or Bhojpuri.

Because of these factors of economics, online information sharing across languages becomes possible in some parts of the world (i.e., the industrialized nations) while *information poverty* continues in other regions (i.e., the developing nations). The gap between the information rich and the information poor decreases in commercially attractive parts of the world because of access to information and knowledge in the languages of the people. Here, localization is not just a viable business; it also supports socioeconomic and democratic development. The same gap not only remains, but it effectively widens in commercially

unattractive parts of the world. In these poorer regions, the lack of localization pushes people and economies even further down to what has been called "the bottom of the pyramid." Rather than supporting the societies most in need of development by providing them with access to digital knowledge and information in their language, the focus of the mainstream localization industry has remained on short-term profits and return on investment (ROI). Ironically, even from a business perspective, more long-term investment in emerging markets promising double-figure growth rates would seem to make sense. According to one recent report (Allen, 2009), two-thirds of the world's mobile phone subscriptions are in developing nations, with the biggest growth rate in Africa – a continent where a quarter of the population now has mobile phones.

The *access* barrier to digital knowledge and information for disadvantaged societies, however, will remain unless the mainstream localization industry recognizes the mid- to long-term growth opportunities it has ignored so far, and unless civil society, supported by government initiatives, introduces development projects targeted at underserved languages. Until that day, the information and knowledge divide will continue to grow with serious consequences for those affected.

LIVES UNDER THREAT

Individuals suffering from information poverty often do not have access to life-saving information on HIV/AIDS prevention, testing, and treatment. Similarly, they often do not have access to "how to" information on accessing alternative sources of fuel for cooking, information describing how to purify water, or information on treating life-threatening diseases such as diarrhoea. Even intergovernmental organizations such as the United Nations make important online content available in just a handful of languages. The Website of "UNAIDS – Uniting the world against AIDS," an organization aimed at the eradication of HIV/AIDS worldwide, is currently available only in English with partial information available in French, Spanish, and Russian – yet a disproportionate number of the world's AIDS victims live in sub-Saharan Africa and speak languages other than these.

Suffering information poverty also means not having access to information on essential services in important areas such as justice (e.g., What are my legal rights in cases of land eviction?), the economy (e.g., What are the current market prices for my agricultural products?), education (e.g., How can I access online learning resources?), and many other areas. An example of how access to digital information and knowledge affects people's livelihood is that of Reuters Market Light (RML). In the case of RML, the provision of crop prices from local markets, localized weather reports, and relevant news using text messages to mobile phones in the local language of the Indian state of Maharashtra, doubled the farmers' yearly income of US$2,000 within months (Prahalad, 2010, p. 147-149).

Information poverty can ultimately be as lethal as other types of poverty. It has long been established – though not widely realized – that tens of thousands of people are dying every day because they do not have access to information that could save their lives (Packenham-Walsh, 2009). Packenham-Walsh (2009), for example, highlights the central role of caregivers, mothers, hospital doctors, and general practitioners in the prevention and treatment of series diseases such as pneumonia, diarrhoea, and hypertension. For any of these individuals, a lack of knowledge of the correct treatment of these diseases – because of lack of access to adequate healthcare information – creates a life-threatening situation.

Aid and development agencies, industry, civil society, and governments are only beginning to realize the need to fight information poverty – particularly as it relates to online media – with equal fervour as other forms of poverty, such as economic poverty, income poverty, or absolute poverty. Examples of these initiatives are have been compiled by The Rosetta Foundation on its Website and include Google.org's HealthSpeaks initiative (Google, 2010c). In addressing the importance of such initiatives, Google quotes Godlee et al.'s 2004 *Lancet* article that highlighted the lack of access to health information as a "major barrier to knowledge-based healthcare in developing countries" (p. 295). Within its recommendations for addressing this issue, Google highlights the fact that "...among currently available technologies, only the Internet has the potential to deliver universal access to up-to-date healthcare information" (Godlee et al., 2004, p. 297). What makes this situation particularly important is the fact that that 90% of the content on the Internet exists in only 12 languages (UNESCO, 2008). It is thus evident that the billions of people who speak other languages are missing out on valuable online information that can help improve their lives.

NEW PERSPECTIVES ON INTERNATIONAL ACCESS TO INFORMATION

As noted, access to essential online knowledge and information in one's native language cannot remain a privilege that is "nice-to-have." Rather, such online information has been recognised as an essential requirement to lift billions of people out of poverty, provide them with access to adequate educational resources, and allow them to deal appropriately with health issues as they arise.

In September of 2009, *The Economist* magazine published a special report on telecoms in emerging markets. The report pointed out how poor countries have already benefited hugely from mobile phones. According to *The Economist*, in 2000, the world's developing countries accounted for around one-quarter of the world's 700m mobile phones. By the beginning of 2009, however, these countries accounted for three-quarters of the globe's 4 billion mobile phone users (Mobile marvels, 2009).

In addition to connecting billions of new users to the digital world, the spread of mobile phones in developing countries is providing home-grown mobile operators in China, India, Africa, and the Middle East that rival existing operations based in industrialized nations. New business models and industry structures have emerged in response to this booming market for mobile phones, and these models enabled providers in developing nations to make a profit by serving low-spending customers with whom Western firms would not bother (Mobile marvels, 2009). Within this new global business context, Indian operators have led the way, and some aspects of the "Indian model" are now being adopted by operators in other countries, both rich and poor (Mobile marvels, 2009).

To help exemplify these trends, *The Economist* report describes the case of Ms. Wokhwale who became a "village phone" operator in Uganda (Mobile marvels, 2009). She bought a basic handset using a microfinance loan and went into business where she sold phone calls to other villagers and made a small profit on each call. She soon repaid her loan and bought a second phone. Today, she is running not just her original phone shop, but also a small business selling beer, as well as a music and video shop – which enabled her to help members of her family pay their children's school fees.

Models such as these could become the key to providing more online content in languages that have remained underrepresented on the Internet. Effectively applying such models to this end, however, requires a change in general perceptions of why online information in multiple languages is important. In sum, the challenge becomes getting more individuals to view aspects of language and online information as not a perk or a privilege, but as a right.

INTERNATIONAL ONLINE ACCESS AS A LEGAL AND DEMOCRATIC RIGHT

Access to essential online knowledge and information in one's native language is increasingly being presented as a basic human right. As De Varennes (2001) points out,

Language rights are not collective rights, nor do they constitute 'third generation' or vague, unenforceable rights: by and large, the language rights of minorities are an integral part of well established, basic human rights widely recognised in international law, just as are the rights of women and children. (p. 15)

Rather, they are seen as both a legal requirement and a democratic necessity in many regions of the world. Recognizing and then acting upon these rights, however, requires individuals to understand certain principles that create the foundations for such rights.

The European Commission (2010a) sees multilingualism and multilingual access to online information as one of the fundamental principles of the European Union (EU). The EU currently recognizes 23 languages as "official" languages of the Union. EU policy also states that equal status for the official languages goes to the heart of what Europe is about, for the Union recognizes language as an important part of both national and personal identity.

In its *Digital Agenda for Europe (DAE)*, published in May of 2010, the European Commission (EC) emphasises the importance of the digital networks for the dissemination of essential information and the collection of core data for the European Union (European Commission, 2010b). The EU considers the *DEA* to be a cornerstone of its strategy for the development of a flourishing digital economy by 2020. The document describes some of the enormous benefits of eGovernment for citizens, businesses, and governments in an increasingly mobile world. For example, in Denmark, electronic invoicing saves taxpayers €150 million and businesses €50 million a year (European Commission, 2010b). In Italy, e-procurement systems cut over €3 billion in costs. The report states that if introduced across the EU, annual savings could exceed €50 billion (European Commission, 2010b).

Organizations in other countries (e.g., South Africa and India) have decided not to have just one, but rather a number of official languages in order to encourage their citizens to express their identity through their own language. This decision allows the citizens of those nations to have direct online access (via digital eGovernment portals) to information and legislation provided to them in their own language. Such an option can be important to using new media – such as mobile phones – as a method for sharing online information with citizens, particularly in developing nations.

South Africa, for example, has eleven official languages. It is also one of the most wired nations on the African continent (Greenwood, 2009). In South Africa, mobile phones outnumber fixed lines by eight to one and are only partially used for making phone calls. According to Greewood (2009), millions of South Africans are now using mobile phones to pay bills, move cash, and buy basic everyday items. Within this context, it is perhaps not surprising that the use of smart phones, which allow for easier access to the Internet and the World Wide Web, is on the rise in South Africa.

This rise in mobile phone use could serve as a mechanism the South African government can use to provide information to the different linguistic groups within its borders. In addition to English and Afrikaans, the nation's other major languages are IsiNdebele, IsiXhosa, IsiZulu, Sepedi, Sesotho, Setswana, SiSwati, Tshivenda, and Xitsonga. While the state has an obligation to make its information available in these languages, this is not always possible. Access to well educated and trained eTranslators is still limited, but

the African Network for Localisation (ANLoc) is attempting to address this problem (Osborn, 2010). Such initiatives, when coupled with the ease and relatively low-cost of providing online (vs. print) information in multiple languages could, in turn, allow the South African government to provide translated materials quickly, easily, and cheaply to a range of language speakers.

Moreover, in Africa decisions to localize based on a human rights perspective are often supported by key policies. These policies, in turn, could be coupled with the rise of mobile phone use to create a context in which multilingual information sharing can be effectively undertaken. In terms of language and information sharing policy, the Cultural Charter for Africa of the Organization of African Unity (1976) is a key document. Agreed to by the Organization of African Unity and adopted by the Heads of States on July 05, 1976 and entering into force on September 19, 1990, the charter contains certain articles that provide a policy initiative for addressing issues of language and localization. Article 17 of Part V of the Charter, for example, states that "the African States recognize the imperative need to develop African languages which will ensure their cultural advancement and accelerate their economic and social development (…)." The charter also recognizes that there is no alternative to the use of the African languages for literacy and for ensuring mass participation in development. This view is re-enforced in the Charter's preamble by the statement "that any human society is necessarily governed by rules and principles based on traditions, languages, ways of life and thought in other words on a set of cultural values, which reflect its distinctive character and personality" (Organization of African Unity, 1976).

The example of Africa and, specifically that of South Africa, demonstrates that the fundamental right to online information access in *one's own* language is not just recognised in the richer parts of the world. Although much work remains to be done to realize this right for the citizens of the

African nations, the enormous and unprecedented boom in the digital mobile markets of Africa has already laid the foundations to make this dream a reality. It is now a matter of time for policy and technology to be integrated into a framework that would make such mobile/online-based multilingualism possible.

India is another country with multiple official languages –22 in total (see Appendix). India has developed a large infrastructure to support the presence and use of Indian languages in the digital world through GIST, a project of the Centre for the Development of Advanced Computing (CDAC) (CDAC, 2010a). Located in Pune and supervised by Mahesh Kulkarni, CDAC's Website offers free downloads of a number of tools supporting Indic language computing. The CDAC's flagship product, BOO, was developed in collaboration with the CDAC team in Bangalore and provides a complete free and open source office software suite, complemented by an email client, browser, and messenger application. The suite is currently available in Assamese, Hindi, Kannada, Malayalam, Marathi, Oriya, Punjabi, Tamil, Telugu, and Urdu (CDAC, 2010b). It can also be downloaded free of charge – thus putting local language access to online information and digital content at the citizens' fingertips. This development is a prerequisite for the Government of India's eGovernment initiatives, and it brings online information closer to the citizens, only 2-3% of which speak English well enough to conduct their everyday business in that language.

Other countries, such as the United States of America, have avoided giving official status to any one language. In the case of the United States, John Adams' 1780 proposal to the Continental Congress that English be declared as the official language of the country was deemed undemocratic and a threat to individual liberty. Today, it is estimated that 322 languages are spoken in the country. Interestingly, in the United States today, there exists legislation requiring all states to make vital materials available in the language of every-

one receiving benefits subsidized by the Federal Government. Meeting this linguistic requirement is also essential in order for an organization to receive federal financial assistance as stipulated in Title VI of the Civil Rights Act of 1964 and 2000 Executive Order 13166.

Executive Order 13166 states that a federal financial recipient has to take steps to ensure that language barriers do not exclude Limited English Proficiency (LEP) persons from effective participation in its benefits and services (United States Department of Justice, 2003; Federal Register, 2000). Implicit in this order is that all online materials developed by all federal agencies in the United States must also be localized for access. The early results of this initiative can already be seen in the current – and increasing – number or state and federal government Websites that have been localized for Spanish (the U.S.'s second most commonly spoken language). For example, the Website of the Department of Motor Vehicles for the state of Maine (over 3,000 miles from the border of Mexico – the US's closest Spanish-speaking neighbor country) offers information in both English and Spanish.

Europe has gone a step further. Officially, texts published online or offline in the official languages do not exist in one original version with 22 translations. Rather, such texts exist in the form of 23 original versions in each of the EU's 23 official languages. Translation is mentioned nowhere in the legislation, and this factor re-enforces the principle that all languages have equal status within the Union. This perspective reflects the desire not to have any one dominant language or culture in the European Union, as explained in the official history of translation at the European Commission (European Commission, 2010a). The idea, as expressed in the policies of the European Union, is to make access to information as easy as possible for all EU citizens (European Commission, 2010b). The EU, in turn, supports this policy by following the dual strategy of eGovernment (i.e., making essential government information available online) and linguistic accessibility (i.e., providing online information in the languages of its citizens).

So what about the cost of maintenance of these complex multilingual online systems? The European Commission's translation services are the largest translation agency in the world and had an operating budget of approximately €1 billion in 2010. However, according to the EU, it is just a myth that a huge proportion of its budget is spent on multilingualism as the costs of translation and interpretation in all the EU institutions account for less than 1% of the EU's total annual budget. From the EU's perspective, the equivalent of spending about €2 per EU citizen on this issue is a modest price to pay for guaranteeing democracy and equal rights among those citizens (European Commission, 2010a).

Legal and democratic rights are important factors when considering multilingualism in the digital knowledge and information society. However, the question of access to information in *one's native* language is projecting way beyond that of *just* legal or democratic rights. Having access to knowledge and information or not can literally become a matter of life and death.

INTERNATIONAL ONLINE ACCESS AS A MATTER OF LIFE OR DEATH

It seems that more important than the cost of multilingualism is the cost of the lack of multilingualism. What price does society have to pay because information is *not* made available online for quick, easy, and free access in the languages of its citizens? Is it possible to calculate the cost to humankind of limiting access to information to those who represent a potential market and deny access to those who do not? In an attempt to quantify these costs, I will examine the question of information access and denial in two important sectors: healthcare and economic development.

Godlee (2004), Pakenham-Walsh (2009), and others have documented that lack of access to adequate healthcare information kills several thousand people every day. While there are multiple causes for this lack of access to adequate online resources (e.g., missing or inadequate Internet and Web connectivity), it is undisputed that the so-called "language barrier" plays an important part in this daily tragedy. Important information might be readily *available* online, but if it is not available in the languages of those who need it, then that information is not *accessible*, and it may as well not exist at all. Easy access to knowledge and information in the global information society must therefore mean both online access *and* linguistic access. One without the other is doomed for certain failure.

According to Sha (2010b), over 24,000 children die every day around the world. This mortality rate is equivalent to:

- 1 child dying every 3.6 seconds.
- 16-17 children dying every minute.
- A 2010 Haiti earthquake occurring almost every 9-10 days.
- A 2004 Asian Tsunami occurring almost every 10 days.
- An Iraq-scale death toll every 16–40 days.
- Just under 9 million children dying every year.
- Some 79 million children dying between 2000 and 2007.

A key statement by Sha is that the silent killers of these children are *poverty, easily preventable diseases, illnesses,* and other related causes. Sadly, many of these situations could be prevented by providing easy mobile online access to relevant health information in the language of the people who need it.

Sha ads that, in our disaster-hungry world, news about earthquakes and tsunami can dominate our news channels for weeks and such coverage can motivate people to donate substantial aid to those affected by these disasters. The scale of the daily and ongoing catastrophe, however, rarely manages to achieve, much less sustain, prime-time headline coverage – probably the main reason why these facts are not more widely known. For example, two decades ago, famine in Africa caught the attention of the global media, and this coverage prompted an outpouring of action and financial assistance. This wide-spread international interest culminated in the spectacle "Live Aid" concert that was covered by most global news services and that appeared on a wide array of international television networks. Shortly after this concert, however, interest in famine relief for African began to wane, and today, the media hardly notes it, yet millions continue to die of starvation across the continent.

James P. Grant, head of UNICEF from 1980 to 1995, launched the child survival revolution with vaccinations and diarrhoea treatment. For Grant, the reason why most children are dying was clear. "There's no great mystery behind the reasons most children are dying. We know why they are dying. They're dying from diseases we have vaccines to prevent. They're dying from unsafe water we have the power to make clean. They're dying from malaria carried by mosquitoes we can block." (Banbury 2008, para. 4).

By the end of the 1980s, it became clear for Grant why tens of thousands of children, women and men died needlessly every day: a lack of available information. *The Healthcare Information for All* campaign and knowledge network, an organization with more than 3,000 members representing 1,800 organizations in 150 countries worldwide, is following in his footsteps (HIFA, 2010). HIFA2015 has provided scientific evidence that the major contributing factor to the worldwide ongoing, enormous tragedy is that the mother, family caregiver, or health worker in many developing nations does not have access to the *information and knowledge* needed, when they need it and in the language they need it to make appropriate decisions and save lives.

In addressing the need for such access to information, the HIFA campaign quotes Pablos-Mendez, Managing Director of the Rockefeller Foundation, who notes "bridging the know-do gap is the foremost challenge and opportunity for public health in the 21st century" (HIFA, 2010, para. 2). The campaign provides concrete examples to back up this claim and cites world leading specialist health and medical journals such as *The Lancet* (Packenham, 2009):

- 8 in 10 caregivers in developing countries are not familiar with the two key symptoms of childhood pneumonia – fast and difficult breathing – which indicate the need for urgent treatment; although antibiotics are often widely available, only 20% of children with pneumonia receive them, and 2 million die each year
- 4 in 10 mothers in India withheld fluids when their baby developed diarrhoea worldwide, 1.8 million children die every year from dehydration due to diarrhoea
- 3 in 4 hospital doctors responsible for sick children in district hospitals in Bangladesh, Dominican Republic, Ethiopia, Indonesia, Philippines, Tanzania, and Uganda had poor basic knowledge of common killers such as childhood pneumonia, severe malnutrition, and sepsis
- 4 in 10 general practitioners in Pakistan used tranquilisers as their standard treatment for hypertension

Shah (2010a) provides additional data and points out inequalities that could be addressed if people only knew and had access to information about alternative methods of cooking or sanitizing water. Sha also reports that indoor air pollution resulting from the use of solid fuels by the poor is a major killer, claiming the lives of 1.5 million people each year, more than half of them below the age of five (i.e., 4,000 deaths a day). This number is higher than that of total deaths from malaria and similar to that from tuberculosis. Thus, as long as access to vital and potentially life-saving online health information in *one's native* language is not made available, tens of thousands of people will continue to face certain death every day.

THE PRACTICE OF INCLUSIVE APPROACHES

Large sections of the mainstream localization and translation industries seem to be locked into yesterday's paradigms. However, many world leaders and those interested in human development issues have recognised the need to bring individuals at the bottom of the global economic pyramid into the digital world. One of the instruments to achieve this end is to make information and knowledge available to individuals in their own language and to do so by using innovative approaches and strategies that disrupt current mainstream thinking. In 2002, Kofi Annan (then President of the United Nations) voiced in what was perceived as his IT challenge to Silicon Valley "On the Digital Divide":

The new information and communications technologies are among the driving forces of globalization. They are bringing people together, and bringing decision makers unprecedented new tools for development. At the same time, however, the gap between information "haves" and "have-nots" is widening, and there is a real danger that the world's poor will be excluded from the emerging knowledge-based global economy. (para. 1)

This challenge has been taken up by some of the large multinational digital content publishers, among them Google and Microsoft.

For some time, translation and multilingual access have been at the core of Google's Internet- and Web-based mission to organize the world's information and to make it universally accessible. Microsoft's approach to localization, by contrast, developed from its desktop-based applications to a point where the company now offers multilingual content and applications on the Web. On the non-commercial side, translation and localization for languages not covered by the mainstream have had a long tradition.. Many of the most popular open source applications have been translated by the community into more than 100 languages, among them Firefox and Open Office. Other initiatives have focused not so much on software applications but on enabling and publishing technologies.

The following section will provide a description and analysis of the main features and the strategies driving Google's and Microsoft's efforts to localize for "out of the ordinary" languages. The author will then examine initiatives supported by the International Development Research Centre (IDRC) of the Canadian Government, the World Wide Web Foundation initiated by the Web's inventor Sir Tim Berners-Lee, and The Rosetta Foundation, founded and supported by sectors of the localization industry itself.

COMMERCIAL APPROACHES

In the past, the localization and translation industries have been careful when committing support for non-commercial projects. As a result, they have been shy in embracing new business models and targeting emerging markets. A number of companies, however, have been making significant investments in localization projects that could not be considered to be part of the mainstream. All of these approaches include attempts to

- Involve communities in the target regions and languages;
- Reduce the effort required to produce the localized content and the translations;
- Remove the tight schedules associated with more traditional approaches while maintaining control and ownership of the content and the overall process.

Two of the corporate leaders in relation to such approaches have been the influential multinational firms of Google and Microsoft.

Google

At the Localization Research Centre's 12th Annual Conference in 2007, Thomas Arend spoke about localization at Google. Arend highlighted his company's mission to organize the world's information and to make it universally accessible and useful. In 2007, for example, 48% of Google's global revenues were already generated through their international business, and the company's main products were available in 117 languages (Arend, 2007). Additionally, Google's search engine supported localized results in over 55 countries and 35 languages (Arend, 2007). The Web Globalization Report Card, published annually by Bytelevel research, listed then – as it did in 2010 – Google in the number one spot of best global Websites.

Arend also insisted on the necessity for businesses to localize their products and services. In so doing, he highlighted his company's view that late localization opens windows of opportunities – for others. Arend also addressed what he called the "linguistic long tail," or those languages of which there are many, but which have not sufficiently large and rich user base to merit localised content.

In 2007, Jeff Howe introduced the notion of "crowdsourcing" to the localization industry at the Localization World Conference in Seattle. At that time, Google had been working with volunteers under the banner "Google in your language" (Google, 2010a). The alphabetical list of languages Google is working on today shows approximately 200 languages (Google, 2010b).

While the 2007 slides presented by Arend showed a screen shot still inviting translators "If you don't see your native language here, you can help Google create it by becoming a volunteer translator." This invitation seems to have disappeared from more recent versions of the Website as the company took back control over which

languages volunteers could work on. "Google in your language" is far from being a perfect approach to solving the digital divide. However, it is an innovative approach, and it involves the users of Google's software and information distribution systems, allowing the company to cover a wider range of languages.

Over the years, Google has been making a growing number of localization and translation technologies available for free. These initiatives include access to Google's machine translation service, a Website translator, a Google word translator as part of the Google toolbar, and Google's 1-click translation tool. The Google Translator Toolkit is a more recent addition to its translation kit, and it is aimed at making translation of digital content easier and more accessible to all. Google.org uses the kit for its HealthSpeaks project (Google, 2010c), which involves volunteer translators and a (voluntary) payment by the company to charities for every word translated by the volunteers. These initiatives by one of the world's richest and most successful digital companies are a good example of what a commercial company can do to support online information sharing across languages.

Microsoft

Unlimited Potential is the program Microsoft has established to help all people benefit from information and communication technology (ICT). The company has so far reached more than one billion people whose life has changed because information is now more easily available to them, commerce is more quickly achieved and success is closer than ever (Microsoft, 2010d). However, Microsoft recognizes that, for more than five billion people, the opportunity to learn, connect, create, and succeed remains elusive (Microsoft, 2010d). The company considers information sharing across languages a major factor in tackling this problem.

A significant development in the search for sustainable models to support commercially not viable languages was the launch of Microsoft's

Localization Interface Pack (LIP) program as part of its Local Language Programme (LLP) (Microsoft, 2010b). The basic idea behind LIP is to translate around 25% of the content (e.g., of Microsoft Office or Microsoft Windows) seen by users 80% of the time (Microsoft, 2010a). So, instead of translating two to three million words, only around 500,000 words of an application are translated. This approach reduces not only the localization effort, but it also cuts the cost of distribution. In 2010, almost 300 LIPs were available in 95 languages from Afrikaans to Yoruba for a range of Microsoft products (Microsoft, 2010a). While LIPs can be downloaded for free, users must still purchase the original version of the product which creates obvious difficulties for users in low income countries. In February of 2010, the company announced that it would help to provide access to technology to more than one billion speakers of endangered languages (Microsoft, 2010a).

According to Microsoft (2010c), providing technology to indigenous speakers of smaller languages not only helps to preserve the language, but it also allows the rest of the world to benefit from the innovation and creativity of the community. Such a practice allows indigenous speakers of these languages to have a voice in the world community and gives them access to the economic benefits of the technology age. However, one road block imposed by Microsoft remains: the decision on which languages are going to be covered by its fully commercial and by its LIP program remains with the company. Notwithstanding, Microsoft's strategy to contribute to information sharing across languages is one of the longest running, most innovative, and the most successful in the industry.

Allowing access to technology for indigenous speakers of smaller languages not only helps to preserve the language, it allows the rest of the world to benefit from the innovation and creativity of the community. In addition, it allows indigenous speakers to have a voice in the world community

and gives them access to the economic benefits of the Technology Age. (Microsoft, 2010c, para. 8)

The company has obviously realised that an investment into underserved languages can only be in its mid- to long-term interests. Narrowing the digital divide can only be in the interest of the world's largest publisher of software.

HUMAN DEVELOPMENT APPROACHES

It was probably to be expected that the non-profit sector would pay more attention to the rights and requirements of underserved languages (i.e., those not covered by commercial mainstream digital publishers). There have been large-scale initiatives to support the localization of open source software into more than 100 languages. There have also been initiatives to enable the use of underserved languages: by encoding their characters, by encoding *locales*, and by creating keyboards and complementary input methods. Other initiatives have tried to provide localization and translation services such as those provided by Translators without Borders, Translations for Progress, and The Rosetta Foundation, and there is the non-profit certification program, Certified Localization Professional (CLP), offered by The Institute of Localization Professionals (TILP). At the same time, initiatives, such as the microfinancing organization KIVA, have built up their own translation infrastructure and enabled the organization to translate up to one million words a month employing only volunteer translators.[1]

The next sections of this chapter will provide some details on two of the programs funded by the IDRC, followed by a short introduction to the World Wide Web Foundation, and, finally, a summary of the activities of The Rosetta Foundation.

The IDRC: PAN Localization and ANLoc

The Information and Communication Technologies division of the Canadian Government's International Development Research Centre (IDRC) has initiated two projects to build local language computing capacity in Asia and Africa. One of these projects is the PAN Localization project that builds local language computing capacity in Asia. In 2005, PAN Localization produced the *Survey of Language Computing in Asia*. This document highlighted the fact that, among the 2,200 languages spoken in Asia, only a fraction had been integrated into the digital world. Although Asians have become the most numerous Internet users worldwide, access to the Internet and the Web – and therefore access to digital information and knowledge – was still largely restricted to those with knowledge of the English language.

PAN Localization's sister project in Africa is the African Network for Localization (ANLoc). Don Osborn (2010) produced a report that summarizes in a very unique way the challenges facing those attempting to develop localization capacities for African languages. In the report, Osborn recognizes that the sheer diversity of the African language scene (some 2,000 languages spoken, or one third of the world's living languages) presents considerable challenges to anyone planning to address it. However, Dwayne Bailey, the project's coordinator, warns that anyone familiar with the United Nation's Millennium Development Goals (MDGs) will soon realize that it is essential to address issues of languages in order to allow for an effective delivery of these goals (IDRC, 2010).

It is a common objective of both of these projects to produce the tools to translate Internet content into local languages, build capacity for local language computing, and advance policy for local language content creation and access provision. The projects focus on the creation of enabling technologies and frameworks that include the development of character sets, fonts, spelling and grammar checkers, speech recognition systems, machine translation, and other related local language applications. Both PAN Localization and ANLoc have so far not addressed the challenge of long-term sustainability of their efforts and will soon need to plan for a future when IDRC funding will no longer be available to them. However, they support a vision of a World Wide Web that speaks "all world languages" and truly facilitates information sharing across languages.

The World Wide Web Foundation

The inventor of the World Wide Web, Sir Tim Berners-Lee, established the World Wide Web Foundation in early 2009, and the Foundation was publically introduced at the 2009 LRC Conference in Limerick, Ireland. "Advance the Web. Empower People." is the slogan of the Foundation, and it was established to promote a Web that empowers "all people, including billions excluded today, by providing new opportunities for creativity, collaboration, teaching, learning, enterprise and a better life" (Bratt, 2010, para. 1). The interesting aspect of the Foundation's work is that it clearly sees the potential for social and economic change around the world by removing barriers to creating and consuming Web content. While the Foundation does not explicitly point to human language issues, its CEO, Steve Bratt, is clear about the central role that language plays when trying to put the World Wide Web in the hands of the people. While the Foundation secured funding to run its first project, concerned with "Regreening in Africa," it relies on the work of volunteers and donations. Promoting and enabling the sharing of information across languages is one of the core interests of the World Wide Web Foundation and its founder Sir Tim Berners-Lee.

The Rosetta Foundation

This organization was established in 2009, to "relieve poverty, support healthcare, develop education and promote justice through access to information and knowledge across the languages of the world" (The Rosetta Foundation, 2010, para. 1). It was established and is supported by individuals and companies including the Localisation Research Centre at the University of Limerick, the Science Foundation Ireland's Centre for Next Generation Localisation, Welocalize, Multilingual, Ontram, and Promt. The founder members, among them Brian Kelly (founder of Ireland's first localization service provider, Softrans International), collectively represent many decades of experience in the localization sector. They had become aware that current mainstream localization approaches actively promoted the exclusion of large numbers of people and languages from access to information and knowledge, information vital for their health, their freedom, their education, and their economic well-being. The Foundation, in turn, was developed to address these issues.

The Foundation is developing The Rosetta Foundation Platform that will allow seamless collaboration of translators on localization and translation projects. The Foundation also offers free translation services to non-profit organisations and has established partnerships with organisations such as the Special Olympics and MediSend. The work of The Rosetta Foundation is exclusively supported by contributions made by donors and its partners.

The non-profit sector serviced by The Rosetta Foundation has, by its very nature, an enormous requirement to share knowledge in every language. Catering for this sector is a massive undertaking that will require significant investment. Such investment, moreover, will be crucial for bridging the global linguistic divide, for making information poverty history.

CONCLUSION

"Language, Money and the Information Society" (2010) is the title that Adel El Zaim, the IDRC's Senior Program Specialist in the Regional Office for the Middle East and North Africa, chose for his foreword to the study on African Language Computing published by his organization. In it, El Zaim advocates the role of translation in socioeconomic development. His assumption that language no longer just serves as a means of communication but also has acquired a strong socio-economic role is supported by the case the author has tried to articulate in this chapter. While money provides access to goods, languages provides access to knowledge and information necessary for survival in the digital information age. Unfortunately, many digital publishers, as well as their mainstream localization and translation service providers, seem to remain focused on the value of money, the main currency of the industrial age. Although they are producing what is the very currency of the information society, they remain stuck in a time warp were "cash is king."

Some leading multinational publishers, such as Microsoft and Google, at least recognize the need to go beyond the pale and serve the underserved language communities in their online materials. These organizations explore new and more inclusive approaches to Web-based localization and translation, but they also continue to very clearly differentiate between more and less "valuable" languages. Within this context, the more valuable languages are those spoken by people with money receive more attention. Their content is localized fully and by professional translators. The less valuable languages, in turn, are those spoken by people with less money receive less attention. Content is dealt with later, and it is generally not localized fully and dealt with by "volunteers" (though often supported by publishers). In a world where cash is king, so is quality. In a world where cash is scarce, "good enough" and "better than nothing" will often have to do when it comes to the translation and localization of Web-based information.

There is no doubt that, at least in the commercial world, we are still a long way away from the day when all languages and their speakers are seen as equal and are dealt with equally. When, as 1997 Nobel Peace Prize winner Muhammad Yunus (2007) put it, "as an IT user, you won't even need to know that other languages exist. When you browse the Internet, you'll see everything in your language" (p. 194). In stating these words, Yunus acknowledges the central role access to technology – and to the information needed to use that technology – will play in the future.

There is, however, a growing realization that information sharing across languages is not a "nice-to-have." It is more than just another instrument of the globalization strategies of multinational digital content publishers or a budget line item to be played with by the accountants whose decisions dominate the global localization and translation strategies. We can no longer afford the cost of the information barrier; the cost of the denial of service to those who do not speak one of the rich people's languages is too high for humanity. The death of tens of thousands of people every day caused by lack of access to information is unacceptable. It goes without saying that equal access to localization and translation services for all languages will not suffice to prevent this suffering but there is no doubt that it has the capacity to save thousands of lives – every day.

The right to access to information in *one's own* language cannot be reduced to a right that can only be redeemed by those who can pay for it. Knowing and understanding the devastating effect that lack of access to information can have on the well-being of people, a denial of service today affecting more than a billion people and thousands of languages cannot be tolerated. There is a golden opportunity for the localization industry to demonstrate to the rest of the world that it takes its role as the enabler of the multi-lingual digital information society seriously and

responsibly, making information sharing across languages possible for all – and especially for those whose lives depend on it. There is also a golden opportunity for researchers, for example those individuals working in the multi-million euro Centre for Next Generation Localization (CNGL), to take the lead and show the world how language technology can be harnessed to make the world a better place for all.

There is a light on the horizon as national and regional initiatives are connecting with each other under the umbrella of the United Nation's Internet Governance Forum to develop a Global Open Localization Platform. However, information sharing across languages – all languages, irrespective of the socioeconomic status of their speakers – remains a major problem. It is a problem that requires a big solution. This can only be provided by a collaboration of all sectors – commercial, political and civil society – on a global scale.

REFERENCES

Allen, P. (2009, March 2). Wired world – The global growth of mobile phone use. *The Guardian*. Retrieved November 25, 2010, from http://www.guardian.co.uk/business/interactive/2009/mar/02/mobile-phones

Annan, K. (2002). *On the digital divide*. Retrieved May 01, 2010, from http://www.un.org/News/ossg/sg/stories/sg-5nov-2002.htm

Arend, T. (2007). *Localization at Google*. LRC XII Conference: The Localization Research Forum. European Foundation Dublin, Ireland. Retrieved May 12, 2010, from http://www.localization.ie/resources/conferences/2007/presentations/TArend/Google_Keynote_LRC_XII_Dublin_Sep_2007_Thomas_Arend.pdf

Banbury, J. (2008). *Jim Grant and the unfinished agenda for children. What "preventable" means.* UNICEF USA. Retrieved May 5, 2010, from http://fieldnotes.unicefusa.org/mt/mt-search.cgi?tag=Jim%20Grant&blog_id=1

Bratt, S. (2010). *Advance the Web. Empower people.* World Wide Web Foundation. Retrieved November 26, 2010, from http://www.Webfoundation.org/2010/03/advance-the-Web-empower-people/

CDAC. (2010a). *Gist- Contributions towards standardization in Indian language computing.* Retrieved May 5, 2010, from http://www.cdac.in/html/gist/research-areas/standardisation.asp

CDAC. (2010b). *Bharateeya Open Office Suite.* Retrieved November 25, 2010, from http://pune.cdac.in/html/gist/products/boo.aspx

De Varennes, F. (2001). Language rights as an integral part of human rights. *IJMS: International Journal on Multicultural Societies, 3*(1), 15–25.

El Zaim, A. (2010). Language, money, and the information society. In Osborne, D. (Ed.), *African languages in a digital age: Challenges and opportunities for indigenous language computing* (pp. ix–xii). Cape Town, South Africa: HSCR Press.

European Commission. (2010a). *Translation at the European Commission – A history.* Luxembourg: Office for Official Publications of the European Communities.

European Commission. (2010b). *E-government on the fast track.* Retrieved November 25, 2010, from http://ec.europa.eu/information_society/activities/egovernment/policy/index_en.htDm

Federal Register. (2000). *Executive order 13166 – Improving access to services for persons with limited English proficiency.* Department of Justice. Enforcement of Title Vi of the Civil Rights Act of 1964 – National Origin Discrimination Against Persons With Limited English Proficiency: Notice. Retrieved May 5, 2010, from http://www.justice.gov/crt/cor/Pubs/eolep.pdf

Godlee, F., Packenham-Walsh, N., Ncayiyana, D., Cohen, B., & Parker, A. (2004). *Can we achieve health information for all by 2015?* Retrieved November 25, 2010, from http://image.thelancet.com/extras/04art6112Web.pdf

Google. (2010a). *Translate Google into your language.* Retrieved May 12, 2010, from https://www.google.com/accounts/ServiceLogin?service=transconsole&passive=true&nui=1&continue=http%3A%2F%2Fwww.google.com%2Ftransconsole&followup=http%3A%2F%2Fwww.google.com%2Ftransconsole

Google. (2010b). *Google in your language. Google translation status report.* Retrieved May 12, 2010, from http://www.google.com/transconsole/giyl/check/status

Google. (2010c). *HealthSpeaks.* Retrieved November 25, 2010, from http://sitescontent.google.com/healthspeaks/about/

Greenwood, L. (2009). Africa's mobile banking revolution. *BBC mobile.* Retrieved November 25, 2010, from http://news.bbc.co.uk/2/hi/8194241.stm.

HIFA2015. (2010). *A global campaign. Healthcare information for all by 2015.* Retrieved May 5, 2010, from http://www.hifa2015.org/about/

IDRC. (2003). *Survey of language computing in Asia.* Retrieved May 12, 2010, from http://www.idrc.ca/uploads/user-S/11446781751Survey.pdf

IDRC. (2010). *African network for localization.* Retrieved May 13, 2010, from http://www.idrc.ca/acacia/ev-122243-201-1-DO_TOPIC.html

Localization, P. A. N. (2010). *PAN localization: Building local language computing capacity in Asia.* Retrieved May 12, 2010, from http://www.idrc.ca/en/ev-51828-201-1-DO_TOPIC.html

Microsoft. (2010a). *Windows language interface pack.* Retrieved May 12, 2010, from http://msdn.microsoft.com/en-us/goglobal/bb688177.aspx

Microsoft. (2010b). *Microsoft local language program: A world of possibilities.* Retrieved May 12, 2010, from http://download.microsoft.com/download/A/2/3/A23A01D2-4B26-4E8B-9A92-F4FD57256404/LLP_Overview_Brochure.pdf

Microsoft. (2010c, February 22). *More than 1 billion speakers of endangered languages get access to technology.* Retrieved May 12, 2010, from http://www.microsoft.com/presspass/press/2010/feb10/02-22mld10pr.mspx

Microsoft. (2010d). *Opening new worlds for everyone.* Retrieved May 13, 2010, from http://download.microsoft.com/download/2/0/A/20AC945C-34D0-4A60-8245-F80E-80FE954F/UP_Factsheet_A4_English_0109.pdf

Mobile marvels. (2009, September 24). *The Economist.* Retrieved November 25, 2010, from http://www.economist.com/node/14483896

Organization of African Unity. (1976). *Cultural charter for Africa.* Retrieved May 4, 2010, from http://www.dfa.gov.za/foreign/Multilateral/africa/treaties/culture.htm

Osborn, D. (2010). *African languages in the digital age: Challenges and opportunities for indigenous language computing.* Cape Town, South Africa: HSCR Press.

Pakenham-Walsh, N. (2009). Lack of access to healthcare information is a hidden killer: Healthcare information for all by 2015. *World Medical Journal, 55*(4), Retrieved May 1, 2010, from http://www.wma.net/en/30publications/20journal/pdf/wmj24.pdf

Prahalad, C. K. (2010). *The fortune at the bottom of the pyramid. Eradicating poverty through profits.* Upper Saddle River, NJ: Pearson Education.

Shah, A. (2010a). *Poverty facts and stats: Global issues.* Retrieved May 2, 2010, from http://www.globalissues.org/article/26/poverty-facts-and-stats

Shah, A. (2010b). *Today, over 24,000 children died around the world: Global issues.* Retrieved May 2, 2010 from http://www.globalissues.org/article/715/today-over-24000-children-died-around-the-world

The Rosetta Foundation. (2010). *Promoting equality through language and cultural diversity.* Retrieved May 12, 2010, from http://www.therosettafoundation.org/

UNESCO. (2008). *Multilingualism in cyberspace.* Retrieved November 25, 2010, from http://portal.unesco.org/ci/en/ev.php-URL_ID=18147&URL_DO=DO_TOPIC&URL_SECTION=201.html

United States Department of Justice. (2003). *Title VI of the Civil Rights Act of 1964. 42 U.S.C. § 2000d et seq. Civil Rights Division. Coordination and Review Section.* Retrieved May 5, 2010, from http://www.justice.gov/crt/cor/coord/titlevi.php

Yunus, M. (2007). *Creating a world without poverty: Social business and the future of capitalism.* New York, NY: Public Affairs.

KEY TERMS AND DEFINITIONS

Localization: The linguistic and cultural adaptation of digital content to the requirements and the locale of a foreign market, includes the provision of services and technologies for the management of multilingualism across the digital global information flow.

Digital Divide: The gap between people with good access to information technology and those with limited or no access.

Language Barrier: The barrier faced by people speaking different languages when they attempt to communicate with each other. In reality, this could be more appropriately be described as a barrier to access of translation and localisation services.

Bottom of the Pyramid: The poorest socio-economic group living on less than US$2.50 a day.

Reuters Market Light (RML): An SMS-based service that provides farmers in India with localised weather forecasts, crop prices, agricultural news and other relevant information.

AGIS - Action for Global Information Sharing: An annual event bringing together non-profit translation agencies, technology gurus and charitable organisation.

ENDNOTE

[1] Information taken from a 13 April 2010 interview the author did with Naomi Baer, KIVA's language coordinator.

APPENDIX

The Offical Languages of the European Union

The European Union has 23 official and working languages: Bulgarian, Czech, Danish, Dutch, English, Estonian, Finnish, French, German, Greek, Hungarian, Irish, Italian, Latvian, Lithuanian, Maltese, Polish, Portuguese, Romanian, Slovak, Slovene, Spanish, and Swedish.

The first Community Regulation determining official languages was passed in 1958. It specified Dutch, French, German and Italian as the first official and working languages of the EU, these being the languages of the Member States at that time. Since then, as more countries have become part of the EU, the number of official and working languages has increased. However, there are fewer official languages than Member States, as some share common languages. In Belgium, for example, the official languages are Dutch, French and German, whilst in Cyprus the majority of the population speaks Greek, which has official status.

There are two main entitlements for languages with "official and working" status:

- Documents may be sent to EU institutions and a reply received in any of these languages;
- EU regulations and other legislative documents are published in the official and working languages, as is the Official Journal.

Due to time and budgetary constraints, relatively few working documents are translated into all languages. The European Commission employs English, French and German in general as procedural languages, whereas the European Parliament provides translation into different languages according to the needs of its Members.

Source:
- Official EU languages. (2009). *EU Languages and EU Language Policy*. Retrieved November 25, 2010, from http://ec.europa.eu/education/languages/languages-of-europe/doc135_en.htm.

The Offical Languages of India

Article 345 of the Indian constitution recognises as "official languages" of the union Standard Hindi or any one or more of the languages adopted by a state legislature as the official language. English is recognised as a secondary official language. Until the Twenty-First Amendment of the Constitution in 1967, the country recognised 14 official regional languages. The Eighth Schedule and the Seventy-First Amendment increased the number of official regional languages of India to 18. The following are the 22 official languages, aside from English, set out in the eighth schedule as of May 2008: Assamese, Bengali, Bodo, Dogri, Gujarati, Standard Hindi, Kannada, Kashmiri, Konkani, Maithili, Malayalam, Manipuri, Marathi, Nepali, Oriya, Punjabi, Sanskrit, Santhali, Sindhi, Tamil, Telugu, Urdu.

Sources:

- ◦ Presidential order, 1960. (1960, April 27). *Ministry of Home Affairs, Government of India.* Retrieved November 25, 2010, from http://www.rajbhasha.gov.in/preseng.htm.
- ◦ *Constitution of India. Articles 29, 30, 120, 210, 343-351 as amended in the 21st and 71st Amendments.* Retrieved November 25, 2010, from http://indiacode.nic.in/coiWeb/welcome. html.

Chapter 16
Linguistic Minorities on the Internet

Jaffer Sheyholislami
Carleton University, Canada

ABSTRACT

This chapter presents the results of an empirical study (done using online ethnography and discourse analysis) of how the Kurds use the Internet. In examining this situation, the author provides suggestions related to the fact that, as much as we need to be concerned with the dominance of a few major languages on the Internet, we also need to map the online presence of linguistic minorities. Such mapping is essential in order to understand the paradoxical nature of a medium that simultaneously homogenizes and fragments linguistic communities and identities.

INTRODUCTION

The Internet represents one of the most interactive, fast-changing, and accessible media forms in human history. Its use is inexorably connected to issues like language and identity – issues that are of great concern to human beings. In fact, scholars such as Appadurai (1996) have suggested that the Internet is a force that is augmenting the spread of cultural globalization, or what Held et al. (1999) refer to as the movement of "objects, signs and

people across regions and intercontinental space" (p. 329). By extension, this situation also often means extending American hegemony and the English language at the expense of other national and regional cultures and other languages and identities (Phillipson, 2009).

Within this context, it has been suggested that the Internet undermines the existence of linguistic minorities[1] (Thussu, 2000). Other studies, however, have illustrated that the Internet can empower marginal groups and speakers of minority languages by enabling them to communicate across geographical, social, and political boundar-

DOI: 10.4018/978-1-60960-833-0.ch016

ies to develop their languages, display their own way of life, and voice their concerns and issues (Castells, 2004; Cunliffe, 2007; Danet & Herring, 2007; Erikson, 2007). Yet still others have warned against "unproblematized" views such as perceiving the Internet as a utopian space where all individuals and all groups have equal access to the production, dissemination, and consumption of information (Wei & Kolko, 2005). Cunliffe and Harries (2005), for example, illustrate that the online use of minority languages could be a very complex activity and, in some cases, even problematic. As the Internet is relatively new and constantly changing, the end of this debate is nowhere in sight. Rather, much more research on Internet usage, especially by speakers of minority languages and members of smaller cultural groups, is needed to flesh out the extent to which language and identity are undermined or fostered by global Internet expansion.

This paper contributes to this line of research by examining the ways Kurds use the Internet to construct, reproduce, and disseminate discursive constructions of their identities. Claiming to be the largest non-state nation in the world (McDowall, 2004), the Kurds' language, territory, culture and political destiny have been fractured among at least four regions, including parts of Turkey, Iraq, Iran and Syria. Much of this fragmentation has been due to the lack of easy communication among Kurds who are divided by harsh terrain and the national and political borders of the states in which they live – factors that have kept them apart for decades, if not centuries. Despite this situation, a sense of Kurdishness and belonging to a common cultural identity has persisted (van Bruinessen, 2000).

The objective of this chapter is to present the results of a study done to examine the extent to which the Kurds have been able to use the Internet to carry out trans-border communication activities and to consolidate their identities. Kurdish identity is often characterised in terms of a language unique to the Kurds – a language that is said to separate the Kurds from neighbouring majority nationalities such as Arabs, Turks, and Persians. Therefore, an examination of the role of the Internet as it relates to the formation of Kurdish identity must involve an examination of the languages the Kurds use on the Internet, how and for what purposes they use these languages, and what implications Internet usage practices might have for not only Kurdish language and identity, but also our understanding of the interfaces between language, identity, and the Internet. Through exploring these issues, the author suggests that, as much as it is valid and necessary to concern ourselves with the socio-political power dimensions of the dominance of English on the Internet and related issues of access to online environments (e.g., the global digital divide), it is also valid to acknowledge and demonstrate that the Internet is enabling marginalized and oppressed minorities to revitalize their languages, reinforce their cultural symbols, and reify their regional and transnational identities in unprecedented ways.

To illustrate these ideas, the chapter will present certain central concepts in order to provide a context for best understanding this study. Several theoretical issues will be outlined and background information on Kurds, Kurdistan, and the Kurdish Internet will be discussed. This discussion will be followed by a description of the methods used for data collection and analysis in relation to studying the Kurdish internet. Data analysis findings, informed by a media discourse analytic approach, will be carried out in two parts. First, the main features of the Internet that are utilised by the Kurds will be identified. In so doing, examples of how Internet resources are used for the construction of group identity will be provided. Second, findings and observations of the socio-cultural and political contexts that bear upon the online activities of the Kurds will be analyzed and discussed. Finally, the main theoretical assumptions about the interface between language, cultural identity, and the Internet will be revisited.

THEORETICAL ISSUES

McLuhan (1962) believed that while print had given birth to nationalism and the modern nation-state (Anderson, 1991), electronic media would undermine nationalism and locality and engender a "global village." In recent years, some scholars have seen electronic media at the forefront of cultural globalization (e.g., Appadurai, 1996) which has meant the spread of English throughout the world (Mair, 2002; Dor, 2004), although this spread has been declining. In 1996, 82% of the world's Websites were in English (Warschauer, 2000). However, according to Internet World Stats (www.internetworldstats.com), by the end of 2007, 30.1% of the information found online was in English, and by the end of September 2009, the percentage had dropped to 27.6%.[2]

Despite this decline in the use of English and the increase in the use of other languages on the Internet (Danet & Herring, 2007), it is evident that, at least for now, English remains the language of "global" communication online. Whereas some individuals see the dominance of a "global English" as inevitable and beneficial to the world (de Swaan, 2001), others view this as "linguistic imperialism," an institutionally-promoted agenda to suppress linguistic and cultural diversity. In this context, the global spread of English online is seen as a means to strengthen the dominance of English-speaking cultures and their cultural, economic, and political values that are indispensable parts of that language (Phillipson, 2009). Other critics have suggested that, alongside English and hundreds of other state languages, minority languages can and should be able to develop and flourish on the Internet (Danet & Herring, 2007; Honeycutt & Cunliffe, 2010). Although some sociolinguists such as Fishman (1991) have been sceptical about the overall positive role of the media in maintaining and developing minority languages, other commentators, such as Crystal (2000), have seen the Internet as a saviour of endangered languages. It is thus perhaps not surprising that, in recent years,

granting linguistic rights to regional and minority languages has also meant supporting minorities to have their own media in their mother tongue (e.g., in the European Charter for Regional or Minority Languages) (Síthigh, 2010). In such situations, online media have been seen as a catalyst for the formation and dissemination of discoursal identity constructs.

There are at least three reasons to underscore the significance of language in defining and constructing cultural identity. First, for the majority of people – especially ethnic or cultural minorities – language is one of the most significant markers of group identity (Edwards, 2009; Fishman, 1989). It has been suggested that the Kurdish language is the most important manifestation of Kurdish identity because it separates the Kurds from their neighbouring peoples (e.g., Arabs, Persians, and Turks) more readily than any other cultural or physical characteristic (van Bruinessen, 2000; Hassanpour, 2003). The second reason is connected to the instrumentality of language. That is, citizens' participation in the cultural, social, and political life of a community depends upon the degree of access they have to their native language (Kymlicka & Straehle, 1999). Finally, language plays a constructivist role in that it enables the reproduction and discursive reconstruction of other components of an ethno-national identity such as a common culture, territory, history, and a host of myths and symbols including the map of an imagined homeland, flag, and heroes (Wodak *et al.*, 2009; Billig, 1995).

This symbolic, instrumental, and constructive power of language is magnified by the Internet, and this situation is especially the case in the context of minorities and peoples without a state of their own. Such groups and individuals generally do not have their own public schools, ministries of culture, and military or other relevant national state-sponsored institutions that fashion national identities (Smith, 1998). Minority language media are similarly deemed important for several reasons. New media such as the Internet provide linguistic minorities with a forum through which they can legitimize the existence of their language and maintain contact with other cultures in a contemporary world. The Internet also enables minority language groups to create public spheres that can be accessed by members from within the same linguistic community. Furthermore, the Internet can be used to boost discursive practices of identity construction and to convey and disseminate these identities (Cormack & Hourigan, 2007; Danet & Herring, 2007). In this context of identity construction, the Internet allows cultural and linguistic minorities to represent themselves rather than being represented by "others."

Far from being a homogenizing influence, the Internet seems suitable for engendering language diversity. The Internet disregards the borders and authorities of states that are often at the forefront of suppressing minority groups and violating language rights with the pretext of preserving the unity and integrity of the nation-state (Billig, 1995; Skutnabb-Kangas, 2000). Moreover, compared to broadcast communication, the Internet is cheaper and far more accessible because it can bypass state or market regulations and constraints (Poster, 1999). Theoretically, anyone who wants to and has the technical means (i.e. access to a computer and to an Internet service provider) should be able to produce and disseminate an unlimited amount of information and do so on a global scale. This situation is especially important for those groups whose voices would otherwise not be heard. While it is essential to keep in mind that the Internet is an instrument used to strengthen transnationalism, globalization (Appadurai, 1996), and English-language dominance, it is equally significant to acknowledge that the Internet fosters national, regional, and local identities. Examples of identity construction through Internet can be found with the Imazighen people from North Africa (Almasude, 1999), the Zapatistas from Mexico (Castells, 2004), the Maori from New Zealand (Muhamad-Brandner, 2009), the Welsh (Cunliffe & Harries, 2005), and Eritreans (Bernal, 2006).

Despite all of these affordances, the Internet has disadvantages that need to be taken into consideration. First, in many parts of the developing world, the majority of people cannot access the Internet (Bargh & McKenna, 2004). New Zealand's Maori speakers, for example, have limited online access (Muhamad-Brandner, 2009). Researchers have also observed limited use of the Internet among some diasporic communities in the West where access may not be a major issue (Benítez, 2006). Thus, investigating minority language Internet use requires a critical analysis of what features of the Internet a linguistic minority can access for both the production and consumption of information. Such an investigation must also consider how the individuals use the features to which they have access, what languages and codes are employed when these individuals interact online, and to what extent these activities are influenced by pertinent socio-economic and political realities, both online and offline.

BACKGROUND

The Kurds and Kurdistan

Numbering between 25 and 35 million people, Kurds are an ethno-national group living in the Middle East, predominantly in Turkey, Iraq, Iran and Syria. About one million Kurds live outside their homeland, Kurdistan, in diasporic communities mainly located in Europe, North America, Australia, Armenia, and Lebanon (Hassanpour & Mojab, 2005). The Kurds have left their homeland for various reasons such as work (e.g., Kurds leaving Turkey in the 1960s), the Iraq-Iran war (1980-1988), political instability and persecution (e.g., the military coup in Turkey in 1980), and wars (e.g., continuous armed conflicts between the military forces of Turkey, Iraq, and Iran and Kurdish armed organizations).

The states of Turkey, Iran, and Syria (and Iraq until 1992) have denied the Kurds some of their most basic human rights. For example, until 1992, Turkey strictly banned Kurdish language use in all public domains (Hassanpour, 2003; Skutnabb-Kangas & Fernandes, 2008). The nation-states of Iran and Syria have never granted the Kurds the right to education in their mother tongue nor have they permitted Kurdish to be taught as a subject in schools. Except in Iraq, the Kurds have been denied the right to publish and broadcast freely in their homeland (Hassanpour, 1992). The Kurds were also the subject of mass killings in Iraq prior to the fall of Saddam Hussein (Black, 1993), and most of the areas inhabited by the Kurds in Turkey, Iran, Iraq, and Syria remain underdeveloped and ravaged by wars (McDowall, 2004).

Given these factors, it should come as no surprise that many Kurds have found diasporic communities in the West as safe havens. Such places allow the Kurds there the freedom of association and communication, and they have become places where Kurds are able to maintain and celebrate their cultural and linguistic identities. This freedom has been facilitated partially through access to digital technology, including the Internet. Through a variety of online media, Kurds today are able to connect not only with Kurds in other diasporic communities but also with Kurds living in Kurdistan, the original homeland.

The Kurdish Internet

The term Kurdish Internet encompasses that area of cyberspace that provides content in Kurdish speech varieties or in other languages that promote Kurdish culture and identity. Similar to many minority and non-Latin languages (Danet & Herring, 2007), the Kurdish Internet had a slow start. In 1997, when this author started a Website devoted to his birthplace, the Kurdish city of Mahabad, there were only a few hundred Websites with content about Kurds and Kurdistan. In the early 2000s, two major changes contributed to a great increase in the number of Kurdish Websites. First, the Kurdish populations in the Middle East started

to be served by relatively sufficient ISP services. Second, Kurd IT Group (www.kurditgroup.org), a technical group of Kurdish volunteers, developed the first Unicode-based Kurdish fonts and a Kurdish Support program for Windows. These developments made Kurdish writing with computers and publishing on the Internet (in both Arabic and Latin-based alphabets) a great deal easier (B. Bardaghani, Personal communication, June 20, 2007). A Yahoo search for Websites including "Kurd," "Kurds," Kurdish," and "Kurdistan" returned less than 2000 hits in June 2001, more than 650,000 in May 2007, and over two million hits in May 2010. These numbers indicate a considerable expansion of online materials in the Kurdish language and substantial growth in online content about the Kurds.

Despite this growth in Kurdish Internet, there has been limited research on the medium. Romano (2002) focuses on the ways in which the Internet enabled many Turkish Kurds living in diaspora to organize demonstrations after the abduction of a Kurdish leader Abdullah Öcalan in 1999. In another study, Mills (2002) observes that, similar to Tibetans and the Zapatistas, the Kurds use the Internet to maintain their "cybernation" known as "Kurdistan" and stay in contact with each other to exchange cultural and political information (p. 82). Van den Bos and Nell (2006), looking at cross-border Internet usage by "Turkish Kurds" (and non-Kurdish Iranians) in the Netherlands, observe that "Turkish-Kurdish" Websites predominantly link these Kurds to other Kurds living either in other diasporic communities or in Turkey. They conclude that "transnational networks and new media need not broaden or dissolve territoriality, but may reinforce it" (p. 202). While this finding is significant, the scope of the study is limited to Turkish Kurds in the Netherlands, and no online content is analyzed. In fact, none of these studies conduct analyses of the actual content of the communication that is said to have taken place. Nor is any close attention paid to the language of

Internet users or to what extent different languages are used in the online activities of the Kurds.

Erikson (2007) is concerned with the languages of the Kurdish Internet and suggests that a Website using English (i.e., www.kurdmedia.com) might be more capable of connecting Kurds in diaspora because the Kurds lack a common language for communication across regional dialects and varieties. (Some of these varieties, moreover, are not mutually intelligible in all contexts.) Erikson concludes that, unlike the nation-state model, "diaspora or virtual nationalism" is unique to nations without a state, and the dynamic online activities of these individuals might only be understood if we abandon the classic notion of the nation as a homogenous entity and instead consider pluralism as a part of the equation (p. 16). Similar to previous studies, Erikson acknowledges that the Internet has enabled the Kurds to engender and reconstruct their "imagined communities" online, but he also adds that such communities, or what he calls "cyber-nations," do not seem to lend themselves to homogeneity and one single national identity. The assertion that Internet usage has fostered nationhood in terms of what Anderson (1991) calls "imagined communities" is also echoed by Candan and Hunger (2008), who investigate how Kurdish immigrants from Germany use the Internet to create a "cyber-nation."

One of the major shortcomings of these studies is that they seem to focus on a handful Websites and Web directories that use European languages, especially English. This factor places a serious limitation on these or other studies that ignore the content of messages that Internet users exchange in their own languages. Content matters.

By not examining Websites in Kurdish and consequently ignoring the complexities of Kurdish language interaction and the cultural and political tensions among Kurds from different countries, these studies, with the exception of Erikson (2007), start from a strong but erroneous assumption that the Kurds are already a homogenous people with "one common language" (Candan & Hunger,

2008, p. 148). Despite the importance of language in defining Kurdish identity, it has never been a unifying force among the Kurds. In fact, in recent memory, we do not know of any single Kurdish language per se. What we have is the concept – a discursive construct of such a language that at best refers to a group of speech varieties consisting of Kurmanji (Northern Kurdish, spoken in all parts of Kurdistan especially in Turkey), Sorani (Central Kurdish, spoken predominantly in Iran and Iraq), Kirmashani, Hawrami, and Zazaki (Southern Kurdish, the first two spoken in Iran and Iraq and the latter in Turkey). The overwhelming majority of the speakers of these language varieties refer to their variety as Kurdish and do not deny their "Kurdishness." At the same time, these individuals also realize that the varieties are not mutually intelligible in many contexts (Kreyenbroek, 1992; Sheyholislami, 2011). The gulf between Kurdish varieties is widened by the fact that they are written in at least three distinct scripts: a Latin-based alphabet (used by Kurds in Turkey), an Arabic-based alphabet (used by Kurds in Iran, Iraq, and Syria), and a Cyrillic alphabet system (used by Kurds in Armenia and Azerbaijan). It is crucial to be aware of these nuances if one is committed to understanding online Kurdish activities and their implications for the language and identity of the Kurds.

DATA AND METHODOLOGY

Data collection is informed by online ethnography (Androutsopoulos, 2006), which is characterised by at least two approaches. In the first approach, researchers carry out a systematic selection of online sources, make systematic observations of online activities and discourse practices, and communicate with group members, online or offline, to elicit further information. The second approach, referred to as "guerrilla ethnography," is less systematic but more fluid and flexible and thus more appropriate and productive for collecting online data (Yang, 2003). A guerrilla ethnographer is required to enter sites with an open mind and be prepared to browse pages, explore links and other elements of a site, make and record observations, take notes, and become involved whenever possible (e.g., leave comments on blogs, post messages on discussion boards, participate in chat rooms and even ask questions). Selected sites are revisited for deeper exploration and more substantial information gathering and exchange. For the purposes of this study, I have drawn on both approaches of online ethnography.

In order to map Kurdish online environments and activities, I have applied several criteria to selected sites. First, following Erikson (2007), I have ensured that the data is representative of various constituents of the Internet including Web directories, Websites, chat rooms, Weblogs, and social networking interfaces such as YouTube and Facebook. Second, I have made certain that the data reflect regional diversity. For example, Kurds from Syria speak the same Kurdish variety (i.e., Kurmanji) as the vast majority of Kurds from Turkey. However, Websites representing both regions have been examined (e.g., www.amude. de belongs to Kurds from Syria, and www.rizgari. com belongs to Kurds from Turkey). The data also represent language diversity in Kurdistan and, as such, include online sources with content in the main Kurdish language varieties (e.g., Kurmanji, Sorani, Hawrami, and Zazaki). I have also chosen sites that are multilingual (e.g., www.peyamner. com) and English-only (e.g., www.kurdmedia. com). In addition to these criteria, I have selected sites that maintain an ongoing online presence and are regularly updated. For example, I have chosen two weblogs (blogs) that were among the very first Kurdish blogs starting in 2002. These blogs were active and updated through 2008. In addition, I have conducted email interviews with bloggers to illicit information about their motivations for blogging, their language choices, and how they felt about their experience blogging in Kurdish.

In order to find sites that meet the afore-mentioned criteria, I have used several strategies. First, I have chosen two of the top Kurdish Web directories on Google (www.koord.com and www. kurdland.com) in order to select appropriate www sources. Next, I have made use of Alexa Internet, Inc. (www.alexa.com), a resource which provides information about Internet site starting dates, traffic, audience distribution, level of popularity, and so forth. Finally, I have conducted telephone or email interviews with the Webmaster of two Kurdish Web directories, moderators of the two most popular chat rooms on *Paltalk*, Webmasters of ten Kurdish language Websites, and the directors/owners of three English-only Websites that deal with the Kurds and Kurdish issues or topics.

FINDINGS: CONSTITUENTS OF THE KURDISH INTERNET AND IDENTITY CONSTRUCTION

Websites

It is not possible to come up with an accurate estimate of the number of Kurdish Websites. However, as suggested earlier, there has been a tremendous increase in the number of sites in recent years. Although the major Kurdish political organizations and mainstream media have a strong presence on the Internet, the vast majority of Websites belong to smaller Kurdish organizations, a variety of groups (e.g., women activists and human rights groups), and ordinary individuals. These sites serve a variety of functions.

Website as Library and Bookstore

Websites serve various purposes. For example, they function as online libraries and distribution systems for print materials. Some of the notable Websites that provide free access to Kurdish books are *Kitêbxaney Kurdî* (www.pertwk.com), *Nefel* (http://nefel.com/epirtuk/epirtuk_overview.

asp?RubricNr=4), *Amude* (www.amude.net/epirtuk.html), and *Koord* (www.koord.com). In January 2010, *Kitêbxaney Kurdî* alone carried 1,300 recent Kurdish books in PDF format available to site visitors at no cost. This factor is very significant when one realises that, in 2006, none of the 2009 public libraries in Kurdistan-Turkey held a single Kurdish book (Malmisanij 2006, p. 40). In addition to books and monographs, many Kurdish periodicals are distributed, redistributed or reproduced on the Internet (e.g., magazine: *Raman*; weekly broadsheet: *Azadiya Welat*; daily newspaper: *Xebat*).

Website as News Agency

The Internet has engendered Kurdish news agencies such as *Peyamnêr News Agency* (www.peyamner.com), *Avesta Kurd* (www.avestakurd.net), and *Rizgarî Online* (www.rizgari.com). Audiences of some of these Websites (e.g., www.renesans.info) are able to engage in Kurdish issues and interact with each other by posting comments. In this way, audiences are able to experience a sense of shared belonging, in Anderson's terms (1991), by reading the same thing simultaneously and by discussing and debating the same issues that concern them. This simultaneous ritual of reading and online interaction enables Web audiences to imagine their belonging to a national identity shared by millions of Kurds who may never see each other face-to-face. Fostering a national identity among Kurdish Internet users is a common objective for many of these sites. For example, *Peyamnêr*, which attracts well over a million visitors in a month, describes itself as follows:

*This website is prepared and launched from the **capital of Kurdistan**. It strives to deliver the news as it happens to the people of **Kurdistan** and the world ... We work around the clock to deliver the truth about **Kurdistan** to the readers from the three major cultures of **Arab, Turk and Persian** so that they become aware of the good intentions of the people of **Kurdistan** ... [Peyamner] wants*

*to be a strong and firm bridge for connecting readers from the **four parts of the homeland** ... (Peyamnêr News Agency, 2005, my translation, my emphasis).*

The Website is managed from the city of Hawler, which the statement recognizes not just as the capital of the Kurdistan Regional Government in Iraq, but also the capital of Kurdistan (i.e., a greater Kurdistan). Secondly, the Website seeks to explain Kurdish issues to the majority of the people in Iraq, Syria, Turkey, and Iran and does so by providing content in the official languages of those countries. In this way, the Website claims to be representing all Kurds and not just the Kurds of Iraq, where *Peyamnêr* is based. Finally, the last sentence leaves no doubt that *Peyamnêr* is committed to the construction of a cross-border Kurdish identity because it "wants to be a strong and firm bridge for connecting readers from the four parts of the homeland," Kurdistan (para 1.).

Website as Broadcasting Facility

Websites also function as broadcasting facilities. Since the mid 1990s, over a dozen radio stations belonging to Kurdish political organizations (e.g., *Dengê Mezopotamya*), private entities (e.g., *Radio Newa*) and Western states (e.g., *Voice of America, Kurdish Service*) can be heard by Kurdish audiences worldwide. Most of these stations archive programs or program selections on their Websites where listeners can tune in at their own convenience. The availability of these shows in MP3 format has also made it easy to download, save, and redistribute them via email. Also, most of the major satellite Kurdish TV stations (e.g., *Roj TV*) can be viewed on the Internet where they provide live streaming broadcast and are able to reach audiences who may not be able to receive their signals via a dish. The Internet is also the easiest and most economical way of broadcasting audio-visual clips that can be created on personal computers and disseminated using social networking tools such as YouTube.

Chat Rooms

While chat rooms are among the most popular sites where a Kurdish cross-border identity is constructed, they are indicative of Kurdish diversification. Text-based chat rooms are predominantly used by youths for casual interaction and not for discussing social or political matters. However, most chat rooms are very restrictive on what language can be used for chatting: Kurdish only. This factor is significant because, in other contexts, the use of minority languages such as Gaelic and Basque have been abandoned to accommodate those who do not speak them, with preference given to the language of the majority – English and Spanish respectively (Fernandez, 2001). However, in most Kurdish chat rooms, the administrators and users have difficulty writing in Sorani Kurdish because the Kurdish Arabic-based alphabet is not supported on these platforms as has also been the case with other non-Latin writing systems such as Greek and Russian (Danet & Herring, 2007). The majority of participants write Kurdish in Roman characters, and this requirement makes communication difficult, at least for people who are not familiar with the writing conventions of a given chat room. If there were a unified Kurdish writing system, the situation might be different.

In contrast to the text-only-based chat rooms, real-time online voice and video chat rooms accommodated by protocols like *Paltalk* are very popular among Kurdish Internet users. Chat rooms are about language use, be it spoken or written. For this reason, chat rooms not only signal but seem to foster language diversification among the Kurds. For example, it is very rare to hear a Sorani Kurdish speaker in rooms where Sorani Kurdish is spoken.

Weblogs (Blogs)

Unlike English, Japanese, and Persian blogs, Kurdish blogs experienced a slow start mainly due to the lack of a blogging platform that would accommodate Kurdish scripts. When the number of Persian blogs reached 6000 by mid-2006, the number of Kurdish blogs was estimated at 150. In addition to technological limitations, Gulagenim, the first Kurdish blogger, believed that the lack of proficiency in writing in the mother tongue among the vast majority of Kurds affected the scanty state of Kurdish Internet (Gulagenim, Personal communication, October 12, 2008). However, the number of Kurdish blogs increased sharply at the end of 2006 and the beginning of 2007 – a time when the Kurdish blogging platform *Kurdblogger* was launched (www.kurdblogger.com). This new platform made it very easy to blog and write in Sorani Kurdish. The number of registered blogs on *Kurdblogger* reached about 6000 by the end of 2008 and over 8700 by February 2010. Blogging and writing in Kurdish has provided many Kurds, mainly from Iraq, Iran, and the diaspora, with the opportunity to represent themselves in their own language. Some bloggers have even claimed that blogging has motivated them to learn how to write in their mother tongue – something the Kurds are not taught in schools in their homeland, particularly under the hegemonies of Persian in Iran, Turkish in Turkey, and Arabic in Syria. On her blog, Gulagenim, a Kurdish woman originally from Iranian Kurdistan but living in diaspora, writes passionately about her experience of writing in Kurdish:

They never taught me [how to write in Kurdish] ... For me, writing in Kurdish is still like a childhood dream that has not come true, and now as an adult I am approaching it with hesitation and trepidation ... (2002, my translation).

Gulagenim uses her blog as a space for practicing writing in Kurdish and overcoming the fear of writing in her mother tongue. After speaking of the same anxiety that she experiences when blogging in Kurdish, Tewar, another Kurdish female blogger, originally from Iran, refuses to give up writing in her mother tongue:

... I cannot quit ... Language is a part of me. Words are mirrors that reflect my ideas and feelings ... Without [our] language we are nothing ... A language is as important as a country, history and flag ... Language is a part of our personality ... Language is identity ... To express your inner thoughts and feelings ... you need the language of feelings and the soul; no language is closer to one's feelings and soul than the mother tongue... When writing we might make mistakes ... We may not have a rich vocabulary... but, let's not quit; let's continue [writing] ... (Tewar, 2002, my translation).

For Tewar, language is important as a national symbol in defining a people; it is also a decisive factor in defining a person. Fishman (1989) states "[t]he essence of a nationality is its spirit, its individuality, its soul. This soul is not only reflected and protected by the mother tongue but, in a sense, *the mother tongue is itself an aspect of the soul*, a part of the soul, if not the soul made manifest" (p. 276, emphasis in original). Fishman has referred to the rediscovering of the mother tongue as an "intellectual rebirth" (p. 283). It seems these two Kurdish bloggers might have experienced this sense of rebirth by blogging in Kurdish.

Other Social Networking Tools

In addition to Websites, chat rooms, and Weblogs, Kurds also use Internet tools such as email, forums, electronic mailing lists, instant messaging services, and social networking tools such as MySpace, Facebook, and YouTube. To show the extent to which Kurds have been able to use a file-sharing facility like YouTube, on October 5, 2007, a search was conducted on YouTube with the query "Kurd or Kurdistan." The search returned over 60,000 hits. This number is a considerable figure compared to the number of hits that on the same day were returned for the following queries: "Canada or Canadian" 155,000, "Iran or Iranian," 145,000, and "Palestine or Palestinian," 44,200. Because of their heavy reliance on audiovisual modes, YouTube clips seem more convenient for crossing linguistic lines that have often hampered communication among the Kurds. This factor is evident in the variety of languages used to make comments on video clips.

Social networking tools in particular foster the construction and dissemination of a Kurdish cross-border identity. The language variety used in these tools is largely suggestive of the geographical location and population size of their users. For example, Kurds from the West, especially the U.K. and the Scandinavian countries, make up the majority of the *Roj Bash Kurdistan* (Good Day Kurdistan) forum's visitors. In contrast, the forum *Kurdish Love,* which uses Sorani Kurdish as its main medium, attracts well over 50% of its users and visitors from Iran and Iraq. Another forum, *Baydigi,* which uses Sorani Kurdish and Turkish as its main languages, has over 80% of its visitors and users from Turkey. Language is thus one of the main factors that determine the type and size of audience that Internet sources attract. It seems that while YouTube contributes to cross-border Kurdish identity, print-language-based interfaces such as forums keep Kurds fragmented along linguistic lines.

DISCUSSION

Overall, the Internet provides a communicative space where emotionally charged, powerful symbols and linguistic constructions of cultural identity are shared by Kurdish Internet users. These symbols and constructions include the Kurdish language, Kurdish flag, maps of a greater Kurdistan, images of a common memory that is both glorious and painful, of common national heroes, of mountains and rural life, and of portrayals of the "free South Kurdistan" (Iraqi Kurdistan). Together, these discourse practices contribute to symbolizing a multiplicity of Kurdish identities divided across linguistic, regional, and political lines on the one hand and fostering the imagination of a common homeland and identity for all Kurds on the other. This paradox is not unique to the Kurdish Internet, but displays characteristics of a medium that is saturated with contradictions (Mills, 2002). The Kurdish Internet, however, is also characterized by some of its own intricacies due to relevant socio-cultural and political realities that bear upon Kurdish online activities and discourses.

Economic and Political Constraints

All language use, discourse practices, and media productions and distributions are inevitably connected to socio-cultural, political and historical contexts and power relations (Fairclough, 1995). Diasporic Kurds still make up the majority of Webmasters, bloggers, forum administrators, and chat room moderators. With the exception of the Kurds living in the autonomous Kurdistan region of Iraq, the Kurds living in Turkey, Iran, and Syria face several difficulties when it comes to using the Internet. There are still millions of people who do not have personal computers in their homes, and of those who do, few have Internet access. When available, Internet connections tend to be slow and expensive in many of the areas where the Kurds live. This situation is similar to many other parts of the developing world (Mills, 2002).

In addition to socio-economic factors, political factors affect access to the Internet. Researchers have underscored the freedom of expression that many diasporic communities enjoy on the Internet (Bernal, 2006). However, Internet users face censorship both inside and outside Kurdistan. As

Mills (2002) notes, many states impose censorship on Internet usage to prevent political and social activism. On April 06, 2004, *Index Online* reported that "[t]wo Kurdish-language news Websites based in Germany, www.amude.com and www.qamislo.com, which provided news, pictures and video clips of demonstrations by the country's Kurdish minority, were banned by the government of Syria" (para. 6). On December 2003, *Reporters without Borders* (2004) reported that a Syrian Kurdish student named Shagouri was arrested "for sending an e-mail newsletter from a banned site www.thisissyria.net" (para. 2). According to the source, Shagouri was kept in solitary confinement and tortured for at least seven months. Furthermore, Kurdish online activities are troubled by hacking. In 2007, close to a dozen popular Websites – such as www.dengekan.com, www.kurdgoal.com, www.kurdmedia.com, and www.rizgari.com – were hacked. These violent virtual activities have turned the Internet into a symbolic battleground between Kurds and their "others." Yet, despite numerous limitations and barriers that Kurdish Internet users have been facing, there has been considerable growth in Kurdish online activities. What are the implications of this growth?

Homogenization and Diversification

Kurdish online activities confirm previous research suggesting that discourses on the Internet are saturated with dichotomies (Mills, 2002). The Internet fosters not only conformity but also diversification in that, while it links and reconnects populations dispersed globally, it fosters the formation of smaller, tight-knit communities locally. This ability might result in further diversification. Kurdish Internet users are fragmented along linguistic lines. The vast majority of Kurds from Iran and Iraq might never visit the Websites of Kurds from Turkey because these Websites are either in Turkish or a different Kurdish variety written in a different script. There are, however, Web

2.0 components such as YouTube and Facebook that seem to bring together Kurds from various regions and diasporas and across linguistic lines.

Kurds from different regions and linguistic communities also seem to be able to communicate more easily when they use English or some other non-Kurdish language as the primary language of a Website. (e.g., www.kurdmedia.com, www.kurdishherald.com, and www.ekurd.net). These Websites seem to be able to overcome linguistic fragmentation more effectively than Web sources that are only in Kurdish (Erikson, 2007). For example, data obtained from www.alexa.com indicate that a Website like www.kurdmedia.com, which is only in English and is based in Britain, attracts audiences primarily from Iraq, Sweden, the United States, the United Kingdom, and Turkey. In this way, the Website connects Kurds from various parts of Kurdistan (e.g., Iraq and Turkey) and Kurds in diaspora. The owner of the Website believes that English is "vital for the Kurdish cause" because English, as he puts it, is a "super language" and a common "communication tool" that helps him and his team to inform the world about the Kurds (R. Fatah, Personal communication, February 5, 2010).

Webmasters and editors at two other major English pro-Kurdish Websites (www.kurdishherald.com and www.ekurd.net) provided similar reasons when asked why they only use English as the language of their Website (G. S., Personal communication, February 21, 2010; Ari, Personal communication, February 22, 2010). In sum, the Kurdish language, with all its varieties, has not been threatened by the dominance of English on the Internet. In fact, online environments have given further legitimacy to the language by facilitating its use, learning, and development. Furthermore, the presence of English on the Internet seems to contribute to the construction of a common Kurdish identity.

CONCLUSION

This chapter began by revisiting the concern over the dominance of a dozen languages, especially English, on the Internet, and set out to examine the assertion that this dominance is at the expense of minority languages and identities. Informed by online ethnography and discourse analysis, this chapter has examined the ways the Kurds, a linguistic minority with very complex socio-cultural and political characteristics, uses the Internet. The chapter has mapped Kurdish Internet features, provided some examples of the ways these online tools contribute to identity formation, and explained some implications of these usages within the relevant socio-cultural contexts. In the chapter, the author has also illustrated that the Internet has enabled the Kurds in their struggle and efforts to legitimate and develop their culture and language, discuss their politics in unprecedented ways, and communicate for personal well-being in building and maintaining relationships across national borders.

The Internet, along with other new media, such as satellite television (Sheyholislami, 2010), has amplified the role of the Kurdish language varieties in practices of identity reconstruction. This is not to suggest that the Internet can alone guarantee the maintenance and vitality of Kurdish, particularly in places such as Turkey, Iran, and Syria where it is threatened. There are limits to what the Internet can do for minority languages (Cormack & Hourigan, 2007). Nor does the author intend to imply that language dominance on the Internet should not be a concern. Instead, the author suggests that critical research cannot afford to lose sight of the significance of cyberspace in the face of cultural globalization and English internationalization. There is also need for further research into Internet use and its possible impact, both online and offline, in more local contexts and with minority language groups. Such examinations can be key to determining how the Internet can be used to its full potential for the maintenance and development of minority languages and identities.

REFERENCES

Almasude, A. (1999). The new mass media and the shaping of Amazigh identity. In Reyhner, J., Cantoni, G., St. Clari, R. N., & Yazzie, E. P. (Eds.), *Revitalizing indigenous languages* (pp. 117–128). Flagstaff, AZ: Northern Arizona University.

Anderson, B. (1991). *Imagined communities: Reflections on the origin and spread of nationalism* (Rev. ed.). London, UK: Verso.

Androutsopoulos, J. (2006). Multilingualism, diaspora, and the Internet: Codes and identities on German-based diaspora websites. *Journal of Sociolinguistics*, *10*(4), 520–547. doi:10.1111/j.1467-9841.2006.00291.x

Appadurai, A. (1996). *Modernity at large: Cultural dimensions of globalization*. Minneapolis, MN: University of Minnesota Press.

Bargh, J. A., & McKenna, K. Y. A. (2004). The Internet and social life. *Annual Review of Psychology*, *55*, 573–590. doi:10.1146/annurev.psych.55.090902.141922

Benítez, J. L. (2006). Transnational dimensions of the digital divide among Salvadoran immigrants in the Washington DC metropolitan area. *Global Networks*, *6*(2), 181–199. doi:10.1111/j.1471-0374.2006.00140.x

Bernal, V. (2006). Diaspora, cyberspace and political imagination: The Eritrean diaspora online. *Global Networks*, *6*(2), 161–179. doi:10.1111/j.1471-0374.2006.00139.x

Billig, M. (1995). *Banal nationalism*. London, UK: Sage.

Black, G. (1993). *Genocide in Iraq: The Anfal campaign against the Kurds: A Middle East Watch report*. New York, NY: Human Rights Watch.

Brouwer, L. (2006). Dutch Moroccan websites: A transnational imagery? *Journal of Ethnic and Migration Studies*, *32*(7), 1153–1168. doi:10.1080/13691830600821869

Candan, M., & Hunger, U. (2008). Nation building online: A case study of Kurdish migrants in Germany. *German Policy Studies*, *4*(4), 125–153.

Castells, M. (2004). *The power of identity* (2nd ed.). Oxford, UK: Blackwell.

Cormack, M., & Hourigan, N. (Eds.). (2007). *Minority language media: Concepts, critiques, and case studies*. Clevedon, UK: Multilingual Matters.

Crystal, D. (2000). *Language death*. Cambridge, UK: Cambridge University Press.

Cunliffe, D. (2007). Minority languages and the Internet: New threats, new opportunities. In M. Cormack & N. Hourigan, N. (Eds.), *Minority language media: Concepts, critiques, and case studies* (pp. 133-150). Clevedon, UK: Multilingual Matters.

Cunliffe, D., & Harries, R. (2005). Promoting minority-language use in a bilingual online community. *New Review of Hypermedia and Multimedia*, *11*(2), 157–179. doi:10.1080/13614560500350750

Danet, B., & Herring, S. (2007). Multilingualism on the Internet. In Hellinger, M., & Pauwels, A. (Eds.), *Handbook of language and communication: Diversity and change* (pp. 554–585). New York, NY: Mouton de Gruyter.

de Swaan, A. (2001). *Words of the world: The global language system*. Cambridge, UK: Polity.

Dor, D. (2004). From Englishization to imposed multilingualism: Globalization, the Internet, and the political economy of the linguistic code. *Public Culture*, *16*(1), 97–118. doi:10.1215/08992363-16-1-97

Edwards, J. (2009). *Language and identity: An introduction*. New York, NY: Cambridge University Press.

Erikson, T. H. (2007). Nationalism and the Internet. *Nations and Nationalism, 13*(1), 1–17. doi:10.1111/j.1469-8129.2007.00273.x

Fairclough, N. (1995). *Media discourse*. London, UK: Longman.

Fernandez, L. (2001). Patterns of linguistic discrimination in discussion forums. *Mercator Media Forum, 5*, 22–41.

Fishman, J. (1989). *Language and ethnicity in minority sociolinguistic perspective*. Clevedon, UK: Multilingual Matters.

Fishman, J. (1991). *Reversing language shift: Theoretical and empirical foundations of assistance to threatened languages*. Clevedon, UK: Multilingual Matters.

Gulagenim. (2002, July 4). Blog entry. Retrieved March 15, 2004, from http://www.gulagenim.blogspot.com/2002_07_04_gulagenim_archive.html

Hassanpour, A. (1992). *Nationalism and language in Kurdistan*. San Francisco, CA: Mellon Press.

Hassanpour, A. (2003). The making of Kurdish identity: Pre-20th century historical and literary discourses. In Vali, A. (Ed.), *Essays on the origins of Kurdish nationalism*. Costa Mesa, CA: Mazda Publishers Inc.

Hassanpour, A., & Mojab, S. (2005). Kurdish diaspora. In Ember, M., Ember, C. R., & Skoggard, I. (Eds.), *Encyclopaedia of diasporas: Immigrant and refugee cultures around the world* (*Vol. 1*, pp. 214–224). New York, NY: Kluwer Academic.

Held, D., McGrew, A., Goldlatt, D., & Perraton, J. (1999). *Global transformations: Politics, economics and culture*. Stanford, CA: Stanford University Press.

Honeycutt, C., & Cunliffe, D. (2010). The use of the Welsh language on Facebook: An initial investigation. *Information Communication and Society, 13*(2), 226–248. doi:10.1080/13691180902914628

Kreyenbroek, P. (1992). On the Kurdish language. In Kreyenbroek, P. G., & Sperl, S. (Eds.), *The Kurds: A contemporary overview* (pp. 68–83). London, UK: Routledge.

Kymlicka, W., & Straehle, C. (1999). Cosmopolitanism, nation-states, and minority nationalism: A critical review of recent literature. *European Journal of Philosophy, 7*(1), 65–88. doi:10.1111/1468-0378.00074

Mair, C. (2002). The continuing spread of English: Anglo-American conspiracy or global grassroots movement? In Allerton, D. J., Skandera, P., & Tschichold, C. (Eds.), *Perspectives on English as a world language* (pp. 159–169). Basel, Switzerland: Schwable.

Malmisanij, M. (2006). *The past and the present of book publishing in Kurdish language in Turkey*. Next Page Foundation. Retrieved July 10, 2007, from http://www.npage.org/article126.html

McDowall, D. (2004). *A modern history of the Kurds* (3rd ed.). London, UK: I. B. Tauris.

McLuhan, M. (1962). *The Gutenberg galaxy: The making of typographic man*. Toronto, Canada: The University of Toronto Press.

Mills, K. (2002). Cybernations: Identity, self-determination, democracy and the "Internet effect" in the emerging information order. *Global Society, 16*(1), 69–87. doi:10.1080/09537320120111915

Muhamad-Brandner, C. (2009). Biculturalism online: Exploring the Web space of Aotearoa/New Zealand. *Journal of Information. Communication and Ethics in Society, 7*(2/3), 182–191. doi:10.1108/14779960910955891

Phillipson, R. (2009). *Linguistic imperialism continued*. New York, NY: Routledge.

Poster, M. (1999). National identities and communications technologies. *The Information Society*, *15*, 235–240. doi:10.1080/019722499128394

Romano, D. (2002). Modern communications technology in ethnic nationalist hands: The case of Kurds. *Canadian Journal of Political Science*, *35*(1), 127–149. doi:10.1017/S0008423902778207

Sheyholislami, J. (2010). Identity, language, and new media: The Kurdish case. *Language Policy*, *9*(4), 289–312. doi:10.1007/s10993-010-9179-y

Sheyholislami, J. (2011). *Kurdish identity, discourse, and new media*. New York, NY: Palgrave Macmillan.

Síthigh, D. M. (2010). More than words: The introduction of internationalised domain names and the reform of generic top-level domains at ICANN. *International Journal of Law and Information Technology*, *18*(3), 274–300. doi:10.1093/ijlit/eaq007

Skutnabb-Kangas, T. (2000). *Linguistic genocide in education - Or worldwide diversity and human rights?* Mahwah, NJ: Lawrence Erlbaum Associates.

Skutnabb-Kangas, T., & Fernandes, D. (2008). Kurds in Turkey and in (Iraqi) Kurdistan: A comparison of Kurdish educational language policy in two situations of occupation. *Genocide Studies and Prevention*, *3*(1), 43–73. doi:10.3138/gsp.3.1.43

Smith, A. (1998). *Nationalism and modernism*. London, UK: Routledge.

Tewar. (2002, July 4). *Blog entry*. Retrieved March 15, 2003, from http://wera.blogspot.com/2002/07/blog-post_04.html

Thussu, D. K. (2000). *International communication: Continuity and change*. London, UK: Arnold.

van Bruinessen, M. (2000). *Kurdish ethno-nationalism versus nation-building states: Collected articles*. Istanbul, Turkey: The ISIS Press.

Van den Bos, M., & Nell, L. (2006). Territorial bounds to virtual space: Transnational online and offline networks of Iranian and Turkish-Kurdish immigrants in the Netherlands. *Global Networks*, *6*(2), 201–220. doi:10.1111/j.1471-0374.2006.00141.x

Warschauer, M. (2000). Language, identity, and the Internet. In Kolko, B. E., Nakamura, L., & Rodman, G. B. (Eds.), *Race in cyberspace* (pp. 151–170). New York, NY: Routledge.

Wei, C. Y., & Kolko, B. E. (2005). Resistance to globalization: Language and Internet diffusion patterns in Uzbekistan. *New Review of Hypermedia and Multimedia*, *11*(2), 205–220. doi:10.1080/13614560500402817

Wodak, R., de Cillia, R., Reisigl, M., & Liebhart, K. (2009). *The discursive construction of national identities* (2nd ed.). Edinburgh, UK: Edinburgh University Press.

Yang, G. (2003). The Internet and the rise of a transnational Chinese cultural sphere. *Media Culture & Society*, *25*, 469–490. doi:10.1177/01634437030254003

KEY TERMS AND DEFINITIONS

Guerrilla Ethnography: Distinguished from ethnography, it is a research methodology that is less systematic but at the same time useful to collect data in situations where practices are more fluid and flexible.

Kurds: Numbering about 25-30 million, the Kurds mainly live in Turkey, Iran, Iraq, and Syria.

Kurdistan: Kurdistan literally means the land of the Kurds.

Kurdish: Of or relating to the Kurds or their language and culture.

Kurdish Language: The language of Kurds. It consists of four main dialect groups that may not be mutually intelligible in all contexts.

Language Rights: See linguistic rights.

Linguistic Rights: Basic human rights in relation to issues of language at both individual and collective levels.

On-Line Ethnography: A research methodology characterized by systematic selection of online sources, making systematic observations, and communicating with group members, online or offline.

ENDNOTES

[1] A linguistic group is identified as minority in terms of two things: power relations and numbers. Although most minority languages are spoken by fewer populations in a polity in the modern world where language use is inseparable from power relations it is the latter factor that determines the status of a language, whether it is minority or majority. Minority languages are often non-dominant.

[2] Despite the decline in the use of English on the Internet, it is alarming to note that, according to the World Internet Stats (www.worldinternetstats.com), 83.3% of the Internet usage was in ten languages of the world (i.e., English, Chinese, Spanish, Japanese, French, Portuguese, German, Arabic, Russian, and Korean) as of September 2009. In other words, only 16.7% of the Internet was being used by about the remaining 6,000 languages. Of course, not all of these languages have a presence on the Internet.

Chapter 17

The Emerging Hispanic Use of Online Health Information in the United States:
Cultural Convergence or Dissociation?

Nicole St. Germaine-McDaniel
Angelo State University, USA

ABSTRACT

As health-information websites become more popular, healthcare corporations have worked quickly to create Spanish-language sites to reach the Spanish-speaking population. However, changes have to be made in order to effectively adapt to the Spanish-speaking audience. In order to be successful, site designers must create a sense of community by having interactive elements and by advertising these sites through radio or television with well-known celebrities or known figures in the healthcare realm. Further, care must be taken to ensure that the information in these sites is culturally appropriate for this audience. The successful health information website can be a strong tool for educating both Spanish and English speakers alike about preventative care, as well as treatment options, which in turn can improve health outcomes.

THE EVOLUTION OF ONLINE HEALTH INFORMATION

Virtually since the dawn of the public Internet, users have been searching for health information online. During the height of the dot com bubble, hundreds of Websites were created to provide patients and physicians with references to health information, as well as to act as online clearinghouses for medical claims, storage archives for medical records, and other related uses. During this time period, "there were grandiose assumptions made about what the Web could do in health care" (Southwick, 2004, par. 8). Developers dreamed of revolutionizing health care by using online media to put health information in the hands of

DOI: 10.4018/978-1-60960-833-0.ch017

the consumer and therefore demystifying medicine and health choices for the patients.

To a large extent, health-related Websites have done exactly that: put the power of information at the fingertips of the user. Americans in particular have become avid consumers of online health information, with 61% of individuals in the U.S. now using the Internet to look for health information online (Pew Internet & American Life Project, 2009). As a result, sites like WebMD, iVillage, Medline, and others have become widely recognized brand names in health information.

Additionally, the use of these health information sites has increased each year (Seper, 2008). Today, these online health sources don't just include the well-established medical sites like Webmd.com. Now, they also include health- and medical-related blogs and message boards. From 2006 to 2008, for example, the number of blogs that discuss brand-name cholesterol treatments more than doubled (2008). These factors reveal that Internet users have evolved from being just consumers of online health information to producers of this information.

This evolution of online health information has been both a blessing and a curse in terms of healthcare outcomes for these users. On one hand, "e-patients" are now able to research their conditions online, connect with others with similar conditions, and read about groundbreaking new treatments. All of these things can be very positive in terms of the health outcomes for patients. Dr. Harrison G. Weed, professor of internal medicine at the Ohio State University's College of Medicine adds, "As a general rule, the squeaky wheel gets the grease – that is, you get better medical care if you're involved – if you ask questions" (Seper, 2008, par. 9). Dr. George Kikano, Chair of Family Medicine at University Hospitals Case Medical Center supports this claim, adding that "It [these medical sites] makes my patients come and ask me the right questions" (2008, par. 7).

These benefits, however, are connected to the access patients have to this information and the conceptual and linguistic frameworks they have for understanding such information. As a result, culture can become an important factor affecting how successfully different groups can use and apply online health information. Such a situation can be particularly interesting if the individuals accessing such information represent a minority culture – and a minority language – accessing this online information within the context of another nation or culture. This situation, however, is increasingly the case in the United States – the world's largest consumer of online health and medical information – where a growing Hispanic population is increasingly turning to the Web for information on health-related or medical issues.

This chapter examines the following factors related to this situation:

- The Hispanic presence on the Web and how that relates to accessing and using health-related information
- Traditional Hispanic attitudes toward health care in general and connect those attitudes toward information seeking behavior for health information
- The healthcare industry's current approaches for getting Hispanic users on their sites and retaining these users
- The ways in which the English-speaking biomedical view of medicine is being imposed on these Spanish-speaking users through these Websites and how that may result in cultural convergence between the English-speaking and Spanish-speaking groups
- The possible health outcomes for Hispanic users that result from greater utilization of these health Websites
- Potential best practices for health writers, managers, and Web developers for attracting and retaining Hispanic audiences

THE HISPANIC PRESENCE ON THE WEB

Until quite recently, Spanish-speakers in the U.S. were often overlooked as an online audience both for e-commerce sites and for health information sites. This factor was due, in large part, to the relatively low rates of Internet use by Hispanics in the U.S., and many organizations assumed that that Hispanics were not a lucrative market for the goods and services that many of these Websites provide (eMarketer, 2009). However, these low rates of Internet use are rapidly changing. eMarketer estimated that, in 2009, 23 million Hispanics were online, which accounts for over 50% of the US Hispanic population.

It is true that Spanish-speakers in the U.S., as a whole, are newer to Internet use, with 79% having used the Internet for five years or less, and 46% having used the Internet for 2 years or less, compared to 17% of English-speaking Americans (Spanish-speakers becoming, 2005). However, Hispanics in the U.S. are increasingly accessing the Internet for the same reasons that English-speaking Americans do: for e-commerce, for news, and to check e-mail. Further, U.S. Spanish-speakers are increasingly spending money both online and off, and as their purchasing power grows, so does the desire to meet their consumer and information needs. By the year 2013, Hispanic buying power (or disposable personal income) in the U.S. is expected to be second only to that of Caucasians, at $1.39 trillion dollars (2009). This economic clout can no longer be ignored.

Hispanics are not just buying products online; they are also looking for information, including health-related information. For instance, the Pew Internet & American Life Project (2009) found that 44% of Hispanic Americans look for health information online. Many of these Spanish-speaking users, including those that identify themselves as bilinguals, actively seek out Web information in Spanish, citing that reading in their native language is more comfortable for them (eMarketer, 2009).

Developers of medical Websites have, in turn, taken notice of this trend and now realize that, just like e-commerce, medical Web information is no longer just for English-speakers.

The current trend for online health information is to develop new sites specifically for Spanish-speakers or to localize existing English-language sites to adapt them for a Spanish-speaking audience. (Localization can be defined as "taking a product that is already designed and adapting it to a local market" (Cronin, 2001, p.13).) Localizing for Spanish-speaking audiences is notoriously difficult, however, because there is no one "Hispanic" audience. Rather, "Hispanic" can mean Mexican-American, Puerto Rican, Ecuadorian, or even Peruvian, and each of these groups has its own set of dialects or nuances in the way individuals use the Spanish language. Similarly, each cultural group can have its own view of what effective health care is as well as what constitutes effective health communication (Pearson, 2010).

In order to accommodate the needs of most Spanish-speakers in the United States, many localizers base their localization choices on the preferences and language styles of Mexican-Americans. This decision is based in large part on the fact that, according to US Census data from the year 2000, ethnic Mexicans are by far the largest group of Hispanics within the United States. In fact, ethnic Mexicans account for some 58.5% of the Hispanic population in the United States (US Census, 2000).

In terms of localizing Websites for use by Spanish-speakers in the United States, many researchers and Web developers hope that increasing Hispanic access to online healthcare information will also lead to more positive health outcomes for the members of this group. Among those outcomes most frequently mentioned are the greater willingness to seek preventative care, the knowledge of local healthcare programs available to Hispanic populations, and greater confidence in making choices about health and medical care (Peña-Purcell, 2008).

Conversely, complications arise from the use of these sites among both English and Spanish-speaking populations. Users from both groups often don't understand the information that they read, or they are unable to distinguish fact from opinion or distinguish good information from "snake oil" sales claims. This issue has led to fraud, distrust of physicians, and at times, harm to the patient (Seper, 2008). These problems have led some researchers and Web site developers to re-examine the use of medical Websites, particularly as they expand and localize the offerings on these sites to other cultural and linguistic groups.

HISPANIC ATTITUDES TOWARD AND USE OF ONLINE HEALTH INFORMATION

Until recently, Hispanics trailed English speakers in their use of online medical information online, and this disparity occurred for a number of reasons. First, in many Hispanic cultures, the advice of family, friends, and trusted individuals that are personally known usually takes precedence over the traditional medical authorities. According to this cultural perspective, physicians are only consulted when other possibilities are exhausted (Byrd, Chavez, & Wilson, 2007). Second, fewer Hispanics were online than Anglo Americans. However, as previously mentioned, these demographics are changing, and the gap is closing between Spanish-speakers' and English-speakers' use of the Internet in the United States.

Furthermore, there is some evidence of cultural convergence in the use and preferences for medical information among U.S. Hispanic populations. This trend can be seen in the increased use of patient information materials by Hispanics as well as the increasing presence of Hispanic "e-patients" online, as noted by the Pew Study (2009). Hispanic users are increasingly likely to view medical information on the Web as well as seek the advice of trusted family members, physi-

cians, and friends. Some researchers (Hispanics and the Internet, 2010) attribute this behavior to increased access to computers and the Internet in schools across the country – a trend that helped to familiarize Hispanic youth with the use of the Internet as a tool for research. This school usage later, presumably, spills over into their personal and professional lives of Hispanic individuals and makes them more likely to view the Internet as an important source of information for all of their needs.

Traditionally, Spanish-speakers would bring a trusted relative or friend with him or her to the hospital, the physician's office, or the clinic, and that friend would generally help interpret the information provided by the attending physician or nurse. However, higher numbers of Hispanics are reporting that they use the Internet to look for health information. This trend indicates more Hispanics are becoming more comfortable with the Internet as a medium for obtaining health and medical information rather than using the traditional "interpretation" method (Peña-Purcell, 2008). Hispanic women in particular have shown higher rates of Internet usage for health information, particularly when looking for information for other family members (2008).

However, the growing use of the Internet and other adaptations to "mainstream" American culture does not indicate that Hispanic users necessarily have completely adopted mainstream American culture. Instead, studies indicate that Hispanics in the United States have become *acculturated* to both communities and to differing extents. Romero (2004) defines acculturation as "a social process where individuals adopt portions of their host's culture" (p.64). According to this perspective, many Mexican-Americans and other Hispanic groups display the "integrative model of acculturation." This factor means Hispanics pick and choose which aspects of the Anglo-American culture to adopt. Such selective adoption includes Anglo technology use and purchasing patterns in some cases, but it also often means retaining important non-Anglo/Hispanic characteristics such as language and worldview (Romero, 2004).

While the proportion of Spanish-speakers online is approaching that of English-speakers, there are also strong markers that indicate online health information is viewed differently by Hispanics than it is by the dominant Anglo-American culture. For instance, a 2008 study by Peña-Purcell indicates that while Hispanics view online medical information favorably and find such medical information empowering, they also often note that referring to online information "worsened" their relationships with their physicians. This factor is probably because the individual search for information is in direct contrast to the principle of *"personalismo"* in which the Hispanic patient develops a personal and trusting relationship with their physician (Kreps & Kunimoto, 2002).

Personalismo, or "personalism," is very important in Hispanic culture, particularly in the context of medicine. *Personalismo* refers to a way of building relationships between the two interlocutors. The Hispanic patient looks for a personal relationship with his or her physician and views the related context as one where he or she can form a rapport and work in a partnership to achieve good health (Kreps & Kunimoto, 1994; García, 2000; Callister & Birkhead, 2002). In many Hispanic cultures, particularly the Mexican-American culture with which most Spanish speakers in the U.S. identify, physicians are not usually consulted unless an illness is untreatable by more traditional means. In such cases, the physician is generally seen as a very strong source of authority. This perspective, in turn, feeds the high power distance relationship between the physician and the patient. In such cases, unless the physician takes care to work with the patient on a personal level, the power distance is reinforced (Kreps & Kunimoto, 1994; García, 2000). If this rapport is not established, Hispanic patients often do not ask questions of the physician due to the perceived gulf in power distance between the patient and the physician (Byrd, Chavez, & Wilson, 2007).

This phenomenon has led to behaviors such as patients not returning for follow-up visits, to errors in taking prescribed medicine, and in a hesitancy to visit the physician when medical attention is needed (Callister & Birkhead, 2002).

This tendency toward avoiding the medical care of a physician until the problem is severe has placed the Spanish-speaking population at the forefront of the current efforts to reform health care. In many cases, such initiatives are driven by the fact that Spanish-speaking patients often do not have insurance or Medicaid coverage (Livingston, et al., 2008). One out of four Hispanics adults in the United States lacks a primary care physician. Moreover, a similar number of Hispanics reports receiving no health information in the past year (2008). Government agencies have often encountered difficulty enrolling eligible Spanish-speaking families in programs such as Medicaid because of the difficulty of advertising such programs with the Spanish-speaking population (2008).

The lack of prioritizing face-to-face interaction for medical care, combined with the growing purchasing power of Hispanics in general, make the Spanish-speaking market a very attractive audience for health and medical Websites. The Hispanic audience in the United States might not necessarily seek face-to-face medical attention, but studies such as the Pew Internet and American Life (2009) project demonstrate that more Hispanics, including Spanish-speakers, are getting online and searching for health-related information.

GETTING THE WORD OUT: ADVERSIGING SPANISH-LANGUAGE HEALTHCARE SITES

Advertising and promoting the Spanish-language healthcare sites has also proven to be a challenge. While Anglo-Americans typically rely on physicians, newspapers, and printed materials for medical information, Hispanics have traditionally received their health information through their social networks, such as from family, friends, or their community (Cheong, 2007). In one Pew Hispanic Research Center report, 83% of Hispanics claimed they received their health information from the media, with television being the most often named venue (Livingston, 2008). Therefore, many states, such as California and Texas, have moved to advertise their health programs in Spanish and on Spanish-language television channels (Cheong, 2007).

The Use of Spokespeople

Health information Websites have followed this pattern of using the media and have advertised their services on Spanish-language networks. For example, when MedlinePlus launched MedlinePlus en español, the company advertised on television and even went one step further: It hired Don Francisco, the star of Sabado Gigante (a popular Spanish-language variety show), to act as the organization's spokesperson (MedlinePlus, 2007). In 2007, Don Francisco began appearing in public service radio and television spots to inform the Spanish-speaking public about MedlinePlus en español (2007).

Advertising on television has proven to be very effective for these Websites, as evidenced by the growing number of Spanish-speakers who review the sites each year. Associating with a recognized Website or "brand" is of particular importance to this audience. This situation is because, in terms of their use of particular sites, Spanish-speakers are more likely to look for particular Websites for information as opposed to search engines. In fact, in one study, 62% of the respondents noted they look for specific names or brands for information when deciding to make an online purchase (Spanish-speakers becoming, 2005).

Part of the reason for such reliance on particular brands vs. an orientation toward search engines (as non-Hispanic Americans tend to have) is due to the cultural dimension of uncertainty avoidance, which Geert Hofstede defines as "The extent to which the members of a culture feel threatened by uncertain or ambiguous situations" (2001, p. 167). Mexico and other Latin American countries tend to rank higher in uncertainty avoidance than Anglos. This pattern is one which Spanish-speakers in the United States also demonstrate (St. Germaine-Madison, 2009). In terms of healthcare information, this tendency to avoid ambiguity means Hispanics often prefer concrete medical information that outlines risk and possible health outcomes. This perspective makes the comprehensive nature of online health information a good match for the Hispanic audience. Additionally, high uncertainty avoidance cultures, such as Mexico, prefer to receive information from and do business with trusted sources. This preference is likely why Spanish-speaking Internet users tend to adhere to particular trusted sources online rather than Engage in the more common Anglo-American practices of using a search engine to review several sources.

This tendency toward uncertainty avoidance also extends beyond the desire for particular Web sources and into the question of who is promoting the site. Using spokespeople such as the widely recognized Don Franciso is one way to establish trust with this audience. Using recognized personalities is also beneficial for this audience because Mexican and Latin-American, as well as US Hispanic, communication tends to display a concern for the relationship between the writer/speaker and the reader/listener. Hispanic cultures tend to be collective in nature, and this factor often means that value in placed on the community as a whole rather than on individual needs or achievements (Hofstede, 2001). When the concept of community is linked to the idea of *personalismo,* or the relationship between the purveyor of medical information and the patient, using a trusted figure from the Hispanic community to advertise medical Websites is a natural fit.

Some sites, such as Vida y Salud (vidaysalud. com) and the National Alliance for Hispanic

Health (www.hispanichealth.org) Websites, go one step further. Instead of having a notable Hispanic figure advertise the site, these organizations have a Hispanic medical authority act as the site sponsor and thus position that medical authority as the narrator and the author of the site. In the case of Vida y Salud (meaning "life and health" in English), "Doctora Aliza" is such a spokesperson. Aliza A. Lifshitz is the editorial director of vidaysalud.com, and her photograph and information appear on virtually every page of vidaysalud.com. "Doctora Aliza" is a graduate of the College of Medicine at la Universidad Nacional Autónoma de México (UNAM), and she currently has a private practice in Los Angeles. However, her greatest claim to fame has been her various appearances on shows such as Hola América, Al Mediodía, and Noticias y Más on Univision, one of the most watched Spanish-language networks in the United States ("Doctora Aliza").

Doctora Aliza's status as a celebrity physician, in effect, replaces the traditional relationship between the physician and the patient in real life consultations. This shift can be seen in how her readers react to her and her authority. On the Facebook page for vidaysalud.com, for example, her photograph is placed prominently by the title of the page, thus reinforcing her ownership of the information presented on that page. Between updates that announce new articles available on the main vidaysalud site, Facebook "fans" of the page give Doctora Aliza praise and often recount their ailments and ask Doctora Aliza for medical advice. One such "e-patient," for example, asks, "Me gustaría saber que alimentos no debo ingerir durante mi embarazo?" (meaning, "I would like to know what foods I should avoid during my pregnancy?"). Others get more personal and detail information such as their blood glucose levels and then ask for specific, related advice.

It is notable that, as far back as one can view the Facebook page's history, Doctora Aliza has never directly answered any such query. Interestingly, this type of medical questioning is the most common post on the page. (Doctora Aliza has, however, replied to requests for articles with links to specific information.) In contrast, the main vidaysalud.com site does have a disclaimer outlined in orange (although in the margin and near the bottom of the page). This disclaimer warns users that the information on the site is not meant to replace the advice of a medical doctor. The contrasts between reinforcing Dr. Aliza's authority yet warning the audience to seek actual face-to-face medical attention marks an interesting tension between the ways in which Spanish-speaking users relate to the information on the page and the English-speaking, dominant-culture's legal system that would allow users to sue the site if it overtly claimed to be the final authority in all things medical for this audience.

In contrast to the Spanish-language fan pages for medical sites on Facebook, English-based health Facebook pages have no such spokespeople. Similarly, they often do not appear to overtly attempt to create a sense of community between the site and the audience. In fact, these pages often have no wall posts by "fans" at all. In contrast, English-speaking readers of healthcare sites tend to read just for information, and are less likely to use one site exclusively. Instead, these Anglo users tend to make greater use of search engines and to view many sites in order to get a broader spectrum of information (Spanish-speakers becoming, 2005). These cultural differences in the way these two audiences use health information Websites indicates a localization effort for an existing English-language site might involve more than just translating the page. It might, in fact, involve using entirely different strategies for each audience. Such a strategy would include using recognized names and building community for the Spanish-language sites as well as focusing on making online information as comprehensive and credible for the English-language sites.

Associative Organization of Content

Another feature that differs in the Spanish-language sites is the organization of the content. Similar to the English versions of popular medical sites, MedlinePlus en español and vidaysalud.com have a navigation system that allows the user to explore by general category, such as "women's health" or "diabetes." Vidaysalud.com and salud.com in particular then depart from this structure on the main page and shift to a loose categorization of topics and articles. This categorization, in turn, is based on a question and answers format rather than on a linear discussion of each topic. For example, at the time of the author's most recent viewing of the site vidaysalud.com, the first article listed on the site stated "¡No te pierdas este reporte gratis sobre la Diabetes Mellitus!" ("Don't overlook this free report about diabetes mellitus!") The next article reads "Próstata crecida: ¿bueno o malo?" ("Enlarged prostate: Good or bad?") While this organization might appear loose to the eyes of the general English-speaking U.S. population, studies indicate that the Spanish-speaking groups often finds this associative organization to be more user-friendly (Ogilvy, 2005).

It is interesting to note that this organizational structure appears only on sites that were specifically launched for the Spanish-speaking public rather than translations of English sites, like MedlinePlus en español or the Spanish version of WebMD. Perhaps this design reflects a different writing strategy from the ground-up rather than an attempt to localize the information later.

CULTURAL CONVERGENCE OR CULTURAL DIVERGENCE: ARE MEDICAL WEBSITES ACCULTURATING SPANISH SPEAKERS?

The difference in how "e-patients" approach on-line information and respond to medical Websites also raises the question of cultural convergence. Many advocates of online medical information for Spanish speakers have touted Spanish-language medical Websites as an answer to the Spanish-speaking population's general reluctance to seek preventative care and an overreliance on emergency care. However, are these sites encouraging Spanish speakers to seek the dominant-culture's biomedical model of care? Or are such materials replacing traditional resources such as community, family, and friends as sources of information about healthcare? To answer these questions, it is helpful to define some basic differences between the English-speaking "biomedical" view of medicine and the Hispanic "holistic" view of medicine.

The Role of Culture in Health Care

Culture plays a considerable role in perspectives on healthcare. Foucault (1973) called culture the "tertiary lens" through which disease must be used:

Tertiary is not intended to imply a derivative or less essential structure. It brings into play a series of options that reveals the way in which a group, in order to protect itself, practices exclusions, establishes the forum of assistance, reacts to poverty and to the fear of death (p.16).

Culture determines what constitutes illness and wellness, as well as how these states of being are treated and by whom (Forslund, 1996). Gary Kreps and Elizabeth Kunimoto (1994) add, "No matter how 'rational' the goals of a health care campaign are, from family planning to organ donation, cultural roots run deep and will influence audience member interpretation" (p.97). For instance, Mexican-American women often consider social aspects as well as personal health before they decide to follow the advice of the physician. If the advice seems difficult to follow in light of one's social obligations, the individual would be unlikely to comply (Browner & Press, 1997, p.126-7). A pregnant Mexican-American woman who is advised to avoid smoke for the health of her baby might not comply if doing so would mean that family members would have to quit smoking in order to accommodate her needs (1997).

In fact, the very concept of health and the wellness/illness dichotomy differs widely among cultures. What one group might consider as well-being, another might consider being illness (Kreps & Kunimoto, 1994; Forslund, 1996). Forslund (1996, p.48) offers the example of a sub-tropical culture where dysentery and malaria are common, and as a result are not expressed in terms of "illness" but rather as a normal (though perhaps unfortunate) state. Brigitte Jordan (1997) refers to this as "cultural authority," or the probability that particular definitions of illness and wellness will be judged to be valid by a particular culture.

Culture also determines who has possession of the knowledge related to and can make determinations about wellness and illness. This concept is widely known in medical rhetoric as "authoritative knowledge," which is defined as:

The knowledge that participants agree counts in a particular situation, that they see as consequential, on the basis of which they make decisions and provide justifications for courses of action. It is the knowledge that within a community is considered legitimate, consequential, official, worthy of discussion, and appropriate for justifying particular actions by people engaged in accomplishing the tasks at hand (Jordan, 1997, p.58).

Authoritative knowledge defines who has the power to make medical decisions and even who can treat patients.

At odds here are two opposite paradigms of health care: the biomedical (or "technocratic") model and the holistic (or "ecological") model (Fiedler, 1997, p. 163). The dominant culture American society places great faith in the biomedical model, which places the authoritative knowledge in the hands of physicians (Lay, 2000; Browner & Press, 1997; Fiedler, 1997). Foucault (1973) went so far as to propose that these views of medicine and science as ways to arrive at knowable truths have become so absolute that they have replaced God, with health replacing salvation, calling doctors the new "priests of the body" (p.163).

Many in dominant-culture Anglo-America believe that technology and science are inherently authoritative knowledge because they are "outside culture" and ways to arrive at absolute truths. However, many critics such as Emily Martin (2001) do not agree, stating that science (and therefore medicine) itself is a hegemonic system that imposes choices upon patients (p.22). Koerber and Lay (2002, p.82) further propose that science and technology are socially constructed cultural products, and that many of the adjectives that describe science, such as "rational," "objective," and "reasonable" are remarkable similar to those used to describe masculinity in dominant American culture. Kreps and Kunimoto (1994) also note that the clinical model is consistent with, and helps reinforce the Anglo-American attachment to individualism and is therefore not necessarily appropriate for other cultures (p.97).

Many scholars have criticized this "medical colonization" or the forcing of the biomedical point of view onto another culture that has different beliefs, such as the Mexican culture. Because of the large potential audience of Spanish-speakers who view medical Websites, they have the great potential to be conduits for such medical colonization for Spanish-speaking populations that might hold different beliefs about the nature of health care.

This "colonization" can already be seen in some topics in health care; for example, Lay (2000) and Floyd-Davis and Johnson (2006) have been particularly vocal in regard to forcing the clinical, biomedical model of birth onto segments of the population that have traditionally used home-birth. It is interesting to note that none of the Spanish-language Websites the author reviewed mention home birth or traditional medicine, yet they do contain "Warnings" about purchasing and using treatments that are not proven or that are based on "brujería," or "witchcraft." In fact, vidaysalud. com has an entire link devoted to "charlatanería," or "charlatanism" and warns users to avoid unproven natural cures, particularly those related to weight loss or abortions. To stress the importance of this message, the discussion itself is phrased as a personal message and is even "signed" "Con Cariño, Doctora Aliza" (with affection, Dr. Aliza). This approach reinforces the community feel of the site and strives to engender trust with the site's Spanish-speaking audience.

In addition to the topics presented, these sites also contain links to and advertisements from organizations that aren't traditionally approved of by the largely Catholic Hispanic cultures including links to Planned Parenthood (see vidaysalud. com's list of links). Birth control is also widely advertised on most of these sites.

In addition to the question of what constitutes illness, the biomedical model departs from the holistic model in terms of how the patient is treated. Specifically, in the biomedical model, the concerns of the individual patient are seen as secondary to the technology and the judgment of the doctor. The holistic vision of the body as part of a person, in turn, gives way to a vision of the body as a collection of parts to be mended or examined (Martin, 1994).

This "biomedical" view of the body and what constitutes wellness and illness is in direct contrast to the traditional Hispanic (most notably Mexi-

can) "holistic" model of medicine. In contrast to the biomedical model, the holistic (or ecological) model considers the patient as the ultimate source of authoritative knowledge. For example, in traditional Hispanic medicine, this "embodied knowledge" has the greatest weight in the health care of the patient. Browner Press (1997) define embodied knowledge as "subjective knowledge derived from a woman's perceptions of her body and its natural processes as these change" (p. 113). In holistic models, technological interventions are used less often and only when the situation calls for them (Szurek, 1997, p.302).

As previously mentioned, one often-cited example of where the biomedical and the holistic models part ways is in the methods used in labor and delivery (Davis-Floyd & Johnson, 2006). In the United States, midwives have been viewed with suspicion as "medical pretenders" who put women and their babies at risk (Lay, 2000; Davis-Floyd & Johnson, 2006). However, the Mexican culture in particular has a long history of using "*parteras,*" or midwives, as opposed to medical doctors (García, 2000). Moreover, most Spanish-speaking cultures have historically depended on their communities rather than a physician when it came time for a pregnant woman to deliver her baby, and therefore parteras were valued sources of knowledge and support (2000).

This same construct can be seen in how Hispanic groups tend to invest less time in preventative health care. Mexican-American women and women from other Hispanic groups are less likely to screen for breast or cervical cancer, to get pap smears, or to return to the physician for follow-up care after labor (Fernandez & Morales, 2007; Byrd, Chavez & Wilson, 2007). These differences might be partially explained by access to health care, as Hispanic groups have the highest uninsured rates in the nation (Hispanic Health, 2002). However, even when access to healthcare and the socio-economic status of the Hispanic groups are controlled for, these differences are still apparent (Callister & Birkhead, 2002).

Many researchers attribute the apparent lack of concern with preventative health care to two cultural elements. First, *fatalismo* (or "fatalism"), in terms of health care (to expand upon the general definition discussed earlier in the chapter), is the view that one's health is ultimately in the hands of God or fate. According to this perspective, modern medicine cannot prevent serious illness (Abraído-Lanza, Viladrich, Florez, Cespedes, Aguirre, & de la Cruz, 2007). Therefore, this fatalistic point of view may prevent Latinos from engaging in various health promotion and disease detection behaviors.

THE IMPACT OF MEDICAL WEBSITES ON HEALTH OUTCOMES FOR SPANISH SPEAKERS

Research indicates that the health information Websites might play a role in convincing Spanish-speaking women to engage in health behaviors that are atypical for their cultural groups. Peña-Purcell (2008) found that, similar to non-Hispanics in the United States, Hispanics considered online information when deciding upon medicines, treatment options, seeking preventative care, and seeking follow-ups to previous medical care. The Internet has become a powerful tool for information dissemination for Hispanic users; however, it is still not cited as the most influential source of information for either Hispanic or non-Hispanic users. For example, among English-speaking women, physicians were cited as the most influential sources to lead them to get a mammogram (Metsch et al, 1998). However, Hispanic women were significantly less likely to mention a physician as being the influencing factor. Instead, they named their interpersonal networks as being the factors that influenced them to seek a mammogram (Oetzel et al, 2007). If Spanish-language healthcare Websites can become integrated into these social networks through the use of spokespeople and other strategies, they could come much

stronger advocates for preventative care, as well as for birth control and other non-traditional (for Hispanics) health practices.

The issue of the acculturation of the Hispanic population to the Western biomedical view of medicine, of which these medical Websites are seemingly playing a part, has been hotly debated in the healthcare community. On one hand, Hispanic women who are highly acculturated (usually identified by fluency in English as well as by identifying strongly with dominant-culture U.S. values) tend to seek more preventative care and engage in other positive health practices advocated by dominant-culture Western medicine (Oetzel et al., 2007). Conversely, they also are more likely to be obese, to smoke, and to use alcohol in excess or to engage in the use of illegal drugs (Murguía et al., 2000).

The challenge for these Websites then becomes to influence Hispanics to seek the positive aspects of the dominant culture medical model (e.g., seeking preventative care), but to retain the positive from their traditional cultural health practices, such as to avoid eating in excess. Clearly, these Spanish-language sites have the attention of the Spanish-speaking population, and the use of popular spokespeople and the adherence to topical organization patterns have been attractive features of these sites for the Spanish-speaking audiences.

BEST PRACTICES: USING ONLINE HEALTH INFORMATION TO BENEFIT HISPANIC AUDIENCES

In summary, some effective practices have emerged in terms of the localization of health information Websites for Spanish-speakers and for advertising these Websites to Hispanic audiences. The best strategy for localizing health Websites for Spanish-speakers might involve changing the information on these sites from the fact-based, linear organization of the English-language version to a more associative format that considers topics either in question-and-answer format (such as that of Vida y salud) or another organization pattern centered around topics rather than in a numbered format.

In addition to the format, instead of resting on its own authority, such sites should have a strong central figure or "narrator" who acts as the host of the sit. This strategy meets the desire of Hispanic audiences to avoid uncertainty by relying on trusted sources. Having this person advertise the site on television or radio would go further to strengthen this association and attract users to the site.

Finally, placing "fan pages" for such sites on social media outlets such as Facebook or Twitter will attract many younger users who are familiar with the Internet and therefore create a loyal fan base for years to come. While this strategy for advertising health information sites has been only marginally effective with English-speakers, the number of fans and the amount of interaction seen on "fan" pages for Spanish-language health sites is encouraging.

Using the Spanish-speaking audience's traditional preference for media and social networks to gather information about healthcare can continue to pay off in terms of positive health outcomes and higher rates of compliance with seeking "appropriate" channels for health care for this audience. The stakes for achieving these outcomes are high as we move forward into a new age of universal healthcare. Future uses of the Internet and medical Websites, in conjunction with traditional media such as television and radio, might include information on how to seek preventative medical care at a low (or no) cost as well as how to select and sign up for a new insurance plan under the new laws. The potential to influence Hispanic health behaviors for the positive that has been opened up with the launching of these Spanish-language medical Websites is enormous, and should continue to be explored.

REFERENCES

Abraído-LanzaA. E.ViladrichA.FlórezK. R.CéspedesA.AguirreA. N. & De

Browner, C. H., & Press, N. (1997). The production of authoritative knowledge in American prenatal care . In Davis-Floyd, R. E., & Sargent, C. F. (Eds.), *Childbirth and authoritative knowledge* (pp. 113–131). Berkley, CA: University of California Press.

Byrd, T. L., Chavez, R., & Wilson, K. M. (2007). Barriers and facilitators of cervical cancer screening among Hispanic women. *Ethnicity & Disease, 17*(1), 129–134.

Callister, L. C., & Birkhead, A. (2002). Acculturation and perinatal outcomes in Mexican immigrant women: An integrative review. *The Journal of Perinatal & Neonatal Nursing, 16*(3), 22–38.

Cheong, H. (2007). Health communication resources for uninsured and insured Hispanics. *Health Communication, 21*(2), 153–163.

Cronin, M. (2001). *Translation and globalization.* New York, NY: Routledge.

Davis-Floyd, R., & Johnson, C. B. (2006). *Mainstreaming midwives: The politics of change.* New York, NY: Routledge.

Doctora Aliza. (2010). *Vidaysalud.* Retrieved March 24, 2010, from http://vidaysalud.com/author/doctoraliza

eMarketer. (2009). *23 million Hispanics now online.* Retrieved November 24, 2009, from http://www.ahorre.com/dinero/Internet/marketing/23_million_hispanics_online_2009/

Fernandez, L. E., & Morales, A. (2007). Language and use of cancer screening services among border and non-border Hispanic women. *Ethnicity & Health, 12*(3), 245–263. doi:10.1080/13557850701235150

Fiedler, D. C. (1997). Authoritative knowledge and birth territories in contemporary Japan . In Davis-Floyd, R. E., & Sargent, C. F. (Eds.), *Childbirth and authoritative knowledge* (pp. 159–179). Berkley, CA: University of California Press.

Forslund, C. J. (1996). Analyzing pictorial messages across cultures . In Andrews, D. C. (Ed.), *International dimensions of technical communication* (pp. 45–58). Arlington, VA: STC.

Foucault, M. (1973). *The birth of the clinic: An archaeology of medical perception*. New York, NY: Vintage Books.

Garcia, N. (2000). *Old Las Vegas: Hispanic memories from the New Mexico meadowlands*. Lubbock, TX: Texas Tech University Press.

Hispanic Tips. (2005). Spanish-speakers becoming more engaged online. Retrieved October 10, 2010, from http://www.hispanictips.com/2005/09/28/spanis-speakers-becoming-more-engaged-online

Hofstede, G. (2001). *Cultures and organizations: Software of the mind*. New York, NY: McGraw-Hill.Jordan, B. (1997). Authoritative knowledge and its construction . In Davis-Floyd, R. E., & Sargent, C. F. (Eds.), *Childbirth and authoritative knowledge* (pp. 55–79). Berkley, CA: University of California Press.

Koerber, A., & Lay, M. (2002). Understanding women's concerns in the international setting through the lens of science and technology . In Lay, M. M., Monk, J., & Rosenfelt, D. S. (Eds.), *Encompassing gender: Integrating international studies and women's studies* (pp. 353–367). New York, NY: Feminist Press.

Kreps, G. L., & Kunimoto, E. N. (1994). *Effective communication in multicultural healthcare settings*. Thousand Oaks, CA: Sage.

La Cruz, A. A. (2007). Fatalismo reconsidered: A cautionary note for health-related research and practice with Latino populations. *Ethnicity & Disease, 17*(1), 153–158.

Lay, M. (2000). *The rhetoric of midwifery: Gender, knowledge, and power*. New Brunswick, NJ: Rutgers University Press.

Livingston, G., Minushkin, S., & Cohn, V. (2008). *Hispanics and health care in the United States*. Retrieved March 13, 2010, from. http://pewhispanic.org/reports/report.php? ReportID=91

Martin, E. (1994). *Flexible bodies: The role of immunity in American culture from the days of polio to the age of AIDS*. Boston, MA: Beacon Press.

Martin, E. (2001). *The woman in the body: A cultural analysis of reproduction*. Boston, MA: Beacon Press.

MedlinePlus. (2010). Retrieved March 13, 2010, from http://medlineplus.gov

MedlinePlus en español. (2010). Retrieved March 13, 2010, from http://medlineplus.gov/spanish

Metsch, L. R., McCoy, C. B., McCoy, V., Pereyra, M., Trapido, E., & Miles, C. (1998). The role of physician as information source in mammography. *Cancer Practice, 6*, 229–236. doi:10.1046/j.1523-5394.1998.006004229.x

Murguía, A., Zea, M. C., Reisen, C. A., & Petersen, R. A. (2000). The development of the Cultural Health Attributions Questionnaire (CHAQ). *Cultural Diversity & Ethnic Minority Psychology, 6*, 268–283. doi:10.1037/1099-9809.6.3.268

National Alliance for Hispanic Health. (2010). Retrieved March 25, 2010, from http://www.hispanichealth.org/

Oetzel, J., DeVargas, F., Ginossar, T., & Sanchez, C. (2007). Hispanic women's preferences for breast health information: Subjective cultural influences on source, message, and channel. *Health Communication, 21*(2), 223–233.

Ogilvy Public Relations Worldwide. (2005). *Human Papillomavirus creative materials testing target audience focus group research: Final report. Gardasil Cervical Cancer Vaccine: Human Papillomavirus essential guide on CD-Rom.* Progressive Management.

Pearson, K. (2010). *New neighbors: A human resource introduction to Latino employees in Georgia's green industry.* Retrieved August 8, 2010, from http://www.uvm.edu/~farmlabr/?Page=multicultural/differences.html&SM=multicultural/submenu_multicultural.html

Peña-Purcell, N. (2008). Hispanics' use of Internet health information: An exploratory study. *Journal of the Medical Library Association, 96*(2), 101–107. doi:10.3163/1536-5050.96.2.101

Pew Internet & American Life Project. (2009). The shared search for health information on the Internet. Retrieved November 24, 2010, from http://pewresearch.org/pubs/1248/americans-look-online-for-health-information

Pew Internet and American Life Project. (2010). *Hispanics and the Internet.* Retrieved March 25, 2010, from http://www.pewInternet.org/Reports/2001/Hispanics-and-the-Internet

Romero, E. (2004). Hispanic identity and acculturation: Implications for management. *Cross Cultural Management, 11*(1), 62–71. doi:10.1108/13527600410797756

Salud.com (2010). Retrieved March 25, 2010, from http://www.salud.com

Seper, C. (2008). *Untangling the web of medical advice.* Retrieved November 19, 2009, from http://blog.cleveland.com/health/2008/02/untangling_the_web_of_medical.html

Southwick, K. (2004). Diagnosing WebMD. *CNET News.* Retrieved November 19, 2010, from http://news.cnet.com/Diagnosing-WebMD/2009-1017_3-5208510.html

St. Germaine-Madison, N. (2009). Localizing medical information for U.S. Spanish-speakers: The CDC campaign to increase public awareness about HPV. *Technical Communication, 47*(3), 235–247.

Szurek, J. (1997). Resistance to technology-enhanced childbirth in Tuscany: The political economy of Italian birth . In Davis-Floyd, R. E., & Sargent, C. F. (Eds.), *Childbirth and authoritative knowledge* (pp. 287–314). Berkley, CA: University of California Press.

United States Census Bureau. (2000). Hispanic population of the United States. Retrieved August 8, 2010, from http://www.census.gov/population/www/socdemo/hispanic/census.html

Vida y Salud. (2010). *Home page.* Retrieved March 6, 2010, from http://www.vidaysalud.com

Vida y Salud. (2010). *Facebook Fan Page.* Retrieved March 22, 2010, from http://www.facebook.com/vidaysalud.

Web, M. D. (2010). *Website.* Retrieved March 17, 2010, from http://Webmd.com

Web, M. D. (2010). *WebMD in Spanish.* Retrieved March 17, 2010, from http://www.Webmd.com/news/spanish/default.htm

(2007). *Welcome to MedlinePlus en español* (pp. 26–27). NIH MedlinePlus.

KEY TERMS AND DEFINITIONS

Acculturation: "A social process where individuals adopt portions of their host's culture" (Romero 2004, p.64).

Biomedical Model of Healthcare: Model of healthcare that places the authoritative knowledge in the hands of physicians.

Cultural Convergence: Phenomenon of two cultures becoming similar in key ways due to contact between the two cultures.

E-Patient: User of online health information.

Fatalismo (or "Fatalism"): In terms of health care is the view that one's health is ultimately in the hands of God or fate, and therefore modern medicine cannot prevent serious illness (Abraído-Lanza, Viladrich, Florez, Cespedes, Aguirre, & de la Cruz, 2007).

Hispanic: Persons of Latin American or South American descent usually of mixed native and European (often Spanish) heritage.

Holistic Model of Healthcare: Model of healthcare that places the authoritative knowledge in the hands of patients and physicians or other alternative healthcare providers together.

Localization: "Taking a product that is already designed and adapting it to a local market" (Cronin, 2001, p.13).

Medical Colonization: Or the forcing of the biomedical point of view onto another culture that has different beliefs.

Personalismo: Principle in which the Hispanic patient develops a personal and trusting relationship with their physician (Kreps & Kunimoto, 2002).

Uncertainty Avoidance: "The extent to which the members of a culture feel threatened by uncertain or ambiguous situations" (Hofstede 2001, p. 167).

Chapter 18
Language as Social Practice on the Chinese Internet

Elaine J. Yuan
University of Illinois at Chicago, USA

ABSTRACT

This chapter presents a discourse analysis of two bulletin board systems (BBS). The analysis was done to identify online linguistic practices within the contextualized parameters of online communities and ongoing sociopolitical development in China. Chinese Internet users employ various discourse strategies to establish community identities, organize online interactions, and defy censorship. These practices demarcate an emergent, public, non-official discourse universe apart from but responsive to the official discourse universe of Chinese political communication.

INTRODUCTION

The rapid diffusion of the Internet has prompted developments in the variety and creativity of language use. Internet users often create new words or appropriate the meanings of existing words in order to express themselves and to communicate with each other. The resultant "Internet language" has unique lexical and discourse features. Existing research on communication in cyberspace, however, typically investigates such language use by analyzing the linguistic characteristics of online texts (e.g. Gao, 2006; Lin 2002; Wu 2003; Yao 2005; C. Yang, 2007). Such research, moreover, often situates language change in narrow technological contexts. In contrast, the discourse analysis of language presented here aims to understand online discourse patterns within the contextualized parameters of online communities. In so doing, the chapter also touches on the broad sociopolitical environment associated with the wide diffusion of the Internet in China.

DOI: 10.4018/978-1-60960-833-0.ch018

Chinese Internet users employ a variety of linguistic and discourse strategies to establish and maintain community identities, organize and sustain online interactions, and avoid and defy censorship. Moreover, unique multi-coded discourse practices on the Chinese Internet delineate an emergent public and non-official discourse universe in which Chinese individuals express themselves and debate social issues. This online discourse differs from the official discourse universe characteristic of mainstream Chinese media, which is tightly controlled by the Chinese government. In fact, online language and discourse practices on the Chinese Internet serve as both a catalyst for and a result of recent technological and social developments in China. As a result, the Internet enables the greater Chinese public to interact with, within, and against an official discourse that demands strict limitations on what one can say or do.

This chapter presents a critical discourse analysis of two distinct BBS forums in two prominent online communities in China. These forums are tianya.cn and jjwxc.net, and they demonstrate vivid examples of online language practices and represent the burgeoning space of online public expression and opinion in China. The use of this approach allows the current findings presented here to be compared with similar studies in other socio-cultural contexts. Such cross-cultural comparisons are the key to understanding and encouraging cross-cultural communication on and about an increasingly multilingual Internet (Danet & Herring, 2007). Additionally, in examining these issues, the author also provides up-to-date information about Internet diffusion, user activities, and Internet regulations in China.

THE CHINESE INTERNET

Since its inception in 1994, the Internet has diffused rapidly in China. Today, with over 384 million users (a group that constitutes 28.9% of the country's total population), China has surpassed the United States as the world's largest Internet market. Over 90% of Chinese Internet users connect to the online environment via broadband, and another 8% can do so through mobile phones. As of 2009, there were 3.23 million Websites registered in China, and the overwhelming majority of these sites were in Chinese (China Internet Network Information Center, CNNIC, 2010).

Like elsewhere in the world, the Internet in China abounds with various user applications ranging from email, news portals, and videocasts to blogs and social networking sites. Online bulletin board systems (BBSs), however, are among the most popular online communication platforms available to Internet users in China. 80% of Chinese Websites, for example, run BBS forums (iResearch, 2007), and BBS-based online activities are popular among 40% of Chinese Internet users in comparison to only 17% of Internet users in the U.S. and 17.1% of Internet users in Japan (Tai, 2006). The total number of daily BBS page views in China, moreover, is over 1.6 billion, with 10 million posts published daily (Lu, 2008). Given their enormous reach and popularity, it is perhaps no surprise that BBS forums have effectively become "mass media" for disseminating formation and crystallizing public opinion among Chinese netizens (Xiao, 2008).

A number of factors contribute to the popularity of this medium. China's Internet population, for example, is young and relatively well educated compared to the China's general population. Over 60% of the Internet users in China are under the age of 30. More than 40% of these individuals are either high school students or high school graduates, and 25% of them are working toward or have completed more advanced degrees (CNNIC, 2010). These demographic characteristics are conducive to the development of a lively online environment for public deliberation.

What sets the Chinese Internet apart from the rest of the online world, however, is the government's extensive control and censorship over the massive network of users and public discourses in China. Not only does the Chinese government directly control the Internet gateway infrastructure, and therefore the online information traffic in and out of China (Xiao, 2008), but it also actively employs various tactics to police the use of the Internet in China. These monitoring tactics include coercive co-option of Internet service providers, filtering, discipline of dissident use, suppression of cyber cafes, and most recently the use of Web commentators to manipulate public opinion (Jiang, in press; Qiu, 2000; Zittrain & Edelman, 2003; Tai, 2006; MacKinnon, 2009).

Yet it would be wrong to conclude that Chinese Internet users are hopelessly trapped behind a great wall of cyber-censorship. Given the ephemeral, anonymous, and networked nature of online communication, the government's control tactics cannot be deployed invariably across all online media or cyberspace access points (Benkler, 2006; Jiang, in press). Consequently, opportunities for public discourses are left open for an increasingly vocal online public in China. In fact, recent years have witnessed a growing number of social incidents that originated from and were sustained by online public opinion in China (e.g., Z. He, 2008; Tai, 2006; G. Yang, 2003, 2006; Zhao, 2008).

In 2006, Baogang He coined the term "authoritarian deliberation" to recognize limited yet lively public debate and discussion of political issues in China. He argues that in contrast to democratic deliberation, which often dwells upon an idealized notion of a public sphere (Habermas, 1989), authoritarian deliberation in China takes place within the boundaries sanctioned and prescribed by the party-state. This concept has been productively applied to the study of public discussion and opinion formation on the Chinese Internet (Jiang, in press).

The development of online public opinion formation and expression signals the revival of a non-official political discourse universe in China (Esarey & Qiang, 2008; Z. He, 2008). That is, two distinct discourse universes have developed

since the inception of the communist regime. One is the official/government-controlled discourse universe, which features "ritualized rhetoric that is characterized by indoctrination, abstractness, vagueness and ambiguity" (Z. He, 2008, p. 183). This discourse universe functions to "legitimize and justify the mandate of the ruling Communist Party, hold the institutionalized state apparatus together, and preempt challenges to the status quo" (Z. He, 2008, p. 183). The other is the private universe characterized by non-hegemonic expressions of ordinary Chinese people (Z. He, 2008, p. 183).

Previously, while the official universe dominated the public spaces of expression carried in the party-state controlled mass media, the private non-official universe primarily existed among trusted friends and family members (Esarey & Qiang, 2008). As the Internet increasingly provided a new channel for information dissemination and public opinion formation, the non-official discourse universe extended its boundaries (Z. He, 2008). As a result, these two discourse universes are increasingly interactive in contemporary Chinese political communication. The dominance of the official universe is often exposed, ridiculed, and challenged by civic-minded Chinese netizens active in the online non-official discourse universe (Z. He, 2008).

LANGUAGE USE ON THE CHINESE INTERNET

Although computer-mediated communication has become increasingly multimodal, online interaction still takes place mainly in textual forms. Early studies of cyberspace interactions mainly focused on identifying common characteristics of online languages and categorizing them according to medium-specific features (Androutsopoulos, 2006). For instance, in his study of "netspeak," a broad term for a homogeneous online language as distinguished from the standard natural language,

Crystal (2001) found online communication was often a hybrid of written and spoken languages. Moreover, the linguistic features of online communiqués varied across different online media such as e-mail and chat groups. Thus, studies such as Crystal's paid less attention to the socially situated discourses in which these features are embedded (Herring, 2004).

Herring (1996), by contrast, argues that the study of online language practices needs to pay more attention to the interplay of contextual and social factors in addition to technological ones. According to Herring, it is essential to study the role of language use in the formation of online social identities and social interaction. In other words, characteristics of "Internet Language" can be further understood as resources that particular groups of users draw upon in their construction of discourse styles used to achieve various social purposes in particular contexts (Herring, 2004).

Although there have recently been an increasing number of studies of online language use in China, these research efforts tend to focus on discovering lexical, syntactic, and distinct discursive features of online Chinese discourse in comparison to standard Chinese interactions (Lin 2002; Wu 2003; Yao 2005; Gao, 2006; C. Yang, 2007). At the lexical level, online Chinese (in the context of this study, the term refers to Mandarin – the official language of Mainland China), much like its foreign counterparts, is anomalous and dynamic in nature. Chinese Internet users often invent new words or expressions, or they appropriate existing words or phrases to represent meanings that differ from their natural language counterparts (Wong, Xia, & Li, 2006).

Common varieties of online Chinese include the following factors:

- Stylized Mandarin (e.g., "东东 (dōng dōng)" for "东西 (dōng xī)" meaning "things")
- Stylized dialect-accented Mandarin (e.g., "偶 (ǒu)" for "我 (wǒ)" meaning "I, me")

- Stylized English (e.g., "酷 (kù) for "cool")
- Stylized initials (e.g., "HX" for "和谐 (hé xié)" meaning "harmony")
- Stylized numbers (e.g., "88 (bā bā)" for "bye-bye") (C. Yang, 2007)

At the sentential level, the most salient feature of Web sentences is that they are short and straightforward. This construction is particularly characteristic of the sentences found in BBS forums in China. At the discourse level, online expressions often feature aspects such as

- Chinese-English code-switching
- A combined written spoken style
- Humor
- Other features such as the use of paralinguistic cues, local dialects and unconventional expressions (Gao, 2007)

Little research, however, goes beyond the mere description of these linguistic characteristics of "online Chinese" in order to examine the social implications of Web-based discourse practices in the contexts of online communities or the broad socio-cultural environment in China. A noted exception is the discussion of the role of language in online identity construction by Gao (2007), who examined the linguistic construction of modern identities by Chinese Internet users.

DISCOURSE ANALYSIS

This study primarily examines linguistic and discourse practices on the Chinese Internet as done within the contexts of online communities and the online social environment. To examine this topic, the author performed a discourse analysis of two Chinese BBS forums. Each of these forums, in turn, had a distinct character and approach to social interaction among its participants. Drawing on the previous literature on online communities and online political deliberation, the author's analysis of this situation focuses on examining how forum participants use different linguistic strategies to maintain community identity and sustain online communication. This analysis also explicates how language practices are shaped by perceived community identities and the broad social environment.

The principle data for the current study are in the form of online discussions from BBS forums, which support public and asynchronous communication. A typical BBS forum often consists of topically related threads of sustained discussions on subjects of shared interest to participants. Such discussion threads usually start with a series of responses to an initial post. These responses then typically evolve into stretches of interaction among various discussants, and this evolution tends to take place when more users start responding to existing posts. Additionally, these forum discussions are often monitored by administrators who review postings for appropriate content and style.

One of the online forums examined in this study is a part of jjwxc.net, a Website where amateur romance authors can write and post their works online for interested audiences to read and comment on. As of this writing, jjwxc.net has 300,000 registered writers and over 5 million registered readers. (The actual reader population might be much larger than that number as registration is not required for reading and commenting in this forum.) On jjwxc.net, writers usually post their works from the beginning of the narrative and then turn the writing into an ongoing and interactive process. As a result, readers are able to comment on and discuss story plots and characters on the BBS forum attached to each story.

In this context, responsive writers often exchange ideas with the readers directly. It is thus not unusual for a writer to modify her or his story according to the popular demand of fans. In fact, popular writers often boast their own homepages where all of their works are often read and followed by thousands of readers and fans. In essence, these BBS forums serve as communicative spaces for writers, readers, and fans to come together not only to write, read, comment, and exchange ideas on a literary work, but also to socialize with each other based on similar interests and viewpoints towards issues related to the writing.

Given the romance nature of the works, it is perhaps not surprising that the writers and readers on the Website are overwhelmingly young females. Additionally, several popular thematic genres have developed based on the tastes of reader populations. *Danmei* (耽美), for example, is a distinctive genre involving romance between male characters. The discussions carried out in a BBS forum hosted by a popular Danmei writer are analyzed below and are referred to as the Romance forum in the remainder of the paper.

The other forum is called *Guoji Guancha* (国际观察), or *Comments on International Affairs*. This forum is affiliated with tiany.cn, which is China's third largest social portal with over 24 million registered users (iUserTracker, 2007). The forum provides a platform for in-depth analysis and comments on China's international relationships as reflected in current news stories. The discussion threads in this forum constitute the data for this part of the analysis and are referred to as the Int'l affairs forum hereafter. In reviewing this resource, relevant news stories in the mainstream press were monitored and consulted to supplement the forum content.

The analysis of online texts as social practice is rooted in the tradition of critical discourse analysis (Fairclough, 1995, 2000; van Dijk, 1997). Going beyond linguistic details of the texts, discourse analysis focuses on the mutually constitutive relationship between discursive practices and their situational and societal contexts. The discourse's text (the written words), which is shaped by and helps to shape social and cultural shifts, provides an empirical basis for study (Fairclough, 1995, 2000; van Dijk, 1997).

The author then systematically analyzed thematic features of the language use in the two forums. This examination identified major themes, and it helped clarify discursive elements within each theme. Excerpts of the discussions that reflect the theoretical framework and the arguments of the study were recorded descriptively or in the form of verbatim quotes. As a result, the analysis presented here accentuates the interactional aspects of online debates over sensitive and controversial issues and their influence on the communicative enactment of group identity.

Internet Language Use for Community Identification

Online messages generated by anonymous or pseudonymous users often demonstrate community identification processes (Herring, 2004). Given its multifaceted nature and the interdisciplinary interests it inspires, the term "online community" has been an elusive concept to define (e.g., Jones, 1995, 1997, 1998; Preece & Maloney-Krichmar, 2005). Researchers have tried to delineate the concept from a sociolinguistic perspective (Androutsopoulos, 2006). Baym, for instance, identifies group-specific vocabulary and humor among the "consistent and distinctive language practices" that indicate the emergence of a coherent online community (Baym 2003, p.1016). She further argues that online communities emerge as participants who "create and codify group-specific meanings, socially negotiate group-specific identities, form relationships [. . .] and create norms that serve to organize interaction and to maintain desirable social climates" (Baym 1998, p 62).

The community identification function of language use is especially acute in the Romance forum, whose participants are female fans of romance stories. Here, the participants embrace this group identity through a set of expressions they use to refer to each other. In the case of a happy story in which a beloved character enjoys an easy life, the writer is called "亲妈 (qīn mā)," meaning "the birth mother." In contrast, "后妈 (hòu mā)" or "the stepmother," refers to the writer of a sad story in which a beloved character suffers greatly.

Finally, the fans call themselves "姨妈 (yí mā)," meaning "the aunts," (which refers to sisters of the mother in Chinese culture) to indicate the close relationship between the readers and the writer. The following are excerpts of forum discussions.

Example 1a

我们要**HE**,XX, 你可要当亲妈啊!
(Translation: We want a *happy ending*. XX, be a *birth (loving) mother*!)

Example 1b

XX是绝对的后妈,总是整一个?昧又混乱的 *NP*局面,
(Translation: XX is absolutely a *stepmother*, (who) always creates a dubious and chaotic romance with *multiple parties* involved in it.)

Example 1c

姨妈们对 *virginity* 嗤之以鼻,一来XX是男生, 二来我们是现代人,偶要是胆敢振臂高 呼XX要守贞,会被姨妈们的唾液淹死。
(Translation: You, the *aunts,* don't give a damn about *virginity* because: One, XX [the main character in the story] is a man; two, we (unlike XX) live in a modern society. If *I* dare to call on XX to preserve his virginity, those aunts would drown me with their saliva.)

Additionally, Table 1 presents some of the special lexicon used in the Romance forum. The creative use of these phrases allows forum participants not only to express their opinions and emotions towards a particular writer or story, but to do so in a personalized and close-knit community atmosphere.

Besides these lexical characteristics, the Romance forum also exhibits a distinctly open yet discrete discourse style. Although the nature of the romance stories in the forum is overwhelmingly light entertainment, the forum participants often find themselves in serious discussions of

Table 1. Online Language Use for Community Identification in the Romance Forum

Online Language	Original Meaning	Appropriated Meaning
NP	"N" is the mathematical notation for an unknown but large quantity. "P" stands for "people"	A multi-party romantic relationship
HE	Short for "happy ending"	--
BL	Short for "boy love"	Gay romance
High	--	Sexual scenes
BT	short for "变态(biàn tài)", perverse, abnormal	--

larger relationship-related issues including love, gender, and sex. These discussions usually originate from particular writings, but they also often go beyond the stories themselves. Interestingly, forum participants, who are young, educated, and open-minded, never shun expressing their innermost feelings towards these issues. However, issues regarding sexual relationships, and especially those concerning gay rights, are still very sensitive, or even taboo, topics in Chinese society. Forum participants are thus acutely aware of the need to balance the tension between the expression of private opinions and the public discussion environment. As a result, these participants often resort to code-switching strategies (i.e., the linguistic practice of alternating between English and other forms of coded words and Mandarin). The resultant codes are often hard for outsiders to decipher. By employing these coded expressions in their discussion, the forum participants keep the discussions viable for the community yet also keep themselves safe from the scrutinizing public or peeping strangers.

Internet Language Use for Interactive Practices

BBS forum posts, varying in length and duration, are more complex than conversational turns (Androutsopoulos, 2006). A single post, for example, might contain replies to one or more previous messages and address specific individuals or the general forum audience. Moreover, a popular discussion thread is often large in scale and long in duration. In the Int'l Affairs forum on tianya.cn, for instance, the most popular thread has remained active for the last two years, has attracted more than 10 million views, and has accumulated over 140,000 replies. Such a thread is often viewed and replied to by many people all at once. As a result, it is often hard to navigate through the conversations and to carry on the discussions in such a complex communicative environment.

In response to situations such as these, Chinese BBS forum participants have developed a set of terms designed to help address these problems. Each thread is referred to as a "楼 (lóu)," meaning a storied building that consists of layered posts termed "stories." Each previous post is referred to as "楼上 (lóu shàng," (i.e., "upstairs") by the author of the immediately following post. To address an old post, discussants may simply identify it by naming the number of the "story" it was posted on. These metaphorical terms give the thread a spatiotemporal reference that is helpful in orienting the discussants. See Table 2 for a summary of such language use in the two forums.

Additionally, a series of relevant terms have been developed to facilitate communication, and they do so by helping the discussants identify and categorize their behaviors and attitudes. A discussant, for example, might show his or her support

Table 2. Online Language Use for Interaction Management in the Two Forums

Chinese Internet Language	Original Meaning	Online Meaning
楼 (lóu)	A storied building; a tower	A thread consisting of many postings on a BBS
楼上 (lóu shàng)	Upstairs	The immediately previous posting
顶 (dǐng)	To prop up; to carry on the head	A short supportive reply in an effort to make the thread appear and stay on the front page of the entire forum for better visibility
歪楼 (wāi lóu)	To tilt	To discuss issues that are not relevant to the main topics (i.e., digress), which may cause the thread to lose its focus thus the attraction to participants
拍砖 (pāi zhuān)	To hit with bricks, to stone	To critique constructively or to attack maliciously a comment or a thread
灌水 (guàn shuǐ)	To water; to flood	To post frequently irrelevant or non-substantive replies, often to bond with other members of the community, which may cause to slow communication if in excess
潜水 (qián shuǐ)	To submerge under the water	To lurk (read without contributing)
楼主 (lóu zhǔ)	The owner of the building	The original author of the thread, who is very often the main contributor of the postings, thus the person with the most discursive power
斑竹 (bān zhú)	The administrator	The person who has the administrative rights to the postings such as deleting inappropriate posts or expelling unruly discussants, thus the person with the most management power
小白 (xiǎo bái)	Newbie; novice	Someone who is new or knows little about the topics being discussed

for the content of a thread or a particular reply by propping it up "顶 (dǐng)" with a short reply that makes the thread reappear on the front page of the forum for better visibility. Or, someone could hit it "with bricks" "拍砖 (pāi zhuān)" to express his or her disagreement. Small talks, or "灌水 (guàn shuǐ)," meaning non-substantive comments, are allowed, but discussants are aware that too much small talk will "tilt the building," "歪楼 (wāi lóu)" and thus place the thread in danger of losing its focus and its ability to attract participants. These popular and unique terms are part of the discourse by which the discussants express their opinions. They are also a kind of meta-discourse through which the discussants consciously characterize and evaluate their conversations.

Online messages generated by anonymous discussants rarely indentify their social status directly. However, this doesn't mean online participants have a uniform status or identity. Research reveals that there is often a hierarchical communicative structure in online communication. Even though this kind of hierarchy is not directly tied to social status or class, it has similar connotations (Androutsopoulos, 2006).

In Chinese BBS forums, a communicative hierarchy is often made visible through the use of labels. For instance, the "楼主 (lóu zhǔ)," or the owner of the building, is the initiator of the thread, and is very often a person who serves as a main contributor of the postings to that thread. Thus, the person becomes the individual with the most discursive power in the discussions. In contrast, "小白 (xiǎo bái)," a newbie, often self-labels him- or herself as such in order to avoid attracting criticisms to his or her inappropriate comments. Both "楼主 (lóu zhǔ)" and "小白 (xiǎo bái)," as well as other respondents, are subject to the supervision of a "斑竹 (bān zhú)," or an administrator who often participates in the discussions and has the most management power.

Because of the complex structure of communication in the forums, this hierarchical structure is very useful in maintaining the exchanges. To stay focused on the topics and to maintain the order of the communications, participants need to respect the appeals from the "楼主 (lóu zhǔ)," obey the ruling of the "斑竹 (bān zhú)," and use the efficient means of expression discussed previously.

Internet Language Use for Authoritarian Deliberation in Segmented Discourse Universes

Although the Int'l Affairs forum focuses on foreign politics, the discussions often slip into discussions of China's domestic political issues. Like most other commercial online spaces that are closely supervised by the Chinese government, tianya. cn (in which the forum resides) mainly relies on keyword-based filtering schemes to self-censor "undesirable" content on its own site. This approach is used in order to avoid troubles with the authorities. However, this censorship does not prevent the forum participants from passionately debating sensitive political issues. Like their counterparts in the Romance forum, the participants in this forum often use coded language to refer to sensitive concepts and to bypass mechanisms for keyword filtering. For instance, the members of this forum use the term "MZ," as shorthand for "mín zhǔ (民主)," meaning "democracy," and "TG," a shorthand for "tǔ gòng (土共)," to mean "the Chinese Communist Party or the CCP."

Example 2a

兄弟我告诉你,*MZ*可是万金油,永远没有错的。

(Translation: Bro, I'm telling you: *Democracy* is a panacea that will never fail.)

Example 2b

A: 如果要实行*MZ*,我只希望是中国特色的党内*MZ*。想玩政治,进党。

(Translation: If (we are) to practice *democracy*, I hope it is a *democracy* with Chinese characteristics, i.e. *democracy* within the CCP. Interested in Politics? Get in the Party.)

B: 党内民主?要不要听党主席的话?若需要听又叫何民主,这还是独裁。

(Translation: *Democracy* within the CCP? Should we listen to the party president then? If so, why call it democracy. It's still dictatorship.)

Example 2c

*TG*愿意与*DL*谈判,但是美国却见*DL*,这就破坏了中央与*DL*的谈判的基础。也就是说,在西藏问题上,美方及*DL*尤其是美国根本没有以谈判解决问题的诚意。因此,美国或者*DL*要承担起破坏谈判的责任,日后*DL*或美方要指责*TG*不想谈判就没有了着力点。

(Translation: *The CCP* is willing to talk to *Dalai Lama (DL)*. But the U.S.'s meeting with *DL* has destroyed the premise on which the talk dwells. In other words, the U.S. and *DL*, especially the U.S., are not sincere about solving the Tibet issues with talks at all.)

In addition to bypassing censorship, phrases and expressions are invented to classify discussants' viewpoints according to the political leanings reflected in the comments they make. This kind of classification helps the discussants not only to evaluate the comments but also to make sense of the complex conversational context where many people are expressing different viewpoints simultaneously. By labeling the comment or the poster in order to classify someone as belonging to a certain political camp (often done in derogatory terms), the discussant signals how he/she understands the comment or author and where he/she stands on the issue. For instance, "FF" (short for "愤怒青年" meaning "angry youth") labels discussants who post emotional comments with extreme political views on social issues. Such discussants are very likely to be young college students who have been deeply influenced by the communist political worldview that is rooted in class struggle and is antagonistic. "JY," or "精英 (jīng yīng)" (meaning "social elites"), is a label for those individuals who often express liberal, right-leaning political views. These discussants are believed to belong to the social elite whose typically well-educated members often have social and capital resources. These individuals usually make comments in favor of the adoption of a Western-style democratic political system and a neo-liberal economy in China – an overall context from which they would benefit most.

Example 3

我算半个新人了,一直潜水乱逛,最近看国关的帖子,真的感觉要感谢无数为了*MZ*奋斗的*JY*们,本来说实话一直对*TG*有很多不满……算个中间偏右派,看了*JY*们越发拙劣的表演,你们生生的把我这与世无争的人给逼迫成个*FF*,在此只能说,你们太NB了

(Translation: I'm fairly new to the forum and have been *lurking under the water*. I have recently come across this thread. I really feel "grateful" to *you, the* (rightist) *social elites,* who "fight diligently for" the *democracy* in China. Honestly, I have many grievances against *the CCP*…And I considered my views middle-of-the-road with a slight right leaning. (However,) The shoddy performances by *you, the elites,* have been so repulsive that I, a fairly apolitical person, have finally turned into *an angry youth* (a supporter of the CCP). So all I can say here is you are really something.)

Table 3 provides additional examples of this approach

Finally, online language on the Chinese Internet provides a way for the online public to interact with the official discourse. As discussed earlier, there are two discourse universes in Chinese political communication: official discourses carried by the mainstream media and private non-official discourse. With the advent of the Internet, private non-official discourse has entered the public domain through various forms of network communication (Z. He, 2008). Moreover, the two discourse universes are increasingly interacting

Table 3. Online Language Use for Authoritarian Deliberation in the Non-Official Discourse Universe

Chinese Internet Language	Original Meaning	Meaning online
MZ	Shorthand for "mín zhǔ (民主)"	Democracy
TD	Shorthand for "tái dú (台独)"	Taiwan independentists
ZD	Shorthand for "záng dú (藏独)"	Tibet independentists
TG	Shorthand for "tǔ gòng (土共)"	The Chinese Communist Party
毛子 (máo zǐ)	俄罗斯 Russia; Russians	
米国 (mǐ guó)	美国 America; Americans	
五毛党 (wǔ máo dǎng)	50 cents party member	Discussant who posts favorable comments in support of government policies and action. The label originated from the rumor that these people are in fact secret online commentators hired by the Chinese Communist Party (CCP) to manipulate public opinion in its favor. These commentators are said to be paid 50 cents for each post they publish.
网特 (wǎng tè)	Short for "网络特务," "online infiltrator"	Discussant who posts comments critical of the government and the CCP. The label originated from the rumor that these discussants are in fact online infiltrators from hostile forces to disseminate incendiary comments with the goal of undermining China's development and the communist political system.

in China's contemporary political environment (Wang, 2008). While reports on a social issue by the mainstream media often set off intense debates in online forums, the mainstream media has also picked up topics hotly debated by netizens (e.g., Tai, 2006; G. Yang, 2003). In most cases, the interaction between the two universes is reflected in the Internet language by Chinese netizens to challenge the hegemony of the official discourse in framing social issues.

One such example is the popularization of the expression "躲猫? (duǒ māo māo)," meaning "(to play) hide and seek." The phrase originated from a mainstream news story about a man who died in local police custody. The police claimed that the man died in "an accident" when he "ran into the wall playing hide and seek blindfolded" in the jail cell. Outraged by the ludicrous explanation, the netizens quickly seized the phrase "hide and seek" in the official account and turned it into a popular expression sarcastically voicing their distrust with the local officials who were believed to be trying to cover the incident.

The phrase has become a generic expression that is widely used online to expose and ridicule official government positions on similar incidents and social issues.

Example 4

为什么一到关键时刻，某些机构总是和我们"躲猫?"?

(Translation: Why is it when it is time for truth, some government agencies always *"play hide and seek"* with us?)

Such popular online phrases often feed back onto the official discourse in the mainstream media. In fact, it is not uncommon to find such phrases appearing in mainstream news reports. In 2009, for example, "hide and seek" was on lists of popular online expressions compiled by the mainstream media outlets such as people.com, xinhuanews.net, Beijing Evening News, and Southern Metropolis Weekly (e.g., Xinhuanet.

com, 2009; People.com.cn, 2009). Researchers argued that such online discourse was often less about resistance to official discourse than the accommodation and appropriation of it. Zhou He (2008), however, points out that such communication nonetheless granted online users semiotic power and a sense of being equal participants in political discourse therefore facilitated political involvement of the online public.

Language Use on a Multilingual Internet in the Greater Online Global Context

Research on language use on the Internet has focused almost exclusively on linguistic practices in English, although about two-thirds of the world's online populations communicate in other languages. Only until recently have we begun to see serious efforts devoted to the analysis of online communication in non-English languages – efforts that reflect the true face of a multilingual Internet (Danet & Herring, 2007). Emerging research on the multilingual Internet covers a number of interesting and important questions including concerns about linguistic imperialism by the English language, the outlook of a global "netspeak," and the prevalence of code-switching in bilingual or multilingual online communication (Crystal, 2001, 2006; Danet & Herring, 2007)

As the Internet becomes a platform that allows people living in different linguistic and cultural regions to come into contact and communicate with each other on an unprecedented scale, the questions to address becomes how does online communication affect and how is it affected by offline socio-cultural environments. Additionally, how much linguistic and cultural diversity does the Internet truly reflect? Before we can provide generalized answers to these broad questions, we first need to do more research on how people actually communicate on the multilingual Internet using languages from their local socio-cultural contexts.

The analysis presented here is one such effort. This analysis is aimed at providing a general and a comprehensive picture of how people in a particular yet vast cultural/linguistic region communicate online. In the analysis, we get a general look into some important questions including how women from a traditional culture take part in online communication and how the general tendency toward informality in online communication interacts with local norms regarding status differences (Danet, B., & Herring, 2007). More importantly, this study constitutes an effort to embed the observed online linguistic practices of Chinese Internet users into China's broad socio-cultural environment in order to achieve a better understanding of both the linguistic practices and the socio-cultural environment.

The current study employs discourse analysis, a qualitative and ethnographic approach, to examine the sociolinguistic research questions. The discourse analysis in this study goes beyond linguistic details of the texts and focuses on the mutually constitutive relationship between discursive practices and their situational and societal contexts (Fairclough, 1995, 2000; van Dijk, 1997). This approach has proven effective and powerful in many similar studies on online sociolinguistic practices in other cultural contexts (see Danet & Herring, 2007; Herring, 1996, 2004). Although the currently study focuses on one singular linguistic and cultural region, the results can be compared with relevant findings in other socio-cultural contexts.

For instance, the current study investigates code switching, which is a common online language practice and a major topic of research on bilingual and multilingual conversation (Crystal, 2001, 2006; Danet, B., & Herring, 2007). In the Mainland Chinese context, code switching is a useful means for free expression in the context of discreet in-group communication (as in the Romance forum) and in the context of restrictive political censorship (as in the Int'l affairs forum). As a comparison, Su (2007) found that the key to

understanding code-switching/mixing practices in two college BBS forums in Taiwan is the popular perceptions associated with the multiple linguistic systems in contemporary Taiwan. For example, English is often seen as potentially arrogant, and the transliteration alphabet is often viewed as simple-minded. However, Su (2007) found that these associations are superseded in the environment of the BBS where playful code-switching practices often generate metalinguistic awareness and cleverness. Additionally, Koutsogiannis & Mitsikopoulou (2007) adopted a similar critical discourse-analytic perspective to study code mixing between English and Greek. They found that such a practice was often viewed as a threat, brought about by globalization, to the Greek language and cultural heritage. Such comparisons across multiple socio-linguistic contexts are the key to the understanding of a multilingual and multicultural Internet.

CONCLUSION AND DISCUSSION

This discourse analysis reveals three dominant themes of linguistic practices on the Chinese Internet. Online users employ highly contextualized lexicons and discourse styles for community identification. As shown in the case of the Romance forum, linguistic practices that mark writer and reader identities and their close affiliation with the community are a part of the construction of group identity for forum participants (Cassell, Huffaker, Tversky & Ferriman, 2006).

Chinese Internet users also actively employ various language strategies to manage their online interactions. Forum participants create phrases to mark spatiotemporal orders that help them navigate through and carry on discussions in the rather disorienting communicative environment of BBS forums. Moreover, hierarchical structures, such as the kind found in the Int'l affairs forum, are made salient by the use of unique terms to facilitate and maintain orderly online communication.

Finally, these unique discourse characteristics are examples of authoritarian deliberation in the segmented discourse universes of China's political communication. In the restrictive online environment, China's Internet users have found creative ways to express their opinions. In both the Romance forum and the Int'l Affairs forum, discussions of sensitive topics, individuals rely on lexicons and discourse strategies unique to the forums to avoid censorship and scrutiny from the authorities. While such public deliberation is authoritarian because the state actively shapes and defines the boundaries of the discourse, it is unmistakably deliberative because citizens do participate in public conversation on issues they are concerned about (Jiang, in press).

Media texts are sensitive barometers of social change (van Dijk, 1997). The dynamic and creative discourse practices on the Chinese Internet, in turn, reflect the currently fluid, unstable, and shifting socio-political environment in China. The unprecedented development of the Internet has been accompanied by other adjustments of the state-society relationship. As a result of the three decades of economic and social reforms, the party-state can no longer monopolize the distribution of social resources and has to allow greater civic and political speech freedom for its own legitimacy and survival (D. Yang, 2004). "Increasingly (albeit cautiously), Chinese are speaking truth to each other, and by doing so in a widely accessible manner, are speaking truth to power" (Esarey & Qiang, 2008, p. 735).

In summary, this critical discourse analysis goes beyond the traditional forms of descriptive linguistic analysis that focuses on lexical, semantic, and grammatical features of a homogeneous "Internet language." It instead employs a user-centered perspective to highlight language use as social practice embedded in communicative and social environments (Herring 2004; Androutsopoulos, 2006). The analyses of online texts on two distinct BBS forums shed light on how contextual parameters shape and are evoked in online discourse in China's changing social environment.

REFERENCES

Androutsopoulos, J. (2006). Introduction: Sociolinguistics and computer-mediated communication. *Journal of Sociolinguistics*, *10*(4), 419–438. doi:10.1111/j.1467-9841.2006.00286.x

Baym, N. K. (1998). The emergence of on-line community . In Jones, S. (Ed.), *CyberSociety 2.0. Revisiting computer-mediated communication and community* (pp. 35–68). London, UK: Sage.

Baym, N. K. (2003). Communication in online communities . In Christiansen, K., & Levinson, D. (Eds.), *Encyclopedia of community* (*Vol. 3*, pp. 1015–1017). Thousand Oaks, CA: Sage.

Benkler, Y. (2006). *The wealth of networks: How social production transforms markets and freedom*. New Haven, CT: Yale University Press.

Bourdieu, P. (1977). The economics of linguistic exchanges. *Social Sciences Information. Information Sur les Sciences Sociales*, *16*(6), 645–668. doi:10.1177/053901847701600601

Cassell, J., Huffaker, D., Tversky, D., & Ferriman, K. (2006). The language of online leadership: Gender and youth engagement on the Internet. *Developmental Psychology*, *42*(3), 436–449. doi:10.1037/0012-1649.42.3.436

China Internet Network Information Center (CNNIC). (2010). *Statistical survey report on the Internet development in China*. Beijing, China: Author.

Crystal, D. (2001). *Language and the Internet*. Cambridge, UK: Cambridge University Press.

Crystal, D. (2006). *Language and the Internet* (2nd ed.). Cambridge, UK: Cambridge University Press. doi:10.1017/CBO9780511487002

Danet, B., & Herring, S. C. (2007). *The multilingual Internet: language, culture, and communication online*. New York, NY: Oxford University Press.

Esarey, A., & Qiang, X. (2008). Political expression in the Chinese blogosphere: Below the radar. *Asian Survey*, *48*(5), 752–772. doi:10.1525/AS.2008.48.5.752

Fairclough, N. (1995). *Media discourse*. London, UK: Edward Arnold.

Fairclough, N. (2000). Critical analysis of media discourse . In Marris, P., & Thornham, S. (Eds.), *Media studies: A reader* (2nd ed., pp. 308–325). New York, NY: New York University Press.

Gao, L. (2006). Language contact and convergence in computer-mediated communication. *World Englishes*, *25*(2), 299–308. doi:10.1111/j.0083-2919.2006.00466.x

Gao, L. (2007). *Chinese Internet language: A study of identity constructions*. Munich, Germany: Lincom GmbH.

Gumperz, J. (1982). *Discourse strategies*. Cambridge, UK: Cambridge University Press. doi:10.1017/CBO9780511611834

Habermas, J. (1989). *The structural transformation of the public sphere*. Cambridge, MA: The MIT Press.

He, B. (2006). Western theories of deliberative democracy and the Chinese practice of complex deliberative governance . In Leib, E., & He, B. (Eds.), *The search for deliberation democracy in China* (pp. 133–148). New York, NY: Palgrave MacMillan.

He, Z. (2008). SMS in China: A major carrier of the non-official discourse universe. *The Information Society*, *24*, 182–190. doi:10.1080/01972240802020101

Herring, S. C. (1996). Introduction . In Herring, S. C. (Ed.), *Computer-mediated communication* (pp. 1–10). Philadelphia, PA: Benjamins.

Herring, S. C. (2004). Computer-mediated discourse analysis: An approach to researching online communities . In Barab, S. A., Kling, R., & Gray, J. H. (Eds.), *Designing for virtual communities in the service of learning* (pp. 338–376). Cambridge, UK & New York, NY: Cambridge University Press.

iResearch. (2007). *A brief report of the study on China's Internet communities*. Retrieved October 10, 2010, from http://www.iresearch.com.cn/Report/Free.asp?classid=&id=1081

iUserTracker. (2007). Mop.com: China's "MySpace"- The SNS for self-proclaimed crazy Chinese people. Retrieved October 10, 2010, from http://www.shanghaiexpat.com/Article1104147.phtml

Jiang, M. (in press). Authoritarian deliberation on Chinese Internet . In Leib, E., & He, B. (Eds.), *In search for deliberative democracy in China*. New York, NY: Palgrave MacMillan.

Jones, S. (Ed.). (1995). *CyberSociety: Computer-mediated communication and community*. London, UK: Sage.

Jones, S. (Ed.). (1997). *Virtual culture*. London, UK: Sage.

Jones, S. (Ed.). (1998). *CyberSociety 2.0. Revisiting computer-mediated communication and community*. London, UK: Sage.

Koutsogiannis, D., & Mitsikopoulou, B. (2007). Greeklish and Greekness: Trends and discourses of "Glocalness." . In Danet, B., & Herring, S. C. (Eds.), *The multilingual Internet: Language, culture, and communication online* (pp. 142–162). New York: Oxford University Press.

Lin, G. (2002). 网络用语的类型及其特征 [Categorization and Characteristics of Internet language]. Xiuci xuexi [Learning Rhetorics], 1, 26-27.

Lu, G. (2008). *Old school BBS: The Chinese social networking phenomenon.* Retrieved October 10, 2010, from http://www.readwriteweb.com/archives/bbs_china_social_networking.php

MacKinnon, R. (2009). China's censorship 2.0: How companies censor bloggers. *First Monday, 14.* Retrieved October 10, 2010, from http://firstmonday.org/htbin/cgiwrap/bin/ojs/index.php/fm/article/view/2378/2089

People.com.cn. (2009). 2009网络新词出炉: "杯具"流行"不差钱"第一 [2009 New online lexicons: "glassware" is popular while "not a penny less" ranks first]. (2009, December). Retrieved October 10, 2010, from http://politics.people.com.cn/GB/1026/10576151.html

Preece, J., & Maloney-Krichmar, D. (2005). Online communities: Design, theory, and practice. Journal of Computer-Mediated Communication, 10(4). Retrieved October 10, 2010, from http://jcmc.indiana.edu/vol10/issue4/preece.html

Qiu, J. L. (2000). Virtual censorship in China: Keeping the gate between the cyberspaces. *International Journal of Communications Laws and Policy, 4,* 1–25.

Su, H.-Y. (2007). The multilingual and multiorthographic Taiwan-based Internet: Creative uses of writing systems on college-affiliated BBSs. In Danet, B., & Herring, S. C. (Eds.), *The multilingual Internet: Language, culture, and communication online* (pp. 46–86). New York, NY: Oxford University Press.

Tai, Z. (2006). *The Internet in China: Cyberspace and civil society.* New York, NY: Routledge.

van Dijk, T. A. (1997). Discourse as interaction in society. In van Dijk, T. A. (Ed.), *Discourse as social interaction* (pp. 1–37). London, UK: Sage.

Wang, S. (2008). Changing models of China's policy agenda setting. *Modern China, 34*(1), 56–87. doi:10.1177/0097700407308169

Wong, K.-F., Xia, Y., & Li, W. (2006 June & Sept.). Linguistics and behavioural studies of Chinese chat language. *International Journal on Computer Processing of Oriental Languages, World Scientific, 19*(2&3), 133-152. doi:10.1142/S0219427906001475

Wu, C. (2003). 中国网络语言研究概观 [A survey of China's cyber-language study]. *Journal of Social Science of Hunan Normal University, 32*(6), 102–105.

Xiao, Q. (2008, June). *The rise of online public opinion and its political impact.* Paper presented at the Chinese Internet Research Conference, HK, China. Retrieved October 10, 2010, from http://jmsc.hku.hk/blogs/circ/files/2008/06/xiao_qiang.pdf

Xinhuanet.com. (2009). 网络新词"另类表达"世情民心 [New online lexicons express public opinion]. (2009, December). Retrieved October 10, 2010, from http://news.xinhuanet.com/politics/2009-12/25/content_12701900.htm

Yang, C. (2007). Chinese Internet language: A sociolinguistic analysis of adaptations of the Chinese writing system. *Language@Internet, 4.* Retrieved October 10, 2010, from http://www.languageatinternet.de/articles/2007/1142/index_html/

Yang, D. (2004). Civil society as an analytical lens for contemporary China. *China: an* International Journal, 21, 1-27.

Yang, G. (2003). The Internet and civil society in China: A preliminary assessment. *Journal of Contemporary China, 12,* 453–475. doi:10.1080/10670560305471

Yang, G. (2006). Activists beyond virtual borders: Internet-mediated networks and informational politics in China. *First Monday, 7*. Retrieved October 10, 2010, from http://firstmonday.org/issues/special11_9/yang

Yao, Z. (2005). 略论网络?言中的词?变异现象 [A brief discussion of lexical deviations in internet language]. *Journal of Luoyang Normal University, 6*, 99–103.

Zhao, Y. (2008). *Communication in China: Political economy, power, and conflict*. New York, NY: Rowman & Littlefield Publishers, Inc.

Zhou, Y., & Moy, P. (2007). Parsing framing processes: The interplay between online public opinion and media coverage. *The Journal of Communication, 57*(1), 79–98.

Zittrain, J., & Edelman, B. (2003). *Empirical analysis of Internet filtering in China*. Cambridge, MA: Berkman Center for Internet and Society, Harvard Law School. Retrieved October 10, 2010, from http://cyber.law.harvard.edu/filtering/china/

KEY TERMS AND DEFINITIONS

Authoritarian Deliberation: Public political discussions that take place within the boundaries sanctioned and prescribed by the party-state.

Bulletin Board System (BBS): Online forums consisted of topically related threads of sustained discussions on shared interests.

Code-Switching: The linguistic practice of alternating between English and other forms of coded words and other languages.

Discourse Analysis: Ethnographic analyses of the mutually constitutive relationship between discursive practices and their societal contexts.

Internet Language: Online expressions with unique lexical and discourse features that differ from those of natural languages.

Netspeak: A broad term for a homogeneous online language as distinguished from the standard natural language.

Online Community: Online groups with group-specific identities and norms to organize interaction and maintain desirable social climates.

Section 3
The New Context for Education:
Who are the Students and
How are They Taught?

Chapter 19
Cultural Considerations of Online Pedagogy

Judith N. Martin
Arizona State University, USA

Pauline Hope Cheong
Arizona State University, USA

ABSTRACT

This chapter provides readers with foundational knowledge of how cultural factors mediate online learning and instruction in global education-based on a review of contemporary scholarship. The authors first describe three approaches--social scientific, interpretive, and critical-- to theorizing the role of culture in online pedagogy. Then, for each approach, the authors review the existing literature and discuss how that theory applies to online pedagogy, specifically identifying the assumptions, the contributions, and the limitations of each theory. The objective of such a review is to highlight pressing issues and theoretical gaps related to cultural factors in the context of online learning. Finally, the authors present practical suggestions that provide readers with the knowledge needed to create effective online materials for students from other countries and cultures.

INTRODUCTION

Online instruction is increasingly prevalent in universities worldwide. An estimated 4.6 million students, more than twenty five percent of all U. S. students in higher education, are now taking at least one course online. This number represents a 17% increase in the number of students in online courses over the previous year, and this number far exceeds the 1.2% growth of the overall student population in U.S. higher education (Allen & Seaman, 2010). The rising popularity of applying a global approach to education (Garcel-avila, 2005) also facilitates the use of online communication technologies in pedagogy in order to extend learning beyond the geographical confines of the classroom (Burbules, 2000).

DOI: 10.4018/978-1-60960-833-0.ch019

This chapter presents a review of the research on online pedagogy. Specifically, the authors critically examine the role of culture in e-learning classes given that theorizing about online pedagogy has not kept pace with the proliferation of online communication and curricula (Herie, 2005; Kelly, Ponton, & Rovai, 2007; Njenga & Fourie, 2010; Price & Oliver, 2007). Moreover, the authors use this review to draw recommendations for integrating intercultural theory and online pedagogical practices. The objective of this approach is to address the increasing use of online media in teaching and the fact that the individuals who develop related instructional materials are often working beyond the realm of their theoretical understanding (Baggaley, 2008; Rogers, Graham, & Mayes, 2007, Johnson, 2010). In this theoretical void, there are the heated voices of both utopian (Wellman, 2004) and dystopian understandings of the Internet (O'Sullivan, 2000) as well as an "equipment centered" view of online pedagogy (Dutton, Cheong, & Park, 2004; Holloway, 1996; Middleton, 2010).[1] The authors, in turn, were motivated to analyze and articulate the cultural considerations of online pedagogy in order to fill a major research lacunae – the "culture and online pedagogy" gap – in the communication literature. In so doing, the authors provide a foundational knowledge needed to communicate effectively with individuals from other countries and cultures via online instruction (Chen, 2007; Herring, 2004).

While there has been an explosion of research investigating various aspects of e-learning in education and technology disciplines, there is far less attention to online pedagogical issues in the communication field. Additionally, scholars suggest that cultural issues impact both the teaching and learning in online courses (Chen, 2007; Moore, 2006; Young, 2008), yet few communication scholars have focused research attention on this topic. Therefore, this chapter reviews the existing literature in communication and related fields on the intersecting topics of communication, culture, and online pedagogy. It also presents both theoreti-

cal and practical implications for communication professionals working in increasingly globalized and mediated educational environments. In this review, the authors strove to be extensive in their search to include qualitative and quantitative articles on online pedagogy published in all major communication journals. This selection included related journals ranked in the social scientific citation index as well as new electronic journals on the topic. In all, the authors reviewed a total of 28 journals and 623 issues of these journals for the past five years. A list of journals reviewed is presented in the Appendix at the end of this chapter.

Culture is a contested definitional arena and has a rich and varied history in communication research (Baldwin, Faulkner, Hecht, & Lindsley, 2006; Collier, Hegde, Lee, Nakayama & Yep, 2002; Hall, 1992; Moon, 1996; Leeds-Hurwitz, 1990). These debates continue to have a profound influence on theoretical and methodological choices and advances in the communication field, including the study of online pedagogy. Such discussions include the postpositive studies where culture is defined almost exclusively in terms of nationality to the more in-depth interpretive studies (Carbaugh, 1988; Shuter, 1990) to the more recent critical conception of culture—where culture is viewed as a contested zone of competing power dynamics (Halualani, Mendoza, & Drzewiecka, 2009). Within the context of these discussions, this chapter does not propose a definitive articulation of the relationship between culture and online pedagogy. Rather, the authors attempt to outline some productive and useful ways to discuss the cultural factors operating in computer-mediated educational settings. In doing so, the intent of the authors is to contextualize emerging debates about online pedagogy, provide heuristic value for further empirical studies on the topic, and describe some practical implications for online instruction in global contexts.

Accordingly, in the chapter, the authors describe social scientific, interpretive, and critical approaches to theorizing the role of culture in online pedagogy – an approach similar to that used by researchers in the fields of education and information technology[2] (Herie, 2005). For each approach, the authors review the existing literature on the topic and then discuss how the approaches they find theorize online pedagogy, specifically identifying the assumptions, the contributions, and limitations of each approach. The objective of such a review is to highlight pressing issues and theoretical gaps concerning this topic as well as identify the practical implication in extant understanding of the relationship between culture and online pedagogy in global contexts.

To afford a systematic review of the literature at the intersections of culture and online pedagogy, the authors extend Saadé, He, and Kira's (2007) proposed framework by measuring *cognitive* and *affective* dimensions of students learning in online courses. Accordingly, the authors discuss students' attitudes toward and perception of online courses. In addition, the authors add a related *behavioral* communicative dimension (i.e., student interaction within online courses). In sum, the authors' intent is to review the communication studies and new media literature with this question in mind:

In each of the dominant research paradigms, how do researchers theorize the relationship between culture and students' cognitive, affective, and behavioral online learning, and what are the applications for contemporary global education?

THE SOCIAL SCIENCE APPROACH TO CULTURE AND ONLINE PEDAGOGY RESEARCH

A review of the literature reveals that the social science approach[3] dominates culture and online pedagogy scholarship with foundations in social psychological research. From this perspective, culture is often viewed as a variable, defined *a priori* by group membership, many times on a national level. This perspective includes an em-

phasis on the stable and orderly characteristics of culture, and the relationship between culture and online pedagogy is usually conceptualized as causal and deterministic (Martin & Nakayama, 1999). That is, group membership and the related cultural patterns (e.g., values like individualism-collectivism) can theoretically predict instructor and student attitudes toward online learning, their effect, and their consequent motivation, as well as their online behavior.

Cognitive and Affective Dimensions of Online Learning

While Saadé, He, and Kira (2007) identify attitudes toward a particular course as an important dimension of online learning, the authors examine student attitudes in the larger sense. That is, the authors focus on student attitudes toward online learning in general, as well as attitudes reflecting cultural values. Social science research investigating the impact of students' cultural membership on their attitudes toward online pedagogy has produced a variety of findings and has largely focused on students from Asian and Western cultures.

Several studies examine students' attitudes toward e-learning within a particular culture. For example, Liaw, Huang and Chen (2007) surveyed the attitudes of Chinese (Taiwan) students and found that these students held positive attitudes toward e-learning. Such attitudes, in turn, were influenced by three factors: e-learning as self-paced learning, e-learning as a form of multimedia instruction, and e-learning as a process that should be instructor led. In a similar study with similar results, van Raaij and Schepers (2008) used several theoretical models to examine the acceptance of online learning in China (PRC). (The models used were the Technology Acceptance Model (TAM), the Unified Theory of Acceptance model, and the Usage of Technology model.) van Raaij and Schepers found, not surprisingly, that perceived usefulness and ease of use has direct effect on use, and ease of use is affected by personal innovativeness and individual computer anxiety. They thus concluded that the TAM model holds for both Chinese and Western settings.

Many social science studies conducted in various countries around the world attempt to identify the predictors of student success in online courses. Such supposed predictors include attitudes (see literature review by Sun, Tsai, Finger, Chen & Yeh, 2008), but largely ignore the role of national or ethnic culture. For example, Yukselturk and Bulut (2007) examined the predictors of student success in an online computer programming course in Turkey and found student success depends upon students self-regulating (e.g., organization, goal setting, planning, memorization, etc.), whereas general personal characteristics (e.g., gender, age, and learning style) did not significantly affect success. Unsuccessful students, it turns out, had motivation and adaptation problems.

Conversely, a few studies explicitly examine the impact of cultural values on student attitudes toward online instruction. For example, Zhu, Valcke and Schellens (2009) compared the attitudes toward e-learning among Chinese students and Flemish students taking a course in instructional sciences. Zhu, Valcke and Schellens found that Chinese students expressed a higher preference for peer learning and interaction. The Flemish students, in turn, were more positive about critical thinking and problem-based learning, and were also more enthusiastic about e-learning in general (Zhu et al., 2009).

Another focus of social science research involves studies that examine the impact of learning styles (sometimes related to cultural attitudes) on student learning. Some scholars also attempt to connect learning style preferences to particular cultural groups. For instance, there is a fair amount of research investigating the implication for teaching to students' various learning styles in the online classroom as well as several different learning style frameworks (Aragon, Johnson, & Shaik, 2003; Saeed, Yang, & Sinnappan, 2009).

Kolb (1985) suggests maximum learning takes place when the learner is taken through four stages of the "learning wheel": having an experience, reflecting on the experience, conceptualizing (applying abstract ideas, deriving theories), and experimenting based on the knowledge derived (which would then lead to new experiences). Most learners have a preference for entering the learning process at one of the four "stages." Specific learning styles based on Kolb's theory are categorized as

- Concrete experiencers (CE)
- Reflective observers (RO)
- Abstract conceptualizers (AC)
- Active experimenters (AE)

For example, in teaching in a traditional classroom, many instructors (consciously or unconsciously) use some form of this cycle. That is, instructors might first provide the students with opportunities for concrete experiences through simulations or other active learning activities. Students are then asked to reflect on their experiences in writing a brief reaction paper (reflective observation), after which the instructor might connect the experience and reflection to theoretical notions through a lecture (abstract conceptualization). Finally, students are asked to apply their knowledge to new contexts via case studies or discussion (experimentation).

Several researchers have alternatively framed learning styles. One way of framing learning styles is according to field independence/dependence (Witkin, Moore, Goodenough, & Cox, 1977). Field independent learners prefer to work alone, with narrow focus; they impose structure on environment and have self-defined goals. In contrast, field-dependent learners rely more on the "field" or context for clues about information. These individuals prefer structure and experience environment more holistically and globally. They are also interested in people and learn better in more holistic, social settings.

Most (particularly early) online learning situations emphasize logical, text-based, passive learning more suited to those students who prefer abstract conceptualization and reflection, as well as field-independent learning (Battalio, 2009; Mestre, 2006). In contrast, field dependent learners and those who prefer learning via active experimentation and concrete experiences might find some online classes challenging and not suited to their learning styles. A recent study confirmed these theoretical suggestions. Using data from students enrolled in nine sections of an online undergraduate technical communication course, Battalio (2009) found that the most successful students were reflective learners, and sequential learners performed better than global learners.[4]

There have been a few attempts to connect learning style preferences to particular cultural groups. Yamazaki (2005), for example, conducted a meta-analysis of six comparative studies and concluded that the Japanese tend to prefer more concrete and reflective learning, and Anglo-Americans tend to be abstract conceptualizers and active experimenters. In comparing French, German, and Quebecois learners, the French and Quebecois seem to prefer more concrete learning styles, while German learners are more abstract and more active in their learning. Finally, Chinese appear to be more reflective and abstract and less active and concrete than Australian student learners. Yamazaki notes that Chinese and Anglo-Americans are in direct contrast—Chinese being more reflective learners and Americans being more active learners. This Chinese-American (or Asian-Western) contrast is a familiar theme throughout the culture and online pedagogy research. More recently, Joy and Kolb (2009), in a study comparing individuals from seven different countries, found a weak relationship between culture and learning styles. This result confirms Yamazaki's findings that individuals from groups high in in-group collectivism tend to have reflective and abstract learning styles.

With a more domestic (U.S.) focus, Mestre (2006) found that African-American students tended to prefer experiential learning and minimal structure, while Native Americans and Latinos preferred relational, social learning. All three groups tended to be field-dependent learners. Asian Americans and white males preferred highly structured tasks and were field independent learners. Mestre points out that Kolb's (1985) Accommodators (learners who prefer concrete and active experimentation) are most at risk in online classes, for they learn best when concrete personal information is presented through interaction with peers and where they can apply what they learn to real situations.

Mestre (2006) also identifies new, emerging types of learners. For example, the "global learners" who follow random sequences through material (the same way that information is presented on Websites and television news channels with the screen divided into several segments with streaming information at various places on the screen (or Website)). "Millennium learners" (sometimes referred to as Gen Y, Net Generation, Echo Boomers, or the Google Generation), by contrast, are ethnically diverse, used to digital environments, used to multi-tasking and visual learning, and prefer what is of personal interest ("is it relevant to me and can I apply it?"). Millennium learners also prefer interactivity, are facile with mobile tools, and are accustomed to social networking through computer-mediated communication (CMC).

Closely related to findings of students' attitudes toward online learning, studies have also examined cultural differences in students' affect and motivation (feelings of joy, pleasure, anxiety, frustration) related to online courses. Some studies examined cultural differences between international and native groups and discovered that international students find online courses rather frustrating and challenging. For example, Smith, Coldwell, Smith, and Murphy (2005) predicted, based on previous research, differences between

Australian and Chinese Heritage students in their willingness and their comfort to participate in online class discussion in a business ethics course. They found that Chinese Heritage students showed a lesser degree of comfort with e-learning based on questionnaire data and objective discussion data (e.g., number of postings, etc.),

While most social science research focuses on culture as nationality or ethnicity, some studies have examined variation along age, gender, and physical ability regarding attitudes toward online learning. For example, several studies find that it may take older learners a little more time to acquire the computer skills needed for successful online learning (Broady, Chan & Caputi, 2010; Chu, 2010). Others stress that age cohorts are not homogenous (e.g., not all young people are digital natives) and a great deal of variation exists in attitudes toward and use of communication technologies (Jones, Ramanau, Cross & Healing, 2010).

There have been similar attempts to identify gender differences in attitudes toward e-learning. Early research found some gender differences in that computers and computer activities were often described as "masculine." Based on this factor, it was speculated that female students would be disadvantaged in online classes. However, recent research reveals few differences in overall attitudes or participation in e-learning. There are some minor differences (e.g., that women tend to show more positive attitudes toward courses), but they tend to focus on the relational aspects of e-learning (e.g. more interaction with instruction, participation in discussion boards) (Chen & Tsai, 2007; Lin & Overbaugh, 2009; Nistor & Neubauer, 2010).

Communication Behavior in Online Learning

Another type of social science study examines the effect of culture on online communication behavior. Using Edward T. Hall's (1959, 1966) concept of low/high context communication style and Geert Hofstede's (1980, 1991, 1997) values framework (individualism/collectivism, power distance, masculinity/femininity, and high/low uncertainty avoidance), some scholars have speculated on the impact of different communication styles in online communication. For instance, Olaniran (2001) hypothesizes conversations between low- and high-context communicators might be difficult online. The idea is that low-context communicators might be comfortable being direct about feelings and opinions, whereas high-context communicators might feel more constrained by CMC (Morse, 2003). Several preliminary studies in online pedagogy confirm this speculation. Warden, Chen, and Caskey (2005) found that Asian students were more likely (than Western students) to engage in small talk online, establishing context in the low-context medium. While Western students were polite in these interactions, they also remained more focused on the topic. In a similar study conducted by Tu (2001), Chinese students studying in the United States reported that it was difficult expressing themselves online because of the lack of context.

In a related study, Morse (2003) compared the online classroom experiences of students from high-context and low-context backgrounds in New Zealand. Though exploratory, the study concluded that there were some interesting differences. High-context students, for example, seem to be more focused on relationships and their own performance. Low-context students, by contrast, were more pragmatically focused and felt that the advantage of the online discussions was the flexibility and the convenience of CMC.

Another cultural difference that plays out in online communication is the preference for high and low power distance. Power distance is the extent to which the less-powerful members in institutions and organizations accept that power is distributed unequally (Hostede, 1991). Cultural groups who value high power distance tend to be more comfortable when lines of hierarchy are clear and prefer to use a more formal communication style, including the use of formal titles. In contrast, cultural groups valuing low power distance (e.g., many cultural groups in the United States) prefer to interact and relate to others more informally. It should be noted that CMC tends to be a status-leveling form of communication in that there are fewer gatekeepers. For example, people with little formal authority can directly contact (through email, SNSs messages, Tweets) those in higher level positions. Bjørge (2007) hypothesizes that a person with a high power distance value might be uncomfortable with the informality and relative disregard for hierarchy expressed online by a person with a low power distance value. There is, moreover, some evidence to support this assertion (Warden, Chen & Caskey, 2005).

Warden, Chen, and Caskey (2005) found cultural differences in their comparisons of Chinese, Southeast Asian, and Western students participating in an online MBA course. Confirming earlier research results, Westerners and Asians demonstrated clear differences in posting behavior, with Asians posting significantly fewer messages. The authors attribute this difference in participation (and motivation) to several sources. These include the fact that, unlike Western cultures, Asian cultures have no real history of debate, and the Asian preference for high power distance relations and the consequent other face-saving strategies commonly employed by Asians.

A similar study measured U. S., Chinese, and South Korean students' preferences for high/low-context communication and collectivistic/individualistic tendencies. These scores were then correlated with students' preferences for a variety of learning activities (Wang, 2007). Results revealed that Chinese and South Korean students preferred asynchronous discussion to live meetings and interactions. Such asynchronous venues permitted time to think through the topics and post more thoughtful contributions to the discussion board. The author also attributes this finding to the "salient Asian cultural trait:

think more, talk less, and think it through before speaking" (Wang, 2007, p. 303). An additional finding was that South Korean students felt the most uncomfortable with the CMC format—apparently based on their cultural perceptions of CMC as impersonal and impolite. Both Chinese and South Korean students felt somewhat lost in live synchronous Web interaction.

Wang (2007), in agreement with previous researchers cited here, attributes these findings to students being accustomed to traditional Asian Confucian-influenced pedagogy, where the instructor is the ultimate authority and students are passive recipients of knowledge. She also found South Korean and Chinese students scored higher than their Anglo-American counterparts on the Hofstede Power Distance index and on the question asking for their perceptions of being equal/unequal to their professor. In addition, the Asian students were very comfortable with collaborative learning and teamwork in the course. Kim and Bonk (2002) compared the online collaborative behaviors of students from Finland, the U.S., and South Korea and found that South Korean students were more social and contextually driven online. Finnish students, by contrast, were more group-focused as well as more reflective and, at times, theoretically driven. Finally, U.S. students were more action-oriented and pragmatic in seeking results or giving solutions. Based on these findings, Kim and Bonk conclude that instructors who require online collaboration projects in their courses need to recognize cultural differences in students' online collaborative behaviors as they (i.e., the instructors) facilitate and evaluate these assignments.

Contributions and Limitations of Social Science Studies

As shown in Table 1, social science research illustrated in the studies described previously has made an important contribution to our understanding of the role of culture in online pedagogy.

These studies heighten our awareness of the need to recognize cultural diversity among online students. Additionally, they illustrate a productive avenue of research to theoretically predict student attitudes and behaviors in online courses. On a more pragmatic level, these studies also demonstrate the need for instructors to adapt to diverse attitudes, motivation, and behavior (Gayton & McEwen, 2007; Menchaca & Bekele, 2008; Wiesenberg & Stacey, 2005).

Scholars have provided useful pedagogical suggestions to reach all types of learners in online courses. For example, Thompson and Ku (2005) urge online instructors to accommodate diverse needs, particularly those of international students, by:

- Holding face-to-face meetings when possible
- Providing explanations when unknown cultural references may emerge in discussions
- Providing opportunities to work in virtual small groups for the experience of giving and receiving feedback
- Providing opportunities for students to work on projects that reflect and reveal their own countries and cultures when possible

Another suggestion is an initial assignment where students describe their own cultural background. Encouraged to think about culture beyond nationality groups, and answering a list of question (where did you grow up? Where did your relatives come from? What intercultural experiences do you have at home, in your job, at school? etc.), students discover the range of intercultural contacts/experiences in their daily lives in terms of gender, age, region, religion etc. In addition, students get to know each other and their instructor in a more personal way – a factor that is particularly important for relational learners (Cheong & Martin, 2009).

Menchaca and Bekele (2008) note the importance of employing a variety of communication tools in online courses (e.g., asynchronous discussion boards, synchronous life chats, virtual team meetings, powerpoints with audio) to accommodate different learning styles, and to especially focus on strategies that accommodate relational, experiential learners—because traditional Virtual Learning Environment (VLE) pedagogical tools do not easily accommodate this type of learning. Additionally, incorporating the more recent Web 2.0 social networking technologies (Facebook, Twitter, blogs, etc) into online courses might provide new opportunities to reach more diverse

Table 1. Three Paradigmatic Approaches to Culture and E-Learning

	Paradigm		
	Social Science	**Interpretive**	**Critical**
Culture conceptualized as	Membership group, primarily nationality	Socially constructed	Site of conflicting meanings and processes
Contributions to Theory and Research	Identification of cultural differences in affect, motivation, and behavior in online courses	In depth descriptions of online student experiences	Analyses of power relations within online pedagogical contexts
	Identification of Learning style differences	Description of complex, ambivalent relations between student and online learning	Examination of larger societal forces on online pedagogy and ethical issues
Limitations	Static conceptualization of culture	Little attention paid to power dynamics	Difficult to directly verify critical notions (e.g. power relations)

learning styles (Brown, 2010; Diaz, 2010; Kelly, 2010; Saeed, Yang, & Sinnappan, 2009).

Instructors and information technology specialists have noted that technological systems are not culture free (Chen, 2007; Young, 2008). McCool (2006), an instructional software designer, describes how U.S. e-learning systems should be adapted for various international audiences. Using the framework of value differences and citing Japanese learners as an example, McCool suggests software developers need to consider Japanese (and others') values (e.g., collectivist, high context, polychronic, etc.) and move beyond the typical educational software structure to a more non-linear sequential structure. He also acknowledges the challenges in doing this – namely that nonlinear programming takes more "screen real estate" and thus is generally less efficient and more costly (p. 336). Specifically, McCool suggests providing more information for Japanese learners on educational websites, and he stresses that outlined material (e.g., bulleted lists) seem simplistic, even offensive, to many Japanese learners. Rather, instructional software designers need to expand information and provide links to other sites and to additional information. Similarly, Faiola and Matei (2006) found that Chinese and Anglo-Americans searching Websites created by both Chinese and American Web designers could find information faster on the sites created by designers from their own cultures. Faiola and Matei point to the underlying cognitive processes that are influenced by culture.

Other scholars, however, caution against using simplistic cultural dichotomies to predict and analyze complex intercultural interaction. They note that, with increased globalization and the resulting prevalence of hybrid identities, the frameworks of Hofstede (1980, 1991, 1997) and Hall (1959, 1966) might be increasingly ill-suited to analyzing intercultural communication online (Ess & Sudweeks, 2006, p. 180; Heaton, 2008). Macfadyen, (2008) identifies three challenges of these frameworks (viewing culture as nation only,

culture as static, and reductionistic nature) and other critics specifically note the colonial discourse of these frameworks (Fougère & Moulettes, 2007).

Hewling (2005) offers some proof in her close analysis of online discussion posts of multicultural students. She found the issues raised by the various students' interaction in her class could not be attributed simply to any one particular national culture. She then offers a useful reminder of the complexity of (online) intercultural communication. Hewling also notes that, on its own, nationality is not entirely an effective predictor of behavior or understanding.

Finally, as Macfadyen (2008) notes, social science studies of technology in general pay more attention to national culture (and occasionally gender and race) as a proxy for culture in comparative studies. For example, much less attention is paid to cultural elements of socioeconomic class, age, and ethnicity – factors that might have a profound effect on student learning and teacher delivery of curricula (Merryfield, 2001). Indeed, students' socioeconomic status might matter in the kinds of courses that are likely to be economically viable for online pedagogy. Such factors, in turn, exacerbate inequalities in the ways different cultural groups access online education locally and globally (Schiller, 1996). A third limitation of these social science studies is they usually focus on actors in the micro level of analysis (i.e., individual student learners), and thus less attention is paid to professors, teaching assistants, administrators, and the broader social, educational, and political contexts in which e-learning takes place. Some research, however, suggests administrators primarily set the tone for Internet use in schools (Levin & Arafeh, 2002). This item is a theoretical and a research lacunae as there might be significant measurable cultural differences in the perceptions and the motivations of administrators toward online pedagogy. Such factors might, in turn, affect syllabus construction and student learning in online contexts.

THE INTERPRETIVE APPROACH TO CULTURE AND ONLINE PEDAGOGY RESEARCH

As described by Martin and Nakayama (1999) and others (e.g., Mumby, 1997), scholars who conduct culture and communication research in the interpretive paradigm[5] are concerned with understanding the world as it is. They focus on describing the subjective, creative communication of individuals and usually use qualitative research methods to do so. Culture, in the interpretive paradigm, is generally seen as socially constructed and emergent, rather than defined *a priori*, and it is not limited to nation-state collectives. Interpretivists thus emphasize the stable, orderly characteristics of culture as reflecting an assumption of the social world as cohesive, ordered, and integrated (Martin & Nakayama, 1999, p. 5). In the context of online pedagogy, the relationship between culture and online learning is seen as more reciprocal than causal, where culture might influence online pedagogy, but is also constructed and enacted through communication.

Cognitive and Affective Dimensions of Online Learning

There are relatively few interpretive studies investigating the cultural implications of online pedagogy, and these studies include in-depth examinations of students' attitudes toward online learning. One previously mentioned study, examines Chinese students' online learning experiences and their attitudes toward online learning using in-depth, qualitative methods, including semi-structured interviews, focus groups and artifacts (Thompson & Ku, 2005). The researchers found the students had mixed reactions. The students recognized some attractive features of online learning, but they also expressed some concerns. They particularly liked easy resource sharing and thought instructors provided more resources online than in a typical class. The students also liked the

written format of online classes. As taking notes in English was sometimes difficult for them in traditional classes, in online courses, they could easily save or print any information they thought important.

The students also liked the discussion boards and felt more comfortable expressing themselves online than in front of classes in traditional classrooms. However, none of the Chinese students said they would like to take all classes online. Rather, they preferred a combination of online work and traditional classroom courses. Some students said they found the written format tedious, for they had trouble understanding some of the language used by instructors or students, thought it too academic, or found that it contained too much slang. Other disadvantages of online classes the students identified were the lack of face-to-face communication and the absence of a community of classmates. Some students also noted the lack of immediate feedback from the instructor as problematic. This in-depth investigation reveals the complex ambivalent relationship that students had with online learning.

A recent in-depth case study conducted by Chen, Bennett, and Maton (2008) both supports and contradicts Thompson and Ku's (2005) earlier findings. This study provides an excellent example of the complementary contribution of interpretive studies to established social science studies. The authors who conducted the study collected qualitative data for one year (multiple interviews, focus groups, study process questionnaire, and document review) on the online course experiences of two Chinese international students studying at an Australian university.

In the course of presenting their findings, the authors clarify misconceptions involved in the Chinese learner "paradox": that is, Chinese students are often seen as passive, rote learners who memorize material and never questioning authority, yet they achieve internationally recognized academic achievements. The researchers explain that the active learning model in

Western contexts requires that students *question* to understand, whereas Chinese learners *listen* to understand. Moreover, the researchers note that Chinese listening is not passive, but instead involves a preference for intense, deep learning. Moreover, another element of Western active learning—collaboration--is viewed and enacted differently by Western and Asian learners. The Western notion of student teamwork is a rather superficial approach to problem solving, whereas the Chinese emphasis is on the collaborative construction of knowledge.

Chen et al. (2008)'s extensive analysis revealed that the Chinese students' primary challenges related to online educational formats involved fundamental differences in epistemic beliefs. That is, the Chinese thought the teacher did not provide sufficient input; they did not see teachers as passing along objective knowledge, but as guides who change and interpret subjective (deep) knowledge through their feedback, reaction, and control of the class discussion. In the Chinese view, knowledge is not legitimate until the teacher has confirmed their fellow students' opinions, and they felt such confirmation could not occur in a solely online learning environment. These findings contradict somewhat previous studies suggesting that Chinese students appreciate the temporal and spatial flexibility afforded by online learning. On the contrary, the Chinese students in this study felt teachers gave up their control in online discussions. These students believe that learning occurs through a teacher's *relationship* with students and that interpersonal interactions represented a prerequisite for intellectual communication.

A similar, though less in-depth qualitative study was conducted by Al-Harthi (2005) who investigated the nature of distance education experiences of Arab graduate students in the U.S. This study used a phenomenological research design and semi-structured qualitative interviews to collect research data. These students had very negative attitudes about online pedagogy prior

to taking their distance education courses. The students also had many fears, concerns, and reservations regarding their mandatory distance education experiences. However, after completing the courses, the students reported greater appreciation and awareness of online options, and with the exception of one, all said they would take another online class in the future. However, they did have some concerns (e.g., the lack of response and direct interaction with instructors). A number of the students also preferred communicating at an individual level with the instructors instead of asking for clarification on the rather public class discussion forum. Similar to findings reported by previous researchers, Al-Harthi notes these attitudes might reflect the students' cultural preference for relatively large power distance between students and teachers where students expect the instructor to initiate all communication and there is less student-student interaction (Hofstede, 1986).

With regards to affect and motivation, Al-Harthi (2005) found that while the students were very anxious prior to taking an online course, they reported feeling much more positive at the end of the course. For example, the lack of physical presence in the online course was viewed positively by the students and seen as reducing the risk of social embarrassment—a factor explained as a reflection of the students' collectivistic views and sensitivity to the possibility of public humiliation. Female students were particularly more comfortable studying online, as it reduced their discomfort with mixing of genders that is less accepted in many Muslim contexts. However, the Arab students were sometimes uncomfortable with the American students' perceived aggressiveness in discussions and in questioning the teacher's authority—a cultural characteristic of U.S. American students described in other studies (Merryfield, 2001; Thompson & Ku, 2005).

In Al-Harthi's (2005) study, the Arabs students' initial reaction was to avoid distance education courses, and they referred to their distance education courses as either a "must" or a "requirement."

The students initially saw distance education as a difficulty – a situation about which they had no choice but to overcome in order to fulfill a degree requirement. However, consonant with findings from other interpretive studies, in the end, they had more positive feelings—again revealing the complex relationship students have with online learning.

Communication Behaviors in Online Learning

In Thompson and Ku's (2005) study, there were also noticeable cultural differences between Chinese and U.S. students in their online interactions. Valuing relational harmony and large power-distance relationships, the Chinese students tended to be more conservative and more agreeable in voicing opinions than U.S. students. Like the Asian students in previous studies, these Chinese students also expressed some concern over not getting feedback from professors, and they reported preferring a more traditional teacher-as-authority model rather than the student-oriented model of online instruction.

A noteworthy interpretive study is Hewling's (2005) work on Australian and international students in an online masters program in an Australian university. Some of the students were physically located in Australia, others were in North America, South East Asia, the Middle East, and Europe. Hewling determined that discussion board messages might be a suitable "nexus" of intercultural communication in this context and set out to identify potential cultural differences and conflicts in the "doing" of online learning. Through close content analysis of discussion postings, she noted some cultural differences early on. For example, Australian students seemed less likely to post messages to the class discussion boards, and when they did, they were much less likely to post messages that actively encouraged readers to respond and continue the discussion.

After analyzing a number of messages, Hewling concludes that the variations in communication behavior did not seem to relate to national/cultural differences. For example, she notes many postings involved the question of authority including who had the authority to speak in this environment, to answer particular questions, and to facilitate discussion. She also observes that students bring their various cultural norms to the issue, but that "it is unlikely that all of the problematic aspects of authority issues raised by analysis of the interaction in this class can be attributed simply to any one particular national culture" (p. 353). Hewling goes on to observe that the online class context itself was a new cultural landscape that all students had to learn to navigate, and that the cultural commonalities they shared in this context did not help them much at all.

In addition to in-depth interpretive studies of the influence of nationality and ethnicity on e-learning dimensions, similar (though fewer) studies have been conducted on other cultural groups, like disabled students. For example, one case study examined blind college students' experiences in online courses and identified their frustration with the Course Management System (Muwanguzi & Lin, 2010). Another case study, by contrast, described software that permits blind students to participate in online courses (e.g using whiteboard software that provides textual descriptions by a live mediator) (Freire, Linhalis, Bianchini, Fortes & Pimentel, 2010).

Contributions and Limitation of Interpretive Studies

As was shown in Table 1, the value of the interpretive studies lies in the in-depth descriptions which provide a rather complex, fluid, and sometimes contradictory picture of students' experiences in online classes. As such, such studies complement the social science research that tends to yield a broader, more static description of the relationships between culture and student online experiences. However, the authors' review and analysis of the extant literature on mediated instructional communication reveal few studies have employed the interpretive paradigm and methodologies to interrogate how students express their cultural selves and understand the meaning of their lived experiences as participants in e-learning courses. As noted previously, interpretive studies can reveal the ambivalence and contradictions experienced by the students in their relationships to cognitive and affective dimensions of online learning. Future studies could further analyze trust and intercultural identity expression in online interactions. Such studies could, for example, involve students from different cultural backgrounds working in virtual teams as they seek to communicate appropriately and build trust amidst the challenges of not being able to directly know or discern the social identity background of their peers (St.Amant, 2002).

Furthermore, given the rise in global education (Gacel-Avila, 2005), future research studies could situate the observation and analysis of cultural variability in communicative behaviors in an expanded array of contexts. Some existing studies yield rather consistent findings concerning cultural influences on behavioral dimensions of online learning. Others (e.g., Chen et al, 2007; Hewling, 2005), however, remind us that case studies of individual class contexts or individual student experiences can highlight the *complexities* of group experiences beyond the rather constrained sightlines of the social science approaches to culture and online pedagogy.

Consequently, interpretive studies provide communication educators with useful insights into the influence of a range of cultural differences in online interactions and highlight some practical suggestions for global educators. For example, educators should be cognizant of the dynamic, contextual, and relational aspects of e-learning. They should also resist tendencies to stereotype on the basis of nationality. Lujan (2008) provides a seemingly contradictory suggestion – that online instructors explore specific communication patterns that significantly impact online learning interactions. Such factors include communication styles, attitudes toward conflict, approaches to completing tasks, decision-making style, attitudes toward disclosure, and approaches to knowing. Zhao and McDougall (2008), in comparison, suggest that Western instructors address these differences explicitly with Asian international students. Zhao and McDougall also suggest that instructors should explain that classroom norms and expectations might be different from those students have experienced in their home countries. Through these explanations, the instructor can discuss how participation is expected and encourage students to share opinions and even disagree with the instructor. Perhaps the primary lesson here is to be aware of the existence and complexities of cultural variations in online student motivation and behavior, but not succumb to easy generalizations and stereotyping.

Cheong and Martin (2009) describe a course assignment designed to help students think in more in-depth and complex ways about culture and its impact on everyday communication and relationships. In the "Intercultural Relationship Interview" assignment, students interview someone they know in an intercultural relationship (again, defining culture inclusively, beyond nationality). Students are provided with a list of potential questions and encouraged to conduct in-depth interviews at multiple meetings (accompanied by a discussion about confidentiality, cultural sensitivity of questioning, etc). The students then write a report on their interviews and in a discussion board assignment, they are asked to explore what they learned that they can apply to their own intercultural relationships. Cheong & Martin (2009) report that students learnt a great deal about culture and communication from this assignment.

THE CRITICAL APPROACH TO CULTURE AND ONLINE PEDAGOGY RESEARCH

The critical paradigm shares many of the same metatheoretical assumptions with the interpretive paradigm. These include an ontological assumption that reality is socially constructed and an emphasis on the voluntaristic characteristic of human behavior (Martin & Nakayama, 1999; Mumby, 1997). However, critical scholars emphasize that human behavior is always constrained by societal ideological superstructures and material conditions that privilege some and disadvantage others. Culture is not a benignly socially constructed variable. Rather, it is a site of struggle where various communication meanings are contested within social hierarchies—the ultimate goal is to examine systems of oppression and ultimately work for system change.

One group of critical scholars--the radical humanists—base their work on Althusser (1971), Gramsci (1971, 1978), and the Frankfurt school (Habermas 1970, 1981, 1987) and focus on the "consciousness" as the basis for a radical critique of society. These scholars attempt to articulate ways in which humans can transcend and reconfigure the larger social frameworks that construct cultural identities in intercultural settings. Another group--the radical structuralists--base their work on the structuralist emphasis of Western Marxists (Lukacs, 1971; Volosinov, 1973), and view the structural hierarchies as less malleable and the human transcendence of such structures less likely (Burrell & Morgan, p. 34).

In the context of online pedagogy, the authors' review reveals two general foci in investigating issues of power and inequity associated with students' motivation, affect and communication behavior. The first body of literature focuses on online pedagogy issues in the context of the larger society (e.g., power relations in the "ecology of games" underpinning e-learning) (Dutton, Cheong & Park, 2004). The second body of literature ex- amines how societal hierarchies are reproduced within the online pedagogical context and identifies strategies for rectifying these inequities.

Cognitive and Affective Dimensions of Online Learning

A number of scholars remind us that that e-learning occurs within significant historical, political, and socioeconomic contexts (always tied to cultural forces). Such contexts, in turn, affect the social shaping of technology, the process of technological change, and innovation. One such approach investigates e-learning as an inherently political process – that is, not as a predetermined techno- logical outcome, but rather as part of the larger "digital academe" of online education, distributed learning, and electronic service delivery in higher education (Amory, 2010; Njenga & Fourie, 2010). The theoretical argument relating culture and online pedagogy is the notion of "teleaccess" whereby the emergent outcomes of e-learning motivation and affect are "anchored in choices that reconfigure access to information, people, services and technologies" (Dutton, Cheong & Park, 2004, p. 134).

This "ecology of games" approach examines everyday decisions and negotiations of the many "players" who often have competing interests in online pedagogy – students, instructors, university administrators, e-learning vendors, courseware specialists. These players can influence outcomes and change rules in unpredictable ways—privileg- ing some and diminishing power of others: "for instance with the role of the teacher diminishing if students spend more time learning directly through e-learning systems" (Dutton, Cheong & Park, 2004, p. 134). Under this critical paradigm, online pedagogy is considered to be "inherently political" (Winner, 2000) as Web-based educa- tional tools facilitate communication patterns that are more compatible with some cultural backgrounds than others.

Several critical scholars have also theorized online pedagogy as "social control" that renders students and educators more susceptible to the manipulations of instructional technology cooperations (Robins & Webster, 1999) amidst local and global competitive environments of higher education. Noble (2002) stridently warns that the top-down, profit driven commercialization of higher education, will lead to "digital diploma mills," undermining educational quality and instructional communication in distance learning courses produced by universities governed by the ideology of private industry. Because universities are increasingly concerned with automation and corporate style efficiency to improve bottom lines and reduce overheads, Noble (2002) believes that online pedagogy represents a commoditized intellectual product produced by professors as "replaceable content providers" and sold to student "consumers." Wilson, Qayyum and Boshier (1998), in particular, argue that educators should counteract "worldwide America" as American corporations and institutions dominate the browsers, search engines, and digitization of content that mediate students' access to online courses and information.

On a more global level, scholars have criticized the online pedagogical "experts" who arrogantly impose their ideas of distance education and e-learning on educational systems in other countries and cultures, particularly those in economically developing countries with different technological and cultural constraints than those found in more economically powerful countries (Hannum, 2009). In this vein, the relationship between culture and online pedagogy is conceived as a contested, contingent, and increasingly commercialized site where students' changing attitudes and perceptions of the educational cyberspace should be tracked as they are perceived, even stereotyped, as customers who expect easy online access to educational services.

Communication Behavior in Online Learning

A related, second body of critical work in online pedagogy examines how societal hierarchies are reproduced within the online pedagogical context, privileging some cultural groups and individuals and marginalizing others. These hierarchies might be based on technological knowledge that is part of cultural capital (Bourdieu 1986) and technological capital (Selwyn, 2004). Those without these skills and knowledge can feel marginalized and disconnected from the center of society (van Dijk, 2004; Rojas, Straubhaar, Roychowdhury, & Okur, 2004), and the notion of "open-access" online pedagogy is contested, noted by Dutton and Loader (2002). Young (1996) argues that the very expression of the potential for online education to extend opportunities across socioeconomic and geographical divides celebrates the value Western cultures place on education as a pathway toward social mobility and equality.

Some scholars have argued that because so much of online communication is conducted in English, speakers of any language other than English are disadvantaged (Keniston, 2001). The linguistic and content aspects of the digital divide are implicated in such critiques, and they might be reproduced via online pedagogy – particularly given the Anglo-American language and cultural bias of cyberspace. The first software developers (technical white elite) of the Internet determined, without much discussion, the basic linguistic conventions (including emoticons and commonly used abbreviations) of the Internet. One implication of this development is students who have not yet learned the new graphic language of emoticons or the "shorthand" of email text can have a powerful sense of being excluded (Rooksby, 2002). Moreover, the emergence of Internet derived neologisms, electronic language or global "netspeak" practices in English (Crystal, 2001) might also be associated with disenfranchisement experienced by students who are less familiar with emerging communication forms afforded by the Internet. On the other hand, some communication researchers point out that online pedagogy may expand educational inclusion by offering learning opportunities to students from disadvantaged groups, for example, First Nations populations (Facey, 2001).

Second, power dynamics in online interactions (e.g., discussion board participation) often mirror social hierarchies outside the classroom. For example, Merryfield (2001) describes how international students and students of color are often marginalized in classroom discussions (even online), while white U.S. students dominate the discussion. This situation can have implications for instructors who may have to negotiate power differently in the online classroom than they do in the traditional classroom (Wood & Fassett, 2003). As noted, computer-mediated communication, in general, is status leveling. That is, there are fewer gatekeepers controlling interaction, determining who talks and when, and for some students, this freedom can be liberating (Kanata & Martin, 2007). Research shows that students who are too shy or anxious to talk in face-to-face classes might feel freer to speak up in online discussion (Al-Harthi, 2005; Merryfield, 2001; Thompson & Ku, 2005). The extent to which intellectual dissent is promoted, however, might be questioned.

Another challenge for online pedagogy is that verbal misunderstanding can be exacerbated because interactors might not be aware of communication problems because confusion or misunderstanding is generally shown nonverbally. In addition to possible misunderstandings of specific words and phrases, nuanced language conventions such as humor can often be misunderstood (Osman & Herring, 2007; St.Amant, 2002; Tolan, 2007). A problem caused by asynchronicity in CMC is silence or non-responses, for the sender has no way of knowing if his or her message has been received (Jarvenpaa, Knoll, & Leidner, 1998).

In face-to-face interaction, silences can be very meaningful, although the meaning of silence might vary from culture to culture (Acheson, 2008; Covarrubias, 2007). Silence could be less acceptable in online classrooms steeped in cybercultures that value "speed, reach, openness, quick response" (Anderson 1995, p. 13). Lack of response to an email or to an online discussion forum might, for example, be taken as lack of interest in low-context cultures where explicit verbal and written contributions are assessed and rewarded. As Newman and Johnson (1999) note, discussions of online pedagogy often fail to recognize the importance of tacit knowledge and values that cannot be codified well and disseminated over the Internet. Yet silence might also mean the person was called away or was experiencing email connection or computer-related problems (Rooksby, 2002; Zembylas & Vrasidas, 2007). Davis (1997) writes that educators should consider technological limitations when setting up listservs or other platforms for online communication.

Contributions and Limitation of Critical Studies

Studies in the critical tradition highlight the importance of understanding established and evolving power differentials and digital inequalities implicated in online pedagogy. Naïve ethnocentrism and the lack of respect for cultural differences might lead to computer-mediated colonization (Ess, 2002), especially in online classes dominated by a "one-to-many" instructional paradigm, despite the advance of interactive, Web-based communication media (Bork, 2001).

Concerning the pedagogical implications, several scholars identify strategies for online instructors to structure discussion assignments so as to ensure equitable power dynamics in online discussion. For example, instructors can "move the center," creating a space wherein all learners feel they are the center of instruction. Merryfield (2001) describes how class interaction changed after she "shifted the center" in her online teacher education course by requiring that each student post the exact same number of discussion messages. As a result, there was then no one group initiating ideas, controlling the discourse, or silencing others. Cheong and Martin (2009) also report a strategy for ensuring a legitimate space for minority students (e.g., non-native speakers, ethnic/racial minorities, and gay students) in class discussions, particularly in early days of the course. This approach is done by quoting these students in instructor discussion summaries and/or explicitly reinforcing the contributions of these students in discussions so no one group of students seems to control the discourse.

Others note that professors are ethically responsible to be on call when dealing with emotional issues online, such as race relations and white privilege, as online discussions about emotional topics do not always lead to productive outcomes (Akintunde, 2006). Sujo de Montes, Oran, and Willis (2002) describe the challenges for instructors facilitating emotional discussions of race and marginality online when well-intentioned students make statements hurtful to other students. Sujo de Montes, Oran, and Willis suggest that an instructor's lack of experience in dealing with issues like racism can lead to silence or interventions that silence students and allow issues of power and racism to remain unchallenged. They conclude their essay with the questions "how do we purposely turn the default 'off' position of race in an online classroom to the 'on' position, and how do we manage the resulting conversations and confrontations?" (p. 268).

In a related essay, Zembylas and Vrasidas (2005) provide an insightful discussion of the ethical issues in learning about "otherness" in online courses and give practical suggestions for how instructors can assist online students in being ethical students of culture. Tolan (2007) discusses the challenges of balancing the freedom of relative anonymity with potential isolation or loss of diversity and suggests that instructors make the invisible (cultural backgrounds/characteristics) visible—in activities that allow students to explore

the impact of their cultural background on their contributions to course content.

Future online pedagogy research using a critical lens should consider the consequences of students' perceptions of online pedagogy in light of the emerging higher education marketplace. That is, they should consider notions such as "advertising" promoting large introductory courses that are economically viable markets versus specialized courses. Given the rising popularity of online pedagogy, there is a need for more critical voices in debates on online pedagogy (Hannon & Bretag, 2010; Jackson & McDowell, 2002). Castell, Bryson and Jenson (2002) note how educational discourse critical of the e-learning imperative are, for the most part, muted as economic interests are prized by a new breed of entrepreneurial academics influenced by commercial and corporate ideologies.

More recently, Njenga and Fourie (2010) describe how "technopositivist ideology" -- the "compulsive enthusiasm" about e-learning -- is being created and promoted by those who are set to gain. In many cases, this situation takes place without giving educators the time and opportunity to examine the dangers and rewards of e-learning on teaching and learning. In order to promote continued dialogue on the topic, Njenga and Fourie identify and discuss ten myths that have been used by technopositivists.

Hannon and Bretag (2010) similarly examine the current discourse in higher education concerning e-learning and find three distinct variations. The first of these is "technology as a bridge to globalised opportunity" -- a utopian vision that ignores the complexity of implementation. The second variation is "technology as delivery of learning," and it also ignores issues of implementation and practice. The third approach --technology as communication and building relationships for learning — was promoted more by instructors and less by administration. Hannon and Bretag see this discourse as most viable in understanding both the possibilities and challenges of learning technologies in practice, as it emphasizes the essential role of student-teacher relationship in learning. Thus, the challenge for global education scholarship entails further critical theorization on the evolving roles, affect, motivations, and communicative behaviors of student learning contingent upon related economic and cultural development within the digital academe.

A limitation of critical studies in online pedagogy is the difficulty in directly verifying these critical notions in real online courses. One might note that the speculations and observations of student marginality and effects of societal forces and macrocontexts are just that. There are rarely empirical verifications of these effects in the critical literature.

CONCLUSION

In conclusion, after the authors' extensive review of research investigating the intersections of culture and online pedagogy in global contexts, they return to fortify their heuristic purpose of this review to summarize ways to enlarge the breadth and depth of online pedagogical research. The key finding of this review was the tangential treatment of the role culture plays in e-learning despite prior scholarly acknowledgement that culture is critical in the social shaping of educational technologies (Bentley, Tinney, & Chia, 2005; Chen, 2007; Young, 2008) and recognition of cultural differences as linked to successful online pedagogical outcomes (Moore, 2006).

What is most striking is that "culture" is so rarely mentioned, particularly in education and technology studies conducted within the social science paradigm.[6] These social science studies investigating various aspects of online pedagogy within particular national, ethnic, regional, institutional contexts make little or no mention of the contextual impact on online learning process and outcomes (e.g., a study on student satisfaction with online course conducted in a university in Taiwan or Turkey), citing previous research and theory (e.g. TAM). It seems, then, that culture is often assumed or subsumed in educational models.

That said, the authors did note the contributions of the various extant paradigmatic approaches and the resulting practical implications. The myriad social science studies do identify some cultural differences in online learning and encourage instructors (and future researchers) to consider the optimum strategies for reaching a broad range of learning styles in designing and implementing online courses. The in-depth interpretive studies remind us of the complexity and heterogeneity of cultural groups and cultural approaches to e-learning. They also call for more studies of this type and as for practical implications, they particularly encourage us as instructors to resist stereotyping our students by nationality, ethnicity/race, etc. They highlight the need for instructors to be aware of and proactively alter conditions that marginalize particular student groups.

Finally, the authors note that extant scholarship is bereft of studies that combine theoretical paradigms. Few scholars consider emerging paradoxes of online pedagogy directly, although there have been suggestions that the very nature of the Internet itself is paradoxical, liberating and dominating, empowering and fragmenting, universalizing but non-totalizing (Levy, 2001; Poster, 2000). Therefore, future research should consider cultural dialectics in order to address the emerging paradoxical nature (Levy, 2001) of online pedagogy, including investigating classroom interactions both offline (Prentice & Kramer, 2006; Holmes, 2005) and online (Perold & Maree, 2003). Such an approach might be useful in moving us toward a more productive comprehensive understanding of the cultural considerations of online pedagogy.

REFERENCES

Acheson, K. (2008). Silence as gesture: Rethinking the nature of communicative silences. *Communication Theory, 18*(4), 535–555. doi:10.1111/j.1468-2885.2008.00333.x

Akdemir, O., & Koszalka, T. A. (2008). Investigating the relationships among instructional strategies and learning styles in online environments. *Computers & Education, 50*(4), 1451–1461. doi:10.1016/j.compedu.2007.01.004

Akintunde, M. (2006). Diversity.com: Teaching an online course on white racism and multiculturalism. *Multicultural Perspectives, 8*(2), 35–45. doi:10.1207/s15327892mcp0802_7

Al-Harthi, A. S. (2005). Distance higher education experiences of Arab Gulf students in the United States: A cultural perspective. *The International Review of Research in Open and Distance Learning, 6*(3). Retrieved July 13, 2010, from http://www.irrodl.org/index.php/irrodl/article/view/263/840

Allen, I. E., & Seaman, J. (2010, January). *Learning on demand: Online education in the United States, 2009*. Needham, MA: The Sloan Consortium. Retrieved June 25, 2010, from http://www.sloan-c.org/publications/survey/pdf/learningondemand.pdf

Althusser, L. (1971). *Lenin and philosophy* (Brewster, B., Trans.). New York, NY: Monthly Review Press.

Amory, A. (2010). Education technology and hidden ideological contradictions. *Journal of Educational Technology & Society, 13*(1), 69–79.

Anderson, J. (1995). Cybarites, knowledge workers and New Creoles on the superhighway. *Anthropology Today, 11*(4), 13–15.

Aragon, S. R., Johnson, S. D., & Shaik, N. (2003). The influence of learning style preferences on student success in online versus face-to-face environments. *American Journal of Distance Education, 16*(4), 227–244. doi:10.1207/S15389286AJDE1604_3

Baggaley, J. (2008). Where did distance education go wrong? *Distance Education, 29*(1), 39–51. doi:10.1080/01587910802004837

Baldwin, J. R., Faulkner, S. L., Hecht, M. L., & Lindsley, S. L. (2006). *Redefining culture: Perspectives across the disciplines*. Mahwah, NJ: Lawrence Erlbaum.

Barnett-Queen, T., Blair, R., & Merrick, M. (2005). Student perspectives of online discussion: Strengths and weaknesses. *Journal of Technology in Human Services, 23*, 229–244. doi:10.1300/J017v23n03_05

Battalio, J. (2009). Success in distance education: Do learning styles and multiple formats matter? *American Journal of Distance Education, 23*(2), 71–87. doi:10.1080/08923640902854405

Bejerano, A. (2008). Raising the question #11: The genesis and evolution of online degree programs: Who are they for and what have we lost along the way? *Communication Education, 57*(3), 408–414. doi:10.1080/03634520801993697

Benbunan-Fich, R., & Hiltz, S. R. (2003). Mediators of effectiveness of online courses. *IEEE Transactions on Professional Communication, 46*(4), 298–312. doi:10.1109/TPC.2003.819639

Benoit, P. J., Benoit, W. L., Milyo, J., & Hansen, G. J. (2006). *The effects of traditional versus Web-assisted instruction on learning and student satisfaction*. Columbia, MO: University of Missouri Graduate School.

Bentley, J. P. H., Tinney, M. V., & Chia, B. H. (2005). International review: Intercultural-Internet-based learning: Know your audience and what it values. *ETR & D, 53*(2), 117–127. doi:10.1007/BF02504870

Bjørge, A. K. (2007). Power distance in English lingua franca email communication. *International Journal of Applied Linguistics, 17*(1), 60–80. doi:10.1111/j.1473-4192.2007.00133.x

Bork, A. (2001). What is needed for effective learning on the Internet? *Journal of Educational Technology & Society, 4*(3). Retrieved from http://ifets.gmd.de/periodical/vol_3_2001/bork.html.

Bourdieu, P. (1986). The forms of capital. In Richardson, J. G. (Ed.), *Handbook of theory and research for the sociology of education* (pp. 241–258). Westport, CT: Greenwood.

Broady, T., Chan, A., & Caputi, P. (2010). Comparison of older and younger adults' attitudes towards and abilities with computers: Implications for training and learning. *British Journal of Educational Technology, 41*(3), 473–485. doi:10.1111/j.1467-8535.2008.00914.x

Brown, S. (2010). From VLEs to learning Web: The implications of Web 2.0 for learning and teaching. *Interactive Learning Environments, 18*(1), 1–10. doi:10.1080/10494820802158983

Burbules, N. C. (2000). Does the Internet constitute a global educational community? In Burbules, N. C., & Torres, C. (Eds.), *Globalization and education: Critical perspectives* (pp. 323–355). New York, NY: Routledge.

Burrell, G., & Morgan, G. (1988). *Sociological paradigms and organizational analysis*. Portsmouth, NH: Heinemann.

Carbaugh, D. (1988). Comments on "culture" in communication inquiry. *Communication Reports, 1*, 38–41.

Carle, A. C. (2009). Evaluating college students' evaluations of a professor's teaching effectiveness across time and instruction mode (online vs. face-to-face) using a multilevel growth modeling approach. *Computers & Education, 53*, 429–435. doi:10.1016/j.compedu.2009.03.001

Castell, S. D., Bryson, M., & Jenson, J. (2002). Object lessons: Toward an educational theory of technology. *First Monday, 7*(1). Retrieved November 25, 2010, from http://131.193.153.231/www/issues/issue7_1/castell/

Chen, C. H. (2007). Cultural diversity in instructional design for technology-based education. *British Journal of Educational Technology, 38*(6), 1113–1116. doi:10.1111/j.1467-8535.2007.00738.x

Chen, R., Bennett, S., & Maton, K. (2008). The adaptation of Chinese international students to online flexible learning: Two case studies. *Distance Education, 29*(3), 307–323. doi:10.1080/01587910802395821

Chen, R.-S., & Tsai, C.-C. (2007). Gender differences in Taiwan university students' attitudes toward Web-based learning. *Cyberpsychology & Behavior, 10*(5), 645–654. doi:10.1089/cpb.2007.9974

Cheong, P. H., & Martin, J. N. (2009). Cultural implications of e-learning access (& divides): Teaching an intercultural communication course online. In Olaniran, B. A. (Ed.), *Cases on successful e-learning practices in the developed and developing world: Methods for global information economy* (pp. 78–91). Hershey, PA: IGI Global. doi:10.4018/978-1-60566-942-7.ch006

Chu, R. J. (2010). How family support and Internet self-efficacy influence the effects of e-learning among higher-aged adults: Analysis of gender and age differences. *Computers & Education, 55*(1), 1–426. doi:10.1016/j.compedu.2010.01.011

Collier, M. J., Hegde, R. S., Lee, W., Nakayama, T. K., & Yep, G. A. (2002). Dialogue on the edges: Ferment in communication and culture. In Collier, M. J. (Ed.), *Transforming communication about culture* (pp. 219–280). Thousand Oaks, CA: Sage.

Covarrubias, P. (2007). (Un)biased in Western theory: Generative silence in American Indian communication. *Communication Monographs, 74*, 265–271. doi:10.1080/03637750701393071

Crystal, D. (2001). *Language and the Internet.* Port Chester, NY: Cambridge University Press.

Davis, M. (1997). Fragmented by technologies: A community in cyberspace. *Interpersonal Computing and Technology, 5*(1-2), 7–18.

Dermo, J. (2009). E-assessment and the student learning experience: A survey of student perceptions of e-assessment. *British Journal of Educational Technology, 40*(2), 203–214. doi:10.1111/j.1467-8535.2008.00915.x

Diaz, V. (2010). Web 2.0 and emerging technologies in online learning. *New Directions for Community Colleges, 150*, 57–66. doi:10.1002/cc.405

Dutton, W. H., Cheong, P. H., & Park, N. (2004). An ecology of constraints on e-learning in higher education: The case of a virtual learning environment. *Prometheus, 22*(2), 131–149. doi:10.1080/0810902042000218337

Dutton, W. H., & Loader, B. D. (2002). Introduction: New media and institution of higher education and learning. In Dutton, W. H., & Loader, B. D. (Eds.), *Digital academe: New media and institution of higher education and learning* (pp. 1–32). London, UK: Routledge.

Ess, C. (2002). Computer-mediated colonization, the renaissance, and educational imperatives for an intercultural global village. *Ethics and Information Technology, 4*(1), 11–22. doi:10.1023/A:1015227723904

Ess, C., & Sudweeks, F. (2005). Culture and computer-mediated communication: Toward new understandings. *Journal of Computer-Mediated Communication, 11*(1), 179–191. doi:10.1111/j.1083-6101.2006.tb00309.x

Facey, E. E. (2001). First nations and education by Internet: The path forward, or back? *Journal of Distance Education, 16*(1). Retrieved December 3, 2010, from http://cade.icap.org/vol16.1/facey.html

Faiola, A., & Matei, S. A. (2006). Cultural cognitive style and Web design: Beyond a behavioral inquiry into computer-mediated communication. *Journal of Computer-Mediated Communication, 11*, 375–394. doi:10.1111/j.1083-6101.2006.tb00318.x

Feintuch, H. (2010, March 18). Keeping their distance. *Diverse: Issues in Higher Education, 27*(3). Retrieved November 25, 2010, from http://www.highbeam.com/doc/1G1-222251349.html

Fougère, M., & Moulettes, A. (2007). The construction of the modern west and the backward rest: Studying the discourse of Hofstede's Culture's Consequences. *Journal of Multicultural Discourses, 2*(1), 1–19. doi:10.2167/md051.0

Freire, A. P., Linhalis, F., Bianchini, S. L., Fortes, R. P. M., & Pimentel, M. da G. C. (2010). Revealing the whiteboard to blind students: An inclusive approach to provide mediation in synchronous e-learning activities. *Computers & Education, 54*(4), 866–876. doi:10.1016/j.compedu.2009.09.016

Gacel-Avila, J. (2005). The internationalization of higher education. A paradigm for global citizenry. *Journal of Studies in International Education, 9*(2), 121–136. doi:10.1177/1028315304263795

Gayton, J., & McEwen, B. C. (2007). Effective online instructional assessment strategies. *American Journal of Distance Education, 21*(3), 117–132. doi:10.1080/08923640701341653

Gramsci, A. (1971). *Selections from the prison notebooks* (Hoare, Q., & Smith, G. N., Trans.). New York, NY: International.

Gramsci, A. (1978). *Selections from cultural writings*. Cambridge, MA: Harvard University Press.

Habermas, J. (1970). On systematically distorted communication. *Inquiry, 13*, 205–218. doi:10.1080/00201747008601590

Habermas, J. (1981). Modernity versus postmodernity. *New German Critique, NGC, 22*, 3–14. doi:10.2307/487859

Habermas, J. (1987). The theory of communicative action: Lifeworld and system: *Vol. 2. T. McCarthy, Trans*. Boston, MA: Beacon Press.

Hall, B. J. (1992). Theories of culture and communication. *Communication Theory, 1*, 50–70. doi:10.1111/j.1468-2885.1992.tb00028.x

Hall, E. T. (1959). *The silent language*. Garden City, NY: Anchor Press.

Hall, E. T. (1966). *The hidden dimension*. Garden City, NY: Anchor Press.

Halualani, R. T., Mendoza, S. L., & Drzewiecka, J. A. (2009). "Critical" junctures in intercultural communication studies: A review. *The Review of Communication, 9*(1), 17–35. doi:10.1080/15358590802169504

Hannon, J., & Bretag, T. (2010). Negotiating contested discourses of learning technologies in higher education. *Journal of Educational Technology & Society, 13*(1), 106–120.

Hannum, W. (2009). Moving distance education research forward. *Distance Education, 30*(1), 171–173. doi:10.1080/01587910902846020

Hara, N., & Kling, R. (2000). Student distress in Web-based distance education course. *Information Communication and Society, 3*(4), 555–579.

Heaton, L. (2008, June 27). *Cultural specificity: When does it matter?* 2008 Cultural Attitudes Towards Communication and Technology Conference.

Herie, M. (2005). Theoretical perspectives in online pedagogy. *Journal of Technology in Human Services, 23*(1/2), 29–52. doi:10.1300/J017v23n01_03

Herring, S. C. (2004). Slouching toward the ordinary: Current trends in computer-mediated communication. *New Media & Society, 6*(1), 26–36. doi:10.1177/1461444804039906

Hewling, A. (2005). Culture in the online class: Using message analysis to look beyond nationality-based frames of reference. *Journal of Computer-Mediated Communication, 11*(1), 337–356. doi:10.1111/j.1083-6101.2006.tb00316.x

Hofstede, G. (1980). *Culture's consequences: International differences in work-related values*. Beverly Hill, CA: Sage.

Hofstede, G. (1986). Cultural differences in teaching and learning. *International Journal of Intercultural Relations, 10*(3), 301–320. doi:10.1016/0147-1767(86)90015-5

Hofstede, G. (1991). *Cultures and organizations: Software of the mind*. London, UK: McGraw-Hill.

Hofstede, G. (1997). *Cultures and organizations: Software of the mind* (Rev. ed.). New York, NY: McGraw-Hill.

Holloway, R. E. (1996). Diffusion and adoption of educational technology: A critique of research design. In D. H. Jonassen (Ed.), *Handbook of research for educational communications and technology* (pp. 1107-1136). New York, NY: Simon & Schuster Macmillan. Jackson, M., & McDowell, S. (2002). Enhancing discourse on new media within higher education. In W. H. Dutton & B. Loader (Eds.), *Digital academe: New media in higher education and learning* (pp. 318-327). London, UK: Routledge.

Holmes, P. (2005). Ethnic Chinese students' communication with cultural others in a New Zealand University. *Communication Education, 54*(4), 289–311. doi:10.1080/03634520500442160

Jarvenpaa, S. K., Knoll, K., & Leidner, D. E. (1998). Is anybody out there? Antecedents of trust in global virtual teams. *Journal of Management Information Systems, 14*(4), 29–64.

Johnson, D. (2010, Mar/Apr). Don't confuse social networking with educational networking. *Library Media Connection, 28*(5), 98–98.

Jones, C., Ramanau, R., Cross, S., & Healing, G. (2010). Net generation or digital natives: Is there a distinct new generation entering university? *Computers & Education, 54*(3), 722–732. doi:10.1016/j.compedu.2009.09.022

Joy, S., & Kolb, D. A. (2009). Are there cultural differences in learning style? *International Journal of Intercultural Relations, 33*, 69–85. doi:10.1016/j.ijintrel.2008.11.002

Kanata, T., & Martin, J. N. (2007). Facilitating dialogues on race and ethnicity with technology: Challenging "otherness" and promoting a dialogic way of knowing. *Journal of Literacy and Technology, 8*(2), 1–40.

Kelly, H. F., Ponton, M. K., & Rovai, A. P. (2007). A comparison on student evaluations of teaching between online and face-to-face courses. *The Internet and Higher Education, 10*(2), 189–101. doi:10.1016/j.iheduc.2007.02.001

Kelly, R. (2010, April). Finding the right community-building tools for your online course. *Online Classroom*, 1-7.

Keniston, K. (2001). Language, power and software. In Ess, C. (Ed.), *Culture, technology, communication: Towards an intercultural global village* (pp. 283–306). Albany, NY: State University of New York Press.

Kim, K., & Bonk, C. J. (2002). Cross-cultural comparisons of online collaboration. *Journal of Computer-Mediated Communication, 8*(1). Retrieved November 25, 2010, from http://jcmc.indiana.edu/vol8/issue1/kimandbonk.html

Kolb, D. (1985). *Learning style inventory*. Boston, MA: McBer and Company.

Leeds-Hurwitz, W. (1990). Notes on the history of intercultural communication: The Foreign Service Institute and the mandate for intercultural training. *The Quarterly Journal of Speech, 76*, 262–281. doi:10.1080/00335639009383919

Levin, D., & Arafeh, S. (2002). *The digital disconnect: The widening gap between Internet-savvy students and their schools*. Washington, DC: Pew Internet & American Life. Retrieved August 14, 2002, from http://www.pewinternet.org

Levy, P. (2001). *Cyberculture*. Minneapolis, MN: University of Minnesota Press.

Liaw, S.-S., Huang, H.-M., & Chen, G.-D. (2007). Surveying instructor and learner attitudes toward e-learning. *Computers & Education, 49*, 1066–1080. doi:10.1016/j.compedu.2006.01.001

Lim, J., Kim, M., Chen, S. S., & Ryder, C. E. (2008). An empirical investigation of student achievement and satisfaction in different learning environments. *Journal of Instructional Psychology, 35*(2), 113–119.

Lin, S., & Overbaugh, R. C. (2009). Computer-mediated discussion, self-efficacy and gender. *British Journal of Educational Technology, 40*(6), 999–1013. doi:10.1111/j.1467-8535.2008.00889.x

Lujan, J. (2008, February). Difference=flavor: Embracing cultural diversity in online learning. *Online Classroom, 2*, 8.

Lukacs, G. (1971). *History and class consciousness: Studies in Marxist dialectics* (Livingston, R., Trans.). Cambridge, MA: The MIT Press.

Macdonald, J. (2004). Developing competent e-learners: The role of assessment. *Assessment & Evaluation in Higher Education, 29*(2), 215–226. doi:10.1080/0260293042000188483

Macfadyen, L. P. (2008). The perils of parsimony: National culture as red herring? In F. Sudweeks, H. Hrachovec & C. Ess (Eds), *Proceedings, 6th International Conference on Cultural Attitudes Towards Communication and Technology, Nimes, France* (pp. 569-580). School of Information Technology, Murdoch University, Australia.

Martin, J. N., & Nakayama, T. K. (1999). Thinking dialectically about culture and communication. *Communication Theory, 9,* 1–25. doi:10.1111/j.1468-2885.1999.tb00160.x

Mavrou, K., Lewis, A., & Graeme, D. (2010). Researching computer-based collaborative learning in inclusive classroom in Cyprus: The role of computer in pupils' interaction. *British Journal of Educational Technology, 41*(3), 486–501. doi:10.1111/j.1467-8535.2009.00960.x

McCool, M. (2006, December). Adapting e-learning for Japanese audiences. *IEEE Transactions on Professional Communication, 49*(4), 335–345. doi:10.1109/TPC.2006.885870

Menchaca, M. P., & Bekele, T. A. (2008). Learner and instructor identified success factors in distance education. *Distance Education, 29*(3), 231–252. doi:10.1080/01587910802395771

Merryfield, M. M. (2001). The paradoxes of teaching a multicultural education course online. *Journal of Teacher Education, 52*(4), 283–299. doi:10.1177/0022487101052004003

Mestre, L. (2006). Accommodating diverse learning styles in an online environment. *Reference and User Services Quarterly, 46*(2), 27–32.

Middleton, D. (2010). Putting the learning into e-learning. *European Political Science, 9*(1), 5–12. doi:10.1057/eps.2009.37

Moon, D. G. (1996). Concepts of culture: Implications for intercultural communication research. *Communication Quarterly, 44,* 70–84. doi:10.1080/01463379609370001

Moore, M. G. (2006). Editorial: Questions of culture. *American Journal of Distance Education, 20*(1), 1–5. doi:10.1207/s15389286ajde2001_1

Morse, K. (2003). Does one size fit all? Exploring asynchronous learning in a multicultural environment. *Journal of Asynchronous Learning Networks, 7*(1), 37–55.

Mumby, D. K. (1997). Modernism, postmodernism, and communication studies: A rereading of an ongoing debate. *Communication Theory, 7,* 1–28. doi:10.1111/j.1468-2885.1997.tb00140.x

Muwanguzi, S., & Lin, L. (2010). Wrestling with online learning technologies: Blind students' struggle to achieve academic success. *International Journal of Distance Education Technologies, 8*(2), 43–57. doi:10.4018/jdet.2010040104

Newman, R., & Johnson, F. (1999). Sites for power and knowledge? Towards a critique of the virtual university. *British Journal of Sociology of Education, 20*(1), 79–88. doi:10.1080/01425699995515

Nistor, N., & Neubauer, K. (2010). From participation to dropout: Quantitative participation patterns in online university courses. *Computers & Education, 55,* 663–672. doi:10.1016/j.compedu.2010.02.026

Njenga, J. K., & Fourie, L. C. H. (2010). The myths about e-learning in higher education. *British Journal of Educational Technology, 41*(2), 199–212. doi:10.1111/j.1467-8535.2008.00910.x

Noble, D. F. (2001). *Digital diploma mills: The automation of higher education.* New York, NY: Monthly Review Press.

O'Sullivan, P. B. (2000). Communication technologies in an educational environment: Lessons from a historical perspective. In Cole, R. A. (Ed.), *Issues in Web-based pedagogy* (pp. 49–64). Westport, CT: Greenwood Press.

Olaniran, B. A. (2001). The effects of computer-mediated communication on transculturalism. In Milhouse, V. H., Asante, M. K., & Nwosu, P. O. (Eds.), *Transcultural realities: Interdisciplinary perspectives on cross cultural relations* (pp. 83–105). Thousand Oaks, CA: Sage.

Osman, G., & Herring, S. (2007). Interaction, facilitation, and deep learning in cross-cultural chat: A case study. *The Internet and Higher Education*, *10*, 125–141. doi:10.1016/j.iheduc.2007.03.004

Park, N., Lee, K. M., & Cheong, P. H. (2008). University instructors' acceptance of electronic courseware: An application of the Technology Acceptance Model. *Journal of Computer-Mediated Communication*, *13*, 163–186. doi:10.1111/j.1083-6101.2007.00391.x

Perold, J. J., & Maree, D. J. F. (2003). Description of novelty, novelty of description: A dialectic analysis of a Web-based course. *Computers & Education*, *41*(3), 225–249. doi:10.1016/S0360-1315(03)00047-2

Prentice, C. M., & Kramer, M. W. (2006). Dialectical tensions in the classroom: Managing tension through communication. *The Southern Communication Journal*, *71*(4), 339–361.

Price, S., & Oliver, M. (2007). A framework for conceptualizing the impact of technology on teaching and learning. *Journal of Educational Technology & Society*, *10*(1), 16–27.

Robins, K., & Webster, F. (1999). *Times of the technoculture*. New York, NY: Routledge.

Rogers, P. C., Graham, C. R., & Mayes, C. T. (2007). Cultural competence and instructional design: Exploration research into the delivery of online instruction cross culturally (International Review). *Educational Technology Research and Development*, *55*, 197–217. doi:10.1007/s11423-007-9033-x

Rojas, V., Straubhaar, J., Roychowdhury, D., & Okur, O. (2004). Communities, cultural capital, and the digital divide. In Bucy, E. P., & Newhagen, J. E. (Eds.), *Media access: Social and psychological dimensions of new technology use* (pp. 107–130). Mahwah, NJ: Erlbaum.

Rooksby, E. (2002). *Email and ethics: Style and ethical relations in computer-mediated communication*. London, UK: Routledge. doi:10.4324/9780203217177

Saadé, R. G., He, X., & Kira, D. (2007). Exploring dimensions to online learning. *Computers in Human Behavior*, *23*, 1721–1739. doi:10.1016/j.chb.2005.10.002

Saeed, N., Yang, Y., & Sinnappan, S. (2009). Emerging Web technologies in higher education: A case of incorporating blogs, podcasts and social bookmarks in a Web programming course based on students' learning styles and technology preferences. *Journal of Educational Technology & Society*, *12*(4), 98–109.

Schiller, H. I. (1996). *Information inequality: The deepening social crisis in America*. New York, NY: Routledge.

Schwartzman, R. (2007). Refining the question: How can online instruction maximize opportunities for all students? *Communication Education*, *56*(1), 113–117. doi:10.1080/03634520601009728

Seale, J., & Cooper, M. (2010). E-learning and accessibility: An exploration of the potential role of generic pedagogical tools. *Computers & Education*, *54*(4), 1107–1116. doi:10.1016/j.compedu.2009.10.017

Selwyn, N. (2004). Reconsidering political and popular understandings of the Digital Divide. *New Media & Society, 6*(3), 341–362. doi:10.1177/1461444804042519

Shuter, R. (1990). The centrality of culture. *Southern Journal of Communication, 55,* 237–249.

Smith, P. J., Coldwell, J., Smith, S. N., & Murphy, K. L. (2005). Learning through computer-mediated communication: A comparison of Australian and Chinese heritage students. *Innovations in Education and Teaching International, 42*(2), 12–134. doi:10.1080/14703290500062441

St.Amant, K. (2002). When cultures and computers collide: Rethinking computer-mediated communication according to international and intercultural communication expectations. *Journal of Business and Technical Communication, 16,* 196–214. doi:10.1177/1050651902016002003

Sujo de Montes, L. E., Oran, S. M., & Willis, E. M. (2002). Power, language, and identity: Voices from an online course. *Computers and Composition, 19,* 251–271. doi:10.1016/S8755-4615(02)00127-5

Sull, E. C. (2007, June). The #1 complaint of online students: Poor instructor feedback! *Online Classroom, 5.*

Sun, P. C., Tsai, R. J., Finger, G., Chen, Y. Y., & Yeh, D. (2007). What drives successful e-learning? An empirical investigation of the critical factors influencing learner satisfaction. *Computers & Education, 50*(4), 1183–1202. doi:10.1016/j.compedu.2006.11.007

Thompson, L., & Ku, H.-Y. (2005). Chinese graduate students' experiences and attitudes toward online learning. *Educational Media International, 42*(1), 33–47. doi:10.1080/09523980500116878

Tolan, D. (2007, July). Making visible the invisible. *Online Classroom, 7-8.*

Tu, C. H. (2001). How Chinese perceive social presence: An examination of interaction in online learning environment. *Educational Media International, 38*(1), 45–60. doi:10.1080/09523980010021235

Urtel, M. G. (2008). Assessing academic performance between traditional and distance education course formats. *Journal of Educational Technology & Society, 11*(1), 322–330.

Uzuner, S. (2009, June). Questions of culture in distance learning: A research review. *International Review of Research in Open and Distance Learning, 10*(3), 1–19.

van Dijk, J. (2004). Divides in succession: Possession, skills, and use of new media for societal participation. In Bucy, E. P., & Newhagen, J. E. (Eds.), *Media access: Social and psychological dimensions of new technology use* (pp. 233–254). Mahwah, NJ: Erlbaum.

van Raaij, E. M., & Schepers, J. J. L. (2008). The acceptance and use of a virtual learning environment in China. *Computers & Education, 50,* 838–852. doi:10.1016/j.compedu.2006.09.001

Volosinov, V. N. (1973). *Marxism and the philosophy of language* (Matejka, L., & Titunik, I. R., Trans.). Cambridge, MA: Harvard University Press.

Wang, M. (2007). Designing online courses that effectively engage learners from diverse cultural backgrounds. *British Journal of Educational Technology, 38*(2), 294–311. doi:10.1111/j.1467-8535.2006.00626.x

Warden, C., Chen, J., & Caskey, D. (2005). Cultural values and communication online: Chinese and Southeast Asian students in a Taiwan international MBA class. *Business Communication Quarterly, 68*(2), 222–232. doi:10.1177/1080569905276669

Wellman, B. (2004). The three ages of Internet studies: Ten, five and zero years ago. *New Media & Society*, *6*(1), 123–129. doi:10.1177/1461444804040633

Wiesenberg, F., & Stacey, E. (2005). Reflections on teaching and learning online: Quality program design, delivery and support issues from a cross-global perspective. *Distance Education*, *26*(3), 385–404. doi:10.1080/01587910500291496

Wilson, M., Qayyum, A., & Boshier, R. (1998). World wide America? Think globally, click locally. *Distance Education*, *19*(1), 109–123. doi:10.1080/0158791980190108

Winner, L. (2000). Do artifacts have politics? In Teich, A. H. (Ed.), *Technology and the future* (8th ed., pp. 150–168). Boston, MA: Bedford/St Martin's.

Witkin, H. A., Moore, C. A., Goodenough, D. R., & Cox, P. W. (1977). Field-dependent and field-independent cognitive styles and their educational implications. *Review of Educational Research*, *47*(1), 1–64.

Wood, A. F., & Fassett, D. (2003). Remote control: Identity, power and technology in the classroom. *Communication Education*, *32*(3/4), 286–296. doi:10.1080/0363452032000156253

Wyatt, G. (2005). Satisfaction, academic rigor and interaction: Perceptions of online instruction. *Education*, *125*(3), 460–468.

Xin, D., Jia, J., & Yanhui, H. (2010). Research on distance education development in China. *British Journal of Educational Technology*, *41*(4), 582–592. doi:10.1111/j.1467-8535.2010.01093.x

Yamazaki, Y. (2005). Learning styles and typologies of cultural differences: A theoretical and empirical comparison. *International Journal of Intercultural Relations*, *29*, 521–548. doi:10.1016/j.ijintrel.2005.07.006

Young, P. A. (2008). The culture based model: Constructing a model of culture. *Journal of Educational Technology & Society*, *11*(2), 107–118.

Yukselturk, E., & Bulut, S. (2007). Predictors for student success in an online course. *Journal of Educational Technology & Society*, *10*(2), 71–83.

Zembylas, M., & Vrasidas, C. (2005). Levinas and the "inter-face": The ethical challenge of online education. *Educational Theory*, *55*(1), 61–78. doi:10.1111/j.1741-5446.2005.0005a.x

Zembylas, M., & Vrasidas, C. (2007). Listening for silence in text-based, online encounters. *Distance Education*, *28*(1), 5–24. doi:10.1080/01587910701305285

Zhao, N., & McDougall, D. (2008). Cultural influences on Chinese students' asynchronous online learning in a Canadian university. *Journal of Distance Education*, *22*(2), 59–80.

Zhu, C., Valcke, M., & Schellens, T. (2009). Cultural differences in the perception of a social-constructivist e-learning environment. *British Journal of Educational Technology*, *40*(1), 164–168. doi:10.1111/j.1467-8535.2008.00879.x

KEY TERMS AND DEFINITIONS

Critical Paradigm: A research belief system that advocates analysis of systemic oppression and systemic change.

Culture: Set of group related perceptions, contextual, symbolic and sometimes contested patterns of meaning.

Intercultural Communication: interactions between people who are culturally different.

Interpretive Paradigm: A research belief system that advocates in depth understanding of human experience.

Online Learning: Acquisition of knowledge, skills, and attitudes through learning environment/learning management system.

Online Pedagogy: Delivery of curriculum through Internet via virtual learning environment/ learning management system.

Research Paradigm: A belief system comprising metatheoretical assumptions and priorities of research processes.

Social Science Paradigm: A research belief system that advocates description and prediction of human behavior.

ENDNOTES

[1] For evidence that online instruction is as effective or more effective than traditional instruction see Allen, Mabry, Mattry, Bourhis, Titsworth & Burrell, 2004; Barnett-Queen, Blair, & Merrick, 2005; Carle, 2009; Feintuch, 2010; Lim, Kim, Chen, & Ryder, 2008; Schwartzman, 2007; Wyatt, 2005; Zembylas & Vrasidas, 2005. For critiques and challenges of online instruction see Allen, 2006; Bejerano, 2008; Benoit, Benoit, Milyo, & Hansen, 2006; Benbunan-Fich & Hiltz, 2003; Dermo, 2009; Hara & Kling, 2000; Liaw, 2008; Haythornthwaite & Kazmer, 2002; Middleton, 2010; Njenga & Fourie, 2010; Sull, 2007; Sun, Tsai, Finger, Chen, & Yeh, 2007; Urtel, 2008.

[2] See Herie (2005) for a review of three major paradigms in pedagogical research on online instruction--positivist and post-positivist (instructivist) paradigms, critical pedagogy, and constructivism—which corresponds very loosely to the three paradigms described in this essay.

[3] Similar terms are the functionalist or post-positivist paradigm. We choose to use the conventional tripartite framework described by Martin, Nakayama & Flores (1998; 2002): Social science, interpretive, and critical.

[4] It should be noted that there are several studies which show no relationship between learning styles and instructional strategies (Akdemir & Koszalka, 2008; Yukselturk. & Bulut, 2007).

[5] Culture and communication research in this tradition has been described and labeled as interpretive (Ting-Toomey, 1984), holistic-contextual-qualitative (Y. Y. Kim, 1984), humanist (Y. Y. Kim, 1988), and subjective (Gudykunst & Nishida, 1989).

[6] One exception is Uzuner's (2009) very recent literature review on the impacts of culture in student engagement and participation in online course discussions.

APPENDIX

Journals Reviewed for this Article

1. Social Science/Interdisciplinary

Cross cultural research
Cultural studies
International Journal of Intercultural Relations
International Social Science journal
Social Sciences Information
Social Science Quarterly
Theory, culture and society

2. Education & Educational Research

American Journal of Distance Education
British Journal of Educational Technology
Computers and Education
Distance Education
Educational Technology and Society
Learning and Instruction

3. Communication

Communication Education
Communication Monographs
Communication Theory
Cyberpsychology & Behavior
Human Communication Research
Journal of Applied Communication Research
Journal of Broadcasting and Electronic Media
Journal of Business and Technical Communication
Journal of Communication
Journal of Computer Mediated Communication
Journal of International and Intercultural Communication*
Media, Culture and Society
New Media & Society
Technical Communication
*This journal has only existed for two years (7 issues)

Chapter 20
Communicating Pragmatics About Content and Culture in Virtually Mediated Educational Environments

Birthe Mousten
Aarhus University, Denmark

John Humbley
Université Paris—Denis Diderot, France

Bruce Maylath
North Dakota State University, USA

Sonia Vandepitte
Hogeschool Gent/University of Ghent, Belgium

ABSTRACT

This chapter examines the interactive communications of geographically distant virtual classrooms, connected via virtual aids ranging from e-mails to videoconferences. The combination is crucial: through diverse filters, virtual teams mediate a final text for a new language and culture. The authors use linguistic pragmatics as a mechanism to analyze and assess the efficiency and the meaningfulness of such communications. They then use this approach to recommend best practices for educators teaching in cross-cultural virtual environments.

INTRODUCTION

This chapter is based on the more-than-decade-long collaborative Trans-Atlantic Project between universities in France, Belgium, Denmark, and the USA. Adult students—mostly in their 20s but some in their 30s and a few in their 40s—have engaged in virtual communication to work on a range of diverse, joint activities. These interactions have involved everything from simple e-mail communication to individual homepages and joint web-based platforms to entire online class video-

DOI: 10.4018/978-1-60960-833-0.ch020

conferences. The Trans-Atlantic Project usually involves students in technical and professional writing courses composing an instructional or procedural text for a North American audience. These students then rework this text for translation. Writers can take certain steps, such as eliminating idioms, to revise their original English-language text in a way that helps translators accurately render that text in another language.

In 1999, students in Bruce Maylath's Technical Writing course at the U.S.'s University of Wisconsin—Stout began an assignment exchange with students in Sonia Vandepitte's Essentials of Translation course at what was then known as Ghent College of Translation and Interpretation in Belgium. UW-Stout students e-mailed their instructions (which had been edited to facilitate translation) to students in Ghent. These Belgian students then tried their hand at translating this text into another language, and the students also noted where they were confused about the meaning or accuracy of the English-language text with which they were working. The Belgian students then sent their questions to the Stout students who were the original authors of the texts begin translated. In response, the technical writing students provided clarification on these translation-related questions, and the translation students used this information to complete the translation of the original instructions. Once these translations were completed, the students in Ghent emailed them back to their Wisconsin – Stout counterparts so the original authors of the instructions could see what their materials looked like in Dutch. In 2000, Birthe Mousten's classes at Business and Social Sciences, Aarhus University, Denmark joined in this translation related-exchange that would soon come to be called the Trans-Atlantic Project. (Another international partner from Université Paris— Denis Diderot joined the group in 2003.)

Although considerable reflection has gone into the ways in which the Project can be set up and assessed (Humbley, Vandepitte, Maylath, Mousten, & Veisblat, 2005; Maylath, Mousten,

& Vandepitte, 2008; Mousten, Vandepitte, & Maylath, 2008; Mousten, Maylath, Vandepitte, & Humbley, 2010), attention to the specific advantages offered by virtual interaction and to the methods of getting the most out of them has been relatively slim. Authors who have brought some attention to the topic include Starke-Meyerring and Andrews, 2006; Herrington, 2008; Fitch, Kirby, and Greathouse Amador, 2008; McCool, 2008; Starke-Meyerring and Wilson, 2008; Starke-Meyerring, 2008; and Flammia, Cleary, and Slattery, 2010. Yet these authors often fail to note that while interaction is possible through virtual teams, virtuality also creates an exchange of cultural input—sometimes unconsciously—that would otherwise not have been possible or would have been exchanged in a different way in a face-to-face exchange. As observers like Olaniran (2008) have noted, the importance of working in virtual teams keeps growing in an increasingly globalized economy, and the problems related to this online intercultural communication have not diminished over the fifteen or so years that virtual teams have been operating in business. Thus, it would appear advisable to expose students to these new practices and incorporate them into their learning environments.

For this chapter, the authors have defined virtual teams as

1. Persons assembled to complete a specific project
2. Members who are functionally diverse
3. Members who depend on technology-mediated communications to connect with each other
4. Persons who are geographically dispersed

In prior publications, the authors have discussed different aspects of their virtual team collaboration, namely the set-up and cross-professional dynamics (Humbley et al., 2005; Maylath et al., 2008), pedagogical theories and practices (Mousten et al., 2008), and group dynamics with best- and worst-case scenarios (Humbley et al., 2005; Mousten et al., 2010).

The notion of knowledge sharing and trust in distributed, virtual teams using information and communication technologies has also been emphasized and discussed by other scholars (e.g., Biggs, 2000; Johnson & Cullen, 2002; Zakaria, Amelinckz, & Wilemon, 2004). Some of the factors important in technological choices in virtual teams (e.g., accessibility, social distance, idea sharing and informing) have also been discussed by researchers (Sivunen & Valo, 2006). Moreover, Garrison (2006) has stressed the importance of having a medium for purely social interaction between group participants, as well as for simply exchanging information.

Important differences, however, exist between virtual teams operating in business and academia. The means of communication in these two areas are similar, but the aims are fundamentally different. In business, the aim is to produce a concrete result. In education and training, the objective is to learn. This difference means the student groups examined in this chapter are communities of inquiry (Garrison, 2006) as well as communities of practice (Wenger, 1998).

This chapter explores and recommends best practices for educators employing cross-cultural virtual teams (CCVTs) in their teaching. The chapter therefore focuses on the knowledge-related problems arising in CCVTs and on what can be done to facilitate and moderate such teams. The authors' experience is that the students involved in CCVT work have come back years later and discussed the merits of the project in relation to their subsequent workplaces. In particular, the interaction between linguistic and cultural aspects in virtual teams at various stages of the task—such as preparing for CCVT work, commenting on each other's work, and following up on each other's comments—has repeatedly surfaced at the core of learning experiences among CCVT members. Therefore, in the first section below, the authors present the various communication modes used

in the project. Then, in the chapter's initial three sections, the authors show how these modes facilitate awareness of regional, personality, and linguistic cultures pervading the task. In the fourth section, the authors discuss cultures' contribution to the exchange of text and ideas. Sections five through eight then focus on the interactive issues of criticism and praise, empathy and power, and the essential role of debriefing in these kinds of international projects. The chapter concludes with a section that examines the main points of the authors' experiences with computer-mediated projects and by identifying the challenges to future interactions in this area.

VIRTUAL MODES OF THE PROJECT

The Project's starting point was the joint aim of

- Raising language awareness among North American students writing technical texts for an international audience
- Introducing European students of translation to communication with the authors of a source text

When the Trans-Atlantic Project began in 1999, virtual exchanges were conducted almost exclusively by email. The students did not see this mode of interaction as impersonal but rather as a natural and expedient way of communicating. What the authors witnessed supported Walther's (1996) claim that "richly social discourse, afforded by personal email exchange is not impersonal, but hyper-personal" (p. 3). The authors can all recall numerous student emails divulging details that were unlikely to have been mentioned in person –a shift that is in part generational, as young people gravitate more and more to screens and electronic messaging (see Twenge, 2006 and Twenge & Campbell, 2009).

Email has continued to be the most commonly used Internet-based communication system in the Trans-Atlantic Project. In the context of the Project, email connects widely separated teams of students where one team in North America typically interacts with another team in Europe. This mode of interaction facilitates the Project's main language-based purpose of technical writing and translation, though the actual form and purpose may vary from institution to institution and more significantly from year to year. (Such differences reflect changes of teaching partners and their individual experiences and wishes.) The fact that the content has changed slightly from year to year and from class pair to class pair is of lesser importance: As Wenger (1998) argues, such communities of practice are valuable simply through the participative nature of the project.

Although this email-based mode of exchange was well-received by the students, basic web pages were later introduced as an alternative medium for the exchange of texts and of accompanying features, such as visuals. In later years, some partners adopted interactive virtual media, such as joint platforms, where the students' comments and work are visible to everyone, and students comment on what they see emerging from these interactions. Videoconferences, through which whole classes can meet virtually, have been useful in allowing students to see that they are working with real human beings like themselves.

Contrary to what has been found in business contexts, where videoconferencing is reported to be of only marginal interest (Gopal & Melkote, 2007; Olaniran, 2008), in an academic setting, the anticipation of an upcoming encounter via videoconferencing can help focus students. Indeed, in contrast to many business communities, students from different countries cannot hope to meet face to face in the course of a semester-long project. However, the logistics of setting up videoconferences has often proven long, complex, and challenging – particularly in dealing with time zone differences. Though much less used in the Trans-Atlantic Project than either e-mail or an interactive web platform, live videoconferences

can promote greater group dynamics through spontaneous commentary in comparison to other media. Videoconferences often also remove the possibly antagonistic sense and rhetoric of "us" versus "them" in Project-related interactions. In cases of a Project follow-up and mutual debriefing, the live videoconference is superb.

Additionally, students have initiated productive sessions on their own, with just their small teams using other modes of communication, like iChat or other streaming video software or inexpensive phone connections like Skype. (Interestingly, all of these media provide closer contact between virtual team members than do email or web platforms.) Because it can be readily downloaded, Skype, or an evolved form of it, might become the dominant means of online international exchange in the future (though it is at present forbidden in French universities for security reasons, thus limiting its international appeal there). For now, however, email remains ubiquitous. It is accessible around the clock, and it allows asynchronous communication at the user's convenience. Moreover, the medium of email is beneficial when students are pressed for time.

In sum, for all virtual activities to work efficiently, the media used must be common enough to be accessible generally, at least at one of the places where students or instructors work, whether at university or home. In their current state, videoconferences or joint web platforms call for an organizational setting in order to allow for easy and common access. Email, iChat, and Skype do not pose such requirements.

For virtual activity to be fruitful, another essential requirement is a common language for interactions. Global communication today is frequently described as fast and efficient, thanks to the technology available and the activities involved. Some words of caution, however, deserve voicing, too. In general, English now serves as a global *lingua franca* by default (Crystal, 2003). As such, it can be used in virtual space with relatively few problems. Yet, even though translation students—all of whom have had many years' experience studying English—share a certain amount of knowledge of communication and culture, they and their instructors nevertheless discover that they need to heed Law and Leonard's (2004) warning: "The notion that English serves as a neutral lingua franca is a dangerous myth" (p. 2). Zakaria et al. (2004) give voice to the same problem and also call for virtual mediation, however in the form of "virtual team leadership" (p. 27). In addition, Zakaria et al. question its effectiveness: "When such teams tend to have more time-consuming decision-making processes and when miscommunication and misunderstandings occur, stress and conflicts among team members are heightened and less easily dispelled" (p. 25). Pantelli and Tucker (2009) also point to mediation, or facilitation, as they call it, as a precondition for efficient virtual teams. Their research concludes, "it is better to be as up front in the project as possible than deal with the vicious, destructive downward spirals that result from team members with conflicting goals and poor levels of trust" (p. 115). This last result comes from long-term industrial global teamwork, whereas the virtual teams examined by the authors were one-time virtual teams. Thus, the authors witnessed the up-front problems and could easily look at short-term results, but cannot say anything about long-term results in virtual groups.

Table 1 shows the different virtual media as well as participatory structures, level of privacy, and activities that have been performed for the Project. Table 1 also displays dependence on time and various restrictions and advantages. In addition, the table includes comments regarding instructors' opportunities for supervision. Apart from these, it is worth mentioning that today's virtual network platforms, such as Facebook or Twitter, also surface in students' exchanges.

From the viewpoints of both linguistic and cultural researchers, it is an advantage if the medium also allows for comments to be collected systematically. In the experiences of the authors, these various media have provided many insights. Students' interactive comments, for instance, gathered electronically by having them send their messages carbon copied (CC) to their instructors, often include text inserted into the bodies of their messages and intra-textual comments inserted either as windowed comments in the texts' margins or as improvements suggested by the word processor's "track-changes" system. These items often clarify what the *topic* of the interaction is.

Logs from web-based platforms, where exchanges are visible to all, allow the instructor even more easily to monitor and study what the students are saying. The fact that some exchanges are completely private and others are completely open to all the members of the group might well influence the type of comments made. This information provides the instructor/observer with direct materials of the negotiation *processes*.

AWARENESS OF CULTURAL AND REGIONAL DIVERSITIES

One important feature of these exchanges is that they heighten students' awareness of cultural specificities. Gradually, understanding of the needs of other cultures in everyday lives dawns upon CCVTs in the Trans-Atlantic Project. Regional differences become apparent to CCVT members and open a forum for discussing and for studying such differences. As an example, many of the European students participating in the Project are amazed at the American students' interest in shooting, which manifests itself in some of the instructions written for the collaborative project assignment (e.g., "How to skin an elk"; "How to clean a rifle"…). This item is partly a difference in North American and European cultures, but it also reflects a difference in rural vs. urban cultures, as the European students in the Project tend to

Table 1. Overview of Virtual Exchange Modes and Their Possibilities

Virtual type	Participants	Private/ public	Possible actions	Time dependence	Restrictions	Advantages	Instructor influence
Email	Team members	Private among team members (and instructors if CC-option is used)	Communication exchanges Exchange of documents	Time-dependent, asymmetric communication	No visual communication Time differences Limited possibility of action	Direct channel of contact between team members Possibility of secrecy	No direct influence May be hard to retrieve email files afterwards
Homepage	The world at large	Public Common information available	Upload of docs Download of docs	Time-independent. Information stays on the homepage for a long time.	Only general information conveyed. Publicly available, must be used with care.	Practical medium for exchange of general information.	Full instructor influence
Joint platforms	Team members and instructors	Public in a limited forum	Comprehensive exchange of discussion, everybody can read everybody's inputs Everything is archived	Symmetric and asymmetric. Information stays on the platform for a long time, but there is a question-answer sequence	Communication available to all participants Hesitant and careful behavior among team members	Great learning opportunity across teams. Everybody benefits from everybody else's communication.	Instructor can follow exchanges and intervene
Logbooks	Team members	Individual	Logging all actions Personal comments on activities and process	Continuous	No interaction with others	Comments which would not be desirable in the other virtual media	Access may be given
Video conferences	Everybody present at the same time Virtual classroom	Public in a limited forum	Free exchange of opinion Presentations Discussions Personal contacts	Time-dependent, very time-limited, but symmetric	Sorting of topics for discussion Ample opportunity for interaction	Oral platform Face-to-face meeting Free discussion	Instructors can join, intervene and facilitate
Skype	Team members	Private among participants	Oral chat Written chat Combination of the above Exchange of docs.	Time-dependent Repeatability	Sorting of topics for discussion Only limited time available	Oral platform Written platform Face-to-face meeting Free discussion	No direct influence May be hard to retrieve written files. Oral files not recorded.

be city dwellers, while many of the Americans (from Minnesota, North Dakota, and Wisconsin) are from the countryside or return to it frequently from their city dwellings. Plenty of people go shooting in France, too, though the average age associated with this activity might be much higher than in the U.S. Another cultural specificity surfaced when Danish students translated texts from technical communication magazines into English for possible publication in an American technical magazine. The U.S. students were amazed at some of the subjects chosen, such as wave-power projects in the North Sea and wood pellets or straw as fuel for hybrid furnaces to supplement indoor heating in private homes.

INTERPERSONAL SKILLS

The reaction of students can depend on the extent to which the teaching staff has prepared them. U.S. teachers in particular comment on the lack of awareness that their American students have of foreigners and the world outside their national borders, which can prove a challenge in communication with a distant partner. For the virtual teams noted here to "quickly become effective upon formation" (Tan, Wei, Huang, & Ng, 2000, p. 151), Århus had the students on both sides of the Atlantic write up an introduction, called a "pre-learning report," about themselves so that their partners knew with whom they are dealing.

Later adopted by other universities in the Project, the pre-learning report does not always fulfill its purpose, for it calls for a degree of openness at the very first stage of the Project, and some students balk at filling out the form completely. Upon reading the form, one American student asked why her Flemish translators in Belgium needed to know her gender. (It was so that they knew whether to refer to their CCVT member as *zij* ["she"] or *hij* ["he"].) Although the American students involved in the Project gave away many details about themselves, this degree of disclosure was less often the case for their European partners. Nevertheless, the authors have all observed that the more frequently the students exchange background information, the better the content of the communication becomes. So, a second solution was for students to exchange basic data about their texts in initial stages through what is called a "translation brief." This document identifies all key communicative elements that might be new content in multilingual versions. In such cases, the importance of teachers as facilitators and mediators becomes manifest, as has been investigated and reported by Pauleen and Yoong (2001), among others.

Tan et al. (2000) argue that electronic communication does not facilitate the building of shared understanding among team members. To do so, they need dialogue techniques (p. 153). When the authors' students continue the process of making acquaintance, they might follow different paths. Some students might use different media for various sorts of communication and, in so doing, clearly separate the class work from private exchanges. In initial student exchanges, however, different cultural preferences to using the online media for Project-related interactions seemed to emerge. Italian students, for example, seem much keener to get down to work and focus on an exclusively professional relationship than do their Trans-Atlantic partners (typically in North America). Other students, notably the Danes, are quick to get going, but they generally stick to email for all exchanges and swap a wide variety of experiences, both personal and professional.

Within these interactions, distinctions between private and public realms surface as important and as closely linked to cultural assumptions. Young American students, for example, tend to mix private and professional to an extent that their American elders find horrifying (Twenge, 2006; Twenge & Campbell, 2009). French students, by contrast, tend to limit any private exchanges to the most stereotypical elements, giving away as little as possible about themselves in what is seen as a university and, therefore, public setting. To overcome this reticence, their instructors generally advise the French students to communicate on an impersonal topic, such as why they chose to work on the subject at hand. Such a focus gives work-related information, but at the same time provides overseas partners with clues about the personality of the person with whom they are working. In all cases, though, a maximum amount of time should be set aside for the exchanges to enhance students' learning.

INSIGHTS INTO MULTILINGUAL PROCESSES

Many students' comments reflect a lack of awareness of the particularities of what is involved in the translation process. For instance, many students have tended to produce translations that are too literal, that lack cultural awareness, or that lack attention to detail or sensitivity to the genre of a text. Quite often, when interacting with writing students, translation students start exchanges by discussing the verb tense they intend to use, thereby revealing that they are not aware that the monolingual American author of the original text cannot possibly have an opinion about a question that solely concerns the details of another language.

On the other hand, students sometimes show heightened awareness, as in the instance where an experienced American student edited a news article a Belgian student had translated from Dutch into English. In the sentence, "McCain rarely elaborated on his program to change the country," the American student substituted "plans" for "program." The Belgians then asked pointedly, "What's wrong with 'program?'" The American explained, "Program sounds wrong to me as a native English speaker. Program usually refers to something that is already established. When politicians are on the campaign trail, they are usually proposing plans to change the country's policies." With this explanation, the Belgian translators came away with a greater sense of both words' nuances. In this sense, the use of virtual classrooms not only makes cooperation closer but can be seen as a quality-enhancing medium as well.

Likewise, comments can let an instructor know that a particular student has discovered something important related to a translation technique. As an example, a Danish group of students had to translate instructions for how to parallel park a car. The instructions were organized in steps. The Danish translation team responded immediately that such instructions could not be divided into steps, as the movement of the car was ongoing.

One translator posed the question, "Maybe the US way of setting up an instruction is more often stepwise compared to what we would naturally do." This comment reveals the kind of reflection which might serve as a general point to investigate further, for it might be a matter of frequency of conventions used in particular areas vs. whether it is possible or not, or even if it is good or not. Learning through an observation like this one might serve as a hypothesis, which can then be tested in discussions with insiders or by empirical observation. The Trans-Atlantic Project has been filled with such discoveries, which cannot be summed up statistically or made into general rules. They form part of the slow realization of cultural differences that have to be internalized through empirical realization. Thus, we support Zakaria et al.'s (2004) statement that new patterns of communication and social exchange can emerge in a computer-mediated team and hence influence the learning process (p. 16).

THE PROCESS OF EXCHANGING TEXTS AND IDEAS

The types of student comments examined in the previous section elicit follow-up comments from partners, thus contributing to a dialogue between CCVT members. In the best cases, the follow-up is complete and satisfactory to all. Most students are aware that working in a CCVT takes an extra effort compared to working, for instance, in a local university virtual team. One American student reported the following about the social skills needed: "The willingness to cooperate with a complete stranger who has a different language, customs, and are [*sic*] living in a different time zone: I am imagining it will take a lot of patience." Occasionally, the follow-up is nonexistent.

One factor to note in virtual exchange is that the use of virtual classrooms, as in trade and industry, results in shorter deadlines and project phases. Industry increasingly practices SimShip (simultaneous shipment), no more so than in the gaming industry. Dietz (2006) observes that "Simultaneous or near-simultaneous release of several language versions requires parallel development.... On the translator's side this parallel development means working with a text that is, despite all assurances to the contrary, still fluid, and sometimes requires frantic re-writing and re-translating during the last few days before the game's ship date" (p. 126). Cronin (2003) likewise points out that "the dissemination of information through globalized mass media or over the web means that potential customers in different parts of the globe are aware of new models as soon as they come out" (p. 15). Most of the case stories in Sprung (2000) also bear witness to the same compressed and globalized time-to-market phenomenon.

The swift exchanges in the virtual classroom call for stricter processes and constant follow-up. When the project has to fit among other regular semester activities, managing the virtual project demands disciplined process planning and stringent follow-up. Because of the sometimes short overlap between U.S. and European semesters (especially those in operation in Germany and much of Austria), the American writing students have often felt pressure to compose their original/source texts in haste. Indeed, the resulting source texts are sometimes barely more than drafts. Translation students in Europe have, in turn, lamented the unfinished nature of such drafts. These translation students have similarly felt rushed to complete a process – in this case, a translation –before the American students leave for the term. When this kind of situation happens, the authors often explain to their students how common a compressed time-to-market situation is in business and industry.

The importance of graphics is sometimes totally underestimated by American students, for the assignment on which they are working generally requires translation of the text only. The lack of graphics, however, might influence the final quality of the text. (In many cases, understanding a given text often depends on the use of pictures, drawings, flow charts, screen shots, or even video sequences to provide examples or clarification.) This situation is where virtual space can be seen as a double-edged sword. Several times, the graphics sent by the American students could not be opened by the computers used by overseas counterparts. So, instead of being a rapid help, the lack of software compatibility essentially reverted the work back to pre-virtual work processes.

VIRTUAL CRITICISM AND PRAISE

Most teams find it easier to give praise than criticism. American and Danish students in particular have revealed themselves quick to praise. An example from the Danish email logs shows U.S. teammates giving praise to their Danish translation partners: "Your translation was very good. The English grammar, punctuation, and spelling were great. Most of our changes were for style, in addition to Americanizing the text." From final comments: "We were very impressed with your command of the English language. We've enjoyed working on the project and look forward to your feedback."

French students, in contrast, have tended to be amazed at what they feel is extravagant praise heaped on their work by their American partners. These French students often also feel a little guilty that they have not been as encouraging when they state the positive or give criticism.

Criticism, however, is generally given with extreme care in all cases, to the point of finding excuses for the mistakes made. Criticism and praise are important in a virtual setting. Fortunately, all partners in the virtual teams have intuitively seemed ready to take to praising and criticizing the geographically distant team members, thereby practicing a complex communicative skill.

The virtual media, especially email, were important in this respect. Figure 1 is an example of a translation rendered by a Belgian student and edited by an American student. The latter's emendations appear in the windowed comments in the margin:

The communication tools within the word processing software not only facilitate interaction, but also enable students to indicate precisely what they would write differently and what they would leave intact. These tools also allow for editorial commentary, such as the second comment in Figure 1. Additionally, the immediacy of the virtual medium means any feedback given or taken has a high degree of relevance to the student. The short time lapse between a task and its feedback and the prospect of having to react immediately bolster learning to a higher extent than with older means of correspondence.

EMPATHY AND POWER

Closely related to praise and criticism are the attitudes and relationships behind them: empathy and power. Empathy inevitably emerges from student-to-student communication, and the degree to which empathy can be felt can influence the efficacy of the learning experience. An advantage of the virtual medium is the rapid, unofficial, almost oral-like exchanges between partners. Empathy is fostered by the students' acknowledging that the work presented by the partner represents a real challenge or commenting on the good quality of a text's rendering. Until embarking on the Trans-Atlantic Project, hardly any technical writing student has ever written anything that had to be translated into another language and used in another culture. One U.S. student wrote in her pre-learning report, "I have never had a document I wrote before translated into another language, so this is a big learning experience for me. I will learn how to prepare a document for translation, and what problems I may encounter because of a different language."

In many situations, empathy seems to be generated by students working on the same topic. In such cases, the empathy is latent rather than expressed, although it may surface in terminological discussions. One writer noted in the translation brief, "The word 'plot' may be hard to translate, but the piece of machinery I wrote the manual for is called a 'plotter' because it produces plots—poster-sized documents. It is important that the words 'plot' and 'plotter' are not 'lost in translation'." In general,

Figure 1. Editing a translation (in Word)

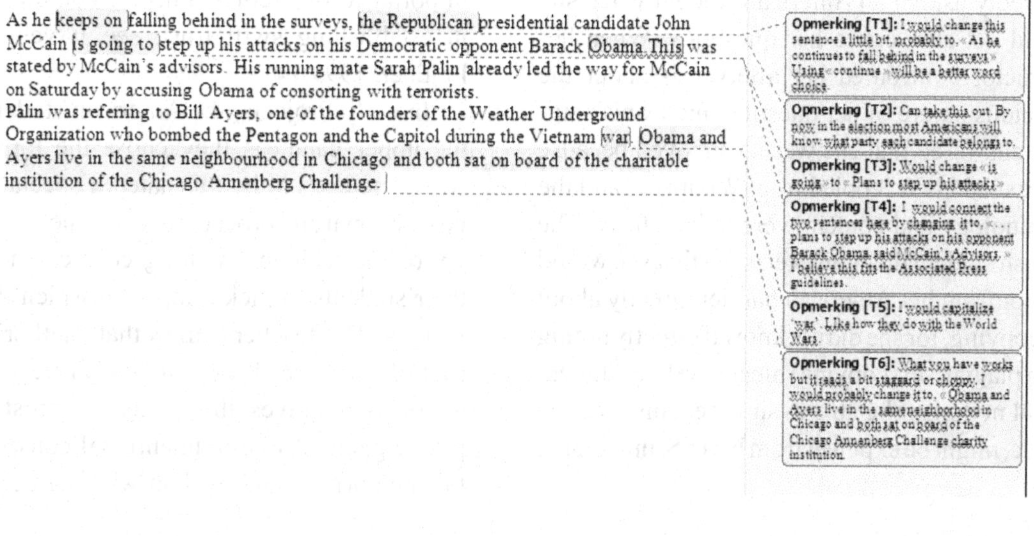
As he keeps on falling behind in the surveys, the Republican presidential candidate John McCain is going to step up his attacks on his Democratic opponent Barack Obama. This was stated by McCain's advisors. His running mate Sarah Palin already led the way for McCain on Saturday by accusing Obama of consorting with terrorists.
Palin was referring to Bill Ayers, one of the founders of the Weather Underground Organization who bombed the Pentagon and the Capitol during the Vietnam war. Obama and Ayers live in the same neighbourhood in Chicago and both sat on board of the charitable institution of the Chicago Annenberg Challenge.

Opmerking [T1]: I would change this sentence a little bit, probably to, « As he continues to fall behind in the surveys » Using « continue » will be a better word choice.

Opmerking [T2]: Can take this out. By now in the election most Americans will know what party each candidate belongs to.

Opmerking [T3]: Would change « is going » to « Plans to step up his attacks »

Opmerking [T4]: I would connect the two sentences here by changing it to, « ... plans to step up his attacks on his opponent Barack Obama, said McCain's Advisors. » I believe this fits the Associated Press guidelines.

Opmerking [T5]: I would capitalize 'war'. Like how they do with the World Wars.

Opmerking [T6]: What you have works but it reads a bit staggard or choppy. I would probably change it to, « Obama and Ayers live in the same neighborhood in Chicago and both sat on board of the Chicago Annenberg Challenge charity institution.

it was difficult for the authors to envision what terms might cause problems.

Among translators, too, terminology has been the most frequent topic of their questions, along with syntax and register. The translation student, faced with a terminology problem, will often ask for more information from the technical writing partner. Such requests, in many cases, lead students to comments on the different ways in which some technical point might be viewed in the two countries concerned.

An example of empathy comes from an exchange between a U.S. student and a Danish student where the U.S. student commented on the use of the document as part of an assignment. Tania writes to Annika, "Annika, overall a very well written essay. I have made some suggestions to make the article more 'Americanized.' *Good luck to you, I know you will do well on this assignment.*" In her pre-learning report, Tania had written the following as one of her learning aims under the question, "What do you expect to learn about cooperation?" Her answer: "Giving constructive criticism without hurting someone's feelings." Although empathy does not often surface so visibly in most student exchanges, this example reveals that the matter of empathy was looming large in the minds of the students.

Another slightly backhanded example from a videoconference featured a Danish student pointedly asking an American student when she would get answers to her questions. When her instructor confronted her afterwards about the ferocious nature of her question, the Danish student answered that she was so annoyed because the text had been copied from Wikipedia and the terminology and content were rather shaky. The Danish student did, however, state that she would not confront her American partner directly about the copying, for she did not know if directly noting such plagiarism (copying) meant the U.S. student might no longer be able to sit for exams, or even worse, might be expelled from his U.S. university.

Another example of the new media resources, notably the web, enabling students to gain empathy comes from a Paris student explaining how to winterize a boat (pleasure craft). Her immediate reaction was to say, "How American, all with their boats…," but she soon found French boat owners using online discussion groups to swap hints on this very question (though admittedly in much less severe climatic conditions). This discovery represents the sort of information that could not be found in the best traditional university library.

All relationships, however, are fraught with matters of power, including international writing and translation projects (Mousten et al., 2010). Such matters are particularly important in understanding group dynamics, as they greatly influence the image that the students have of their partners and themselves. The assumption that group members carry expertise is common in what Meyerson, Weick, and Kramer (1996) have dubbed "swift trust." This phrase seems to encapsulate nicely what happens in Trans-Atlantic CCVTs, where there seems to be an instant recognition of the expertise of the partner. Typically, these situations involve the technical writers as native English-speakers and the subject-matter experts, their translation partners as multilingual language experts. (For a thorough-going examination of the importance of trust to group functioning, see Fukuyama, 1995; for an examination of the importance of predictability in communication in establishing swift trust, see Jarvenpaa and Leidner, 1999.)

In early Projects, the American students had the upper hand, as they chose the topics and wrote the texts to be translated. Especially with instructional and procedural texts, the U.S. teachers of the technical writing courses encourage their students to pick a topic on which they are experts. The teachers stress that "author" is the root of "authority." The student's role as author undoubtedly gives the writers a boost in the power game. As an unintentional consequence, this authority could explain why the translation students often seem to take a relatively uncritical approach toward the texts to be translated.

Various steps have since been taken to redress the balance of power. Aarhus and Ghent have instituted exchanges whereby the Danish and Belgian students translate a text into English, which the American students edit (as in Figure 1). When the direction of text travel is reversed in this way, students in the U.S. react to a text on a topic that they do not necessarily know much about. For their part, the instructors in Paris have taken to asking their students to write a text on the same subject as that which they are about to translate for their American partner, and to draft such an item *before* they receive the American text. To do so, the French students first research the topic themselves and decide how they would present the topic to others. Generally, the French students' decisions are quite different from what they later see made by their American partners. As a result, when the French students initially write their own text on the topic, they are generally much more questioning about the source text provided by U.S. authors, and therefore less submissive than students who were simply given a text to translate.

One aspect of power in these Projects can manifest itself in the use of language, particularly as it relates to English. American students can hide behind their status as native speakers. When questioned on a particular formulation, they will reply that it "sounded better," which—although never accepted as a valid argument in academic translation circles—effectively stops any further discussion. As a result, European students are often hesitant to think that native speakers can make mistakes in a text written in their native language.

Issues of power also surface in the editing of texts. Some criticism can be met by explaining the context and the author's attitude—especially important in a translation situation. In her pre-learning report, a Danish student wrote, "I need to be polite and not get offended by corrections." In her translation brief, the same student wrote an idea for editing the translated article (in reference to the article's "code"): "There is a slight touch of irony in the section about heredity. Please notice if this has been kept in your version." This statement was one of the rare examples the authors saw where the translator and the text editor communicated on the tenor of the text.

DEBRIEFING THE PROCESS

The debriefing of the process is important, but it sometimes ends up being the stage that is often neglected in such projects. There are at least two phases of debriefing: one external, with the distant partner, and one internal, with the students' classmates on campus. To these can be added an exchange between the teaching staff involved in the exchange. Admittedly, some of the exchanges for the Project were terminated without any debriefing. Often, this situation was due to other projects having taken over, by the semester having concluded at one end of the exchange, or by exams looming in the minds of students and instructors.

However, debriefing with the distant partner might actually constitute the culmination of the project. A videoconference is particularly well suited to this purpose. Discussions run freely: The virtual project has come to an end, and, successful or not, there is the feeling that "we did it." In this respect, the virtual classroom draws people into the same emotional sphere, and the geographical divide becomes a curiosity rather than a problem. The virtual classroom essentially removes the "us" versus "them" rhetoric.

When a videoconference cannot be conducted, the participating classes have used a written post-learning report or a general report on the process. Although perhaps primitive in nature, such a report can be composed fairly quickly, posted on the web learning platform, or forwarded as an attachment to an email. Such action can counter the timing problems caused by different starts and stops to partners' semesters, exam schedules, holidays, etc. Again, the virtual media have been helpful in lowering hurdles in the communication process and ensuring some kind of debriefing.

Debriefing students within their own classroom is also useful. Not only are technical points mentioned, thereby giving hints to improve communications for the next time around, but students can be encouraged to reflect on their success in communicating with their distant partners and to analyze why certain strategies proved more productive than others. With guidance from their instructor, students learn to think carefully about what they have experienced in doing the project. As a result, student achievements and lessons drawn from these projects can be transferred to other situations. This learning process can be carried out either as a final stage of the logbook previously mentioned or as a wrap-up activity at the end of the semester.

Finally, it is important for the teaching staff to review the successes and failures. This situation is particularly useful when more than two instructors are involved or when an instructor is participating in the exchange for the first time. Newcomers are invariably surprised by the amount of planning necessary for a successful outcome to be achieved. In such cases, a review of the steps involved, as well as identifying what was successful and what went wrong, is a great help in planning for the next session.

LEARNING FROM THESE DIVERSE VIRTUAL COLLABORATIONS

The effects of virtual collaborative projects for students are still felt long after the projects have been completed. All of the authors leading the Trans-Atlantic Project have experienced chance encounters years later with former students and have listened to these former students recount what they had gained from their involvement. Collaborative projects with intensive international student interaction are highly profitable means of encouraging learning in the field of intercultural communication. Instructors, as project leaders, can help students understand the pragmatics of cross-cultural virtual team exchanges by analyzing pragmatics themselves.

From this study on the virtual collaborative project, the participating instructors have learned that essential human exchanges that prompt students to give their partners praise, to accept their partners' criticism, and to negotiate issues of power with their partners in a *common* language are most relevant to the learning experience and that they are enhanced in the collaborative exchanges that the authors have arranged for students. However, the task-oriented aspects of human communication are also a crucial element of the exchanges. The instructors take care to put in place a stringent process of project management, which is crucial as the windows of time are so narrow and the virtual exchanges of communication so fast.

It is important that the staff initiating the exchange have a clear and detailed idea of the project's schedule well before it commences. Timelines for the exchange end up being incredibly tight. In most cases, specific instruction, such as introducing principles of technical writing to both writers and translators, precedes the exchange itself and involves setting still more time aside.

The new media that have made virtual teamwork possible have also made apprentice writers and translators realize the differences between cultures. On the other hand, the students' performance in CCVTs has shown that what they may initially perceive as alien and peculiar is in fact known and practiced in other countries and very often in the students' home country, too. The new media have provided a ubiquity and swiftness of virtual space that has made communication, awareness, and subsequent understanding so much easier: globalization has made the world smaller. The main challenge for educators in countries that have already started computer-mediated practices is to assume responsibility and apply the new media to their fullest.

Finally, this examination of the Trans-Atlantic Project also highlights some factors that have not yet been discussed in the literature on virtual cross-cultural communication. As an educational project, the Trans-Atlantic Project is different from the industrial projects that have so far been discussed in the literature. A theory on cross-cultural virtual teams should not only explore virtual teams in industry but also teams in other areas of society, such as services, government, or education. In fact, the differences in terms of aims, management, procedures, means, and results may be so great that not only the tools used in computer-mediated cross-cultural communication but also their impact on the collaboration itself will differ.

REFERENCES

Biggs, M. (2000). Enterprise toolbox: Assessing risks today will leave corporate leaders well prepared for the future of work. *InfoWorld, 22*(3), 100–101.

Cronin, M. (2003). *Translation and globalization.* New York, NY: Routledge.

Crystal, D. (2003). *English as a global language* (2nd ed.). Cambridge, UK: Cambridge University Press. doi:10.1017/CBO9780511486999

Dietz, F. (2006). Issues in localizing computer games. In Dunne, K. J. (Ed.), *Perspectives on localization* (pp. 121–134). Amsterdam, The Netherlands & Philadelphia, PA: John Benjamins Publishing Company.

Fitch, B., Kirby, A., & Greathouse Amador, L. M. (2008). In Starke-Meyerring, D., & Wilson, M. (Eds.), *Designing global learning environments: Visionary partnerships, policies, and pedagogies* (pp. 145–155). Rotterdam, The Netherlands: Sense Publishers.

Flammia, M., Cleary, Y., & Slattery, D. M. (2010). Leadership roles, socioemotional communication strategies, and technology use of Irish and US students in virtual teams. *IEEE Transactions on Professional Communication, 53,* 89–101. doi:10.1109/TPC.2010.2046088

Fukuyama, F. (1995). *Trust.* New York, NY: The Free Press.

Garrison, D. R. (2006). Online collaborative principles. *Journal of Asynchronous Learning Networks, 10*(1), 25–33.

Gopal, Y., & Srinivas, M. (2007, May 23). *New work paradigms? Implication for communication and coordination.* Paper presented at the Annual Meeting of the International Communication Association, San Francisco, CA. Retrieved November 23, 2010, from http://www.allacademic. com/meta/p169097_index.html

Herrington, T. (2008). The global classroom project. In Starke-Meyerring, D., & Wilson, M. (Eds.), *Designing global learning environments: Visionary partnerships, policies, and pedagogies* (pp. 37–51). Rotterdam, The Netherlands: Sense Publishers.

Humbley, J., Vandepitte, S., Maylath, B., Mousten, B., & Veisblat, L. (2005). Learning localization through trans-Atlantic collaboration. In G. F. Hayhoe (Ed.), *Proceedings of the IEEE International Professional Communication Conference,* (pp. 578-595). New York, NY: IEEE.

Jarvenpaa, S. L., & Leidner, D. E. (1999). Communication and trust in global virtual teams. *Organization Science, 10,* 791–815. doi:10.1287/ orsc.10.6.791

Johnson, J. L., & Cullen, J. B. (2002). Trust in cross-cultural relationships. In Cannon, M. J., & Newman, K. L. (Eds.), *The Blackwell handbook of cross-cultural management.* Malden, MA: Blackwell Publishing.

Law, S. F., & Leonard, D. P. (2004). *Culture, language and online dispute resolution*. RMIT University and Dispute Settlement Centre Victoria, Department of Justice. Retrieved November 15, 2010, from http://www.odr.info/unforum2004/law_leonard.htm

Maylath, B., Vandepitte, S., & Mousten, B. (2008). Growing grassroots partnerships: Trans-Atlantic collaboration between American instructors and students of technical writing and European instructors and students of translation. In Starke-Meyerring, D., & Wilson, M. (Eds.), *Designing global learning environments: Visionary partnerships, policies, and pedagogies* (pp. 52–66). Rotterdam, The Netherlands: Sense Publishers.

McCool, M. (2008). Negotiating the design of globally networked learning environments: The case of a collaborative online learning module about the Sonoran biosphere. In Starke-Meyerring, D., & Wilson, M. (Eds.), *Designing global learning environments: Visionary partnerships, policies, and pedagogies* (pp. 200–217). Rotterdam, The Netherlands: Sense Publishers.

Meyerson, D., Weick, K., & Kramer, R. (1996). Swift trust and temporary groups. In Kramer, R. M., & Tyler, T. R. (Eds.), *Trust in organizations: Frontiers of theory and research* (pp. 166–195). Thousand Oaks, CA: Sage.

Mousten, B., Maylath, B., Vandepitte, S., & Humbley, J. (2010). Learning localization through trans-Atlantic collaboration: Bridging the gap between professions. *IEEE Transactions on Professional Communication, 53*, 401–411. doi:10.1109/TPC.2010.2077481

Mousten, B., Vandepitte, S., & Maylath, B. (2008). Intercultural collaboration in the trans-Atlantic project: Pedagogical theories and practices in teaching procedural instructions across cultural contexts. In Starke-Meyerring, D., & Wilson, M. (Eds.), *Designing global learning environments: Visionary partnerships, policies, and pedagogies* (pp. 129–144). Rotterdam, The Netherlands: Sense Publishers.

Olaniran, B. (2008). Team leaders' technology choice in virtual teams. *IEEE Transactions on Professional Communication, 49*, 1–25.

Pantelli, N., & Tucker, R. (2009). Power and trust in global virtual teams. *Communications of the ACM, 52*(12), 113–115. doi:10.1145/1610252.1610282

Pauleen, D. J., & Yoong, P. (2001). Relationship building and the use of ICT in boundary-crossing virtual teams: A facilitator's perspective. *Journal of Information Technology, 16*, 205–220. doi:10.1080/02683960110100391

Sivunen, A., & Valo, M. (2006). Team leaders' technology choice in virtual teams. *IEEE Transactions on Professional Communication, 49*, 57–68. doi:10.1109/TPC.2006.870458

Sprung, R. C. (Ed.). (2000). *Translating into success: Cutting-edge strategies for going multilingual in a global age*. Amsterdam, The Netherlands & Philadelphia, PA: John Benjamins.

Starke-Meyerring, D. (2008). Genre, knowledge and digital code in web-based communities: An integrated theoretical framework for shaping digital discursive spaces. *International Journal of Web-Based Communities, 4*, 398–417. doi:10.1504/IJWBC.2008.019547

Starke-Meyerring, D., & Andrews, D. (2006). Building a shared virtual learning culture: An international classroom partnership. *Business Communication Quarterly*, *69*, 24–49. doi:10.1177/1080569905285543

Starke-Meyerring, D., & Wilson, M. (2008). Globally networked learning environments: Shaping visionary futures. In Starke-Meyerring, D., & Wilson, M. (Eds.), *Designing global learning environments: Visionary partnerships, policies, and pedagogies* (pp. 218–230). Rotterdam, The Netherlands: Sense Publishers.

Tan, B. C. Y., Wei, K. K., Huang, W. W., & Ng, G. N. (2000). A dialogue technique to enhance electronic communication in virtual teams. *IEEE Transactions on Professional Communication*, *43*, 153–165. doi:10.1109/47.843643

Twenge, J. M. (2006). *Generation me: Why today's young Americans are more confident, assertive, entitled—And more miserable than ever before*. New York, NY: The Free Press.

Twenge, J. M., & Campbell, W. K. (2009). *The narcissism epidemic: Living in the age of entitlement*. New York, NY: The Free Press.

Walther, J. B. (1996). Computer-mediated communication: impersonal, interpersonal and hyperpersonal. *Communication Research*, *23*(1), 3–43. doi:10.1177/009365096023001001

Wenger, E. (1998). *Communities of practice: Learning meaning and e-dentity*. Cambridge, UK: Cambridge University Press.

Zakaria, N., Amelinckz, A., & Wilemon, D. (2004). Working together apart? Building a knowledge-sharing culture for global virtual teams. *Creativity and Innovation Management*, *13*, 15–29. doi:10.1111/j.1467-8691.2004.00290.x

KEY TERMS AND DEFINITIONS

Cross-Cultural Teams: Consist of student members from a European university and a US university.

Mediation: The process of negotiating text content between cultures and audiences.

Linguistic Pragmatics: Discussions of system-bound and cultural differences and finding solutions.

Best Practices: How a text transfer process can be optimized through dialogue.

Virtual Classroom: Teams dispersed geographically working on the same project through virtual means.

Multilingual Process: Dealing with language differences between team members.

Power Issues: Imbalances in virtual teams, evolvement and solutions.

Chapter 21
Using the Cultural Challenges of Virtual Team Projects to Prepare Students for Global Citizenship

Madelyn Flammia
University of Central Florida, USA

ABSTRACT

Global citizens are those individuals who understand the complex and interdependent nature of the world and who take action to address global issues at a local level. Many faculty members recognize the need to prepare students for the demands of global work and citizenship. In this chapter, the author demonstrates how virtual team projects are an ideal means to help students develop global competency and offers suggestions for faculty seeking to structure projects geared to civic engagement.

INTRODUCTION

Global changes in society are occurring rapidly. Developments in telecommunications, computing, and transportation have increased the ease and frequency of communication among members of different cultures. Similarly, international trade agreements have opened up opportunities and new avenues of commerce. At the same time, the global marketplace is also influenced by developments in international politics and the rise of ecommerce and multinational corporations. Trends in immigration and an increasing number of multinational corporations employing a globally distributed workforce have blurred the distinctions between national and cultural boundaries (Suárez-Orozco & Sattin, 2007). All of these changes have led to an increased need for effective communication to facilitate cooperation and collaboration among the peoples of the world. They have also led to

DOI: 10.4018/978-1-60960-833-0.ch021

the rise of a new concept of citizenship: that of the global citizen. As a result, today's educators now recognize the need to prepare students for the challenges associated with such global citizenship.

The purpose of this chapter is to demonstrate how virtual team projects – projects in which students located in different nations use online media to collaborate – are an ideal means to help students develop global competency. For this reason, the author recommends that virtual team projects be more fully integrated into the curriculum of many different educational programs. In addressing this issue, the author demonstrates how virtual teaming can foster global competency and produce students who are actively engaged citizens. The author then concludes the chapter by offering suggestions educators can use for developing virtual team projects geared toward civic engagement.

GLOBAL EDUCATION AND THE TECHNICAL COMMUNICATION CURRICULUM

As the higher education curriculum becomes "internationalized," faculty members across campus have sought ways to prepare students for citizenship in the twenty-first century. Faculty members in the field of technical communication – the author's own academic discipline – are no exception, and as a result, their experiences in addressing this issue can serve as an example for other disciplines. Like the members of many other fields, technical communication faculty agree that students need to be prepared for global work (DeVoss, Jasken, & Hayden, 2002; Giammona, 2004; Miles, 1997; Schafer, 2009; St.Amant, 2002b; Starke-Meyerring & Andrews, 2006; Weiss, 1998). Reporting on a survey of global partnerships in technical communication programs, Starke-Meyerring, Duin, and Palvetzian (2007) argue that changes brought about by globalization call for the creation of learning environments to foster the develop-

ment of the skills students will need for today's workplace and for *global citizenship*. The key then is to understand what global citizenship means in order to develop educational approaches and opportunities to help students become effective citizens in the global age.

Hobbs and Chernotsky (2007) define global citizens as individuals who are skilled in intercultural communication, respectful of cultural differences, and aware of the complex and interdependent nature of the world. Global citizens are people who are aware of the relationship between global and local events. They are individuals who recognize their actions at a local level have the potential to affect international events (Stevens & Campbell, 2006).

To be prepared for the challenges of global citizenship, technical communication students – like students in most disciplines – need to understand how to communicate and collaborate with members of other cultures (Sapp, 2004). St.Amant (2002a) points out it is not enough to give students the opportunity to interact with individuals from other cultures. Rather, students must participate in structured activities that will allow them to communicate online with diverse others. Students also need to become skilled in using technology – particularly online communication technologies – for collaboration with global teammates. Additionally, today's students need to know how to develop shared understandings with team members from other cultures and how to work across both national and disciplinary boundaries (Starke-Meyerring & Andrews, 2006).

Like their peers in other fields, technical communication students also need to understand how to prepare documentation for global audiences and to write documentation that is translation ready (Maylath, 1997; Maylath & Thrush, 2000; Thrush, 2001; Weiss, 1998). They should be prepared to face the ethical and legal challenges of communication with global audiences (Dragga, 1999; St.Amant, 2001).

Opportunities to develop the skills for working effectively in global contexts need to be integrated into the technical communication curriculum. To achieve this objective, faculty should create assignments that allow students to engage in collaborative and experiential learning. Furthermore, the curriculum should enable students to understand the connections between global and local events. Students should be given the opportunity to participate in projects that require them to act as engaged global citizens. Within this context, virtual team projects are particularly well suited to helping students develop global competency. The literature of the technical communication field, for example, contains many examples of virtual team projects designed to help technical communication students improve their intercultural communication and collaboration skills. However, a need persists for projects designed to help students develop all aspects of global competency, particularly civic engagement.

VIRTUAL TEAM PROJECTS AND GLOBAL COMPETENCY

Technical communication faculty can use virtual team projects to foster the development of global competency in their students, and such projects can easily be adapted for use in other educational units or academic disciplines. Specifically, virtual team projects can help students develop these components of global competency:

- Cultural sensitivity and knowledge
- Effective skills for communicating in diverse environments
- Technology skills, specifically facility using collaborative technologies for global work
- Essential knowledge of global events
- A foundational understanding of the interconnectedness of global and local events

- Critical thinking skills that can be applied to global events and can be used to view such events from an interdisciplinary perspective
- Civic engagement, taking action to address global issues

Such components collectively provide students with the range of skills needed to observe, interpret, and communicate about key developments affecting a range of global work practices. The key, however, is finding mechanisms to help students develop such skills and foundations of knowledge.

Global virtual team projects are particularly well suited to addressing the development of each of these components of global competency.

Intercultural Competence

Globally competent individuals are culturally sensitive and have an understanding of cultural differences (Hunter, White, & Godbey, 2006). Intercultural competence involves a *mindful* approach to communication across cultures. A mindful approach to the study of intercultural and international communication means that an individual approaches information about other cultures with an open mind and breaks free of stereotypical categorizations of members of cultures that are different from his/her own. Mindful individuals also strive to see the world from the different perspectives of other cultures (Ting-Toomey, 1999). This approach can go a long way toward decreasing and even preventing unintentional conflict. A mindful approach is also necessary for successful virtual collaboration among members of diverse cultures.

While part of the study of intercultural communication does involve knowledge of and respect for cultural differences, too great an emphasis on differences can be reductive and can lead to forming stereotypical views of members of other cultures (Brislin, 2000). On the other hand, some knowledge of different cultural perceptions of time, leadership, and communication are likely to be vital to the success of any global virtual collaboration. The concept of mindfulness, as explained by Stella Ting-Toomey (1999), emphasizes the importance of creating a feeling of "being understood, supported, and respected" in the individual(s) with whom you are communicating (p. 46). This approach is consistent with the call for a broader intercultural understanding that can be transferred from culture to culture (Hunter, White, & Godbey, 2006).

The challenge of global teaming requires that students negotiate cultural differences as they affect group knowledge sharing and knowledge creation (Sole & Edmondson, 2002; Vogel et al., 2001). Students will have to address misunderstandings and communication problems caused by different cultural perspectives or different notions of leadership and authority (Maznevski & Chudoba, 2000; Robey, Khoo, & Powers, 2000; Sarker, Sarker, & Schneider, 2009; Tan, Wei, Watson, Clapper, & McLean, 1998). In a fast-paced world where cultures are evolving, a global virtual team project will give students a much more meaningful understanding of how different cultural perspectives may affect global work. It will also present a much more realistic view of the complexity of cultures and an understanding of members of diverse cultures as individuals, often culturally diverse individuals, than a classroom discussion of different cultural perspectives on time or leadership could ever do.

Effective Communication in Diverse Environments

Communication skills are vital to global competency, specifically the ability to communicate in diverse situations and work outside one's "cultural comfort zone" (Hunter, White, & Godbey, 2006). Globally competent individuals are able to work outside their own environment; that is, they are prepared for global work. For U.S. students, this kind of preparedness means being ready to work

outside the United States. While study abroad has long been the primary means through which students gained this type of preparation, advocates of global education call attention to the fact that the percentage of students who study abroad is only a fraction of the student population (Guerin, 2009). Further, study abroad programs are generally an "add-on" to most curricula rather than being an integral part of every student's course of study (Starke-Meyerring, Duin, & Palvetzian, 2007).

Due to technological developments, virtual team collaborations are potentially available to all students and can provide students with the experience of working outside their "cultural comfort zone" while they remain at their home universities. For this reason, virtual team projects need to be more fully integrated into the curriculum of many programs since they have the potential to provide an intercultural experience to all students rather than just to the small number of students who have the opportunity to participate in study abroad programs.

Technology Skills

Clearly global virtual team projects are an ideal means for helping students develop mastery of collaborative technologies. In addition to gaining facility using various software programs and other collaborative media, such projects will also help students develop an understanding of the challenges of using online media to communicate with members of other cultures. These projects will also allow students to experience firsthand how reliance on technologies that do not allow for nonverbal cues may lead to miscommunication, for a lack of nonverbal cues creates much greater potential for cultural misunderstandings (Furamo & Pearson, 2006; Watson-Manheim & Belanger, 2002).

Virtual projects can be structured to require student teams to use many different types of technology for communication among team members (e.g., Skype™, videoconference, chat, discussion forums). Teams, for example, may begin their collaboration with an initial videoconference and then conduct meetings using Skype™, online chat, virtual workspaces, and other suites of collaborative technologies. Through such activities, students can gain an understanding of the strengths and the weaknesses of these technologies when used to communicate with individuals from other cultures. Through such experiences, students can become more adept at selecting the appropriate technology for different phases of an international project (Anawati & Craig, 2006; Starke-Meyerring & Andrews, 2006) and for different types of global communication (Deluca & Valacich, 2005; Sivunen & Valo, 2006).

Knowledge of World Events

While students can and should develop an interest in world events without participation in a global project, it is more likely that students will develop an interest in learning about world events when they are in communication with members of other cultures. As teammates from other cultures might hold different perspectives of an event, such international discussions can enliven students' interest in and enrich their understanding of these events. For example, faculty in the College of Business at Southern Arkansas University structure student work teams to include international students. By forcing students out of their "comfort zone and into teams that are diverse" faculty from Southern Arkansas University have found that students arrive at solutions to business cases that are "more creative and varied than those that would be produced by more homogenous student groupings" (White & Toms, 2009, p. 12).

Instructors can also create team projects that require international teams of students to examine and discuss world events and the role of effective communication in helping citizens address global issues in a meaningful way. Student teams can, for example, be required to develop websites that present information on environmental concerns from multiple perspectives. Students can then use these websites to explain how members of different cultures strive to live "green" lives. Such projects, in turn, can lead students to important discoveries. U.S. students, for example, might be surprised to learn that their Japanese teammates consider the use of dishwashers environmentally unfriendly (Katsunori, 2010). The U.S. students may counter by explaining that the dishwashers used in the United States are very energy efficient. Student teams might then collaborate to provide information for consumers who wish to avoid buying products that have a negative environmental impact. According to this approach, once students are required to address a global issue with teammates, they will greatly expand their understanding of it.

Connecting the Local and the Global

In addition to knowledge of world events, to be globally competent students need to be aware of the connection between global and local events. For example, students can become aware of how the actions they take in their local communities can affect demand in the global market, and how such demand might affect the local communities where the resources necessary for the products they purchase are extracted (Stevens & Campbell, 2006). Students can also become aware of the local-level power they have to address global issues, particularly when they are partnering with fellow students in other cultures who are also seeking to address these issues.

The first step in addressing these factors is for students to understand the connection between local and global events and then to share their understanding of such events with teammates who see the connections from different but related perspectives (i.e., from the perspective of another culture). Students may learn that some of the products that they buy locally have a negative impact on the environment or on the lives of workers who produce them (Hytten & Bettez,

2008). Students might then wish to disseminate this understanding to other college students or to an even broader audience.

A Critical and Interdisciplinary View of Global Events

One benefit of global teams in the workplace is that they allow companies to create cross-functional teams; cross-functional teams are typically composed of employees from diverse areas in a corporation. For example, a cross-functional team working on a software development project might include human factors experts, marketing personnel, customer support representatives, and technical communicators in addition to software developers. Technical communicators frequently find themselves working on teams with subject matter experts and other colleagues.

A virtual team project can give students the experience of working with fellow students from other majors. When students work with teammates from other disciplines, they have an opportunity to view global issues from an interdisciplinary perspective. Their critical thinking skills will be developed when they are challenged to negotiate with diverse teammates to create a group consensus on their understanding of the key considerations at stake in a particular global issue. Moreover, when students participate in virtual teams, they are engaging not only in collaborative work, but also in collaborative learning (Rutkowski, Vogel, van Genuchten, & Saunders, 2001). Students must therefore negotiate with one another to create shared meanings (Ulijn & St.Amant, 2000).

When addressing a global issue in an interdisciplinary team, students will be challenged to create a shared understanding that encompasses the perspective of all the disciplines/cultures represented by team members. In doing so, they begin by learning about each other's perspectives on the issue and will be forced to think critically in order to forge the team's unified understanding of the issue and their consensus on the best way to

offer a local solution to some aspect of the issue (Reimers, 2010).

For example, a team studying world hunger might lean heavily on the commonality of its members (i.e., all members being college students) and decide to create a website offering college students advice about how they can take small local actions to address world hunger. Or a team might elect to address the issue in the region where one or more team members reside. For example, an interdisciplinary team composed of Honors students at the University of Central Florida created a handbook for the Educational Concerns for Hunger Organization (ECHO) located in Fort Myers, Florida. ECHO is an organization combats hunger in 140 developing nations and does so by distributing seeds and educational literature in these nations. For this particular project, the members of this team wrote a manual describing the seed plants which ECHO cultivates and provides to its clients in developing nations. These students also translated the manual into Spanish and Haitian Creole because most of ECHO's clients speak one of these two languages (Sadri & Flammia, 2009).

The particular approach that students decide to take to the project is not as significant as the fact that they will be engaged in collaborative learning. Moreover, such projects will require students to negotiate with diverse teammates in order to create a shared understanding of a global issue and to formulate a plan for taking local action to address that issue.

Civic Engagement

The concept of the citizen diplomat is an extension of the concept of global citizenship. The globally competent citizen is aware of the complex interrelationship between local and global issues and recognizes that many global issues require the efforts of all nations to address them. A citizen diplomat, in comparison, is an ordinary citizen (as opposed to a political leader or government representative) who seeks to take action to address global issues and to foster understanding and cooperation with diverse others across national boundaries. In today's interconnected world, it is increasingly possible for individuals to effect global change. The accessibility of information via electronic media has made it possible for citizens to become active participants in international politics (Melissen, 2005). For this reason, the actions of both non-governmental organizations (NGOs) and individuals can be cited as examples of citizen diplomacy.

Within this context, students are much more likely to become engaged citizens when they have an awareness of global issues (Hanson, 2010; Stevens & Campbell, 2006). Awareness alone, however, might not be enough to facilitate engagement because global issues are quite complex and students could feel daunted when facing serious global concerns (Hytten & Bettez, 2008). For example, students in an interdisciplinary global health course found it difficult to resolve the tension between being reflective and taking action (Hanson, 2010). One student said that "It is hard to be a good global citizen. There's too much information and you need to find a balance between being realistic and acting meaningfully" (Hanson, 2010, p. 80).

However, participation in a global project wherein students address a global issue will provide them with more confidence regarding their ability to effect global change—even if they do so at a very limited local level. The experiential learning that takes place in such a project will give students a framework they can apply to future civic engagement. Such projects help students understand how to think about global issues from a critical perspective and how to collaborate with diverse others to negotiate meaning and to formulate and execute a plan of action. Once students have been part of a successful collaborative international project, and once they have become active global citizens through their involvement with these projects, they are much

more likely to want to be fully engaged citizens in their lives beyond the university (Stevens & Campbell, 2006).

STRUCTURING VIRTUAL TEAM PROJECTS

Global virtual team projects have the potential to foster global competency in students studying in a range of disciplines. When participating in such a project, students will need to engage in mindful intercultural communication and will face the challenge of functioning in an unfamiliar environment (Cogburn & Levinson, 2008). To do so, they will need to develop facility with collaborative technologies and use these technologies to communicate with others outside their "cultural comfort zone." Further, when the team project requires students to address a global issue, team members will be required to develop an understanding of the relationship between global and local events and will need to think critically about global events, often from an interdisciplinary perspective. Beyond thinking about events, students will engage in collaborative learning as they formulate a local project to address a global concern (Suárez-Orozco & Sattin, 2007).

As Starke-Meyerring, Duin, and Palvetzian (2007) have pointed out, global partnerships frequently require a great deal of initiative from faculty. Unfortunately, faculty members often receive little or no institutional support for undertaking such efforts. As a result, the prospect of establishing a global project for students may seem daunting to faculty members—even when they are deeply committed to preparing students for the demands of global citizenship.

While a detailed discussion of how to locate international partners and seek institutional support is beyond the scope of this chapter, faculty members might explore certain avenues when looking for international partners. These include

- *Seeking assistance from the International Office at one's university.* Many universities have international offices that administer international agreements with universities abroad. Frequently, these international agreements deal with student and faculty exchanges. Such agreements may also cover shared programs of study and curricular exchanges. Faculty whose departments are unable to support their international collaboration may gain support from their university's international studies office. A faculty member in an English department may find that his/her university already has a general agreement with a university in Spain and that art professors at the two universities are working collaboratively. Through a colleague in the art department, a faculty member may have the opportunity to make a personal connection with a faculty member in English. Personal connections are crucial to the success of international collaboration (Sapp, 2004).
- *Using professional organizations like the Society for Technical Communication to locate colleagues abroad.* Since both the Society for Technical Communication and the IEEE Professional Communication Society are international organizations, they are a good place to seek colleagues who may be interested in collaborating.
- *Making connections with international colleagues when attending conferences.* Professional conferences are an excellent place to meet with international colleagues. The author began a successful ongoing collaboration with two colleagues in Ireland when she attended the 2005 International Professional Communication Conference (IPCC) at the University of Limerick.
- *Drawing on local resources (international students, international businesses).* Faculty members who are having difficulty finding an international partner to conduct

a virtual team collaboration with might still find ways to add international elements to student projects by drawing on local resources. For example, as mentioned previously, faculty in the College of Business at Southern Arkansas University structure student work teams to include international students. Students may also work on local projects for an international client and/or audience. Local branches of international corporations and volunteer organizations that have an international scope, such as Habitat for Humanity, are a good place to find projects.

Locating an international partner is the first step to developing international collaborative projects for students. Once an international partner has been located, the next step is planning and structuring the project. Faculty members who collaborate to design virtual team projects for their students are themselves participating in a virtual team, often for the first time. As a result, these faculty members are likely to face challenges related to communication and project management (Gavidia, Mogollón, & Baena, 2005).

Communication

Consistent and frequent communication among collaborating faculty is important. Faculty members should try to establish "routines of interaction"; that is, they should have set meetings and guidelines for how frequently each team member should check the project website, message board, or email (DeSanctis, Fayard, Roach, & Jiang, 2003). Before beginning a virtual collaboration, faculty should get to know one another's teaching philosophies and the goals they have for their courses generally and the virtual team project specifically. Faculty also need to know something about the work environment, the work load, and the personal situation of the peers with whom they are collaborating on a virtual team project.

Reflecting on ten years of experience with the HKNET, a long-term collaboration between teachers in Hong Kong, the Netherlands, China, and the United States, Rutkowski, Vogel, van Genuchten, & Saunders (2001) state that for student virtual team projects to succeed the communication between professors is equally as important as the communication among students.

Project Management

Faculty members need to set up a clear division of responsibilities for all aspects of the project. It is important that students are given consistent responses to questions about the project. For this reason, one faculty member should be responsible for answering student questions or faculty members should take time to discuss answers to any unanticipated student questions in order to prevent inconsistent or even contradictory responses to student questions. Responding to students' requests for technical support is a potentially time-consuming task. Therefore, the responsibility for handling technical questions should be addressed before the project begins. In some cases, the use of a mutually-shared technology might make this issue less of a concern, particularly if the students can seek technical support from an outside office or agency on the campus (Flammia, Cleary, & Slattery, 2010).

A virtual team project is likely to require a significant commitment of time and effort from faculty members. Thus, faculty members need to have a strong presence to guide students through the project (Gavidia, Mogollón, & Baena, 2005). When faculty members neglect their responsibilities, the virtual team collaboration will suffer. Rutkowski, Vogel, van Genuchten, & Saunders (2001), for example, report that in their ten years with the HKNET project when collaborations with some universities failed, the reason was a lack of engagement on the part of the faculty members, not the students.

PROJECTS TO FOSTER GLOBAL COMPETENCY

If a virtual team project is going to help students develop global competency, it should require students to collaborate across national boundaries, and ideally also across disciplinary boundaries. The project should require students to examine and to discuss world events and then formulate a meaningful response to one local aspect of a particular global issue. For these reasons, Dubinsky (2002) argues that instruction in business and professional communication should be linked to pedagogies of civic engagement so that students become aware of the concerns of the global community.

Fortunately, global virtual team projects can be structured to help students develop as mindful global citizens. While faculty might face some limitations because of the particular class or topic being taught, there are some key principles that can be applied successfully in nearly all situations and that relate to the various components of global competency discussed earlier in this chapter. Educators can, in turn, use these principles to structure a global virtual team project. For example, some of the actions that should be performed before beginning the actual collaboration include the following:

Action 1. Begin by Helping Students Develop Global Awareness

Faculty should begin by explaining the concept of global citizenship to students and should emphasize the fact it is possible to be a global citizen without leaving one's local environment. An initial assignment could be to have students write a reflection piece on their current level of global involvement. This level might vary greatly among members of a given class, and having students share their experiences in small groups or with the whole class is one way of beginning a dialogue regarding global civic engagement. Faculty might plan to have students revisit their initial reflective essay at the end of the semester after they have participated in a global team project. In fact, students may write an updated version of the piece at the end of the semester as part of a reflection on the team project (Hanson, 2010).

Fortunately, faculty can use a number of resources to demonstrate the concept of citizen diplomacy. For example, faculty can introduce students to the website for TakingITGlobal (see www.tigweb.org). TakingITGlobal is an organization that strives to get young people (between the ages of 13 and 30) actively engaged in creating a more inclusive, peaceful, and sustainable world. TakingITGlobal offers students six steps to becoming a global citizen. The first step is for students to reflect on the changes they would like to see happen either in their local community or in the world. The steps offered by TakingITGlobal can be used in structuring the global project. The steps are

- Reflect on desired changes.
- Identify skills and interests.
- Gather information and seek inspiration.
- Create a plan of action to address the desired changes.
- Implement the plan.
- Reflect on what was accomplished and what could be done differently/better next time (http://www.takingitglobal.org/action/guide/Guide_to_Action.pdf).

These steps can be linked to specific assignments as students work on their project. Steps 1 and 2, for example, can be connected to the initial reflection piece. Similarly, Step 3 can be related to a research assignment that requires students to learn about a particular global issue. Faculty can also help students develop their understanding by bringing in guest speakers and providing students with classroom exercises that will enlarge their understanding. Step 4 can, in turn, be linked to the creation of a proposal by the student teams for a documentation project to address a particular

global issue, and Step 5 can be connected to the documentation project itself. Finally, Step 6 can be linked to a wrap-up report in which students reflect on their team experience and evaluate their work.

Action 2. Use Public Figures to Introduce the Concept of Citizen Diplomacy

Public figures like the entrepreneur Bill Gates and the singer Bono are excellent examples of what an individual citizen diplomat can accomplish, and such examples can be used to inspire students. However, students might quite rightly point out that they lack the resources and media stardom of these individuals. For this reason, once students have heard of the efforts of public figures to address global challenges, faculty can go on to give students examples that are closer to home. Educators can, for example, discuss Alternative Spring Break programs. They can also tell students about opportunities to volunteer online to address global concerns and note that many non-profit organizations offer opportunities to individuals who want to volunteer online. Additionally, students can find volunteer opportunities through the United Nations database (onlinevolunteering.org). Each of these programs provides students with the opportunity to benefit society by taking part in experiential learning and community service. Students might also consider volunteering locally with international organizations like Earthwatch and Habitat for Humanity. Even when volunteering in the United States, students will still be part of international programs and will be acting in the spirit of global citizenship. Once educators have introduced students to such ideas and opportunities, the next step is to get students thinking about ways they can use the skills or knowledge base of their particular discipline to address global issues.

Action 3. Involve Faculty from Other Disciplines and International Scholars (in Addition to Global Teammates) to Provide Students with a Broader View of a Particular Issue

Before students begin to collaborate with global teammates, faculty can prepare them for the project by exposing them to multiple perspectives on global issues. Faculty can invite colleagues from other disciplines and international scholars to serve as guest speakers who provide different views on a given issue. For example, for a discussion of world hunger guest speakers from international relations, global health, economics, and environmental science could be brought in to discuss the issue from various perspectives.

Faculty can also invite international scholars on campus to provide students with an intercultural context for understanding a global issue. For example, an international scholar from Russia can discuss censorship and governmental control in his/her nation. An international scholar from Norway can discuss the attitudes toward "green living" in his/her country.

In addition to other faculty and visiting scholars, international business people can also serve as guest speakers. These business people can be located through local branches of multinational corporations, local consular offices, or local chambers of commerce. For example, the author of this chapter invited the Vice President of the Metro Orlando Economic Development Commission to speak to her class about connections between Orlando and Dubai. If these options are not fruitful, faculty can consider using technology to provide students with opportunities to participate in webinars or videoconferences with scholars in other locations.

Action 4. Have Students Research a Particular Global Issue to Stimulate their Critical Thinking About It

Before having students participate in a team project, faculty members can have students or student teams research global issues. The research assignment can allow students to further investigate aspects of a particular topic that they learned about from guest speakers. A student's interest in learning more about microfinance programs, for example, might grow out of class discussion of the programs Bono started in Africa, out of hearing an economics professor discuss how such programs are structured and funded, or out of hearing an international scholar from Mozambique explain how such programs enhance the quality of life in his/her country. The student might then wish to pursue further research on the topic.

The research phase of the project will help students develop their information fluency at the same time that it gives them an opportunity to develop a broader understanding of a given global issue. Of course, the research can also serve as a basis for a documentation project that students will create with their global teammates.

Action 5. Have Students Use Collaborative Technologies for Team Work

Once students have developed an awareness of world events and an ability to think about them critically from multiple perspectives, they will be ready to engage in global collaboration. If possible, faculty should provide students participating in a virtual collaboration with a mutually shared workspace, for such shared resources are an important component of successful virtual collaborations (Roberts, Lowry, & Sweeney, 2006). In addition to a shared workspace, students will be likely to use email, chat, instant messaging, and Skype™.

Most students will have access to the peripheral technologies either on their own or through their universities. It is the shared group workspace that must be provided by or at least chosen by the faculty members because it less likely that all students will have access to collaborative technologies like Blackboard and Sakai unless they are provided by their universities (Flammia, Slattery, & Cleary, 2010).

Action 6. Require that Students Produce a Documentation Project that Addresses a Particular Global Issue

Generally, students will want to put their newly-enlarged understanding of global issues into practice. The virtual team project can require that students create documentation to address a global issue either at a local, regional, national (in more than one nation simultaneously), or international level. A project that requires students to focus on global issues can also help students develop the competencies necessary for global citizenship. Further, this type of project will give students a framework for civic engagement and greater confidence in their ability to effect change (Hanson, 2010).

For example, student teams researching world hunger might collaborate to create documentation to be disseminated at their individual universities to raise the awareness of the campus community about how they can take steps as individuals to address world hunger. Or students might decide to create documentation to serve a regional non-governmental organization whose mission is to address world hunger. Alternatively, students could create a website that disseminates information on how individuals can help developing nations. For example, students in an anthropology course at Portland State University worked with a public-health organization in Oaxaca to study the prevalence of diabetes in migrant workers from Mexico. These students then returned to Oregon and wrote research papers on the relationship between migration and health (Fischer, 2007). Their research papers had relevance in the local community since a large number of the migrant workers who come to Oregon are from Oaxaca.

CONCLUSION

Educators across disciplines agree that students need to be prepared to function as global citizens in the twenty-first century. Students must be given opportunities to develop global competency. Faculty in many disciplines can use global virtual team projects to help students develop global competency and to produce students who are actively engaged citizens.

It is true that faculty members will face some challenges when structuring virtual team projects. The benefits to students, however, greatly outweigh these challenges. Successful projects will give students the opportunity to participate in experiential learning and to develop documentation products that will contribute solutions to global concerns.

REFERENCES

Anawati, D., & Craig, A. (2006). Behavioral adaptation within cross-cultural virtual teams. *IEEE Transactions on Professional Communication*, *49*(1), 44–56. doi:10.1109/TPC.2006.870459

Brislin, R. (2000). *Understanding culture's influence on behavior*. Ft. Worth, TX: Harcourt.

Cogburn, D. L., & Levinson, N. S. (2008). Teaching globalization, globally: A 7-year case study of South Africa-U.S. virtual teams. *Information Technologies and International Development*, *4*(3), 75–88. doi:10.1162/itid.2008.00018

Deluca, D., & Valacich, J. S. (2005). Outcomes from conduct of virtual teams at two sites: Support for media synchronicity theory. *Proceedings of the 38th Hawaii International Conference on Systems Sciences*, (pp. 1-10). Los Alamitos, CA: IEEE Computer Society.

DeSanctis, G., Fayard, A., Roach, M., & Jiang, L. (2003). Learning in online forums. *European Management Journal, 21*(5), 565–577. doi:10.1016/S0263-2373(03)00106-3

DeVoss, D., Jasken, J., & Hayden, D. (2002). Teaching intercultural and intercultural communication: A critique and suggested method. *Journal of Business and Technical Communication, 16*(1), 69–94. doi:10.1177/1050651902016001003

Dragga, S. (1999). Ethical intercultural technical communication: Looking through the lens of Confucian ethics. *Technical Communication Quarterly, 8*, 365–381.

Dubinsky, J. (2002). Service-learning as a path to virtue: The ideal orator in professional communication. *Michigan Journal of Community Service Learning, 9*, 62–74.

Fischer, K. (2007). Flat world lessons for real-world students. *The Chronicle of Higher Education*, 35.

Flammia, M., Cleary, Y., & Slattery, D. M. (2010). Leadership roles, socioemotional communication strategies, and technology use of Irish and US students in virtual teams. *IEEE Transactions on Professional Communication, 53*(2), 89–101. doi:10.1109/TPC.2010.2046088

Furamo, K., & Pearson, J. M. (2006). An empirical investigation of how trust, cohesion, and performance vary in virtual and face-to-face teams. *Proceedings of the 39th Hawaii International Conference on Systems Sciences*. Honolulu, HI: Computer Society Press.

Gavidia, J. V., Mogollón, R. H., & Baena, C. (2005). Using international virtual teams in the business classroom. *Journal of Teaching in International Business, 16*(2), 51–74. doi:10.1300/J066v16n02_04

Giammona, B. (2004). The future of technical communication: How innovation, technology, information management, and other forces are shaping the future of the profession. *Technical Communication, 51*(3), 349–366.

Guerin, S. H. (2009). Internationalizing the curriculum: Improving learning through international education: Preparing students for a success in a global society. *Community College Journal of Research and Practice, 33*(8), 611–614. doi:10.1080/10668920902928945

Hanson, L. (2010). Global citizenship, global health, and the internationalization of curriculum: A study of transformative potential. *Journal of Studies in International Education, 14*(1), 70–88. doi:10.1177/1028315308323207

Hobbs, H. H., & Chernotsky, H. I. (2007). Preparing students for global citizenship. *Proceedings of the American Political Science Conference*. Retrieved November 20, 2010, from www.apsanet.org/ tlc2007/ TLC07HobbsChernotsky.pdf

Hunter, B., White, G. P., & Godbey, G. C. (2006). What does it mean to be globally competent? *Journal of Studies in Intercultural Education, 10*(3), 267–285. doi:10.1177/1028315306286930

Hytten, K., & Bettez, S. C. (2008). Teaching globalization issues to education students: What's the point? *Equity & Excellence in Education, 41*(2), 168–181. doi:10.1080/10665680801957295

Katsunori, M. (2010, February 3). Experiences of an international scholar from Japan. Lecture given in the class ENC 4262: International Technical Communication, University of Central Florida, Orlando, FL.

Maylath, B. (1997). Writing globally: Teaching the technical writing student to prepare documents for translation. *Journal of Business and Technical Communication*, *11*(3), 339–352. doi:10.1177/1050651997011003006

Maylath, B., & Thrush, E. (2000). Café, thé, ou lait? Teaching technical communicators to manage translation and localization. In Hager, P. J., & Schreiber, H. J. (Eds.), *Managing global communication in science and technology* (pp. 233–254). New York, NY: John Wiley & Sons.

Maznevski, M. L., & Chudoba, K. M. (2000). Bridging space over time: Global virtual team dynamics and effectiveness. *Organization Science*, *11*(5), 473–492. doi:10.1287/orsc.11.5.473.15200

Melissen, J. (2005). *Wielding soft power: The new public diplomacy*. The Hague, The Netherlands: Netherlands Institute of International Relations Clingendael.

Miles, L. (1997). Globalizing professional writing curricula: Positioning students and re-positioning textbooks. *Technical Communication Quarterly*, *6*, 179–200. doi:10.1207/s15427625tcq0602_4

Reimers, F. (2010). Educating for global competency. In Coehn, J. E., & Malin, M. B. (Eds.), *International perspectives on the goals of universal basic and secondary education* (pp. 183–202). New York, NY: Routledge.

Roberts, T., Lowry, P. B., & Sweeney, P. (2006). An evaluation of the impact of social presence through group size and the use of collaborative software on group member voice in face-to-face and computer-mediated task groups. *IEEE Transactions on Professional Communication*, *49*(1), 28–43. doi:10.1109/TPC.2006.870460

Robey, D., Khoo, H. M., & Powers, C. (2000). Situated learning in cross-functional virtual teams. *Technical Communication*, *47*(1), 51–66.

Rutkowski, A., Vogel, D., van Genuchten, M., & Saunders, C. (2001). Communication in virtual teams: Ten years of experience in education. *IEEE Transactions on Professional Communication*, *51*(3), 302–312. doi:10.1109/TPC.2008.2001252

Sadri, H., & Flammia, M. (2009). Using technology to prepare students for the challenges of global citizenship. *Journal of Systemics, Cybernetics, and Informatics*, *7*(5), 66–71.

Sapp, D. A. (2004). Global partnerships in business communication: An institutional collaboration between the United States and Cuba. *Business Communication Quarterly*, *67*(3), 267–280. doi:10.1177/1080569904268051

Sarker, S., Sarker, S., & Schneider, C. (2009). Seeing remote team members as leaders: A study of U.S.-Scandinavian teams. *IEEE Transactions on Professional Communication*, *52*(1), 75–94. doi:10.1109/TPC.2008.2007871

Schafer, R. (2009). Introducing heuristics of cultural dimensions into the service-level technical communication classroom. *Journal of Technical Writing and Communication*, *39*(3), 305–319. doi:10.2190/TW.39.3.f

Sivunen, A., & Valo, M. (2006). Team leaders' technology choice in virtual teams. *IEEE Transactions on Professional Communication*, *49*(1), 57–68. doi:10.1109/TPC.2006.870458

Sole, D., & Edmondson, A. (2002). Situated knowledge and learning in dispersed teams. *British Journal of Management*, *13*, 517–534. doi:10.1111/1467-8551.13.s2.3

St.Amant, K. (2001). Considering China: A perspective for technical communicators. *Technical Communication*, *48*(4), 385–388.

St.Amant, K. (2002a). Integrating intercultural online learning experiences into the computer classroom. *Technical Communication Quarterly*, *11*, 289–315. doi:10.1207/s15427625tcq1103_4

St.Amant, K. (2002b). When cultures collide: Rethinking computer-mediated communication according to international and intercultural expectations. *Journal of Business and Technical Communication, 16*(2), 196–214. doi:10.1177/1050651902016002003

Starke-Meyerring, D., & Andrews, D. (2006). Building a shared virtual learning culture: An international classroom partnership. *Business Communication Quarterly, 69*(1), 25–49. doi:10.1177/1080569905285543

Starke-Meyerring, D., Duin, A. H., & Palvetzian, T. (2007). Global partnerships: Positioning technical communication programs in the context of globalization. *Technical Communication Quarterly, 16*, 139–174. doi:10.1207/s15427625tcq1602_1

Stevens, C. R., & Campbell, P. J. (2006). Collaborating to connect global citizenship, information literacy, and lifelong learning in the global studies classroom. *References Services Review, 34*(4), 536–556. doi:10.1108/00907320610716431

Suárez-Orozco, M. M., & Sattin, C. (2007). Wanted: Global citizens. *Educational Leadership, 64*(7), 58–62.

Taking, I. T. Global. (n.d.) *Guide to action: Simple steps toward change.* Retrieved November 20, 2010, from http://www.tigweb.org/ action/ guide/

Tan, B. C. Y., Wei, K., Watson, R. T., Clapper, D. L., & McLean, E. R. (1998). Computer-mediated communication and majority influence: Assessing the impact in an individualistic and collectivistic culture. *Management Science, 44*(9), 1263–1278. doi:10.1287/mnsc.44.9.1263

Thrush, E. A. (2001). Plain English? A study of plain English vocabulary and international audiences. *Technical Communication, 48*(3), 289–296.

Ting-Toomey, S. (1999). *Communicating across cultures.* New York, NY: The Guilford Press.

Ulijn, J., & St.Amant, K. (2000). Mutual intercultural perception: How does it affect technical communication? *Technical Communication, 47*(2), 220–237.

Vogel, D. R., van Genuchten, M., Lou, D., Verveen, S., van Eekout, M., & Adams, A. (2001). Exploratory research on the role of national and professional cultures in a distributed learning project. *IEEE Transactions on Professional Communication, 44*(2), 114–124. doi:10.1109/47.925514

Watson-Manheim, M. B., & Belanger, F. (2002) Support for communication-based work processes in virtual work. *e-Service Journal, 1*(3), 61-82.

Weiss, E. H. (1998). Technical communication across cultures: Five philosophical questions. *Journal of Business and Technical Communication, 12*(2), 253–269. doi:10.1177/1050651998012002005

White, G. W., & Toms, L. (2009). Preparing college of business students for a global world. *The Delta Kappa Gamma Bulletin, 75*(4), 11-13, 26.

KEY TERMS AND DEFINITIONS

Citizen Diplomat: An ordinary citizen who takes action to address global issues and to foster understanding and cooperation with diverse others across national boundaries.

Civic Engagement: Taking action to address global issues. (NOTE: I realize there are many more complex definitions of this term. I included a definition related specifically to how I used the term in the chapter.)

Global Citizenship: An awareness of the relationship between global and local events and a willingness to take actions at a local level to impact international issues.

Global Competency: An array of skills and abilities including cultural sensitivity, knowledge of global events, technological proficiency, and the ability to communicate in diverse environments.

Internationalization: The integration of global perspectives in the curriculum.

Mindful Approach: Bringing an open mind to the study of intercultural communication, break-ing free of stereotypes, and striving to see things from the perspectives of diverse others.

Virtual Teams: Groups of individuals who use technology to collaborate across time, distance, and national and organizational boundaries.

Chapter 22
Studying Locally, Interacting Globally:
Demographic Change and International Students in Australian Higher Education

Angela T. Ragusa
Charles Sturt University, Australia

Emma Steinke
Charles Sturt University, Australia

ABSTRACT

This chapter uses findings from an online survey of international onshore undergraduate and post-graduate students enrolled in an Australian university in 2009 to critically examine and compare their expectations, experiences, and levels of satisfaction. This research yielded a plethora of unique and vital concerns that were further affected by variables such as students' age and geographic location in regional/rural versus metropolitan areas. Moreover, the results of this study, in turn, can offer educators important initial insights they can then use to develop online educational materials or online courses for such internationally diverse groups of students. This chapter argues the gap between expectations and experiences requires further attention if the delivery of academic excellence to students from divergent cultural backgrounds, with different language skills and varying social norms is to be achieved within an environment that supports and reflects cultural diversity. The chapter also provides suggestions on how such factors can and should be addressed when devising online educational materials and environments for such students.

The general trend towards freely circulating capital, goods and services, coupled with changes in the openness of labour markets, has translated into growing demands for an international dimension of education and training. Indeed, as world economies become increasingly inter-connected, international skills have grown in importance for operating on a global scale. Globally oriented firms seek internationally-competent workers versed in foreign languages and having mastered basic inter-cultural skills to successfully interact with international partners. Governments as well as individuals are looking to higher education to play a role in broadening students' horizons and allowing them to develop a deeper

DOI: 10.4018/978-1-60960-833-0.ch022

understanding of the world's languages, cultures and business methods. One way for students to expand their knowledge of other societies and languages, and hence leverage their labour market prospects, is to study in tertiary educational institutions in countries other than their own. Several OECD [Organisation for Economic Co-operation and Development] governments – especially in countries of the European Union (EU) – have set up schemes and policies to promote mobility as a means of fostering intercultural contacts and building social networks for the future. (Organisation for Economic Co-operation and Development, 2009, p. 310)

INTRODUCTION

Enrolment numbers of international students, defined as "those who left their country of origin and moved to another country for the purpose of study" (OECD, 2009, p. 324), at Australian universities has increased with the development and improved capacity of information communication technologies. Some Australian universities, such as Deakin, have tried to address such international interests in education via the development of online classes and curricula designed for such an international student base. In other cases, Australian educators and administrators have sought to use online media to find new ways to address the educational needs of on-site students attending brick and mortar campuses. At Charles Sturt University (CSU), a rural and regional university in inland Australia, international students are receiving increased interest from university administrators and marketers as a unique sub-culture within the student population. This approach, in turn, affects how online media are used to connect with and provide education to such students.

Historically, the use of technologically-driven communication systems, as a foundational component of educational systems, is a recent phenomenon (Schifter, 2004). Recent changes in the structure of higher education, in Australia and globally, have vastly changed the development, range and use of information technologies, particularly computer mediated communications (CMC). As recently as 2005, the vast majority of distance education courses offered in Australia existed as correspondence degrees (Ragusa, 2007).

The growth in primary and supplementary learning materials based upon electronic resources has increased exponentially, partially in response to internationalisation of the tertiary education sector and more generally in response to broad social changes in technical skills, required proficiencies and cross-cultural communications. As Adeoye and Wentling (2007) explain, "Demographic change, technological advances and globalization have forced corporations throughout the world to re-examine their policies, programs, and practices" (p. 119)

Yet, while "the spread of information and communication technology lowered the information and transaction costs of study abroad and boosted demand for international education" (OECD, 2009, p. 313), the proliferation of academic research investigating the cultural relevance, not to mention the access, uptake and competence with use of these computer-based resources, remains minimal at best. Equally important, the use of such resources remains largely nonexistent for international students in Australian universities. The introduction and widespread adoption of CMC in university education in Australia has contributed to the globalization of classrooms, virtual and physical (Ragusa, 2007) and is fundamentally altering the degree and nature of how individuals from divergent cultures interact in formal educational environments. As a result of these factors, the time has now come to examine how international, on-campus students make use of such CMC-based resources to determine the efficacy of such resources and to consider what modifications might need to be made. The implications of such an examination, moreover, are of import not only to educators in Australia, but to educators at any physical institution with a large or a growing on-site population of international students. Furthermore, the insights focused research can provide about students' use of CMC within educational contexts can offer new perspectives and ideas that could be used to revise or refine exclusively online approaches to using CMC technologies. Such insights may facilitate interactions among students from different nations and cultures.

This chapter builds upon previous research (Ragusa, 2010a; Ragusa, 2009; Ragusa, 2007) examining the cultural and academic environment of universities as social institutions undergoing social change. By taking an in-depth look at international students' expectations and experiences with communicating, interacting, and learning at an Australian university, the chapter draws upon primary-collected 2009 survey data of all international onshore students enrolled at CSU and examines perspectives and attitudes that can affect or influence their perspectives on and uses of CMC in educational contexts. Using a range of demographic variables, this chapter aims to identify, from the perspective of international students, how the unique position of being an international student has impacted their interactions and communications with peers, professors, administrators and others during their pursuit of higher education at CSU. All of these factors, in turn, have important implications for how such students might use CMC to interact in educational contexts and in online learning environments.

Quantitative and qualitative data analysis presented in this chapter reveals international students' expectations and perceptions of various academic and socio-cultural resources. Topics examined include opinions about the quality and value of their university courses/subjects, lecturers/professors and course resources/materials delivered in online and face-to-face education; opportunities for and satisfaction with social

interactions (with peers and teachers); ability to make local friends and/or fit within their new community; skills required and acquired, and support available, relating to language competency, amenities and employment opportunities. Findings are contextualized within the existing international and national literature to discuss the implications key insights may hold for relevant theories, research and policies. Finally, the authors conclude this presentation with a discussion of how these results can be applied to create best practices for both using CMC to provide effective educational experiences to on-site international students as well as suggested practices for creating effective online learning environments for such students.

BACKGROUND

International Students in Australian Higher Education: Market Growth and Focus

Since the 1970s, worldwide growth in international students has risen exponentially, from 0.8 million in 1975 to more than 3 million in 2007, and "has accelerated during the past 12 years, mirroring the growth in the globalisation of economies and societies" (OECD, 2009, p. 312). Growth in international student enrolment is also arguably fuelled by higher education institutions actively courting foreign markets in an environment shaped by the push-pull factors of global economics. According to 2007 statistics compiled by UNESCO and the OECD, more than 3 million tertiary students were enrolled in degrees outside of their country of citizenship, with the United States and Europe claiming 48% of the global market which predominantly consisted of Chinese and Indian students (OECD, 2009).

The internationalisation of tertiary education and rapid expansion "has intensified the financial pressures on education systems and led to greater interest in the recruitment of foreign students. As tertiary institutions increasingly rely on revenues from foreign tuition fees, some countries actively recruit foreign students" (OECD, 2009, p. 310). More recently, a range of public and private universities have begun to develop online classes that could tap this growing international market from afar. (St.Amant, 2007). Indeed, international students have become big business for Western countries, as the British experience exhibits, and its continued growth looks uninhibited for Australia, the U.K. and United States (Huang, 2008). In many cases, these international students will be required to use a range of online media to participate in such educational settings. Factors of culture, however, could affect how these students uses of such media in learning contexts, and this notion of how culture affects the uses of CMC technologies is one that needs to be examined in order to determine the most effective methods for providing such students with a quality education in the wired age of the 21st century.

In Australia, in order to meet government-mandated challenges imposed on the higher education sector, and to achieve growth in an extremely competitive environment, Charles Sturt University's (CSU's) 2007-2011 Strategic Plan aims to increase the number of international students enrolled in its on- and off-shore courses to 19% by 2011 (Charles Sturt University [CSU], 2009). International students presently comprise more than 10% of undergraduate enrolment figures in Australia, Austria, New Zealand, Switzerland and the United Kingdom and more than 20% in advanced research programs in Australia, Belgium, Canada, New Zealand, Switzerland, the United Kingdom and the United States (OECD, 2009, p. 309). Moreover, this number of international students is poised to grow from 1.25 million in the year 2000 to 7.25 million by 2025 (Bohm, Davis, Meares, & Pearce, 2002). In 2009, full-fee paying international students in Australia grew by 16.8% in comparison with 2008 statistics, with the majority of students originating from China

and India (Department of Education, Employment & Workplace Relations, 2009).

Despite interest in this sub-group of students as a new "market" by institutions of higher education, little research into the cultural and lifestyle issues associated with international students in Australia has been conducted. The primary focus of research into the Australian tertiary education sector, and to some extent globally, has been on understanding the student experience (Universities Australia, 2009) by focussing on items such as quality of learning and teaching, student living arrangements, finances, graduate outcomes and student safety. News media coverage in 2009 of attacks on Indian students in Melbourne highlighted safety concerns of international students (Universities Australia, 2009) and resulted in the announcement of a Senate enquiry (IEAA Secretariat, 2009). Unfortunately, such studies miss crucial points such as why and how the cultural environment created a setting for these instances to occur in the first place and what changes need to be made to improve interactions amongst diverse cultures beyond merely ensuring physical safety. Given that Australia, the United Kingdom and the United States are the top three destinations for Indian students, representing "82.6% of Indian citizens enrolled abroad" (OECD, 2009, p. 323), this lack of more focused research on international students is particularly disturbing.

Increased publicity of international students, coupled with global growth in international students studying offshore, has increased the desire to understand international students' experiences. However, the research motivation remains largely fiscal because the goal is to attract more international "onshore" students to Australia. Education is the third highest export earner for Australia (Australian Bureau of Statistics, 2008) and the number of international students studying in Australia has grown from 273,703 students in 2002 to 541,187 in 2008, representing a 98% increase for that period (Australian Education International, 2009). Of those students, the number of international students enrolled in higher education grew from 115,404 in 2002 to 181,528 in 2008, which is a 57% increase.

Growth in targeting the international student market is in part fuelled by government policy. Over the past decade, Australia moved away from high levels of government funding for universities and higher education institutions in favour of increased privatization. Along with tertiary graduation and entry rates, the proportion of private funding can be influenced by the incidence of international students which form a relatively high proportion in Australia and New Zealand (see OECD, 2009, *Table B3.2a and Table B3.2b* p. 322). As policy forced educational institutions to find alternative funding sources, admitting more fee-paying students proved lucrative. Australian enrolment statistics confirm the forecasted growth predicted by Bohm et al. (2002) as international student rates grew by 12.1% between 2008-2009 in higher education (Australian Education International, 2010 March) which contributed $18.6 billion in export revenue, which was an 8.1% increase for the national economy in 2009 (Australian Education International, 2010 May).

In a speech made May 26, 2009, Australia's then Education Minister, and current Prime Minister, Julia Gillard (2009), stated international education generated $15.5 billion for the national economy and over 125,000 jobs in 2008. Following the election of the Rudd Government, higher education institutions were prevented from enrolling domestic fee paying undergraduates. This left postgraduate and international fee-paying students as the main source of fee-paying income. The financial imperative imposed by the government for institutions to become increasingly self-funded, combined with an emerging opportunity to attract an increasingly mobile global student population, resulted in heightened competition among Australian higher education providers seeking to attract international students.

In both Australia and New Zealand, the high proportion and impact of international students has been described as "so huge that their entry rate dropped significantly when international students were excluded, causing them to lose their top two ranking positions" (OECD, 2009, p. 45). With "adjustments of 23 and 14 percentage points respectively, the impact is so great that their entry rates slip from the top 2 ranking positions to fall behind the United States" (OECD, 2009, p. 52). What these figures demonstrate is that the importance of international students to universities in Australia and New Zealand supersedes mere fiscal income. Indeed, the quality of higher education, as measured by university rankings based on multiple indicators including students' entry scores, measurably declined when international students were not included in calculations. In national comparisons, Australia's (84%) and New Zealand's (72%) overall highest entry rates to "tertiary-type A" education, both which are well above the OECD average, are attributed to their high proportion of international students (OECD, 2009). Again, what this reveals is that international students are better prepared to commence university study than domestic students. This phenomenon continues throughout students' experience of higher education.

The scope and importance of the international student cohort to the overall quality of student cohort in terms of both academic performance and retention in these countries can be further evidenced by the impact of graduation rates, which drop by 15% in Australia and 10% in New Zealand when only domestic students are included for tertiary-type A first degrees (OECD, 2009). Therefore, given the fiscal imperative for higher education institutions to be self-funding, as promoted by government policy, and the importance of international students to higher levels of academic quality, retention and graduation rates, it is imperative that universities identify and nurture the learning environment which is best suited to supporting this important social group. This requires universities provide them with effective educational experiences and reconsider how the

CMC technologies recently developed and relied upon provide international students with satisfactory materials and instruction.

Culture and Multiculturalism in Higher Education Learning Environments

Although commencement of higher education typically entails exposure to previously un-encountered ideas, beliefs and ways of knowing, or epistemologies, rapid global growth in the higher education sector has witnessed increased student diversity, including participation by individuals from disadvantaged backgrounds – persons who might find new ways of thinking particularly confronting (Brownlee, Walker, Lennox, Exley, & Pearce, 2009). "In every era, knowledge is based upon assumptions that the current worldview is "normal." These normative assumptions guide what individuals consider commonplace and varies greatly by culture, ethnicity, class, gender and a range of other socio-demographic variables" (Ragusa, 2010a, p. 3). These culture shock experiences can be particularly acute in relation to technology, particularly if the technologies used to provide educational experiences are drastically different from the contexts of teaching and learning with which students are accustomed. Interestingly, the impact of culture, and the effect of cultural differences on worldviews, perceptions and experiences, is well articulated in disciplines such as sociology and cultural studies. Yet, the impact cultural diversity has in institutions of higher education, especially in relation to an information society and knowledge-based economy, is a historically new area of research. Such factors, however, need to be considered, examined, and, if needed, addressed in order to provide effective educational experiences, particularly experiences involving CMC technologies, to international students.

Typically, the theoretical underpinnings of cultural difference are grounded in simultaneously political and personal conceptions of nationhood and citizenship. In our global society, demarcation of national identity is increasingly problematic as individuals, such as employees of multinational corporations, military institutions and international students spend significant portions of their lives outside their country of origin. In our "Information Age" (Castells, 2000), the contentious concept of "globalisation" (Hirst & Thompson, 1996) has not only been bantered and debated; globalization has also been accompanied by widespread social anxiety and fear of "others," commonly termed "xenophobia." Ethical issues surround seemingly simple sociological concepts, such as "multiculturalism," and remind us that national and trans-national/global identities and "culture" are imperative to examinations of higher education today.

Growth in global communication technologies has increased the frequency in which people of diverse nationalities are coming into contact with one another (OECD, 2009). Increased interpersonal contact, along with either the internationalization (Hirst & Thompson, 1996), or globalization of the world's economies, has subsequently lead to an "increased emphasis on internationalization of the curriculum" (Barjis, 2003, p.1). Excluding variables such as culture (see Bowles, 2004, Monolescu, Schifter, & Greenwood, 2004; Palloff & Pratt, 2001; Brooks, Nolan, & Gallagher, 2001) in the development, delivery, and evaluation of education technologies, and higher education in general, may foster undesirable learning, economic and communicative consequences, especially where international participants are involved (Ragusa, 2007). Australian higher education environments with multinational and international students have recently advocated the development and use of learning resources that utilize technology to democratize the learning experience. For example, microbiologists that created vodcasts to demonstrate laboratory techniques to university students noted such learning tools would be particularly useful for English-as-a-second-language students with English language skills that impinged on their comprehension of relevant information in the laboratory/classroom environment (Crampton, Vanniasinkam, & Milic, 2010). Without consideration of students' cultural background, international students may remain disadvantaged.

Within the higher education academic research literature, examinations of how international students adjust to the demands placed upon them by their new socio-cultural environments, whilst pursuing higher education, have tended to focus on a relatively narrow range of issues. According to Sovic (2009), the majority of research has related to academic and/or cultural adjustment, which predominates over explorations of the social psychological mechanisms students use to cope with experiences such as isolation in classrooms or alienation. The integration and adjustment of international students, in other words the socialization process, was found in several studies (Sovic, 2009; Lee & Rice, 2007; Ramsay et al., 2007; Volet & Ang, 1998; Gerdes & Mallinckrod, 1994) to be pivotal for the retention, adaptation, cultural learning and ultimately success of students experiencing multiculturalism at institutions of higher education. Although researchers' perceptions varied regarding which variables were attributed as most important for fostering successful student experiences, several highlighted the centrality of social interactions and support received from friends or peers (Paswan & Ganesh, 2009; Ramsay, Jones, & Barker, 2007; Wilcox et al., 2005) or a combination of individual and structural practices (Volet & Ang, 1998; Perrucci & Hu, 1995). In some instances, the growth of international students resulted in overall increased perceptions of student dissatisfaction, although there is a dearth of research examining levels of students' satisfaction with specific components of the higher education experience (Zhao, Kuh, & Carini, 2005).

This section has demonstrated the importance of the international student market to universities in Australian and New Zealand because of the contribution this cohort makes both economically and academically to the national functioning of higher education. Simultaneously it has identified some of the undesirable consequences which result when culturally diverse individuals come together in physical and virtual environments. Although a limited body of research has identified the importance of cultural awareness in higher education settings, sociological analysis remains largely absent despite the widespread increase in use of CMC which increases social interactions amongst culturally diverse learners. Pragmatically, priority has been given to the economic interests of institutions, such as higher education, and analysis of student experiences are marginalized to a limited range of nationally-driven set of quantitative questions that fail to incorporate either student experiences with CMC or examine how or if the ethnic status of students affects learning satisfaction. Therefore, this chapter seeks to fill the existing knowledge gap by prioritizing focus on international students to better understand some of the cultural factors which may affect why and how individuals from diverse backgrounds approach learning in an environment that is increasingly technologically mediated.

Cultural Diversity and International Student Experiences

A number of structural and socio-political factors affect international students' choices about where to study abroad. Key determining criteria include use of the English language in instruction, tuition fees and living costs, and immigration policies. For example, although the majority of countries charge international students higher tuition fees than are paid by their domestic students (see OECD, 2009, Box C2.3. *Tuition fees structure for a cross-national comparison*), some countries, such as the Nordic countries, do not charge for education at all. Countries such as Australia, Canada, and New Zealand have immigration policies that encourage their international students to remain in the country after graduation whereas the United States discourages this practice. Other influential factors include the academic reputation of an institution, the flexibility of credit transfer for coursework, educational availability in the student's country of origin, geography and political relationships among nations, and future employment options (OECD, 2009).

International research has identified cultural factors, specifically the challenges international students' face with successful social interactions and social integration, that are of even greater importance than academic factors in determining student retention (Sovic, 2009). Although quality audits reveal international students at CSU progress at rates higher than domestic students, whereby progress is defined as, "the proportion of completed subjects that have been undertaken successfully, calculated in terms of Equivalent Full Time Student Load (EFTSL) and expressed as a percentage" (Clemson, 2009, p. 1), analyses of international students' satisfaction with their higher degree experience remains limited. Part of this limitation stems from contention regarding the term "student experience."

In the recent Australian University Quality Audit (AUQA) report on the tertiary student experience, student diversity factored into the difficulty associated with arriving at a single mechanism for determining a successful student experience (Alcock, Cooper, Kirk, & Oyler, 2009) as each student brings his or her own particular expectations and perspectives for viewing the world (1994 Group [U.K. universities], 2007). Student experience has been described as diverse and multi-faceted. Understanding it requires requiring definitions that encompass various quality measures of academics, courses and programs, support mechanisms for learning, well-being, academic integrity and equity, and appropriate facilities for social and academic activities – all while managing individuals' transition from entry to graduation (Alcock et al., 2009). Cultural adaptation, or acculturation, also factors into

students' perceived satisfaction and is related to student experiences (Campbell & Li, 2008; Sawir, Marginson, Deumert, Nyland, & Ramia, 2008; Wadsworth, Hecht, & Jung, 2008) with intercultural communication, language ability, interaction with local students and understanding Australian academic norms. Research into study-related stress extended the concept of cultural adaptation, proposing the "acquisition of sociocultural skills will offset culture shock" and noted the sooner one could overcome culture shock, the more likely one would have a positive experience (Brown, 2008, p. 11). Furthermore, an ability to form and maintain networks, both locally and with those back home, were critical to international students having a positive experience in Australia (Sawir et al., 2008). Consequently, when asking international students to participate in learning environments that use CMC, the cultural factors described mentioned here require consideration. Such consideration, moreover should take place during the developmental phase of learning aims and objectives and prior to students engaging in culturally diverse CMC environments.

Applying a Business Model to a Previously Public Good: Student Expectations

As the socioeconomic shift in the relative importance of education increases, due to its status as an export industry with significant capacity to impacting national revenue, an associated paradigm shift is occurring. Historically, education was proclaimed a public good vs. today's business model of education (Simpson & Tan, 2009) in which students assume the role of customers first and learners second. The shift from public to private good has seen the enactment of consumer protection legislation for international students by the Australian Government, specifically the Education Services for Overseas Students Act 2000. The application of business principles to the operations of higher education institutions, combined with legislative changes requiring a higher level of self-funding (Currie, 2005; Grebennikov & Skaines, 2006; Scott, 2005; Soutar & Turner, 2002), has led institutions to focus on understanding student (customer) experiences for effective marketing and competitive advantage (Alcock et al., 2009; Krause, Hartley, James, & McInnis, 2005) despite that most fail to focus on international students.

When students identify themselves as consumers more than learners, not only do their expectations change, but the focus of educational providers changes as well. In the United States, for example, universities have shifted toward focusing more on amenity provision in order to gain a competitive advantage over their "competition." Doing so involves promoting services relating to quality-of-life, financial aid, and housing – all which were traditionally supra-educational provisions (Paswan & Ganesh, 2009). However, research has found the alignment of student expectations with lived experiences is extremely complex (Nelson, Kift, & Clarke, 2008), dynamic, and in transition as expectations are confirmed and new expectations are formed (Nelson et al., 2008). James' (2002) classification of student expectations into specific expectations (i.e. value for money, or personal significance) and timed expectations (i.e. short- vs. long-term expectations).

This approach distinguishes between the types of expectations a student might have, but does not comment extensively on the relative importance of the different types of expectations. For example, are long-term expectations such as career goals more important than short-term expectations such as campus facilities? Although a number of studies (Dalgleish & Chan, 2005; Krause et al., 2005) have found differences in expectations between cultures, academic achievement, as well as original expectations verses subsequent perception of overall experience (Ahmad, 2006), the researchers pointed out student expectations might or might not be aligned with the goals of higher education (James, 2002). Thus, disjunction between student expectations and experiences might even be a positive, liberating, component of education (Krause et al., 2005; James, 2002). Finally, it is not simply expectations students have of themselves that affects outcomes. Rather, the expectations academic staff hold for students also affects student experiences (Kingston & Forland, 2008). In brief, student expectations and experiences are shaped and influenced by a complex web of social psychological and structural factors that form a dialectical relationship which is difficult to deconstruct. To the extent that international students are increasingly required to use CMC as a method for obtaining a university education, it is increasingly important that understanding the socio-demographic characteristics of this unique sub-group of students is prioritized. Understanding if and how the cultural backgrounds of international students affect their perceptions of education will enable universities to create more effective learning environments, particularly if CMC-related educational materials continue to be used as an alternative to, or augmentation of face-to-face classroom environments.

METHODOLOGY

Sample, Response Rate, and Survey

In Session 2 of 2009, an invitation to complete an anonymous online survey was distributed via email to all international onshore undergraduate students (N=2,538) enrolled at each of CSU's regional campuses (N=1,397) and study centres (N=1,141). Onshore locations consisted of five primary regional campuses in the state of New South Wales (NSW), three smaller regional campuses, and two metropolitan study centres – one in Victoria, and the other in NSW.

The survey contained 36 open- and close-ended questions that enabled the collection of both qualitative and quantitative data. Along with a range of demographic and experience-based questions, six multiple-question items were used to generate attitudinal responses for two 6-point Likert scales ("strongly disagree-strongly agree" and "not important-extremely important") and one 4-point scale (low importance-high importance). After four weeks, the online survey was closed. A total of 139 surveys were completed, representing a 5.5% response rate. Consequently, the findings reported in this chapter are indicative of the perceptions of onshore international students who completed the survey and cannot be generalised as representative of the entire population. The survey is the first to provide such data for Australia and the insights yielded are informative for current international academic literature, university policy and future research.

FINDINGS

This chapter provides a demographic profile of the sample and presents findings related to international students' perceptions about the factors involved with

- Selecting an international institution of higher education
- The expectations held regarding the course/ program and academic environment
- The type and quality of communication and interaction experienced
- Beliefs regarding their cultural fit within local communities.

Demographic Profile: Gender, Age, and Country of Origin

The majority (68%/N=95) of completed surveys came from the metropolitan study centres. Forty-one students from regional campus locations returned their survey and a further 3 students failed to report their location. Despite that women comprised 52% of the international student population at CSU in 2008, men were far more likely to complete the survey (71% men versus 29% women). Eighty-four percent of respondents were between 20-29 years old. Only 7% of participants were over the age of 35. For most (68%) students, this instance was the first time they had enrolled in an educational course in Australia which, for 98%, was to pursue either a Bachelor's or Master's Degree. Although the majority (57%) were undergraduates, 29% came to pursue a master's degree and 12% to earn a Ph.D. (the remaining 2% were pursuing diplomas). For those completing advanced degrees, 39% came to Australia with a bachelor's degree and 18% already had a master's degree prior to arriving. Ninety percent of the students who completed this survey were the first in their family to study in Australia and 74% were the first generation to pursue higher education overseas.

By far, the most popular courses were in the fields of information technology (IT), accounting and business. Collectively, these three disciplines attracted over 76% (N=106) of the students who completed the survey. This finding is unsurprising given that more than 60% of all international students in Australia are enrolled in arts, business, humanities, law, services, or social sciences courses (see OECD, 2009, Chart C2.4. *Distribution of international students by field of education (2007)*). The remaining courses pursued included education, natural and medical sciences, policing, art history, and psychology, each of which attracted between one and eight students. For most (82%) of the students surveyed, Australia was their first choice for geographic location, and CSU was the preferred higher education institution for 63% of the respondents.

Students migrated from 31 countries, with the most originating from China, India, and Nepal respectively. The overall breakdown of students by region of origin was

- Asia – 74%
- E. Europe – 7%
- W. Europe – 5%

- N. America – 4%
- Undisclosed – 4%
- Pacific/Island – 3%
- S. America – 2%
- Africa – 1%

This demographic profile is consistent with broader global trends whereby Asian students, particularly Chinese students, represent the largest percentage of international students for countries contributing to OECD or UNESCO statistics. According to OECD (2009), Asian students account for 75% of all international students studying in Australia, Japan and Korea. Sixty-three percent of the students from Asia were pursuing a bachelor's degree. With the exception of one undergraduate from Africa, every other continent represented had more than 50% of their students pursuing a graduate degree, with the highest percentage of Ph.D. students coming from the Americas.

Descriptive Statistics and Qualitative Feedback

Students' Choice of Institution and Information Desired

The most important factor in international students' decision about where to study was the safety of the geographic location. Thirty-nine percent of respondents rated a country's degree of safety as "extremely important" when considering where to study. Second and third in importance were the cost of tuition (36%) and availability of part-time work (35%). Despite the popularity of tuition and part-time work availability in deliberations about where to study, only 12% of respondents received any information relating to the availability of part-time work. Student anxiety about finding employment was a prominent theme, "The job crisis is very important part because most student can't work within the area they stay. CSU must provide facilities in getting job for students of all categories" (Student 76).

Nevertheless, 92% found the material provided prior to commencement at least moderately useful. Qualitative feedback revealed a broad range of other information prospective students would like to receive. The majority of information sought related to lifestyle concerns: obtaining driver's licenses and visas, regional information and recreation, services and accommodation for family and children, work, and internships. As one student put it, "Aussie living cultures in general, life of overseas students in general" (Student 58). For others, the ability to locate those with similar cultural preferences was important, "Information on religion activities, prayer facilities, community from the same religion background, food/groceries shops availability" (Student 125). Academically, some students sought knowledge about the university's scientific facilities and expertise, where to study English, and coursework. For many subjects, the university's status was important, "The quality of study, reliable fees and the most important thing is the status of CSU" (Student 59). For others, the cost of higher education was a key concern: "increasing fee in every semester should be stop" (Student 120).

Interestingly, students appeared to make up their own minds about where to study as "agent's recommendation" was the least important factor for 33% of the sample – well ahead of not having friends or family in the country of destination (13%) and ability of future migration (11%) – despite that 52% first found out about their course of study from an agent. Newspaper advertisements, open days, and educational fairs produced the fewest recruits (8% collectively), whereas recommendations from friends or family (28%) and the university's website (17%) were responsible for providing many international students with information about the course in which they ultimately enrolled.

Students' Perceptions of Academic Quality

Expectations of University Life

Most international students (62%) reportedly expected to experience a high level of interaction with their lecturers and this expectation was highly important (66%) to the majority. However, while there existed a general expectation that the quality of education delivered would be high, as reflected by course materials (60%) and quality of teaching (62%), and this was very important to most (76%), only 32% expected to spend most of their learning time in physical classrooms and 57% expected to spend much study time working independently. These findings were anticipated given the number of higher degree research students and distance education courses offered by the university. Ninety-two percent stated having quality online learning resources was important to them, yet 97% expected good-quality on-campus facilities as well. Most (69%) expected to be able to find a job in their chosen career upon graduation, believed their degree would make this possible (64%) and 92% stated employment was an important goal. This factor indicates a pragmatic, utilitarian, rationale for obtaining degrees. Such utilitarian ideology extended to student expectations of subject content as well. For example, one student requested, "I wish that there should be some practicle subject or activities in subject because by learning and studying just theory no one will survive in his career so if there is a practicle scenario then it will easy to find job after graduation and also easy store in mind" (Student 133).

Consistent with the findings reported about choice of institution and information desired, international students expected a range of lifestyle accommodations. In particular, the majority (62%) expected to be able to afford the cost of living in Australia. Yet, even though part-time employment was an important consideration and concern for 81% of respondents, only 41% expected to easily gain such work. In contrast, the majority (57%) expected to be able to make friends with local Australians, with 87% saying this was important to them, and they expected to find accommodations easily.

Qualitative responses advising of other expectations international students had prior to commencement of their university degree were nearly all related to either social support expectations, either from administrators and peers, or teachers. Social support expectations entailed requests for student study groups (Student 12), research networks (Student 23), library services, and generally a "multicultural atmosphere" (Student 51). Unfortunately, as one student revealed, expectations of multiculturalism do not always up to individuals' ideals: "I was expecting the Australian people to be too friendly with the foreign students, but what I have seen here is otherwise" (Student 125).

Qualitative comments regarding the support expected from teachers ranged from requests to improve teacher" (Student 38), provide "more better lectures" (Student 59), to issues which capture key issues for delivery on higher education without enrolment caps: "class room are with more than 60-80 students and the lecture gets stress easily and don't give the proper answer and feedback that we are looking which decrease the quality of education" (Student 128). As one detailed comment revealed, insufficient support for international students directly relates not only to staff, but also student stress and perceptions of inequality:

CSU should have an oversea student special care system. There are few (2~3) students who studies Medical Science and they need a lot of help and understanding. For first year student, they should give us extra mark for exams or some special consideration. It's easy to fail one oversea student, but if they fail, they might have to go back to their country or transfer to another university. Some of us have a lot of money so failing doesn't mat-

ter to them, but student like me, I made a budget for 2 yrs, If I fail, It means I have to do part time job, but as we know it's really hard to make few grands during school, as if I can, I'm not sure I can concentrate in my studying. (Student 11).

When asked to comment on lifestyle aspects of their experience, nearly all comments reflected a need for changing social interactions and culture. For some students, the Australian drinking culture is problematic, "Most activities revolved around drinking...would be nice to have more student clubs and organizations that do not involve this sort of culture" (Student 23). For another, cultural norms relating to gender, sanitation, and food were sources of discomfort, "Bowen Hall for an established university would be considered close to poverty conditions where I am from. Unisex bathhouses in a university setting I feel are asking for problems to develop. Dining halls have an abhorrently limited selection available, the food is clean and edible but like Paul Hogan says, you can live on it" (Student 44). Other facilities some students expected were family-friendly accommodation (Student 59) and medical facilities because a "Medical doctor is not available on campus" (Student 112).

Still others noted issues with social interactions in general, such as the cost, "opportunities for social interaction require high expense in cash" (Student 70) and ethnic relations, "The weakest area I would like to say about CSU is the lack of social interaction among the students of different racial groups" (Student 122). Students' propensity to focus on the need for improved social interactions continued in other than to questions, with some articulating they, "didn't do any experience with local students, would be nice for a change" (Student 129) or desired, "more social activities, more foreigners friendly activities" (Student 122) and "more chance to interact with local peer students" (Student 47).

Differences in cultural norms featured in a range of other qualitative comments international students provided. For instance, customer service expectations were reflected in comments about the lack of emotional labour some staff put into their job, "staff are not smiling all the time as they were rendering a service" (Student 70). Other comments increasingly reflected a consumerist ideology regarding the delivery of higher education: "Library should be open till late until the classes finishes. i have no access to library when i need it in the evening classes" (Student 107); "CSU should open at 24 hours so student can study in study center" (Student 136); "outdoor activities, indoor activities like pool, billiard, snooker. There is no service and facilities given by CSU. It dose not have standerd level comparing to other universities" (Student 125). Increasingly, perhaps due to the instantaneous nature of our technocratic society, students articulated high expectations of service delivery, preferably of an immediate nature:

study materials are not provided by csu. we had to print it our selves. we expect them to be provided. assignments take along time to be marked. we expect a quick feed back. though there are lot of computer labs at times we have to stop our important assignments and leave the lab for a lecturer's lessons. that is really annoying. if there are computer labs they should be available for the students at anytime to do there assignments. specially while doing a online assignment we have to leave the lab. we as student dont expect that to happen in future. (Student 79)

Realities of University Life

Students' expectations prior to commencement of their degrees were contrasted with the realities associated with studying as international students. While respondents indicated a desire for more information relating to life in Australia, those who attended orientation activities reported the information received about "living in Australia" was less useful (29%) then the "study skills sessions" attended (63%), which related to such topics as plagiarism and essay writing, or online resource information (49%). Nevertheless, when asked what other information would have been useful, students again reported lifestyle-related details, listing items such as banking and regional/local information, how to make friends, learning the expectations of scientific work in Australia and how to receive support or assistance with living in communities.

Eighty percent of respondents believed they had sufficient English skills to succeed in their degrees, yet 43% found their assessment tasks were at a level of difficulty they had not expected. Further, 49% failed to agree their course materials were relevant to international students. Fifty-three percent of international students pursuing a bachelor's degree who responded to the query about whether "there are a good mix of students from different backgrounds" in their course "agreed" or "strongly agreed." However, satisfaction with the level of student diversity declined at the Master's level to 50% and dropped further to only 30% amongst responding Ph.D. students. International students who felt the most encouraged to participate in class discussions were in IT (82%) and medical science (75%), whereas students in education (66%) and accounting/business (60%) felt the most ambivalent or discouraged.

No bachelor's or Master's degree students reported the quality of their course as unimportant to them, and just one Ph.D. student believed course quality was unimportant, revealing the importance of student perceptions to course enrolment. When further analysed by specific course, the quality of the course was most important to students in policing and education, with 100% of the participating students in those courses reporting course quality as "very important" or "extremely important" to them. In contrast, students in accounting/business, information technology and medical science reported course quality as "slightly" or "not important" at all.

International students exhibited differing opinions regarding the helpfulness, versus quality, of experience they received from various staff members and resources. In particular, administrative staff was found to be more helpful or interested (76%) than academic staff (57%). Online resources were perceived to be reasonably helpful by most (68%), albeit of less use than the administrative staff. Unfortunately, just 61% thought their lecturers were knowledgeable on the subject matter they taught, 56% were dissatisfied with the overall quality of university facilities and 53% failed to agree that the level of library resources available was appropriate. Dissatisfaction with the quality of the University's library was further confirmed by the repeated request for better library facilities in open-ended questions that asked about other services that would improve their experience. "Put more books in liabrery" (Student 35) and "more textbooks in library" (Student 56) accompanied other students' (Student 52) vague articulations about the "liberary" (Student 135).

When asked to further comment on any aspects of their academic experience, aside from one student who noted there were, "very friendly, helpful, and polite academic staff" (Student 112). A number of students again took the opportunity to articulate their disapproval of the university's library resources, reputation, and quality of teaching. Comments such as, "improve acknowledge of lectures in their teaching areas" (Student 56) and "lecture to be more cooperative with the students about the study rather than saying 'I don't know'" (Student 125) demonstrate there is a need to decrease the gap between student expectations and experiences of academic quality. Students' perceptions of quality relate not only to discrepancies within institutions, but also reflect the need to benchmark performance across institutions:

Two things need to be improved: quality of academic staffs and the international reputation of CSU. First, quality of teaching staffs could have wide differecnes. Also, students notice that

*excellent lecturers are thinking abuot leaving...
Secondly, the reputation of CSU in the business
area is not so popular compare to Macquarie,
UNSW, Uni of Sydney. etc. I think this is something
CSU need to work on. (Student 87).*

At least four students felt sufficiently disgruntled to elaborate in some detail the dissatisfaction with the level of quality, cultural understanding and sensitivity exhibited towards international students:

- It is a good uni to study independently but only focus on local students. If international students are not able to keep up with class, then it should be language issues rather than lack of understanding. I wish lecturers could concern of this. To study in different language is not that easy! (Student 9)
- Im sorry to say that but the academic staff they are very bad with international student. Of course not all of them, but my supervisor is the worst Dr. ive ever seen. its really shame. im realy very disappointed and i'll report that back in my country. (Student 28)
- Bad experiecne. Quality of students in master course are quite unstable. Some students definitly are incapable (lack of knowledge of the course, and they are not motivated to study. They are in Master course becasue of the Permanent residency or other reasons.) to study the course but they are in the class which affect the motivated students. (Student 87)
- I was not told about a core subject, so as a result I haven't done it yet. One of my classes, the lecturer hadn't read the slides prior to giving the lecture. Most of the slides were skipped through. Another lecturer treated me like I was stupid. I have questions but don't know who to address them to so they never got asked. The es-

say writing workshop is laughable. For the structure of a reports it is good, for grammar not quite. (Student 92)

At a quantitative level, when student age was taken into account, those aged 35 and over expressed the greatest expectation for high levels of interaction with lecturers, 50% "strongly agree[ing]" in contrast with 0% of 18-19, 6% of 20-24, 12% of 25-29 and 20% of 30-34 which shows a linear progression in expectation of interaction with age. Likewise, the oldest students exhibited the highest expectations for quality of teaching, learning resources and facilities, as well as believed the majority of their study would be done independently. In other words, older students had the highest expectations of their experience. As expected, the youngest students, those 18-19, were most likely to expect much of their learning to occur within classroom environments, with 100% choosing "agree" in contrast with 60% or less of the other age groups having the same expectation of their higher education environment.

Realities of Living in Australia

A range of questions were asked to gauge international students' satisfaction with lifestyle concerns associated with living and studying in Australia. Overall, more than half of students agreed they felt they belonged to the university community, enjoyed their campus experience, had a good work-study balance, could afford living in Australia and had sufficient access to support when needed. However, when the data was examined more closely, a number of nuances emerged, especially in relation to geographic location.

Not one respondent "strongly agreed" that living in Australia was affordable and 57% were unable to find sufficient part-time employment. As expected, locating part-time work was harder for those living in regional/rural Australia than in the cities. Sixty-two percent of international students in regional Australia were unable to locate desirable levels of part-time employment in contrast with 43% of those in cities. Thus, the difference in urban/rural student attribution of importance to living expenses, with 32% of rural versus 17% of urban students noting such concerns were "extremely important" to them appears well-grounded. Still, overall, financial concerns were an ongoing issue for many international students in Australia.

Geographic location affected a range of socio-cultural factors in perceptions of satisfaction amongst international students. For example, 27% of respondents "strongly disagreed" or "disagreed" they felt they belonged to the university community in regional/rural Australia. In contrast, none of those studying at the metropolitan campuses expressed the same opinion. Interestingly, 67% of urban students felt they belonged to the university community. Given this factor, it is surprising that the majority (52%) of urban students did not enjoy their campus environment while the majority (52%) of regional/rural students said they did.

Lifestyle factors that students were least satisfied with included perceptions of a good interaction between local and international students, whereby 63% failed to agree this was achieved, and opportunities for social interaction, for which 54% did not agree there were many. In addition to overall dissatisfaction with these lifestyle factors, international students living in the city seemed to experience fewer challenges with these issues than their rural counterparts. Specifically, 62% of regional/rural students did not agree there were many opportunities for social interaction in contrast with 45% of those in urban centres. Yet, the interaction between local and international students was perceived to be worse among those in one metropolitan location than another, with 42% disagreeing or strongly disagreeing interactions were "good," in contrast with 17% in regional/rural Australia.

FUTURE TRENDS

In our global economy, international students today approach higher education with a broad range of expectations relating to academic and lifestyle amenities in the country where they pursue degrees. This research has found student expectations vary by age, location, culture and a range of other sociological and demographic variables. As universities seek to expand their global market, it is becoming increasingly important to prioritize understanding the unique needs and expectations individuals bring to the classroom, whether that is virtual, face-to-face or both. Historically, administrators have tended to focus on supra-academic factors, such as housing, finance and facilities, whilst academics concentrated on academic learning objectives. This research highlights neither alone is sufficient to guaranteeing international students achieve a positive and successful educational experience. Student dissatisfaction with any of a range of complex and interrelated academic and lifestyle factors can have deleterious impacts on both the individual and the institution's reputation and operation.

Researches in America (Paswan & Ganesh, 2009) have argued international students wish to be perceived holistically. Our findings confirm international students in Australia also desire (indeed, expect) a far-reaching array of amenities and services to be delivered at the highest level of quality. Therefore, institutions of higher education worldwide striving for excellence would do well to take a holistic approach to their provision of all services, if they indeed seek to retain or establish "brand loyalty" and satisfaction amongst their consumers/learners.

Over the past few years, cultural considerations have filtered into research about higher education. The research presented in this chapter adds to the growing body of literature highlighting the centrality of social interactions and cultural relativity in expectations, experiences and perceptions of satisfaction among university students.

Future trends analyses predict continuing growth in international student numbers globally. Thus, it is imperative that socio-cultural research continue and expand, not only to avoid repeating past mistakes, but to facilitate cultural understanding and improve inter-cultural relations.

Finally, with an awareness that increased use of CMC in educational settings may impact international students' expectations, perspectives and reactions to university life and the realities of living abroad, we recommend a number of best practices be developed. Although our recommended best practices are pedagogically driven, future researchers may wish to consider how such media may address an entire range of issues that accompany migration, such as homesickness or culture shock. Crucial to successful development and implementation of CMC, and moreover of central importance to fostering satisfaction, is the ability to take an integrated and holistic approach to supporting international students in higher education. Whether this entails using CMC for pedagogical imperatives or supporting interactions amongst locals and/or those back home, clear articulation of the resources available, support for their use and guidelines about best practice may work to alleviate culturally-driven anxieties and foster a more nurturing, inclusive environment.

Suggested Best Practices for Using CMC with On-Site International Students

In light of the research findings, this section offers a range of pedagogically-driven "best practices" for educators and administrators wishing to utilize CMC in their work with international, or other, students who are living away from their country of origin. As a cautionary note, we wish to advise that any use of CMC for teaching and learning purposes should be informed by the desired learning outcomes. Some authors have been critical of the push for more CMC-based practices and have

noted the delivery mode is irrelevant as long as the teacher uses best practice (Larson & Chung-Hsien, 2009). With this idea in mind, along with our conclusions about cultural considerations, we offer six best practice suggestions for using CMC with on-site international students:

1. Ensure there is adequate training available for both staff and students to support use of the designated CMC tools that takes into account varying levels of prior experience with technology. Computer literacy varies widely by gender and age (Cohen & Kennedy, 2007). As such, the digital divide (Homes, Hughes, & Julian, 2007) that exists within and across nations and individuals requires consideration.

2. Inform students clearly about what tools will be used and the purpose each tool will serve. Setting foundational guidelines about appropriate and acceptable modes of communication for dialogue occurring between teaching-administrative staff, teacher-students and/or student-student is likely to reduce confusion or role ambiguity.

3. Ensure staff participating or assisting with such educational activities have a level of cultural competency about the cultures represented in the cohort they are serving. Therefore, staff will have sufficiently developed social capital (Coleman, 1988) to ensure their pedagogy considers the cultural differences in communication and interpersonal interaction norms likely to arise among staff and/or students.

4. Structure group work so each group contains a mix of international and domestic students when collaboration is driving the use of CMC. This practice will facilitate multiculturalism. Sociologically, multiculturalism refers to interaction amongst cultures and politically multiculturalism remains the preferred practice guiding Australian

government immigration policy (Holmes et al., 2007).

5. Take into consideration the time it takes students from different cultural backgrounds to use CMC, such as those for whom English is a second language (ESOL) who may require more time to digest information and integrate it into their existing knowledge base. The use of CMC has been found to encourage increased "time on task," a key consideration for ESOL, while increased "time on task" was the only variable significantly associated with the use of CMC and better academic performance (U.S. Department of Education, Office of Planning, Evaluation, and Policy Development, 2009).

6. Ensure the selection of tools used is sufficiently diverse to cater to the vast majority's learning needs. For instance, applications such as Skype and webinars may not be well received by the more reflexive learners who prefer to view proceedings and think about content before engaging with teaching staff and peers. On the other hand, tools should be not so diverse that they promote confusion among students about how to access content and/or communicate with staff or peers.

Readers can use these best practices both in creating or modifying classes for online delivery to internationally diverse student groups or as the foundation for future research on the topic of CMC in global contexts.

Suggested Best Practices for Developing Online Classes/Learning Environments for Internationally Dispersed Students

In addition to the best practices noted in the previous section, a range of practices also need to be considered when working online with internationally dispersed students. This section offers six best practices for developing online classes or learning environments when teaching students who are geographically dispersed, particularly internationally dispersed:

1. Consider international variations in Internet speeds when designing the CMC platform of a subject or course. For example, web-hosted quizzes may not be appropriate when you have a cohort with low bandwidth or an unreliable Internet connection. In such instances, resources that can be downloaded quickly and used offline may be more suitable.

2. Develop a strategy to account for differences in time zones when planning synchronous communications that encompass multiple zones. This may involve rotating the timing of the synchronous session or recording the synchronous session and encouraging those unable to attend to comment via an alternative asynchronous mode at a later time.

3. Create multimedia resources that are culturally sensitive to national laws. In other words, make sure that the viewing or downloading of learning materials will not contravene any laws for all countries involved. For example, an anthropology vodcast that included images of naked or semi-naked women undertaking tribal ceremonies may be deemed unsuitable for viewing in some countries.

4. Provide CMC-related technical support for staff and students that is as flexible as the learning environment. For example, at CSU, IT support is only available between 9am-5pm Australian Eastern Standard Time. This fails to meet the needs not only of internationally dispersed students but also of some staff teaching outside of standard business time, especially to non-traditional students. Similarly, it is important to consider the mode used to provide support. Offering a technical support service that

requires telephone communication in order to troubleshoot is unlikely to well serve individuals internationally dispersed. Although a 24-hour support centre would be ideal, alternatives, such as a regularly updated frequently-asked-questions page, notices of known issues and a policy of responding to international students' emailed requests for support within a 24-hour response time should comprise the minimum standards provided.

5. Be conscious of local jargon and irregular uses of language and remove them from all learning materials to ensure comprehension by an international audience. Where possible, make a conscious effort to include international examples, perhaps some provided by past students if applicable, to foster greater inclusiveness and give all students a deeper understanding of the learning material being presented.

6. Do not be afraid of professional debate, or the exercise of culturally-relative differences being acted out in a culturally-sensitive fashion. The presence of off-shore students in a domestic cohort should be embraced and international dialogue and debate (where relevant) encouraged. This may provide students not only with a novel of engaging with learning material from diverse points-of-view, but is likely to foster development of graduate attributes, such communication skills in international relations, which may be invaluable in global workplaces yet unpronounced in primary learning objectives.

Again, these practices can serve as a foundation for the development of more effective online learning environments for culturally diverse or globally dispersed students. They can also serve as foci for engaging in further research in the area of globalizing online education.

CONCLUSION

This study set out to investigate the expectations and experiences of international students pursuing higher education degrees within the context of Australian culture. When expectations were compared with "real life" experiences, gaps emerged in levels of satisfaction with

*   Lecturer interest in students' progress
*   Course materials relevant to international students
*   Ability to obtain sufficient part-time employment
*   Appropriate levels of multiculturalism in classroom environments
*   Adequate opportunities for social interaction between local and international students
*   Ability to achieve good interactions between local and international students

Students' age and geographic location, particularly in urban or regional/rural Australia, further affected levels of satisfaction on a range of measures. In total, 15% of respondents expressed dissatisfaction with their campus environment and did not feel as if they belonged to the university community. Given that prior studies indicate levels of cultural adaptation have implications for international students' overall experience (Brown, 2008; Campbell & Li, 2008; Sawir et al., 2008), this situation remains an area for improvement. Regional/rural Australia has long been noted for its "country mindedness" and lack of amenities in contrast with its metropolitan cities (Ragusa, 2010b). Those subjects most dissatisfied with the university's facilities were studying at regional, non-metropolitan campuses. Rurality continues to pose challenges for meeting amenity provision and service delivery expectations. International students found attainment of part-time employment hardest in regional/rural Australia and were the most dissatisfied with university facilities at regional campuses. They expressed the greatest dissatisfaction with perceived community "fit" and felt country Australia offered few opportunities for social interaction.

Students at regional/rural campuses also placed greater importance on shorter term expectations, such as making friends with local Australians and being able to afford the cost of living, whereas urban students prioritized long-term expectations of gaining employment and careers post-graduation. This yields limited support for James (2002) findings. The desire or expectation to have degrees materialize into discipline-specific careers upon graduation indicates a pragmatic, utilitarian rationale for international students' pursuit of higher education in this study. Nevertheless, 98% of respondents reportedly expected to obtain increased general knowledge and learning skills from their efforts. Age also affected student satisfaction. International students aged 30-34 were least satisfied with their academic and lifestyle experiences in the Australian higher education system, with 57% stating it was "below expectations." In contrast, the youngest and oldest students, those between 18-19 years of age and those individuals age 35 or older were the most satisfied, with 100% and 89% respectively noting it either met or exceeded their expectations. These findings exist in contrast with Krause et al. (2005) who found age was not a significant factor in determining student satisfaction.

This research confirms the general trends reported by the OECD in 2009 relating to the demographic composition of international students in Australia and factors affecting their decision about where to study. Safety, English language, tuition fees and living costs, immigration policies, and institutional reputation all factored into the surveyed students considerations. At an institutional level, qualitative comments revealed the importance of high-quality teaching and library facilities and identified socio-cultural factors deemed important by international students. Similar to Huang's (2008) survey of international students in the U.K.

which found 39% were motivated by friends' recommendations, our research confirmed the vital importance of friends or family recommendations to institutional selection and course decisions. However, whereas students seeking to study in the U.K. identified the country's attractiveness as a tourist destination, international students in Australia prioritised safety and economics over tourism.

The centrality of importance social interactions assume as a component of the overall higher education experience cannot be overstated. In addition to high academic expectations and concerns about the English language, international students in the U.K. (Huang, 2008) and Australia identified social interactions as a key component of their education, expected to make local friends and have cultural experiences, and though institutional policy and staff should be sensitive to differing cultural needs. In the U.S., research found "social interaction augmenters," i.e. opportunities for international students to interact with American students and Americans in general, enhanced international students' university loyalty (Paswan & Ganesh, 2009). Yet, social integration across cultures remains an obstacle, with inadequate opportunities for social interaction reported by the majority in rural locations and many in the city reporting the existing interactions were poor in quality. Just as 80% of international students in the U.K. were dissatisfied with integration levels between international and domestic students (Huang, 2008), between half and two-thirds in our study were dissatisfied with the cultural diversity in their courses. These findings are problematic.

In Britain, research into international students' experiences is said to offer "a strong message to British universities that international students are keen to integrate with domestic students but dissatisfied with current efforts made by universities in this direction" (Huang, 2008, p. 1014). This chapter reveals the same for Australia. Despite national variation, research outcomes collectively make a compelling case for the underwhelming rate at which institutions of higher education have met the expectations of international students and advocates prioritizing re-examination of the unique academic and socio-cultural needs and desires of international students in developed countries globally to improve the disparity between expectation and reality, as learners, customers and social beings.

As universities increasingly adopt CMC as a systemic component of higher education's infrastructure, learning and teaching technologies need to be planned, included and evaluated in a fashion that takes into consideration cultural relativity. The high expectations international students hold for both the provision of quality learning materials and the broader social environment were articulated by many participants. Yet, satisfaction varied for structural and cultural aspects of the Australian learning environment analysed. Students' expectations and perceived realities of university life hold many insights for the enhancement of CMC technologies used in higher education.

That only 32% of international students expected to spend most of their learning time in physical classrooms evidences widespread social change in higher education norms and practices. With the increased adoption of CMC technologies, as required or supplemental learning materials, it is timely universities also prioritize identifying and exceeding the socio-cultural expectations that accompany a culturally diverse student body. Admission of international students, in the opinion of the researchers, also entails a commitment to facilitate dialogue and the interactions in culturally diverse learning environments in both face-to-face and virtual classrooms.

ACKNOWLEDGMENT

The authors would like to acknowledge the contribution made by each international student who took the time to share their thoughts and recommendations as research participants. It is our hope the insights you shared will effect positive social change via improving cross-cultural understanding and increasing the delivery of academic excellence. We also wish to warmly thank Dr. Heather Cavanagh, Sub-Dean International, for her support of this chapter.

REFERENCES

Adeoye, B., & Wentling, R. (2007). The relationship between national culture and the usability of an e-learning system. *International Journal on E-Learning*, *6*(1), 119–146.

Ahmad, S. (2006). International student experiences: The voice of Indian students. Paper presented at the Australian International Education Conference. WA: Perth. Retrieved August 4, 2010, from www.idp.com/ aiec

Alcock, C., Cooper, J., Kirk, J., & Oyler, K. (2009). *The tertiary student experience: A review of approaches based on the first cycle of AUQA audits 2002-2007*. Australian Universities Quality Agency.

Australian Bureau of Statistics. (2008). *Education export statistics*. Retrieved November 10,

Australian Education International. (2009). *International student data for 2009*. Retrieved November 10, 2009, from http://www.aei.gov.au/ AEI/ MIP/ Statistics/ StudentEnrolmentAndVisaStatistics/ 2009/ Default.htm#Pivot

Australian Education International. (2010, March). *International student enrolments in higher education*. Retrieved August 4, 2010, from http://aei.gov.au/ AEI/ PublicationsAndResearch/ Snapshots/ 20100416HE_pdf.pdf

Australian Education International. (2010, May). *Export income to Australia from education services in 2009*. Retrieved August 9, 2010, from http://aei.gov.au/ AEI/ PublicationsAndResearch/ Snapshots/2010052810_pdf.pdf

Barjis, J. (2003). An overview of virtual university studies: Issues, concepts, trends. In Albaloshie, F. (Ed.), *Virtual education: Cases in learning and teaching technologies* (pp. 1–20). Hershey, PA: IRM Press.

Bohm, A., et al. (2002). *Global student mobility 2025: Forecasts of the global demand for international higher education*. Retrieved August 4, 2010, from http://www.aiec.idp.com/ PDF/ Bohm_2025 Media_p.pdf

Bowles, M. S. (2004). *Relearning to e- learn: Strategies for electronic learning and knowledge*. Carlton, Victoria, Australia: Melbourne University Press.

Brooks, D. W., Nolan, D. E., & Gallagher, S. M. (2001). *Web-teaching: A guide to designing interactive teaching for the World Wide Web* (2nd ed.). New York, NY: Kluwer Academic/Plenum.

Brown, L. (2008). The incidence of study-related stress in international students in the initial stage of the international sojourn. *Journal of Studies in International Education, 12*(1), 5–28. doi:10.1177/1028315306291587

Brownlee, J., Walker, S., Lennox, S., Exley, B., & Pearce, S. (2009). The first-year university experience: Using personal epistemology to understand effective learning and teaching in higher education. *Higher Education, 58*, 599–618. doi:10.1007/ s10734-009-9212-2

Campbell, J., & Li, M. (2008). Asian student's voices: An empirical study of Asian student's learning experiences at a New Zealand university. *Journal of Studies in International Education, 12*(4), 375–395. doi:10.1177/1028315307299422

Castells, M. (2000). *The Information Age* (*Vol. 1-3*). Oxford, UK: Blackwell.

Charles Sturt University. (2009). *Charles Sturt University internationalisation strategy*. Retrieved November 10, 2009, from http://www.csu.edu.au/ division/ oir/ docs/ strategy.pdf

Clemson, N. (2009). *2008 progress rates report*. NSW, Australia: Charles Sturt University, Office of Planning & Audit.

Cohen, R., & Kennedy, P. (2007). *Global sociology*. London, UK: Macmillan.

Coleman, J. S. (1988). Social capital in the creation of human capital. *American Journal of Sociology, 94*, S95–S120. doi:10.1086/228943

Crampton, A., Vanniasinkam, T., & Milic, N. (2010). Vodcasts! How to unsuccessfully implement a new online tool. In Ragusa, A. T. (Ed.), *Interaction in communication technologies & virtual learning environments: Human factors (preface)*. Hershey, PA: IGI Global. doi:10.4018/978-1-60566-874-1.ch008

Currie, J. (2005). *Organisational culture of Australian universities: Community or corporate?* Paper presented at the 2005 HERDSA Annual Conference. NSW, Sydney, 3-6 July.

Dalgleish, D. C., & Chan, M. A. (2005). *Expectations and reality - International student reflections on studying in Australia*. Paper presented at the Australian International Education Conference Retrieved 10 November 2009, from http://www.aiec.idp.com/ past_papers/ 2005.aspx

Department of Education. Employment & Workplace Relations. (2009). *End of year summary of international student enrolment data – Australia – 2009*. Retrieved August 4, 2010, from http://aei.gov.au/ AEI/ Statistics/ StudentEnrolmentAndVisaStatistics/ 2009/ MonthlySummary_Dec09_pdf. pdf

Gerdes, H., & Mallinckrod, B. (1994). Emotional, social, and academic adjustment of college students: A longitudinal study of retention. *Journal of Counseling and Development, 72*, 281–288.

Gillard, J. (2009). *International education – Its contribution to Australia.* Retrieved August 4, 2010, from http://www.deewr.gov.au/ Ministers/ Gillard/ Media/ Speeches/ Pages/ Article_090527 _093411.aspx

Grebennikov, L., & Skaines, I. (2006). *International students in higher education: Comparative analysis of student surveys on international student experience in higher education.* Paper presented at the Australasian Association for Institutional Research. Retrieved November 10, 2009, from http://www.aair.org.au/ 2006Papers/ Skaines.pdf

1994 Group [UK Universities] (2007). *Enhancing the student experience: Policy report.*

Hirst, P., & Thompson, G. (1996). *Globalisation in question: The international economy and the possibilities of governance.* London, UK: Polity.

Holmes, D., Hughes, K., & Julian, R. (2007). *Australian sociology: A changing society* (2nd ed.). NSW, Australia: Pearson Education Australia.

Huang, R. (2008). Mapping educational tourists' experience in the UK: Understanding international students. *Third World Quarterly, 29*(5), 1003–1020. doi:10.1080/01436590802106247

James, R. (2002). *Students' changing expectations of higher education and the consequences of mismatches with reality.* Retrieved October 12, 2010, from http://www1.oecd.org/ publications/ e-book/ 8902041E.pdf

Kingston, E., & Forland, H. (2008). Bridging the gap in expectations between international students and academic staff. *Journal of Studies in International Education, 12*(2), 204–220. doi:10.1177/1028315307307654

Krause, K.-L., Hartley, R., James, R., & McInnis, C. (2005). *The first year experience in Australian universities: Findings from a decade of national studies.*

Larson, D. G., & Chung-Hsien, S. (2009). Comparing student performance: Online versus blended versus face to face. *Journal of Asynchronous Learning Networks, 13*(1), 31–42.

Lee, J. J., & Rice, C. (2007). Welcome to America? International student perceptions of discrimination. *Higher Education, 53*, 381–409. doi:10.1007/ s10734-005-4508-3

Monolescu, D., Schifter, C. C., & Greenwood, L. (2004). *The distance education evolution: Issues and case studies.* Hershey, PA: Information Science Publishing.

Nelson, K., Kift, S., & Clarke, J. (2008). *Expectations and realities for first year students at an Australian university.* Paper presented at the First Year in Higher Education Conference 2008. Retrieved November 10, 2009, from http://www. fyhe.qut.edu.au/ past_papers/ papers08/ FYHE08/ content/ pdfs/ 6a.pdf

Organisation for Economic Co-operation and Development. (2009). *Education at a glance 2009.* OECD. Retrieved February 22, 2010, from www. oecd.org/ publishing

Palloff, R. M., & Pratt, K. (2001). *Lessons from the cyberspace classroom: The realities of online teaching.* San Francisco, CA: Jossey-Bass Inc.

Paswan, A. K., & Ganesh, G. (2009). Higher education institutions: Satisfaction and loyalty among international students. *Journal of Marketing for Higher Education, 19*, 65–84. doi:10.1080/08841240902904869

Perrucci, R., & Hu, H. (1995). Satisfaction with social and educational experiences among international graduate students. *Research in Higher Education, 36*(4), 491–508. doi:10.1007/BF02207908

Ragusa, A. T. (2007). The impact of socio-cultural factors in multi-cultural virtual communication environments: A case example from an Australian university's provision of distance education in the global classroom. In St. Amant, K. (Ed.), *Linguistic and cultural online communication issues in the global age* (pp. 306–327). Hershey, PA: Idea Group Inc. doi:10.4018/978-1-59904-213-8.ch018

Ragusa, A. T. (2009). Asynchronous communication forums: Improving learning & social engagement among distance education students. In Dumova, T. (Ed.), *Handbook of research on social interaction technologies and collaboration software* (pp. 181–193). Hershey, PA: IGI Global. doi:10.4018/978-1-60566-368-5.ch017

Ragusa, A. T. (2010a). Communication and social interactions in a technologically-mediated world. In Ragusa, A. T. (Ed.), *Interaction in communication technologies & virtual learning environments: Human factors* (pp. 1–6). Hershey, PA: IGI Global. doi:10.4018/978-1-60566-874-1.ch001

Ragusa, A. T. (2010b). Seeking trees or escaping traffic? Socio-cultural factors and tree change migration in Australia. In Luck, G., Black, R., & Race, D. (Eds.), *Demographic change in rural landscapes: What does it mean for society and the environment?* (pp. 71–99). New York, NY: Springer. doi:10.1007/978-90-481-9654-8_4

Ramsay, S., Jones, E., & Barker, M. (2007). Relationship between adjustment and support types: Young and mature-aged local and international first-year university students. *Higher Education*, *54*, 247–265. doi:10.1007/s10734-006-9001-0

Sawir, E., Marginson, S., Deumert, A., Nyland, C., & Ramia, G. (2008). Loneliness and international students: An Australian study. *Journal of Studies in International Education*, *12*(2), 181–203.

Schifter, C. (2004). Faculty participation in DE programs: Practices and plans. In Monolescu, D., Schifter, C. C., & Greenwood, L. (Eds.), *The distance education evolution: Issues and case studies* (pp. 1–21). Hershey, PA: Information Science Publishing. doi:10.4018/9781591401209.ch002

Scott, G. (2005). *Promoting student retention and productive learning in universities: Research and action at UWS 2004-05*. Unpublished manuscript. Office of Planning and Quality. Penrith, NSW: University of Western Sydney.

Secretariat, I. E. A. A. (2009). *Australian senate inquiry into international education*. Retrieved July 4, 2009, from www.ieaa.org.au/ NewsArticles/ NewsArticle.asp? articleNo=38

Simpson, K., & Tan, W. S. (2009). A home away from home? Chinese student evaluations of an overseas study experience. *Journal of Studies in International Education*, *13*(1), 5–21. doi:10.1177/1028315308317694

Soutar, G. N., & Turner, J. P. (2002). Students' preference for university: A conjoint analysis. *International Journal of Educational Management*, *16*(1), 40–45. doi:10.1108/09513540210415523

Sovic, S. (2009). High-bye friends and the herd instinct: International and home students in the creative arts. *Higher Education*, *58*, 747–761. doi:10.1007/s10734-009-9223-z

St. Amant, K. (2007). Online education in an age of globalization: Foundational perspectives and practices for technical communication instructors and trainers. *Technical Communication Quarterly*, *16*(1), 13–30. doi:10.1207/s15427625tcq1601_2

Universities Australia. (2009). *Enhancing the student experience & student safety: A position paper*. Canberra, Australia: Universities Australia.

U.S. Department of Education, Office of Planning, Evaluation, and Policy Development. (2009). *Evaluation of evidence-based practices in online learning: A meta-analysis and review of online learning studies.* Washington, D.C., 2009. Retrieved April 6, 2010, from www.ed.gov/ about/ offices/ list/ opepd/ ppss/ reports.html

Volet, S. E., & Ang, G. (1998). Culturally mixed groups on international campuses: An opportunity for inter-cultural learning. *Higher Education Research & Development, 17*(1), 5–23. doi:10.1080/0729436980170101

Wadsworth, B. C., Hecht, M. L., & Jung, E. (2008). The role of identity gaps, discrimination, and acculturation in international students' educational satisfaction in American classrooms. *Communication Education, 57*(1), 64–87. doi:10.1080/03634520701668407

Wilcox, P., Winn, S., & Fyvie-Gauld, M. (2005). It was nothing to do with the university, it was just the people: The role of social support in the first-year experience of higher education. *Studies in Higher Education, 30*(6), 707–722. doi:10.1080/03075070500340036

Zhao, C. M., Kuh, G. D., & Carini, R. M. (2005). A comparison of international student an American student engagement in effective educational practices. *The Journal of Higher Education, 76*(2), 209–231. doi:10.1353/jhe.2005.0018

KEY TERMS AND DEFINITIONS

Computer Mediated Communications: Social interactions which are technologically assisted.

International Students: Individuals who move to a country for higher education.

Culture: Values, ideas, questions, and norms which are shared by members of a group.

Multiculturalism: Sociological concept describing social interactions among different cultures.

Culture Shock: The experience of norm violation when members of one culture come into contact with other cultures.

Globalization: Complex system of formal and informal interactions among nations on economic, cultural, political, and social issues.

Student Experience: Range of standardized satisfaction measures for evaluating higher education processes in Australia.

Educational Technologies: Range of information technologies used in higher education.

Utilitarian Ideology: Belief that practical objectives are the most worthwhile.

Quantitative Research: Social research methodology that produces numerical data for statistical analysis.

Chapter 23
Computer–Mediated Cross–Cultural Communication:
Creating Cultural Exchange through Articulated Studies

William Klein
University of Missouri - St. Louis, USA

Bernard E. La Berge
Modern College of Business and Science, UAE

ABSTRACT

This chapter describes a case of Internet-mediated collaboration between writing classes in the U.S. and in Oman. In the chapter, the authors examine the challenges they experiences including differences in time, culture, academic preparation, language skills, and technological capabilities and literacies. The authors also discuss how such challenges let do their rethinking pedagogical practices and uses of technology and through the structure of institutional affiliation agreements.

INTRODUCTION

Before the development of web-based learning technologies, cross-cultural academic exchanges in higher education were severely constrained by time and resources. For example, the typical international exchange – the semester study abroad – would send students across the globe to learn while immersed in a different culture. These exchanges could take a single semester or even two and it could encompass sixteen to thirty-two weeks of regular semester study or involve a four to ten week summer session. Such experiences, however, can be quite expensive, and for some students – especially self-supporting students and students with families of their own – participation in such programs can be difficult if not impossible. Some students simply cannot afford to pay

DOI: 10.4018/978-1-60960-833-0.ch023

the tuition associated with these study abroad programs, and because of ever shrinking budgets at colleges and universities, financial aid is not always available to help them cover such costs. Other students cannot afford to take the time off and sacrifice the income they might make from work, and still others cannot spend that much time away from their responsibilities and dependents at home. Yet, the value of providing access for students to other cultures, especially through structured, reflective learning experiences, to improve cultural sensitivity and meaningful global citizenship is great and certainly worth the effort (Anderson, Lawton, Rexeisen, & Hubbard, 2006; Boehm & Aniola-Jedrzejek, 2006; Pedersen, 2010). This chapter examines how educational institutions can use online media to provide students with viable and cost- and time-effective options for engaging with individuals in other cultures in a way that provides for meaningful educational experiences.

A CONTEXT FOR CONSIDERATION

Like other institutions, the University of Missouri-St. Louis (UMSL) in the U.S. and the Modern College of Business and Science (MCBS) in Oman, have been experiencing rising budget cuts, and these cuts have threatened opportunities for cultural exchanges. As a result, we – an UMSL English professor and an MCBS Dean and Writing Professor – looked for a collaborative solution. We wanted to find a way to make cultural exchanges less expensive and more accessible. Within this context, an online writing class in which students could gain first-hand experience interacting with people from another culture seemed quite obvious to us. Cross-cultural communication in educational settings, however, was not one of our specialties. Thus, we had limited knowledge of its literature. We did, however, have a great deal of experience with writing instruction, and one of us had experience in online education in writing classes. For these reasons, we decided to plunge ahead with

a plan to collaborate on something that would be interesting and beneficial for our students in the U.S. and Oman, as well as provide them with an inexpensive and convenient option to engage with individuals from other cultures.

Traditional semester study abroad formats are prescribed in part by the distance between institutions and the related travel time, expense, and convenience associated with traveling to a different land. Because of these factors, a U.S. student studying an academic subject in Italy might as well stay in Italy for an entire semester and take advantage of cultural experiences outside the classroom because. Otherwise, it would be too expensive, too time-consuming, and too inconvenient to send the student abroad for only a week here and/or a week there. If, however, the constraint of distance and its related costs were removed, other possibilities for different cross-cultural experiences could open up.

Within this context, online learning technologies and practices offer faculty opportunities to create learning experiences that can take place in the traditional formats of a semester or an academic year – or within a *fraction* of a semester, such as within a few weeks or days, or at several times at strategic points during a semester. The costs associated with such experiences, moreover, could be minimal. An online option means that students would not have to engage each other on a continuous 24/7 basis, but could instead interact at select times. Such interactions could be synchronous or asynchronous, depending on the learning strategies needed to produce the desired learning outcomes. These options mean that students who have full-time jobs or have dependents could meaningfully experience other cultures and still earn their livings and pick up their children from school.

Granted, such situations are not necessarily perfect. Online cultural exchanges cannot replicate face-to-face study abroad experiences where total immersion in the culture and place provides unique thickness and depth. Computer-mediated educational experiences can, however, be rich and valuable in their own ways (Rivera & Rice, 2002; Mentzer, Cryan, Teclehaimanot, 2007; Tallent-Runnels et al., 2006). In fact, according to a June 2009 U.S. Department of Education report on the effectiveness of online learning, instructional strategies have more influence on the effectiveness of online learning than the online medium of delivery (Means, Toyama, Murphy, Bakia, Jones, 2009). The report concludes by noting, "on average, students in online learning conditions performed better than those receiving face-to-face instruction" (Means et al., 2009, *ix*).

INSTITUTIONAL RELATIONSHIPS

The relationship underlying the items discussed here was structured through legally binding agreements and a history of collaboration. These facts proved to be critical in the online cultural exchange developed between the U.S. and Oman. UMSL, a public research university located the most populous metropolitan area in Missouri (U.S.), is the largest university in the region and is the third largest in the state of Missouri. UMSL offers several degree programs that are nationally ranked as being in the top twenty within their respective fields. Although the student body represents 49 states and 68 countries, 87% of students come from the surrounding area, and the average student is 27 years of age. Seventy seven percent of UMLS students are Caucasian, and 23% claim other ethnic backgrounds. Additionally, many UMSL students have full-time jobs and have families of their own (Student Body Profile, 2010).

MCBS is a private college in Muscat, the most populous and economically significant metropolitan area in the Sultanate of Oman on the Arabian Peninsula. Oman is a Muslim country, yet it is very oriented toward doing business. As a result, Oman tends to be more tolerant of Western culture than most of its neighbors in the region. MCBS is fully licensed and sanctioned by Oman's Ministry of Higher Education, but because it is a private institution, it has some flexibility that other institutions in Oman do not. These include a strong English as a Second Language (ESL) program that is designed to support the college's emphasis on business, international business, and computer science. The student body of MCBS is made up of students from Muscat and from throughout rural Oman. A significant number of students also come from India, Pakistan, and other Middle Eastern countries. Some students have British English language skills, while others acquire what English-language skills can through the College's ESL program.

Through its Center for International Studies, UMSL entered into affiliation and articulation agreements with MCBS in 1996, when MCBS was first established (see About MCBS, 2010). These agreements made it possible for UMSL to extend its educational agenda into the Middle East, and to provide its students with a mechanism for cultural explorations. For MCBS, these agreements were primarily focused on institution building, curriculum development, and quality assurance. Through these agreements, MCBS was able to develop its curricula and programs on UMSL examples and offer UMSL-approved courses and programs taught by both visiting UMSL faculty and local MCBS professors. The agreements also made it possible to offer quality private higher education in Oman, but to do so in a way that is not as encumbered by governmental control as other colleges. Additionally, these agreements enabled the professional and cultural development of faculty and staff, and made it possible for the study abroad program to develop and mature. As a result of these achievements, MCBS governing body awarded the College provisional accreditation in 2004, and MCBS passed its first successful quality audit in 2009.

PROJECTS AND OUTCOMES

Within the context of this UMSL-MCBS relationship, our project involved using UMSL's course management system to develop a Business Writing course at each institution. The courses, in turn, would take place through a shared, online learning environment involving students from both universities. The idea was that courses at UMSL and at MCBS would require students to use online media to discuss and respond to international business case studies from their different cultural perspectives. Because the local time in St. Louis was ten hours behind that of Muscat, and because the semester at MCBS was to begin five weeks after UMSL's began, the most convenient way to organize this project would be through asynchronous exchanges and that would last over a maximum window of six weeks.

We, the participating instructors, anticipated that the outcomes of these exchanges would be straightforward. We also assumed students would learn about communication genres common in doing business, and that they would have the opportunity to write and learn under the guidance of their professors. Moreover, we expected students to experience some of the cultural dimensions of international business and that through these encounters, students could examine (and perhaps to negotiate) the language and tone of international communications with counterparts in another culture. To facilitate these objectives, the project would feature frequent peer-review interactions. Such interactions, in turn, would allow students to offer each other feedback that could help them learn how to make their writing more appropriate for an international audience.

We saw that there were opportunities for other possible outcomes, and we hoped that these might also materialize. First, the Business Writing course had been a challenge to MCBS' affiliation with UMSL for some time, and we hoped that our project might help improve relations among the two entities. In essence, the challenges relating to the class had to do with scheduling and timing. According to the articulation agreement between the two institutions, MCBS must offer courses that satisfy all UMSL degree requirements. The UMSL Business Writing course, which comes at the third year, is one of these requirements. The MCBS course, which was to be UMSL's equivalent, comes at the second year. However, the differences between these two courses and their students are considerable.

The third year UMSL course attracts students at a later point in their academic careers where they are immersed (or beginning to immerse themselves) in upper division studies in their majors. As a result, these students are able to draw on learning from other courses to read and write more like knowledgeable professionals in their fields. At this point, the students are beginning to transition from college to professional life. For these reasons, they are often more academically mature than, have experienced more advanced academic class work than, and have a better sense of the contexts of their professions that do first or second year students.

The MCBS course, by contrast, is a second year course that appears during general education studies in which students are still developing the academic skills that will carry them into more advanced studies and make them successful in college. The students in this course are typically still transitioning from high school to college and from a sense of the working world contextualized by low-level positions in their family businesses and villages in the country. As a result, these students often do not understand yet what a professional knows or how a professional must think. Rather, these students are just getting ready to learn. Our objective was to use our particular course to try to bridge the academic and professional differences between these two groups of students. We hoped that the collaboration offered by our linking our course objectives would provide a step that would lead to a more advanced course at MCBS, one that would fully meet the requirements of the articulation agreement.

A second opportunity we hoped would materialize from such a course would be a chance for better reflection related to the writing process. That is, we knew the asynchronous nature of student interactions, made necessary by the ten-hour difference between students, would slow down the cycles of communication so that students could more closely observe and discuss their writing and its cultural aspects. This delay meant more time could be devoted to face-to-face meetings on discussion about business and international business processes. Additionally, the instructors hoped that more time could be dedicated to introducing MCBS students to their majors and to pushing UMSL students further along in theirs. This approach had never been done before in either institution's international business programs, and the collaborating instructors knew that if the project worked well, it would set a precedent that could be used to develop other courses.

A third opportunity involved getting more students interested in the classes. Both institutions were committed to helping their students develop advanced writing competencies in business. For this reason, the Business Writing courses were made a graduation requirement by UMSL and MCBS. Students, however, tend to resist courses they see as being forced upon them, especially when they see those courses as being outside their field of interest. We hoped that by including an element of cultural exchange, especially for International Business students, we could make the required course seem even more valuable and attractive to students at both institutions.

INFLUENCES ON COURSE DESIGN

The literature suggests that no one model exists that is exclusive to effective online learning (Mayes & de Freitas, 2004; Postle, Stunman, Mangubhai, Cronk, Carmichael, McDonald, 2003). However,

online environments seem well suited for teaching and learning strategies derived from constructionist epistemologies and from approaches that emphasize the social aspects of learning (Kehrwald, 2008; Reil & Polin, 2004). These strategies and approaches are student-centered and view learning as an active, dynamic matter of constructing meaning through social, interactive events. The students, in turn, benefit greatly online through the promotion of social presence in the learning environment – that is, through activities and processes that enable them to make their presence know and to sense the presence of others in the learning environment (Kehrwald, 2008).

"Time on task," which is the notion that equates student achievement with a student's sustained attention during the learning event, was a concern for us in our course design because we did not expect our students to spend long periods of time on any single activity. Peters (2004) echoes the conclusion many scholars have made for years that students' time on task is one of the most influential factors in learning. He, in turn, calls on instructors to find ways to maximize student time on task. This perspective, in fact, has been a major justification for arguments that call for extending the school day and year for U.S. public schools. The argument was raised again in September 2009 as President Obama called for lengthening the school year in order to make U.S. students more competitive in the global marketplace (Associated Press, 2009). Research, however, has long established that simply extending time on task alone will not raise test scores (Quartarola, 1984). Rather, other factors, including instructor feedback and active learning strategies, must also help to define the quality of the time spent on task (Chickering & Gamson, 1987).

More relevant to our concern, quality time on task had been conceptualized physically in terms of the amount of time spent in the, together with the amount of time spent on reading and homework. Arbaugh and Hornik (2006), however, have challenged this notion by suggesting traditional concepts of time and space in terms of learning are different online and that online-based technologies can address time on task in ways that are not constrained by physically-based concepts of learning.

A joint report by the American Association for Higher Education, American College Personnel Association, and the National Association of Student Personnel Administrators (Learning principles, 1998) also informed our course design. The report synthesizes a host of learning studies and initiatives published over the last 20 years. For our purposes, particularly important to us among the conclusions drawn by the task force were first, that *learning takes place formally in traditional venues, but also informally and incidentally*. Students, in fact, construct understandings of what they are exposed to whether those understandings are prescribed by a teacher or not. Students, moreover, will construct such understanding anywhere they feel comfortable and interested enough to think, talk, and reflect on that learning. This idea was something we had long recognized intuitively from our experience working with students in and out of the classroom, but the report helped us more clearly realize what we should do.

A second task force conclusion, that *learning is all about making and maintaining connections*, suggested to us that the potential for learning occurs whenever students interact with each other, with objects, materials, ideas, and experience, and process new information with old. The possibilities for students to interact with each other and their course materials online are vast through text, video, audio, images, and a variety of interactive technologies. For this reason, we planned units with shared readings, assignments, and activities, and whenever possible, we planned to draw dotted lines in our classroom discussions to guide students to make connections between those materials.

A third task force conclusion, that *learning occurs most effectively when students are actively involved in the process*, underscored what we knew from experience: as student involvement increases, the extent of their processing of information increases, and so does their learning. We have heard the virtues of active learning so often in our professional conversations, conferences, and classrooms, and it was a point we took quite seriously.

Closely allied to this idea was the task force conclusion that *learning occurs in a social context*. Social networks enable people to learn from and through each other. Moreover, they can provide a place for emotional support and a shared feeling of trust and safety among those who bond with each other through their participation in the group. This support and connection helps individuals to build social presence.

Within this context, trust is a key element: students will learn through social and other kinds of networks only when they feel that being social is safe and welcome. The online environment is often depicted as cold and dehumanizing. By contrast, our experiences with online relationships, both professional and casual, have told us that technologies such as email, instant messaging, Facebook, Twitter, and other such systems can enable the humanization of online interaction.

STUDENTS

Sixteen UMSL students (14 male and two female) and 17 MCBS students (eight male and nine female) participated in our educational project. Students ranged between 19 and 26 years in age, with the MCBS students generally younger than their UMSL counterparts. The UMSL students were American, Midwestern, day students majoring in International Business. Most worked part-time jobs as laborers or clerks; two were lower-level managers, and one owned his own business. Many had not traveled outside of the Midwest, and only three had traveled outside of the United States. Their perspectives on culture, especially culture as remote to them as that of the Middle East, were limited.

MCBS students, by contrast, were characteristically Gulf Arab students and Muslim. They tended to be better at verbal communication than written communication, were culturally shy, and were unaccustomed to cross-gender relationships in school. (Note: Classes at MCBS, and in Oman in general, are not gender-segregated, as they are in many gulf Arab countries.) Many of these students came from the Muscat area, but some had moved to Muscat from the countryside in order to go to school at MCBS.

APPROACH

A formal collaboration between the faculty members (based on the shared course) was incorporated into the annual agreement between UMSL and MCBS. This inclusion provided a legal structure for collaboration to take place and for the roles and responsibilities of the participants to be known. A course site was constructed on UMSL's course management system, and content was uploaded to the site. MCBS students were then given UMSL student status and IDs in order to logon to the course management site. UMSL students, in turn, were prepared for the collaboration through a live presentation about the culture and language of Oman. (The presentation was given by two Omani exchange students who were at UMSL that semester.) The presentation was followed by a writing assignment in which students were asked to reflect upon the presentation and discuss their expectations about doing business with Omani counterparts.

To promote social presence and meaningful interaction, a class-wide blog was made available, so all students could talk freely to each other about themselves and about the course.

Students were also provided with instructions to help them learn how to use the blog. Groups were then created, and two to three students from each institution were assigned to each group and were given email capabilities through UMSL's server. In addition, class photographs were taken and posted side-by-side on the course site homepage so UMSL and MCBS students could see themselves and their counterparts whenever they logged on to the course site. Next, UMSL students made a streaming video in which they introduced themselves and welcomed the MCBS students to the collaboration. This video was then posted to the course site. Finally, the instructors planned an icebreaker blog assignment in which students were asked to introduce themselves and share something about their backgrounds.

Four international business cases were written or adapted for students to study, and assignments were written to encourage students to discuss the cases and respond in defined ways to the cases. Wikis were created for each student group, and group members were asked to post their rough drafts of assignments to the wiki. Peer review assignments were then added to the wiki in order to encourage students to comment on their group members' drafts. Students were provided with instructions to guide them through the processes of posting drafts and of peer reviewing papers.

Because UMSL students met on Mondays and Wednesdays and MCBS students met on Thursdays and Saturdays, UMSL students decided to blog first on the assignments and submit the first drafts. The MCBS students would then blog second and discuss the pros and cons of these initial drafts. We hoped this process would enable UMSL students to provide their MCBS counterparts with models of how to respond to assignments and how to talk about drafts. Finally, both instructors made plans to stay in constant contact with each other by email and cell phone in order to troubleshoot the project as it progressed.

RESULTS

UMSL's semester began on August 24, and over its first five weeks, the UMSL students studied rhetorical situations and contexts and international business in the Middle East. The students also made an introductory video and wrote about Oman and about ways of doing business in the Middle East. On Tuesday, Oct. 6, two Omani students studying at UMSL visited class and gave a presentation about the culture and the people of Oman. That same week, MCBS students began their semester, had their English-language skills assessed, and were given IDs and passwords to log on to UMSL's course management system. Unfortunately, the MCBS students encountered difficulties with the system, and it took over two weeks before most of them were able to log onto the system (some never did). In the meantime, the MCBS students studied rhetorical situations and contexts and international business in the United States, and how to use UMSL's course management system.

By the end of MCBS' third week (and UMSL's eighth week), all 16 UMSL students and all eight MCBS students had posted an introductory message to the class blog. There were 10 responses, or "comments," to these initial postings. Six of these comments were by UMSL students, and four were posted by MCBS students. At that time, it was determined that only two of the case studies would be used, and both cases would involve exercises in communicating negative messages. This decision was based on the difficulty the MCBS students encountered when using the course management system, and because of the time lost in logging the MCBS students onto UMSL's system.

On the Monday of UMSL's ninth week of class (and MCBS' fourth week of class), the UMSL students were given the two case studies designed for the collaboration. By that Wednesday, they had posted rough drafts for peer review to their group wikis. They then posted their comments on these drafts by Friday of that same week. The

MCBS students, in turn, were asked to post their rough drafts by Saturday, and then join UMSL students in the peer reviews. Over the two weeks that followed this initial posting, two students responded to "Case A" and three responded to "Case B." The collaboration ended at the beginning of the UMSL's 12th week of class (MCBS' 7th week of class).

DISCUSSION

In terms of the outcomes we expected, the collaboration was a partial success. Students learned about genres of business writing and how they functioned in the processes of doing business writing. Students also learned about and had a chance to examine language and tone in relation to cross-cultural communications. Perhaps most valuable to the students, though, was the chance to talk to someone from a different culture. The peer review process also allowed participating students to get feedback about their responses to assignments.

However, after the icebreaker assignment, UMSL and MCBS students had little interaction. We had hoped that peer review would provide the kind of feedback that would help students learn how to make their writing more appropriate for an international audience. Instead, discussions rarely reached that level of sophistication, or discussions focused mainly on stylistic issues and questions about the assignments themselves. We believe this focus was based upon the differences in the academic preparation of the groups of students and the infrequent attempts at interaction across students.

Academic Preparation

MCBS students come from two principal streams and thus two contrasting levels of knowledge of and use of English. One stream is by way of the College Foundation Program (see About UMSL,

2010), which is an intensive ESL program run by the College[1]. The other is by way of having learned and used English as a medium of instruction in private high schools in Oman. The members of the second group tended to be better prepared; their fluency in English was greater and more complete in terms of both academic writing and social discourse. Unfortunately, more of the students at MCBS tend to start in the College Foundation Program than those who learned English in private high schools. In our study, approximately 80% of the Omani participants came through the Foundation program and the Academic Writing preparatory program.

UMSL students found some MSBS students very difficult to understand because of their language skills. Other students were considered inappropriate. Greetings such as "whats cracken guys, my name is _____ im 25 years old im half turkish half omani and this is my first time bloging" made UMSL students chuckle because the Omani's rhetorical knowledge and experience failed to measure up to UMSL students' expectations. The American students had to learn to move past their rather parochial (and somewhat arrogant) notions of discourse community to engage in respectful, meaningful communication with their Omani counterparts. Although difficult, this experience became a valuable lesson in the cultural exchange. The UMSL students learned that using English, their first language, in the cultural exchange enabled them a position by which they could develop certain unfair expectations of the Omanis. The Omani student's levels of language proved good enough, however, for blogging activity and there seemed to be a genuine interest in getting to know their American counterparts. The Americans recognized this factor and appreciated it.

Furthermore, few second year MCBS students had academic experience in the study of business beyond a smattering of entry-level general education courses. Many of these students were working at jobs, but the jobs were lower-level ones that did not require much knowledge of business. The UMSL students, by contrast, had taken at least some upper-level business courses. These students took some of these courses in the last semester of their senior years, and so their knowledge of doing business at a higher level and the potential of what they could bring to discussions with MCBS students was somewhat greater than their MCBS counterparts. This difference was significant. One case study, in which an English businessperson disputed a complex set of credit card charges from a computer supply business in Dubai, it was difficult for the MCBS students to follow and to understand the dispute because they had a less-developed understanding of business practices in the credit card industry. UMSL students also found it difficult to follow such exchanges, but they were usually able to grasp concepts more readily. The second assignment, in which a supervisor at Monsanto Europe N.V. had to explain why a trusted employee was not promoted, proved to be easier for Omani students, and they were able to interact more effectively in relation to the subject because it didn't require as much specialized business knowledge.

Infrequent Interactions

The low numbers of interactions, we believe, were due partly to the topics discussed and in part to the lack of familiarity with the technology used. The greatest number of interactions by far occurred during the icebreaker assignment on the blog. In this instance, students on both sides seemed at ease in talking to each other about themselves. The number of interactions declined, though, as soon as students began talking in their wikis about case studies and written responses to case studies (such discussions required more specialized knowledge).

Students were also more familiar with blogs than they were wikis. Although no one on either the UMSL or the MCBS side had actually blogged before, most had read blogs prior to starting the class and many were at least somewhat familiar with their rhetorical qualities. Although we provided ample instructions on both the course site and in the classroom, students – especially MCBS students – struggled with the wikis. While MCBS students were familiar with the idea of peer review in a writing class, doing such reviews in groups and online with wikis proved to be a significant cultural leap. None of the MCBS students had used wikis prior to the class, and commenting on someone's writing proved far more difficult (i.e., requiring comfort with rules of grammar, etc.) than a simple introduction within a student blog. Moreover, while MCBS students were largely familiar with social networking software such as Facebook, they were not familiar with the complexities and possibilities of the course management software they were using. As a result, navigating such things as wikis and blogs was a foreign concept to them. Rather, their knowledge was limited to simple, content management software available at MCBS that did not have the advanced features.

Students might also have experienced significant frustration in relation to different aspects of the class. Enrolling MCBS students into UMSL's course management system, for example, proved to be time consuming and frustrating because of the complicated layers of safeguards and procedures that identify and protect student information. Guest access accounts that cut through these safeguards had to be given to each student, and temporary randomized passwords had to be issued. MCBS students, however, had trouble recognizing the random English letters and numbers of these passwords, or simply they did not know what to do with them. This lack of understanding lead to significant frustration. Without a legally binding agreement in place that outlined responsibilities and roles, we instructors might not have been able to draw on the resources necessary to overcome these obstacles. Because of the agreement between our institutions, however, we were able to appeal to IT professionals at UMSL to jump in to work on solutions, which they did. Without the cross-institutional agreement, it would have been

difficult to persuade these senior administrators to drop what they were doing to help us.

Additionally, for students in Oman, Internet learning is still in its formative stages, and Omani society is not yet information-based. MCBS students, however, were quite familiar with cell phone texting processes, and so texting rhetoric (e.g., "how r u" and "do u know how 2...") and emoticons showed up frequently in MCBS student writing. The frustration Omani students experienced with the technology and Internet-based learning strategies also showed up occasionally in their comments to UMSL students. For example, one student, not knowing how to find comments on her paper, wrote, "y don't u mark on my paper?" UMSL students (who were more familiar with the technology and with blogs and wikis because of their use in previous classes) often misinterpreted such structures, which MCBS students were using to indicate frustration, as aggressive, shrill tones.

In spite of the obstacles we encountered, there are no major "down sides" to undertaking a program such as the one we've described here. Students learned valuable lessons and were able to interact with people they would not have otherwise encountered. For us instructors, the lessons we learned from this experience will enable us to better define additional collaborative opportunities for the future.

REFERENCES

About, M. C. B. S. (2010). *Modern College of Business and Science*. Retrieved September 2, 2010, from http://www.mcbs.edu.om/ aboutmcbs.html

ACPA. (1998). Learning principles and collaborative action. In Berson, J. (Ed.), *Powerful partnerships: A shared responsibility for learning* (pp. 3–10). Washington, DC: ACPA.

Anderson, P. H., Lawton, L., Rexeisen, R. J., & Hubbard, A. C. (2006). Short-term study abroad and intercultural sensitivity. *International Journal of Intercultural Relations*, *30*(4), 457–469. doi:10.1016/j.ijintrel.2005.10.004

Arbaugh, J. B., & Hornik, S. (2006). Do Chickering and Gamson's seven principles also apply to online MBAs? *The Journal of Educators Online, 3*(2). Retrieved December 10, 2010, from http://www. thejeo.com/ Volume3Number2/ ArbaughFinal.pdf

Associated Press. (2009). President Obama wants to keep kids in school longer: extended days, weekend hours, shorter summers. *NY Daily News*. Retrieved December 10, 2010, from http://www. nydailynews.com/ news/ national/ 2009/ 09/ 28/ 2009-09-28_president_obama_wants_to_keep _kids_in_school_longer_extended _days_week-end_hours_.html#ixzz0grS3TH6Z

Boehm, D., & Aniola-Jedrzejek, L. (2006). Seven principles of good practice for virtual international collaboration. In Ferris, S. P., & Godar, S. H. (Eds.), *Teaching and learning with virtual teams* (pp. 1–31). Hershey, PA: Information Science Publishing. doi:10.4018/9781591407089.ch001

Chickering, A. W., & Gamson, Z. (1987). Seven principles for good practice in undergraduate education. *AAHE Bulletin*, *40*(7), 3–7.

Kehrwald, B. A. (2008). Understanding social presence in text-based online learning environments. *Distance Education*, *29*(1), 89–106. doi:10.1080/01587910802004860

Mayes, J. T., & de Freitas, S. (2004). *Review of e-learning theories, frameworks and models*. JISC e-Learning Models Desk Study. Retrieved December 10, 2010, from http://www.jisc.ac.uk/ uploaded_documents/ Stage%202%20Learning% 20Models%20(Version%201).pdf

Means, B., Toyama, Y., Murphy, R., Bakia, M., & Jones, K. (2009). *Evaluation of evidence-based practices in online learning: A meta-analysis and review of online learning studies*. Washington, DC: U. S. Department of Education.

Mentzer, G. A., Cryan, J., & Teclehaimanot, B. (2007). Two peas in a pod? A comparison of face-to-face and Web-based classrooms. *Journal of Technology and Teacher Education*, *15*(2), 233–246.

Pedersen, P. (2010). Assessing intercultural effectiveness outcomes in a year-long study abroad program. *International Journal of Intercultural Relations*, *34*(1), 70–80. doi:10.1016/j. ijintrel.2009.09.003

Peters, E. (2004). Maximize student time on task. *Science Scope*, *28*(1), 38–39.

Postle, G., Sturman, A., Mangubhai, F., Cronk, P., Carmichael, A., & McDonald, J. (2003). *Online teaching and learning in higher education: A case study*. Canberra, Australia: Department of Education, Science and Training.

Quartarola, B. (1984). *A research paper on time on task and the extended school day/year and their relationship to improving student achievement*. ERIC, ED245347.

Reil, M., & Polin, L. (2004). Online learning communities: Common ground and critical differences in designing technical environments. In Barab, S. A., Kling, R., & Gray, J. H. (Eds.), *Designing for virtual communities in the service of learning* (pp. 16–50). Cambridge, UK: Cambridge University Press.

Rivera, J. C., & Rice, M. L. (2002). A comparison of student outcomes & satisfaction between traditional and Web based course offerings. *Online Journal of Distance Learning Administration*, *5*(3). Retrieved December 10, 2010, from http:// www.westga.edu/ ~distance/ ojdla/ fall53/ rivera53.html

Tallent-Runnels, M. K., Thomas, J. A., Lan, W. Y., Cooper, S., Ahern, T. C., Shaw, S. M., & Liu, X. (2006). Teaching courses online: A review of the research. *Review of Educational Research*, *76*(1), 93–135. doi:10.3102/00346543076001093

University of Missouri – St. Louis. (2010). *Student body profile fall 2009*. Retrieved September 2, 2010, from http://www.umsl.edu/ about/ student-profile.html

KEY TERMS AND DEFINITIONS

Study Abroad: Academic program that involves travel to another country.

Cultural Exchange: Experience that enables mutual exploration of other cultures.

Communication Education: Teaching and learning of verbal and non-verbal codes and cues occurring in message exchange.

Online Learning: Computer-mediated learning that occurs over the Internet.

Social Presence: A sense of self and of others expressed and interpreted through social activity in online situations.

Institutional Relationships: Legal, curricular, functional, and structural ties between institutions.

Middle East: Countries in and around the Arabian Peninsula.

International Business Writing: Written communication that occurs in business across cultural and national boundaries.

Course Design: The content, processes, and arrangement of learning materials and activities.

ENDNOTE

[1] Students in the Foundation Program study English intensively for 78 hours per semester for three academic semesters. In these cases, instruction is divided into four levels of proficiency. Only students who pass all levels can begin their regular academic language study.

Chapter 24

New Era, New Media, and New Strategies for Cross-Cultural Collaborative Learning

Chun-Min Wang
National Hsinchu University of Education, Taiwan

Jinn-Wei Tsao
University of Georgia, USA

Gretchen Bourdeau Thomas
University of Georgia, USA

ABSTRACT

The purpose of this chapter is to share a cross-cultural project between Taiwan and the United States for educational practitioners. Taking advantage of Web 2.0 applications as facilitators, the project served as action research to discover better strategies for conducting online cross-cultural collaboration. Specifically, the authors describe the evolution of the instructional design of the project and the difficulties encountered during the cross-cultural collaboration.

INTRODUCTION

With increasing globalization and the exponential growth of communication technologies, people with a global vision and the ability to collaborate internationally are increasingly becoming sought-after members of society. Thus, the question becomes how can institutions provide higher education students with the training needed to become global citizens who have cross-cultural empathy? Although the strategy of global learn-ing through short-term study abroad can achieve this goal (Donnelly-Smith, 2009), due to limited resources, it is almost impossible for students to go abroad on a regular basis. Thus, an increasingly important issue has become how to use online technologies to link students in higher education in order to fostering intercultural awareness. The major issue is if higher education, through the use of technology, can prepare students to become culturally responsive global citizens. Underlying this question is the challenge of adopting

DOI: 10.4018/978-1-60960-833-0.ch024

appropriate pedagogical and learning activities to infuse technology into the learning process (McRae, 2006).

Out of a desire to discover which strategies would work in the virtual learning environment, the authors of this chapter initiated a project to connect – via online media – over one hundred college students in Taiwan and the United States in the winter of 2007. The cross-cultural collaboration begun at that time has continued every fall semester since. From the start of this relationship, the project involved Web 2.0 applications, and the intention was they would decrease the burden of administrative work on school technology staff and encourage conversations among students after the class had ended. More importantly, Web 2.0 applications are generally free for use and their interfaces are continually improving in order to make them more accessible to everyone. As a result, in this new era of globalization, it is a meaningful challenge for educators to take advantage of Web 2.0 applications and create a virtual environment for cross-cultural student collaboration.

The purpose of this chapter is to introduce how the project was conducted and what instructional design was applied throughout the project. In examining these issues, we share the evolution of the instructional design of the project as well as the difficulties we encountered and the compromises we made during the cross-cultural collaboration. The chapter also presents student feedback and recommendations for improvement as well as reflections from the teachers and facilitator involved in this project. The chapter then concludes by suggesting components readers might consider in order to conduct more successful cross-cultural collaborations in educational contexts.

BACKGROUND

Although culture has been acknowledged as an important factor to be considered during the process of instructional design (Henderson, 1996;

McLoughlin, 1999; Reeves & Reeves, 1997; Wang, 2004), a need exists to translate these cultural considerations into practice (Rose, 2005). In the cross-cultural setting of this project, cultural differences actually became learning materials for nurturing intercultural competence related to a range of activities (Byram, 1995).

Interestingly, for almost 20 years, educators have been exploring the application of technology to connect students and teachers from different nations and cultures (Davis, Cho, & Hagenson, 2005). As Davis (1999) pointed out, the motivation for making such connections was the belief that education was now operating in a global context, and technology could increase access to education on an international scale. As a result, providing pre-service teachers with an opportunity to learn from peers in other cultures could equip those teachers with the skills needed to become effective educators within global contexts. These same experiences could be used to provide students with similar kinds of experiences in order to make them more effective global citizens.

Culture and Communication in Cyberspace

For example, a study conducted by Shaughnessy, Ross, and Jackson (2008) examined 18 specialist primary and secondary teachers in the Teachers' International Professional Development Programme in UK. The researchers found that, in addition to mutual commitment and enthusiasm, factors important to the success of collaborative international projects included the development of a good working partnership in a short space of time, the ability to collaborate effectively on projects, and an underlying belief that the project could support realistic curriculum goals. The same study also identified workload and time commitments as two frequently cited reasons for lack of success of collaborative international projects.

Other research in this area reveals additional factors to consider in creating such relationships.

For example, when conducting a cross-cultural collaborative project, instructors also need to overcome the problem of different time zones for an instant communication (Murphy, 2005), as well as be aware of different levels of familiarity the participating groups might have in terms of the technologies being used to facilitate interactions (Lajoie et al., 2006). There is also the issue of language being a barrier to international collaborations (Cifuentes & Shih, 2001; Wang & Reeves, 2007). Although some general tips for online cross-cultural collaboration (e.g., "be mindful, be comfortable with silence, encourage differing viewpoints, avoid debates, observe, know themselves, and normalize diversity") have been proposed (Saphiere, 2000), more guidelines for interacting in online cross-cultural collaborative projects are needed.

As Tutty and Klein (2008) point out, no matter if the collaboration is happening in a traditional classroom or in a virtual space, the learning goals can be achieved if the teaching strategy is appropriately adopted and executed. The only difference is that the instructors need to consider the course content and the design of the assignment more carefully in virtual space than they might in a face-to-face setting. The key to success in such cases can often involve providing students with a clear understanding of the benefits (and skills) they can gain from such virtual projects (Sweeney, Weaven, & Herington, 2008, p.129). Such an understanding can be particularly important to motivating students involved in cross-cultural collaborative projects (Chen, Hsu, & Caropreso, 2005). Unfortunately, there is no concise definition of what exactly "collaboration" means in these settings due to the fact that collaboration is a dynamic and context-contingent process (Sammons, 2007). However, according to Hathorn and Ingram (2002), there are three characteristics of collaboration:

1. Interdependence in the communication patterns of the learners
2. Syntheses of what is known with the result that new ideas are formed
3. Independence from the teacher as they work out a synthesis among themselves

By practicing these characteristics in the classrooms and using them to build a collaborative learning environment, researchers have found that teachers can encourage higher-order thinking, create reciprocating learning environments, and enhance new knowledge building in the classrooms (Cohen, 1994; Lai & Law, 2006). Researchers have also indicated that collaboration can improve students' learning performance in different settings (Rohrbeck, Ginsburg-Block, Fantuzzo, & Miller, 2003; Springer, Stanne, & Donovan, 1999). The value of collaborative learning was also deemed important in online environments (Jung, Choi, Lim, & Leem, 2002).

Knowing the benefits of cross-cultural projects and collaboration in education, more universities and colleges ought to work together to provide programs and expand the number of both online courses involving international collaboration and the requirement that students participate in such courses (Webber & Robertson, 2003). By taking full advantage of the characteristic of networking technologies that can cross borders, teachers could have more opportunities to develop cross-cultural online learning collaboration. These collaborations, in turn, can expand students' views of multiculturalism as well as enhance students' self-identification and their empathy with different cultures (Cifuentes & Murphy, 2000). Moreover, in today's context of globalization, requiring students to collaborate in such international teams can be an effective way to prepare them for future interactions they might have in similar kinds of international work or social settings (Krishnamurthi, 2003; Webber & Robertson, 2003).

Working with Web 2.0

With the growth of networking technologies, more and more Web 2.0 applications have been adopted by teachers for educational purposes (Richardson, 2009). Although the application of Web 2.0 technologies in higher education has created some challenges (Collis & Moonen, 2008), the potential for Web 2.0 applications to improve teaching and learning remains (Churchill, 2009). Additionally, it seems reasonable that a combination of Web 2.0 applications could be used to facilitate online learning in order to enhance students' global perspectives and their intercultural communication skills. The proper mix of applications for achieving such objectives, however, remains unclear. Applications that are less dependent on reading and writing are preferred by students. The students in a study reported by Cifuentes and Shih (2001), for example, indicated that software that would provide audio or visual aids would have been helpful, for email is limited to text-based messages. Web 2.0 technologies, by contrast, often offer more visual guidance within communication. And the use of Web 2.0 applications is growing quickly.

The rapid adoption of Web 2.0 technologies can be seen in the marked growth of social networking sites such as LinkedIn, Twitter, Facebook, and Ning. Moreover, the use of these social networking technologies in training and learning will only increase over time even though we still do not fully understand the best way to apply them (Livingston, 2010). In terms of the use of Web 2.0 applications in different socio-cultural contexts, Olaniran (2009) pointed out that learner control is essential to Web 2.0, but this situation could be limited by learning styles and cultural value preferences. As a result, conflicts could arise when teachers and students from different cultures have different expectations of learner control in online learning contexts. Students from high power distance cultures (Hofstede, 1984), for example, might not be willing to share individual ideas and instead expect the teacher to act as the knowledge

provider. However, this potential situation does not mean Web 2.0 applications cannot be applied in certain cultures. As Herold (2009) argued, "communities on the Internet create their own online culture that draws on multiple influences to produce unique amalgamations of cultural, political, and technological practices that are constantly redefining the relationship between the local and the global for its users" (p.92). Cultures could thus find different ways to adapt Web 2.0 applications to their communication expectations. More work, however, is needed to further investigate how Web 2.0 applications can be implemented appropriately within cross-cultural contexts (Olaniran, 2009).

The Role of the Teacher

Within online educational contexts, teachers are the key to successful collaborations (Sammons, 2007). In addition to understanding and addressing the abilities of the technologies being used, teachers must also develop pedagogical frameworks that provide students with meaningful learning experiences within international online contexts (Laurillard, 2009). Most researchers, however, have focused on describing what occurred during a cross-cultural online course (Ali, 2007). As a result, there is a lack of research that addresses the issues of instructional design for cross-cultural collaboration. As McRae (2006) pointed out, with the rapid growth of technology, one of the primary challenges among educators is to engage in effective global collaboration in education. Yet there is a lack of understanding as to the appropriate pedagogical and learning activities necessary to integrate technology into such learning processes. This situation could be attributed to the reality that it is much more difficult to conduct cross-cultural online learning collaboration. A major challenge is that instructors involved in such international projects need to communicate and negotiate with instructors from other countries. Moreover, instructors in such situations also need access to online technology that will support effective (and, ideally, equal) collaboration in international contexts. Despite these challenges, cross-cultural online collaboration for learning will remain a valuable and meaningful goal to pursue as the world is becoming "flat" beyond what we might be able to imagine (Friedman, 2005).

THE PROJECT

The important rationale embedded in the project reported here is the belief that providing students with cross-cultural learning opportunities can help them appreciate multiculturalism and diversity. Such experience can also better equip students for future participation in our modern global society. The basic prerequisites of the success of the project were enthusiasm and commitment, and the project involved three primary investigators: Arthur Wang, Michael Tsao, and Gretchen Thomas. Wang is a faculty member at a public university in Taiwan and a graduate of the same public university in the United States where Tsao is currently a doctoral student and Thomas is an instructor.

The initiation of this cross-cultural collaboration project began with a conversation during an international conference held in Orlando, Florida in 2007. At the conference, Wang and Tsao discussed a shared research interest in cultural issues in online learning environment; they also chatted about possible opportunities for collaborating. Upon returning to Taiwan, Wang proposed that Tsao use his undergraduate course to conduct such a cross-cultural collaboration. Tsao, in turn, was excited about the idea and quickly connected Thomas's undergraduate "Introduction to Computers for Teachers" class in the United States with Wang's students in Taiwan. At the beginning of the collaboration, none of the participants had the experience needed to run this kind of project. However, all of us believed this collaboration would provide all involved students with an important learning opportunity.

Project Design

This collaborative project involved action research in that, every semester, the participating instructors designed and redesigned the collaboration to improve student learning outcomes. Two main questions, in turn, guided the action research for these projects. Those questions are

1. How should students be grouped to ensure better learning satisfaction?
2. How should the assignments be designed in order to create better collaborative learning environments?

Based on these two questions, the collaborating instructors grouped the Taiwanese students and the U.S. students in different formats each semester. In one instance, one Taiwanese student was paired with one U.S. student, while in another situation, two Taiwanese students were grouped with one U.S. student. The purpose of this grouping was to compare learning satisfaction and analyze the group interaction in different formats. Additionally, the collaborating instructors designed different major assignments each semester in order to gain insights about what kinds of assignments seem more suited to a cross-cultural setting.

To decrease the burden of students, we used an online survey and reflection essays to collect project-related data. We asked the students to fill out the online survey and write a reflection essay at the end of collaboration. We also interviewed 1 to 2 students from both cultures involved in the collaboration in order to gain further information on their perceptions of the project. Surveys were analyzed quantitatively in order to determine the levels of students' learning satisfaction as well as student preferences regarding the grouping formats and activities held during the collaboration. The reflection essays were analyzed qualitatively in order to gather perspectives from the students regarding the learning experience. Thus far, we have conducted the collaboration three times and are planning to continue with these international projects every fall semester in the foreseeable future. Although the model of this project may not be directly applicable to every cross-cultural collaboration, the factors examined in this project could be of benefit to educators or instructional designers interested in conducting this type of collaboration.

Project Implementation

There were three main issues considered during each iteration of this project:

1. Where is the Students' Virtual Meeting Space?

As mentioned, in comparison to commercial course management platforms such as Blackboard, Web 2.0 applications provide free and user-friendly social networks for conducting cross-cultural collaboration. As a result, the collaborating instructors adopted the popular social networking application Facebook as the platform from the beginning of this project. On Facebook, students were asked to join a group that was created for the project. An advantage of adopting Facebook is that the students can continue their interaction even after the completion of a given course. Although some students did note concerns about the instant message function in Facebook, after three iterations of this project, Facebook has proven to be a good platform for the purpose of this particular project.

2. What Project Should be Assigned to the Students?

To design a meaningful assignment and allow students to truly collaborate and learn from one another is not an easy task. In addition to ice breaking activities (e.g., creating a self-introduction video that was posted on YouTube), answering questions on the Facebook discussion board, and holding synchronous online meetings through Skype,

students were also assigned a major project that required cross-cultural collaboration. Fortunately, we were able to identify existing projects within our courses that would lead themselves well to such collaboration. These projects included the following items:

- **WebQuest:** WebQuests are inquiry-oriented lesson plans in which all or most the information that learners work with comes from the Internet (see www.webquest.org/). In the design of the classes described here, student-created WebQuests were presented in the format of a webpage. In order to make this project meaningful to both Taiwanese and U.S. students, Taiwanese students were asked to design the webpage, and U.S. students were asked to design the lesson plan. This project format helped the Taiwanese students meet their course curricular goals of learning to design a website and addressed the US students' curricular goals of designing WebQuests to learn about inquiry-based activities. In addition, because of the limited English proficiency of the Taiwanese students, it would have been difficult for them to write a lesson plan in English. In other words, in this project Taiwanese students were making the "shell" for the U.S. students' lesson plan. Our hope was that through the negotiation associated with creating these different components, these students would learn from each other.

After the tryout during the first semester, we realized we were too optimistic about the design of this project, for the students merely sent materials to each other without much interaction. As a result, we redesigned the project for the next collaboration and asked the students to work on a wiki chapter together to increase their level of interaction in our second trial.

- **Wiki chapter:** Taiwanese students and U.S. students paired up to use a free Wiki platform to write a chapter related to a selected learning technology. Each class had curricular goals of having students explore and write about various tools, so this project fit well with the objectives of both courses. Each group was asked to discuss its topic and to collaboratively draft answer to several guiding questions, such as: "What are the educational applications of this particular technology in Taiwan and the United States?"

Because of their limited English proficiency, the Taiwanese students found it time consuming to write in English. We also found this assignment resulted in a degree of plagiarism in producing texts with some Taiwanese students copying certain English sentences from the Internet and putting these sentences into their wiki chapter. As a result, we redesigned the project and asked students to instead work on an individual PowerPoint game.

- **PowerPoint Game:** The students were required to use Microsoft PowerPoint to design and develop a game about their partner's culture. Taiwanese students and U.S. students were paired up to form international teams, and the teams had to provide information their foreign partners would use to design a game for the members of that "other" culture. The assignment turned out to be more interesting than previous projects, and the students felt less stress completing the project. Additionally, students also had the chance to learn about another culture during the game development. Based on these successes, we plan to continue adopting PowerPoint games as our major assignment for future semesters.

3. How to Manage the Collaboration?

Each semester, approximately 120 students participated in these collaborative projects. The collaborations involved two classes of 40 Taiwanese students and two classes of 20 students from the United States. Forming the cross-cultural groups and maximizing students' learning satisfaction has been a challenge, and for the past three semesters, we have tried different ratios of Taiwanese students to U.S. students. Experience creating such teams indicates the best configuration involves groupings of one Taiwanese student to one U.S. student. We plan to further explore such groupings by trying different requirements, such as weekly online discussion, and to investigate how to lead the group discussion in order to reach a better interaction.

In addition to these three main questions described here, the collaborating instructors had to develop a schedule that would allow the participating classes to mirror one another. This is a difficult task when one must bridge time differences, differing holiday schedules, and variances in curriculum. But through the use of the online video chat tool Skype, we were able to coordinate a range of activities and interactions. As we have moved through different iterations of these collaborative projects, we have begun to develop activities that allow students to provide assistance and feedback to each other and to build projects that would interest each group. We have also started the international interactions earlier in the semester and have increased the frequency of these interactions so students can have the opportunity to interact a bit more before they are expected to collaborate on the main project for a class.

FINDINGS

The objective of this section is to provide readers with a general overview of students' thoughts, the challenges they encountered, and the recommendations they provided on how to improve the project.

Overall Thoughts

Both Taiwanese and U.S. students were initially interested in the idea of learning about communicating and collaborating with peers in a foreign country. Some students were a bit apprehensive about the group work aspect of the class and the language issues that could arise, but most participants were excited about the project. Interactions between student groups varied. Some students, for example, did not have the chance to engage in the level of interaction they expected through Facebook. A number of groups, however, interacted frequently and prompted one U.S. student to note, "*I really enjoyed [the project] and I learned that while Taiwan and the US have many differences, there are a lot of ways in which we are alike. Plus, I made a friend in the process.*"

The Taiwanese students, in general, reported that this project broadened their view of the world, and they felt they learned about a foreign culture through their communication with their U.S. partners. Moreover, many Taiwanese students noted that this project motivated them to improve their English comprehension in order to express their thoughts more precisely and easily with U.S. counterparts. Generally, the students from both cultures thought this project helped them expand their world view and make friends from foreign countries. Students did, however, suggest that more structured guidelines could be used to focus the discussions and improve the quality of interactions among students.

Challenges

Students reported that the primary challenges they encountered during the implementation of the project involved time differences and language barriers. Many U.S. students, for example, noted they would have had the opportunity to participate in more video conference activities had they not needed to compensate for the 12-hour time difference by moving the video conference to late evening U.S. time. The U.S. students also noted that while they were looking for more conversations with their Taiwanese partners, the fact that some of the Taiwanese students were uncomfortable speaking in English prohibited interaction to a degree.

Despite the fact that Taiwanese students begin learning English in early elementary school, the findings from the observations showed that the Taiwanese students' English proficiency was not good enough to successfully communicate unassisted with their U.S. partners. One reason for this situation is that English education in Taiwan mainly focuses on memorizing vocabulary and grammar and lacks a focus on speaking and listening skills. As a result, the Taiwanese students became nervous and seemed to show a lack of confidence when speaking to a native English speaker from the United States. Additionally, communicating in English sometimes became a burden for the Taiwanese students, and this factor tended to cause Taiwanese students to procrastinate when replying to U.S. partners. Frustration also occurred when Taiwanese students did not understand what U.S. students were talking about or when Taiwanese students could not get their message across because of limited vocabulary.

From the perspectives of Taiwanese students, language barriers did not only limit the quality of their interaction, but also required them to spend more time on reading and writing messages. However, due to the fact that the Taiwanese students need to pass certain English comprehension tests in order to receive their undergraduate degree (a common requirement in the universities in Taiwan), many students felt these collaborations provided them with a good opportunity to practice their English. Thus, a number of Taiwanese students felt the project was difficult, but they appreciated the unique learning opportunity it offered.

An additional challenge to the collaborations was the assumption many U.S. students had that the Taiwanese students would be on Facebook as often as the U.S. students were. While use of Facebook by Taiwanese undergraduates has grown since this project began - the almost addictive use of Facebook by most of the participating U.S. students was difficult for the Taiwanese students to match when these collaborations first began in 2007. However, the situation has changed dramatically since that time. Taiwan now has one of the world's fastest growing populations of Facebook users, and as of this writing, there are over five million registered Facebook users in Taiwan (see: http://www.checkfacebook.com/). Thus, the use of Facebook as the platform for cross-cultural collaboration for these Taiwan-U.S. projects will continue in the future.

Recommendations from the U.S.

Feedback from U.S. students suggested that, in future collaborations, the course instructors provide more opportunities for communication among students from different cultures and allow the students to be more like true pen pals than partners on class assignments. U.S. students, in general, believed that more required interaction might encourage both U.S. and Taiwanese students to become more comfortable talking with each other more frequently. U.S. students, however, also warned the instructors to be cautious of using suggested discussion topics so conversations among groups did not seem "forced."

Surprisingly, one of the highlights for the U.S. students was the day they received gifts from their Taiwanese partners. It was like a child's holiday as the students' eyes lit up when their names were called to pick up their gifts (The Taiwanese students had created beautiful handmade gifts and found unusual trinkets that the U.S. students loved). While the gift exchange required no technology, it was a wonderful capstone to the cross-cultural collaboration.

Recommendations from Taiwan

Although the language barrier was a major concern noted by the Taiwanese students, they also recommended that future collaboration involve scheduling more synchronous online meetings so ideas can be communicated more quickly and directly. The Taiwanese students also noted that in addition to the discussion on Facebook, certain requirements to chat with their foreign partner on Skype or MSN could be of benefit for later collaboration. Additionally, the Taiwanese students recommended that students be allowed to their own international partners so that the project could become more interesting. The Taiwanese students also advocated a one Taiwanese student to one U.S. student format, so participants could have more in-depth interactions with their partners. The Taiwanese participants also suggested in-class activities that do not need a lot time to complete, but would allow them to work together more closely with their U.S. partners. Like the U.S. students, Taiwanese participants also liked the gift exchange activity and were very excited to find out what their gifts were. However, this moment was also a time to learn how well they maintained their collaborative relationships, for students who received big package were usually seen as having good communications with their U. S. partners.

THE REFLECTION

In this section, we reflect on our experiences conducting these cross-culture collaboration projects.

Michael Tsao (The U.S. Facilitator)

Being a facilitator who coordinated the overall project turned out to be harder than initially expected. Not only did I have to maintain close contact and make negotiations with both instructors in two countries, I also had to monitor the

U.S. and Taiwanese students' interactions on Facebook. However, the process was enjoyable, and as a doctoral student, I felt privileged to have the opportunity to work with practitioners and conduct action research in a real educational setting. This project allowed me to see what really occurs during a cross-cultural collaboration and challenged me to come up with better methods of improving the course. Since I am fluent in both English and Chinese, I also served as an interpreter and tech support person for students during the video conference and on Facebook.

Gretchen Thomas (The U.S. Instructor)

I felt this project provided a unique opportunity for U.S. students to encounter peers from another culture. The positive feedback from U.S. students was surprising and overwhelming. I initially expected students to complain about the extra time and effort required by the project, but most comments were highly positive and enthusiastic. In reflecting on this project, I found that students had benefited in ways that the project's organizers had not anticipated. Moreover, while these applications were modeled for all of the participating students - what really benefited all of the instructors was the collaborative experiences we gained from the process and achieving a true level of cross-cultural collaboration.

Arthur Wang (The Taiwanese Instructor)

When I surveyed similar projects before beginning this particular venture, the research revealed the majority of the Taiwanese students involved in this kind of project were majoring in English or taking some courses related to English learning. For this reason, I realized from the very beginning that a language barrier would be a major problem for students in terms of collaborating with U.S. counterparts. However, I also noticed that this linguistic

situation would serve as an innovative learning experience for Taiwanese student participants. Despite the prospects of receiving poor student evaluations for the class, I decided to proceed with the collaborative project. Fortunately, the overall feedback from Taiwanese students was very positive, and these results encouraged me both to continue with this project and to look for ways to make it an even better learning experience for the students. While the whole process requires more effort on the course management than other courses, I believe once the procedures of this project have become more standardized and familiar to the participating instructors, the overall process will become much easier.

Suggestions

Based on a combination of student feedback and instructor experiences, we believe the following suggestions can help in creating similar kinds of cross-cultural online collaboration for a wider range of students from a broader range of nations:

1. *Create ice breaker activities.* We suggest a self-introduction video created at the beginning of the collaboration. In the case of the collaborations reported in this chapter, Photo Story, free video production software, was introduced to the students so they could use it to produce their own introduction. The videos were then added to a free YouTube channel created for this project.

2. *Use Google Map as a mechanism for allowing students to learn the geography of where their collaborative partners are from.* This application can be a simple in-class demonstration, but using such tools can increase students' motivation to know more about their partners.

3. *Use a gift exchange to motivate students and to establish a personal connection across cultures.* However, depending on the location and carrier selected for transport-

ing gifts, sending packages oversea can be quite expensive. It is advised that instructors try to secure some funding for this activity prior to starting these kinds of collaborative projects.

4. *Use both asynchronous and synchronous technologies for student interaction.* For synchronous discussion, we suggest using a video chat tool like Skype to allow participants to engage in multiple voice chats at the same time. For asynchronous discussions, a free-access online bulletin board or blog site can suffice.

5. *Inform native English speakers of the limitations their overseas partners might have when communicating in English as well as the behaviors those individuals might adopt when communicating in English (e.g., giggling when speaking or using short, seemingly terse answers).*

These suggestions represent an initial foundation upon which instructors can build or add to in order to develop collaborative, cross-cultural learning experiences for their particular students or for different cultural groups.

CONCLUSION

In this chapter, we shared the instructional design and strategies adopted for the cross-cultural collaboration between undergraduate students in Taiwan and the United States. As of now, we continue to believe language barriers remain the main problem area in such collaborations. However, the good news is that even though this issue is a challenge, students' feedback indicates such projects can be successful despite such factors. Based on our experiences, perhaps an effective strategy for reducing the pressure of language barriers might be to assign projects that require more multimedia development than collaborative writing. Additionally, we believe that increasing

the familiarity between partners can also reduce the embarrassment of communicating by using a second language. Some ice breaking activities like self-introduction videos and synchronous online meetings in the early stage of the course can be very beneficial for active participation of the learners in later collaboration.

In addition to language, time differences can be an issue that affects cross-cultural interactions, but such differences are not necessarily a problem. Rather, by making online interactions a part of the course requirements, instructors can provide students with a reasonable method for communicating effectively and regularly across time zones. Nevertheless, instructors should continually provide student collaborators with encouragement and learning support through the overall collaborative process.

In this new era of globalization, and with the help of new media and new strategies, we encourage educators to establish cross-cultural collaboration. We believe that, by expanding students' world vision and cultural sensitivity, educators can help students become global citizens who will be ready to create a better society in the future. After all, with the rapid growth of Web 2.0 applications, people are only limited by their imagination to think of new strategies for cross-cultural collaboration in this era. Some might argue that using Web 2.0 applications could compromise students' privacy. Yet the concept of "sharing" will continue to be the trend in this era, and initiations such as the Open Course project in MIT and the Open Source Software movement will only continue to expand in the future. Thus, when adopting Web 2.0 applications for cross-cultural collaboration, the first task for the instructors should be changing their mind-set to be open to share their course to the world. However, the bottom line is respecting the intellectual property and giving necessary credits to the contributors.

REFERENCES

Ali, A. (2007). Modern technology and mass education: A case study of a global virtual system. In Edmundson, A. (Ed.), *Globalized e-learning cultural challenges* (pp. 327–339). Hershey, PA: Information Science Publishing.

Byram, M. (1995). Cultural studies in foreign language teaching. In Basnett, S. (Ed.), *Studying British cultures: An introduction* (pp. 56–67). London, UK: Routledge.

Chen, S.-J., Hsu, C., & Caropreso, E. (2005). *Cross-cultural collaborative online learning: When the West meets the East.* Paper presented at the World Conference on E-Learning in Corporate, Government, Healthcare, and Higher Education 2005, E-Learn 2005-World Conference on E-Learning in Corporate, Government, Healthcare, and Higher Education.

Churchill, D. (2009). Educational applications of Web 2.0: Using blogs to support teaching and learning. *British Journal of Educational Technology, 40*(1), 179–183. doi:10.1111/j.1467-8535.2008.00865.x

Cifuentes, L., & Murphy, K. L. (2000). Promoting multicultural undestanding and positive self-concept through a distance learning community: Cultural connections. *Educational Technology Research and Development, 48*(1), 69–83. doi:10.1007/BF02313486

Cifuentes, L., & Shih, Y.-C. D. (2001). Teaching and learning online: A collaboration between U.S. and Taiwanese students. *Journal of Research on Technology in Education, 33*(4), 456–474.

Cohen, E. G. (1994). *Designing groupwork: Strategies for the heterogeneous classroom* (2nd ed.). NY: Teachers College, Columbia University.

Collis, B., & Moonen, J. (2008). Web 2.0 tools and processes in higher education: Quality perspectives. *Educational Media International, 45*(2), 93–106. doi:10.1080/09523980802107179

Davis, N. E. (1999). The globalization of education through teacher education with new technologies: A review informed by research through teacher edcuation with new technologies. *Educational Technology Review, 1*(12), 8–12.

Davis, N. E., Cho, M. O., & Hagenson, L. (2005). Editorial: Intercultural competence and the role of technology in teacher education. *Contemporary Issues in Technology & Teacher Education, 4*(4), 384–394.

Donnelly-Smith, L. (2009). Global learning through short-term study abroad. *Peer Review, 11*(4), 12–15.

Friedman, T. L. (2005). *The world is flat: A brief history of the twenty-first century* (1st ed.). NY: Farrar Straus and Giroux.

Hathorn, L. G., & Ingram, A. L. (2002). Co-operation and collaboration using computer-mediated communication. *Journal of Educational Computing Research, 26*(3), 325–347. doi:10.2190/7MKH-QVVN-G4CQ-XRDU

Henderson, L. (1996). Instructional design of interactive multimedia: A cultural critique. *Educational Technology Research and Development, 44*(4), 85–104. doi:10.1007/BF02299823

Herold, D. (2009). Cultural politics and political culture of Web 2.0 in Asia. *Knowledge. Technology & Policy, 22*, 89–94. doi:10.1007/s12130-009-9076-x

Hofstede, G. (1984). Hofstede culture dimensions - An independent validation using Rokeach value survey. *Journal of Cross-Cultural Psychology, 15*(4), 417–433. doi:10.1177/0022002184015004003

Jung, I., Choi, S., Lim, C., & Leem, J. (2002). Effects of different types of interaction on learning achievement, satisfaction and participation in Web-based instruction. *Innovations in Education and Teaching International, 39*(2), 153–162. doi:10.1080/14703290252934603

Krishnamurthi, M. (2003). Assessing multicultural initiatives in higher education institutions. *Assessment & Evaluation in Higher Education, 28*(3), 263–277. doi:10.1080/0260293032000059621

Lai, M., & Law, N. (2006). Peer scaffolding of knowledge building through collaborative groups with differential learning experiences. *Journal of Educational Computing Research, 35*(2), 123–144. doi:10.2190/GW42-575W-Q301-1765

Lajoie, S., Garcia, B., Berdugo, G., Márquez, L., Espíndola, S., & Nakamura, C. (2006). The creation of virtual and face-to-face learning communities: An international collaboration experience. *Journal of Educational Computing Research, 35*(2), 163–180. doi:10.2190/1G77-3371-K225-7840

Laurillard, D. (2009). The pedagogical challenges to collaborative technologies. *International Journal of Computer-Supported Collaborative Learning, 4*(1), 5–20. doi:10.1007/s11412-008-9056-2

Livingston, B. (2010). Using Web 2.0 technologies. *Infoline, 1001*(27), 1–14.

McLoughlin, C. (1999). Culturally responsive technology use: Developing an online community of learners. *British Journal of Educational Technology, 30*(3), 231–243. doi:10.1111/1467-8535.00112

McRae, P. (2006). *Transcendent opportunities for global communication & collaboration in education.* Paper presented at the Society for Information Technology & Teacher Education International Conference 2006, Orlando, Florida, USA.

Murphy, E. (2005). Issues in the adoption of broadband-enabled learning. *British Journal of Educational Technology, 36*(3), 525–536. doi:10.1111/j.1467-8535.2005.00490.x

Olaniran, B. A. (2009). Culture, learning styles, and Web 2.0. *Interactive Learning Environments, 17*(4), 261–271. doi:10.1080/10494820903195124

Reeves, T. C., & Reeves, P. (1997). Effective dimensions of interactive learning on the World Wide Web. In Khan, B. H. (Ed.), *Web-based instruction* (pp. 59–66). Englewood Cliffs, NJ: Educational Technology Publications.

Richardson, W. (2009). *Blogs, wikis, podcasts, and other powerful Web tools for classrooms* (2nd ed.). Thousand Oaks, CA: Corwin Press.

Rohrbeck, C. A., Ginsburg-Block, M. D., Fantuzzo, J. W., & Miller, T. R. (2003). Peer-assisted learning interventions with elementary school students: A meta-analytic review. *Journal of Educational Psychology, 95*(2), 240–257. doi:10.1037/0022-0663.95.2.240

Rose, E. (2005, March-April). Cultural studies in instructional design: Building a bridge to practice. *Educational Technology, 45*, 5–10.

Sammons, M. (2007). Collaborative interaction. In Moore, M. G. (Ed.), *Handbook of distance education* (2nd ed., pp. 311–321). Mahwah, NJ: L. Erlbaum Associates.

Saphiere, D. H. (2000). Online cross-cultural collaboration. *Training & Development, 54*(10), 71–72.

Shaughnessy, J., Ross, P., & Jackson, A. (2008). Baptism by firewall? Computer-mediated collaborative projects as professional development opportunities for teachers. *Contemporary Issues in Technology & Teacher Education, 8*(4), 367–393.

Springer, L., Stanne, M. E., & Donovan, S. S. (1999). Effects of small-group learning on undergraduates in science, mathematics, engineering, and technology: A meta-analysis. *Review of Educational Research, 69*(1), 21–51.

Sweeney, A., Weaven, S., & Herington, C. (2008). Multicultural influences on group learning: A qualitative higher education study. *Assessment & Evaluation in Higher Education, 33*(2), 119–132. doi:10.1080/02602930601125665

Tutty, J., & Klein, J. (2008). Computer-mediated instruction: A comparison of online and face-to-face collaboration. *Educational Technology Research and Development*, *56*(2), 101–124. doi:10.1007/s11423-007-9050-9

Wang, C. M. (2004). Taking online courses in the United States: The perspectives of Asian students from China, Korea, Singapore, and Taiwan. In J. Nall & R. Robson (Eds.), *Proceedings of the E-Learn 2004 Conference: World Conference on e-learning in corporate, government, healthcare, & higher education* (pp. 2466-2468). Norfolk, VA: Association for the Advancement of Computing in Education (AACE).

Wang, C. M., & Reeves, T. C. (2007). Synchronous online learning experiences: The perspectives of international students from Taiwan. *Educational Media International*, *44*(4), 339–356. doi:10.1080/09523980701680821

Webber, C., & Robertson, J. (2003). Developing an international partnership for tomorrow's educational leaders. *International Studies in Educational Administration*, *31*(1), 15–32.

KEY TERMS AND DEFINITIONS

Action Research: A reflective process of problem solving aims to improve the way to address issues and solve problems.

Intercultural Competence: The ability of successful communication with people of other cultures.

Online Cross-Cultural Collaboration: Collaborative activities in online environment that involve people from more than one culture.

Web 2.0 Applications: Web-based applications that adopt the concept of user-generated, interoperability, and information sharing.

Chapter 25
Maximizing Multicultural Online Learning Experiences with the Social Presence Model, Course Examples, and Specific Strategies

Aimee L. Whiteside
University of Tampa, USA

Amy E. Garrett Dikkers
University of North Carolina at Wilmington, USA

ABSTRACT

This chapter presents Whiteside's (2007) Social Presence Model, course examples, and specific strategies and explains how such factors help facilitators maximize interactions in multicultural, online learning environments. The model provides a framework rooted in socio-cultural learning, linguistic nuances, learning communities, prior experiences, and instructor investment. The chapter also illustrates how the Social Presence Model, coupled with examples from a Human Rights Education case study and research-based strategies, can make significant differences in online interactions.

INTRODUCTION

Years ago, May and Short (2003) urged online facilitators to embrace a more fruitful, constructive, and transformative metaphor for online

learning opportunities rather than be consumed by the technological angst and time pressures often associated with online education. The *gardening in cyberspace* metaphor invoked by these authors allows individuals to focus on the unique milieu from which facilitators can reconsider and transform the online learning experience. May

DOI: 10.4018/978-1-60960-833-0.ch025

and Short suggest, "The practices of good gardening—positioning, conditioning soil, watering, and controlling weeds and pests—all serve as useful analogues to good online pedagogical practices, addressing individual differences, motivating the student, providing feedback, and avoiding information overload" (p. 673). This metaphor provides online facilitators with a healthy perspective from which they can cultivate meaningful learning experiences.

This chapter couples this transformative metaphor with Whiteside's (2007) Social Presence Model, course examples, and specific strategies to help academics, practitioners in industry, students, and other professionals around the world maximize their online interactions. This model provides a simple framework rooted in the social aspects of learning, linguistic nuances, and the importance of developing learning communities. The course examples presented in this chapter extend from three iterations of a one-semester higher education course entitled *Human Rights Education*. The overall objective of this chapter, in turn, is to provide a framework supported by case study examples and additional strategies that illustrates how simple it is to make significant advances in online interactions and relationships among participants.

IMPORTANCE OF SOCIAL PRESENCE ONLINE

The social dimensions of learning have long been discussed in the educational literature across time (Dewey, 1910, 1916; Bandura, 1973, 1977, 1986; Wenger, 1998). Educational theorist and practitioner Etienne Wenger (1998) notes, "We are social beings…this fact is a central aspect of learning" (p. 4). Likewise, *social presence* can contribute to learners' construction of knowledge and help them engage more in their learning process.

Historically, the concept of social presence emerged in the late 1960s and early 1970s where

Mehrabian (1969) and Short, Williams, and Christie (1976) examined social presence from a social psychological perspective within the area of telecommunication. These researchers found social presence to be "the degree to which a person is perceived as a 'real person' in mediated communication" (qtd. in Polhemus, Shih, & Swan, 2001, p. 5). Then as various interactive and other communication media evolved over time into options such as teleconferencing, interactive television, and online learning environments, a flurry of additional yet similar definitions for social presence emerged. These definitions helped to position social presence as the resulting phenomenon within a particular technological medium.

In contrast, contemporary researchers find that social presence has emerged as a concept much larger than any individual medium (Gunawardena & Zittle, 1997; Rourke, Anderson, Garrison, & Archer, 2001; Tu, 2002; Whiteside, Hughes, & McLeod, 2005; Whiteside, 2007). These researchers see social presence as an affectively-charged connectedness that motivates participants to take an active role in their own and their peers' construction of knowledge and meaning-making processes (Whiteside, 2007; Whiteside, Hughes, & McLeod, 2005). This category extends beyond isolated individual perceptions, behaviors, and attitudes in a cross-cultural communication medium. Thus, this category addresses trust, interaction, and group dynamics in emerging learning environments.

Today, contemporary social presence research has branched into a number of exciting, related directions including

- Blended learning (Garrison & Kanuka, 2004; Jusoff & Khodabandelou, 2009; Whiteside, 2007; Whiteside, Hughes, & McLeod, 2005)
- Collaborative learning (Kerhwald, 2007)
- Community building (Shen & Khalifa, 2008; Ubon & Kimble, 2003; Vesely, Bloom, & Sherlock, 2007)

- Content management systems (Marcus, 2006)
- Emerging and mobile technologies (Hodge, Tabrizi, Farwell, & Wuensch, 2007; Kekwaletswe, 2007)
- Engagement and social interaction (Lu, Huang, Ma, & Luce, 2007; Swan, 2002; Wise, Chang, Duffy, & delValle, 2004)
- Learner characteristics and personality types (Hingorani, 2008; Mykota & Duncan, 2007)
- Learner satisfaction and awareness (Gunawardena & Zittle, 2003; Rettie, 2003; Stacey, 2002; Stein & Wanstreet, 2003; Swan & Richardson, 2003; Wise, Chang, Duffy, & Valle, 2004)
- Performance and cognitive engagement (Bai, 2003; Picciano, 2002)
- Social networking tools (Anderson, 2008; Dunlap & Lowenthal, 2009; Duvall, Powell, Hodge, & Ellis, 2007; Joyce & Brown, 2009;)
- Synchronous learning (Chen, Kinshuk, Wei, Wang, 2009)

With all this vital research available, it can be difficult for online facilitators to know how to consolidate important research into simple, practical advice for both them and their online participants. Furthermore, when one compounds multicultural considerations and global dimensions in an online environment, the facilitator's role becomes even more intricate. As a result, it becomes more difficult to find quick, intuitive solutions early-on in the learning experience.

Fortunately, social presence research sheds some light on multicultural considerations for online interactions. Tu (2001; 2002) found that Chinese participants were more likely to respond to more emotive discussion responses. She also found that when her Chinese participants were able to integrate more personal anecdotes into their responses, there was greater participation for those topics/units.

Additionally, Yildiz (2009) found, contrary to many instructors' views, "the Web-based forum *decreases* the distance that might occur between domestic and international students in the face-to-face classroom" (p. 63). Thus, the non-native participants [including Taiwanese, Korean, and Turkish EFL students] felt more ease and comfort in expressing themselves in an online environment than they felt in a face-to-face classroom environment. This sensation seemed to be because these students did not have to physically face their classmates after expressing an opinion.

There were also notable cultural differences mentioned in Yildiz's (2009) study. For example, "Although Taiwanese students indicated that they needed a caring expression such as appreciation, approval, or encouragement, they found some of the American students too direct, which they interpreted as being impolite" (p. 61). Yildiz (2009) also suggests, "American students tended to directly address the business, international students like Korean and Turkish students usually started their e-mails with a caring question or comment such as 'How are you?' or 'I hope your classes are going well'" (p. 62). Overall, with regard to May and Short's (2003) gardening in cyberspace metaphor, Yildiz found that cultivating and integrating both social presence and cultural awareness at the beginning of the online learning experience will yield a better overall course experience. This is because such an approach makes facilitators and participants aware of and accountable for individual differences. The next section of this chapter, in turn, introduces an online course that serves as a case study to provide examples that illustrate how the notion of social presence as noted by these authors can help online facilitators.

ABOUT THE CASE STUDY

The case study involves a Human Rights Education course developed through a partnership between the University of Minnesota's Department of Organizational Leadership, Policy, and Development (OLPD) and the Human Rights Center. This online course was originally designed for an audience of

K-12 practitioners, but the course has wider appeal across many different constituent groups including

- Community practitioners
- Educational practitioners (including K-12 and higher education)
- Graduate students (M.A., Ed.D., and Ph.D.) in educational disciplines
- Graduate students in other disciplines, including Law, Public Policy, or the International Education minor
- Undergraduates, often majoring in Global Studies or completing the Leadership minor offered in the OLPD Department
- Volunteer community human rights experts (who are not taking the course for credit – just volunteering their time and expertise)

Although the majority of the students in the course have been based in and around the metropolitan area of the University of Minnesota-Twin Cities, there are several students outside of this area and around the world. These individuals have selected the course because of an interest in the topic and because it is one of the few courses in the College of Education and Human Development offered entirely online.

One of the main tenets of Human Rights Education (HRE) is that it is participant-guided and context-driven. As such, the course instructors create an authentic experience for students by bringing in as many real-life experiences of HRE advocates and practitioners from around the world as possible. The course is co-taught completely in the Moodle online learning environment. The course includes the following three major themes: Introduction to Human Rights; The need for Human Rights Education; and Human Rights Education in P-16 and the Community. See Figure 1

for an illustration of the Moodle online learning environment for this course.

This study focuses on three subsequent iterations of the Human Rights Education course (Spring 2008, Spring 2009, and Spring 2010). The majority of the coursework is conducted asynchronously with posts in discussion forums and blogs as well as the completion of activities through other Websites. In each of the three years the course has been taught, the instructors have integrated opportunities for additional online interactions. Such opportunities include synchronous sessions recorded through a conferencing software program and archived online for students to view asynchronously as their busy schedules allow.

One unique aspect of this course is that experts from the community – individuals who are practitioners in the field (and not students in the course) – voluntarily provide content for the students (lectures, PowerPoint presentations, articles, drafts of chapters). These experts also engage in dialogue with the students in discussion forums and/or participate in the recorded synchronous presentations and discussions. Finally, the course culminates in a final project of the students' own choosing that situates their learning about human rights and human rights education in their own personal, professional, or academic contexts. Experts also give feedback on these projects based on their experience in the Human Rights Education field. The chapter's next section examines how Whiteside's (2007) Social Presence Model as a framework to maximize online learning experiences involving these individuals.

SOCIAL PRESENCE MODEL WITH CASE EXAMPLES

Whiteside's (2007) Social Presence Model provides a simple framework that helps academics, practitioners from industry, students, and other professionals around the world to maximize their

Figure 1. Human rights education course overview

BLOCK 1: Introduction to Human Rights and Human Rights Education

(Weeks 2 to 4)

- KNOWLEDGE: Foundations of Human Rights
- ATTITUDES AND SKILLS: The Building Blocks for Human Rights Education
- ACTION: Curriculum and Action Planning Tools
- ACCOUNTABILITY: Evaluation, Assessment, and Rippling Impact

BLOCK 1: Introduction
BLOCK 1: DISCUSSION FORUM   4 unread posts
BLOCK 1: Assignment

January 25–January 31

Week 2
Foundations of Human Rights and Why Do We Need Them?
Block 1: Introduction to Human Rights and Human Rights Education

Introduction

Introduction: Week 2

Human Rights Foundations: What are Human Rights? Who are Human Rights leaders?

Introduction to Human Rights
Human Rights Foundations - Presentation

online exchanges. This is done through increasing participant awareness of linguistic nuances, social interaction, learning communities, instructor involvement, and prior knowledge and experiences. In relation to May and Short's (2003) *gardening in cyberspace* metaphor, the Social Presence Model is analogous to "conditioning the soil" in the online learning environment. This benefit is due to the fact the Model paves the way for developing critical connections and cultivating relationships among and between facilitators and participants. In so doing, it increases student motivation and fostering good online pedagogical practices.

This Model is based on programmatic research in social presence (Whiteside, 2007) that inte-

grated the coding schemes of Rourke, Anderson, Garrison, and Archer (2001) and Swan and Shih (2005). Rourke, Anderson, Garrison, and Archer (2001) focused their research and coding scheme in three distinct social presence categories: Affective, Cohesive, and Interactive categories. The Affective category involves emotive responses, such as openness, humor, and warmth. The Cohesive category involves learners seeing themselves as part of a larger community. Examples of this category include sharing additional resources, greeting each other, and referring to each other by name. Finally, the Interactive category involves learners' interaction with each other, such as direct quotes, questions, and agreements. Swan and Shih (2005) build and refine on this existing three-prong coding scheme. These experts added codes for emotion, value, course reflection, approval, and personal advice.

Appendix A shows how Whiteside (2007) integrated the coding schemes of Rourke, Anderson, Garrison, and Archer (2001) and Swan (2002). In the course of her social presence study involving two iterations of a 13-month blended program on School Technology Leadership, Whiteside found that "two other important factors emerged that affect social presence: a) knowledge and experience and b) instructor involvement" (p. 249). Thus, Whiteside's Social Presence Model integrates five key elements that can help instructors maximize the learning experience (See Figure 2). The Social Presence Model and its five key elements seeks to help facilitators increase the level of trust and respect in an online community, which can motivate participants to take a more active role in their own and their peers' construction of knowledge.

The rest of this section offers examples from the discussion responses and blog reflections in the Human Rights Education course to help online facilitators better identify the five elements of the Social Presence Model: affective association, community cohesion, interaction intensity, knowledge and experience, and instructor investment. Please note that because many of the discussion posts and blog reflections in the course included self-disclosure and personal information, the authors used both pseudonyms and masking techniques that did not change the intent of the entry. This approach instead prevented individual identities from being disclosed. An example of a masking technique would be changing or deleting the name of a school a student wrote about in a post.

Association

Affective Association addresses the emotional connections in the course. Affection Association examines Emotion, Humor and Sarcasm, Paralanguage, and Self-Disclosure (See Table 1).

For example, in the second week of class of the first year of the Human Rights Education course, one student shared experiences of discrimination in her life:

Okay, so I just wrote a book about my own experiences and maybe it sounded a little mad... sorry

Figure 2. The Social Presence Model

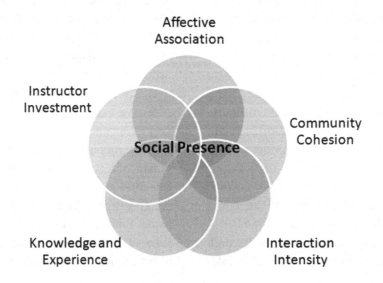

about that, but I get kind of passionate about that topic, and my own personal experiences are largely what have led me to [my graduate] program. All people have worth and should be valued for their differences and are deserving of the respect of others and I am going to do whatever I can to make that happen. And THAT is why Human Rights are important.

This student's responses exemplifies Affective Associate in form of emotion (e.g., mad, sorry, passionate), paralanguage (e.g., THAT), and self-disclosure (e.g., my own personal experiences are largely what have led me to [my graduate] program).

Community Cohesion

Community Cohesion represents the extent to which participants see the group as a community. This concept is examined through Additional Resources, Experiential Sharing, Greetings or Salutations, Social Sharing, Group Reference, and Vocatives (See Table 2).

The following instructor response in the Human Rights Education course provides an example of Community Cohesion:

It's wonderful to hear, Stephanie, that your peers' reflections have spurred you to think more and challenge yourself to do something... hopefully the rest of the class will provide you with lots of answers as to WHAT you can do about it. We should revisit this later in the course. Please remind me if it gets lost in the myriad of other things we do. Isabel

In this example, one of the Human Rights Education co-instructors warmly refers to her student by name, adds some Affective Association (emotion, paralanguage), connects her student's comment to the learning community as a whole, and signs her post with her first name.

Interaction Intensity

Interaction Intensity refers to the level of interaction among participants. Interaction includes

Table 1. Expressions Related to Affective Association

Affective Association	
Emotion	"Conventional expressions of emotion, or unconventional expressions of emotion" (Rourke, Anderson, Garrison, & Archer, 2001).
Humor or sarcasm	"Teasing, cajoling, irony, understatements, sarcasm" (Rourke, Anderson, Garrison, & Archer, 2001).
Paralanguage	Features of text outside formal syntax used to convey emotion (e.g., emoticons, punctuation, exclamation, and capitalization).
Self-Disclosure	"Presents details of life outside of class, or expresses vulnerability" (Rourke, Anderson, Garrison, & Archer, 2001).

Table 2. Expressions Related to Community Cohesion

Additional Resources	Participant provides additional readings, URLs, or other resources to help another participant or the entire group.
Greetings or Salutations	Uses "communication that serves a purely social function: greetings, closures" (Rourke, Anderson, Garrison, & Archer, 2001).
Group References	"Addresses the group as we, us, our" (Rourke, Anderson, Garrison, & Archer, 2001).
Social Sharing	Sharing information relating to their work and/or home life. Also includes phatics, such as Happy Birthday!
Vocatives – Refers to by Name	Addresses or refers "to participants by name" (Rourke, Anderson, Garrison, & Archer, 2001).

Acknowledgement, Compliment or Agreement, Disagreement, Inquiry, and Opinions or Comments. (See Table 3).

The following student response to another student showcases the Interaction Intensity of the Model:

I agree very much with your response, especially about showing 'problems associated with' the videos. Though you point out that the girl's perfect English undermines reality. Would your response have differed if she had a heavy/thick accent"

In this response, the student expresses acknowledgement and agreement in the opening sentence, and she poses a question back to her classmate, which shows a high-level of interaction intensity.

Knowledge and Experience

One of important themes that emerged from the literature and the research is that sharing prior knowledge and experiences can be an important element for overall social presence. The following example exemplifies the how one student's experience can help deepen the discussion:

In my school right now, I think of a student who has her human rights violated daily by fellow staff members. This student is one of a handful of minority students in our school yet in a school of over 1000 students, she accounts for a third of all office referrals in our building - I checked. When something happens, she is usually sought out and

blamed for crimes she didn't commit. She's been kicked off a sporting team because she lost her uniform and doesn't have the money to replace it. Interestingly enough, three minority students have been kicked off teams in the last two years for one reason or another, while white students who lose their uniforms are still allowed to participate use without being reprimanded.

The value of this response is that it provides students without a lot of content-level experience the opportunity to comment on one of their peer's direct experiences. It also creates an open opportunity for other students with similar or differing experiences to freely share their knowledge to support the entire learning community.

Instructor Investment

Instructor Investment refers to the extent to which the instructor is an invested, active partner in the learning community. Collison, Elbaum, Haavind, and Tinker (2000) stress the importance of instructor investment, which the instructor can mitigate through active involvement. The following instructor response in the HRE course provides an example of Instructor Investment:

Stephanie,

Please share with us "Why do your students think there hasn't been a female US president? What might they think, feel, know are the reasons?" I really wonder where we may have failed in engaging

Table 3. Expressions Related to Interaction Intensity

Acknowledgement	Quotes or refers to others posts (Rourke, Anderson, Garrison, & Archer, 2001; Swan, 2002).
Compliments or Agreement	"Compliments others or the contents of others' messages." (Rourke, Anderson, Garrison, & Archer, 2001; Swan, 2002).
Disagreement	Responds to others with a respectful, supported disagreement.
Inquiry	Asks questions of "other students or the moderator" (Rourke, Anderson, Garrison, & Archer, 2001). Or requests ideas from students without asking questions.
Opinions or Comments	Expresses an opinion or comment based on the class material or their experience.

women in the US into political leadership. I was your students' age when the Equal Rights Amendment (ERA) - http://www.equalrightsamendment. org/era.htm -failed to pass in the US. I haven't reviewed much of this history, so I found it interested to look back in time today. I came across a link of a speech by Shirley Chisholm on the ERA.

In this example, the instructor's response addresses the importance of instructor involvement as she refers to the student by name, asks for further information about her post, makes a personal connection with the student, and provides more resources that might be interesting.

SPECIFIC STRATEGIES TO MAXIMIZE ONLINE INTERACTIONS

Asynchronous online environments can offer learners and facilitators a number of unique, positive characteristics, such as autonomy in when to contribute to the learning environment, a chance to connect more deeply with more people. It also allows time to reflect and refine responses, allows for equal participation among participants, some anonymity and distance from other participants, and permits shared authority among facilitators and participants.

For many online facilitators, these positive attributes make online learning experiences worthy of the challenges they face, such as meeting participants' round-the-clock expectations in environments that are inherently more demanding of their time. Additionally, facilitators are challenged to keep their participants' attention from a myriad of competing, online distractions, not to mention the pervasive everyday, real-time demands, including work schedules, family responsibilities, social commitments, professional development opportunities, and untimely emergencies. Thus, there is a tremendous need for specific, simple strategies that might maximize online interactions and meaningful learning outcomes. This section

presents a potential issue that online facilitators might face, connects it to the Social Presence Model, and provides strategies or examples to help maximize online interactions and the overall learning experience.

Strategy One: Affective Association by Assuming the Social Negotiator Role

Online learning experts, Conrad and Donaldson, introduced the Phases of Engagement in their 2004 work entitled *Engaging the Online Learner*. The first phase of their Phases of Engagement framework introduced the learner's role as a *Newcomer* in the learning community and the facilitator's role as that of the *Social Negotiator*. These experts stress that this initial Social Negotiation phase "is actually the essence of the course" and that "the rest of the course will go much more smoothly if care is taken to promote the appropriate frame of mind" in this first phase of the process (p. 10). The Social Negotiation phase, thus, involves cultivating the foundation of the online learning experience. In relation to May and Short's (2003) cybergarden metaphor, the phase involves tilling and preparing the "soil" of the online learning environment before planting the seeds (the academic content).

Therefore, instead of leaping right into the academic content, Conrad and Donaldson (2004) strongly suggest that the facilitator provide activities that "help the learners get to know one another" (p. 11). These activities include icebreakers, individual introductions, and discussions concerning community issues. Conrad and Donaldson also urge that this earliest phase of engagement is ultimately important because it sets the "initial tone of the course" and helps the learners understand "that others in the community will be just as important as the instructor, if not more so at times" (p. 10). Finally, Conrad and Donaldson provide a helpful checklist to help create effective icebreakers. For example, they ask "Does it request a person to be imaginative or express genuine emotions or openness?" (p. 47). These authors devote several chapters to example activities, such as Bingo, Classmate Quiz, Lost in Space, One Word, What Kind of Animal, and Portrait (p. 48).

In the Human Rights Educations course studied by the authors, one such introductory activity involves starting with a Moodle scavenger hunt to provide students with a fun, risk-free list of tasks to complete to familiarize themselves with the online course management system. One task as part of that list is to post a introductory biography (profile) in the Bio Forum. Another task involves following the directions on how to post an image as one's profile picture. Luckily, one of the more personable features in the Moodle online learning environment (but not in all course management systems) is that every time a participant posts in a discussion forum, his or her chosen photo displays. This feature helps to build more community and social presence into the online learning environment.

Strategy Two: Interaction Intensity with Extended Introductory Profiles

To help alleviate any feelings of isolation that an online learner might feel, a second strategy involves online facilitators assigning an extended introductory profile. These profiles are more than a quick two-minute, one-sentence introduction. Instead, they are a deep, rich profile that is several paragraphs long. The rationale behind extended introductory profiles is that they allow learners to gain a better sense of each other to enable them to interact more with each other in the discussion forums. To help new online learners get started, the facilitator(s) should provide a rich model for their participants. Here's an example from one of the instructors of the Human Rights Education course:

Welcome!! I am really looking forward to this Human Rights Education course with you. I hope that we can share our own hopes, dreams, learn-

ings, and struggles to work for justice, equality, and human rights for all. When I was younger, I remember constantly being challenged as an idealist, which hit hard. I would respond back, 'I know the realities of the world only too well.' Yet, each confrontation was difficult. I reflected on whether I was being an unrealistic, idealist. Through my journey, I now agree with my grandfather, who tried to support me with his words, 'Carly, I'm an idealist. Once you stop being an idealist, you might as well stop living.' My grandfather's words of wisdom have kept me going, working to educate for and about human rights. I have been very fortunate to have worked for justice from grade school forward.

I have facilitated prejudice reduction workshops for teachers, taught decision groups and parenting classes for fathers in prison and for mothers on the outside, and developed a self-esteem class for young children with parents in prison. I also edited the first report for Article 19, a freedom of expression organization in London, and assisted economically disadvantaged individuals obtain legal assistance with a justice foundation in the upper Midwest. In 1989, I became the Co-Director of the Human Rights Center at the University of Minnesota. Within this capacity, I have developed a number of human rights education programs and initiatives that I hope to share with you throughout the course. Thanks again for your participation!

Here's an example of an extended introduction from one of the Human Rights Education students:

Hi! My name is Hilda Johannsen and I'm in my second semester of master's studies in Comparative & International Development Education in EdPA here at the U.

I hail from Grand Forks, North Dakota, but I attended college in this area. In 2005 I graduated with a B.A. in English from St. Olaf College in Northfield, MN.

From 2005-08, I taught English in Slovakia, one year at the primary level and two at the secondary level. While I truly miss teaching, the Slovak language and people, and the European way of life, I am enjoying being a student again quite a bit. I love the distinct four seasons that Minnesota offers and relish in the outdoor beauty which surrounds us: cycling the Grand Rounds trails, cross-country skiing, and jogging. I really enjoy studying in small groups or pairs in coffee shops, so if any of you ever feel the need for face-to-face interaction, I'd like meeting [sic] you!

I am not very well-versed in human rights, but for that reason I am eager to learn more about our topic. After graduation, I hope to work in foreign policy or for an NGO that assists developing nations with their education systems. I presume that knowledge of this topic will be pertinent, and I'm looking forward to learning from all of you and your diverse backgrounds.

Each extended introduction offers a number of ways (e.g., hometown, educational program, background, interests, future plans) to connect with other learners to increase the level of social presence.

Strategy Three: Community Cohesion by Early Cultural Awareness

Both Tu (2001) and Yildiz (2009) found in their social presence research that cultural differences definitely impact the online learning situation. Therefore, participants should be made aware of these nuances at the very beginning of their course experience in the form of a "netiquette" to "avoid misunderstandings and unnecessary conflicts" (Yildiz, 2009, p. 63). Yildiz suggests that student learn about "possible implications of delayed responses" and that they should be "warned about the potential misunderstandings caused by the absence of social context cues" (p. 63).

Additionally, to help build community, participants in a multicultural online environment should be introduced to a multicultural framework. Such a framework might be Hofstede's (2001) five cultural dimensions where they can gain knowledge about cultural dynamics in the form of indicators – e.g., Power Distance Index (PDI), Individualism, Masculinity, Uncertainty Avoidance Index (UAI), and Long-Term Orientation (LTO). Online facilitators should consider developing icebreaker activities that allow students to learn more about cultural differences and potential misunderstandings before addressing the course content.

In this response early in the Human Rights Education course, a student explains her Jewish heritage and how it impacts her interest in the topic:

Ever since I was little, I have been interested in human rights…I became particularly interested when I studied the Holocaust, both because half of my relatives are Jewish and because I just didn't understand how something like the Holocaust could happen. During college, I studied political philosophy, and had a teacher that had us read authors such as Vaclav Havel and Hannah Arendt. This literature, coupled with my political science background, led me to realize that while inherent rights do exist, there have not been enough political actions taken to secure them. I studied in depth the Civil Rights and Black Power Movements, as well as the Constitution and the Bill of Rights, and have grown quite dissapointed (sic) with the attention paid to human rights. Because of this, for me, I have grown to look at human rights from a very political and legal standpoint. To me, it's interesting to look at what has been done by the legislature to protect human rights, and to look at what still needs to be done legislatively.

In this example, the student shares her cultural background, which gives her classmates an early understanding of her experience and background, which could affect their responses and potentially avoid cultural misunderstandings as the course progresses.

As another example, one of the early activities in the Human Rights Education course involved Building a Culture of Human Rights. In this discussion post, the course instructors explained how much she learned from the experience and diversity of the two course participants, and she then invited other students to share their experiences:

Sandra and Crystal,

I concur. I have learned so much from your forum discussions. It is really interesting to have these discussions in written format, because I am able to see the diverse ways and learning web for your thoughts and comments.

The course participants come from so many different disciplines with such a wide range of experiences, we really represent The Village Video that was shared by Luisa.

In terms of your peers in the class, do you think that you benefit by seeing someone apply their experiences through HRE in a different educational setting and program area? If so, how does this expand your learning? If not, why do you think that you learn better with a more homogenous learning environment?

Strategy Four: Knowledge and Experience Through the K-W-L Activity

One challenge that often arises in online learning is identifying the range of knowledge and experience of your participants while also being able to meet the needs of your audience. This aspect is perhaps more noted in online courses than face-to-face ones, for some students actively seek online courses and might choose based on course availability and interest rather than their level of background knowledge or experience. As

mentioned, the course was originally designed for K-12 practitioners, but the actual participants in the course have come from a broad range of backgrounds, disciplines, and professional experience levels.

One strategy that has been successful in the Human Rights Education course involves requiring students to post a series of responses gauged to identify their background knowledge in the content and the reasons why they have chosen the course. The basic outline of the activity follows:

- The forum is called the K-W-L forum. The *K* stands for *What do you KNOW*? The *W* relates to *What do you WANT to know?* The *L* pertains to *What did you LEARN*?
- In the first week of class, students post in the K-W-L forum in answer to the first two questions.
- In the last week of the class, students return to their initial posts in the K-W-L forum and reflect on what they knew when they came to the class, what they said they wanted to learn, and whether or not they learned it.

The following is an example of a student's initial post:

I wish I could say I know quite a bit about human rights, but that is not the case. As I have seen from other postings, we are all claiming to know very little. I am familiar with the Universal Declaration of Human Rights as I read it for a class last semester. It reinforced the idea that we all, as humans regardless of our class, gender, race, age, etc, should have equal rights. While I was reading it, I remember thinking that this is all well and good, but the reality is we do not have equal rights and they vary greatly across borders.

I want to know more about how, in an age of globalization, we can better achieve universal human rights and what are the barriers preventing it?

In the closing weeks of the course, this same student's final post in the K-W-L forum shows the power of this activity for student learning:

With one week left in the semester, I wanted to revisit the K-W-L forum from the first week of the course. In my initial post I admitted that I didn't quite know much when it came to human rights... I learned a lot. I learned about the history of human rights and the birth of the UDHR. I learned about the rights of children. I learned that it goes beyond just the color of your skin, but having something as simple as adequate housing or working conditions. I learned that there is a pressing need to integrate human rights into curriculum at ALL levels and not just in K-12 lesson plans. The learning continued with different ways to teach, different learning styles and how to effectively integrate human rights into a classroom

Perhaps the biggest 'L' of all, was that I learned I could be an agent of change. Going forward, my work in higher education can be shaped and influenced from the human rights perspective. Working with students on a daily basis, I am fortunate to be in a position to inspire change. It takes one to make a difference, and I in a field that is full of many "ones," each who has the ability to change the world in a positive way if given the rights tools. My toolbox grew a little larger this semester.

Strategy Five: Instructor Investment with Early and Iterative Feedback

Another challenge that online instructors face is providing feedback on student progress and their course activities and discussion posts early-on in the term to help them understand the course and instructor expectations as soon as possible. Feedback serves as the fertilizer for the online learning experience (May & Short, 2003). Students need feedback to understand how to improve their work and how to gain critical skills. Additionally, feedback is critical because it is perceived by students as a direct reflection of how much the instructor is invested in their learning experience.

The instructors of Human Rights Education course employed the following strategies to achieve a balance of instructor investment and peer interaction to better meet students' needs for early and iterative feedback:

- In the third iteration of the course, the instructors reorganized the course content into manageable chunks or blocks, consisting of a three-week period of time with one major assignment due.
- Another strategy involved moving from a mid-term paper to two smaller response papers, due at times of the students' choosing in the middle one-third of the course. This change both empowers the students to choose weeks that work with their personal and professional responsibilities, and it also spreads out the grading so the instructor has fewer papers to grade at any one point in time and can provide more feedback more often.
- The course instructors restructured the discussion forums into small groups where group members take turns synthesizing and posting a response for the entire group each week. The instructor and students in other groups can then read fewer, more thoughtful responses that allow all participants to save time and to provide more focus and depth in the discussion.

Strategy Six: Instructor Investment Through Individual Email Check-Ins with Participants

The appeal of online courses is often that students can more easily juggle personal, academic, and professional responsibilities. They do not need to be on campus at the same time every week. They do not have to shift family duties in the evening to attend night classes. Accordingly, online facilitators often use broad due dates for discussions to aid in that flexibility, such as post by midnight on a given Saturday. But, as a result, there might be few postings early in the unit and a flurry of postings later in the week. As a result, gaps can appear at certain points in participation. These participation gaps can align with the Instructor Involvement piece of Whiteside's (2007) Social Presence Model, as it requires investment on the part of the instructor to check-in with the students, something that is rarely done in a face-to-face class.

The following excerpt illustrates a simple strategy used by the online facilitators in the Human Rights Education course of sending an individual "check-in" email addressed by name and customized to each course participant at approximately one-third and two-thirds through the course:

We realize that every participant in the class has a full plate and is involved in many different academic, professional, and personal activities at once. Therefore, we realize that participation rates in the course will vary somewhat over the course of the semester...Below is individualized feedback on your progress. We have also included our thoughts on your response rates and overall participation in the course activities.

In this example, the instructors explained the course expectations in a caring, affective way, which illustrated their high level of investment in the overall learning experience. Overall, by using the Social Presence Model and these simple strategies, we suggest that academics, practitioners, students/participants, and other professionals can make more effective decisions related to the uses and design of online media when interacting with individuals from other cultures.

CONCLUSION

This chapter offers Whiteside's (2007) Social Presence Model with course examples from the Human Right Education course, and specific related strategies to help academics, practitioners, students, and other professionals around the world maximize their online interactions. As individuals continue to learn more about cultivating online interactions in the spirit of May and Short's (2003) gardening metaphor, social presence might help us discover additional connections and alignments to institutional goals and strategies, such as learning outcomes, student engagement, instructor/student roles and responsibilities, and retention rates. The authors welcome additional studies that apply qualitative, quantitative, and mixed-methods approaches to social presence research and that extend its rich history to other disciplines.

In sum, the authors suggest that social presence represents an imperative literacy for facilitators and participants alike. The authors find it to be akin to any influential literacy, such as technological literacy, rhetorical literacy, and media literacy. It is a literacy that requires careful consideration, cultivation, and continued exploration.

REFERENCES

Anderson, T. (2008). Social software to support distance education learners. In Anderson, T. (Ed.), *Theory and practice of online learning* (2nd ed., pp. 221–244). Edmonton, Alberta: Athabasca University Press.

Bai, H. (2003). Student motivation and social presence in online learning: Implications for future research. In C. Crawford et al. (Eds.), *Proceedings of Society for Information Technology & Teacher Education International Conference 2003* (pp. 2714-2720). Albuquerque, NM: Association for the Advancement of Computing in Education.

Bandura, A. (1973). *Aggression: A social learning analysis*. Englewood Cliffs, NJ: Prentice-Hall.

Bandura, A. (1977). *Social learning theory*. New York, NY: General Learning Press.

Bandura, A. (1986). *Social foundations of thought and action*. Englewood Cliffs, NJ: Prentice-Hall.

Chen, N. S. Kinshuk, Wei, C. W., & Wang, M. J. (2009). A framework for social presence in synchronous cyber classrooms. In *Proceedings of the 9th IEEE International Conference on Advanced Learning Technologies* (pp. 40-44). Riga, Latvia: IEEE Computer Society Press.

Collison, G., Elbaum, B., Haavind, S., & Tinker, R. (2000). *Facilitating online learning: Effective strategies for moderators*. Madison, WI: Atwood Publishing.

Conrad, R., & Donaldson, A. (2004). *Engaging the online learner: Activities and resources for creative instruction*. San Francisco, CA: Jossey-Bass.

Dewey, J. (1910). *How we think*. Boston, MA: D. C. Heath. doi:10.1037/10903-000

Dewey, J. (1916) *Democracy and education: An introduction to the philosophy of education* (1966 ed.). New York, NY: Free Press.

Dunlap, J. C., & Lowenthal, P. R. (2009). Tweeting the night away: Using Twitter to enhance social presence. *Journal of Information Systems Education, 20*(2), 129–136.

DuVall, J. B., Powell, M. R., Hodge, E., & Ellis, M. (2007). Text messaging to improve social presence in online learning. *Educause Quarterly, 3*, 24-28. Retrieved October 10, 2010, from http://net.educause.edu/ ir/ library/ pdf/ EQM0733.pdf

Garrison, D. R., & Kanuka, H. (2004). Blended learning: Uncovering its transformative potential in higher education. *The Internet and Higher Education, 7*(2), 95–105. doi:10.1016/j.iheduc.2004.02.001

Gunawardena, C. N., & Zittle, F. J. (1997). Social presence as a predictor of satisfaction within a computer-mediated conferencing environment. *American Journal of Distance Education, 11*(3), 8–26. doi:10.1080/08923649709526970

Hingorani, K. K. (2008). Social presence, personality types, and IT-supported teaching methods. *Issues in Information Systems, 9*(2), 56–62.

Hodge, E. M., Tabrizi, M. H. N., Farwell, M. A., & Wuensch, K. L. (2007). Virtual reality classrooms: Strategies for creating a social presence. *International Journal of Social Sciences, 2*, 105–109.

Hofstede, G. (2001). *Culture's consequences: Comparing values, behaviors, institutions, and organizations across nations*. Thousand Oaks, CA: Sage.

Joyce, K. M., & Brown, A. (2009). Enhancing social presence in online learning: Mediation strategies applied to social networking tools. *Online Journal of Distance Learning Administration, 12*(4). Retrieved October 10, 2010, from http://www.westga.edu/ ~distance/ ojdla/ winter124/ joyce124.html

Jusoff, K., & Khodabandelou, R. (2009). Preliminary study on the role of social presence in blended learning. *International Education Studies, 2*(4), 79–83.

Kehrwald, B. (2007). The ties that bind: social presence, relations, and productive collaboration in online learning environments. In *Proceedings of ASCILITE Conference*, Singapore. Retrieved October 10, 2010, from http://www.ascilite.org.au/ conferences/ singapore07/ procs/ kehrwald.pdf

Kekwaletswe, R. M. (2007). Social presence awareness for knowledge transformation in a mobile learning environment. *International Journal of Education and Development using Information and Communication Technology, 3*(4), 102-109.

Lu, J., Huang, W., Ma, H., & Luce, T. (2007). Interaction and social presence in technology-mediated learning: A partial least squares model. In *Proceedings IEEE 3rd International Conference on Wireless Communications, Networking and Mobile Computing* (pp.4411-4414). Shanghai, China.

Marcus, S. (2006). Measure by measure: How WBT can help create a social online presence. *Campus-Wide Information Systems, 23*(2), 56–67. doi:10.1108/10650740610654447

May, G. L., & Short, D. (2003). Gardening in cyberspace: A metaphor to enhance online teaching and learning. *Journal of Management Education, 27*, 673–693. doi:10.1177/1052562903257940

Mehrabian, A. (1969). Some referents and measures of nonverbal behavior. *Behavior Research Methods and Instruction, 1*(6), 205–207.

Mykota, D., & Duncan, R. (2007). Learner characteristics as predictors of online social presence. *Canadian Journal of Education, 30*(1), 157–170. doi:10.2307/20466630

Na Ubon, A., & Kimble, C. (2003). Supporting the creation of social presence in online learning communities using asynchronous text-based CMC. In *Proceedings of the 3rd International Conference on Technology in Teaching and Learning in Higher Education* (pp.295-300). Heidelberg, Germany.

Picciano, A. G. (2002). Beyond student perceptions: Issues of interaction, presence, and performance in an online course. *Journal of Asynchronous Learning Networks, 6*(1), 21–40.

Polhemus, L., Shih, L. F., & Swan, K. (2001). *Virtual interactivity: The representation of social presence in an online discussion.* Paper presented at the annual meeting of the American Educational Research Association, Seattle, WA.

Rettie, R. (2003). *Connectedness, awareness and social presence.* 6th International Presence Workshop. Aalborg, Denmark. Retrieved November 8, 2009 http://www.presence-research.org/ papers/ Rettie.pdf.

Richardson, J., & Swan, K. (2003). Examining social presence in online courses in relation to students' perceived learning and satisfaction. *Journal of Asynchronous Learning Networks, 6*(1), 76–90.

Rourke, L., Anderson, T., Garrison, D. R., & Archer, W. (2001). Assessing social presence in asynchronous textbased computer conferencing. *Journal of Distance Education, 14*(2), 51–70.

Shen, K. N., & Khalifa, M. (2007). Exploring multi-dimensional conceptualization of social presence in the context of online communities. In Jacko, J. (Ed.), *Human-computer interaction: HCI applications and services* (pp. 999–1008). New York, NY: Springer. doi:10.1007/978-3-540-73111-5_110

Short, J., William, E., & Christie, B. (1976). *The social psychology of telecommunications.* Toronto, ON: Wiley.

Stacey, E. (2002). Social presence online: Networking learners at a distance, education and Information Technologies. *Education and Information Technologies, 7*(4), 287–294. doi:10.1023/A:1020901202588

Stein, D., & Wanstreet, C. (2003). *Role of social presence, choice of online or face-to-face group format, and satisfaction with perceived knowledge gained in a distance learning environment.* Paper Presented at the 2003 Midwest Research to Practice Conference in Adult Continuing and Community Education.

Swan, K. (2002). Building communities in online courses: The importance of interaction. *Education Communication and Information, 2*(1), 23–49. doi:10.1080/1463631022000005016

Tu, C. (2001). How Chinese perceive social presence: An examination inline learning environment. *Educational Media International, 38*(1), 45–60. doi:10.1080/09523980010021235

Tu, C. (2002). The measurement of social presence in an online learning environment. *International Journal on E-Learning, 1*(2), 34–45.

Vesely, P., Bloom, L., & Sherlock, J. (2007). Key elements of building online community: Comparing faculty and student perceptions. *Journal of Online Learning and Teaching, 3*, 234–246.

Wenger, E. (1998). *Communities of practice: Learning, meaning, and identity.* Cambridge, UK: Cambridge University Press.

Whiteside, A. L. (2007). *Exploring social presence in communities of practice within a hybrid learning environment: A longitudinal examination of two case studies within the School Technology Leadership graduate-level certificate program.* Unpublished doctoral dissertation, University of Minnesota.

Whiteside, A. L., Hughes, J. E., & McLeod, S. (2005, September). *Opening the shades of isolationism: An examination of social presence in a hybrid-model certificate program.* Paper presented at the New Media Research @ UMN Conference, Minneapolis, MN.

Wise, A., Chang, J., Duffy, T., & Del Valle, R. (2004). The effects of teacher social presence on student satisfaction, engagement, and learning. *Journal of Educational Computing Research, 31*(3), 247–271. doi:10.2190/V0LB-1M37-RNR8-Y2U1

Woods, R., & Ebersole, S. (2003). Becoming a communal architect in the online classroom—Integrating cognitive and affective learning for maximum effect in Web-based learning. *Online Journal of Distance Learning Administration, 6*(1). Retrieved October 10, 2010, from www.westga.edu/~distance/ojdla/spring61/woods61.htm

Yildiz, S. (2009). Social presence in the Web-based classroom: Implications for intercultural communication. *Journal of Studies in International Education, 13*, 46–67. doi:10.1177/1028315308317654

KEY TERMS AND DEFINITIONS

Affective Association: One of the elements used in measuring social presence; the level of emotive connectedness exemplified by paralanguage, feelings, and self disclosure.

Authentic Learning: Incorporation of activities, professionals, issues, and contexts of the field into educational environments.

Community Cohesion: One of the elements used in measuring social presence; the level of community connectedness exemplified by references to the course community as "we" as well as when participants suggest additional resources for each other.

Blended Learning: Also called hybrid learning, describes a learning experience that takes place in a combination of online and face-to-face environments.

Instructor Investment: One of the elements used in measuring social presence—the extent to which the students perceive the instructor(s) of the course is invested in their unique learning needs.

Interaction Intensity: One of the elements used in measuring social presence characterized by quoting or paraphrasing responses as well as referring to each other by name.

Knowledge and Experience: One of the elements used in measuring social presence—the collective and individual knowledge and experiences available within a course community.

Online Learning: Learning experiences conducted solely through the Internet.

Social Presence in Education: The degree of connectedness among students and instructors that creates a level of trust, respect, and comfort that affects the learning experience.

Technology-Enhanced Learning: Learning supported, supplemented, and/or reinforced by technologies. Includes technology use in face-to-face, blended, and online learning environments.

APPENDIX: WHITESIDE'S (2007) SOCIAL PRESENCE CODING SCHEME

Affective Association	
Emotion	"Conventional expressions of emotion, or unconventional expressions of emotion" (Rourke, Anderson, Garrison, & Archer, 2001).
Humor or sarcasm	"Teasing, cajoling, irony, understatements, sarcasm" (Rourke, Anderson, Garrison, & Archer, 2001).
Paralanguage	Features of text outside formal syntax used to convey emotion (e.g., emoticons, punctuation, exclamation, and capitalization).
Self-Disclosure	"Presents details of life outside of class, or expresses vulnerability" (Rourke, Anderson, Garrison, & Archer, 2001).

Community Cohesion	
Additional Resources	Participant provides additional readings, URLs, or other resources to help another participant or the entire group.
Greetings or Salutations	Uses "communication that serves a purely social function: greetings, closures" (Rourke, Anderson, Garrison, & Archer, 2001).
Group References	"Addresses the group as we, us, our" (Rourke, Anderson, Garrison, & Archer, 2001).
Social Sharing	Sharing information relating to their work and/or home life. Also includes phatics, such as Happy Birthday!
Vocatives – Refers to by Name	Addresses or refers "to participants by name" (Rourke, Anderson, Garrison, & Archer, 2001).

Interaction Intensity	
Acknowledgement	Quotes or refers to others posts (Rourke, Anderson, Garrison, & Archer, 2001; Swan, 2002).
Compliments or Agreement	"Compliments others or the contents of others' messages." (Rourke, Anderson, Garrison, & Archer, 2001; Swan, 2002).
Disagreement	Responds to others with a respectful, supported disagreement.
Inquiry	Asks questions of "other students or the moderator" (Rourke, Anderson, Garrison, & Archer, 2001). Or requests ideas from students without asking questions.
Opinions or Comments	Expresses an opinion or comment based on the class material or their experience.

Chapter 26

Language Abilities and Culture Clashes in Cyberspace:
Potential Problems for ESL/EFL Students in Hybrid Mainstream Classes

Anna M. Harrington
Edison State College, USA

ABSTRACT

An increasing number of ESL/EFL students are expected to enroll in hybrid (i.e., mixed on-site and online) mainstream courses populated by a majority of native-English-speaking students. However, due to varying language abilities and cultural clashes, the TESOL community has not yet explored the potential online communication problems for ESL/EFL students. This chapter examines issues of differences in language proficiency and cultural norms, identity, community, and muting that can affect computer-based education. The chapter also provides readers with teaching strategies that can be applied in hybrid mainstream courses that include ESL/EFL students.

INTRODUCTION

The recent proliferation of Internet access has led to an explosive growth in the use of hybrid course delivery (i.e., part of the course is conducted online and part is conducted on-site) by a number of colleges and universities. Current estimates, for example, note that between 5% and 21% of all college courses offered in the U.S. are now in some form of hybrid format (Sener, 2003; Allen,

Seaman, & Garrett, 2007). Unlike traditional on-site/face-to-face classes held only on campus or exclusively online courses conducted completely outside the traditional classroom, hybrid courses blend elements of both. In hybrid courses, 20% to 80% of face-to-face class meetings are replaced with online activities students complete outside the classroom and on their own time (Kaleta & Aycock, 2004; Kurthen & Smith, 2005/2006; Allen, Seaman, & Garrett, 2007). Yet, unlike participants in exclusively online classes, students in hybrid courses are required to maintain a limited

DOI: 10.4018/978-1-60960-833-0.ch026

on-campus presence and complete some assignments or activities in person/face-to-face with fellow classmates and in a traditional classroom setting. This on-site/online blend of course offering is predicted to increase as educators worldwide increasingly recognize this delivery method has the potential to offer the higher success rates of online-only courses coupled with the higher retention rates of on-site courses (Aycock, Garnham, & Kaleta, 2002; Duhaney, 2004; Garnham & Kaleta, 2002; Welker & Berardino, 2005-2006). Such thinking has led researchers to proclaim hybrid delivery to be "the best of both worlds: the infinite freedom of the Internet enhanced and made manageable by regular classroom interactions" (Stine, 2004, p. 66).

At this same time, the enrollment numbers for English as a second language (ESL) and English as a foreign language (EFL) students in U.S. schools are increasing. During the last two decades, the number of U.S. English language learners (ELLs) over age five has grown from 23 million to 47 million persons – or by an equivalent of 103 percent (Fu & Matoush, 2006, p. 10). Currently, one in every five K-12 students nationwide resides in a household where a language other than English is spoken, and by 2030, this number is projected to double (Urban Institute, 2005). Furthermore, the international education association NAFSA (2007) predicts continued slow growth in international student enrollment in the U.S., with 55% of its surveyed institutions reporting growth. This trend could result in more opportunities for intercultural interaction within U.S. college settings as more ESL/EFL students find themselves enrolled in mainstream classes along with a majority of native English-speaking (NES) students. Moreover, as the growth trend of hybrid educational delivery overlaps with increased ESL/EFL enrollment, it is not unrealistic to expect a higher number of ESL/EFL students to enroll in these hybrid classes.

Despite this impending intersection of increased hybrid offerings and ESL/EFL enrollment, the Teachers of English to Speakers of Other Languages (TESOL) education community has not yet opened a discussion of the implications of hybrid delivery for ESL/EFL students in mainstream classes. Some researchers have conducted studies that follow the experiences of students in hybrid ESL/EFL-only courses. (In such courses, ESL/EFL students only encounter other ESL/EFL students vs. in mainstream classes where the majority of their peers will be native English speakers/NES students.) The experiences these students have faced in mainstream classes, however, have been largely ignored. Such an examination, however, is needed now – as the numbers of ESL/EFL students who might participate in mainstream hybrid classes is only starting to increase.

In an effort to start a discussion of these issues, this chapter investigates potential problems ESL/EFL students might encounter when enrolled in hybrid classes comprised of a majority of NES students. The potential problem areas involve language abilities and cultural clashes, participation in academic communities, creation of academic and authorial identities, and muting (the silencing of others). The chapter then concludes with a discussion of items instructors of hybrid mainstream courses might wish to consider in order to create a more inclusive, more welcoming environment and a safe learning space for both ESL/EFL and NES students.

THE NEED FOR RESEARCH

Within the large body of literature on educational technology, research on the effects of hybrid delivery on ESL/EFL students is minimal. Lai and Kritsonis (2006) wrote of the advantages and disadvantages generally associated with computer technology and computer-assisted language learning (CALL) programs. The disadvantages they list, however, are problems faced by all students enrolled in hybrid courses and are not specific to ESL/EFL students. While Al-Jarf's (2004a) work deals specifically with ESL students, the online activities he describes are in addition to, not in place of, the regular ESL-only face-to-face sessions. Thus, he does not address true hybrid delivery. Three more recent articles specifically address language learning with true hybrid delivery, but all three focus on non-ESL/EFL students. Blake, Wilson, Cetto, and Pardo-Ballister (2008) and Chenoweth, Ushida and Murday (2006), for example, focus on oral proficiency among English-speaking American students who are studying a second language. By contrast, Long, Vignare, Rappold, and Mallory (2007) examine hybridity and communication access primarily for deaf students.

DePew's (2006) work addresses the use of technology as instructional aides, but does so mostly from the perspective of coping strategies for international teaching assistants and not as a type of instruction delivery. Similarly, Campbell (2007) examines ESL/EFL student performance using technology in a mainstream class and the benefits it brings, but as with Al-Jarf (2004a), such technologies were used in addition to regular class sessions and not in place of instructional delivery. Even Stephen Thorne (2005 and 2007) and Mark Warschauer (1996 and 1998), researchers known for exploring technology and its effects on language learners, have yet to address the effects of hybrid's dual deliveries on ESL/EFL students. While both individuals have detailed the uses and effects of various individual technologies in ESL/ EFL classes, neither has examined the issue of using technology *to replace* part of the face-to-face instruction delivery[1].

These factors give rise to an odd educational situation. Much research shows positive results when using technology to enhance language learning for ESL/EFL students (e.g., Sykes, Oskoz, & Thorne, 2008; Thorne & Black, 2007; Thorne & Payne, 2005; Warschauer, 2006). Research on the potential of hybrid instruction delivery for ESL/EFL students in mainstream classes, by contrast, has found itself in a metaphorical

"No Man's Land," stuck between research on individual technologies and research in ESL/ EFL-only classes. In fact, the effect of dual instruction delivery and the effects of intercultural interaction in a mixed learning environment have been largely ignored. As Villalva (2006) notes, while "studies often explore what a person can do under particular circumstances, the circumstances themselves often are neglected" (p. 32). Campbell (2007) also acknowledges this neglected when writing "although there is a sizable volume of literature on the pedagogic use of online discussion in general, there is comparatively little that focuses on how the medium could benefit ESL/ EFL students in a mainstream class" (p. 38). As a result, instructors will find there is little available research to assist them as they attempt to create effective hybrid courses for students from different cultural backgrounds and with varying language abilities. This lack of research on hybrid's dual instruction deliveries is an oversight which needs to be corrected. One key starting point for such investigation is that educators need to recognize the potential for conflict between ESL/EFL and native English-speaking (NES) students in mainstream courses.

CULTURAL CONFLICT IN MAINSTREAM COLLEGE CLASSES

Many U.S. colleges and universities offer ESL/ EFL-only courses, which restrict enrollment to ESL/EFL students, but some schools lack the resources to offer such classes. As a result, ESL/ EFL students attending these schools must instead enroll in mainstream courses, which have open enrollment for all students and can often be populated by a majority of NES students. These mainstream courses have the potential for creating a class community comprised of students with various English language abilities, cultural backgrounds, and differing ways of interacting and communicating. The result is a global educational context created through the various cultures of the students participating in the class. The online activities of a hybrid class also carry the potential for more intercultural interaction than traditional ground classes, as the assigned activities can be extended beyond the classroom community to interact with people from different cultures around the world through the use of email, real-time chat, Skype, and other technologies. Moreover, the potential for the types of activities, which comprise the online portion of a hybrid course, are virtually unlimited (Stine, 2004).

Few individuals would argue the benefits of a class with both ESL/EFL and NES students. The opportunity to interact with and learn from and about others from different cultures is a vital experience and skill in an increasingly diverse society and workforce (Offsite learning: On target? Pt. 1, 2002; Offsite learning: On target? Pt. II, 2002). This factor is particularly important given increased globalization, advances in technology, increased and easier mobility between countries and work assignments, and the resulting need to learn to interact sensitively with different cultures.

The proliferation of the Internet and other computer-mediated communication technologies has increased opportunities for cross-cultural interactions in a way previously unmatched in history. The global scope of today's online environment has quite possibly made the ability to interact with people from different countries an essential life skill because as Goodwin (1995) asserts, "so many of the problems that we face today within the United States are multinational in their origin and solution" (p. 78) but if solutions are to be found then "we must understand other places and peoples" (p. 78).

Unfortunately, such classes also have the potential for conflict due to differences in communication abilities between ESL/EFL students and their NES classmates. As Braine (1996), Harklau (1994), and Matsuda and Silva (1994), and Matsuda and Silva (2006) conclude, ESL/EFL students often feel threatened, afraid, or embarrassed in mainstream classes. "Some ESL/

EFL students," according to Matsuda and Silva (2006), "tend not to do well in mainstream courses partly because many of them feel intimidated by their NES peers who are obviously more proficient in English and comfortable with the U.S. classroom culture" (p. 248). Harklau (1994) reported that discussions in mainstream classes are generally dominated by NES students. This dominance results in some ESL/EFL students being afraid or embarrassed to speak up in mainstream classes. As a result, these students are not able to engage as fully in discussions as they want because they expected negative reactions from classmates and teachers (Braine, 1996). This fear and embarrassment is compounded by "a lack of awareness and sensitivity towards their needs among some NES students and teachers" (Matsuda & Silva, 2006, p. 248).

The online portion of hybrid classes compounds problems associated with lack of proficiency by forcing ESL/EFL students to communicating in a second language without the benefit of non-verbal cues. Because computer-mediated communication in an educational environment is dominated by writing (i.e., typing), the online portion of a hybrid class eliminates the use of nonverbal communication as a mechanism for clarifying meaning. The text-based online portion of the class removes body language, gestures, eye contact, physical distance, silences, and other forms of non-verbal communication that many ESL/EFL students find essential when communicating with NES students. This situation is problematic for ESL/EFL students who are learning both academic and American cultures while also working on increasing language proficiency: "The expression of culture is so bound up in nonverbal communication that the barriers to culture learning are more nonverbal than verbal" (Brown, 2007, p. 237). Even when students communicate with other members of their same culture and in a common native language, it has been recognized that the lack of non-verbal cues in online communication increases the possibility for misunderstanding and conflict. As a result, an entire system for expressing emotions—emoticons—has been developed in an attempt to address this limitation. ESL/EFL students who lack English proficiency might find it equally difficult to express themselves clearly, and even the use of emoticons or other such coping strategies might not be enough to prevent conflict and frustration. The confusion and frustration experienced by ESL/EFL students in online contexts is compounded by language problem related to the use of slang by NES students and the more informal tone used in much of U.S. education (as opposed to the more formal discourse expectations ESL/EFL students might have come to associate with education in their native countries).

Differing cultural norms and expectations also present the possibility for conflict. In a thought-provoking article from 1986, Geert Hofstede presented the results of a study of cultural communication norms in fifty different countries. Hofstede used four categories to present the aggregated results of his research: individualist/collectivist, power distance, uncertainty avoidance, and masculinity. The two categories that apply most in an online learning environment are individualist/collectivist cultures and uncertainty avoidance. *Individualist* cultures assumes that a person primarily looks after his or her own interests, as opposed to *collectivist* cultures which assumes that people belong to groups from which they cannot detach themselves, whether as a result of birth or later life events (Hofstede, 1986). *Uncertainty avoidance* is the extent to which people within a culture are made anxious by situations which they perceive as unclear, unstructured, or unpredictable. Members of cultures Hofstede identified as having a high level of uncertainty avoidance would, therefore, try to avoid perceived unclear or unstructured situations by maintaining beliefs in absolute truths and strict codes of behavior (Hofstede, 1986). Such factors, however, can have a pronounced effect on how individuals from different cultures interact in online contexts.

Individualism and Online Communication Behavior

The individualistic culture inherent in U.S. college courses can cause problems for ESL/EFL students whose native cultures might tend toward group participation and harmonization, rather than individuality, dissent, and argumentation. In a hybrid class, this forced individualism is further heightened by an instructional approach that tends to single individuals out from the group (e.g., calling on individual students to provide in-class answers to instructor question). Thus, the same online component which gives an opportunity for inclusion for those who are too shy to speak up in class discussions can also create an individualistic, sometimes isolated, learning environment. Similarly, the completion of online tasks is usually done alone with the student sitting at a computer and isolated from his or her fellow classmates. Such tasks require the individual student to call upon his or her own thoughts and experiences to complete a given assignment or activity (Lai & Kritsonis, 2006; Al-Jarf, 2004b).

Furthermore, hybrid classes usually require the public posting of individual opinions to online discussion boards, where discussions and postings can often become heated and argumentative. In such situations, students from collectivist cultures who value group decisions and consensus-building can clash with those students whose cultures prize individualism and argumentation when discussing different topics and ideas. In such cases, students from collectivist cultures might agree with classmates in online discussions even when they do not believe in what they are saying in order to avoid conflict or embarrassment. When this kind of behavior occurs, true discussion is thwarted, and full participation in the online community is impossible.

Forced individualism is particularly problematic in hybrid college writing classes. As Ramanathan and Atkinson (2006) point out, individualism is strongly favored in U.S. academic settings, especially in writing courses. This tendency toward individualism is implied in such elements as voice, peer review, critical thinking, and textual ownership. Peer review, especially, holds difficulties for ESL/EFL students, whose native cultures might prompt individuals to see these practices as alien (Campbell, 2007). When students are asked to participate in peer review sessions, especially when those sessions are held online and comments posted for all classmates to read (see Kastman Breuch, 2004), a situation might result in which ESL/EFL students feel compelled to agree with other classmates and resist giving criticism. This behavior could lead to a frustrating situation for all involved students. In such situations, ESL/EFL students are forced into a situation which runs counter to the norms of their native cultures, and the NES writer does not receive the criticism he or she needs to revise the paper.

Uncertainty Avoidance and Online Communication Behavior

Students from cultures with high uncertainty avoidance might find an online discussion too unpredictable or uncomfortable to take part for a variety of reasons. These reasons could range from unfamiliarity with the technology to self-consciousness over language proficiencies and expressing opinions. The result could be turning to avoidance as a coping mechanism. The result is that ESL/EFL students in mainstream classes might not take part in any online activities involving their NES counterparts. This behavior could result in a frustrating situation for all involved students. ESL/EFL students might find themselves struggling with the conflict between their native cultural norms and the new norms being asked of them by their instructors. NES students, on the other hand, could be struggling to understand the cultures of their ESL/EFL classmates and to determine how to appropriately interact with them. As Brown (2007) reminds us, effective learning "may be considerably clouded by what students see as

contradictory expectations for their participation, and as a result, certain unnecessary blocks stand in the way of their success" (p. 202).

ISSUES OF CLASSROOM COMMUNITY AND ACADEMIC IDENTITY

The unique feature of hybrid classes is that they offer two instruction delivery methods, in effect creating two separate classroom communities. When ESL/EFL students enroll in hybrid classes, they unknowingly enter the debate surrounding the extent to which these communities are established and of the social interactions of their members. Educators who advocate online-only instruction often cite the Internet as a safe space where students who might normally be shy or feel intimidated in a face-to-face classroom find their voice. This aspect of online classes, they claim, allows marginalized students to establish themselves as part of the classroom community (see Palmer, Holt, & Bray, 2008). Others, however, argue that an online-only academic environment produces a different set of anxieties and problems (see Stine, 2004). These critics also note that students who feel self-conscious or encounter difficulties working in an online environment will either limit their online participation or stop it completely (Yena & Waggoner, 2003).

What this debate suggests is that two distinct, and often exclusionary, classroom communities exist. There are, in effect, a community of face-to-face interaction and an online community. Both of these communities have their own social dynamics, interactions, and communication signals – such as body language in face-to-face encounters and emoticons in online communication. Those individuals who champion hybrid instruction believe that hybrids learning environments provide a middle ground by giving students the opportunity to interact in both communities. Advocates of hybrid education argue that combining face-to-face interaction with online discussion solidifies the classroom community in ways that only online or only face-to-face instruction cannot. Hybrid approaches thus provide students with the opportunity to engage in both mediums or choose between them, as necessary, for the best way to express themselves (Aycock, Garnham, & Kaleta, 2002; Stine, 2004). If we problematize this participation in two communities, however, we can see that the opportunity to choose between communities might result not so much in a positive choice for involvement. Rather, it could result in a negative self-exclusion from half of the academic discussions that are necessary to be a full participant in the classroom community.

Even for those students who are able and willing to participate in both communities, the requirement to constantly switch between the two might stifle the development of their academic identities. The development of one's academic identity is, in turn, a dynamic process linked to gaining discourses and literacy, and literacy is a social practice born in community (Street, 1984; Barton, 1994; Barton & Hamilton, 2000; Harklau, 2000; Heath 1983; Villalva, 2006). Gee (1994) posits that literacy cannot be separated from its cultural context. Thus, in school, which is a cultural institution, "academic literacy facilitates the transmission of norms, values, and beliefs of the specific discourse community in which is it rooted" (Bao, 2006, p.2). According to this perspective, ESL/EFL students' academic literacy results from not only becoming literate in English, but also in becoming literate in the norms and values of U.S. culture and U.S. academic discourse (Bao, 2006). Therefore, for a complete formation of academic literacy within a hybrid class, it is important for students to engage in both communities and learn the different academic discourses provided by each delivery method. For students unfamiliar with U.S. academic discourse, however, the time split between the two communities limits exposure to both. To what extent, then, can ESL/EFL students learn these two academic discourses and establish

their own academic identity when the time spent in each is effectively halved?

Constant switching between the two social communities might result in a fragmented and incomplete development of academic identity. This situation is a sort of instructional schizophrenia in which ESL/EFL students remain in neither community long enough to establish their identities within the group. If we work from Harklau's (2000) premise that "identities are locally understood and constantly remade in social relationships" (p.104), and that there exists two separate and disparate communities within the hybrid course, then students in hybrid classes must create two separate identities: one for the online community and one for the face-to-face community.

Additionally, these identities are constantly being shaped by their communities. Despite perceptions that identity is stable, unitary, and self-evident in a given context, identity formation is actually characterized as highly unstable, disjunct, and interactionally rendered (Harklau, 2000). As Harklau explains, even though an identity or representation "may seem self-evident, its meanings are in fact constantly renegotiated and reshaped by particular educators and students working in specific classrooms, institutions, and societies" (p.104). Thus, switching between communities can create changes in identity based upon changes in perceived representations by teachers and fellow students. Within this context, what becomes of the identity and representation of an ESL/EFL student who is forced to switch constantly between two academic communities and two communication formats on a daily basis?

While it is true that most ESL/EFL students, like their NES counterparts, are technologically savvy and spend much time communicating online, this communication is not within an academic setting. As a result, these kinds of interactions do not lead to the formation of an academic identity essential for educational success. Rather, the switching within an academic setting, with its unique tensions and stressors, could cause the interrupted creation of academic identity. The results of such interruption, moreover, could be a disjointed, incomplete sense of self that is unable to function fully in either community.

AUTHORIAL SELF-IDENTITY

With hybrid courses, ESL/EFL students face two distinct learning environments. One is a face-to-face environment in which physical differences are impossible to hide. The other is an online environment in which language proficiency differences are highlighted. Each of these learning environments, however, requires its own set of communication tools and discourse. These two learning environments both have the potential to negatively affect development of the authorial self for ESL/EFL students and influence academic success in hybrid classes.

The authorial self is a concept which describes to what extent students see and present themselves as authors (Ivanic, 1998). It is shaped by social context: selfhood "does not exist in a vacuum" but is "shaped by individual acts of writing in which people take on particular discoursal identities" (Ivanic, 1998, p. 27). Ultimately, then, writing is a presentation of the self (Canagarajah, 2002), inseparable from issues of identity (Ivanic, 1998). This perspective is particularly problematic given a hybrid course's dependence upon computer-mediated communication. The overwhelming majority of online activities are writing-based and shared with the overall class. As a result, what these activities all have in common is the potential for highlighting the differences in language proficiency of ESL/EFL students for all community members to see. Ivanic (1998) highlights how these differences relate to identity construction when she writes that "individuals do not define themselves entirely in terms of group membership(s). They also have a sense of themselves as defined by their difference from others they encounter" (Ivanic, 1998, p. 14). The self-consciousness of

being different, along with unrealistic comparisons of language use to their native-speaking or more proficient ESL/EFL peers, can led to negative effects on the development of the authorial self.

This perception could create feelings of inadequacy not only as a writer, but also as a student (Canagarajah, 2002). ESL/EFL students who could employ various coping strategies to hide their language deficiencies in face-to-face activities now find that their weaknesses are on display for all in a computer-mediated environment. Their self-valuation as participants in the classroom community is affected, as well as their ability to become full members within the larger academic community (Mays, 2008). This situation, in turn, has the potential to restrict the creativity and risk-taking necessary to acquire advance literacy skills and develop as a writer and scholar (Scarcella, 2002).

MUTING

The large number of online activities in a hybrid class might pose a minefield of challenges for ESL/EFL students when interacting with NES classmates. Online discussion boards, streaming audio and video, real-time chatrooms, electronic portfolios, blogs, micro-blogs, and websites such as a SecondLife have all found their way into online course instructional materials. These media, moreover, exist in addition to the "old" technologies of email, PowerPoint presentations, databases, and electronic comments in Microsoft Word (DePew, 2006). This proliferation of technology is potentially problematic for ESL/EFL students, for the use of these technologies increasingly creates a learning environment which is "mediated through the written word" (DePew, 2006, p. 175). For ESL/EFL students who lack proficiency writing in English, a difference can immediately be seen between them and their NES counterparts in online activities involving such technologies. As a result, ESL/EFL students might develop a sense of self-conscious about their lack of proficiency might develop which makes participation in the class community difficult and encourages silence—or *muting*—rather than participation. This muting is especially likely in the online environment where language differences are difficult if not impossible to hide and draw attention to the differences of ESL/EFL students rather working toward their inclusion in the classroom community. Such muting takes two forms: *self-muting* and *imposed muting*.

Self-muting is something ESL/EFL students do to themselves; they make a conscious choice to either limit their participation or to exclude themselves from participating in the community, muting their voices completely. In the online component of a hybrid course, discussion boards show promise for ESL/EFL participation (Campbell, 2007). However, student perceptions of their technology skills, their ability to complete assignments, and their insecurities stemming from the ephemeral nature of online instruction—such as, worry that they may have missed important information—has the potential to create communication anxiety that can contribute to muting behavior (Yena & Waggoner, 2003). Communication anxiety is also created by the lack of social cues in online exchanges; without these cues, students experience anxiety over whether their communication is being understood or not (Hara & Kling, 1999; Kurthen & Smith, 2005/2006). This anxiety is increased when the student is aware of the fact that the communication likely affects their course grade (Yena & Waggoner, 2003). ESL/EFL students are also likely to experience increased anxiety, stemming from insecurities over language proficiency and self-consciousness about accents to conflicts of culture (Campbell, 2007; Ramanathan & Atkinson, 1999/2006). This anxiety could create a failure to engage, whether partially or completely, in the classroom communities. And, again, the student has decided to mute his or her voice in an online exchange.

Imposed-muting occurs as a result of others' actions toward ESL/EFL students, and it is much more insidious. At its best, imposed-muting is a result of insensitivity, and at its worst, it instills feelings of intimidation and inferiority in ESL/EFL students. Imposed-muting can involve NES students excluding ESL/EFL students from discussions, ignoring their posted comments or questions, or actively discouraging them from participation in an exchange. Braine (1996) found examples of imposed-muting in the students he followed in his study:

Many [ESL] students stated, generally, the [NES] students did not help them or even speak to them in class and that the teacher did little to encourage communication. During peer review of papers in groups, these [ESL] students felt that the students were impatient with them, and one [ESL] student said that he overheard a [NES] student complain to the teacher about her inability to correct the numerous grammatical errors in the [ESL student's] paper. (p. 98).

Harklau (1994) cited similar reactions from ESL/EFL students, who did not speak up in class, blaming negative reactions from both the teacher and the NES students, and Campbell (2007) noticed that, while ESL/EFL students had no trouble interacting with each other, they often fell silent around NES students. These behaviors are problematic enough in a conventional classroom. In an online class, they can further contribute to feelings of isolation associated with the student sitting at a lone computer terminal while trying to interact with others.

CONSIDERATIONS FOR HYBRID INSTRUCTORS

As ESL/EFL enrollment in hybrid mainstream courses increases, it will not be enough for instructors to simply take into consideration the variety of language proficiencies while planning and evaluating class activities. Rather, instructors must also learn to recognize situations in which potential conflicts resulting from differing cultural expectations might occur, for such conflicts might not only hamper learning, but possibly stop it all together. Until further research is conducted on the potential of hybrid delivery for ESL/EFL students, however, instructors can take certain steps to make hybrid courses more inclusive, productive, and culturally rewarding for all students involved:

- Make certain that all students have access to the necessary technology and the skills to use it for all the required course activities. Although this suggestion seems like an obvious point, currently in the United States, ethnic and language minority students are least likely to have computer/Internet access or to use them for challenging, problem-solving activities (Rainie, 2010; U. S. Dept. of Commerce, 2004; Warschauer, 1998). Determining student access to technology can be accomplished by administering a short survey on the first day of class, and this survey would ask students about their access to the technology associated with class participation, their ability to use that technology, and their comfort level in using it.
- Monitor the online participation of ESL/EFL students and gently prompt those students who are not participating to engage with the community. As Al-Jarf (2004b) discovered, some ESL/EFL students are so self-conscious about their English-language abilities that they will not post to online discussions unless the instructor directly prompts them to do so. Some students will actually fail to write a follow-up post to an ongoing discussion thread unless the instructor posts a new topic and a sample response. In such cases, ESL/EFL students often cut and paste from previous posts rather than writing a new response or starting new threads (Al-Jarf, 2004b). Still others will "lurk"—that is, they read all the discussion posts but do not respond (Al-Jarf, 2004b).

- Discourage NES students from dominating the discussions and muting ESL/EFL students. Instead, encourage NES students to be supportive of fellow classmates and to give others equal time during online chats or on online discussion boards.
- Consider taking a non-participatory role once the discussions are underway. Students from cultures where it is considered inappropriate to challenge authority might be hesitant to disagree with instructor's views (Campbell, 2007). In such cases, attempting to interact with students could wind up muting discussion rather than encouraging it.
- Assign the creation of a list of "Rules of Online Discussion" as the first online discussion task (Campbell, 2007). This task helps to reduce the potential for problems by asking students to develop an awareness of "netiquette"—that is, rules of civility when interacting online—as well as giving the instructor a document to refer back to when students break the rules. It also helps students work toward building a sense of online community by giving them a group task to complete and find consensus.
- Consider designing activities in which students explore cultural differences in communication and social interaction. Then, have students work together to solve problems created by the lack of visual cues in cyberspace. This type of activity uses self-reflection to solve the problems, enhance communication between students from different cultures, and works to create a meta-cognitive learning situation. H. Douglas Brown (2007) provides a checklist of considerations for instructors designing cul-

ture-based assignments (p. 213), and this checklist could serve as a starting point for such activities. Also, for other ideas on interjecting culture into the classroom, instructors could review DeCapua and Wintergerst's (2004)*Crossing Cultures in the Language Classroom.*

CONCLUSION

Hybrid classes hold great potential for all students. In addition to providing opportunities to learn various technologies, these classes offer students more flexible schedules, and the focus on writing offers ESL/EFL students and struggling writers with more opportunities for improving writing skills for (Al-Jarf, 2004a; Bao, 2006; Lam, 2000; Stine, 2004). Hybrid classes also have the potential to remove many socio-economic obstacles, such as problems with childcare, transportation, and parking; scheduling class time around family and work obligations. As a result, such educational approaches can allow a wider range of students to feel like part of the academic community (Carpenter, Brown & Hickman, 2004). Based upon growth projections and a very favorable reception by administrators, this instructional delivery method will be a growing part of higher education for a long time to come.

But we must not become so enamored of the benefits of hybrid classes that we overlook the potential problems that such delivery brings, especially in relation to ESL/EFL students. The same technologies that hold the promise of improving ESL/EFL students' learning experience also have the potential for creating feelings of acute self-consciousness and anxiety. In sum, increased opportunities for open discussion and sharing of ideas also create increased opportunities for intimidation. Thus, the same classroom social community which should allow for the creation of an academic self also has the potential for

fragmenting that self, perhaps even preventing its creation all together.

Despite these potential problems, ESL/EFL students should not be restricted from participating in mainstream hybrid course. On the contrary, all students need to be exposed to the technology used in such deliveries. Likewise, all students should be given the opportunity to develop an online academic discourse and to interact with fellow students from various cultural backgrounds. What I advocate in this chapter a increased instructor and administrator awareness of the potential problems ESL/EFL students could encounter in hybrid classes. These problems must be anticipated when designing online assignments, requiring task-based and peer response work, evaluating student participation and/or performance, and monitoring student interaction online. To assist instructors and administrators with this objective, researchers must begin investigating issues regarding identity, academic community development, forced individualism, and muting as they relate to offering hybrid classes. Otherwise, the dual elements of hybrid delivery – elements Stine (2004) posits as having infinite possibilities – might prove not to be the best of both worlds for ESL/EFL students after all—but the worst.

REFERENCES

Al-Jarf, R. (2004a). The effects of Web-based learning on struggling EFL college writers. *Foreign Language Annals, 37*(1), 49–57. doi:10.1111/j.1944-9720.2004.tb02172.x

Al-Jarf, R. S. (2004b). *Differential effects of online instruction on a variety of EFL classes.* Paper presented at 3rd Asia CALL: Perspectives on Computers in Language Learning, Penang, Malaysia.

Allen, I. E., Seaman, J., & Garrett, R. (2007, March). *Blending in: The extent and promise of blended education in the United States.* Needham, MA: Sloan Consortium. Retrieved June 11, 2009, from http://www.sloan-c.org/ publications/ survey/ blended06.asp

Aycock, A., Garnham, C., & Kaleta, R. (2002, March 20). Lessons learned from the hybrid course project. *Teaching with Technology Today, 8*(6). Retrieved September 2, 2008, from http://www.uwsa.edu/ ttt/ articles/ garnham2.htm

Bao, H. (2006). Computer means/changes my life: ESL students and computer-mediated technology. *Electronic Magazine of Multicultural Education, 8*(1), 1–9.

Barton, D. (1994). *Literacy: An introduction to the ecology of written language.* Malden, MA: Blackwell.

Barton, D., & Hamilton, M. (2000). Literacy practices. In Baron, D., Hamilton, M., & Ivanic, R. (Eds.), *Situated literacies: Reading and writing in context* (pp. 7–15). New York, NY: Routledge.

Blake, R., Wilson, N. L., Cetto, M., & Pardo-Ballister, C. (2008). Measuring oral proficiency in distance, face-to-face, and blended classrooms. *Language Learning & Technology, 12*(3), 114–127.

Braine, G. (1996). ESL students in first-year writing courses: ESL versus mainstream classes. *Journal of Second Language Writing, 5*, 91–107. doi:10.1016/S1060-3743(96)90020-X

Brown, H. D. (2007). *Principles of language learning and teaching* (5th ed.). White Plains, NY: Pearson.

Campbell, N. (2007). Bringing ESL students out of their shells: Enhancing participation through online discussion. *Business Communication Quarterly, 70*(1), 37–43. doi:10.1177/108056990707000105

Canagarajah, A. S. (2002). Understanding critical writing. In Canagarajah, A. S. (Ed.), *Critical academic writing and multilingual students* (pp. 1–22). Ann Arbor, MI: University of Michigan Press.

Carpenter, T. G., Brown, W. L., & Hickman, R. C. (2004). Influences of online delivery on developmental writing outcomes. *Journal of Developmental Education, 28*(1), 14–35.

Chenoweth, N. A., Ushida, E., & Murday, K. (2006). Student learning in hybrid French and Spanish courses: An overview of language online. *CALICO Journal, 24*(1), 115–146.

DeCapua, A., & Wintergerst, A. (2004). *Crossing cultures in the language classroom.* Ann Arbor, MI: University of Michigan Press.

DePew, K. E. (2006). Different writers, different writing: Preparing international teaching assistants for instructional literacy. In Matsuda, P. K., Ortmeier-Hooper, C., & You, X. (Eds.), *The politics of second language writing* (pp. 168–187). West Lafayette, IN: Parlor.

Duhaney, D. C. (2004). Blended learning in education, training and development. *Performance Improvement, 43*(8), 35–39. doi:10.1002/pfi.4140430810

Fu, D., & Matoush, M. (2006). Writing development and biliteracy. In Matsuda, P. K., Ortmeier-Hooper, C., & You, X. (Eds.), *The politics of second language writing* (pp. 5–29). West Lafayette, IN: Parlor Press.

Garnham, C., & Kaleta, R. (2002, March 20). Introduction to hybrid courses. *Teaching with Technology Today, 8*(6). Retrieved June 16, 2009, from http://www.uwsa.edu/ ttt/ articles/ garnham.htm

Gee, J. (1994). Orality and literacy: From the savage mind to ways with words. In Maybin, J. (Ed.), *Language and literacy in social practice* (pp. 168–192). Clevedon, UK: The Open University Press.

Goodwin, C. D. (1995). Fads and fashions on campus: Interdisciplinarity and internationalization. In Deneef, A. L., & Goodwin, C. D. (Eds.), *The academic's handbook* (pp. 73–80). Durham, NC: Duke UP.

Hara, N., & Kling, R. (1999) Students' distress with a web-based distance education course: An ethnographic study of participants' experiences. *Center for Social Informatics.* Retrieved June 11, 2009 from http://www.slis.indiana.edu/ csi

Harklau, L. (1994). ESL versus mainstream classes: Contrasting L2 learning environments. *TESOL Quarterly, 28,* 241–272. doi:10.2307/3587433

Harklau, L. (2000). From the "good kids" to the "worst": Representations of English language learners across educational settings. *TESOL Quarterly, 34*(1), 35–67. doi:10.2307/3588096

Heath, S. B. (1983). *Ways with words: Language, life, and work in communities and classrooms.* New York, NY: Cambridge University Press.

Hofstede, G. (1986). Cultural differences in teaching and learning. *International Journal of Intercultural Relations, 10,* 301–320. doi:10.1016/0147-1767(86)90015-5

Irvine, T. (2006). *Hybrid works best: Looking to professional research to understand why and how hybrid classes best foster basic skills development.* Unpublished raw data, Johnston Community College, Smithfield, NC. Retrieved October 14, 2008, from http://www.mymathlab.com/ redesign_ppts/ jcc.ppt

Ivanic, R. (1998). *Writing and identity: The discoursal construction of identity in academic writing.* Amsterdam, The Netherlands: John Benjamins.

Kaleta, R., & Aycock, A. (2004). *Getting faculty ready for hybrid/blended teaching.* Paper presented at the conference EduCause, Denver, CO.

Kastman Breuch, L. (2004). *Virtual peer review: Teaching and learning about writing in online environments.* Albany, NY: SUNY Press.

Kurthen, H., & Smith, G. G. (2005/2006). Hybrid online face-to-face teaching: When is it an efficient learning tool? *International Journal of Learning, 12*(5), 237–245.

Lai, C. C., & Kritsonis, W. A. (2006). Advantages and disadvantages of computer technology in second language learning. *National Journal for Publishing and Mentoring Doctoral Student Research, 3*(1), 1–6.

Lam, W. S. E. (2000). L2 literacy and the design of the self: A case study of a teenager writing on the Internet. *TESOL Quarterly, 34*(3), 457–482. doi:10.2307/3587739

Long, G. L., Vignare, K., Rappold, R. P., & Mallory, J. (2007). Access to communication for deaf, hard-of-hearing and ESL students in blended learning courses. *International Review of Research in Open and Distance Learning, 8*(3), 1–13.

Matsuda, P. K., & Silva, T. (2006). Cross-cultural composition: Mediated integration of U.S. and international students. In Matsuda, P., Cox, M., Jordan, C., & Ortmeier-Hooper, C. (Eds.), *Second language writing in the composition classroom: A critical sourcebook* (pp. 246–259). New York, NY: Bedford/St. Martin's Press.

Mays, L. (2008). The cultural divide of discourse: Understanding how English-language learners' primary discourse influences acquisition of literacy. *The Reading Teacher, 61*(5), 415–418. doi:10.1598/RT.61.5.6

NAFSA. Association of International Educators. (2007, Nov. 12). *Press Release: Latest survey indicates continued slow growth in international enrollments.* Retrieved June 11, 2009, from http://www.nafsa.org/ press_releases.sec/ press_releases.pg/ latest_survey_indicates

Offsite learning: On target? Pt. I. (2002, October 7). *The Economist*. Retrieved Sept. 1, 2010, from http://www.economist.com/ displaystory.cfm?story_id=1377339

Offsite learning: On target? Pt. II. (2002, October 7). *The Economist*. Retrieved Sept. 1, 2010, from http://www.economist.com/ displaystory.cfm?story_id=1377324

Palmer, S., Holt, D., & Bray, S. (2008). Does the discussion help? The impact of a formally assessed online discussion on final student results. *British Journal of Educational Technology, 39*(5), 847–858. doi:10.1111/j.1467-8535.2007.00780.x

Rainie, L. (2010, January 5). *Pew Internet & American life project: Internet, broadband, and cell phone statistics.* Retrieved February 6, 2010 from http://www.pewinternet.org/ reports/ 2010/ Internet-broadband-and- cell-phone-statistics. aspx?r=1

Ramanathan, V., & Atkinson, D. (2006). Individualism, academic writing, and ESL writers. In Matsuda, P., Cox, M., Jordan, C., & Ortmeier-Hooper, C. (Eds.), *Second language writing in the composition classroom: A critical sourcebook* (pp. 159–185). New York, NY: Bedford/St. Martin's Press.

Scarcella, R. (2002). Some key factors affecting English learners' development of advanced literacy. In Schleppegrell, M. J., & Colombi, M. C. (Eds.), *Developing advanced literacy in first and second languages: Meaning with power* (pp. 209–228). Mahwah, NJ: Lawrence Erlbaum.

Sener, J. (2003). Improving access to online learning: Current issues, practices, and directions. In Bourne, J., & Moore, J. (Eds.), *Elements of quality online education: Practice and direction* (pp. 119–136). Needham, MA: Sloan Consortium.

Stine, L. (2004). The best of both worlds: Teaching basic writers in class and online. *Journal of Basic Writing, 23*(2), 49–69.

Street, B. (1984). *Literacy in theory and practice.* New York, NY: Cambridge University Press.

Sykes, J., Oskoz, A., & Thorne, S. L. (2008). Web 2.0, synthetic immersive environments, and mobile resources for language education. *CALICO Journal, 25*(3), 528–546.

Thorne, S. L., & Black, R. (2007). Language and literacy development in computer-mediated contexts and communities. *Annual Review of Applied Linguistics, 27*, 133–160. doi:10.1017/S0267190508070074

Thorne, S. L., & Payne, S. (Eds.). (2005). Computer-mediated communication and foreign language learning: Context, research and practice [Special issue]. *CALICO Journal, 22*(3).

U. S. Department of Commerce. (2004). *A nation online: Entering the broadband age.* Retrieved June 15, 2009, from http://www.ntia.doc.gov/reports/ anol/ NationOnlineBroadband04.htm

Urban Institute. (2005). *High concentration of limited-English students challenges implementation of No Child Left Behind Act.* Retrieved June 11, 2009, from http://www.urban.org/url.cfm?ID=900884

Villalva, K. E. (2006). Reforming high school writing: Opportunities and constraints for Generation 1.5 writers. In Matsuda, P., Ortmeier-Hooper, C., & You, X. (Eds.), *The politics of second language writing: In search of the promised land* (pp. 30–55). West Lafayette, IN: Parlor Press.

Warschauer, M. (1996). Computer assisted language learning: An introduction. In Fotos, S. (Ed.), *Multimedia language teaching* (pp. 3–20). Tokyo, Japan: Logos International.

Warschauer, M. (1998). Online learning in sociocultural context. *Anthropology & Education Quarterly, 29*(1), 68–88. doi:10.1525/aeq.1998.29.1.68

Warschauer, M. (2006). *Laptops and literacy: Learning in the wireless classroom.* New York, NY: Teachers College.

Welker, J., & Berardino, L. (2005-2006). Blended learning: Understanding the middle ground between traditional classroom and fully online instruction. *Journal of Educational Technology Systems, 34*(1), 33–55. doi:10.2190/67FX-B7P8-PYUX-TDUP

Yena, L., & Waggoner, Z. (2003). *One size fits all? Student perspectives on face-to-face and online writing pedagogies.* Computers & Composition Online. Retrieved June 13, 2009, from http://www.bgsu.edu/ cconline/ yena-waggoner/ index.html

KEY TERMS AND DEFINITIONS

ESL: English as a Second Language.

EFL: English as a Foreign Language.

Hybrid Classes: 20% to 80% of face-to-face class meetings are replaced with online activities completed outside the classroom on the students' own time. Also known as blended classes or dual delivery.

Mainstream classes: Classes which do not have restricted enrollment and enroll both ESL/EFL and NES.

Netiquette: Rules of civility when interacting online.

Native English Speakers (NES): Students for whom English is their first language.

Muting: A conscious choice to either limit or completely exclude oneself from class participation; can be self-muting or imposed-muting.

English Language Learner (ELL): Non-NES students who are learning English, either as ESL or EFL students.

Computer-Assisted Language Learning (CALL): Learning situation in which technology assists but does not replace traditional course delivery. Often interchangeable with CALI.

Computer-Assisted Language Instruction (CALI): Learning situation in which technology assists but does not replace traditional course delivery. Often interchangeable with CALL.

Authorial Self: A concept which describes to what extent students see and present themselves as authors.

Individualist Culture: A culture in which a person primarily looks after his or her own interests, as opposed to collectivist cultures.

Collectivist Culture: A culture in which people belong to groups from which they cannot detach themselves, whether as a result of birth or later life events.

Uncertainty Avoidance: When people are made anxious by situations which they perceive as unclear, unstructured, or unpredictable and try to avoid them.

ENDNOTES

[1] At this point, it is also important to draw on Warschauer (1996) in order to mark a distinction between the research conducted on computer-assisted language learning (CALL) or computer-assisted language instruction (CALI) classes and hybrids; CALL and CALI are instructional tools, not instruction deliveries, and while it is possible for a hybrid course to incorporate CALL or CALI technologies, CALL or CALI by itself cannot constitute a hybrid course.

Chapter 27
International Collaboration and Design Innovation in Virtual Worlds:
Lessons from Second Life

Pete Rive
Victoria University of Wellington, New Zealand

Aukje Thomassen
Auckland University of Technology, New Zealand

ABSTRACT

Second Life is a popular virtual world that can provide us with valuable lessons about international collaboration and design innovation. This chapter will explore how design practice and design education can assist geographically dispersed design teams working on collaborative designs in a shared virtual space, using real-time 3D constructions and communication tools. We contend that Second Life can provide solutions to collaborative international design and enable knowledge creation and innovation through tacit knowledge exchange.

INTRODUCTION

This chapter examines the dynamics and the features of international collaboration and design innovation in the virtual world, Second Life. Many writers have recognized innovation as an important contributor to the global economy (Von Krogh,

Nonaka, & Ichijo, 2000; Sunstein, 2006; Bryan & Joyce, 2007; Hamel, 2007; Hunter, 2008; Sebell, 2008). Three of the biggest drivers of innovation have been global mobility, information technology, and communications, (Kurzweil, 2005; Salzman & Matathia, 2007). These three mega trends have created an unprecedented convergence of diverse people, ideas, and cultures. They have formed a global "network society," creating intersections

DOI: 10.4018/978-1-60960-833-0.ch027

never seen before in the history of the planet (Castells, 2000; Shavinina, 2003; Kurzweil, 2005; Benkler, 2006; Salzman & Matathia, 2007). Many writers have recognized innovation as an important driver of education, economic development, and scientific discovery (Peters, 1997; Teece, 2000; Von Krogh, et al., 2000; Shavinina, 2003).

UNDERSTANDING INNOVATION

At the heart of the innovation process is a design team who collaborates to contribute novel solutions to user problems (Mau, Leonard, & Institute without Boundaries, 2004; Suri & IDEO, 2005). The designer, Bruce Mau, has commented that design is no longer about one designer, one solution, one place, and one client, but is "distributed, plural, and collaborative" (Mau, et al., 2004). Therefore, the ability to innovate is closely related to one's ability to collaborate (Tapscott & Williams, 2006; Bryan & Joyce, 2007; Hamel, 2007; Managing risks, 2008).

Fredrick Johansson (2004) describes how cross-cultural and international collaboration can contribute to surprising, rule-changing breakthrough innovations, or what he defines as "intersectional" innovations. This situation contrasts with the more common and pedestrian directional and incremental innovation processes typified by the formal Stage Gate™ model (Cooper, 2003; Rickards, 2003; Johansson, 2004; Koch & Leitner, 2008; Sebell, 2008).

However, a tension exists between the ability of a network society to collaborate and intersect as never before and the acknowledgement that innovative ideas often reside in people's heads and is tacit rather than explicit. A number of writers have described how difficult it is to share expert knowledge that has been accumulated over years of experience and requires extended conversations within a shared spatial context, providing a rich sensory and emotional experience face-to-face (Nonaka & Takeuchi, 1995; Dixon, 2000; Teece & Nonaka, 2000; Von Krogh, et al., 2000; Ben-

kler, 2006; Rive, 2008; Rive, Thomassen, Lyons, & Billinghurst, 2008). From a design innovation perspective, it often requires multiple experts in cross-functional conversations to explore intersectional ideas, and that demands rich, emotional, and full sensory input to achieve knowledge creation, knowledge transfer, and knowledge sharing (Von Krogh, et al., 2000; Leonard & Swap, 2004; Benkler, 2006).

KNOWLEDGE CREATION AND KNOWLEDGE MANAGEMENT

If we place the plural, distributed, and collaborative design trend within the context of two other mega-trends – globalization and the virtualization of the office – we can understand how organizations now face the demand to somehow simulate the advantages of face-to-face communications in order to keep up with the accelerating pace of change to achieve timely innovations (Shields, 2003; Sunstein, 2006; Tapscott & Williams, 2006; Friedman, 2006; Cascio & Paffendorf, 2007; Yankelovich, 2007).

Given the importance of knowledge creation and tacit knowledge exchange in the design innovation process, it is important to be clear about the definitions of these terms. Knowledge creation was defined by Nonaka and Takeuchi (1995) as "justified true belief" and is unlike information because it is about beliefs and commitments (p. 58). Second, order cyberneticists, such as Maturana and Varela (1992), also state that knowledge is about action and has some end goal (Nonaka & Takeuchi, 1995). Third, knowledge is about meaning, and it is context specific and relational (Maturana & Varela, 1992; Nonaka & Takeuchi, 1995). Thus, knowledge creation is both an individual and a social process. An individual can create knowledge, but such creation takes place within the context of social behavior (Bateson & Donaldson, 1991; Maturana & Varela, 1992; Von Krogh, et al., 2000).

Up until relatively recently, the field of knowledge management has over emphasized information processing, information technology, and explicit knowledge (Firestone & McElroy, 2003; Firestone, 2008). This emphasis is despite what Michael Polanyi (1967) described as the importance of tacit knowledge in creative thinking. Polanyi defined tacit knowledge as things that we know, but cannot say. Leonard and Swap (2004), in turn, define tacit knowledge as "deep smarts," or knowledge that is accumulated from years of experience and activity in a field and is also difficult to write down or quickly explain. Rather, conveying such knowledge requires long conversations, contextual observation, and rich emotional communications in order to convert tacit knowledge into explicit knowledge (Polanyi, 1967; Von Krogh, et al., 2000; Hussi, 2003; Leonard & Swap, 2004).

The importance of tacit knowledge and its creation are recognized as essential to the creative innovation process (Dixon, 2000; Von Krogh, et al., 2000; Rive, et al., 2008). Many commentators have remarked that such tacit knowledge can only be transferred through face-to-face conversations and contextual observation (Polanyi, 1967; Von Krogh, et al., 2000; Dixon, 2000; Leonard & Swap, 2004). Von Krogh did, however, admit that cyberspace could create a virtual context for tacit knowledge creation, or "cyber ba" (Von Krogh, et al., 2000). Elsewhere, the authors have argued that it is within a virtual space, such as Second Life, that the individual can achieve some tacit knowledge creation through simulated face-to-face communications (Rive, 2008; Rive, et al., 2008).

KNOWLEDGE CREATION IN VIRTUAL WORLDS

Virtual worlds such as Second Life can provide simulated face-to-face communications in an environment that moves beyond phone conference calls and video conferencing. In contrast to these two more common approaches, Second Life provides participants with a 3D experience of "being there" during an exchange. It is a context in which participants can feel an emotional sense of presence, or consciousness, in a shared virtual environment (Riva, Davide, & Ijsselsteijn, 2003; Boellstorff, 2008). This situation is known as "social presence," and it is a perception activated through a combination of sensory stimulation and social immersion in this alternative reality. In other words, the feeling of social presence created in Second Life is a psychological and emotional state – a state that meets the central requirements of tacit knowledge creation (Botella, Baños, & Alcañiz, 2003). Thus, the degree to which Second Life can simulate face-to-face communications will determine the success of tacit knowledge exchange and creative collaboration as a precursor to design innovation. In so doing, it allows users to bridge physical distance to create effective venues for effective tacit knowledge creation in international contexts.

The Gartner Technology Group has predicted that, by 2011, 80% of the world's Internet users, or 1.63 billion persons, will have a presence in virtual worlds such as Second Life (Gartner, 2007). Despite a decline in media hype, Second Life has continued to grow (Livingstone, 2009). Second Life has proven to be the most popular non-game virtual world on the Internet, and it attracts approximately 70,000 concurrent users at once, and has over 1 million regular users. As a result, Second Life is responsible for creating over 270 terabytes of user-generated content, and it represents economic transactions of approximately $US 1.5 million every 24 hours (a factor that makes the virtual world of Second Life equivalent to the 168th largest economy in the world).

A number of scientists and researchers have postulated that technological evolution will result in full sensory, photorealistic, virtual worlds by the end of the decade. Some individuals, moreover, believe such online environments will become indistinguishable from physical reality by 2030 (Tiffin & Terashima, 2001; Kurzweil, 2005; Goertzel, 2007). New tools that enable trust, creativity, and communication in real-time and in international contexts are being developed through virtual worlds that will assist in greater trans-global design innovation in the near future (Tapscott & Williams, 2006).

SECOND LIFE CASE STUDY SUMMARIES

The authors will use two case studies of design innovation in Second Life to illustrate examples that support theoretical generalizations made throughout this chapter. The reviews of these cases are not, however, intended to be comprehensive. Rather, they are used to present initial evidence that this topic area as it relates to knowledge creation is one ripe for further investigation.

The first case study involves a second year student design class taught in a mixed reality environment. That is, the students all occupied a large media lab that consisted of

- 35 high-end Apple workstations
- 3 large projection units (equipped with stereo sound) showing the tutor's view

Once a week, one tutor would conduct the class remotely, while other tutors were physically present in the lab. This approach is called a "mixed reality experience" because the digital design students and the educators were both physically and virtually co-located, sometimes at the same time, and at other times only virtually.

The class explored the effectiveness of creative collaboration in Second Life through a machinima exercise. "Machinima" is a neologism that comes from "machine + cinema" and uses the 3D graphics engine in a game or virtual world to make animated movies with avatars and create a virtual environment. The students were divided into 3-4 person teams that had to write, direct, design, and build a 2-3 minute machinima in Second Life.

The second case study examines the Studio Wikitecture group in Second Life. The group is an open architecture community that uses a 3D object known as a Wikitree to collaboratively design and build architecture in Second Life. The project has won the 2009 Founders Prize, which is awarded by the Second Life developers, Linden Lab. Many of the group's designers are enthusiastic amateurs, but the group also includes professional designers and architects as members. The 3D Wikitree, in turn, is based on the concept of a collaborative text website that allows contributors to edit, change, comment on, and vote on the contributions of other participants. This structure provides a means to use the Second Life 3D building and design tools while simultaneously using a voting and comments site to complete a collaborative architectural design.

In examining these two cases, the authors will discuss how international collaboration in the virtual world Second Life can contribute to creativity and innovation in design, education, and practice. The objective of this chapter is to provide theory, using case study evidence, to support our contention that Second Life can enable international collaboration, knowledge creation, and innovative design. In addressing this objective, the authors will first provide some practical examples of the tools of Second Life and explain how these tools can enable greater international collaboration and innovation. The authors will then quickly move to a more abstract level, as the Second Life platform is constantly evolving. Next, the authors will explore how knowledge creation is enabled in Second Life and what factors regulate international collaboration in education and other organizations via Second Life. Finally, the authors will outline the main lessons learned from the two small-scale case studies in Second Life. The authors will also discuss the limitations of the virtual environment in contrast to face-to-face contexts.

Tools for International Collaboration in Second Life

Many commentators on innovation and knowledge management have argued that "deep smarts" and tacit knowledge are not only the source of truly breakthrough innovation. Rather, the claim goes, these essential elements can only be communicated face-to-face (Dixon, 2000; Von Krogh, et al., 2000; Leonard & Swap, 2004). The distinction between tacit knowledge and explicit knowledge was first made by the polymath Michael Polanyi in 1967, and it remans an important foundational factor in the field of knowledge management to this day (Firestone & McElroy, 2003). In his classic, *The Tacit Dimension,* Polanyi wrote, "we can know more than we can tell" (Polanyi, 1967, p. 4). However, with computer-mediated-communications, we might be able to *show* what we cannot say, (Rive, et al., 2008).

Tacit knowledge exchange requires prolonged conversations, and often involves multiple communication channels that use all the senses –visual, aural, tactile, taste, and olfactory (Dixon, 2000; Von Krogh, et al., 2000; Leonard & Swap, 2004). Tacit knowledge relies on emotional responses, and it needs to take place between people (or AI's in the future). Such a situation exists in opposition to explicit information that can be exchanged between machines. Tacit knowledge creation contrasts with explicit knowledge exchange that can take place through documentation, such as text based manuals. Such information can, in turn, be comfortably handled through information technology. A large number of commentators in the field of knowledge management have, however, expressed disappointment with the return on investment that information technology and global communications has contributed to measurable innovation (Teece, 2000; Von Krogh, et al., 2000; Stewart, 2001; Firestone & McElroy, 2003; Hussi, 2003; Firestone, 2008).

It is the authors' contention that virtual worlds can simulate face-to-face communication, and in so doing, can go a long way toward substituting actual meetings when it is not practical, cost effective, or in terms of carbon miles, not environmentally desirable to travel to meet with a colleague (Rive, et al., 2008). Second Life already provides a number of tools that can assist international collaborators who want to work together on innovative designs.

Connections to the Cases

To explore these ideas, the students in the machinima class created a shared virtual context in which to communicate their intention and design purpose. Second Life provides a 3D virtual world which includes a sky and a sea that can also be navigated, explored, and constructed or modified. The student's first task was to self-organize into micro-communities, or teams of 3-4. The tutor was remote from the class and met them all on MediaZone, the design school's island/area in Second Life. The tutor had been teaching the basics of Second Life, and despite the students being second year digital design undergraduates, they found the learning curve of the design tools and machinima challenging. The ability for designers to easily self-organize around a project or shared interest is a strong aspect of cross-functional teams, and such self organization has been praised as an enabler of innovation (Tapscott & Williams, 2006; Lessig, 2008).

For the machinima projects, a virtual platform, a 10 x 10 meter grid, was built 150 meters in the air above the Second Life island, and this space was used to provide visual cues to the students to assemble in teams and to choose their own roles as directors, producers, and designers. Another advantage of doing this in Second Life is that, due to the fact that the students were instructed to keep their avatar identity private, teams formed amongst students who did not usually socialize or associate with one another.

Knowledge Creation in Second Life

With respect to innovation, Von Krogh et al. (2000) describe five programs that can enable knowledge creation:

1. Instill a knowledge vision
2. Manage a conversation
3. Mobilize knowledge activists
4. Create right context
5. Globalize local knowledge

As the interests of education and industry increasingly intersect around the topic of knowledge creation, theses aspects become points of interest and collaboration for both groups. Studies involving educational processes and practices associated with knowledge creation, thus, have important insights to offer industry and vice versa.

Interestingly, design education institutions are facing a growing challenge as they work to try and keep pace with the accelerating pace of change dictated by professional design (Kurzweil, 2005). Design education also shares many of the concerns of professional practice in the area of innovation, knowledge sharing, and collaboration, for "Learning is a process of creating knowledge" (Weick, 1991, p. 2). In a case study that researched students who were learning machinima in Second Life, the authors were able to understand how the tools of Second Life contributed to knowledge creation as a necessary precursor to innovative design (Rive, et al., 2008).

Machinima is an art form that uses the 3D render engine of a game (or Second Life in the case studied here) to make movies. By examining the dynamics of interaction in this hybrid environment, this case study of second year design students from Victoria University provides helpful examples of how Second Life enables knowledge creation. The authors first activity with the students was to provide them with a knowledge vision, (1st enabler) instilled by outlining the importance of

working together as teams, sharing knowledge, and helping each other.

During the conversion process of tacit to explicit knowledge related to collaborative design, there can be a many-to-many learning experiences enabled through the tools of Second Life. Second Life, in turn, is particularly good at creating the right context (the 4th enabler) for knowledge creation by allowing informal groups or design teams to emerge without central control from a teacher (or, in the business context, a corporate manager). A group can be formed in Second Life by anyone for $L100 linden dollars, which is less than US$1. This feature provides users with a powerful means to organize roles, a group charter, group ownership, and group communication in Second Life. Another powerful tool is the ability to have a simultaneous and spontaneous group conference using text or voice chat in real-time, and this option is something that no other social network currently offers. This option helps to create the right context for conversations, and it allows emergent self-organization to evolve – a context very beneficial to innovation (Root-Bernstein, 2003; Benkler, 2006; Sunstein, 2006; Tapscott & Williams, 2006; Hamel, 2007; Bryan & Joyce, 2007; Page, 2007).

The flexible permissions system associated with Second Life means group members can edit each other's virtual objects if such objects are shared with the group. One student commented on the design process during the machinima project:

We made all our objects editable by each other, and so it was fun working with each other's designs. One person made an object, then another improved it, then another had their hand at making it look better, until the final product was really impressive.

Bureaucracy, monocultures, lack of diversity, and inflexible attitudes tend to inhibit creativity and stifle innovation,(Hussi, 2003; Johansson, 2004; Sunstein, 2006; Page, 2007; Hamel, 2007). Self-organizing teams, by contrast, can establish clusters of creativity around a new idea suggested by an individual (Von Krogh, et al., 2000; Koch & Leitner, 2008). Such benefit is based on the fact that chaos is often fertile ground for knowledge creation and innovation (Peters, 1987, 1997). From relative simplicity and disorder can emerge novel patterns and useful ideas at the intersections of organizational structure and formal strategies and emerging from self-organization (Johansson, 2004; Koch & Leitner, 2008). Such intersections also provide an exponential increase in concept combinations once disciplines are combined in unique ways; these combinations, in turn, often produce a massive mathematical jump in opportunities for innovations (Johansson, 2004). Emergence and self-organisation are considered to be beneficial to innovation as they allow for the formation of harmonious groups that are more likely to share interests, get along, and contribute a random grouping of individuals who do not know each other that well before hand (Koch & Leitner, 2008).

These beneficial factors are all attributes of Second Life, and they can help to enhance emergent ideas and self-organization through informal meetings and the serendipity created when people bump into each other by the virtual water cooler or in an informal gathering by the beach (Farshchian, 2003; Bryan & Joyce, 2007; Au, 2008). In many of the Studio Wikitecture projects, the group of designer is made up of individuals with diverse backgrounds. In a recursive process the Studio Wikitecture group meets to discuss how they might improve collaboration and engage more designers in the next project. Community building is often seen as the next most important priority, after the project's content for open source projects (Goldman & Gabriel, 2005). Studio Wikitecture has a clear knowledge vision to be an open architectural design group and assist designers with the tools to enable this process. The leaders of the group can also be seen as knowledge activists (3rd enabler) who actively manage the conversations, (2nd enabler).

In the machinima case study, the students had some technical difficulty using voice chat, and so most "inworld" communication was conducted using text chat and IM within Second Life. One member of each team, usually the Producer or Director, assumed the role of knowledge activist (the 3rd enabler) and managed the conversation (the 2nd enabler) in order to assist in the production of the movie and thus enable knowledge creation. This approach varied from team to team, and it was also often shared by team members at different times. The students were not explicitly instructed to appoint someone as the knowledge activist, but all teams carried out this function during the course of their production.

This ability to distribute the management functions related to knowledge creation can be an important aspect when Second Life is used to work in international contexts. The ability to globalize local knowledge (the 5th enabler) is, in fact, another strength of the Second Life environment. As access to Second Life is not limited by traditional boundaries of time and location, the students and tutors could interact to create knowledge in a shared, common virtual environment, even though they were often separated geographically. The shared virtual environment with commonly understood virtual objects was thus another major enabler of knowledge creation through, for it created the right context (the 4th enabler) for learning. Rather than creating fantastical buildings or virtual objects, it is common in a learning, or knowledge sharing situation for the creator to build a virtual simulation of an actual environment (e.g., a lecture theatre with a large screen for presentations in Second Life). This versatility, in turn, has the benefit of creating shared symbols and facilitating shared understanding through mutual learning experiences that span national borders (Johnson, 2006). Thus, Second Life has the ability to present real-world contexts for knowledge creation in a virtual environment accessible to individuals scattered across the globe.

Localization in Second Life

Second Life specifically addresses two knowledge creation enablers. First, it gives participants the right context for conversations through a shared virtual space. Second it gives participants the ability to exchange each individual's local knowledge across a globally distributed team. Participants from other cultures can then re-purpose or revise this knowledge to then share with other members of their native culture according to the norms of that culture (i.e., localize the information). Conversely, international groups can work to create a new form of common knowledge that could work across all of the participating cultures involved. In this way, globalized or internationalized knowledge can be created in a Second Life context.

What is central in either situation is that through the international exchange of knowledge exchange, the virtual group can globalize the fragmented knowledge of individual participants it through a shared co-presence in common place in the virtual world. In such contexts, the language of the collaborators embodies their cultural backgrounds, and their tacit assumptions provide other participants with a rich source of diverse experiences and innovative ideas – both of which are essential to the knowledge creation process (Maturana & Varela, 1992; Von Krogh, et al., 2000; Johansson, 2004).

Moreover, Second Life not only provides a means to communicate with others who might not share your language, but it also provides individuals with a user interface that offers a choice of languages. In a global economy, this option is an important tool that enables a greater number of cultural intersections, and more chances of innovative breakthroughs (Teece, 2000; Von Krogh, et al., 2000; Johansson, 2004; Page, 2007). An accurate and understandable real-time translator enables Second Life residents to have "prolonged conversations'" with individuals who are communicating in another language within a shared virtual context. This option thus allows Second Life users to transcend the traditional barrier of language and greatly enhances their ability to share their local knowledge in a much wider range of international interactions (Von Krogh, et al., 2000). The likely outcome of this Second Life tool is a conversion that shifts an individual's personal tacit knowledge into explicit globalized knowledge that can be applied by collaborators living elsewhere. The breadth of the global access – particularly access that can transcend language to a degree – greatly enhances the chances for innovative novelty essential to knowledge creation (Von Krogh, et al., 2000; Johansson, 2004).

In a recent build of the open source Second Life client Snow Globe version 1.2.4.0, there was the addition of a new translation feature built into the user interface. This feature is turned on in the software preferences, and the user can choose the language into which they would like their messages to be translated. In producing such translations, Second Life uses Google Translate to retype the voice chat of one language to another language and does so on-the-fly in real time. This new feature has the potential to encourage and enable more conversations with people who speak different languages including English, Danish, German, Spanish, French, Italian, Hungarian, Dutch, Polish, Portuguese, Russian, Turkish, Ukrainian, Chinese, Japanese, and Korean. It is expected that Google Translate will continue to improve, and so will international collaborations in Second Life.

CREATING GLOBAL CONVERSATIONS IN SECOND LIFE

Von Krogh et al. (2000) wrote it was ironic that while corporate executives and knowledge officers focused on expensive databases and measurement tools, they were ignoring one of the best means of sharing and creating knowledge through conversations. Managing conversations need not be restricted to voice. Rather, it could include non-verbal, text, gestures, and other means of sensory communication (Rive, et al., 2008). The introduction of voice chat into Second Life in early 2007 was an important milestone in the evolution of this virtual world. It also provides us with some clues as to some of the subtleties of this form of computer-mediated-communications. Because Second Life uses avatars (3D representations of people), a meeting or communication "inworld" currently has some important limitations.

Tacit knowledge creation is reliant on emotional responses, and Second Life is a powerful means of eliciting such responses. Voice is not simply a data communication medium. Rather, it conveys subtle tones and inflections that transmit emotions, geographical origins, socio-cultural cues, and subconscious messages that greatly benefit tacit knowledge creation and exchange. Second Life can convey subtle emotional responses via sensory communications channels, and thereby it can enhance tacit knowledge sharing and learning through knowledge creation (Von Krogh, et al., 2000; Rive, et al., 2008). In Second Life, a user can decide to simply leave their computer microphone open, toggle it on and off, or leave it off permanently.

When international collaborators are attempting to discuss innovative ideas, voice can be an important tool to help convey complex tacit knowledge. It can also be essential to establishing a sense of being together in a shared, albeit virtual, space at the same time. Moreover, the Second Life interface provides users with useful visual cues as to which avatar is talking, and such cues include an obvious pattern of green waves emanating from above the speaker's head. 3D spatial audio also contributes to a sense of presence and gives other listeners cues as to who is talking and where that person's avatar is standing. With both the text chat and voice chat, it is possible to get a sense of virtual proximity that enhances presence. In the Second Life context, the further away an avatar stands from you, the quieter the related person sounds. Similarly, in the case of text exchanges,

you do not receive text messages beyond a certain distance from another avatar.

Such communication features offered by Second Life are important additions to making virtual interactions mirror those of the real world. As Bailenson et al. (2003) note, human communication is not just verbal: "Living, breathing humans socially respond to virtual humans in IVEs, (immersive virtual environment), in a naturalistic way regarding personal space, social presence, and affect" (p. 13). Research has shown that people maintain a similar virtual distance in Second Life with their avatars as they do with physical proximity. This factor would suggest that individuals have a strong sense of presence "in-world" (Bailenson, et al., 2003; Bailenson, Beall, Loomis, Blascovich, & Turk, 2004; Yee, Bailenson, Urbanek, Chang, & Merget, 2007).

In both case studies conducted by the authors, the persistence of the Second Life environment has been an important aspect of the design innovation process. In the machinima projects, each group was given land that was subdivided on the virtual island MediaZone. Only members of the appropriate group could build on that land, place objects there, or run interactive scripts there. Thus, one group member could begin to build a set for the movie, and due to the persistence of the virtual environment, another member could work on the same set at another time. In this way, maintaining the simulated context of the design allowed designers to carry out asynchronous design collaboration without needing to be present at the same time. (The implications for such delayed design in global contexts are manifold and mindboggling.)

The Studio Wikitecture Wikitree is heavily dependent on persistence as its leaves (i.e., design iterations) are permanently present during the course of the collaborative design. Each leaf that was clicked on would "rez" or recreate one designers work to enable a voter or collaborator to assess its value. The tree and the leaves remained in place while designs would instantly come and go according to which leaf was selected. The open source Wikitree is engineered to encourage individual designs that "rift" on the previous work performed by others, and the votes of the community. This situation was typically an asynchronous activity, although community meetings were called to discuss the progress of the project and decide which design branch to follow based on votes and comments.

The Importance of Presence

Many individuals who have not spent time in a virtual world might not comprehend the advantages such a virtual environment has to offer over other computer-mediated-communications. Without experience in Second Life, simply using instant messaging or voice over IP applications such as Skype can be perceived as equally effective. In order to understand and value Second Life, one needs to be in the world and experience an emotional response. This kind of psychological experience is known as *presence*. Presence in cyberspace has been noted by a number of authors that it takes time for a user to associate closely with their avatar (Castronova, 2005; Dibbell, 2006; Taylor, 2006; Malaby, 2009). This subjective state might not be instantly recognized by a new "resident" of Second Life as the technical demands of the software client can undermine a sense of presence. Yet presence determines if an individual is participating in a shared (albeit constructed) reality and is able to communicate while suspending their skepticism that they are somehow sharing the same space. A simulated shared space can enable knowledge creation through Von Krogh et al.'s (2000)'s fourth enabler: a managed context.

According to the psychologist's perspective, virtual worlds are simply alternative realities to be understood from the point of view of consciousness and perception (Riva, Davide, & Ijsselsteijn, 2003). Contrary to popular opinion, all perception is mediated by our senses, and so the distinction of computer-mediated-communications only has

meaning if we consider what psychologists Lombard and Ditton called, the "perceptual illusion of non-mediation" (Riva & Ijsselsteijn, 2003, p. 7). The most profound implication of this argument is that there is a false dichotomy between the virtual vs. the real as the virtual is all based on subjective perception (Botella, et al., 2003). This argument is not only supported by a growing number of psychology researchers, but it is also supported in the fields of cyber-ethnography, anthropology, biology, and even quantum physics (Maturana & Varela, 1992; Shields, 2003; Chown, 2007; Boellstorff, 2008).

The etymology of the word virtual suggests it is not juxtaposed to the real, but it is in fact co-joined with the real or the essence of the real (Shields, 2003). Botella et al. (2003) argue that presence is not usually a reflexive act, of which a person is conscious, but rather is one they only become aware of when they return from a state of absent minded day dreaming (Botella, et al., 2003). Lombard and Ditton (1997) suggested six concepts of presence: realism, immersion, transportation, social richness, social actor within medium, and medium as social actor. Riva and Ijsselsteijn (2003) further simplified this into social and physical presence with co-presence intersecting the two. Co-presence is defined by Riva and Ijsselsteijn as being together in a shared space in the intersection between the physical and social. By their definition, Second Life would offer participants co-presence. This situation is also similar to what is described as the "co-action field" by Tiffin and Terashima (2001). Riva and Ijsselsteijn (2003) also considered the importance of fidelity of media in relation to presence and how the more interactive, immersive, and perceptually realistic something is, the more convincing the experience of presence would be.

It has been repeatedly observed and reported by other researchers that people do not make the clear distinction between the real and the virtual, or online/offline presence. Perhaps as a result of this situation, residents of SL often discuss a blurring of the actual and the virtual (Fornas, 2002; Castronova, 2004, 2005, 2007; Guimaraes, 2005; Boellstorff, 2008). The machinima students studied by the authors created alternative realities that were fictions layered upon virtual shared spaces. This behavior suggests that design collaborators in Second Life are already experiencing a high level of presence and tacit knowledge creation and exchange – the two necessary prerequisites of design innovation.

Challenges of Co-Presence in Second Life

The technical difficulty of achieving co-presence in a multi-user virtual environment has seen an historical emphasis on enhancing individual presence in a virtual environment (Davies, 2003; Farshchian, 2003). This emphasis tends to focus on technology that enhanced physical presence and sensory fidelity (Botella, et al., 2003). Recently, there has been research into the psychosocial dimensions of presence, and this research has identified the importance of social presence and perception (Riva, et al., 2003). This perspective has revealed virtual worlds are simply alternative realities, and all reality, in turn, is mediated by our perceptions (Riva & Ijsselsteijn, 2003). Virtual worlds like Second Life are typically social constructs that have first focused on social presence with limited technological capability in the area of physical presence. Therefore, it is social presence that will reveal the strengths of Second Life's face-to-face simulation. While technical features enhancing physical presence in Second Life are currently limited, the ongoing ambition to achieve "hyperreality" in Second Life is very likely to bear fruit (Tiffin & Terashima, 2001).

The residents of Second Life have collaborated in building a co-presence through a common virtual environment that goes a long way toward constructing a shared context for knowledge exchange. Place is the underlying element that establishes a context for people to understand each other. The lack of place, in turn, has been shown to be a difficulty with many computer mediated communication technologies (Moon, 1999; Cottone & Montavani, 2003). Tacit knowledge exchange, or meaning based learning, is more sensitive to distance than learning based on codified or explicit information. Additionally, studies have shown teams that are collocated in a shared physical space have less problems building a "common ground" than remote teams using phones or computers that lack a representation of a common place (Olsen & Olsen, 2002). Yet, the residents of Second Life often work together to build shared "realities" and can form groups that are sustained over a long period of time.

The very act of designing, and creating the software and hardware that can conjure a virtual world into existence requires imagination, and in the case of Second Life, such creation is an act of innovation in itself (Bartle, 2004). The advantages of a virtual world environment are that teams can share "situational awareness" that is enhanced through both the common graphical interface and the process by which they have created their virtual space together. As William Gibson (1986) described it, this cyberspace becomes a "consensual hallucination" as the participants willingly suspend their disbelief (Botella, et al., 2003). These non-verbal cues are very helpful in allowing members of a group to understand the context of their conversations and actions in that virtual space. These factors, in turn, allow participants in online groups to assume a shared reality for those individuals (Johnson, 2006).

Knowledge Creation and Design Education in Second Life

As explained in the previous section, Second Life enables the residents to construct a shared and persistent 3D graphical reality that extends the imagination beyond the limitations of the written word. It is an environment in which individuals can even augment physical reality to depict concepts that cannot be physically shown in the "real world." Second Life is being used by students and design professionals to collaboratively build prototypes and architectural models of virtual, and physical constructions, (Au, 2008; Rive, et al., 2008).

There are two such examples of how Second Life is being used in education and professional practice, SLoodle and Studio Wikitecture, according to these ideas. Both of these projects are open source, and the international collaboration of the developers and users of these projects continue to push the boundaries of design innovation and what a self-organizing team can achieve. SLoodle is a Second Life extension of the popular learning management tool Moodle, and it provides teachers with a way to use constructivist methods to teach in Second Life (Livingstone, 2009). The Studio Wikitecture Wikitree provides an open source tool that allows international collaborators to cross cultural boundaries and share in the process of designing virtual architecture. The current evaluation process of voting is considered by some to lack granularity and could be improved with better tracking processes and a more flexible point system.

The success or failure of innovative technology is not so much rational and deterministic as a complex adaptive system within a social context, and it is based on the discursive nature of user led design, "produsage," and early adopters (Hine, 2000; Lipartito, 2003; Hippel, 2005). The Studio Wikitecture project can be seen as an agile software project that is in constant beta, and continually being adapted to suit the design innovators. As a result of factors such as these, academic organizations are becoming increasingly challenged by the fast pace of technological change, revealing a gap between education and professional practice and the competitive nature of knowledge creation that is taking place in virtual worlds such as Second Life.

OPEN INNOVATION AND DESIGN EDUCATION

All those participating in the learning experience create knowledge tentatively and in networks and create both tacit and non-tacit knowledge. Ubiquitous ways of learning entrepreneurial approaches and industry pressure are currently mapping out other ways of knowledge exchange procedures. Any tertiary educational institute and in particular design institutes are deeply involved in the current groundswell of open and shared creative processes. The key drivers for this relationship are the Internet, economic turmoil, and a changing cultural zeitgeist that prizes fluid and non-hierarchical creative dialogue between individuals with common goals and interests (Tapscott & Williams, 2006).

Virtual worlds, such as Second Life, provide a test bed for those individuals who are willing to experiment with new methods of design education, design innovation and rapid prototyping (Au, 2008). The low cost and relative ease of experimentation in Second Life contributes to the suitability of using the virtual world for agile design and innovation, and it encourages informal conversations (Farshchian, 2003; Highsmith, 2004). Further research is required to examine whether and how tertiary educational institutes can support design innovation and how technology-enhanced learning leads to innovations. Within this context, openness is an essential characteristic of an innovative and creative environment as it allows for achieving new combinations (Chesbrough, 2003). This characteristic not only helps the creative production within the creative industries themselves, but it also encourages the exploitation of creativity in divergent sectors of the economy.

The current economic climate also provides opportunities for generating successes coming out of the Net generation and includes virtual worlds and Twitter, which brings us back to Weiser's (1995) ubiquitous way of interacting. New forms of creative outputs will not be standardized to a "one size fits all" model solution. (In fact, the global context for interaction crated by Second Life would make such a restrictive approach almost impossible.) Therefore, systems need to be configured and developed according to the project, discipline, and preferences of the user. From a global context, this means that to interact is to localize, almost by virtue of the nature of the interaction. Moreover, the flexibility of design tools in Second Life and collaborative tools such as machinima cameras and the Wikitree suggest ways to encompass the future of design innovation. In some instances, however, the system requires certain approaches from its users to be successful. The ability of design institutes to remain relevant to the future of design will hinge on their ability to stay conversant with the latest experiments in design practice and design innovation. This factor strongly suggests a knowledge of virtual worlds and real-time shared virtual environments as essential to such success.

MAIN LESSONS LEARNED FROM SECOND LIFE CASE STUDIES

The authors have argued that design innovation and knowledge creation should be judged against the criteria of tacit knowledge exchange and the ability of Second Life to simulate face-to-face communications. The lessons learned from the case studies done by the authors provide practical advice for those looking to use Second Life for design innovation in education and a design practice. These lessons include the following factors:

Mixed Reality: The Advantages

The case study of the mixed reality machinima design class provides us with some valuable les-

sons in design education. The expense of the media lab and the physical requirement of the students to attend other classes makes this experience not uncommon. In the future, however, there are likely to be more university design courses that are totally virtual classes (Tiffin & Rajasingham, 2003). This mixed reality learning, or knowledge creation environment, is superior for most design innovation ecologies as it overcomes the limitations of either the strictly virtual or the strictly physical shared environment. Yet within this context, there is one area of weakness in the mixed reality shared space illustrated by the machinima case study. In Second Life, there is the ability for designers to create a digital identity that is anonymous. This characteristic can have profound implications for creativity, team contributions, and ultimately design innovation.

When a pool of designers is physically collocated, there are limitations on their ability to freely associate with others. This factor limits the abilities for novel teams to emerge in a process of self-organization. This case study of the machinima class is also supported by group theory and collective decisionmaking that shows that status and reputation of individuals in a group can diminish the diversity of ideas and lead to groupthink (Surowiecki, 2004; Sunstein, 2006; Page, 2007; Shirky, 2008). In the machinima case study, for example, the students were instructed not to inform their classmates or educators as to their actual identity. In a number of the design teams, the diversity of the members were quite apparent; however, it was also noted that some students had ignored the instruction of anonymity, and so their teams were comprised of close friends who associated together in their physical lab. The anonymity of digital identity and the open nature of avatar appearance meant that ethnic, age, gender, and even disability issues are not to the fore, and so there is the greater likelihood for avatars to associate with a greater diversity of people.

Second Life's Design Innovation Advantages

During the course of four years of ethnographic field work in Second Life, one of the authors has had the opportunity to research the design innovation advantages of working in a virtual shared ecology. They can be summarized in noting that Second Life

- Gives designers the ability to own their own creation.
- Gives designers the tools to allow a flexible ownership.
- Gives designers the ability to collaborate and work on a virtual object in real-time.
- Is a rich, programmable, and interactive shared virtual 3D space. The ability to communicate non-verbally and with easily malleable virtual objects surpasses the slow, expensive process of physical prototypes.
- Provides a rich communications platform to communicate concepts with design colleagues from around the world enabling global localization.
- Allows designers to quickly establish a group based on common interests and facilitate self-organization encouraging diversity in groups.
- Facilitates intersectional ideas by allowing cross-functional teams to easily come together to discuss prototypes.

There is insufficient space here to discuss each of these items in detail and illustrate them with examples. Instead, the authors have selected two important examples, or cases, of design innovation that have enabled knowledge creation in Second Life.

In the first example, the authors consider design innovation in general in Second Life. The authors also consider how flexible digital rights management software has enabled designers to own and share digital content – a factor resulting in a massive amount of user created content. The Second Life economy grew 68% from 2008 to 2009, and it was worth $567 million dollars in user-to-user transactions (C. R. Ondrejka, 2006; Au, 2008; C. Ondrejka, 2008; Lab, 2010). This large amount of "resident" design far exceeded any other multi-player online (MMO) virtual environment and has been largely attributed to allowing residents to own their own creations (C. R. Ondrejka, 2006; Au, 2008; C. Ondrejka, 2008; Lab, 2010).

All of the user-generated content in Second Life will not be innovative design; however, in the case study of Studio Wikitecture and its architectural wikitree, it can be illustrated how designers from remotely separated countries as Belgium, the United States, New Zealand, and the United Kingdom have managed to collaborate on a project that won an Open Architecture Award for the Tibetan Medical Centre in the Himalayas. The Wikitree, together with a web based voting and comment tool, enabled diverse designers to experiment freely with concepts and share ideas in Second Life in order to complete a complex and pleasing final innovative design.

Face-to-Face Advantages

It is important to understand the current advantages of face-to-face design innovation in order to suggest a blueprint for improving how virtual worlds such as Second Life can be more successful in the future. The case studies overviewed in this chapter provide some initial evidence of the current limitations of Second Life and the areas where face-to-face provides a design innovation advantage.

These limitations can be summarized as

- Physical presence currently provides the maximum sensory and emotional communications bandwidth to design collaborators. Second Life must also include high fidelity touch, smell, and taste to match actual presence.

- Physical presence is learned from birth and is intuitive. Second Life tools are complex and require extensive learning and use to become comfortable in design.
- Gestural and facial expressions are high-bandwidth communication modes that are tightly integrated with meaning and context. These aspects are primitive in Second Life and retard tacit knowledge creation.
- Regular physical meetings build up communal knowledge faster due to the higher sensory bandwidth.

In both the machinima and Wikitree case studies, the design innovation capability of the projects would have been enhanced if Second Life had been more closely simulated an actual face-to-face communication situation. It could be argued that as technology continues to shrink and improve these objectives will be eventually met. The current state of the rapidly improving technology already provides Second Life advantages over face-to-face meetings that simply use physical design processes with no technological augmentation.

Future Trends and Opportunities in Virtual Worlds

Virtual worlds should not be regarded as a recent fad or fashion because of an ancient art history in both the visual and literal arts (Wertheim, 1999; Grau, 2003). It is common practice for recent writers on virtual worlds to only look back as far as the first MUDs (multi user dungeons) or 3D graphical virtual game environments. However, even in the early part of the 20th century, there were writers and early technologists who were interested in virtual worlds and virtual reality (Packer & Jordan, 2001; Bartle, 2004; Au, 2008). Even if Second Life does not survive long into the future, it will remain a part of a long history that shows humanity's abiding philosophical, artistic, and scientific interest in virtual worlds (Heim, 1993; Wertheim, 1999; Grau, 2003). The current investments in 3D visualization, 3D gaming, 3D movies, and social networks on the Internet all point to a future that is likely to include some evolution of virtual worlds. The criteria with which we should assess their effectiveness as a design innovation environment involve asking the key questions

- To what extent do they simulate a face-to-face and physical environment?
- To what extent they exceed that experience by augmenting that physical process, and take us far beyond those current limitations?

The questions of who are the current gatekeepers and how will design innovation in Second Life be kept open are important for the future of a global knowledge economy. The complexity of these issues are beyond the scope of this chapter as they entail discussions around intellectual property and the regulation of knowledge creation as discussed by the likes of Lawrence Lessig in his books, *The Future of Ideas, Free Culture, Code 2.0*, and *Remix,* (Lessig, 2001, 2004, 2006, 2008). As Stewart Brand (1988) once said, information may want to be free, but information also wants to be expensive. Suffice to say, that virtual worlds like Second Life will have at their disposal either the means of ensuring open innovation or effectively controlling knowledge creation and the free flow of ideas.

REFERENCES

Au, W. J. (2008). *The making of Second Life: Notes from the new world* (1st ed.). New York, NY: Harper Collins.

Bailenson, J. N., Beall, A. C., Loomis, J., Blascovich, J., & Turk, M. (2004). Transformed social interaction: Decoupling representation from behavior and form in collaborative virtual environments. *Presence (Cambridge, Mass.), 13*(4), 428–441. doi:10.1162/1054746041944803

Bailenson, J. N., Blascovich, J., Beall, A. C., & Loomis, J. M. (2003). Interpersonal distance in immersive virtual environments. *Personality and Social Psychology Bulletin, 29*(7), 819–833. doi:10.1177/0146167203029007002

Bartle, R. A. (2004). *Designing virtual worlds.* Indianapolis, IN: New Riders.

Bateson, G., & Donaldson, R. E. (1991). *A sacred unity: Further steps to an ecology of mind* (1st ed.). New York, NY: Cornelia & Michael Bessie Book.

Benkler, Y. (2006). *The wealth of networks: How social production transforms markets and freedom.* New Haven, CT: Yale University Press.

Boellstorff, T. (2008). *Coming of age in second life: An anthropologist explores the virtually human.* Princeton, NJ: Princeton University Press.

Botella, C., Baños, R. M., & Alcañiz, M. (2003). *A psychological approach to presence.* Paper presented at the PRESENCE 2003, 6th Annual International Workshop on Presence. Retrieved December 5, 2010, from http://www.presence-research.org/ papers/ Botella.html

Brand, S. (1988). *The media lab: Inventing the future at MIT.* New York, NY: Penguin Books.

Bryan, L. L., & Joyce, C. I. (2007). *Mobilizing minds: Creating wealth from talent in the 21st-century organization.* New York, NY: McGraw-Hill.

Cascio, J., & Paffendorf, J. (2007). *Metaverse roadmap overview.* Retrieved October 1, 2010, from http://metaverseroadmap.org/ overview/

Castells, M. (2000). *The rise of the network society* (2nd ed.). Malden, MA: Blackwell Publishers.

Castronova, E. (2004). Right to play. *New York Law School Law Review. New York Law School, 49*(1), 185–210.

Castronova, E. (2005). *Synthetic worlds: The business and culture of online games.* Chicago, IL: University of Chicago Press.

Castronova, E. (2007). *Exodus to the virtual world: How online fun is changing reality.* New York, NY: Palgrave Macmillan.

Chesbrough, H. W. (2003). *Open innovation: The new imperative for creating and profiting from technology.* Boston, MA: Harvard Business School Press.

Cooper, R. G. (2003). Profitable product innovation: The critical success factors. In Shavinina, L. V. (Ed.), *The international handbook on innovation* (pp. 139–157). Boston, MA: Elsevier. doi:10.1016/ B978-008044198-6/50010-3

Cottone, P., & Montavani, G. (2003). Grounding subjective views: Situation awareness and co-reference in distance learning. In Riva, G., Davide, F., & Ijsselsteijn, W. A. (Eds.), *Being there: Concepts, effects and measurements of user presence in synthetic environments* (pp. 249–260). Washington, DC: IOS Press.

Davies, R. (2003). Virtual reality hardware and software: Complex usable devices? In G. Riva & F. Davide (Eds.), *Communications through virtual technology: Identity, community and technology in the Internet age.* Retrieved 2nd March, 2008, from http://www.emergingcommunication.com/ volume5.html

Dibbell, J. (2006). *Play money: Or, how I quit my day job and made millions trading virtual loot.* New York, NY: Basic Books.

Dixon, N. M. (2000). *Common knowledge: How companies thrive by sharing what they know.* Boston, MA: McGraw-Hill.

Farshchian, B. A. (2003). Presence technologies for informal collaboration. In Riva, G., Davide, F., & Ijsselsteijn, W. A. (Eds.), *Being there: Concepts, effects and measurements of user presence in synthetic environments* (pp. 209–222). Washington, DC: IOS Press.

Firestone, J. M. (2008). On doing knowledge management. *Knowledge Management Research & Practice*, 6(1), 13–22. doi:10.1057/palgrave. kmrp.8500160

Firestone, J. M., & McElroy, M. W. (2003). *Key issues in the new knowledge management*. Boston, MA: Butterworth-Heinemann.

Fornas, J. (2002). *Digital borderlands: Cultural studies of identity and interactivity on the Internet*. New York, NY: Peter Lang.

Friedman, T. L. (2006). *The world is flat: A brief history of the twenty-first century* (1st updated and expanded ed.). New York, NY: Farrar, Straus and Giroux.

Gartner. (2007). *Gartner says 80 percent of active Internet users will have a "Second Life" in the virtual world by the end of 2011*. Gartner Newsroom. Retrieved April 24, 2007, from http://www. gartner.com/ it/ page.jsp? id=503861

Gibson, W. (1986). *Neuromancer*. London, UK: Grafton.

Goertzel, B. (2007). *AI meets the metaverse: Teachable AI agents living in virtual worlds*. Kurzweil Articulating Intelligence. Retrieved October 1, 2010, from http://www.kurzweilai.net/ meme/ frame.html? main=/ articles/ art0710.html

Goldman, R., & Gabriel, R. P. (2005). *Innovation happens elsewhere: Open source as business strategy*. Boston, MA: Morgan Kaufmann.

Grau, O. (2003). *Virtual art: From illusion to immersion* (Rev. and expanded ed.). Cambridge, MA: The MIT Press.

Guimaraes, M. J. L. J. (2005). Doing anthropology in cyberspace: Fieldwork boundaries and social environments. In Hine, C. (Ed.), *Virtual methods: Issues in social research on the Internet* (pp. 141–156). New York, NY: Berg.

Hamel, G. (2007). *The future of management*. Boston, MA: Harvard Business School Press.

Heim, M. (1993). *The metaphysics of virtual reality*. New York, NY: Oxford University Press.

Highsmith, J. A. (2004). *Agile project management: Creating innovative products*. Boston, MA: Addison-Wesley.

Hine, C. (2000). *Virtual ethnography*. Thousand Oaks, CA: Sage.

Hippel, E. v. (2005). *Democratizing innovation*. Cambridge, MA: The MIT Press.

Hunter, I. (2008). *Imagine: What Wedgwood, Da Vinci, Mozart, Eiffel, Disney (and many others) can teach us about innovation*. North Shore, New Zealand: Penguin.

Hussi, T. (2003). Reconfiguring knowledge management: Combining intellectual capital, intangible assets and knowledge creation. *Journal of Knowledge Management*, 8(2), 36–52. doi:10.1108/13673270410529091

Johansson, F. (2004). *The Medici effect: Breakthrough insights at the intersection of ideas, concepts, and cultures*. Boston, MA: Harvard Business School Press.

Johnson, D. R. (2006). The new virtual literacy: How the screen affects the law. In Balkin, J. M., & Noveck, B. S. (Eds.), *The state of play: Law, games, and virtual worlds* (pp. 245–256). New York, NY: New York University Press.

Koch, R., & Leitner, K.-H. (2008). The dynamics and functions of self-organization in the fuzzy front end: Empirical evidence from the Austrian semiconductor industry. *Creativity and Innovation Management, 17*(3), 216–226. doi:10.1111/j.1467-8691.2008.00488.x

Kurzweil, R. (2005). *The singularity is near: When humans transcend biology*. New York, NY: Viking.

Lab, L. (2010). *Second Life blogs: Features: 2009 end of year Second Life economy wrap up (including Q4 economy in detail)*. Second Life. Retrieved May 3, 2010, from http://blogs.secondlife.com/ community/ features/ blog/ 2010/ 01/ 19/ 2009-end-of-year-second-life-economy-wrap-up-including-q4- economy-in-detail

Leonard, D., & Swap, W. (2004). *Deep smarts: How to cultivate and transfer enduring business wisdom*. Cambridge, MA: Harvard Business Press.

Lessig, L. (2001). *The future of ideas: The fate of the commons in a connected world* (1st ed.). New York, NY: Random House.

Lessig, L. (2004). *Free culture: How big media uses technology and the law to lock down culture and control creativity*. New York, NY: Penguin Press.

Lessig, L. (2006). *Code: Version 2.0* (2nd ed.). New York, NY: Penguin Press.

Lessig, L. (2008). *Remix: Making art and commerce thrive in the hybrid economy*. New York, NY: Penguin Press.

Lipartito, K. (2003). Picturephone and the information age: The social meaning of failure. *Technology and Culture, 44*(1), 50–81. doi:10.1353/tech.2003.0033

Livingstone, D. (2009). *Online learning in virtual environments with SLOODLE*. San Jose, CA: San José State University School of Library and Information Science.

Malaby, T. M. (2009). *Making virtual worlds: Linden Lab and Second Life*. Ithaca, NY: Cornell University Press.

Maturana, H. R., & Varela, F. J. (1992). *The tree of knowledge: The biological roots of human understanding*. New York, NY: Shambhala.

Mau, B., Leonard, J., & Institute without Boundaries. (2004). *Massive change*. London, UK: Phaidon.

Moon, Y. (1999). The effects of physical distance and response latency on persuasion in computer-mediated communication and human-computer communication. *Journal of Experimental Psychology, 5*, 379–392.

Nonaka, I. O., & Takeuchi, H. (1995). *The knowledge-creating company*. New York, NY: Oxford University Press.

Olsen, G. M., & Olsen, J. S. (2002). Distance matters. In J. M. Carroll (Ed.), *Human-computer interaction in the new millennium* (pp. pp 139-178). New York, NY: Addison-Wesley.

Ondrejka, C. (2008). Education unleashed: Participatory culture, education, and innovation in second life. In Salen, K. (Ed.), *The ecology of games: Connecting youth, games, and learning* (pp. 229–251). Cambridge, MA: The MIT Press.

Ondrejka, C. R. (2006). Escaping the gilded cage: User created content and building the metaverse. In Balkin, J. M., & Noveck, B. S. (Eds.), *The state of play: Law, games, and virtual worlds* (p. viii). New York, NY: New York University Press.

Page, S. E. (2007). *The difference: How the power of diversity creates better groups, firms, schools, and societies*. Princeton, NJ: Princeton University Press.

Peters, T. J. (1997). *The circle of innovation: You can't shrink your way to greatness* (1st ed.). New York, NY: Knopf.

Polanyi, M. (1967). *The tacit dimension*. London, UK: Routledge.

PricewaterhouseCoopers. (2008). *Managing the risks and rewards of collaboration*. Retrieved October 1, 2010, from http://www.pwc.com/ gx/ en/ technology/ technology-executive-connections/ index.jhtml

Reeves, B., & Read, J. L. (2009). *Total engagement: Using games and virtual worlds to change the way people work and businesses compete*. Boston, MA: Harvard Business Press.

Rickards, T. (2003). The future of innovation. In Shavinina, L. V. (Ed.), *The international handbook on innovation* (pp. 1094–1112). Boston, MA: Elsevier. doi:10.1016/B978-008044198-6/50071-1

Riva, G., Davide, F., & Ijsselsteijn, W. A. (2003). *Being there: Concepts, effects and measurements of user presence in synthetic environments*. Washington, DC: IOS Press.

Rive, P. B. (2008). Knowledge transfer and marketing in Second Life. In Zemliansky, P., & St.Amant, K. (Eds.), *Handbook of research on virtual workplaces and the new nature of business practices* (pp. 424–438). Hershey, PA: Information Science Reference. doi:10.4018/978-1-59904-893-2.ch030

Rive, P. B., Thomassen, A., Lyons, M., & Billinghurst, M. (2008). *Face to face with the white rabbit: Sharing ideas in Second Life*. Paper presented at the IEEE International Professional Communications Conference.

Salzman, M. L., & Matathia, I. (2007). *Next now: Trends for the future*. New York, NY: Palgrave Macmillan.

Sebell, M. H. (2008). *Stage gates: Good or bad for innovation*. Creative Realities. Retrieved October 29, 2008, from http://www.creativerealities.com/ knowledgeArticles.html

Shavinina, L. V. (2003). *The international handbook on innovation*. Boston, MA: Elsevier.

Shields, R. (2003). *The virtual*. New York, NY: Routledge.

Shirky, C. (2008). *Here comes everybody: The power of organizing without organizations*. New York, NY: Penguin Press.

Stewart, T. A. (2001). *The wealth of knowledge: Intellectual capital and the twenty-first century organization* (1st ed.). New York, NY: Currency.

Sunstein, C. R. (2006). *Infotopia: How many minds produce knowledge*. New York, NY: Oxford University Press.

Suri, J. F., & IDEO. (2005). *Thoughtless act: Observations on intuitive design* (1st ed.). San Francisco, CA: Chronicle Books.

Surowiecki, J. (2004). *The wisdom of crowds: Why the many are smarter than the few and how collective wisdom shapes business, economies, societies, and nations* (1st ed.). New York, NY: Doubleday.

Tapscott, D., & Williams, A. D. (2006). *Wikinomics: How mass collaboration changes everything*. New York, NY: Portfolio.

Taylor, T. L. (2006). *Play between worlds: Online multiplayer games and contemporary play*. Cambridge, MA: The MIT Press.

Teece, D. J. (2000). *Managing intellectual capital: Organizational, strategic, and policy dimensions*. New York, NY: Oxford University Press.

Teece, D. J., & Nonaka, I. O. (2000). *Managing industrial knowledge*. London, UK: Sage.

Tiffin, J., & Rajasingham, L. (2003). *The global virtual university*. New York, NY: Routledge Falmer. doi:10.4324/9780203464670

Tiffin, J., & Terashima, N. (2001). *HyperReality: Paradigm for the third millenium.* New York, NY: Routledge.

Von Krogh, G., Nonaka, I., & Ichijo, K. (2000). *Enabling knowledge creation: How to unlock the mystery of tacit knowledge and release the power of innovation.* New York, NY: Oxford University Press.

Weick, K. E. (1991). The nontraditional quality of organizational learning. *Organization Science, 2*(1), 116–124. doi:10.1287/orsc.2.1.116

Wertheim, M. (1999). *The pearly gates of cyberspace: A history of space from Dante to the Internet.* New York, NY: W. W. Norton.

Yankelovich, N. (2007). *MPK20: Sun's virtual workplace.* Oracle. Retrieved October 1, 2010, from http://research.sun.com/ projects/ mc/ mpk20.html

Yee, N., Bailenson, J. N., Urbanek, M., Chang, F., & Merget, D. (2007). The unbearable likeness of being digital: The persistence of nonverbal social norms in online virtual environments. *Cyberpsychology & Behavior, 10*(1), 115–121. doi:10.1089/cpb.2006.9984

KEY TERMS AND DEFINITIONS

Second Life: An online 3D virtual world developed by Linden Lab.

Virtual World: An online simulation in which users can interact with each other and virtual objects.

Avatar: A representation of a person or artificial intelligence in a virtual world.

Machinima: A movie made using a 3D gaming engine or virtual world.

Digital Rights Management (DRM): A means of controlling permissions and access to digital files.

Massively Multiplayer Online (MMO): An online environment that could be a game, or a virtual world, such as Second Life.

Presence: A sense of 'being there,' either in a virtual world, or in a psychological state.

Rez: To render a 3D object in real-time in Second Life.

Chapter 28

Immigration Reform:
Re[forming] Theories and Cyber–Designs

Barbara Heifferon
Louisiana State University, USA

ABSTRACT

This chapter focuses on the theoretical preparation of students who design digital media for other cultural groups. Some designers of cross-cultural e-communication assume that the localization of document design is no longer preferable. However, the fact that we have the technical capability to distribute documents universally does not mean we cannot localize content. Universalizing some projects, such as online health care materials to address Spanish-speakers, when audiences with different needs speak Spanish in the U.S., can be less than effective. To address these ideas, this chapter first articulates the theoretical preparation of students to design online materials for different cultural audiences. Secondly, the author also discusses local application and pedagogy related to this process.

INTRODUCTION

This chapter focuses on the theoretical preparation necessary for students to design digital media for other cultures. In so doing, the author uses a case study of a project designed for Spanish-speakers from Latin and South America, particularly for recent arrivals from Mexico, *Mexicanos*[1] to examine issues related to this process. The overarching

DOI: 10.4018/978-1-60960-833-0.ch028

idea is to argue against the tendency to assume global or universal applications. In fact, localization of cultural communication is usually the most effective message-design process.

Within this context, some designers assume that the Internet means localization of document design is no longer viable or preferable over leaving materials "as they already are." However, because we have the technical capability to make documents accessible to wider audiences does not mean that approach is best. Rather, much effectiveness could be lost in universalizing some projects. For instance, one online health care site used for all U.S.-based Spanish-speakers can be problematic, for the U.S. actually contains a range of Spanish-speaking users from a variety of cultures and in need of different kinds and types of information.

The purpose of this chapter is to examine these issues in order to help readers better understand their complexity. Such an understanding is, in turn, essential to creating effective online materials for users from different cultures and countries. To examine these issues, the author first articulates the theoretical preparation necessary for students of cross-cultural health communication to understand and address such factors. The author then uses a case study to briefly discuss a local application of these ideas to the design of online health information for different cultural groups. In examining these issues, the chapter focuses predominately on theoretical preparation and appropriate pedagogy for preparing students to more effectively design online materials for cross-cultural interactions.

SIGNIFICANCE AND TERMINOLOGY

Most professional communication students are aware of translation issues in U.S. workplaces. In many cases, these translation issues involve not creating materials for overseas audiences, but developing texts for U.S.-based workers who are not native speakers of English. One particularly important kind of information within this context is health-related information that workers/individuals must have access to in order to get the treatment needed to address a variety of medical conditions and situations. In the U.S., the largest population most in need of non-English-language health materials and translators is Spanish-speakers.[2] This particular population, moreover, continues to grow – and to grow rapidly – in relation to other cultural and linguistic groups in the U.S.

Immigration from Latin and South America, for example, is still growing, and as a result, "the diversity of the United States population continues to change at a rapid pace" (Nelson, Brownson, Remington, & Parvanta, 2002, p. 209). In 2000, for example, an estimated ten percent of the U.S. population was not born in this country. At the same time, figures from 2005 show approximately 42,687,224 Hispanics in the U.S, out of which one in five speak English (U.S. Census Bureau, 2006). English is then a second or even third language for most of those persons born outside of the United States (Gudykunst & Mody, 2002). As a result, a growing number of individuals in direct need of medical attention are arriving at emergency rooms and doctors' offices where they are unable to understand English and provide the answers needed to receive effective medical care. (This communication disconnect is only made more complex by the use of medical jargon in such contexts.) In such scenarios, translators are not always available or are often not available in the numbers needed to provide effective translation (i.e., effective care) to all non-English-speaking patients. These factors reveal a need for our students to learn how to develop effective online materials – particularly health and medical materials – for the increasingly diverse local workplace.

The first step in preparing students for such tasks involves defining the terms of cross-culture work, as the terms themselves carry political implications. For example, how do we talk about *international, global, cross-cultural* and *intercultural* issues? These terms are used interchangeably, and we often use them unreflectively, even as language and communication scholars. In this chapter, the terms *international* and *cross-cultural* will be used, but not the word *global*. The term, *global*, for many people outside the U.S., has become associated with the Americanization of their countries. As a result, the term represents a political agenda – that of *globalism* – which is often viewed negatively and not accepted as neutral by members of non-U.S. cultures.[3] Additionally, the chapter uses the term *cross-cultural* as it reflects work across cultures: one culture found in a predominately Anglo-American sector in the U.S. and one culture found among recent immigrants from Mexico. Making such distinctions for our students is of key importance. In working with future professional communicators, our work as teachers involves communicating our language choices to build awareness of students working in increasingly cross-cultural or multicultural settings.

Once these terms are clarified for students, the next step involves interacting with them to consider the meanings – and the implications – of other terms associated with cross-cultural communication tasks. For example, some of the questions the author and her students have undertaken, and continue to undertake, are the following:

- As health and international technical communicators, should we attempt to compose online messages that are more "universal" or should we design online messages that are more local?
- What theoretical frames work best if we decide to localize our e-media?
- What do "high-context" and "low-context" cultures mean and why are they important concepts related to online communication and design?
- Which methods work best in participatory, community-based research associated with designing online materials?
- How do we apply the theory and methods in our professional/health communication classrooms to understand the design of online materials?

This chapter articulates the theory and the *praxis* of one case: a localized application in bilingual design. The overarching idea is that without putting appropriate theoretical lenses into place before gathering participatory data, field notes and observations, we cannot hope to design the most effective digital materials for our audience.

SHOULD WE DESIGN MESSAGES THAT ARE "UNIVERSAL" OR LOCAL?

In *Writing in the Health Professions* (2005), the author argues that this question has often been at the center of a debate in international professional communication (Heifferon, p. 206). Shome and Hegde (2002) agree that "Globalism challenges our understanding of culture and identity in ways that both open up new directions for communication scholarship and invite a rethinking of current ones" (p. 172). They maintain that rethinking the study of culture for those of us in communication is "urgent" (p. 172). Bourges-Waldegg and Scrivener (1998) also suggested that the "internationalization-localization process is the most common means by which culturally determined usability problems are approached in HCI" (p. 287). Hawisher and Selfe (2000) go further and claim that the "global village" is a myth and that our technology maps Western cultural assumptions onto unsuspecting and unwitting cultures (p. 292).

In an earlier (1999) article, Selfe argues that in fact the global village narrative "is shaped by American and western cultural interests" (Selfe, "Lest," p. 292). This narrative, Selfe maintains, "has been criticized by technology studies scholars who question its accuracy and point to the specific national and cultural interests" of those countries who impose culturally insensitive practices on others (p. 2). In addition to seeing this myth negatively, people of other cultures often interpret "the global expansion of the Web within the historical context of colonialism" (p. 9). Hawisher and Selfe (2000) suggest that we need to look at the local cultural contexts to discover the "culturally specific literacy practices" rather than using global village metaphor that could erase important, cultural differences.

Additionally, Hawisher & Selfe (2000) suggest that the global emphasis "provides a convenient and ideologically effective way of making efforts to expand free-market economic development, provide active support of fledgling democratic political efforts and intervene militarily in the affairs of non-western countries" (p. 9). The myth can conceal the actuality that Western countries stand to gain financially more than other countries gain technologically. Issues like culture, literacy, and accessibility become factors for many countries at the receiving end of Western technology. Shome and Hegde (2002), on the other hand, don't see globalism as a continuation of colonialism, but rather globalism creates new configurations of empowerment and disempowerment (p. 175). They, too, suggest that their caveat does not imply colonialism doesn't matter within the context of globalism (p. 175). Rather, students should be made aware of these distinctions as they approach digital design for other cultures.

Today, when immigration issues are dividing many in the U.S., individuals who design online materials need to be especially sensitive to cross-cultural communication. This situation is particularly the case for projects that teach a participatory research method, one in which the "target audience" becomes the experts. In examining such issues, educators have the opportunity to show that our interests are not to interfere with but to bridge to another culture without dictating to and being disrespectful of the eventual users of the online information we create.

The other side in this debate is represented in another collection of essays.[4]

In C. Lovitt's and D. Goswami's text (1999) on international professional communication, Jane Perkins does not advocate universalism per se. Rather, she proposes using generic lenses within professional communication to construct communication across cultures. Perkins does acknowledge that communication will "benefit from 'inter' [inter-cultural or between cultures] research that helps us understand what confuses and what offends – verbally, visually, proxemically, socially, and so forth" (Perkins, p. 17).[5] However, Perkins (1999) also believes "Professional communication teachers and researchers need to consider

additional metaphors, new ways of thinking about international communication; we can begin from an understanding of some current changes in corporations—changes toward borderless, yet multicultural, professional communication" (p. 18).[6] Such ideas have powerful implications for how educators teach students to develop online materials for individuals from other cultural and linguistic groups.

In marketing and advertising literature, scholars are beginning to address cross-cultural issues in digital work. Singh and Baack (2004), for example, argue, "very few studies have addressed the issue of Web site standardization or localization" (para. 1). In the recent past, a debate has raged over whether websites are culturally neutral or sensitive documents, and we have had few examples to see how representations of cultures and their values are depicted or reflected in websites from other countries.

Interestingly, Singh's and Baack's study (2004) of Mexican and American websites found significant differences between Mexican and American web pages in their content analyses. Bourges-Waldegg and Scrivener (2000), in comparison, suggest that many user problems are representational (p. 112). These scholars also suggest a quantitative research model – Meaning in Mediated Action (MIMA) – to use in determining user problems. This model, however, is one students might or might not find useable. This chapter, in turn, suggests a more qualitative approach to such situations. Yet both approaches, if used together, might prove to be the most effective way to examine such sites.

One problem with designing online materials for other cultures emerges even when we choose a local application of communication strategies to problem-solve: That is, we still use predominately Western or American practices to examine the problems faced by *other* cultures. For this reason, we must be very clear in how we define and position such terms as *local* and *global*. As Yi-Jokipii (2001) explains

The terms local and global are increasingly used to refer to the problems emerging from the fact that variations in professional communication conventions and expectations derive from linguistic and cultural differences. Indeed, the term localization has been used to refer to the strategy of a company to adjust its documents to the local culture of the market area. However, LOCALIZATION is considered an unsophisticated strategy that has largely been ignored in practice and in research. It is no surprise then, that much of the current research in the past few years has looked only into how primarily American strategies are translated to accommodate local cultures, their conditions and expectations. (p. 105) (See also Hofstede, 1991; Hofstede, Neuijen, Ohayv, & Sanders, 1990; Trompenaars & Hampden-Turner, 1998; Weiss and Stripp, 1998; Pinker, 1994; and Hall, 1983). (Emphasis mine).

Given the debate briefly outlined above, how are digital communicators and designers of online materials for international and multicultural audiences supposed to respond? Instead of seeing these positions as either/or, it might be better to find a balance and approach the question from a both/and viewpoint. A move from unsophisticated, untheorized localization as translation to theoretically rich, carefully researched and grounded localization is in order. From a medical communication perspective, individuals need to be culturally sensitive to persuade target audiences to employ or cease certain health behaviors. If the goal of online medical and health communication is the overall health and quality of life of individuals, the individuals designing such materials must be sensitive to issues within the populations they hope to reach and not just put a local gloss on their usual practices. If the persons creating such online materials do not attempt specific, audience

analyses and have audience members participate in the design process, they risk either alienating the very people they had hoped to reach or designing ineffective materials for those users.

Realistically speaking, time and resources prevent individuals from being able to customize each particular application to each, specific audience member. Some of the choices designers make cannot help but be based on a more generalized view of someone else's culture or of cultures overall. One learns through the process of trial and error and also reviews what someone else tried unsuccessfully to implement in a different cultural context.

WHAT IS THE HISTORY OF LOCAL KNOWLEDGE?

This section examines the history of local knowledge and its theories. The combination of theories reviewed here represents "a rethinking... of the communication of cultural politics in ways that exceed some of the dominant cultural frameworks through which we usually tend to map cultural politics" (Shome & Hegde, 2002, p. 178).

Local knowledge has long been a research term and practice among anthropologists. This is due in large part to Clifford Geertz's work in the 1970s and his more recent work. In *Local Knowledge* (2000), Geertz writes that "To an ethnographer sorting through the machinery of distant ideas, the shapes of knowledge are always ineluctably local, indivisible from their instruments and encasements" (p. 4). As designers, we lose the surety of how our digital designs and e-media will work within new contexts, although we might feel confident about many of our choices and decisions within a familiar culture. Although he is talking about theory itself here, Geertz's comments are apropos: "To turn from trying to explain social phenomena by weaving them into grand textures of cause and effect to trying to explain them by placing them in local frames of awareness is to exchange a set of well-charted difficulties for a set of largely uncharted ones" (*Local,* p. 6). In sum, using participants as cultural guides helps.

In *Power/Knowledge* (1980), Michel Foucault also addressed the use of local knowledge, although in a more tangential way. Foucault defines a subjugated knowledge, that of the persons not in positions of power, as the "whole set of knowledges... disqualified as inadequate to their task or insufficiently elaborated: naive knowledges, located low down on the hierarchy, beneath the required level of cognition or scientificity" (p. 82). In that same definition, Foucault includes what he characterizes as local or particular knowledges, those attitudes that have been "disqualified," including those of the psychiatric patient and the ill person (p. 82).

This category is useful in relation to the case study presented here because *Mexicano* patients and their families' knowledge (i.e., understandings, preferences, and biases) are often subjugated and "disqualified" in health care settings. These factors can cause further problems in triaging, treating, educating, and communicating with individuals from this culture. The more careful our audience analysis and recovery of local attitudes towards health, illness, pregnancies and U.S. medical practices are, the better the design and the implementation of online health information. Because of our hierarchy of knowledges, the influence of science and logic and their epistemic roles in systems of knowledge are privileged (Heifferon, 1998). While scientific knowledge is crucial in health care, the role of patients and their reactions and cooperation is key. In short, individuals who design online health care information need to know what patients are thinking and how health communications will be received by those patients. The case study presented here supports such theory.

HOW DOES FREIREAN THEORY AND PRACTICE AFFECT *PRAXIS* IN AND OUT OF THE CLASSROOM?

Although it might seem unusual to begin a Master's seminar in professional communication by assigning Freire's (1993) *Pedagogy of the Oppressed,* composition scholars in service learning have also used his work (1996Cushman and others, 1996!, 1999, pp. 376 & 382). Freire also practiced recovery of local knowledge from those with whom he developed projects. He articulated this factor in his various pedagogical works. Within the context (i.e., case) of the aforementioned graduate seminar, Freire's (1993) work was useful both as a background for the research methodology (grassroots and bottom up rather than top-down) used by the students and the population for and with whom the students designed online materials.

Freire's ideas (1993) made it possible for seminar participants to discuss the conditions that drove people to come to our country in order to do back-breaking manual labor for long hours and under conditions few U.S. citizens would tolerate. Freire's (1993) pedagogical theories interrogating the "banking model" of education also provided seminar participants with a critique of a top-down approach to education and research. It allowed them to imagine a real community-participation model of research and design. Just as Freire would ask the villagers with whom he worked to articulate and decide on how to solve their own problems using him as a facilitator and resource person, the instructor (i.e., the author) prepared students to think as the author of *Pedagogy of the Oppressed* thought. Before participants even began their project work, they needed to believe that their audience had its own expertise to bring to the table.

Although the instructor expected student resistance to Freire's (1993) use of the terms *revolution* and *oppression,* ironically perhaps, Freire's religious stance (liberation theology) gave the South Carolina students raised in the Bible Belt a common religious belief (in Christianity) with Freire. Also, using a local problem with a real exigency creates a classroom in which students are less threatened by and have less resistance to ideas that could potentially create cognitive dissonance (e.g., immigration, liberation, or revolution). Input about other cultures unnerves students and expands their horizons, especially as future international professional and health communicators. Students often resist having to read about other races and classes and can resent service learning. Such students, however, tend to not resist projects that make sense to them. Students are also more motivated when they have some beliefs in common with the theorists they study, and/or clients' knowledge is seen as valuable.

In his *CCC* article (1994) and CCCC presentation (1999), Bruce Herzberg critiqued service learning. He argued it did not encourage cultural critiques. In so doing, Herzberg referred to students who do volunteerism, wrote about their experience in journals, and reflected only on how good they felt about themselves. He appropriately urged educators to move beyond such pedagogy. Ellen Cushman also urged educators (in her essay reprinted in *The Braddock Essays*, 1996, p. 376) to move beyond self-congratulation and *noblesse oblige*. The author, in fact, observed examples of students beginning to question and critique cultural patterns as their understanding of the various factors affecting farm workers grew. By using readings from Foucault (1980), Freire (1993), Geertz (2000), and others, students understood how community-based, participatory research interrupts the normal top-down power relations. As they learned to record and recover the particular and local knowledges that Foucault (1980), Geertz (2000), and Freire (1993) emphasized, students recognized they would learn as much or more from their clients as those clients would learn from them.

After focusing on the theoretical understanding about what the class was going to undertake (participating in online design with another cul-

tural group), it was necessary for the students to develop an understanding of how cultures might differ from their own. A useful taxonomy for this is that of a high/low context grid. The version presented in this chapter does not differ greatly from that first introduced by Edward Hall (1983).

ARE "HIGH-CONTEXT" AND "LOW-CONTEXT" TAXONOMIES USEFUL IN DESIGNING ONLINE MATERIALS FOR OTHER CULTURES?

Because the author's students, both graduates and undergraduates, had not usually had or taken advantage of opportunities to travel widely outside of the U.S., they had little knowledge of cultural differences. Their assumptions were based on their own culture and more narrowly within the confines of their particular region and state. In spite of media access to many online international and cross-cultural sources, the author's experience with students at the medium-sized, rural Southeastern university where she was teaching continually supported this view of students' provincialism and cultural isolation. although students in large Northern universities in big urban centers could also be isolated from cultural differences.

However, with immigration pushed to the front burner and Latin Americans often targeted as "Other" as a political strategy, students living in such contexts were more apt to disrespect another cultural group within their communities. [7] As G. Spivak pointed out, even the migrant is implicated in "dominant global capital," but, I would argue, is still more of a pawn than a player (qtd. in Shome and Hegde, 2002, p. 177). Even graduate students need much foundational work in cross-cultural and international communication to begin to understand how to design online materials for such audiences.

Cultural characteristics mapped onto a continuum between high and low context can give very basic understandings of cultural difference, especially for students and online designers who have not yet experienced other cultures directly. It might seem contradictory to be promoting localization and then use a device which divides cultures into dichotomous groups. The need to educate students, however, necessitates a funnel approach. This approach moves from theoretical lenses in support of participatory practice to an entry way into cultural difference to actual involvement in a small and local cultural group, members of which participated in the digital design process. While the cultural taxonomy serves as a guideline for students, it does not pretend to substitute for good, qualitative research into particular groups and the local knowledge of participants. Yet, the brief overview of culture does help student begin to frame an understanding of cultural difference before they interview and work with audience members. In examining such factors with students, the author usually starts with a continuum and as she and her students study various cultures, they

place these factors on the continuum (acknowledging our "approximations").

High Context   Low Context

Table 1 shows the characteristics that make-up high- and low-context cultures.

When given this matrix, students understand very quickly that U.S. culture is a low-context one. It is a culture that emphasizes open and informal communication and values competitive and individualistic attitudes. U.S. economic structure based on capitalism and private enterprise reinforces the communicative styles used by members of that culture and vice versa. Perhaps it was the history of the U.S. as a country of immigrants arriving in a large and sparsely populated land that created a scene for such low-context attitudes to flourish. Waves of immigrants from many different classes and countries arrived in the U.S. and attempted to assimilate. Perhaps

Table 1. Traits of Low-vs. High-Context Cultures[8]

	Low Context	**High Context**
Approach to Disagreement	Resolution via conflict	Resolution via consensus
Business Affiliations	Based on monetary benefits	Based on tradition & personal relationships
Conflict Resolution Style	Face-to-face	Through liaisons & intermediaries
Discourse Groups & Communities	Belonging to many communities & groups	Belonging to and identifying with one predominant group
Interpersonal Relationships	Informal	Formal
Life Goals	Achievement up to the individual	Achievement up to the group or in the hands of Fate
Motivation	Individual goals	Group goals
Play & Work	Kept separate	Integrated
Relationship to Nature	Separated from nature & the environment	Integrated with or a part of nature
Self Concept	Thinks of self as a single individual	Thinks of self as a part of a group
Status in Relationships	Egalitarian	Hierarchical
Time	Future orientation	Past & present orientation
Trust Level	Open	Closed except to group members
Usual Behavior	Independent, oriented toward self	Dependent, oriented toward group
Values	Active - doing	Passive - being

because these immigrants could not be so easily blended, an individualistic orientation developed in which a person was no longer identified with his or her former culture or even the new one. Instead, he or she felt free to develop as an individual and that individualism became the cultural marker that many later generations did have in common with each other.

In contrast, high-context cultures evolved over time to value more group-oriented and formal methods of communication. These cultures created stricter rules of social conduct and less direct, more subtle rhetorical interactions. This indirect communication style presents one of the most difficult challenges for digital designers striving to create effective online health communication across cultures.

Anglo-American communicators, for example, issue very direct orders and requests, while members of high-context cultures generally neither compose nor respond well to the same type of such direct commands. Additionally, members of high-context cultures can often feel reluctant to directly refuse or deny requests. "It has been said that Japanese don't have a word for *no*. While this is not true, it is true that the Japanese, like many other people, are reluctant to give a direct refusal" (Thrush, 2001, p. 34).

These characteristics of high-context cultures hold true for many of the *Mexicano* patients with whom the students in the author's class worked. While these *Mexicano* participants were somewhat less formal than Japanese, they often view many of the direct health care messages created by Anglo-Americans as rude and invasive. Similarly, they sometimes view Anglo-American graphics and digital interfaces as offensive or problematic. All of these factors, however, needed to be understood, considered, and addressed by individuals creating online materials for today's increasingly diverse U.S. workplace.

The use of the high- and low-context matrix has proven useful to other scholars teaching e-design for multicultural audiences. Nitish Singh

and Arun Pereira (2005) use these concepts in their student-friendly textbook on customizing websites for a global market. In the book, the two similarly argue for localizing our web design, although much of their analysis and advice is transferable to other e-media.

Throughout their text, Singh and Pereira use the various characteristics of Hall's (1983) taxonomy to instill good methods to research the audience for web design. Singh and Pereira's chapter on individualization and collectivism, for example, is especially helpful in teaching the concepts. Throughout the text these two authors have specific examples for how to analyze the audience. As a result, using their text in addition to the theoretical work is ideal. Interestingly, it is not until one of the last chapters in the book that Singh and Pereira introduce the actual terms *high* and *low context* as useful tools for web design. While the text is an excellent and effective overview of localizing ("customizing" in their terms), this chapter argues for even more in-depth involvement and activism in which community-based participation informs the project throughout its development.

While designing electronic and visual programs for Latin American cultures, it is important for individuals to remember that many of the cultures south of the U.S. emphasize oral language. In particular, "... Latin American [cultures], place a high value on personal and oral communication" (Lewis, 1996, p. 20). Singh's and Baack's (2004) research, moreover, clearly shows how "cultural values are reflected in American and Mexican Web sites" and found "significant differences in the depiction of local cultural values on the Web" (para. 1). Exposing students to such examples, thus, reinforces the theory and their text is particularly useful for this purpose. In fact, by giving students examples of other cultures, instructors can help students begin to understand the need for cultural analysis (a more general approach at first) using a matrix such as the one presented earlier in this chapter. Such a matrix, moreover, can be an essential tool for them to consult before they begin qualitative research relating to culture and communication.

In addition to using Singh and Baack, instructors in the areas of professional and of online communication can explain and reinforce the concept of direct and indirect communication efforts. To do so, they can use articles about various cultures before going out in the field. They learn that "German business people... prefer factual detail in documents and are likely to thoroughly read and absorb written documents. Consequently, Germans may be likely to tolerate a substantial amount of textual material [even] in web documents" (Zahedi, Van Pelt, & Song, 2001, p. 86).

Because many high-context cultures see written language as the end of negotiating, they tend to also see written documents as the end of a discussion and not as a part of it. Thus, when Anglo-American individuals now modify the online deliverables for our various health education and triage software for a *Mexicano* audience, they must think in terms of more oral and audio media.

In the previously mentioned study by Singh and Baack (2004), for example, the authors found "that Mexico is a highly collectivistic society, with a high power distance structure, and with a relatively low tolerance for uncertainty, while the United States is an individualistic society, low on power distance structure and relatively high on tolerance for uncertainty" (para. 16). Thus, if students can begin to understand these differences before they go into a community, they can be more sensitive to the differences and have some cultural sensitivity and real literacy before working with the community. However, the job of instructors must then be directed toward creating an understanding without also biasing students in case a local group might have developed some other hybrid cultural values as a result from dwelling in the U.S. over longer periods of time. To address some of these factors, the author's own students have turned more toward DVDs with photo-novellas featuring health information and web-based programs downloadable to cell phones

with primarily digitized audio presentations. Such media are popular among the target group of users in the area in which the students are working, and local focus groups help the students assess access and preferences of media choices related to these design decisions.

HOW WAS THEORY APPLIED TO THIS PROJECT?

The project that served as the focus of this case had evolved over numerous semesters into a health education system that will feature a Web-based delivery of graphic interfaces for tablets, P.D.A.s., cell phones, and DVDs for physician waiting rooms. For this project, students used ethnographic research methods involving farm workers from Mexico and the families of those workers. The individuals who participated in the design process with the students revealed important cultural differences that informed content and design choices related to online media. The methods students used to collect this information included field notes, interviews, usability tests (in the field, not in labs), site-testing, focus groups, and follow-up interviews. Rather than translating previously developed web content for English-speaking audiences (a choice many digital designers make), the students, *Mexicanos,* and the instructor developed original, culturally sensitive visuals, charts, and graphic surveys to aid in health screening and education. Based on this successful experience, the students and the instructor are now designing materials for digital formats only.

The overall project began in a graduate seminar in summer of 1999, and it continued for numerous semesters. The Joseph F. Sullivan Center of Nursing and Wellness asked the author and her class to design bilingual health diagnostic materials for Latino farm workers and for a related health care mobile unit. The center not only delivered primary health care, but it also taught nurse practitioner, nursing, and health science students as it served a local rural area. The author and her class did the first phase of the project in an intensive 5-week period. The project has spun off a series of other iterations, including the planning for a digital, prenatal health education module for local Latinas.

The Sullivan Center on Clemson's campus has been a frequent partner for service-learning or client-based projects. In addition to an onsite clinic in the nursing building, the Center has a state-of-the-art mobile van that is equipped with all the necessities to provide primary health care to people in rural areas in the upstate of South Carolina.[9] This interdisciplinary collaboration spanned eight years and involved several disciplines spread across four of our five colleges. The emphasis the author has taken on problem-based learning to address such situations has worked well in taking on communication problems for this nursing center.

In summer of 1999, the author's international professional communication class was to solve a problem that involved inventing a triage system that could be used across languages and cultures. In the Round Mountain apple orchards in Long Creek, SC, the mobile unit often worked in the evenings, because the farm workers who picked the apple crops in Long Creek worked from dawn to dusk. The Sullivan Center contracted with the orchard owners and growers to deliver health care to the farm workers, the majority of whom were *Mexicanos* who followed the crops from Florida to Maine.

Typically the mobile unit arrived, plugged into the electrical source at a sorting and packaging facility near the orchards, and set up portable tables that serve to process and triage patients.[10] A nurse practitioner heading the team along with nurse practitioner students, nursing students, and sometimes a few health science students, served both inside the large mobile unit to administer care and outside to assess and do paperwork on arriving patients. A truck or bus would then pull up with some 30-60 farm workers who spoke Spanish and not English. The majority of students spoke no Spanish, although once the patients completed a pre-screening and got into the van for treatment, practitioners inside the mobile unit did speak Spanish.

The challenge faced by the author and her students was to facilitate the triage and early diagnosis process in which neither health student nor patient could communicate with each other. This situation was no small task. To figure out how to solve the problem and facilitate this process, the author and her students needed their theoretical background, outlined earlier, and intensive audience analysis, including a careful and sensitive look at the culture of the patients with whom and for whom we were designing. Because the author and her students had chosen a local approach, although they read and analyzed various texts for some background information, they did the ethnographic research for their case study locally (Bosley, 2001; Geertz, 2000; Lovitt & Goswami, 1999).

Putting into practice the theories they had studied, in interviews and focus groups, the author and her students asked the *Mexicanos* what health materials to design that would meet their needs. The author and her students then used the suggestions provided by these interviewees as a guide for what they would do on this project.

The deliverables for the overall project came mainly from two *Mexicanos*. One suggested the design of charts and graphics to help identify symptoms. This idea developed into an 85-page, graphic, diagnostic booklet of culturally sensitive graphics. One *Mexicana*, who had settled in this area, became a regular attendee of the class in which the chart was developed. This person, in turn, acted as both consultant and designer; she helped design a female chart, and the students then designed a male chart, resulting in separate charts for men and for women. These 11x17 laminated charts could then be used in the field, for Long Creek, SC had no shelter outside the mobile unit for its screenings. They could also serve as an initial template from which individuals could develop similar kinds of web-based visual charts to be downloaded and used on mobile phones in a variety of rural contexts.

From our interviews, students learned *Mexicanas* would be more comfortable with a separate chart, one for each gender that was sensitively and subtly designed, not as explicit as a typical chart seen in U.S. doctors' offices. The students set up the interviews so that female students and translators interviewed women workers while male students interviewed male farm workers. In addition, the students also interviewed growers to understand their constraints: governmental, economic, ethical and practical. Unlike the students in the health classes, many of my students spoke Spanish, and also a native speaker and Spanish professor from the college assisted in translations. The students and the author conducted site visits to the mountains and took voluminous field notes. Each student also followed a patient through the mobile unit to understand the history and physical following the initial triage.

In the semester following this data collection, the author set up site tests for the three deliverables. The materials (two charts and an 85-page diagnostic booklet) were field tested at five *Mexicano* health care sites in South Carolina. Teams from an undergraduate technical writing class in another semester took the charts and books to clinics and to health fairs in order to get further feedback from Spanish-speaking patients and English-speaking health workers. A graduate student then took the project and began to incorporate feedback to revise the project deliverables as part of his Master's project.[11] He supervised intensive interviews at the five field sites, again relying on both patients and practitioners for revision strategies. Again the results of these activities could easily be translated into a series of visual materials that could be created for online delivery via websites or that could be accessed by or downloaded to mobile phones.

As students work with community groups, they gain experience in ethical judgment –especially if instructors foreground this component in their courses as students analyze and reflect. The author's own students agonized over the construction of site-specific surveys, over choices of graphics, over document designs, challenging each other to find ethical ways to relate to and connect with our Long Creek workers. In terms of the design choices, students were faced with difficult cultural and health-related representations. How, for example, does one represent digestive disorders? How can one be culturally sensitive and respond appropriately to a high-context culture that is much more modest and less exhibitionist in many ways than an American culture in which almost anything goes, especially for a young audience brought up on Bart Simpson and South Park?

After many false and sometimes very humorous iterations, students settled on representing a certain digestive disorder by depicting a person with lines indicating a fast motion headed toward a bathroom door. At first the students marked the door with the word *bano*, but because some of the local farmworkers spoke Nhautl, they chose instead the universal sign for male on a door. The community members then approved this graphic for inclusion in the digitized health materials. With animation, these projects will now be able to show the figure in motion toward the door and not just have a stationary figure with action lines. Each of the 87 figures the students designed went through a similar process, some more quickly than others. Such a process, moreover, can easily be adapted to create a wide variety of visual information for online dissemination. It can also be used to convert existing online visual materials designed for one particular cultural audience to visual communiqués that can work effectively with persons from several other cultures.

After conducting focus groups, the students identified a number of community members to help by working with them one-on-one (students paired up with a community member) to give feedback on specific designs. The students did not conduct formal, laboratory usability testing because many community members felt more comfortable not coming onto campus and meeting instead in their familiar settings. They, however, did do what the author and the students considered "field testing." For future digital work relating to this project, the mobile unit will be upgrading its computer and wireless access in order to field test our digital designs as community members come in for their more routine health care.

Once the theory was laid out, further, extensive discussion went on without any initiation on the part of the instructor because students were engaged at a deep level. The students began to care about the project and the audience they were trying to reach. Students learned that working closely with their audience yielded better and more culturally sensitive projects. They also became aware of their own roles and that they need to take a backseat to the people who would actually be using their materials. The students began to question the power relations in the situation. They also moved from bottom-up not top-down – the model of power Foucault came to value in his later work (1977), as he moved beyond his earlier views of power relations as always autocratic and coming from the center.

WHAT LESSONS WERE LEARNED?

The students in the classes learned a great deal from their interactions with *Mexicano*, Spanish-speaking farm workers about a culture different from their own. They also learned which communication strategies to use to more sensitively approach other cultures on a micro level. They learned that an appreciation of difference is one of the keys to understanding another culture. They also learned the localization of online projects means much more work for them than staying in a computer lab and finding source materials on the Internet. But the work was also more engaging and it incorporated good research methods, not just good design work.

Students grappled with theoretical constructs continually during the early classes. They also grappled with the preparation for field research, audience analyses, document design decisions, field testing, and the actual production of deliverables. Teachers and future developers of the digital deliverables, must therefore also work continually to incorporate theory and cultural critiques into our *praxis*.

Freire (1993) suggests theory without action leads to armchair revolutionaries (p. 107). Action without reflection leads to some of the blind activism we see other groups guilty of (p. 108). Reflection plus action equal *praxis* -- one that can make fundamental changes. "... [A] revolution is achieved with neither verbalism nor activism, but rather with praxis, that is with *reflection* and *action* directed at the structures to be transformed" (Freire, 1993, p. 107). Educators thus need to reflect on the critiques and change their pedagogy carefully. Educators need to keep the danger of *noblesse oblige* foremost in their minds, lest they end up supporting rather than challenging the power relations of researcher and subject (Cushman, 1996).

In this type of class, there is a blurring of the line between pedagogy and activism. This concern is an important one, both literally and theoretically. With the use of Freire in the classroom, the boundaries are indeed erased because the pedagogy is an activist one, one in which the teaching methods are themselves empowering. This theory can quickly migrate to create an active participation on the part of students and community members; its endpoint, in addition to better student experience, more in-depth research and more effective design could involve (on a limited basis with a few classes and deliverables) the active solving of social problems (ideally those involving poverty, disempowerment and endemic inequality of power relations).

With service learning, the boundaries are always already blurred. The instructor in using such pedagogy will be modeling a type of activist agenda for the empowerment of both students and community members. Yet, when National Institutes of Health (NIH) also advocates for community-based, participatory research (CBPR), and, as designers of online materials, individuals know that more involvement of actual users improves a "product" exponentially, this approach can be easily justified. If time permitted, a thorough literature review going back to pedagogical theorists would build a case for *education* (from Latin *educare: to lead out or forward*), that would indeed see education and activism as synonymous and not in conflict. Cultures, however, have separated these practices over the centuries.

APPLICATION AND PEDAGOGY

From the beginning of any digital/online project, it is incumbent on the designer to find out which media are most preferred by the targeted clients. Various large public health campaigns are replete with failures caused by assumptions that "everyone" has access to certain media. Have client participants weigh in on whether to use computers, cell phones, computer kiosks in waiting rooms, "apps," text messages, CDs, or DVDs to deliver information. When online beta models are tested among the participants, are developers being sensitive to and garnering data that reveals the impact of various media in the home? For example, the research project described in this chapter notes a cultural dilemma when televisions were brought into *Mexicano* homes. That is, the family was expected to spend time together in the same room after dinner at the end of the day. Often, when the family in the main room of the home was centered around the television, the schoolchildren could no longer do homework because of the distraction of the programs. In this particular cultural context, it would have been thought of as unusual and rude to go off to one's room alone to do schoolwork. Thus, with the use of digital health education delivery systems via home computers, our research will

need to include follow-ups to determine if there are negative implications by participants' choice of media. In short, developers and designers will need to use the same participatory-based research to determine if jointly-developed projects present problems to a culture in which oral communication and verbal transmission of health advice within the local community are the norm. Potentially, traditional methods of community-building could be disrupted. Thus far, plans are to implement the most recently developed digital projects in waiting rooms of local doctors, in which pregnant *Mexicanas* already negotiate cultural differences once they walk through the door.

In the focus groups discussed earlier in this chapter, the students and the author were working on identifying which media are most comfortable and least invasive for *Mexicanas*. The idea is to prepare to move from the older triage project to educational modules delivering prenatal health care. The software individuals develop as well as the online delivery methods they use is customizable. Designers can make such online materials local to a given situation and yet can share them across the state and further to other health care facilities that can in turn *customize* for their local populations. As Bourgess-Waldegg and Scrivener (2000) note, "It is crucial, therefore, to distinguish between designing interfaces that will be used exclusively within a particular culture... and those that will be *shared* by users from different cultures" (p. 288). Individuals thus design locally *and* enable other groups to do so using online media. To build in flexibility and the ability to localize sets apart both theory and practice, or *praxis,* as health message, digital designers. For example, in the online surveys the author's students are designing, the content for the questions can be easily changed, added, and deleted. For example, a community group living and working in a local area in the Blue Ridge Mountains might prefer information on contraception with an emphasis on persuading spouses to prevent another pregnancy shortly after the birth of the new baby. Conversely, a group working in the chicken factories in west Columbia, one of the largest cities in the area, might prefer an online survey for contraception to prevent STDs. The community members have been and will be continually encouraged to work with individuals in designing online surveys, Websites, DVDs, and other digital materials that address their specific and local issues.

Again, the author recognizes it would not be good professional communication *praxis* to ignore the ethical issues inherent both in the theoretical frames advocated in this project and in ignoring the future effect computer-mediated health education might have for the *Mexicanos* in her local area. The theoretical frames advocated by Geertz (2000), Foucault (1980), and Freire (1993) seem more ethical than ignoring or not honoring and valuing the local knowledge contributed by the patients we work with and for. Individuals can certainly posit that their understandings and subsequent designs when informed by the users will be more culturally sensitive and less stereotypical than those based on others' case studies. Designers of online materials run the risk, however, of skewing e-documents in ways that reflect too narrow a point of view of a few more articulate or assertive members of a particular group. The designers of such materials must therefore make sure the views expressed in their online materials are truly representative. To do so, they must conduct participatory research in their local community.

The author does plan to return to her research model again and again to include the audience members in our designs. This process would include target audience members not just to give feedback on designs she and her students develop, but to also participate in the design process itself by suggesting colors, scripts and content for the photo novellas we develop for delivery of prenatal advice. In so doing, the author plans to integrate the good advice from grandmothers, midwives, and *curanderas* to honor the prenatal and midwifery practices that produce healthy babies among our *Mexicanas* in this area. As faculty, students,

researchers, we must continue to balance the needs of the local community and keep our own voices at a minimum, offering bridges to often misinterpreted Western obstetrical practices rather than rigid prescriptions.

In essence, health communicators need to move away from functional, *pro forma* and over-scripted testing of materials on users/patients to a true participatory model of design practices related to creating online materials. In working with various organizations, designers can use the aforementioned arguments to explain to them the value added through careful analyses, making results even more persuasive to various workplaces. Using the powerful theories already developed in different fields, researchers and designers need to extend these lenses and bring the clients into the design studios with them or take the designing to them, so the *local* in *localization* is truly realized... even in cyberspace.

REFERENCES

Bosley, D. S. (2001). *Global contexts: Case studies in international communication*. Needham Heights, MA: Allyn & Bacon.

Bourges-Waldegg, P., & Scrivener, S. A. R. (1998). Meaning, the central issue in cross-cultural HCI design. *Interacting with Computers, 9*, 287–309. doi:10.1016/S0953-5438(97)00032-5

Bourges-Waldegg, P., & Scrivener, S. A. R. (2000). Applying and testing an approach to design for culturally diverse user groups. *Interacting with Computers, 13*, 111–126. doi:10.1016/S0953-5438(00)00029-1

CDC. (2005, July 1). *Birth rates*. Retrieved October 14, 2006, from http://www.census.gov/Press-Release/ www/ 2006/ cb06-123table1.xls

Clemson University. (2006). *Master of Arts in professional communication program*. Retrieved October 14, 2006, from http://www.clemson.edu/caah/ mapc

Cushman, E. (1996). The rhetorician as an agent of social change. *College Composition and Communication, 47*(1), 7–28. doi:10.2307/358271

Cushman, E. (1999, March 27). *Activist methods in service learning: Overcoming noblesse oblige.* Conference on College Composition and Communication (CCCC). Atlanta, GA.

Dirven (Eds.), *The cultural context in business communication* (pp. 51-118). Amsterdam, The Netherlands: John Benjamins.

Foucault, M. (1980). *Power/knowledge.* New York, NY: Pantheon.

Freire, P. (1971). *Pedagogy of the oppressed.* New York, NY: Herder.

Freire, P. (1988). The adult literacy process as cultural action for freedom. In Kintgen, E., Kroll, B., & Rose, M. (Eds.), *Perspectives on literacy* (pp. 398–409). Carbondale, IL: Southern Illinois University Press.

Geertz, C. (2000). *Local knowledge.* New York, NY: Basic.

Gudykunst, W. B., & Mody, G. (2002). *Handbook of international and intercultural communication* (2nd ed.). Thousand Oaks, CA: Sage.

Hall, E. T. (1983). *The dance of life: The other dimension of time.* New York, NY: Doubleday.

Hall, E. T. (1992). *Beyond culture.* Gloucester, MA: Peter Smith Publisher.

Hall, E. T., & Hall, M. (1990). *Understanding cultural differences: Germans, French, and Americans.* Boston, MA: Intercultural Press.

Hawisher, G. E., & Selfe, C. L. (2000). *Global literacies and the World-Wide Web.* London, UK: Routledge.

Heifferon, B. A. (1998). *Look who's not talking: Recovering the voice of the patient in the clinique.* Unpublished dissertation. U of Arizona.

Heifferon, B. A. (2005). *Writing in the health professions. The Allyn/Bacon series in technical communication.* Boston, MA: Allyn-Bacon/Longman.

Herzberg, B. (1994). Community service and critical teaching. *College Composition and Communication, 45,* 307–319. doi:10.2307/358813

Herzberg, B. (1994, March 27). *Service learning and civic education.* Conference on College Composition and Communication (CCCC). Atlanta, GA.

Hofstede, G. (1991). *Culture and organization: The software of the mind.* New York, NY: McGraw-Hill.

Hofstede, G., Neuijen, B., Ohayv, D., & Sanders, G. (1990). Measuring organizational cultures: A qualitative and quantitative study of twenty cases. *Administrative Science Quarterly, 35,* 286–316. doi:10.2307/2393392

Joseph, F. Sullivan Center. (2005). *Clemson wellness.* Retrieved October 14, 2006, from http://virtual.Clemson.edu/ groups/ wellness/

Lewis, R. D. (1996). *When cultures collide.* London, UK: Nicholas Brealey.

Lovitt, C. with Goswami, D. (1999). *Exploring the rhetoric of international professional communication: An agenda for teachers and researchers.* Amityville, NY: Baywood.

Nelson, D. E., Brownson, R. C., Remington, P. L., & Parvanta, C. (Eds.). (2002). *Communicating public health information effectively: a guide for practitioners.* Washington, DC: American Public Health Association.

Perkins, J. (1999). Communicating in a global, multicultural corporation: Other metaphors and strategies. In Lovitt, C., & Goswami, D. (Eds.), *Exploring the rhetoric of international professional communication: An agenda for teachers and researchers* (pp. 17–38). Amityville, NY: Baywood.

Pinker, S. (1994). *The language instinct: How the mind creates language*. New York, NY: William Morrow.

Selfe, C. L. (1999). Lest we think the revolution is a revolution: Images of technology and the nature of change. In Hawisher, G. E., & Selfe, C. L. (Eds.), *Passions, pedagogies, and the 21ˢᵗ century technologies* (pp. 292–322). Logan, UT: Utah State University Press.

Shome, R., & Hegde, R. S. (2002). Culture, communication, and the challenge of globalization. *Critical Studies in Media Communication, 19*(2), 172–189. doi:10.1080/07393180216560

Singh, N., & Baack, D. W. (2004). Web site adaptation: A cross-cultural comparison of U.S. and Mexican websites. Journal of Computer-Mediated Communication, 9(4). Accessed May 4, 2007, from http://www.indiana.edu/ vol.9/ issue4/index.html

Singh, N., & Pereira, A. (2005). *The culturally customized website: Customizing websites for the global marketplace*. Burlington, MA: Elsevier Butterworth Heinemann.

Thrush, E. A. (2001). High-context and low-context cultures: How much communication is too much? In Bosley, D. (Ed.), *Global contexts: Case studies in international communication* (pp. 27–41). Boston, MA: Allyn-Bacon.

Trompenaars, F., & Hampden-Turner, C. (1998). *Riding the waves of culture: Understanding diversity in global business* (2nd ed.). New York, NY: McGraw-Hill.

U. S. Bureau of the Census. (2006, July 1). Race chart. Retrieved October 14, 2006 from http://www.census.gov/ Press-Release/ www/ 2006/ cb06-123table1.xls

U.S. Bureau of the Census. (2001). *Statistical abstract of the United States*. Washington, DC: U.S. Census Bureau.

Weiss, S., & Stripp, W. (1998). Negotiating with foreign business persons: An introduction for Americans with propositions for six cultures. In *S. Niemeier*. C. P. Campbell, & R.

Xiaobo, L. (2006, February 20). Communist Internet censorship an internationally common practice? *The Epoch Times*. Retrieved October 15, 2006, from http://www.theepochtimes.com/ news/ 6-2-20/ 38388.html

Yi-Jokipii, H. (2001). The local and the global: An exploration into the Finnish and English websites of a Finnish company. *IEEE Transactions on Professional Communication, 44*(2), 104–113. doi:10.1109/47.925512

Zahedi, F. M., Van Pelt, W. V., & Song, J. A. (2001). Conceptual framework for international Web design. *IEEE Transactions on Professional Communication, 44*(2), 83–103. doi:10.1109/47.925509

ENDNOTES

[1] I am grateful to Juan Guerra for suggesting some years ago that in fact people from Latin and South America usually prefer to be called by the name of the country they come from rather than lumped together into such terms as *Hispanic* and *Latino*.

[2] The first class that took on this design project included a graduate student in our graduate program who had been an exchange student in South America, and like several students in this class, was fluent in Spanish. During the course, he developed acute appendicitis and was treated at a local hospital. The need for translators was so critical in this small rural area that the student was pulled from his hospital bed, in his patient gown and trailing his I.V. pole, to go to another patient's bedside and translate for the English-speaking health professionals.

[3] While teaching in Genoa, Italy in 1999, I observed a demonstration in the city center, in which speakers and signs denounced *Globalism* as an American, hegemonic conspiracy.

[4] Hawisher's and Selfe's text is *Global literacies and the world wide web.* Lovitt's and Goswami's text is: *Exploring the rhetoric of international professional communication: an agenda for teachers and researchers.*

[5] "Proxemically" refers to distance or space between and among people. If you have known someone from another country who stands closer to you than you are comfortable with, this is a matter of proxemics. People from the U.S. typically feel more comfortable with a larger personal space.

[6] Perkins claims that the boundary metaphor is problematic.

[7] Hispanic immigration to South Carolina has increased by 200% in the last few years.

[8] This chart is reprinted by permission from Allyn/Bacon Longman. Although the table is based on one originally developed by anthropologists, this author varied it for her classroom purposes.

[9] There are mostly rural areas in the Upstate (northwestern corner) of South Carolina.

[10] Triage refers to quickly assessing medical needs and prioritizing them.

[11] Our university offers a Master of Arts in Professional Communication: http://www.clemson.edu/caah/mapc/

Compilation of References

About, M. C. B. S. (2010). *Modern College of Business and Science*. Retrieved September 2, 2010, from http://www.mcbs.edu.om/ aboutmcbs.html

Abrams, Z. I. (2003). Flaming in CMC: Prometheus' fire or Inferno's. *CALICO Journal, 20*(2), 245–260.

Acheson, K. (2008). Silence as gesture: Rethinking the nature of communicative silences. *Communication Theory, 18*(4), 535–555. doi:10.1111/j.1468-2885.2008.00333.x

Adeoye, B., & Wentling, R. (2007). The relationship between national culture and the usability of an e-learning system. *International Journal on E-Learning, 6*(1), 119–146.

Adomi, E. (2008). Combating cybercrime in Nigeria. *The Electronic Library, 26*(5), 716–725. doi:10.1108/02640470810910738

Ahmad, S. (2006). International student experiences: The voice of Indian students. Paper presented at the Australian International Education Conference. WA: Perth. Retrieved August 4, 2010, from www.idp.com/ aiec

Aitchison, J., Gilchrist, A., & Bawden, D. (2000). *Thesaurus construction and use: A practical manual* (4th ed.). Chicago, IL: Fitzroy Dearborn.

Ajjan, H., & Hartshorne, R. (2008). Investigating faculty decisions to adopt Web 2.0 technologies: theory and empirical tests. *The Internet and Higher Education, 11*, 71–80. doi:10.1016/j.iheduc.2008.05.002

Akdemir, O., & Koszalka, T. A. (2008). Investigating the relationships among instructional strategies and learning styles in online environments. *Computers & Education, 50*(4), 1451–1461. doi:10.1016/j.compedu.2007.01.004

Akintunde, M. (2006). Diversity.com: Teaching an online course on white racism and multiculturalism. *Multicultural Perspectives, 8*(2), 35–45. doi:10.1207/s15327892mcp0802_7

Al-Badi, A., & Naqvi, S. (2009). A conceptual framework for designing localized business websites. *Journal of Management & Marketing Research, 2*, 113–120.

Alcock, C., Cooper, J., Kirk, J., & Oyler, K. (2009). *The tertiary student experience: A review of approaches based on the first cycle of AUQA audits 2002-2007*. Australian Universities Quality Agency.

Alexander, B. (2008). Social networking in higher education. In Katz, R. N. (Ed.), *The tower and the cloud: Higher education in the age of cloud computing* (pp. 197–201). Boulder, CO: Educause E-Books.

Al-Harthi, A. S. (2005). Distance higher education experiences of Arab Gulf students in the United States: A cultural perspective. *The International Review of Research in Open and Distance Learning, 6*(3). Retrieved July 13, 2010, from http://www.irrodl.org/index.php/irrodl/article/view/263/840

Ali, A. (2007). Modern technology and mass education: A case study of a global virtual system. In Edmundson, A. (Ed.), *Globalized e-learning cultural challenges* (pp. 327–339). Hershey, PA: Information Science Publishing.

Al-Jarf, R. (2004a). The effects of Web-based learning on struggling EFL college writers. *Foreign Language Annals, 37*(1), 49–57. doi:10.1111/j.1944-9720.2004.tb02172.x

Al-Jarf, R. S. (2004b). *Differential effects of online instruction on a variety of EFL classes*. Paper presented at 3rd Asia CALL: Perspectives on Computers in Language Learning, Penang, Malaysia.

Allemang, D., Coyne, R., & Hodgson, R. (2003). *Solution envisioning for ontology-based applications.* Paper presented at the Technology Appreciation Webinar, Beaver Falls, PA.

Allen, I. E., & Seaman, J. (2010, January). *Learning on demand: Online education in the United States, 2009.* Needham, MA: The Sloan Consortium. Retrieved June 25, 2010, from http://www.sloan-c.org/publications/survey/pdf/learningondemand.pdf

Allen, I. E., Seaman, J., & Garrett, R. (2007, March). *Blending in: The extent and promise of blended education in the United States.* Needham, MA: Sloan Consortium. Retrieved June 11, 2009, from http://www.sloan-c.org/publications/ survey/ blended06.asp

Allen, P. (2009, March 2). Wired world – The global growth of mobile phone use. *The Guardian.* Retrieved November 25, 2010, from http://www.guardian.co.uk/business/interactive/2009/mar/02/mobile-phones

Allik, J., & Realo, A. (2004). Individualism-collectivism and social capital. *Journal of Cross-Cultural Psychology, 35,* 29–49. doi:10.1177/0022022103260381

Almasude, A. (1999). The new mass media and the shaping of Amazigh identity. In Reyhner, J., Cantoni, G., St. Clari, R. N., & Yazzie, E. P. (Eds.), *Revitalizing indigenous languages* (pp. 117–128). Flagstaff, AZ: Northern Arizona University.

Al-Olayan, F. S., & Karande, K. (2000). A content analysis of magazine advertisements from the United States and the Arab world. *Journal of Advertising, 29,* 69–82.

Althusser, L. (1971). *Lenin and philosophy* (Brewster, B., Trans.). New York, NY: Monthly Review Press.

Alwitt, L. F., & Prabhaker, P. R. (1994). Identifying who dislikes television advertising: Not by demographics alone. *Journal of Advertising Research, 34*(5), 17–29.

Amar, S. (2008, June 29). *India's Internet matchmakers see potential boom.* Retrieved July 6, 2010, from www.internetevolution.com/ author.asp?section_id=687&doc_id=160162

Amory, A. (2010). Education technology and hidden ideological contradictions. *Journal of Educational Technology & Society, 13*(1), 69–79.

An, D. (2007). Advertising visuals in global brand's local websites: A six-country comparison. *International Journal of Advertising, 26*(3), 303–332.

Anawati, D., & Craig, A. (2006). Behavioral adaptation within cross-cultural virtual teams. *IEEE Transactions on Professional Communication, 49*(1), 44–56. doi:10.1109/TPC.2006.870459

Anderson, S. R. (2004). *How many languages are there in the world?* Washington, DC: Linguistic Society of America.

Anderson, B. (1991). *Imagined communities: Reflections on the origin and spread of nationalism* (Rev. ed.). London, UK: Verso.

Anderson, J. (1995). Cybarites, knowledge workers and New Creoles on the superhighway. *Anthropology Today, 11*(4), 13–15.

Anderson, P. H., Lawton, L., Rexeisen, R. J., & Hubbard, A. C. (2006). Short-term study abroad and intercultural sensitivity. *International Journal of Intercultural Relations, 30*(4), 457–469. doi:10.1016/j.ijintrel.2005.10.004

Anderson Analytics. (2008). *Blogging increasing in popularity among generation Y.* Retrieved November 20, 2010, from http://www.andersonanalytics.com /index.php?mact=News,cntnt01,detail,0&cntnt01articleid=56&cntnt01origid=47&cntnt01detail template=newsdetail.tpl&cntnt 01dateformat=%25m.%25d.%25Y&cntnt01returnid=46

Anderson, T. (2008). Social software to support distance education learners. In Anderson, T. (Ed.), *Theory and practice of online learning* (2nd ed., pp. 221–244). Edmonton, Alberta: Athabasca University Press.

Androutsopoulos, J. (2006). Multilingualism, diaspora, and the Internet: Codes and identities on German-based diaspora websites. *Journal of Sociolinguistics, 10*(4), 520–547. doi:10.1111/j.1467-9841.2006.00291.x

Androutsopoulos, J. (2006). Introduction: Sociolinguistics and computer-mediated communication. *Journal of Sociolinguistics, 10*(4), 419–438. doi:10.1111/j.1467-9841.2006.00286.x

Annan, K. (2002). *On the digital divide.* Retrieved May 01, 2010, from http://www.un.org/News/ossg/sg/stories/sg-5nov-2002.htm

Anonymous. (2010, March 10). Moneymaker: Internet – Zocken, Shoppen, Daddeln. *Focus Money,* 10-12.

Appadurai, A. (1996). *Modernity at large: Cultural dimensions of globalization.* Minneapolis, MN: University of Minnesota Press.

Appadurai, A. (1996). *Modernity at large: Cultural dimensions of globalization.* Minneapolis, MN: University of Minnesota Press.

Aragon, S. R., Johnson, S. D., & Shaik, N. (2003). The influence of learning style preferences on student success in online versus face-to-face environments. *American Journal of Distance Education, 16*(4), 227–244. doi:10.1207/S15389286AJDE1604_3

Arbaugh, J. B., & Hornik, S. (2006). Do Chickering and Gamson's seven principles also apply to online MBAs? *The Journal of Educators Online, 3*(2). Retrieved December 10, 2010, from http://www.thejeo.com/ Volume3Number2/ ArbaughFinal.pdf

Arend, T. (2007). *Localization at Google.* LRC XII Conference: The Localization Research Forum. European Foundation Dublin, Ireland. Retrieved May 12, 2010, from http://www.localization.ie/resources/conferences/2007/ presentations/TArend/Google_Keynote_LRC_XII_Dublin_Sep_2007_Thomas_Arend.pdf

Arikan, A. (2009). *A closer look into prospective English language teachers' social-networking activities.* Paper presented at the Second International Online Language Conference, 25-26 June 2009.

Armstrong, D. J., & Cole, P. (2002). Managing distances and differences in geographically distributed work groups. In Hinds, P., & Kiesler, S. (Eds.), *Distributed work* (pp. 167–186). Cambridge, MA: The MIT Press.

Associated Press. (2009). President Obama wants to keep kids in school longer: extended days, weekend hours, shorter summers. *NY Daily News.* Retrieved December 10, 2010, from http://www.nydailynews.com/ news/ national/ 2009/ 09/ 28/ 2009-09-28_president_obama_wants_to_ keep _kids_in_school_longer_extended _days_weekend_hours_.html#ixzz0grS3TH6Z

Atkin, D. (1993). Adoption of cable amidst a multimedia environment. *Telematics and Informatics, 10,* 51–58. doi:10.1016/0736-5853(93)90017-X

Atkin, D., & Larose, R. (1994). Profiling call-in poll users. *Journal of Broadcasting & Electronic Media, 38,* 217–227.

Au, W. J. (2008). *The making of Second Life: Notes from the new world* (1st ed.). New York, NY: Harper Collins.

Australian Bureau of Statistics. (2008). *Education export statistics.* Retrieved November 10,

Australian Education International. (2009). *International student data for 2009.* Retrieved November 10, 2009, from http://www.aei.gov.au/ AEI/ MIP/ Statistics/ StudentEnrolmentAndVisaStatistics/ 2009/ Default.htm#Pivot

Australian Education International. (2010, March). *International student enrolments in higher education.* Retrieved August 4, 2010, from http://aei.gov.au/ AEI/ PublicationsAndResearch/ Snapshots/ 20100416HE_pdf.pdf

Australian Education International. (2010, May). *Export income to Australia from education services in 2009.* Retrieved August 9, 2010, from http://aei.gov.au/ AEI/ PublicationsAndResearch/ Snapshots/2010052810_pdf.pdf

Aycock, A., Garnham, C., & Kaleta, R. (2002, March 20). Lessons learned from the hybrid course project. *Teaching with Technology Today, 8*(6). Retrieved September 2, 2008, from http://www.uwsa.edu/ ttt/ articles/ garnham2.htm

Baack, D. W., & Singh, N. (2006). Culture and Web communications. *Journal of Business Research, 60*(3), 181–188. doi:10.1016/j.jbusres.2006.11.002

Babu, M. (2005). *The business of online matchmaking.* Retrieved March 10, 2007, from http://www.garamchai. com/ mohan/ITP05Apr04.htm

Baggaley, J. (2008). Where did distance education go wrong? *Distance Education, 29*(1), 39–51. doi:10.1080/01587910802004837

Bai, H. (2003). Student motivation and social presence in online learning: Implications for future research. In C. Crawford et al. (Eds.), *Proceedings of Society for Information Technology & Teacher Education International Conference 2003* (pp. 2714-2720). Albuquerque, NM: Association for the Advancement of Computing in Education.

Bailenson, J. N., Beall, A. C., Loomis, J., Blascovich, J., & Turk, M. (2004). Transformed social interaction: Decoupling representation from behavior and form in collaborative virtual environments. *Presence (Cambridge, Mass.)*, *13*(4), 428–441. doi:10.1162/1054746041944803

Bailenson, J. N., Blascovich, J., Beall, A. C., & Loomis, J. M. (2003). Interpersonal distance in immersive virtual environments. *Personality and Social Psychology Bulletin*, *29*(7), 819–833. doi:10.1177/0146167203029007002

Bal, J., & Foster, P. (2000). Managing the virtual team and controlling effectiveness. *International Journal of Production Research*, *38*(17), 4019–4032. doi:10.1080/00207540050204885

Baldwin, J. R., Faulkner, S. L., Hecht, M. L., & Lindsley, S. L. (2006). *Redefining culture: Perspectives across the disciplines*. Mahwah, NJ: Lawrence Erlbaum.

Ballesteros, L., & Croft, W. B. (1998). *Resolving ambiguity for crosslanguage retrieval.* Paper presented at the the 21st Annual International ACM SIGIR Conference on Research and Development in Information Retrieval, New York.

Bambauer, D. E. (2009). Filtering in Oz: Australia's foray into Internet censorship. *The University of Pennsylvania Journal of International Law*, *31*, 493–513.

Banbury, J. (2008). *Jim Grant and the unfinished agenda for children. What "preventable" means.* UNICEF USA. Retrieved May 5, 2010, from http://fieldnotes.unicefusa.org/mt/mt-search.cgi?tag=Jim%20Grant&blog_id=1

Bandura, A. (1973). *Aggression: A social learning analysis*. Englewood Cliffs, NJ: Prentice-Hall.

Bandura, A. (1977). *Social learning theory*. New York, NY: General Learning Press.

Bandura, A. (1986). *Social foundations of thought and action*. Englewood Cliffs, NJ: Prentice-Hall.

Bao, H. (2006). Computer means/changes my life: ESL students and computer-mediated technology. *Electronic Magazine of Multicultural Education*, *8*(1), 1–9.

Barakat, H. (1993). *The Arab world: Society, culture, and state*. Berkeley, CA: University of California Press.

Bargh, J. A., & McKenna, K. Y. A. (2004). The Internet and social life. *Annual Review of Psychology*, *55*, 573–590. doi:10.1146/annurev.psych.55.090902.141922

Bargh, J. A., & McKenna, K. Y. A. (2004). The Internet and social life. *Annual Review of Psychology*, *55*, 573–590. doi:10.1146/annurev.psych.55.090902.141922

Barjis, J. (2003). An overview of virtual university studies: Issues, concepts, trends. In Albaloshie, F. (Ed.), *Virtual education: Cases in learning and teaching technologies* (pp. 1–20). Hershey, PA: IRM Press.

Barkho, L. (2007). Advertising resources in oil rich Arab Gulf states—Implications for international marketers. *International Journal of Business Studies*, *19*(2), 1–24.

Barnes, S. B. (2003). *Computer-mediated communication: Human-to-human communication across the internet*. Boston, MA: Allyn and Bacon.

Barnett-Queen, T., Blair, R., & Merrick, M. (2005). Student perspectives of online discussion: Strengths and weaknesses. *Journal of Technology in Human Services*, *23*, 229–244. doi:10.1300/J017v23n03_05

Barthes, R. (1977). The death of the author. In Heath, S. (Ed.), *Image, music, text* (pp. 101–105). New York, NY: Hill & Wang.

Bartle, R. A. (2004). *Designing virtual worlds*. Indianapolis, IN: New Riders.

Barton, D. (1994). *Literacy: An introduction to the ecology of written language*. Malden, MA: Blackwell.

Barton, D., & Hamilton, M. (2000). Literacy practices. In Baron, D., Hamilton, M., & Ivanic, R. (Eds.), *Situated literacies: Reading and writing in context* (pp. 7–15). New York, NY: Routledge.

Bateson, G., & Donaldson, R. E. (1991). *A sacred unity: Further steps to an ecology of mind* (1st ed.). New York, NY: Cornelia & Michael Bessie Book.

Battalio, J. (2009). Success in distance education: Do learning styles and multiple formats matter? *American Journal of Distance Education*, *23*(2), 71–87. doi:10.1080/08923640902854405

Batteau, A. W. (2004). Anthropology and HCI. In Sims Bainbridge, W. (Ed.), *Berkshire encyclopedia of human-computer interaction* (*Vol. 1*, pp. 17–25). Great Barrington, MA: Berkshire.

Baym, N. K. (2003). Communication in online communities. In Christiansen, K., & Levinson, D. (Eds.), *Encyclopedia of community* (*Vol. 3*, pp. 1015–1017). Thousand Oaks, CA: Sage.

Baym, N. K. (1998). The emergence of on-line community. In Jones, S. (Ed.), *CyberSociety 2.0. Revisiting computer-mediated communication and community* (pp. 35–68). London, UK: Sage.

Beeston, A. (1974). *The Arab language today*. London, UK: Hutchinson & Co Ltd.

Bejerano, A. (2008). Raising the question #11: The genesis and evolution of online degree programs: Who are they for and what have we lost along the way? *Communication Education, 57*(3), 408–414. doi:10.1080/03634520801993697

Belk, R. W., Devinney, T. M., & Eckhardt, G. (2005). Consumer ethics across cultures. *Consumption. Markets and Culture, 8*(3), 275–289. doi:10.1080/10253860500160411

Belk, R. W. (2000). Are we what we own? In A. L. Benson (Ed.), *I shop, therefore I am: Compulsive buying and the search for self* (pp. 27-53). Northvale, NJ: Jason Aronson Inc. boyd, d., & Ellison, N. B. (2007). Social network sites: Definition, history, and scholarship. *Journal of Computer-Mediated Communication, 13*(1), 210-230.

Bell, D., & Kennedy, B. M. (2007). *The cybercultures reader* (2nd ed.). New York, NY: Routledge.

Benbunan-Fich, R., & Hiltz, S. R. (2003). Mediators of effectiveness of online courses. *IEEE Transactions on Professional Communication, 46*(4), 298–312. doi:10.1109/TPC.2003.819639

Benítez, J. L. (2006). Transnational dimensions of the digital divide among Salvadoran immigrants in the Washington DC metropolitan area. *Global Networks, 6*(2), 181–199. doi:10.1111/j.1471-0374.2006.00140.x

Benkler, Y. (2006). *The wealth of networks: How social production transforms markets and freedom*. New Haven, CT: Yale University Press.

Benoit, P. J., Benoit, W. L., Milyo, J., & Hansen, G. J. (2006). *The effects of traditional versus Web-assisted instruction on learning and student satisfaction*. Columbia, MO: University of Missouri Graduate School.

Bentley, J. P. H., Tinney, M. V., & Chia, B. H. (2005). International review: Intercultural-Internet-based learning: Know your audience and what it values. *ETR & D, 53*(2), 117–127. doi:10.1007/BF02504870

Bernal, V. (2006). Diaspora, cyberspace and political imagination: The Eritrean diaspora online. *Global Networks, 6*(2), 161–179. doi:10.1111/j.1471-0374.2006.00139.x

Berry, M. (1987). What is theme? – A(nother) personal view. In Halliday, M. A. K., & Fawcett, R. P. (Eds.), *New developments in systemic linguistics* (pp. 1–64). London, UK: Pinter.

ACPA. (1998). Learning principles and collaborative action. In Berson, J. (Ed.), *Powerful partnerships: A shared responsibility for learning* (pp. 3–10). Washington, DC: ACPA.

Bhagat, R. B. (2002). *Early marriages in India: A socio-geographical study*. New Delhi, India: Rajat Publications.

Bhat, P. N. M., & Halli, S. S. (1999). Demography of brideprice and dowry: Causes and consequences of the Indian marriage squeeze. *Population Studies, 53*(2), 129–148. doi:10.1080/00324720308079

Biggs, M. (2000). Enterprise toolbox: Assessing risks today will leave corporate leaders well prepared for the future of work. *InfoWorld, 22*(3), 100–101.

Bijker, W. E., & Law, J. (1992). General introduction. In Bijker, W. E., & Law, J. (Eds.), *Shaping technology – building society. Studies in sociotechnical change* (pp. 1–16). Cambridge, MA: The MIT Press.

Billig, M. (1995). *Banal nationalism*. London, UK: Sage.

Biocca, F. (2003). Preface. In *Being there: Concepts, effects and measurements of user presence in synthetic environments*, Retrieved April 28, 2010, from http://www.emergingcommunication.com /volume5.html

Bjørge, A. K. (2007). Power distance in English lingua franca email communication. *International Journal of Applied Linguistics, 17*(1), 60–80. doi:10.1111/j.1473-4192.2007.00133.x

Black, G. (1993). *Genocide in Iraq: The Anfal campaign against the Kurds: A Middle East Watch report.* New York, NY: Human Rights Watch.

Blake, R., Wilson, N. L., Cetto, M., & Pardo-Ballister, C. (2008). Measuring oral proficiency in distance, face-to-face, and blended classrooms. *Language Learning & Technology, 12*(3), 114–127.

Blake, B. F., & Neuendorf, K. (2004). Cross-national differences in website appeal: A framework for assessment. *Journal of Computer-Mediated Communication, 9*(4). Retrieved October 10, 2010, from http://jcmc.indiana. edu/vol9/ issue4/blake_neuendorf.html

Bliss Classification Association. (1998). *The Bliss bibliographic classification.* Retrieved September 15, 2005, from http://www.sid.cam.ac.uk/ bca/bchist.htm

Blommaert, J., & Omoniyi, T. (2006). Email fraud: Language, technology, and the indexicals of globalization. *Social Semiotics, 16*(4), 573–605. doi:10.1080/10350330601019942

Blumler, J. G., & Katz, E. (1974). *The uses of mass communications: Current perspectives on gratifications research.* Beverly Hills, CA: Sage.

Boase, J. (2008). Personal networks and the personal communication system: Using multiple media to connect. *Information Communication and Society, 11,* 490–508. doi:10.1080/13691180801999001

Boehm, D., & Aniola-Jedrzejek, L. (2006). Seven principles of good practice for virtual international collaboration. In Ferris, S. P., & Godar, S. H. (Eds.), *Teaching and learning with virtual teams* (pp. 1–31). Hershey, PA: Information Science Publishing. doi:10.4018/9781591407089.ch001

Boellstorff, T. (2008). *Coming of age in second life: An anthropologist explores the virtually human.* Princeton, NJ: Princeton University Press.

Bohm, A., et al. (2002). *Global student mobility 2025: Forecasts of the global demand for international higher education.* Retrieved August 4, 2010, from http://www. aiec.idp.com/ PDF/ Bohm_2025 Media_p.pdf

Bork, A. (2001). What is needed for effective learning on the Internet? *Journal of Educational Technology & Society, 4*(3). Retrieved from http://ifets.gmd.de/periodical/vol_3_2001/bork.html.

Bosley, D. S. (2001). *Global contexts: Case studies in international communication.* Needham Heights, MA: Allyn & Bacon.

Botella, C., Baños, R. M., & Alcañiz, M. (2003). *A psychological approach to presence.* Paper presented at the PRESENCE 2003, 6th Annual International Workshop on Presence. Retrieved December 5, 2010, from http://www. presence-research.org/ papers/ Botella.html

Bourdieu, P., & Wacquant, L. (1992). *An invitation to reflexive sociology.* Chicago, IL: University of Chicago Press.

Bourdieu, P. (1977). The economics of linguistic exchanges. *Social Sciences Information. Information Sur les Sciences Sociales, 16*(6), 645–668. doi:10.1177/053901847701600601

Bourdieu, P. (1986). The forms of capital. In Richardson, J. G. (Ed.), *Handbook of theory and research for the sociology of education* (pp. 241–258). Westport, CT: Greenwood.

Bourges-Waldegg, P., & Scrivener, S. A. R. (1998). Meaning, the central issue in cross-cultural HCI design. *Interacting with Computers, 9,* 287–309. doi:10.1016/ S0953-5438(97)00032-5

Bourges-Waldegg, P., & Scrivener, S. A. R. (2000). Applying and testing an approach to design for culturally diverse user groups. *Interacting with Computers, 13,* 111–126. doi:10.1016/S0953-5438(00)00029-1

Bowles, M. S. (2004). *Relearning to e- learn: Strategies for electronic learning and knowledge.* Carlton, Victoria, Australia: Melbourne University Press.

Boyd, D. (2008). Why youth (heart) social network sites: The role of networked publics in teenage social life. In Buckingham, D. (Ed.), *Youth, identity, and digital media* (pp. 119–142). Cambridge, MA: MIT Press.

Boyd, D., & Ellison, N. B. (2007). Social network sites: Definition, history, and scholarship. *Journal of Computer-Mediated Communication, 13*(1), article 11. Retrieved November 20, 2010, from http://jcmc.indiana.edu/vol13 /issue1/boyd.ellison.html

Braine, G. (1996). ESL students in first-year writing courses: ESL versus mainstream classes. *Journal of Second Language Writing*, *5*, 91–107. doi:10.1016/S1060-3743(96)90020-X

Brand, S. (1988). *The media lab: Inventing the future at MIT*. New York, NY: Penguin Books.

Branon, R. F., & Essex, C. (2001). Synchronous and asynchronous communication tools in distance education: A survey of instructors. *TechTrends*, *45*, 36–42. doi:10.1007/BF02763377

Branzei, O., Vertinsky, I., & Camp, R. D. II. (2007). Culture-contingent signs of trust in emergent relationships. *Organizational Behavior and Human Decision Processes*, *104*(1), 61–82. doi:10.1016/j.obhdp.2006.11.002

Bratt, S. (2010). *Advance the Web. Empower people.* World Wide Web Foundation. Retrieved November 26, 2010, from http://www.Webfoundation.org/2010/03/advance-the-Web-empower-people/

Brislin, R. (2000). *Understanding culture's influence on behavior*. Ft. Worth, TX: Harcourt.

Broady, T., Chan, A., & Caputi, P. (2010). Comparison of older and younger adults' attitudes towards and abilities with computers: Implications for training and learning. *British Journal of Educational Technology*, *41*(3), 473–485. doi:10.1111/j.1467-8535.2008.00914.x

Brooks, D. W., Nolan, D. E., & Gallagher, S. M. (2001). *Web-teaching: A guide to designing interactive teaching for the World Wide Web* (2nd ed.). New York, NY: Kluwer Academic/Plenum.

Brouwer, L. (2006). Dutch Moroccan websites: A transnational imagery? *Journal of Ethnic and Migration Studies*, *32*(7), 1153–1168. doi:10.1080/13691830600821869

Brown, T. J. (2004). Deconstructing the dialectical tensions in *The Horse Whisperer*: How myths represent competing cultural values. *Journal of Popular Culture*, *38*(2), 274–295. doi:10.1111/j.0022-3840.2004.00112.x

Brown, S. (2010). From VLEs to learning Web: The implications of Web 2.0 for learning and teaching. *Interactive Learning Environments*, *18*(1), 1–10. doi:10.1080/10494820802158983

Brown, L. (2008). The incidence of study-related stress in international students in the initial stage of the international sojourn. *Journal of Studies in International Education*, *12*(1), 5–28. doi:10.1177/1028315306291587

Brown, H. D. (2007). *Principles of language learning and teaching* (5th ed.). White Plains, NY: Pearson.

Browner, C. H., & Press, N. (1997). The production of authoritative knowledge in American prenatal care. In Davis-Floyd, R. E., & Sargent, C. F. (Eds.), *Childbirth and authoritative knowledge* (pp. 113–131). Berkley, CA: University of California Press.

Brownlee, J., Walker, S., Lennox, S., Exley, B., & Pearce, S. (2009). The first-year university experience: Using personal epistemology to understand effective learning and teaching in higher education. *Higher Education*, *58*, 599–618. doi:10.1007/s10734-009-9212-2

Bruns, A. (2008). *Blogs, Wikipedia, Second Life, and beyond: From production to produsage*. New York, NY: Peter Lang.

Bryan, L. L., & Joyce, C. I. (2007). *Mobilizing minds: Creating wealth from talent in the 21st-century organization*. New York, NY: McGraw-Hill.

Buda, R., & Elsayed-Elkhouly, S. (1998). Cultural differences between Arabs and Americans: Individualism-collectivism revisited. *Journal of Cross-Cultural Psychology*, *29*(3), 487–492. doi:10.1177/0022022198293006

Burbules, N. C. (2000). Does the Internet constitute a global educational community? In Burbules, N. C., & Torres, C. (Eds.), *Globalization and education: Critical perspectives* (pp. 323–355). New York, NY: Routledge.

Burcher, N. (2010). *Facebook usage statistics: March 2010*. Retrieved April 23, 2010, from http://www.nickburcher.com/2010/03/facebook-usage-statistics-march-2010.html

Burke, K. (1950). *A rhetoric of motives*. Berkeley, CA: University of California Press.

Burrell, G., & Morgan, G. (1988). *Sociological paradigms and organizational analysis*. Portsmouth, NH: Heinemann.

Bush, V. D., & Gilbert, F. W. (2002). The Web as a medium: An explanatory comparison of Internet users versus newspaper readers. *Journal of Marketing Theory & Practice, 10*, 1–10.

Byram, M. (1995). Cultural studies in foreign language teaching. In Basnett, S. (Ed.), *Studying British cultures: An introduction* (pp. 56–67). London, UK: Routledge.

Byrd, T. L., Chavez, R., & Wilson, K. M. (2007). Barriers and facilitators of cervical cancer screening among Hispanic women. *Ethnicity & Disease, 17*(1), 129–134.

Cabe, T. (2002). Regulation of speech on the Internet: Fourth time's the charm? *Media Law and Policy, 11*(1), 50–61.

Callister, L. C., & Birkhead, A. (2002). Acculturation and perinatal outcomes in Mexican immigrant women: An integrative review. *The Journal of Perinatal & Neonatal Nursing, 16*(3), 22–38.

Campbell, J., & Li, M. (2008). Asian student's voices: An empirical study of Asian student's learning experiences at a New Zealand university. *Journal of Studies in International Education, 12*(4), 375–395. doi:10.1177/1028315307299422

Campbell, N. (2007). Bringing ESL students out of their shells: Enhancing participation through online discussion. *Business Communication Quarterly, 70*(1), 37–43. doi:10.1177/108056990707000105

Canagarajah, A. S. (2002). Understanding critical writing. In Canagarajah, A. S. (Ed.), *Critical academic writing and multilingual students* (pp. 1–22). Ann Arbor, MI: University of Michigan Press.

Candan, M., & Hunger, U. (2008). Nation building online: A case study of Kurdish migrants in Germany. *German Policy Studies, 4*(4), 125–153.

Carbaugh, D. (1988). Comments on "culture" in communication inquiry. *Communication Reports, 1*, 38–41.

Cardon, P. W., Marshall, B., Norris, D. T., Cho, J., Choi, J., & Cui, L. (2009). Online and offline social ties of social network website users: An exploratory study in eleven societies. *Journal of Computer Information Systems, 50*, 54–64.

Cardon, P. W. (2008). A critique of Hall's contexting model: A meta-analysis of literature on intercultural business and technical communication. *Journal of Business and Technical Communication, 22*(4), 399–428. doi:10.1177/1050651908320361

Carle, A. C. (2009). Evaluating college students' evaluations of a professor's teaching effectiveness across time and instruction mode (online vs. face-to-face) using a multilevel growth modeling approach. *Computers & Education, 53*, 429–435. doi:10.1016/j.compedu.2009.03.001

Carleta, J., Anderson, A., & McEwan, R. (2000). The effects of multimedia communication technology on non-collocated teams: A case study. *Ergonomics, 43*(8), 1237–1251. doi:10.1080/00140130050084969

Carpenter, T. G., Brown, W. L., & Hickman, R. C. (2004). Influences of online delivery on developmental writing outcomes. *Journal of Developmental Education, 28*(1), 14–35.

Cascio, J., & Paffendorf, J. (2007). *Metaverse roadmap overview*. Retrieved October 1, 2010, from http://metaverseroadmap.org/ overview/

Cassell, J., Huffaker, D., Tversky, D., & Ferriman, K. (2006). The language of online leadership: Gender and youth engagement on the Internet. *Developmental Psychology, 42*(3), 436–449. doi:10.1037/0012-1649.42.3.436

Castell, S. D., Bryson, M., & Jenson, J. (2002). Object lessons: Toward an educational theory of technology. *First Monday, 7*(1). Retrieved November 25, 2010, from http://131.193.153.231/www/issues/issue7_1/castell/

Castells, M. (2009). *Communication power*. Oxford, England: Oxford University Press.

Castells, M. (2004). *The power of identity* (2nd ed.). Oxford, UK: Blackwell.

Castells, M. (2000). *The Information Age* (Vol. 1-3). Oxford, UK: Blackwell.

Castells, M. (2000). *The rise of the network society* (2nd ed.). Malden, MA: Blackwell Publishers.

Castronova, E. (2004). Right to play. *New York Law School Law Review. New York Law School, 49*(1), 185–210.

Castronova, E. (2005). *Synthetic worlds: The business and culture of online games*. Chicago, IL: University of Chicago Press.

Castronova, E. (2007). *Exodus to the virtual world: How online fun is changing reality*. New York, NY: Palgrave Macmillan.

CDAC. (2010a). *Gist- Contributions towards standardization in Indian language computing*. Retrieved May 5, 2010, from http://www.cdac.in/html/gist/research-areas/standardisation.asp

CDAC. (2010b). *Bharateeya Open Office Suite*. Retrieved November 25, 2010, from http://pune.cdac.in/html/gist/products/boo.aspx

CDC. (2005, July 1). *Birth rates*. Retrieved October 14, 2006, from http://www.census.gov/ Press-Release/ www/ 2006/ cb06-123table1.xls

Charles Sturt University. (2009). *Charles Sturt University internationalisation strategy*. Retrieved November 10, 2009, from http://www.csu.edu.au/ division/ oir/ docs/ strategy.pdf

Charney, T., & Greenberg, B. S. (2003). Uses and gratifications of the Internet. In Lin, C. A., & Atkin, D. J. (Eds.), *Communication technology and society: Audience adoptions and uses* (pp. 379–409). New Jersey: Hampton Press, Inc.

Chatterjee, J. S. (2007). *The Internet as matchmaker: A study of why young Indians are seeking marriage alliances online*. Paper presented at the annual meeting of the International Communication Association, San Francisco, CA.

Chen, C. C., Meindl, J. R., & Hunt, R. G. (1997). Testing the effects of vertical and horizontal collectivism: A study of reward allocation preferences in China. *Journal of Cross-Cultural Psychology, 28*, 44–70. doi:10.1177/0022022197281003

Chen, C. H. (2007). Cultural diversity in instructional design for technology-based education. *British Journal of Educational Technology, 38*(6), 1113–1116. doi:10.1111/j.1467-8535.2007.00738.x

Chen, R., Bennett, S., & Maton, K. (2008). The adaptation of Chinese international students to online flexible learning: Two case studies. *Distance Education, 29*(3), 307–323. doi:10.1080/01587910802395821

Chen, R.-S., & Tsai, C.-C. (2007). Gender differences in Taiwan university students' attitudes toward Web-based learning. *Cyberpsychology & Behavior, 10*(5), 645–654. doi:10.1089/cpb.2007.9974

Chen, G. (2002). Communication in intercultural relationships. In Gudykunst, W. B., & Mody, B. (Eds.), *Handbook of international and intercultural communication* (2nd ed., pp. 241–258). Thousand Oaks, CA: Sage.

Chen, N. S. Kinshuk, Wei, C. W., & Wang, M. J. (2009). A framework for social presence in synchronous cyber classrooms. In *Proceedings of the 9th IEEE International Conference on Advanced Learning Technologies* (pp. 40-44). Riga, Latvia: IEEE Computer Society Press.

Chen, S.-J., Hsu, C., & Caropreso, E. (2005). *Cross-cultural collaborative online learning: When the West meets the East*. Paper presented at the World Conference on E-Learning in Corporate, Government, Healthcare, and Higher Education 2005, E-Learn 2005-World Conference on E-Learning in Corporate, Government, Healthcare, and Higher Education.

Chenoweth, N. A., Ushida, E., & Murday, K. (2006). Student learning in hybrid French and Spanish courses: An overview of language online. *CALICO Journal, 24*(1), 115–146.

Cheong, H. (2007). Health communication resources for uninsured and insured Hispanics. *Health Communication, 21*(2), 153–163.

Cheong, P. H., & Martin, J. N. (2009). Cultural implications of e-learning access (& divides): Teaching an intercultural communication course online. In Olaniran, B. A. (Ed.), *Cases on successful e-learning practices in the developed and developing world: Methods for global information economy* (pp. 78–91). Hershey, PA: IGI Global. doi:10.4018/978-1-60566-942-7.ch006

Chesbrough, H. W. (2003). *Open innovation: The new imperative for creating and profiting from technology*. Boston, MA: Harvard Business School Press.

Chickering, A. W., & Gamson, Z. (1987). Seven principles for good practice in undergraduate education. *AAHE Bulletin, 40*(7), 3–7.

Chickering, A. W., & Ehrmann, S. C. (1997). *Implementing the seven principles: Technology as lever.* Retrieved May 1, 2010, from http://www.aahe.org/technology/ehrmann.htm

Chiluwa, I. (2009). The discourse of digital deceptions and email "419" solicitations. *Discourse Studies, 11*(6), 1–26. doi:10.1177/1461445609347229

China Internet Network Information Center (CNNIC). (2010). *Statistical survey report on the Internet development in China.* Beijing, China: Author.

Cho, B., Kwan, U., Gentry, J. W., Jun, S., & Kropp, F. (1999). Cultural values reflected in theme and execution: A comparative study of U.S. and Korean television commercials. *Journal of Advertising, 28*, 59–73.

Cho, C. H., & Hongsik, J. C. (2005). Cross-cultural comparisons of interactivity on corporate websites: The United States, the United Kingdom, Japan, and South Korea. *Journal of Advertising, 34*(2), 99–115.

Choi, R. E., Nisbett, R., & Norenzayan, A. (1999). Causal attribution across cultures: Variation and universality. *Psychological Bulletin, 125*, 47–63. doi:10.1037/0033-2909.125.1.47

Chu, R. J. (2010). How family support and Internet self-efficacy influence the effects of e-learning among higher-aged adults: Analysis of gender and age differences. *Computers & Education, 55*(1), 1–426. doi:10.1016/j.compedu.2010.01.011

Chuang, R. (2003). Postmodern critique of cross-cultural and intercultural communication. In W. J. Storosta & G. M. Chen (Eds.), *Ferment in the intercultural field* (International and Intercultural Communication Annual, Vol 26) (pp. 24-53). Thousand Oaks, CA: Sage.

Churchill, D. (2009). Educational applications of Web 2.0: Using blogs to support teaching and learning. *British Journal of Educational Technology, 40*(1), 179–183. doi:10.1111/j.1467-8535.2008.00865.x

Cifuentes, L., & Murphy, K. L. (2000). Promoting multicultural undestanding and positive self-concept through a distance learning community: Cultural connections. *Educational Technology Research and Development, 48*(1), 69–83. doi:10.1007/BF02313486

Cifuentes, L., & Shih, Y.-C. D. (2001). Teaching and learning online: A collaboration between U.S. and Taiwanese students. *Journal of Research on Technology in Education, 33*(4), 456–474.

Clemson, N. (2009). *2008 progress rates report.* NSW, Australia: Charles Sturt University, Office of Planning & Audit.

Clemson University. (2006). *Master of Arts in professional communication program.* Retrieved October 14, 2006, from http://www.clemson.edu/ caah/ mapc

Cleveland, W. L. (1964). *A history of the modern Middle East.* Boulder, CO: Westview Press.

CNNIC. (2009). *2009 Chinese social networking service research report.* Retrieved November 20, 2010, from http://www.cnnic.cn/html/ Dir/2009/11/11/5721.htm

Cogburn, D. L., & Levinson, N. (2003). U.S.-Africa virtual collaboration in globalization studies: Success factors for complex cross-national learning teams. *International Studies Perspectives, 4*, 34–52. doi:10.1111/1528-3577.04103

Cogburn, D. L., & Levinson, N. S. (2008). Teaching globalization, globally: A 7-year case study of South Africa-U.S. virtual teams. *Information Technologies and International Development, 4*(3), 75–88. doi:10.1162/itid.2008.00018

Cohen, R., & Kennedy, P. (2007). *Global sociology.* London, UK: Macmillan.

Cohen, E. G. (1994). *Designing groupwork: Strategies for the heterogeneous classroom* (2nd ed.). NY: Teachers College, Columbia University.

Cohen, L. I. (2007, April 5). *Social scholarship on the rise.* Retrieved December 3, 2010, from http://liblogs.albany.edu/library20 /2007/04/social_scholarship_on_the_rise.html

Coleman, J. S. (1988). Social capital in the creation of human capital. *American Journal of Sociology, 94*, S95–S120. doi:10.1086/228943

Colley, A., & Maltby, J. (2008). Impact of the Internet on our lives: Male and female personal perspectives. *Computers in Human Behavior, 24*, 2005–2013. doi:10.1016/j.chb.2007.09.002

Collier, M. J., Hegde, R. S., Lee, W., Nakayama, T. K., & Yep, G. A. (2002). Dialogue on the edges: Ferment in communication and culture. In Collier, M. J. (Ed.), *Transforming communication about culture* (pp. 219–280). Thousand Oaks, CA: Sage.

Collier, M. J. (2005). Theorizing cultural identifications: Critical updates and continuing evolution. In Gudykunst, W. (Ed.), *Theorizing about intercultural communication* (pp. 235–256). Thousand Oaks, CA: Sage.

Collis, B., & Moonen, J. (2008). Web 2.0 tools and processes in higher education: Quality perspectives. *Educational Media International, 45*(2), 93–106. doi:10.1080/09523980802107179

Collison, G., Elbaum, B., Haavind, S., & Tinker, R. (2000). *Facilitating online learning: Effective strategies for moderators*. Madison, WI: Atwood Publishing.

ComScore. (2008). *Social networking explodes worldwide as sites increase their focus on cultural relevance*. Retrieved November 20, 2010, from http://www.comscore.com/Press_Events/Press_Releases/2008/08/Social_Networking_World_Wide

ComScore. (2009). *93 percent of Internet users in Turkey visited Google sites in September 2009: Facebook popularity highlights rapid emergence of social networking*. Retrieved April 28, 2010, from http://www.comscore.com/Press_Events/Press_Releases/2009/11/93_Percent_of_Internet_Users_in_Turkey_Visited_Google_Sites_in_September_2009/(language)/eng-US

Conklin, J. (1987). Hypertext: An introduction and survey. *IEEE Computer, 20*(9), 17–41.

Connolly, T., Jessup, L. M., & Valacich, J. S. (1990). Effects of anonymity and evaluative tone on idea generation in computer-mediated groups. *Management Science, 36*, 97–120. doi:10.1287/mnsc.36.6.689

Conrad, R., & Donaldson, A. (2004). *Engaging the online learner: Activities and resources for creative instruction*. San Francisco, CA: Jossey-Bass.

Constant, D., Spoull, L., & Kiesler, S. (1996). The kindness of strangers: The usefulness of electronic weak ties for technical advice. *Organization Science, 7*(2), 119–135. doi:10.1287/orsc.7.2.119

Contractor, N. S., & Eisenberg, E. M. (1990). Communication networks and new media in organizations. In Fulk, J., & Steinfield, C. W. (Eds.), *Organizations and communication technology* (pp. 143–172). Newbury Park, CA: Sage.

Cools, C. A. (2006). Relational communication in intercultural couples. *Language and Intercultural Communication, 6*(3&4), 262–274. doi:10.2167/laic253.0

Cooper, R. G. (2003). Profitable product innovation: The critical success factors. In Shavinina, L. V. (Ed.), *The international handbook on innovation* (pp. 139–157). Boston, MA: Elsevier. doi:10.1016/B978-008044198-6/50010-3

Cormack, M., & Hourigan, N. (Eds.). (2007). *Minority language media: Concepts, critiques, and case studies*. Clevedon, UK: Multilingual Matters.

Cottone, P., & Montavani, G. (2003). Grounding subjective views: Situation awareness and co-reference in distance learning. In Riva, G., Davide, F., & Ijsselsteijn, W. A. (Eds.), *Being there: Concepts, effects and measurements of user presence in synthetic environments* (pp. 249–260). Washington, DC: IOS Press.

Coulmas, F. (2008, May 15). Mobiles Internet: Handy verrückt. *Zeit Online*.

Covarrubias, P. (2007). (Un)biased in Western theory: Generative silence in American Indian communication. *Communication Monographs, 74*, 265–271. doi:10.1080/03637750701393071

Crampton, C. D. (2002). Attribution in distributed work groups. In Hinds, P., & Kiesler, S. (Eds.), *Distributed work* (pp. 191–212). Cambridge, MA: The MIT Press.

Crampton, A., Vanniasinkam, T., & Milic, N. (2010). Vodcasts! How to unsuccessfully implement a new online tool. In Ragusa, A. T. (Ed.), *Interaction in communication technologies & virtual learning environments: Human factors (preface)*. Hershey, PA: IGI Global. doi:10.4018/978-1-60566-874-1.ch008

Crane, D. (1972). *Invisible colleges: Diffusion of knowledge in scientific communities*. Chicago, IL: University of Chicago Press.

Cronin, M. (2001). *Translation and globalization*. New York, NY: Routledge.

Crystal, D. (2006). *Language and the Internet* (2nd ed.). Cambridge, UK: Cambridge University Press. doi:10.1017/CBO9780511487002

Crystal, D. (2000). *Language death*. Cambridge, UK: Cambridge University Press.

Crystal, D. (2001). *Language and the Internet*. Cambridge, UK: Cambridge University Press.

Crystal, D. (2003). *English as a global language* (2nd ed.). Cambridge, UK: Cambridge University Press. doi:10.1017/CBO9780511486999

Cullen, P. P. (2009). Irish pro-migrant nongovernmental organizations and the politics of immigration. *Voluntas*, *20*, 99–128. doi:10.1007/s11266-009-9084-1

Cummings, J. N., & Kraut, R. (2002). Domesticating computers and the Internet. *The Information Society*, *18*, 221–231. doi:10.1080/01972240290074977

Cunliffe, D., & Harries, R. (2005). Promoting minority-language use in a bilingual online community. *New Review of Hypermedia and Multimedia*, *11*(2), 157–179. doi:10.1080/13614560500350750

Cunliffe, D. (2007). Minority languages and the Internet: New threats, new opportunities. In M. Cormack & N. Hourigan, N. (Eds.), *Minority language media: Concepts, critiques, and case studies* (pp. 133-150). Clevedon, UK: Multilingual Matters.

Currie, J. (2005). *Organisational culture of Australian universities: Community or corporate?* Paper presented at the 2005 HERDSA Annual Conference. NSW, Sydney, 3-6 July.

Cushman, E. (1996). The rhetorician as an agent of social change. *College Composition and Communication*, *47*(1), 7–28. doi:10.2307/358271

Cushman, E. (1999, March 27). *Activist methods in service learning: Overcoming noblesse oblige*. Conference on College Composition and Communication (CCCC). Atlanta, GA.

Cutter, C. A. (1875). *Rules for a printed dictionary catalogue*. Washington, DC: Government Printing Office.

Daft, R. L., & Lengel, R. H. (1986). Organizational information requirements, media richness and structural design. *Management Science*, *32*, 554–571. doi:10.1287/mnsc.32.5.554

Daft, R. L., Lengel, R. H., & Trevino, L. K. (1987). Message equivocality, media selection, and manager performance: Implications for information systems. *Management Information Systems Quarterly*, *11*, 355–366. doi:10.2307/248682

Dalgleish, D. C., & Chan, M. A. (2005). *Expectations and reality - International student reflections on studying in Australia*. Paper presented at the Australian International Education Conference Retrieved 10 November 2009, from http://www.aiec.idp.com/ past_papers/ 2005.aspx

Danet, B., & Herring, S. C. (2007). *The multilingual Internet: language, culture, and communication online*. New York, NY: Oxford University Press.

Danet, B., & Herring, S. (2007). Multilingualism on the Internet. In Hellinger, M., & Pauwels, A. (Eds.), *Handbook of language and communication: Diversity and change* (pp. 554–585). New York, NY: Mouton de Gruyter.

Danet, B. (2004). Flaming. In V. P. Bouisaac (Ed.), *The Garland encyclopaedia of semiotics*. New York, NY: Garland. Retrieved June 12, 2009, from http://pluto.mscc.huji.ac.il /~msdanet/flame.html

Davidson, R., & Vreede, G. (2001). The global application of collaborative technologies. *Communications of the ACM*, *44*(12), 69–70.

Davies, R. (2003). Virtual reality hardware and software: Complex usable devices? In G. Riva & F. Davide (Eds.), *Communications through virtual technology: Identity, community and technology in the Internet age*. Retrieved 2nd March, 2008, from http://www.emergingcommunication.com/ volume5.html

Davis, M. (1997). Fragmented by technologies: A community in cyberspace. *Interpersonal Computing and Technology*, *5*(1-2), 7–18.

Davis, N. E. (1999). The globalization of education through teacher education with new technologies: A review informed by research through teacher edcuation with new technologies. *Educational Technology Review*, *1*(12), 8–12.

Davis, N. E., Cho, M. O., & Hagenson, L. (2005). Editorial: Intercultural competence and the role of technology in teacher education. *Contemporary Issues in Technology & Teacher Education, 4*(4), 384–394.

Davis-Floyd, R., & Johnson, C. B. (2006). *Mainstreaming midwives: The politics of change.* New York, NY: Routledge.

de Mooij, M. (2004). *Consumer behavior and culture. Consequences for global marketing and advertising.* Thousand Oaks, CA: Sage.

de Swaan, A. (2001). *Words of the world: The global language system.* Cambridge, UK: Polity.

De Varennes, F. (2001). Language rights as an integral part of human rights. *IJMS: International Journal on Multicultural Societies, 3*(1), 15–25.

DeCapua, A., & Wintergerst, A. (2004). *Crossing cultures in the language classroom.* Ann Arbor, MI: University of Michigan Press.

Deibert, R. J. (2002). Dark guests and great firewalls: The Internet and Chinese security policy. *The Journal of Social Issues, 58,* 143–159. doi:10.1111/1540-4560.00253

Deibert, R. J., & Villeneuve, N. (2005). Firewalls and power: An overview of global state censorship of the Internet. In Klang, M., & Murray, A. (Eds.), *Human rights in the digital age* (pp. 111–124). London, UK: The GlassHouse Press.

Deluca, D., & Valacich, J. S. (2005). Outcomes from conduct of virtual teams at two sites: Support for media synchronicity theory. *Proceedings of the 38ᵗʰ Hawaii International Conference on Systems Sciences,* (pp. 1-10). Los Alamitos, CA: IEEE Computer Society.

Dennis, A. R., & Kinney, S. T. (1998). Testing media richness theory in the new media: The effects of cues, feedback, and task equivocality. *Information Systems Research, 9*(3), 256–274. doi:10.1287/isre.9.3.256

Department of Education. Employment & Workplace Relations. (2009). *End of year summary of international student enrolment data – Australia – 2009.* Retrieved August 4, 2010, from http://aei.gov.au/ AEI/ Statistics/ StudentEnrolmentAndVisaStatistics/2009/ MonthlySummary_ Dec09_pdf.pdf

DePew, K. E. (2006). Different writers, different writing: Preparing international teaching assistants for instructional literacy. In Matsuda, P. K., Ortmeier-Hooper, C., & You, X. (Eds.), *The politics of second language writing* (pp. 168–187). West Lafayette, IN: Parlor.

Dermo, J. (2009). E-assessment and the student learning experience: A survey of student perceptions of e-assessment. *British Journal of Educational Technology, 40*(2), 203–214. doi:10.1111/j.1467-8535.2008.00915.x

Desanctis, G., & Poole, M. S. (1994). Capturing the complexity in advanced technology use: Adapative structuration theory. *Organization Science, 5*(2), 121–147. doi:10.1287/orsc.5.2.121

DeSanctis, G., Fayard, A., Roach, M., & Jiang, L. (2003). Learning in online forums. *European Management Journal, 21*(5), 565–577. doi:10.1016/S0263-2373(03)00106-3

DeVoss, D., Jasken, J., & Hayden, D. (2002). Teaching intercultural and intercultural communication: A critique and suggested method. *Journal of Business and Technical Communication, 16*(1), 69–94. doi:10.1177/1050651902016001003

Dewey, J. (1910). *How we think.* Boston, MA: D. C. Heath. doi:10.1037/10903-000

Dewey, J. (1916) *Democracy and education: An introduction to the philosophy of education* (1966 ed.). New York, NY: Free Press.

Diaz, V. (2010). Web 2.0 and emerging technologies in online learning. *New Directions for Community Colleges, 150,* 57–66. doi:10.1002/cc.405

Dibbell, J. (2006). *Play money: Or, how I quit my day job and made millions trading virtual loot.* New York, NY: Basic Books.

Dietz, F. (2006). Issues in localizing computer games. In Dunne, K. J. (Ed.), *Perspectives on localization* (pp. 121–134). Amsterdam, The Netherlands & Philadelphia, PA: John Benjamins Publishing Company.

Dillon, E. (2008). *The fraudsters: How con artists steal your money.* London, UK: Merlin Publishing.

Dirven (Eds.), *The cultural context in business communication* (pp. 51-118). Amsterdam, The Netherlands: John Benjamins.

Dixon, N. M. (2000). *Common knowledge: How companies thrive by sharing what they know*. Boston, MA: McGraw-Hill.

Dobrin, D. N. (1983). What's technical about technical writing? In Johnson-Eilola, J., & Selber, S. (Eds.), *Central works in technical communication* (pp. 108–123). Oxford, UK: Oxford University Press.

Doctora Aliza. (2010). *Vidaysalud*. Retrieved March 24, 2010, from http://vidaysalud.com/author/doctoraliza

Doing Business. (2009). *Doing Business 2010: Reforming through difficult times- International Finance Corporation*. Retrieved December 10, 2010, from http://www.doingbusiness.org/Documents/CountryProfiles/ARE.pdf

Donath, J., & Boyd, D. (2004). Public displays of connection. *BT Technology Journal*, *22*, 71–82. doi:10.1023/B:BTTJ.0000047585.06264.cc

Donath, J. S. (1999). Identity and deception in the virtual community. In Smith, M., & Kollock, P. (Eds.), *Communities in cyberspace* (pp. 27–58). London, UK: Routledge.

Donnelly-Smith, L. (2009). Global learning through short-term study abroad. *Peer Review*, *11*(4), 12–15.

Dor, D. (2004). From Englishization to imposed multilingualism: Globalization, the Internet, and the political economy of the linguistic code. *Public Culture*, *16*(1), 97–118. doi:10.1215/08992363-16-1-97

Dragga, S. (1999). Ethical intercultural technical communication: Looking through the lens of Confucian ethics. *Technical Communication Quarterly*, *8*, 365–381.

Druyd, M. A. (2005). "I brought you a good news": An analysis of Nigerian 419 letters. *Proceedings of the 2005 Association of Business Communication Annual Convention*, 1-11.

Dubai eGovernment. (2009). *Dubai economy*. Retrieved December 4, 2010, from http://www.dubai.ae/en.portal? topic,Article_000239,0,&_nfpb =true&_pageLabel=home

Dube, L., & Pare, G. (2001). Global virtual teams. *Communications of the ACM*, *44*(12), 71–73. doi:10.1145/501317.501349

Dubinsky, J. (2002). Service-learning as a path to virtue: The ideal orator in professional communication. *Michigan Journal of Community Service Learning*, *9*, 62–74.

Dubrovsky, V. J., Kiesler, S., & Sethna, B. N. (1991). The equalization phenomenon: Status effects in computer-mediated and face-to-face decision-making groups. *Human-Computer Interaction*, *6*, 119–146. doi:10.1207/s15327051hci0602_2

Ducheneaut, N., Yee, N., Nickell, E., & Moore, R. (2006). "Alone together?" Exploring the social dynamics of massively multiplayer online games. In *Proceedings of the CHI 2006, ACM* (pp. 407-416). New York, NY: Association for Computing Machinery.

Ducoffe, R. H. (1996). Advertising value and advertising on the Web. *Journal of Advertising Research*, *36*(5), 21–35.

Duhaney, D. C. (2004). Blended learning in education, training and development. *Performance Improvement*, *43*(8), 35–39. doi:10.1002/pfi.4140430810

Dunlap, J. C., & Lowenthal, P. R. (2009). Tweeting the night away: Using Twitter to enhance social presence. *Journal of Information Systems Education*, *20*(2), 129–136.

Dutton, W. H., Cheong, P. H., & Park, N. (2004). An ecology of constraints on e-learning in higher education: The case of a virtual learning environment. *Prometheus*, *22*(2), 131–149. doi:10.1080/0810902042000218337

Dutton, W. H., & Loader, B. D. (2002). Introduction: New media and institution of higher education and learning. In Dutton, W. H., & Loader, B. D. (Eds.), *Digital academe: New media and institution of higher education and learning* (pp. 1–32). London, UK: Routledge.

DuVall, J. B., Powell, M. R., Hodge, E., & Ellis, M. (2007). Text messaging to improve social presence in online learning. *Educause Quarterly*, *3*, 24-28. Retrieved October 10, 2010, from http://net.educause.edu/ir/library/pdf/EQM0733.pdf

Economides, A. A. (2008). Culture-aware collaborative learning. *Multicultural Education & Technology Journal*, *2*(4), 243–267. doi:10.1108/17504970810911052

Edelson, E. (2003). The 419 scam: Information warfare on the spam front and a proposal for local filtering. *Computers & Security, 22*(5), 392–401. doi:10.1016/S0167-4048(03)00505-4

Edwards, J. (2009). *Language and identity: An introduction*. New York, NY: Cambridge University Press.

El Zaim, A. (2010). Language, money, and the information society. In Osborne, D. (Ed.), *African languages in a digital age: Challenges and opportunities for indigenous language computing* (pp. ix–xii). Cape Town, South Africa: HSCR Press.

Ellis, D. G. (1999). *Crafting society: Ethnicity, class, and communication theory*. Mahwah, NJ: Lawrence Erlbaum.

Ellison, N. B., Steinfield, C., & Lampe, C. (2007). The benefits of Facebook friends: Social capital and college students' use of online social network sites. *Journal of Computer-Mediated Communication, 12*(4), 1143–1168. doi:10.1111/j.1083-6101.2007.00367.x

Elsidafy, M. (2009). E-commerce in UAE to hit $36bn by 2010. *Emirates Business 24-7*. Retrieved December 3, 2010, from http://www.business24-7.ae/Articles/2009/7/Pages/04072009/07052009_ b30f3ffaa4d94a639dc703fcdcf5264b.aspx

eMarketer. (2008). Social network marketing: Ad spending update. Retrieved December 3, 2010, from http://www.emarketer.com

eMarketer. (2009). *23 million Hispanics now online*. Retrieved November 24, 2009, from http://www.ahorre.com/dinero/Internet/marketing/23_million_hispanics_online_2009/

Encyclopedia of Nations. (2009). *United Arab Emirates: Country overview*. Retrieved December 3, 2010, from http://www.nationsencyclopedia.com /economies/Asia-and-the-Pacific/ United-Arab-Emirates.html

Erard, M. (2004, May 17). When technology ignores the East-West divide. *The New York Times*, p. 4.

Erikson, T. H. (2007). Nationalism and the Internet. *Nations and Nationalism, 13*(1), 1–17. doi:10.1111/j.1469-8129.2007.00273.x

Esarey, A., & Qiang, X. (2008). Political expression in the Chinese blogosphere: Below the radar. *Asian Survey, 48*(5), 752–772. doi:10.1525/AS.2008.48.5.752

Esra'a. (2008). Online social networking: The strength of weak ties. *Mideast Youth*. Retrieved December 10, 2010, from http://www.mideastyouth.com/ 2008/11/15/online-social -networking-the-strength-of-weak-ties/

Ess, C. (2002). Cultures in collision philosophical lessons from computer-mediated communication. *Metaphilosophy, 33*(1-2), 229–253. doi:10.1111/1467-9973.00226

Ess, C. (2002). Computer-mediated colonization, the renaissance, and educational imperatives for an intercultural global village. *Ethics and Information Technology, 4*(1), 11–22. doi:10.1023/A:1015227723904

Ess, C., & Sudweeks, F. (2005). Culture and computer-mediated communication: Toward new understandings. *Journal of Computer-Mediated Communication, 11*(1), 179–191. doi:10.1111/j.1083-6101.2006.tb00309.x

European Commission. (2010a). *Translation at the European Commission – A history*. Luxembourg: Office for Official Publications of the European Communities.

European Commission. (2010b). *E-government on the fast track*. Retrieved November 25, 2010, from http://ec.europa.eu/information_society/activities/egovernment/policy/index_en.htDm

Faber, B. (2002). *Community action and organizational change: Image, narrative, identity*. Carbondale, IL: Southern Illinois University Press.

Facebook. (2010). *Facebook statistics*. Retrieved May 11, 2010, from http://www.facebook.com/press /info.php?statistics

Facey, E. E. (2001). First nations and education by Internet: The path forward, or back? *Journal of Distance Education, 16*(1). Retrieved December 3, 2010, from http://cade.icap.org/vol16.1/facey.html

Faiola, A., & Matei, S. A. (2005). Cultural cognitive style and Web design: Beyond a behavioral inquiry into computer-mediated communication. *Journal of Computer-Mediated Communication, 11*(1). Retrieved October 10, 2020, from http://jcmc.indiana.edu/vol11 /issue1/faiola.html

Fairclough, N. (1995). *Media discourse*. London, UK: Longman.

Fairclough, N. (2000). Critical analysis of media discourse. In Marris, P., & Thornham, S. (Eds.), *Media studies: A reader* (2nd ed., pp. 308–325). New York, NY: New York University Press.

Faris, R., & Villeneuve, N. (2008). Measuring global Internet filtering. In Deibert, R. (Eds.), *Access denied: The practice and policy of global Internet filtering* (pp. 5–27). Cambridge, MA: The MIT Press.

Farkas, D. K. (1999). The logical and rhetorical construction of procedural discourse. *Technical Communication, 46*(1), 42–54.

Farrell, K. (2007). The big mamas are watching: China's censorship of the Internet and the strain on freedom of expression. *Michigan State Journal of International Law, 15*, 577–603.

Farshchian, B. A. (2003). Presence technologies for informal collaboration. In Riva, G., Davide, F., & Ijsselsteijn, W. A. (Eds.), *Being there: Concepts, effects and measurements of user presence in synthetic environments* (pp. 209–222). Washington, DC: IOS Press.

Federal Register. (2000). *Executive order 13166 – Improving access to services for persons with limited English proficiency*. Department of Justice. Enforcement of Title Vi of the Civil Rights Act of 1964 – National Origin Discrimination Against Persons With Limited English Proficiency: Notice. Retrieved May 5, 2010, from http://www.justice.gov/crt/cor/Pubs/eolep.pdf

Feintuch, H. (2010, March 18). Keeping their distance. *Diverse: Issues in Higher Education, 27*(3). Retrieved November 25, 2010, from http://www.highbeam.com/doc/1G1-222251349.html

Fernandez, L. (2001). Patterns of linguistic discrimination in discussion forums. *Mercator Media Forum, 5*, 22–41.

Fernandez, L. E., & Morales, A. (2007). Language and use of cancer screening services among border and non-border Hispanic women. *Ethnicity & Health, 12*(3), 245–263. doi:10.1080/13557850701235150

Fiedler, D. C. (1997). Authoritative knowledge and birth territories in contemporary Japan. In Davis-Floyd, R. E., & Sargent, C. F. (Eds.), *Childbirth and authoritative knowledge* (pp. 159–179). Berkley, CA: University of California Press.

Firestone, J. M. (2008). On doing knowledge management. *Knowledge Management Research & Practice, 6*(1), 13–22. doi:10.1057/palgrave.kmrp.8500160

Firestone, J. M., & McElroy, M. W. (2003). *Key issues in the new knowledge management*. Boston, MA: Butterworth-Heinemann.

Fischer, K. (2007). Flat world lessons for real-world students. *The Chronicle of Higher Education, 35*.

Fishman, J. (1989). *Language and ethnicity in minority sociolinguistic perspective*. Clevedon, UK: Multilingual Matters.

Fishman, J. (1991). *Reversing language shift: Theoretical and empirical foundations of assistance to threatened languages*. Clevedon, UK: Multilingual Matters.

Fitch, B., Kirby, A., & Greathouse Amador, L. M. (2008). In Starke-Meyerring, D., & Wilson, M. (Eds.), *Designing global learning environments: Visionary partnerships, policies, and pedagogies* (pp. 145–155). Rotterdam, The Netherlands: Sense Publishers.

Flammia, M., Cleary, Y., & Slattery, D. M. (2010). Leadership roles, socioemotional communication strategies, and technology use of Irish and US students in virtual teams. *IEEE Transactions on Professional Communication, 53*(2), 89–101. doi:10.1109/TPC.2010.2046088

Fong, M., & Chuang, R. (2004). *Communicating ethnic and cultural identity*. Lanham, MD: Rowman & Littlefield.

Foot, K. A., & Schneider, S. M. (2002). Online action in campaign 2001: An exploratory analysis of the US political Web sphere. *Journal of Broadcasting & Electronic Media, 42*(2), 222–244. doi:10.1207/s15506878jobem4602_4

Fornas, J. (2002). *Digital borderlands: Cultural studies of identity and interactivity on the Internet*. New York, NY: Peter Lang.

Foronda, C. L. (2008). A concept analysis of cultural sensitivity. *Journal of Transcultural Nursing, 19*(3), 207–212. doi:10.1177/1043659608317093

Forslund, C. J. (1996). Analyzing pictorial messages across cultures. In Andrews, D. C. (Ed.), *International dimensions of technical communication* (pp. 45–58). Arlington, VA: STC.

Foucault, M. (1973). *The birth of the clinic: An archaeology of medical perception.* New York, NY: Vintage Books.

Foucault, M. (1980). *Power/knowledge.* New York, NY: Pantheon.

Fougère, M., & Moulettes, A. (2007). The construction of the modern west and the backward rest: Studying the discourse of Hofstede's Culture's Consequences. *Journal of Multicultural Discourses, 2*(1), 1–19. doi:10.2167/md051.0

Freire, A. P., Linhalis, F., Bianchini, S. L., Fortes, R. P. M., & Pimentel, M. da G. C. (2010). Revealing the whiteboard to blind students: An inclusive approach to provide mediation in synchronous e-learning activities. *Computers & Education, 54*(4), 866–876. doi:10.1016/j.compedu.2009.09.016

Freire, P. (1971). *Pedagogy of the oppressed.* New York, NY: Herder.

Freire, P. (1988). The adult literacy process as cultural action for freedom. In Kintgen, E., Kroll, B., & Rose, M. (Eds.), *Perspectives on literacy* (pp. 398–409). Carbondale, IL: Southern Illinois University Press.

Friedman, T. L. (2000). *The Lexus and the olive tree: Understanding globalization.* New York, NY: Anchor Books.

Friedman, T. L. (2006). *The world is flat: A brief history of the twenty-first century* (1st updated and expanded ed.). New York, NY: Farrar, Straus and Giroux.

Fryer, J. (2009, December 30). Mobile-phone culture: The Aparatgeist calls. *The Economist.* Retrieved January 2, 2010, from http://www.economist.com/ displaystory. cfm?story_id =15172850

Fu, D., & Matoush, M. (2006). Writing development and biliteracy. In Matsuda, P. K., Ortmeier-Hooper, C., & You, X. (Eds.), *The politics of second language writing* (pp. 5–29). West Lafayette, IN: Parlor Press.

Fukuyama, F. (1995). *Trust.* New York, NY: The Free Press.

Fulk, J., Schmitz, J., & Steinfield, C. W. (1990). A social influence model of technology use. In Fulk, J., & Steinfield, C. W. (Eds.), *Organization and communication technology* (pp. 117–140). Newbury Park, CA: Sage.

Furamo, K., & Pearson, J. M. (2006). An empirical investigation of how trust, cohesion, and performance vary in virtual and face-to-face teams. *Proceedings of the 39th Hawaii International Conference on Systems Sciences.* Honolulu, HI: Computer Society Press.

Furnas, G. W., Landauer, T. K., Gomez, L. M., & Dumais, S. T. (1987). The vocabulary problem in human-system communication. *Communications of the ACM, 30*(11), 964–971. doi:10.1145/32206.32212

Gacel-Avila, J. (2005). The internationalization of higher education. A paradigm for global citizenry. *Journal of Studies in International Education, 9*(2), 121–136. doi:10.1177/1028315304263795

Gajjala, R. (1998). *The sawnet refusal: An interrupted cyberethnography.* Dissertation Abstracts International, (pp. 99-131).

Galasinki, D. (2000). *The language of deception: A discourse analytic study.* London, UK: Sage.

Galtung, J. (1981). Structure, culture and intellectual style: An essay comparing Saxonic, Teutonic, Gallic and Nipponic approaches. *Social Sciences Information. Information Sur les Sciences Sociales, 20*(6), 817–856. doi:10.1177/053901848102000601

Gao, L. (2006). Language contact and convergence in computer-mediated communication. *World Englishes, 25*(2), 299–308. doi:10.1111/j.0083-2919.2006.00466.x

Gao, L. (2007). *Chinese Internet language: A study of identity constructions.* Munich, Germany: Lincom GmbH.

Gao, J., Nie, J. Y., Zhang, J., Xun, E., Su, Y., & Zhou, M. (2001). *TREC-9 CLIR experiments at MSRCN.* (NIST Special Publication 500–249). Paper presented at the The Ninth Text REtrieval Conference, Gaithersburg, MD.

Garcia, N. (2000). *Old Las Vegas: Hispanic memories from the New Mexico meadowlands.* Lubbock, TX: Texas Tech University Press.

Garnham, C., & Kaleta, R. (2002, March 20). Introduction to hybrid courses. *Teaching with Technology Today, 8*(6). Retrieved June 16, 2009, from http://www.uwsa.edu/ ttt/ articles/ garnham.htm

Garrison, D. R. (2006). Online collaborative principles. *Journal of Asynchronous Learning Networks, 10*(1), 25–33.

Garrison, D. R., & Kanuka, H. (2004). Blended learning: Uncovering its transformative potential in higher education. *The Internet and Higher Education, 7*(2), 95–105. doi:10.1016/j.iheduc.2004.02.001

Garshol, L. (2005). *Topic maps and information design*. Majorstuen, Norway: Ontopia.

Garshol, L. M. (2004). Metadata? Thesauri? Taxonomies? Topic maps! Making sense of it all. *Journal of Information Science, 30*(4), 378–391. doi:10.1177/0165551504045856

Gartner. (2007). *Gartner says 80 percent of active Internet users will have a "Second Life" in the virtual world by the end of 2011*. Gartner Newsroom. Retrieved April 24, 2007, from http://www.gartner.com/ it/ page.jsp? id=503861

Garton, L., & Wellman, B. (1995). Social impacts of electronic mail in organizations: A review of the research literature. In Burleson, B. R. (Ed.), *Communication yearbook, 18* (pp. 434–453). Thousand Oaks, CA: Sage.

Gasner, A. (1999). Globalization: The changing face of the workforce. *Business Today, 36*(3), 43–44.

Gavidia, J. V., Mogollón, R. H., & Baena, C. (2005). Using international virtual teams in the business classroom. *Journal of Teaching in International Business, 16*(2), 51–74. doi:10.1300/J066v16n02_04

Gayton, J., & McEwen, B. C. (2007). Effective online instructional assessment strategies. *American Journal of Distance Education, 21*(3), 117–132. doi:10.1080/08923640701341653

Gee, J. (1994). Orality and literacy: From the savage mind to ways with words. In Maybin, J. (Ed.), *Language and literacy in social practice* (pp. 168–192). Clevedon, UK: The Open University Press.

Geertz, C. (2000). *Local knowledge*. New York, NY: Basic.

Genesereth, M. R., & Nilsson, N. J. (1987). *Logical foundations of artificial intelligence*. San Mateo, CA: Morgan Kaufmann Publishers.

Gerdes, H., & Mallinckrod, B. (1994). Emotional, social, and academic adjustment of college students: A longitudinal study of retention. *Journal of Counseling and Development, 72*, 281–288.

Gevorgyan, G., & Manucharova, N. (2009). Does culturally adapted online communication work? A study of American and Chinese Internet users' attitudes and preferences toward culturally customized Web design elements. *Journal of Computer-Mediated Communication, 14*(2), 393–413. doi:10.1111/j.1083-6101.2009.01446.x

Gezo, T., Oliverson, M., & Zick, M. (2000). Managing global projects with virtual teams. *Hydrocarbon Processing, 79*, 112c–112i.

Giammona, B. (2004). The future of technical communication: How innovation, technology, information management, and other forces are shaping the future of the profession. *Technical Communication, 51*(3), 349–366.

Gibson, W. (1986). *Neuromancer*. London, UK: Grafton.

Gibson, J. J. (1977). The theory of affordances. In Shaw, R. E., & Bransford, J. (Eds.), *Perceiving, acting, and knowing* (pp. 67–82). Hillsdale, NJ: Erlbaum.

Gillard, J. (2009). *International education – Its contribution to Australia*. Retrieved August 4, 2010, from http:// www.deewr.gov.au/ Ministers/ Gillard/ Media/ Speeches/ Pages/ Article_090527 _093411.aspx

Gimenez, J. (2002). New media and conflicting realities in multinational corporate communication: A case study. *IRAL, 40*, 323–343. doi:10.1515/iral.2002.016

Godlee, F., Packenham-Walsh, N., Ncayiyana, D., Cohen, B., & Parker, A. (2004). *Can we achieve health information for all by 2015?* Retrieved November 25, 2010, from http://image.thelancet.com/extras/04art6112Web.pdf

Goel. (2006, November 2). Online marriages are a runaway success. *Knight Rider Tribune Business News*, 1.

Goertzel, B. (2007). *AI meets the metaverse: Teachable AI agents living in virtual worlds*. Kurzweil Articulating Intelligence. Retrieved October 1, 2010, from http:// www.kurzweilai.net/ meme/ frame.html? main=/ articles/ art0710.html

Goldman, R., & Gabriel, R. P. (2005). *Innovation happens elsewhere: Open source as business strategy.* Boston, MA: Morgan Kaufmann.

Goldsmith, J., & Wu, T. (2006). *Who controls the internet: Illusions of a borderless world. New York.* NY: Oxford University Press.

Goodwin, C. D. (1995). Fads and fashions on campus: Interdisciplinarity and internationalization. In Deneef, A. L., & Goodwin, C. D. (Eds.), *The academic's handbook* (pp. 73–80). Durham, NC: Duke UP.

Google. (2010b). *Google in your language. Google translation status report.* Retrieved May 12, 2010, from http://www.google.com/transconsole/giyl/check/status

Google. (2010c). *HealthSpeaks.* Retrieved November 25, 2010, from http://sitescontent.google.com/healthspeaks/about/

Gopal, Y., & Srinivas, M. (2007, May 23). *New work paradigms? Implication for communication and coordination.* Paper presented at the Annual Meeting of the International Communication Association, San Francisco, CA. Retrieved November 23, 2010, from http://www.allacademic.com/meta/p169097_index.html

Gore, M. S. (1969). *Urbanization and family change.* Bombay, India: Popular Prakash.

Grabowsky, P., Smith, R. G., & Dempsy, G. (2001). *Electronic theft: Unlawful acquisition in cyberspace.* Cambridge, UK: Cambridge University Press.

Gramsci, A. (1978). *Selections from cultural writings.* Cambridge, MA: Harvard University Press.

Gramsci, A. (1971). *Selections from the prison notebooks* (Hoare, Q., & Smith, G. N., Trans.). New York, NY: International.

Granovetter, M. S. (1983). The strength of weak ties: A network theory revisited. *Sociological Theory, 1,* 201–233. doi:10.2307/202051

Grau, O. (2003). *Virtual art: From illusion to immersion* (Rev. and expanded ed.). Cambridge, MA: The MIT Press.

Gray, K., Thompson, C. R., Sheard, J., & Hamilton, M. (2008). Web 2.0 authorship: Issues of referencing and citation for academic integrity. *The Internet and Higher Education, 11,* 112–118. doi:10.1016/j.iheduc.2008.03.001

Grebennikov, L., & Skaines, I. (2006). *International students in higher education: Comparative analysis of student surveys on international student experience in higher education.* Paper presented at the Australasian Association for Institutional Research. Retrieved November 10, 2009, from http://www.aair.org.au/ 2006Papers/ Skaines.pdf

Greenwood, L. (2009). Africa's mobile banking revolution. *BBC mobile.* Retrieved November 25, 2010, from http://news.bbc.co.uk/2/hi/8194241.stm.

Group [UK Universities] (2007). *Enhancing the student experience: Policy report.*

Gruber, T. (1993a). *A translation approach to portable ontology specifications.* Stanford, CA: Stanford University Press.

Gruber, T. (1993b). *What is an ontology?* Retrieved December 12, 2004, from http://www-ksl.stanford.edu/kst /what-is-an-ontology.html

Gu, R., & Higa, K. (2009). A study on communication media selection in IT and service work groups. *International Journal of Services Sciences, 2*(3-4), 381–397. doi:10.1504/IJSSCI.2009.026548

Gudykunst, W. B., & Ting-Toomey, S. (1988). *Culture and interpersonal communication.* Newbury Park, CA: Sage.

Gudykunst, W. B., & Kim, Y. Y. (1992). *Communicating with strangers: An approach to intercultural communication* (2nd ed.). New York, NY: McGraw Hill.

Gudykunst, W. B., & Mody, G. (2002). *Handbook of international and intercultural communication* (2nd ed.). Thousand Oaks, CA: Sage.

Gudykunst, W. B., & Lee, C. (2002). Cross-cultural communication theories. In Gudykunst, W. B., & Mody, B. (Eds.), *Handbook of international and intercultural communication* (pp. 19–24). Thousand Oaks, CA: Sage.

Guerin, S. H. (2009). Internationalizing the curriculum: Improving learning through international education: Preparing students for a success in a global society. *Community College Journal of Research and Practice, 33*(8), 611–614. doi:10.1080/10668920902928945

Guha, R. (2007). *India after Gandhi: The history of the world's largest democracy.* New York, NY: Ecco.

Guimaraes, M. J. L. J. (2005). Doing anthropology in cyberspace: Fieldwork boundaries and social environments. In Hine, C. (Ed.), *Virtual methods: Issues in social research on the Internet* (pp. 141–156). New York, NY: Berg.

Gulagenim. (2002, July 4). Blog entry. Retrieved March 15, 2004, from http://www.gulagenim.blogspot.com/2002_07_04_gulagenim_archive.html

Gumperz, J. (1982). *Discourse strategies*. Cambridge, UK: Cambridge University Press. doi:10.1017/CBO9780511611834

Gunawardena, C. N., & Zittle, F. J. (1997). Social presence as a predictor of satisfaction within a computer-mediated conferencing environment. *American Journal of Distance Education, 11*(3), 8–26. doi:10.1080/08923649709526970

Gupta, G. R. (1979). Love, arranged marriage and the Indian social structure. In Kurian, G. (Ed.), *Cross-cultural perspectives of mate-selection and marriage* (pp. 11–32). Connecticut: Greenwood Press.

Habermas, J. (1989). *The structural transformation of the public sphere*. Cambridge, MA: The MIT Press.

Habermas, J. (1970). On systematically distorted communication. *Inquiry, 13*, 205–218. doi:10.1080/00201747008601590

Habermas, J. (1981). Modernity versus postmodernity. *New German Critique, NGC, 22*, 3–14. doi:10.2307/487859

Habermas, J. (1987). The theory of communicative action: Lifeworld and system: Vol. 2. T. McCarthy, Trans. Boston, MA: Beacon Press.

Hachigian, N. (2001). China's cyber-strategy. *Foreign Affairs (Council on Foreign Relations), 80*(2), 118–133. doi:10.2307/20050069

Halavais, A. (2000). National borders on the World Wide Web. *New Media & Society, 1*, 7–28. doi:10.1177/14614440022225689

Hall, E. T. (1959). *The silent language*. Garden City, NY: Anchor Press/Doubleday.

Hall, E. T. (1976). *Beyond culture*. Garden City, NY: Anchor Press/Doubleday.

Hall, E. T., & Hall, M. R. (1990). *Understanding cultural differences: Keys to success in West Germany, France and the United States*. Yarmouth, ME: Intercultural Press.

Hall, B. J. (1992). Theories of culture and communication. *Communication Theory, 1*, 50–70. doi:10.1111/j.1468-2885.1992.tb00028.x

Hall, E. T. (1966). *The hidden dimension*. Garden City, NY: Anchor Press.

Hall, E. T. (1983). *The dance of life: The other dimension of time*. New York, NY: Doubleday.

Hall, E. T. (1992). *Beyond culture*. Gloucester, MA: Peter Smith Publisher.

Halliday, M. A. K. (1973). *Explorations in the functions of language*. London, UK: Edward Arnold.

Halliday, M. A. K. (1985). *An introduction to functional grammar*. London, UK: Longman.

Halualani, R. T., Mendoza, S. L., & Drzewiecka, J. A. (2009). "Critical" junctures in intercultural communication studies: A review. *Review of Communication, 9*, 17–35. doi:10.1080/15358590802169504

Hamel, G. (2007). *The future of management*. Boston, MA: Harvard Business School Press.

Hampton, K., & Wellman, B. (2001). Long distance community in the network society: Contact and support beyond Netville. *The American Behavioral Scientist, 45*(3), 476–495. doi:10.1177/00027640121957303

Han, Y. (2010). Wangyou pinglun liangze yu wangjin (Two pieces of comments from net friends and Internet censorship). Retrieved February 18, 2010, from http://www.hanyimin.com /post/1173.html

Hannon, J., & Bretag, T. (2010). Negotiating contested discourses of learning technologies in higher education. *Journal of Educational Technology & Society, 13*(1), 106–120.

Hannum, W. (2009). Moving distance education research forward. *Distance Education, 30*(1), 171–173. doi:10.1080/01587910902846020

Hanson, L. (2010). Global citizenship, global health, and the internationalization of curriculum: A study of transformative potential. *Journal of Studies in International Education, 14*(1), 70–88. doi:10.1177/1028315308323207

Hara, N., & Kling, R. (2000). Student distress in Web-based distance education course. *Information Communication and Society, 3*(4), 555–579.

Hara, N., & Kling, R. (1999) Students' distress with a web-based distance education course: An ethnographic study of participants' experiences. *Center for Social Informatics*. Retrieved June 11, 2009 from http://www.slis.indiana.edu/ csi

Hardesty, S., & Sugarman, T. (2007). Academic librarians, professional literature, and new technologies: A survey. *University Library Faculty Publications, Paper 3*. Retrieved May 17, 2010 from http://digitalarchive.gsu.edu /univ_lib_facpub/3

Harklau, L. (1994). ESL versus mainstream classes: Contrasting L2 learning environments. *TESOL Quarterly, 28*, 241–272. doi:10.2307/3587433

Harklau, L. (2000). From the "good kids" to the "worst": Representations of English language learners across educational settings. *TESOL Quarterly, 34*(1), 35–67. doi:10.2307/3588096

Harrison, R., & Thomas, M. (2009). Identity in online communities: Social networking sites and language learning. *International Journal of Emerging Technologies and Society, 7*(2), 109–124.

Hassanpour, A. (1992). *Nationalism and language in Kurdistan*. San Francisco, CA: Mellon Press.

Hassanpour, A., & Mojab, S. (2005). Kurdish diaspora. In Ember, M., Ember, C. R., & Skoggard, I. (Eds.), *Encyclopaedia of diasporas: Immigrant and refugee cultures around the world* (*Vol. 1*, pp. 214–224). New York, NY: Kluwer Academic.

Hassanpour, A. (2003). The making of Kurdish identity: Pre-20th century historical and literary discourses. In Vali, A. (Ed.), *Essays on the origins of Kurdish nationalism*. Costa Mesa, CA: Mazda Publishers Inc.

Hathorn, L. G., & Ingram, A. L. (2002). Cooperation and collaboration using computer-mediated communication. *Journal of Educational Computing Research, 26*(3), 325–347. doi:10.2190/7MKH-QVVN-G4CQ-XRDU

Hauser, R. (2010). *Technisierte Kultur oder kultivierte Technik: Das Internet in Deutschland und Russland. Cultural diversity and new media* (*Vol. 14*). Berlin, Germany: Trafo.

Hawisher, G. E., & Selfe, C. L. (2000). *Global literacies and the World-Wide Web*. London, UK: Routledge.

He, Z. (2008). SMS in China: A major carrier of the non-official discourse universe. *The Information Society, 24*, 182–190. doi:10.1080/01972240802020101

He, B. (2006). Western theories of deliberative democracy and the Chinese practice of complex deliberative governance. In Leib, E., & He, B. (Eds.), *The search for deliberation democracy in China* (pp. 133–148). New York, NY: Palgrave MacMillan.

Heath, S. B. (1983). *Ways with words: Language, life, and work in communities and classrooms*. New York, NY: Cambridge University Press.

Heaton, L. (2008, June 27). *Cultural specificity: When does it matter?* 2008 Cultural Attitudes Towards Communication and Technology Conference.

Heifferon, B. A. (2005). *Writing in the health professions. The Allyn/Bacon series in technical communication*. Boston, MA: Allyn-Bacon/Longman.

Heifferon, B. A. (1998). *Look who's not talking: Recovering the voice of the patient in the clinique*. Unpublished dissertation. U of Arizona.

Heim, M. (1993). *The metaphysics of virtual reality*. New York, NY: Oxford University Press.

Hein, K. (2004, November 29). Matchmaker e-Harmony makes note of successes. *Brandweek New York, 45*(43), 13.

Held, D., McGrew, A., Goldlatt, D., & Perraton, J. (1999). *Global transformations: Politics, economics and culture*. Stanford, CA: Stanford University Press.

Henderson, L. (1996). Instructional design of interactive multimedia: A cultural critique. *Educational Technology Research and Development, 44*(4), 85–104. doi:10.1007/BF02299823

Herie, M. (2005). Theoretical perspectives in online pedagogy. *Journal of Technology in Human Services, 23*(1/2), 29–52. doi:10.1300/J017v23n01_03

Hermeking, M. (2001). *Kulturen und Technik: Techniktransfer als Arbeitsfeld der interkulturellen Kommunikation. Beispiele aus der arabischen, russischen und lateinamerikanischen Region.* Münster/München, Germany: Waxmann.

Hermeking, M. (2010). Kultur und Technik: Schnittstellen für die Interkulturelle Kommunikation. In Banse, G., & Grunwald, A. (Eds.), *Technik und Kultur: Bedingungs- und Beeinflussungsverhältnisse* (pp. 163–178). Karlsruhe: KIT Scientific Publishing.

Hermeking, M. (2008). Kulturelle Kommunikationsstile in der Mensch-Maschine-Interaktion: Einflüsse auf technische Bedienungsanleitungen und Internet-Webseiten. In Rösch, O. (Ed.), *Technik und Kultur* (pp. 163–185). Berlin, Germany: News&Media.

Hermeking, M. (2007). Global Internet usage, website design, and cultural communication preferences: Contributions from cross-cultural marketing and advertising research. In St.Amant, K. (Ed.), *Linguistic and cultural online communication issues in the global age* (pp. 160–176). Hershey, PA: Information Science Reference. doi:10.4018/978-1-59904-213-8.ch011

Hermeking, M. (2005). Culture and Internet consumption: Contributions from cross-cultural marketing and advertising research. *Journal of Computer Mediated Communication, 11*(1). Retrieved January 15, 2010, from http://jcmc.indiana.edu/vol11 /issue1/hermeking.html

Herold, D. (2009). Cultural politics and political culture of Web 2.0 in Asia. *Knowledge. Technology & Policy, 22*, 89–94. doi:10.1007/s12130-009-9076-x

Herring, S. D. (2001). Using the World Wide Web for research: Are faculty satisfied? *Journal of Academic Librarianship, 27*(3), 213–219. doi:10.1016/S0099-1333(01)00183-5

Herring, S. C. (2004). Slouching toward the ordinary: Current trends in computer-mediated communication. *New Media & Society, 6*(1), 26–36. doi:10.1177/1461444804039906

Herring, S. C. (2004). Computer-mediated discourse analysis: An approach to researching online communities. In Barab, S. A., Kling, R., & Gray, J. H. (Eds.), *Designing for virtual communities in the service of learning* (pp. 338–376). New York, NY: Cambridge University Press.

Herring, S. C. (1996). Introduction. In Herring, S. C. (Ed.), *Computer-mediated communication* (pp. 1–10). Philadelphia, PA: Benjamins.

Herring, S. C. (1999). Interactional coherence in CMC. *Journal of Computer Mediated Communication, 4*(4). Retrieved December 23, 2008, from http://jcmc.indiana.edu/vol4/ issue4/herring.html

Herrington, J., Herrington, A., Mantei, J., Olney, I., & Ferry, B. (Eds.). (2009). *New technologies, new pedagogies: Mobile learning in higher education.* Wollongong, Australia: University of Wollongong.

Herrington, T. (2008). The global classroom project. In Starke-Meyerring, D., & Wilson, M. (Eds.), *Designing global learning environments: Visionary partnerships, policies, and pedagogies* (pp. 37–51). Rotterdam, The Netherlands: Sense Publishers.

Herzberg, B. (1994). Community service and critical teaching. *College Composition and Communication, 45*, 307–319. doi:10.2307/358813

Herzberg, B. (1994, March 27). *Service learning and civic education.* Conference on College Composition and Communication (CCCC). Atlanta, GA.

Hewling, A. (2005). Culture in the online class: Using message analysis to look beyond nationality-based frames of reference. *Journal of Computer-Mediated Communication, 11*(1), 337–356. doi:10.1111/j.1083-6101.2006.tb00316.x

Hiemstra, G. (1982). Teleconferencing, concern for face, and organizational culture. In Burgoon, M. (Ed.), *Communication yearbook* (Vol. 6, pp. 874–904). Beverly Hills, CA: Sage.

HIFA2015. (2010). *A global campaign. Healthcare information for all by 2015*. Retrieved May 5, 2010, from http://www.hifa2015.org/about/

Highsmith, J. A. (2004). *Agile project management: Creating innovative products*. Boston, MA: Addison-Wesley.

Hiltz, S. R., Johnson, K., & Turoff, M. (1986). Experiment in group decision making communication process and outcome in face to face vs. computerized conference. *Human Communication Research, 13*, 225–252. doi:10.1111/j.1468-2958.1986.tb00104.x

Hinduja, S., & Patchin, J. W. (2008). Cyberbullying: An exploratory analysis of factors related to offending and victimization. *Deviant Behavior, 29*(2), 1–29. doi:10.1080/01639620701457816

Hine, C. (2000). *Virtual ethnography*. Thousand Oaks, CA: Sage.

Hingorani, K. K. (2008). Social presence, personality types, and IT-supported teaching methods. *Issues in Information Systems, 9*(2), 56–62.

Hippel, E. v. (2005). *Democratizing innovation*. Cambridge, MA: The MIT Press.

Hirst, P., & Thompson, G. (1996). *Globalisation in question: The international economy and the possibilities of governance*. London, UK: Polity.

Hispanic Tips. (2005). Spanish-speakers becoming more engaged online. Retrieved October 10, 2010, from http://www.hispanictips.com/2005/09/28/spanis-speakers-becoming-more-engaged-online

Hobbs, H. H., & Chernotsky, H. I. (2007). Preparing students for global citizenship. *Proceedings of the American Political Science Conference*. Retrieved November 20, 2010, from www.apsanet.org/ tlc2007/ TLC07HobbsChernotsky.pdf

Hodge, G. (2000). *Systems of knowledge organization for digital libraries: Beyond traditional authority files*. Washington, DC: Council on Library and Information Resources.

Hodge, E. M., Tabrizi, M. H. N., Farwell, M. A., & Wuensch, K. L. (2007). Virtual reality classrooms: Strategies for creating a social presence. *International Journal of Social Sciences, 2*, 105–109.

Hofstede, G. (1980). *Culture's consequences*. Beverly Hills, CA: Sage.

Hofstede, G. (1984). *Culture's consequences: International differences in work-related values*. Beverly Hills, CA: Sage.

Hofstede, G. (1997). *Cultures and organizations, software of the mind: Intercultural cooperation and its importance for survival* (Rev. ed.). New York, NY: McGraw-Hill.

Hofstede, G. (1980). *Culture's consequences: International differences in work-related values*. Beverly Hill, CA: Sage.

Hofstede, G. (1986). Cultural differences in teaching and learning. *International Journal of Intercultural Relations, 10*(3), 301–320. doi:10.1016/0147-1767(86)90015-5

Hofstede, G. (1991). *Cultures and organizations: Software of the mind*. London, UK: McGraw-Hill.

Hofstede, G. (1984). Hofstede culture dimensions - An independent validation using Rokeach value survey. *Journal of Cross-Cultural Psychology, 15*(4), 417–433. doi:10.1177/0022002184015004003

Hofstede, G. (2001). *Culture's consequences: Comparing values, behaviors, institutions, and organizations across nations*. Thousand Oaks, CA: Sage.

Hofstede, G. (1986). Cultural differences in teaching and learning. *International Journal of Intercultural Relations, 10*, 301–320. doi:10.1016/0147-1767(86)90015-5

Hofstede, G., Neuijen, B., Ohayv, D., & Sanders, G. (1990). Measuring organizational cultures: A qualitative and quantitative study of twenty cases. *Administrative Science Quarterly, 35*, 286–316. doi:10.2307/2393392

Holloway, R. E. (1996). Diffusion and adoption of educational technology: A critique of research design. In D. H. Jonassen (Ed.), *Handbook of research for educational communications and technology* (pp. 1107-1136). New York, NY: Simon & Schuster Macmillan.

Holmer, T. (2008). Discourse structure analysis of chat communication. *Language@Internet*. Retrieved March 29, 2009 from: http://www.languageatinternet.de /articles/2008/1633

Holmes, P. (2005). Ethnic Chinese students' communication with cultural others in a New Zealand University. *Communication Education, 54*(4), 289–311. doi:10.1080/03634520500442160

Holmes, D., Hughes, K., & Julian, R. (2007). *Australian sociology: A changing society* (2nd ed.). NSW, Australia: Pearson Education Australia.

Holton, J. A. (2001). Building trust and collaboration in a virtual team. *Team Performance Management, 7*(3/4), 36–47. doi:10.1108/13527590110395621

Holts, T. J., & Graves, D. C. (2007). A qualitative analysis of advance free fraud email schemes. *International Journal of Cyber Criminology, 1*(1), 137–154.

Honeycutt, C., & Cunliffe, D. (2010). The use of the Welsh language on Facebook: An initial investigation. *Information Communication and Society, 13*(2), 226–248. doi:10.1080/13691180902914628

House, R. J., Quigley, N. R., & Sully de Luque, M. (2010). Insights from project GLOBE: Extending global advertising research through a contemporary framework. *International Journal of Advertising, 29*(1), 111–139. doi:10.2501/S0265048709201051

Houston, M. (2004). When black women talk with white women: Why the dialogues are difficult. In Gonzales, A., Houston, M., & Chen, V. (Eds.), *Our voices* (pp. 119–125). Los Angeles, CA: Roxbury Publishing Company.

Hoy, M. G., & Milne, G. (2010). Gender differences in privacy-related measures for young adult Facebook users. *Journal of Interactive Advertising, 10*(2), 28–45.

Hsieh, C. H., Holland, R., & Young, M. (2009). A theoretical model for cross-cultural Web design. *Human-Computer Interaction, 10*, 712–721.

Huang, R. (2008). Mapping educational tourists' experience in the UK: Understanding international students. *Third World Quarterly, 29*(5), 1003–1020. doi:10.1080/01436590802106247

Huang, J. (2010, February 11). 2009 liuxing yuwen yipian: toukecai songgei 2010 (A glimpse of the buzz words in 2009: Stealing a vegetable and present it to 2010 as a gift). *Nanfang Zhoumo (Southern Weekly)*. Retrieved February 18, 2010, from http://nf.nfdaily.cn/nfzm/content/2010-02/11/ content_9188181.htm

Huffaker, D. A., & Calvert, S. L. (2005). Gender, identity, and language use in teenage blogs. *Journal of Computer-Mediated Communication, 10*(2), article 1. Retrieved from http://jcmc.indiana.edu/vol10/issue2/huffaker.html

Hughes, C. R., & Wacker, G. (Eds.). (2003). *China and the Internet: Politics of the digital leap forward*. London, UK & New York, NY: Routledge Curzon.

Human Rights Watch. (2006). *Race to the bottom: Corporate complicity in Chinese Internet Censorship*. New York, NY: Human Rights Watch.

Humbley, J., Vandepitte, S., Maylath, B., Mousten, B., & Veisblat, L. (2005). Learning localization through trans-Atlantic collaboration. In G. F. Hayhoe (Ed.), *Proceedings of the IEEE International Professional Communication Conference*, (pp. 578-595). New York, NY: IEEE.

Hunter, B., White, G. P., & Godbey, G. C. (2006). What does it mean to be globally competent? *Journal of Studies in Intercultural Education, 10*(3), 267–285. doi:10.1177/1028315306286930

Hunter, I. (2008). *Imagine: What Wedgwood, Da Vinci, Mozart, Eiffel, Disney (and many others) can teach us about innovation*. North Shore, New Zealand: Penguin.

Hussi, T. (2003). Reconfiguring knowledge management: Combining intellectual capital, intangible assets and knowledge creation. *Journal of Knowledge Management, 8*(2), 36–52. doi:10.1108/13673270410529091

Hutchby, I. (2001). Technologies, texts and affordances. *Sociology, 35*, 441–456.

Hytten, K., & Bettez, S. C. (2008). Teaching globalization issues to education students: What's the point? *Equity & Excellence in Education, 41*(2), 168–181. doi:10.1080/10665680801957295

IDRC. (2003). *Survey of language computing in Asia*. Retrieved May 12, 2010, from http://www.idrc.ca/uploads/user-S/11446781751Survey.pdf

IDRC. (2010). *African network for localization*. Retrieved May 13, 2010, from http://www.idrc.ca/acacia/ev-122243-201-1-DO_TOPIC.html

Imamichi, T. (1998). The character of Japanese thought. In Imamichi, T., Wang, M., & Liu, F. (Eds.), *The humanization of technology and Chinese culture* (pp. 279–296). Washington, DC/Tokyo, Japan: Kluwer.

Inden, R. B. (1976). *Marriage and rank in Bengali culture: A history of caste and clan in middle period Bengal*. Berkeley, CA: University of California Press.

Inside Facebook. (2009). *College students' Facebook use easing up over the summer, while parents logging on in record numbers*. Retrieved November 20, 2010 from http://www.insidefacebook.com/ 2009/07/06/college-students -facebook-use-easing-up-over -the-summer-while-parents-logging -on-in-record-numbers/

Internet & Mobile Association of India. (2008). *Website*. Retrieved November 23, 2009, from http://www.iamai.in/

Internet World Stats. (2009). *Top 20*. Retrieved November 25, 2009, from http://www.internetworldstats.com / top20.html

Internet World Stats. (2009). *Top ten languages used on the Web*. Retrieved Febuary 1, 2010, from http://www. internetworldstats.com /stats7.htm

Internet.gov.sa. (2010). *Internet in Saudi Arabia*. Retrieved November 15, 2010, from http://www.internet.gov.sa/ learn-the-web/guides/ internet-in-saudi-arabia

Internetworldstats.com. (2009). *United Arab Emirates: Internet usage and marketing report*. Retrieved December 10, 2010, from http://www.internetworldstats.com / me/ae.htm

iResearch. (2007). *A brief report of the study on China's Internet communities*. Retrieved October 10, 2010, from http://www.iresearch.com.cn/Report/Free. asp?classid=&id=1081

Irvine, T. (2006). *Hybrid works best: Looking to professional research to understand why and how hybrid classes best foster basic skills development*. Unpublished raw data, Johnston Community College, Smithfield, NC. Retrieved October 14, 2008, from http://www.mymathlab. com/ redesign_ppts/ jcc.ppt

iUserTracker. (2007). Mop.com: China's "MySpace"-The SNS for self-proclaimed crazy Chinese people. Retrieved October 10, 2010, from http://www.shanghaiexpat.com/ Article1104147.phtml

Ivanic, R. (1998). *Writing and identity: The discoursal construction of identity in academic writing*. Amsterdam, The Netherlands: John Benjamins.

Jackson, L. A., Ervin, K. S., Gardner, P. D., & Schmitt, N. (2008). Gender and the Internet: Women communicating and men searching. *Sex Roles, 44*, 363–380. doi:10.1023/A:1010937901821

Jackson, M., & McDowell, S. (2002). Enhancing discourse on new media within higher education. In W. H. Dutton & B. Loader (Eds.), *Digital academe: New media in higher education and learning* (pp. 318-327). London, UK: Routledge.

Jacobs, M. (2008). Multiculturalism and cultural issues in online gaming communities. *Journal for Cultural Research, 12*(4), 317–334. doi:10.1080/14797580802561182

James, M., & Ward, K. (2001). Leading a multinational team of change agents of Glaxo Welcome. *Journal of Change Management, 2*(2), 148–159. doi:10.1080/714042500

James, R. (2002). *Students' changing expectations of higher education and the consequences of mismatches with reality*. Retrieved October 12, 2010, from http://www1.oecd.org/ publications/ e-book/ 8902041E.pdf

Jana, R. (2000, August 17). Arranged marriages, minus the parents [Electronic version]. *New York Times*. Retrieved September 1, 2009, from http://tech2.nytimes.com/mem /technology/techreview.html?res=940CE7DA163EF934 A2575BC0A9669C8B63

Jansen, D. E., & Riemer, M. J. (2003). Interkulturelle Kommunikation für den globalen Ingenieur. *Global Journal of Engineering Education, 7*(3), 303–310.

Jansen, B. J., Spink, A., & Saracevic, T. (2000). Real life, real users, and real needs: A study and analysis of user queries on the Web. *Information Processing & Management, 36*(2), 207–227. doi:10.1016/S0306-4573(99)00056-4

Jarvenpaa, S. L., & Leidner, D. E. (1999). Communication and trust in global virtual teams. *Organization Science, 10*, 791–815. doi:10.1287/orsc.10.6.791

Jarvenpaa, S. K., Knoll, K., & Leidner, D. E. (1998). Is anybody out there? Antecedents of trust in global virtual teams. *Journal of Management Information Systems, 14*(4), 29–64.

Jha, S., & Adelman, M. (2009). Looking for love in all the white places: A study of skin color preferences on Indian matrimonial and mate-seeking websites. *Studies in South Asian Film and Media, 1*(1), 65–83. doi:10.1386/safm.1.1.65_1

Jiang, M. (in press). Authoritarian deliberation on Chinese Internet. In Leib, E., & He, B. (Eds.), *In search for deliberative democracy in China*. New York, NY: Palgrave MacMillan.

Johansson, F. (2004). *The Medici effect: Breakthrough insights at the intersection of ideas, concepts, and cultures*. Boston, MA: Harvard Business School Press.

Johnson, D. (2010, Mar/Apr). Don't confuse social networking with educational networking. *Library Media Connection, 28*(5), 98–98.

Johnson, D. R. (2006). The new virtual literacy: How the screen affects the law. In Balkin, J. M., & Noveck, B. S. (Eds.), *The state of play: Law, games, and virtual worlds* (pp. 245–256). New York, NY: New York University Press.

Johnson, J. L., & Cullen, J. B. (2002). Trust in cross-cultural relationships. In Cannon, M. J., & Newman, K. L. (Eds.), *The Blackwell handbook of cross-cultural management*. Malden, MA: Blackwell Publishing.

Johnson, D. R., & Post, D. G. (1997). The rise of law on the global network. In Kahin, B., & Nesson, C. (Eds.), *Borders in cyberspace information policy and the global information infrastructure* (pp. 3–47). Cambridge, MA: The MIT Press.

Joinson, A. (1998). Causes and implications of disinhibited behavior on the internet. In Gackenbach, J. (Ed.), *Psychology and the Internet: Intrapersonal, interpersonal and transpersonal implications* (pp. 43–60). San Diego, CA: Academic Press.

Jones, S. (Ed.). (1995). *CyberSociety: Computer-mediated communication and community*. London, UK: Sage.

Jones, S. (Ed.). (1997). *Virtual culture*. London, UK: Sage.

Jones, S. (Ed.). (1998). *CyberSociety 2.0. Revisiting computer-mediated communication and community*. London, UK: Sage.

Jones, C., Ramanau, R., Cross, S., & Healing, G. (2010). Net generation or digital natives: Is there a distinct new generation entering university? *Computers & Education, 54*(3), 722–732. doi:10.1016/j.compedu.2009.09.022

Jordan, A. (2003). *Business anthropology*. Long Grove, IL: Waveland Press.

Joseph, F. Sullivan Center. (2005). *Clemson wellness*. Retrieved October 14, 2006, from http://virtual.Clemson.edu/ groups/ wellness/

Joy, S., & Kolb, D. A. (2009). Are there cultural differences in learning style? *International Journal of Intercultural Relations, 33*, 69–85. doi:10.1016/j.ijintrel.2008.11.002

Joyce, K. M., & Brown, A. (2009). Enhancing social presence in online learning: Mediation strategies applied to social networking tools. *Online Journal of Distance Learning Administration, 12*(4). Retrieved October 10, 2010, from http://www.westga.edu/ ~distance/ ojdla/ winter124/ joyce124.html

Jung, T., Youn, H., & McClung, S. (2007). Motivations and self-presentation strategies on Korean-based "Cyworld" weblog format personal homepages. *Cyberpsychology & Behavior, 10*, 24–31. doi:10.1089/cpb.2006.9996

Jung, I., Choi, S., Lim, C., & Leem, J. (2002). Effects of different types of interaction on learning achievement, satisfaction and participation in Web-based instruction. *Innovations in Education and Teaching International, 39*(2), 153–162. doi:10.1080/14703290252934603

Ju-Pak, K.-H. (1999). Content dimensions of Web advertising: A cross-national comparison. *International Journal of Advertising, 18*(2), 207–231.

Jusoff, K., & Khodabandelou, R. (2009). Preliminary study on the role of social presence in blended learning. *International Education Studies, 2*(4), 79–83.

Kahin, B., & Nesson, C. (Eds.). (1997). *Borders in cyberspace: Information policy and the global information infrastructure*. Cambridge, MA: The MIT Press.

Kalawsky, R. S., Bee, S. T., & Nee, S. P. (1999). Human factors evaluation techniques to aid understanding of virtual interfaces. *BT Technology Journal, 17*, 128–241. doi:10.1023/A:1009687227736

Kaleta, R., & Aycock, A. (2004). *Getting faculty ready for hybrid/blended teaching.* Paper presented at the conference EduCause, Denver, CO.

Kalliny, M., & Gentry, L. (2007). Cultural values reflected in Arab and American television advertising. *Journal of Current Issues and Research in Advertising, 29*(1), 15–32.

Kalyanam, C. (2004). *Seeking an alliance: A psychiatrist's guide to the Indian matrimonial process in America.* Bloomington, IN: iUniverse.

Kamat, V. (2005). *India's arranged marriages.* Retrieved from http://www.kamat.com/indica/ culture/sub-cultures/arranged_marriage.htm

Kanata, T., & Martin, J. N. (2007). Facilitating dialogues on race and ethnicity with technology: Challenging "otherness" and promoting a dialogic way of knowing. *Journal of Literacy and Technology, 8*(2), 1–40.

Kang, D., & Mastin, T. (2008). How cultural difference affects international tourism public relations websites: A comparative analysis using Hofstede's cultural dimensions. *Public Relations Review, 34*(1), 54–56. doi:10.1016/j.pubrev.2007.11.002

Kapiszewski, A. (2006). *Arab versus Asian migrant workers in the GCC countries, United Nations expert group meeting on international migration and development in the Arab region.* New York, NY: Department of Economic and Social Affairs, United Nations Secretariat.

Kapoor, G. (2003). *Partners online.* Retrieved from http://www.rediff.com/netguide /2003/apr/17nri.htm

Karande, K., Almurshide, K. A., & Al-Olayan, F. (2006). Advertising standardisation in culturally similar markets: Can we standardise all components? *International Journal of Advertising, 25*(4), 489–511.

Karson, E. J., McCloy, S., & Bonner, P. G. (2006). An examination of consumer' attitudes and beliefs towards website advertising. *Journal of Current Issues & Research in Advertising, 28*(2), 77–91.

Kasper-Fuehrer, E. C., & Ashkanasy, N. M. (2001). Communicating trustworthiness and building trust in interorganizational virtual organizations. *Journal of Management, 27*, 235–254.

Kastman Breuch, L. (2004). *Virtual peer review: Teaching and learning about writing in online environments.* Albany, NY: SUNY Press.

Katsunori, M. (2010, February 3). Experiences of an international scholar from Japan. Lecture given in the class ENC 4262: International Technical Communication, University of Central Florida, Orlando, FL.

Katz, E., Blumler, J. G., & Gurevitch, M. (1974). Ulilization of mass communication by the individual. In Blumler, J. G., & Katz, E. (Eds.), *The uses of mass communications: Current perspectives on gratifications research* (pp. 19–32). Beverly Hills, CA: Sage.

Kaynay, J. (1998). Contexts of uninhibited online behavior: Flaming in social newsgroups on usenet. *Journal of the American Society for Information Science American Society for Information Science, 49*, 1135–1141. doi:10.1002/(SICI)1097-4571(1998)49:12<1135::AID-ASI8>3.0.CO;2-W

Kehrwald, B. A. (2008). Understanding social presence in text-based online learning environments. *Distance Education, 29*(1), 89–106. doi:10.1080/01587910802004860

Kehrwald, B. (2007). The ties that bind: social presence, relations, and productive collaboration in online learning environments. In *Proceedings of ASCILITE Conference*, Singapore. Retrieved October 10, 2010, from http://www.ascilite.org.au/ conferences/ singapore07/ procs/ kehrwald.pdf

Kekwaletswe, R. M. (2007). Social presence awareness for knowledge transformation in a mobile learning environment. *International Journal of Education and Development using Information and Communication Technology, 3*(4), 102-109.

Kelly, G. A. (1955). *The psychology of personal constructs.* New York, NY: Norton.

Kelly, H. F., Ponton, M. K., & Rovai, A. P. (2007). A comparison on student evaluations of teaching between online and face-to-face courses. *The Internet and Higher Education, 10*(2), 189–101. doi:10.1016/j.iheduc.2007.02.001

Kelly, R. (2010, April). Finding the right community-building tools for your online course. *Online Classroom*, 1-7.

Keniston, K. (2001). Language, power and software. In Ess, C. (Ed.), *Culture, technology, communication: Towards an intercultural global village* (pp. 283–306). Albany, NY: State University of New York Press.

Kesan, J. P., & Shah, R. C. (2005). Shaping code. *Harvard Journal of Law & Technology, 18*, 319–399.

Kiesler, S., Siegel, J., & McGuire, T. W. (1984). Social psychological aspects of computer-mediated communication. *The American Psychologist, 39*, 1123–1134. doi:10.1037/0003-066X.39.10.1123

Kim, H., & Papacharissi, Z. (2003). Cross-cultural differences in online self-presentation: A content analysis of personal Korean and US home pages. *Asian Journal of Communication, 13*(1), 100–119. doi:10.1080/01292980309364833

Kim, K.-H., & Yun, H. (2007). Cying for me, Cying for us: Relational dialectics in a Korea social network site. *Journal of Computer-Mediated Communication, 13*(1), 298–318. doi:10.1111/j.1083-6101.2007.00397.x

Kim, H., Coyle, J. R., & Gould, S. J. (2009). Collectivist and individualist influences on website design in South Korea and the U.S.: A cross-cultural content analysis. *Journal of Computer Mediated Communication, 14*(3), 581-601. Retrieved January 10, 2011 from http://onlinelibrary. wiley.com /doi/10.1111/j.1083-6101.2009.01454.x/full

Kim, K. H., & Yun, H. (2007). Cying for me, cying for us: Relational dialectics in a Korean social network site. *Journal of Computer-Mediated Communication, 13*(1), article 15. Retrieved November 20, 2010, from http:// jcmc.indiana.edu/vol13 /issue1/kim.yun.html

Kim, K., & Bonk, C. J. (2002). Cross-cultural comparisons of online collaboration. *Journal of Computer-Mediated Communication, 8*(1). Retrieved November 25, 2010, from http://jcmc.indiana.edu/vol8/issue1/kimandbonk.html

Kingston, E., & Forland, H. (2008). Bridging the gap in expectations between international students and academic staff. *Journal of Studies in International Education, 12*(2), 204–220. doi:10.1177/1028315307307654

Kiser, K. (1999, March). Working on world time. *Training (New York, N.Y.), 36*(3), 28–34.

Kishi, M. (2008). Perceptions and use of electronic media: Testing the relationship between organizational interpretation differences and media richness. *Information & Management, 45*(5), 281–287. doi:10.1016/j. im.2008.02.008

Kluver, R. (2005). US and Chinese policy expectations of the Internet. *China Information, 19*(2), 299–324. doi:10.1177/0920203X05054685

Koch, R., & Leitner, K.-H. (2008). The dynamics and functions of self-organization in the fuzzy front end: Empirical evidence from the Austrian semiconductor industry. *Creativity and Innovation Management, 17*(3), 216–226. doi:10.1111/j.1467-8691.2008.00488.x

Kock, N. (1998). Can communication medium limitations foster better group outcomes? An action research study. *Information & Management, 34*(5), 295–305. doi:10.1016/ S0378-7206(98)00066-4

Koerber, A., & Lay, M. (2002). Understanding women's concerns in the international setting through the lens of science and technology. In Lay, M. M., Monk, J., & Rosenfelt, D. S. (Eds.), *Encompassing gender: Integrating international studies and women's studies* (pp. 353–367). New York, NY: Feminist Press.

Kohima, K. (2005). A decade in the development of mobile communication in Japan (1993-2002). In Ito, M., Okabe, D., & Matsuda, M. (Eds.), *Personal, portable, pedestrian: Mobile phones in Japanese life* (pp. 61–75). Cambridge, MA: The MIT Press.

Kolb, D. (1985). *Learning style inventory*. Boston, MA: McBer and Company.

Kollock, P., & Smith, M. A. (1999). Communities in cyberspace. In Smith, M. A., & Kollock, P. (Eds.), *Communities in cyberspace* (pp. 1–26). New York, NY: Routledge.

Korgaonkar, P. K., & Wolin, L. D. (1999). A multivariate analysis of Web usage. *Journal of Advertising Research, 39*(2), 53–68.

Koutsogiannis, D., & Mitsikopoulou, B. (2007). Greeklish and Greekness: Trends and discourses of "Glocalness.". In Danet, B., & Herring, S. C. (Eds.), *The multilingual Internet: Language, culture, and communication online* (pp. 142–162). New York: Oxford University Press.

Krause, K.-L., Hartley, R., James, R., & McInnis, C. (2005). *The first year experience in Australian universities: Findings from a decade of national studies.*

Kreps, G. L., & Kunimoto, E. N. (1994). *Effective communication in multicultural healthcare settings.* Thousand Oaks, CA: Sage.

Kreyenbroek, P. (1992). On the Kurdish language. In Kreyenbroek, P. G., & Sperl, S. (Eds.), *The Kurds: A contemporary overview* (pp. 68–83). London, UK: Routledge.

Krishnamurthi, M. (2003). Assessing multicultural initiatives in higher education institutions. *Assessment & Evaluation in Higher Education, 28*(3), 263–277. doi:10.1080/0260293032000059621

Kulkarni, K. G. (2005). *Effect of globalization on India's economic growth.* Paper presented in the Oxford Roundtable Conference. Oxford University, UK.

Kurian, G. (1961). *The Indian family in transition: A case study of Kerala Syrian Christians.* The Hague, the Netherlands: Mouton and Company.

Kurop, M. C. (1998). Greece and Turkey: Can they mend fences? *Foreign Affairs (Council on Foreign Relations), 77*(1), 7–12. doi:10.2307/20048357

Kurthen, H., & Smith, G. G. (2005/2006). Hybrid online face-to-face teaching: When is it an efficient learning tool? *International Journal of Learning, 12*(5), 237–245.

Kurzweil, R. (2005). *The singularity is near: When humans transcend biology.* New York, NY: Viking.

Kymlicka, W., & Straehle, C. (1999). Cosmopolitanism, nation-states, and minority nationalism: A critical review of recent literature. *European Journal of Philosophy, 7*(1), 65–88. doi:10.1111/1468-0378.00074

La Cruz, A. A. (2007). Fatalismo reconsidered: A cautionary note for health-related research and practice with Latino populations. *Ethnicity & Disease, 17*(1), 153–158.

Lab, L. (2010). *Second Life blogs: Features: 2009 end of year Second Life economy wrap up (including Q4 economy in detail).* Second Life. Retrieved May 3, 2010, from http://blogs.secondlife.com/ community/ features/ blog/ 2010/ 01/ 19/ 2009-end-of-year-second-life-economy-wrap-up-including-q4- economy-in-detail

Lai, M., & Law, N. (2006). Peer scaffolding of knowledge building through collaborative groups with differential learning experiences. *Journal of Educational Computing Research, 35*(2), 123–144. doi:10.2190/GW42-575W-Q301-1765

Lai, C. C., & Kritsonis, W. A. (2006). Advantages and disadvantages of computer technology in second language learning. *National Journal for Publishing and Mentoring Doctoral Student Research, 3*(1), 1–6.

Lajoie, S., Garcia, B., Berdugo, G., Márquez, L., Espíndola, S., & Nakamura, C. (2006). The creation of virtual and face-to-face learning communities: An international collaboration experience. *Journal of Educational Computing Research, 35*(2), 163–180. doi:10.2190/1G77-3371-K225-7840

Lam, W. S. E. (2000). L2 literacy and the design of the self: A case study of a teenager writing on the Internet. *TESOL Quarterly, 34*(3), 457–482. doi:10.2307/3587739

Lanigan, R. L. (1988). *Phenomenology of communication: Merleau-Ponty's thematics in communicology and semiology.* Pittsburgh, PA: Duquesne University Press.

Larson, D. G., & Chung-Hsien, S. (2009). Comparing student performance: Online versus blended versus face to face. *Journal of Asynchronous Learning Networks, 13*(1), 31–42.

Laurillard, D. (2009). The pedagogical challenges to collaborative technologies. *International Journal of Computer-Supported Collaborative Learning, 4*(1), 5–20. doi:10.1007/s11412-008-9056-2

Lavidge, R. J., & Steiner, G. A. (1961). A model for predictive measurements of advertising effectiveness. *Journal of Marketing, 25*, 59–62. doi:10.2307/1248516

Law, S. F., & Leonard, D. P. (2004). *Culture, language and online dispute resolution.* RMIT University and Dispute Settlement Centre Victoria, Department of Justice. Retrieved November 15, 2010, from http://www.odr.info/unforum2004/law_leonard.htm

Lay, M. (2000). *The rhetoric of midwifery: Gender, knowledge, and power.* New Brunswick, NJ: Rutgers University Press.

Lea, M., O'Shea, T., Fung, P., & Spears, R. (1992). "Flaming" in computer-mediated communication: Observations, explanations, implications. In M. Lea (Ed.), *Context of computer-mediated communication* (pp. 89-112). London, England: Harvester- Wheatsheaf.

Lee, O. (2002). Cultural differences in email use of virtual teams a critical social theory perspective. *Cyberpsychology & Behavior, 5*(3), 227–232. doi:10.1089/109493102760147222

Lee, J. J., & Rice, C. (2007). Welcome to America? International student perceptions of discrimination. *Higher Education, 53*, 381–409. doi:10.1007/s10734-005-4508-3

Lee, W.-N., & Choi, S. M. (2007). Classifying web users: A cultural value based approach. In St.Amant, K. (Ed.), *Linguistic and cultural online communication issues in the global age* (pp. 45–62). Hershey, PA: Idea Group, Inc.doi:10.4018/978-1-59904-213-8.ch004

Leeds-Hurwitz, W. (1990). Notes on the history of intercultural communication: The Foreign Service Institute and the mandate for intercultural training. *The Quarterly Journal of Speech, 76*, 262–281. doi:10.1080/00335639009383919

Lenhart, A. (2009). Adults and social network websites. *Pew Internet & American Life Project*. Retrieved November 20, 2010, from http://www.pewinternet.org/PPF /r/272/report_display.asp

Lenhart, A., & Madden, M. (2007). *Social networking websites and teens: An overview*. Pew Internet & American Life Project. Retrieved November 20, 2010, from http://www.pewinternet.org

Leonard, D., & Swap, W. (2004). *Deep smarts: How to cultivate and transfer enduring business wisdom*. Cambridge, MA: Harvard Business Press.

Lessig, L. (2006). *Code and other laws of cyberspace version*. New York, NY: Basic Books.

Lessig, L. (2006). *Code: And other laws of cyberspace, version 2.0*. New York, NY: Basic Books.

Lessig, L. (2001). *The future of ideas: The fate of the commons in a connected world* (1st ed.). New York, NY: Random House.

Lessig, L. (2004). *Free culture: How big media uses technology and the law to lock down culture and control creativity*. New York, NY: Penguin Press.

Lessig, L. (2008). *Remix: Making art and commerce thrive in the hybrid economy*. New York, NY: Penguin Press.

Levin, D., & Arafeh, S. (2002). *The digital disconnect: The widening gap between Internet-savvy students and their schools*. Washington, DC: Pew Internet & American Life. Retrieved August 14, 2002, from http://www.pewinternet.org

Levy, P. (2001). *Cyberculture*. Minneapolis, MN: University of Minnesota Press.

Lewis, C. C., & George, J. F. (2008). Cross-cultural deception in social networking sites and face-to-face communication. *Computers in Human Behavior, 24*, 2945–2964. doi:10.1016/j.chb.2008.05.002

Lewis, R. D. (2000). *When cultures collide: Managing successfully across cultures*. London, England: Nicholas Brealy Publishing.

Li, H., Li, A., & Zhao, S. (2009). Internet advertising strategy of multinationals in China: A cross-cultural analysis. *International Journal of Advertising, 28*(1), 125–146. doi:10.2501/S0265048709090441

Li, S., Hsieh, H., & Sun, I. (2003). *An ontology-based knowledge management system for the metal industry*. Retrieved April 23, 2004, from http://www2003.org/ cdrom/ papers/alternate/P620 /p620-li.html

Liaw, S.-S., Huang, H.-M., & Chen, G.-D. (2007). Surveying instructor and learner attitudes toward e-learning. *Computers & Education, 49*, 1066–1080. doi:10.1016/j.compedu.2006.01.001

Lim, J., Kim, M., Chen, S. S., & Ryder, C. E. (2008). An empirical investigation of student achievement and satisfaction in different learning environments. *Journal of Instructional Psychology, 35*(2), 113–119.

Lim, T. (2002). Language and verbal communication across cultures. In Gudykunst, W., & Mody, B. (Eds.), *Handbook of international and intercultural communication* (pp. 69–87). Thousand Oaks, CA: Sage.

Lin, C. A. (1998). Exploring personal computer adoption dynamics. *Journal of Broadcasting & Electronic Media, 42*, 95–112.

Lin, S., & Overbaugh, R. C. (2009). Computer-mediated discussion, self-efficacy and gender. *British Journal of Educational Technology, 40*(6), 999–1013. doi:10.1111/j.1467-8535.2008.00889.x

Lin, G. (2002). 网络用语的类型及其特征 [Categorization and Characteristics of Internet language]. Xiuci xuexi [Learning Rhetorics], 1, 26-27.

Lipartito, K. (2003). Picturephone and the information age: The social meaning of failure. *Technology and Culture, 44*(1), 50–81. doi:10.1353/tech.2003.0033

Livingston, B. (2010). Using Web 2.0 technologies. *Infoline, 1001*(27), 1–14.

Livingston, G., Minushkin, S., & Cohn, V. (2008). *Hispanics and health care in the United States.* Retrieved March 13, 2010, from. http://pewhispanic.org/reports/report.php? ReportID=91

Livingstone, S. (2008). Taking risky opportunities in youth content creation: Teenagers' use of social networking sites for intimacy, privacy and self-expression. *New Media & Society, 10*, 393–411. doi:10.1177/1461444808089415

Livingstone, D. (2009). *Online learning in virtual environments with SLOODLE.* San Jose, CA: San José State University School of Library and Information Science.

Localization, P. A. N. (2010). *PAN localization: Building local language computing capacity in Asia.* Retrieved May 12, 2010, from http://www.idrc.ca/en/ev-51828-201-1-DO_TOPIC.html

Loch, K. D., Straub, D. W., & Kamel, S. (2003). Diffusing the Internet in the Arab World: The role of social norms and technological acculturation. *IEEE Transactions on Engineering Management, 50*(1), 45–63. doi:10.1109/TEM.2002.808257

Long, G. L., Vignare, K., Rappold, R. P., & Mallory, J. (2007). Access to communication for deaf, hard-of-hearing and ESL students in blended learning courses. *International Review of Research in Open and Distance Learning, 8*(3), 1–13.

Lovitt, C. with Goswami, D. (1999). *Exploring the rhetoric of international professional communication: An agenda for teachers and researchers.* Amityville, NY: Baywood.

Lu, G. (2008). *Old school BBS: The Chinese social networking phenomenon.* Retrieved October 10, 2010, from http://www.readwriteweb.com/archives/bbs_china_social_networking.php

Lu, J., Huang, W., Ma, H., & Luce, T. (2007). Interaction and social presence in technology-mediated learning: A partial least squares model. In *Proceedings IEEE 3rd International Conference on Wireless Communications, Networking and Mobile Computing* (pp.4411-4414). Shanghai, China.

Lujan, J. (2008, February). Difference=flavor: Embracing cultural diversity in online learning. *Online Classroom, 2*, 8.

Lukacs, G. (1971). *History and class consciousness: Studies in Marxist dialectics* (Livingston, R., Trans.). Cambridge, MA: The MIT Press.

Lum, T. (2006). Internet development and information control in the People's Republic of China.

Luna, D., Peracchio, L. A., & de Juan, M. D. (2002). Cross-cultural and cognitive aspects of website navigation. *Journal of the Academy of Marketing Science, 30*(4), 397–410. doi:10.1177/009207002236913

Macdonald, J. (2004). Developing competent e-learners: The role of assessment. *Assessment & Evaluation in Higher Education, 29*(2), 215–226. doi:10.1080/0260293042000188483

Macfadyen, L. P. (2008). The perils of parsimony: National culture as red herring? In F. Sudweeks, H. Hrachovec & C. Ess (Eds), *Proceedings, 6th International Conference on Cultural Attitudes Towards Communication and Technology, Nimes, France* (pp. 569-580). School of Information Technology, Murdoch University, Australia.

MacKenzie, D. A. (1996). *Knowing machines: Essays on technical change.* Cambridge, MA: The MIT Press.

MacKinnon, R. (2008). Blogs and China correspondence: Lessons about global information flows. *Chinese Journal of Communication, 1*(2), 242–257. doi:10.1080/17544750802288081

MacKinnon, R. (2008). Flatter world and thicker walls? Blogs, censorship and civic discourse in China. *Public Choice, 134*(1/2), 31–46.

MacKinnon, R. (2009). China's censorship 2.0: How companies censor bloggers. *First Monday, 14.* Retrieved October 10, 2010, from http://firstmonday.org/htbin/cgiwrap/bin/ojs/index.php/fm/article/view/2378/2089

Maedche, A., & Staab, S. (2001). Ontology learning for the Semantic Web. *IEEE Intelligent Systems, 16*(2), 72–79. doi:10.1109/5254.920602

Mair, C. (2002). The continuing spread of English: Anglo-American conspiracy or global grassroots movement? In Allerton, D. J., Skandera, P., & Tschichold, C. (Eds.), *Perspectives on English as a world language* (pp. 159–169). Basel, Switzerland: Schwable.

Malaby, T. M. (2009). *Making virtual worlds: Linden Lab and Second Life.* Ithaca, NY: Cornell University Press.

Malmisanij, M. (2006). *The past and the present of book publishing in Kurdish language in Turkey.* Next Page Foundation. Retrieved July 10, 2007, from http://www.npage.org/article126.html

Marcus, S. (2006). Measure by measure: How WBT can help create a social online presence. *Campus-Wide Information Systems, 23*(2), 56–67. doi:10.1108/10650740610654447

Markus, H. R., & Kitayama, S. (1991). Culture and the self: Implications for cognition, emotion, and motivation. *Psychological Review, 98*(2), 224–253. doi:10.1037/0033-295X.98.2.224

Marshall, T. C. (2008). Cultural differences in intimacy: The influence of gender-role ideology and individualism-collectivism. *Journal of Social and Personal Relationships, 25*(1), 143–168. doi:10.1177/0265407507086810

Martin, J. N., & Nakayama, T. K. (1999). Thinking dialectically about culture and communication. *Communication Theory, 9*, 1–25. doi:10.1111/j.1468-2885.1999.tb00160.x

Martin, J. N., & Nakayama, T. K. (2009). *Intercultural communication in contexts* (5th ed.). Boston, MA: McGraw Hill.

Martin, E. (1994). *Flexible bodies: The role of immunity in American culture from the days of polio to the age of AIDS.* Boston, MA: Beacon Press.

Martin, E. (2001). *The woman in the body: A cultural analysis of reproduction.* Boston, MA: Beacon Press.

Martin, J. N., & Nakayama, T. K. (1999). Thinking dialectically about culture and communication. *Communication Theory, 9*, 1–25. doi:10.1111/j.1468-2885.1999.tb00160.x

Martin, J. N., & Nakayama, T. K. (2011). Intercultural communication dialectics revisited. In Halualani, R. T., & Nakayama, T. K. (Eds.), *The handbook of critical intercultural communication* (pp. 59–83). Malden, MA: Blackwell.

Martinez, J. (2000). *Phenomenology of Chicana experience and identity.* Lanham, MD: Rowman & Littlefield.

Martinez, J. (2006). Semiotic phenomenology and intercultural communication scholarship: Meeting the challenge of racial, ethnic, and cultural difference. *Western Journal of Communication, 70*(4), 292–310. doi:10.1080/10570310600992103

Martinez, J. (2008). Semiotic phenomenology and the dialectical approach to intercultural communication: Paradigm crisis and the actualities of research practice. *Semiotica, 169*, 135–153. doi:10.1515/SEM.2008.028

Mason, R., & Rennie, F. (2007). Using Web 2.0 for learning in the community. *The Internet and Higher Education, 10*, 196–203. doi:10.1016/j.iheduc.2007.06.003

Massey, A. P., Montoya-Weiss, M., Hung, C., & Ramesh, V. (2001). Cultural perceptions of task-technology fit. *Communications of the ACM, 44*(12), 83–84. doi:10.1145/501317.501353

Matsuda, P. K., & Silva, T. (2006). Cross-cultural composition: Mediated integration of U.S. and international students. In Matsuda, P., Cox, M., Jordan, C., & Ortmeier-Hooper, C. (Eds.), *Second language writing in the composition classroom: A critical sourcebook* (pp. 246–259). New York, NY: Bedford/St. Martin's Press.

Mattelart, A. (1995). Unequal voices. *The Unesco Courier, 48*(2), 11.

Maturana, H. R., & Varela, F. J. (1992). *The tree of knowledge: The biological roots of human understanding.* New York, NY: Shambhala.

Mau, B., Leonard, J., & Institute without Boundaries. (2004). *Massive change.* London, UK: Phaidon.

Maureen, E. H., Detlor, B., Toms, E., & Trifts, V. (2009). *Online information seeking: Understanding individual differences and search contexts.* Paper presented at the The annual Americas' Conference on Information Systems (AMCIS) 2009, San Francisco, California.

Mavrou, K., Lewis, A., & Graeme, D. (2010). Researching computer-based collaborative learning in inclusive classroom in Cyprus: The role of computer in pupils' interaction. *British Journal of Educational Technology, 41*(3), 486–501. doi:10.1111/j.1467-8535.2009.00960.x

May, G. L., & Short, D. (2003). Gardening in cyberspace: A metaphor to enhance online teaching and learning. *Journal of Management Education, 27,* 673–693. doi:10.1177/1052562903257940

Mayer-Schönberger, V., & Foster, T. E. (1997). A regulatory Web: Free speech and the global information infrastructure. In Kahin, B., & Nesson, C. (Eds.), *Borders in cyberspace: Information policy and the global information infrastructure* (pp. 235–254). Cambridge, MA: The MIT Press.

Mayes, J. T., & de Freitas, S. (2004). *Review of e-learning theories, frameworks and models.* JISC e-Learning Models Desk Study. Retrieved December 10, 2010, from http://www.jisc.ac.uk/ uploaded_documents/ Stage%202%20 Learning% 20Models%20(Version%201).pdf

Maylath, B. (1997). Writing globally: Teaching the technical writing student to prepare documents for translation. *Journal of Business and Technical Communication, 11*(3), 339–352. doi:10.1177/1050651997011003006

Maylath, B., & Thrush, E. (2000). Café, thé, ou lait? Teaching technical communicators to manage translation and localization. In Hager, P. J., & Schreiber, H. J. (Eds.), *Managing global communication in science and technology* (pp. 233–254). New York, NY: John Wiley & Sons.

Maylath, B., Vandepitte, S., & Mousten, B. (2008). Growing grassroots partnerships: Trans-Atlantic collaboration between American instructors and students of technical writing and European instructors and students of translation. In Starke-Meyerring, D., & Wilson, M. (Eds.), *Designing global learning environments: Visionary partnerships, policies, and pedagogies* (pp. 52–66). Rotterdam, The Netherlands: Sense Publishers.

Mays, L. (2008). The cultural divide of discourse: Understanding how English-language learners' primary discourse influences acquisition of literacy. *The Reading Teacher, 61*(5), 415–418. doi:10.1598/RT.61.5.6

Maznevski, M. L., & Chudoba, K. M. (2000). Bridging space over time: Global virtual team dynamics and effectiveness. *Organization Science, 11*(5), 473–492. doi:10.1287/orsc.11.5.473.15200

McCool, M. (2006, December). Adapting e-learning for Japanese audiences. *IEEE Transactions on Professional Communication, 49*(4), 335–345. doi:10.1109/TPC.2006.885870

McCool, M. (2008). Negotiating the design of globally networked learning environments: The case of a collaborative online learning module about the Sonoran biosphere. In Starke-Meyerring, D., & Wilson, M. (Eds.), *Designing global learning environments: Visionary partnerships, policies, and pedagogies* (pp. 200–217). Rotterdam, The Netherlands: Sense Publishers.

McDowall, D. (2004). *A modern history of the Kurds* (3rd ed.). London, UK: I. B. Tauris.

McGonigal, J. (2007). The puppet master problem: Design for real-world, mission-based gaming. In Harrigan, P., & Wardrip-Fruin, N. (Eds.), *Second person: Role-playing and story in games and playable media* (pp. 251–264). Cambridge, MA: The MIT Press.

McLoughlin, C. (1999). Culturally responsive technology use: Developing an online community of learners. *British Journal of Educational Technology, 30*(3), 231–243. doi:10.1111/1467-8535.00112

McLuhan, M. (1962). *The Gutenberg galaxy: The making of typographic man.* Toronto, Canada: University of Toronto Press.

McPhail, T. L. (2006). *Global communication: Theories, stakeholders and trends* (2nd ed.). Malden, MA: Wiley-Blackwell.

McRae, P. (2006). *Transcendent opportunities for global communication & collaboration in education.* Paper presented at the Society for Information Technology & Teacher Education International Conference 2006, Orlando, Florida, USA.

Means, B., Toyama, Y., Murphy, R., Bakia, M., & Jones, K. (2009). *Evaluation of evidence-based practices in online learning: A meta-analysis and review of online learning studies.* Washington, DC: U. S. Department of Education.

Meddah, M. M. (2009). *Active Facebook users in Middle East & North Africa.* Retrieved December 10, 2010, from http://www.startuparabia.com/ 2009/08/active-facebook -users-in-middle-east-north-africa/

MedlinePlus en español. (2010). Retrieved March 13, 2010, from http://medlineplus.gov/spanish

MedlinePlus. (2010). Retrieved March 13, 2010, from http://medlineplus.gov

Mehra, B., Merkel, C., & Bishop, A. P. (2004). The Internet for empowerment of minority and marginalized users. *New Media & Society, 6,* 781–802. doi:10.1177/146144804047513

Mehrabian, A. (1969). Some referents and measures of nonverbal behavior. *Behavior Research Methods and Instruction, 1*(6), 205–207.

Melissen, J. (2005). *Wielding soft power: The new public diplomacy.* The Hague, The Netherlands: Netherlands Institute of International Relations Clingendael.

Melrose, R. (1991). *The communicative syllabus: A systemic functional approach to language teaching.* London, UK: Pinter.

Menchaca, M. P., & Bekele, T. A. (2008). Learner and instructor identified success factors in distance education. *Distance Education, 29*(3), 231–252. doi:10.1080/01587910802395771

Meng, Z., & Zuo, M. (2008). Why MSN lost to QQ in China market? Different privacy protection design. *International Journal of Security and Its Applications, 2,* 81–87.

Menon, V. (2008). *UAE second in world list for online social networking.* Retrieved December 10, 2010, from http://www.arabianbusiness.com/532785-uae-second-in-world-list-for-online-social-networking?ln=en.

Mentzer, G. A., Cryan, J., & Teclehaimanot, B. (2007). Two peas in a pod? A comparison of face-to-face and Web-based classrooms. *Journal of Technology and Teacher Education, 15*(2), 233–246.

Merryfield, M. (2003). Like a veil: Cross-cultural experiential learning online. *Contemporary Issues in Technology & Teacher Education, 3,* 146–171.

Merryfield, M. M. (2001). The paradoxes of teaching a multicultural education course online. *Journal of Teacher Education, 52*(4), 283–299. doi:10.1177/0022487101052004003

Mesdag, M. V. (2000). Culture-sensitive adaptation or global standardization-the duration of usage hypothesis. *International Marketing Review, 17,* 74–84. doi:10.1108/02651330010314722

Mestre, L. (2006). Accommodating diverse learning styles in an online environment. *Reference and User Services Quarterly, 46*(2), 27–32.

Metsch, L. R., McCoy, C. B., McCoy, V., Pereyra, M., Trapido, E., & Miles, C. (1998). The role of physician as information source in mammography. *Cancer Practice, 6,* 229–236. doi:10.1046/j.1523-5394.1998.006004229.x

Meyerson, D., Weick, K., & Kramer, R. (1996). Swift trust and temporary groups. In Kramer, R. M., & Tyler, T. R. (Eds.), *Trust in organizations: Frontiers of theory and research* (pp. 166–195). Thousand Oaks, CA: Sage.

Microsoft. (2010a). *Windows language interface pack.* Retrieved May 12, 2010, from http://msdn.microsoft.com/en-us/goglobal/bb688177.aspx

Microsoft. (2010b). *Microsoft local language program: A world of possibilities.* Retrieved May 12, 2010, from http://download.microsoft.com/download/A/2/3/A23A01D2-4B26-4E8B-9A92-F4FD57256404/LLP_Overview_Brochure.pdf

Microsoft. (2010c, February 22). *More than 1 billion speakers of endangered languages get access to technology.* Retrieved May 12, 2010, from http://www.microsoft.com/presspass/press/2010/feb10/02-22mld10pr.mspx

Microsoft. (2010d). *Opening new worlds for everyone.* Retrieved May 13, 2010, from http://download.microsoft.com/download/2/0/A/20AC945C-34D0-4A60-8245-F80E80FE954F/UP_Factsheet_A4_English_0109.pdf

Middleton, D. (2010). Putting the learning into e-learning. *European Political Science, 9*(1), 5–12. doi:10.1057/eps.2009.37

Miksa, F. L. (1998). *The DDC, the universe of knowledge and the post-modern library.* Albany, NY: OCLC Forest Press.

Miles, L. (1997). Globalizing professional writing curricula: Positioning students and re-positioning textbooks. *Technical Communication Quarterly, 6,* 179–200. doi:10.1207/s15427625tcq0602_4

Mills, J., & Clark, M. S. (1982). Exchange and communal relationships. *Review of Personality and Social Psychology, 6,* 91–127.

Mills, K. (2002). Cybernations: Identity, self-determination, democracy and the "Internet effect" in the emerging information order. *Global Society, 16*(1), 69–87. doi:10.1080/09537320120111915

Mittal, B. (1994). Public assessment of TV advertising: Faint praise and harsh criticism. *Journal of Advertising Research, 34*(1), 35–53.

Mizoguchi, R. (2003). Tutorial on ontological engineering. *New Generation Computing, 21*(4), 365–384. doi:10.1007/BF03037311

Mo, P., Malik, S., & Coulson, N. (2009). Gender differences in computer-mediated communication: a systematic literature review of online health-related support groups. *Patient Education and Counseling, 75*(1), 16–24. doi:10.1016/j.pec.2008.08.029

Mo, P. K., Malik, S. H., & Coulson, N. S. (2009). Gender differences in computer-mediated communication: A systematic literature review of online health-related support groups. *Patient Education and Counseling, 75*(1), 16–24. doi:10.1016/j.pec.2008.08.029

Mobile marvels. (2009, September 24). *The Economist.* Retrieved November 25, 2010, from http://www.economist.com/node/14483896

Moenaert, R. K., Caeldries, F., Lievens, A., & Wauters, E. (2000). Communication flows in international product innovation teams. *Journal of Product Innovation Management, 17,* 360–377. doi:10.1016/S0737-6782(00)00048-5

Monolescu, D., Schifter, C. C., & Greenwood, L. (2004). *The distance education evolution: Issues and case studies.* Hershey, PA: Information Science Publishing.

Mooij, M. (1998). *Global marketing and advertising: Understanding cultural paradoxes.* Thousand Oaks, CA.

Moon, D. G. (1996). Concepts of culture: Implications for intercultural communication research. *Communication Quarterly, 44,* 70–84. doi:10.1080/01463379609370001

Moon, Y. (1999). The effects of physical distance and response latency on persuasion in computer-mediated communication and human-computer communication. *Journal of Experimental Psychology, 5,* 379–392.

Moore, M. G. (2006). Editorial: Questions of culture. *American Journal of Distance Education, 20*(1), 1–5. doi:10.1207/s15389286ajde2001_1

Moore, C. (2002). Diving into data. *InfoWorld.* Retrieved November 14, 2004, from http://www.infoworld.com/article/02/10/25/021028 feundata_1.html

Morse, K. (2003). Does one size fit all? Exploring asynchronous learning in a multicultural environment. *Journal of Asynchronous Learning Networks, 7*(1), 37–55.

Mortensen, T. E. (2009). *Perceiving play: The art and study of computer games.* New York, NY: Peter Lang.

Mousten, B., Maylath, B., Vandepitte, S., & Humbley, J. (2010). Learning localization through trans-Atlantic collaboration: Bridging the gap between professions. *IEEE Transactions on Professional Communication, 53,* 401–411. doi:10.1109/TPC.2010.2077481

Mousten, B., Vandepitte, S., & Maylath, B. (2008). Intercultural collaboration in the trans-Atlantic project: Pedagogical theories and practices in teaching procedural instructions across cultural contexts. In Starke-Meyerring, D., & Wilson, M. (Eds.), *Designing global learning environments: Visionary partnerships, policies, and pedagogies* (pp. 129–144). Rotterdam, The Netherlands: Sense Publishers.

Muhamad-Brandner, C. (2009). Biculturalism online: Exploring the Web space of Aotearoa/New Zealand. *Journal of Information. Communication and Ethics in Society*, *7*(2/3), 182–191. doi:10.1108/14779960910955891

Mumby, D. K. (1997). Modernism, postmodernism, and communication studies: A rereading of an ongoing debate. *Communication Theory*, *7*, 1–28. doi:10.1111/j.1468-2885.1997.tb00140.x

Munkvold, E. (2005). Experiences from global e-collaboration: Contextual influences on technology adoption and use. *IEEE Transactions on Professional Communication*, *48*(1), 78–86. doi:10.1109/TPC.2005.843300

Murguía, A., Zea, M. C., Reisen, C. A., & Petersen, R. A. (2000). The development of the Cultural Health Attributions Questionnaire (CHAQ). *Cultural Diversity & Ethnic Minority Psychology*, *6*, 268–283. doi:10.1037/1099-9809.6.3.268

Murphy, E. (2005). Issues in the adoption of broadband-enabled learning. *British Journal of Educational Technology*, *36*(3), 525–536. doi:10.1111/j.1467-8535.2005.00490.x

Muwanguzi, S., & Lin, L. (2010). Wrestling with online learning technologies: Blind students' struggle to achieve academic success. *International Journal of Distance Education Technologies*, *8*(2), 43–57. doi:10.4018/jdet.2010040104

Mykota, D., & Duncan, R. (2007). Learner characteristics as predictors of online social presence. *Canadian Journal of Education*, *30*(1), 157–170. doi:10.2307/20466630

Na Ubon, A., & Kimble, C. (2003). Supporting the creation of social presence in online learning communities using asynchronous text-based CMC. In *Proceedings of the 3rd International Conference on Technology in Teaching and Learning in Higher Education* (pp.295-300). Heidelberg, Germany.

NAFSA. Association of International Educators. (2007, Nov. 12). *Press Release: Latest survey indicates continued slow growth in international enrollments*. Retrieved June 11, 2009, from http://www.nafsa.org/ press_releases.sec/ press_releases.pg/ latest_survey_indicates

National Alliance for Hispanic Health. (2010). Retrieved March 25, 2010, from http://www.hispanichealth.org/

Naughton, J. (2000). *A brief history of the future*. Woodstock, NY: The Overlook Press.

Nawyn, M. D. (2007). *Code red: Responding to the moral hazards facing U. S. Information*.

Nelson, M. R., & Shavitt, S. (2002). Horizontal and vertical individualism and achievement values: A multimethod examination of Denmark and the United States. *Journal of Cross-Cultural Psychology*, *33*, 439–458. doi:10.1177/0022022102033005001

Nelson, M., & Otnes, C. C. (2005). Exploring cross-cultural ambivalence: A netnography of intercultural wedding message boards. *Journal of Business Research*, *58*(1), 89–95. doi:10.1016/S0148-2963(02)00477-0

Nelson, D. E., Brownson, R. C., Remington, P. L., & Parvanta, C. (Eds.). (2002). *Communicating public health information effectively: a guide for practitioners*. Washington, DC: American Public Health Association.

Nelson, K., Kift, S., & Clarke, J. (2008). *Expectations and realities for first year students at an Australian university*. Paper presented at the First Year in Higher Education Conference 2008. Retrieved November 10, 2009, from http://www.fyhe.qut.edu.au/ past_papers/ papers08/ FYHE08/ content/ pdfs/ 6a.pdf

Newman, R., & Johnson, F. (1999). Sites for power and knowledge? Towards a critique of the virtual university. *British Journal of Sociology of Education*, *20*(1), 79–88. doi:10.1080/01425699995515

Nielsen NetRatings. (n.d.). *Active digital media universe: Home panel*. Retrieved January 12, 2010, from http://www.nielsennetratings.com /news.jsp?section=dat_to

Nielsen Online. (2009*). Global faces* and networked places. *A Nielsen report on social networking's new global footprint*. Retrieved November 20, 2010, from http://blog.nielsen.com/nielsenwire /wp-content/uploads/2009/03/nielsen_globalfaces_mar09.pdf

Nisbett, R. E. (2003). *The geography of thought: How Asians and Westerners think differently... and why*. New York, NY: The Free Press.

Nistor, N., & Neubauer, K. (2010). From participation to dropout: Quantitative participation patterns in online university courses. *Computers & Education*, *55*, 663–672. doi:10.1016/j.compedu.2010.02.026

Njenga, J. K., & Fourie, L. C. H. (2010). The myths about e-learning in higher education. *British Journal of Educational Technology, 41*(2), 199–212. doi:10.1111/j.1467-8535.2008.00910.x

Noble, D. F. (2001). *Digital diploma mills: The automation of higher education.* New York, NY: Monthly Review Press.

Nonaka, I. O., & Takeuchi, H. (1995). *The knowledge-creating company.* New York, NY: Oxford University Press.

Norton, M. J. (2000). *Introductory concepts in information science.* Medford, NJ: Information Today, Inc.

O'Connor, B. (1993). Myths and mirrors: Tourist images and national identity. In B. O'Connor & M. Cronin (Eds.), *Tourism in Ireland: A critical analysis* (pp/ 68-85). Cork, Ireland: Cork University Press.

Oetzel, J., DeVargas, F., Ginossar, T., & Sanchez, C. (2007). Hispanic women's preferences for breast health information: Subjective cultural influences on source, message, and channel. *Health Communication, 21*(2), 223–233.

Offsite learning: On target? Pt. I. (2002, October 7). *The Economist.* Retrieved Sept. 1, 2010, from http://www.economist.com/ displaystory.cfm? story_id=1377339

Offsite learning: On target? Pt. II. (2002, October 7). *The Economist.* Retrieved Sept. 1, 2010, from http://www.economist.com/ displaystory.cfm? story_id=1377324

Ofulue, I. C. (2010). A digital forensic analysis of advance fee fraud (419). In Taiwo, R. (Ed.), *Handbook of research on discourse behavior and digital communication: Language structures and social interaction* (pp. 296–317). Hershey, PA: IGI Global. doi:10.4018/978-1-61520-773-2.ch019

Ogden, C. K., & Richards, I. A. (1923). *The meaning of meaning.* New York, NY: Harvest Books.

Ogilvy Public Relations Worldwide. (2005). *Human Papillomavirus creative materials testing target audience focus group research: Final report. Gardasil Cervical Cancer Vaccine: Human Papillomavirus essential guide on CD-Rom.* Progressive Management.

Ohlms, C. (2002). *The business potential of ontology-based knowledge management.* New York, NY: McKinsey & Company.

Olaniran, B. A. (1994). Group performance and computer-mediated communication. *Management Communication Quarterly, 7,* 256–281. doi:10.1177/0893318994007003002

Olaniran, B. A. (1995). Perceived communication outcomes in computer-mediated communication: An analysis of three systems among new users. *Information Processing & Management, 31,* 525–541. doi:10.1016/0306-4573(95)00006-3

Olaniran, B. A. (1996). A model of satisfaction in computer-mediated and face-to-face communication. *Behaviour & Information Technology, 15,* 24–36. doi:10.1080/014492996120373

Olaniran, B. A. (2009c). Discerning culture in e-learning and in the global workplaces. *Knowledge Management & E-Learning: An International Journal, 1*(3), 180–195.

Olaniran, B. (2008). Team leaders' technology choice in virtual teams. *IEEE Transactions on Professional Communication, 49,* 1–25.

Olaniran, B. A. (2009). Culture, learning styles, and Web 2.0. *Interactive Learning Environments, 17*(4), 261–271. doi:10.1080/10494820903195124

Olaniran, B. A. (2004). Computer-mediated communication in cross-cultural virtual groups. In Chen, G. M., & Starosta, W. J. (Eds.), *Dialogue among diversities* (pp. 142–166). Washington, DC: National Communication Association.

Olaniran, B. A. (2007a). Challenges to implementing e-learning and lesser developed countries. In Edmundson, A. L. (Ed.), *Globalized e-learning cultural challenges* (pp. 18–34). Hershey, PA: Idea Group, Inc.

Olaniran, B. A. (2001). The effects of computer-mediated communication on transculturalism. In Milhouse, V., Asante, M., & Nwosu, P. (Eds.), *Transcultural realities* (pp. 83–105). Thousand Oaks, CA: Sage.

Olaniran, B. A. (2009b). A proposition for developing trust and relational synergy in international e-collaborative groups. In Salmons, J., & Wilson, L. (Eds.), *Handbook of research on electronic collaboration and organizational synergy* (pp. 472–486). Hershey, PA: IGI-Global.

Olaniran, B. A. (2007b). Culture and communication challenges in virtual workspaces. In St.Amant, K. (Ed.), *Linguistic and cultural online communication issues in the global age* (pp. 79–92). Hershey, PA: Idea Group, Inc.doi:10.4018/978-1-59904-213-8.ch006

Olaniran, B. A., & Edgell, D. (2008). Cultural implications of collaborative information technologies (CITs) in international online collaborations and global virtual teams. In Zemliansky, P., & St.Amant, K. (Eds.), *Handbook of global virtual workspaces* (pp. 118–133). Hershey, PA: IGI Global.

Olsen, G. M., & Olsen, J. S. (2002). Distance matters. In J. M. Carroll (Ed.), *Human-computer interaction in the new millennium* (pp. pp 139-178). New York, NY: Addison-Wesley.

Ondrejka, C. R. (2006). Escaping the gilded cage: User created content and building the metaverse. In Balkin, J. M., & Noveck, B. S. (Eds.), *The state of play: Law, games, and virtual worlds* (p. viii). New York, NY: New York University Press.

Ondrejka, C. (2008). Education unleashed: Participatory culture, education, and innovation in second life. In Salen, K. (Ed.), *The ecology of games: Connecting youth, games, and learning* (pp. 229–251). Cambridge, MA: The MIT Press.

Ono, H., & Zavodny, M. (2003). Gender and the Internet. *Social Science Quarterly*, *84*, 111–121. doi:10.1111/1540-6237.t01-1-8401007

OpenNet Initiative. (2005). *Internet filtering in Tunisia in 2005: A country study*. Retrieved

OpenNet Initiative. (2007). *Internet filtering in China: 2006-2007*. Retrieved March 26, 2010, from http://opennet.net/studies/china2007

Orbe, M. P. (2008). Theorizing multidimensional identity negotiation: Reflections on the lived experiences of first-generation college students. In Azmitia, M., Syed, M., & Radmacher, K. (Eds.), *The intersections of personal and social identities. New directions for child and adolescent development* (pp. 81–95). New York, NY: Jossey-Bass.

Orgad, S. (2006). The cultural dimensions of online communication: A study of breast cancer patients' Internet spaces. *New Media & Society*, *8*, 877–899. doi:10.1177/1461444806069643

Organisation for Economic Co-operation and Development. (2009). *Education at a glance 2009*. OECD. Retrieved February 22, 2010, from www.oecd.org/ publishing

Organization of African Unity. (1976). *Cultural charter for Africa*. Retrieved May 4, 2010, from http://www.dfa.gov.za/foreign/Multilateral/africa/treaties/culture.htm

Osborn, D. (2010). *African languages in the digital age: Challenges and opportunities for indigenous language computing*. Cape Town, South Africa: HSCR Press.

Osman, G., & Herring, S. (2007). Interaction, facilitation, and deep learning in cross-cultural chat: A case study. *The Internet and Higher Education*, *10*, 125–141. doi:10.1016/j.iheduc.2007.03.004

O'Sullivan, P., & Flanagan, A. (2003). Reconceptualizing "flaming" and other problematic messages. *New Media & Society*, *5*(1), 69–94. doi:10.1177/1461444803005001908

O'Sullivan, P. B. (2000). Communication technologies in an educational environment: Lessons from a historical perspective. In Cole, R. A. (Ed.), *Issues in Web-based pedagogy* (pp. 49–64). Westport, CT: Greenwood Press.

Oyelaran-Oyeyinka, B., & Lal, K. (2005). Internet diffusion in sub-Saharan Africa: A cross-country analysis. *Telecommunications Policy*, *29*, 507–527. doi:10.1016/j.telpol.2005.05.002

Page, S. E. (2007). *The difference: How the power of diversity creates better groups, firms, schools, and societies*. Princeton, NJ: Princeton University Press.

Pakenham-Walsh, N. (2009). Lack of access to healthcare information is a hidden killer: Healthcare information for all by 2015. *World Medical Journal*, *55*(4), Retrieved May 1, 2010, from http://www.wma.net/en/30publications/20journal/pdf/wmj24.pdf

Palda, K. S. (1966). The hypothesis of a hierarchy of effects: A partial evaluation. *JMR, Journal of Marketing Research*, *3*, 13–24. doi:10.2307/3149430

Palloff, R. M., & Pratt, K. (2001). *Lessons from the cyberspace classroom: The realities of online teaching.* San Francisco, CA: Jossey-Bass Inc.

Palmer, S., Holt, D., & Bray, S. (2008). Does the discussion help? The impact of a formally assessed online discussion on final student results. *British Journal of Educational Technology*, *39*(5), 847–858. doi:10.1111/j.1467-8535.2007.00780.x

Pan, P., & Xu, J. (2009). Online strategic communication: A cross-cultural analysis of U.S. and Chinese corporate websites. *Public Relations Review*, *35*(3), 251–253. doi:10.1016/j.pubrev.2009.04.002

Pantelli, N., & Tucker, R. (2009). Power and trust in global virtual teams. *Communications of the ACM*, *52*(12), 113–115. doi:10.1145/1610252.1610282

Papacharissi, Z. (2009). The virtual geographies of social networks: A comparative analysis of Facebook, LinkedIn and ASmallWorld. *New Media & Society*, *11*, 199–220. doi:10.1177/1461444808099577

Parekh, B. (2000). *Rethinking multiculturalism: Cultural diversity and political theory.* Cambridge, MA: Harvard University Press.

Park, H. S., & Guan, X. (2009). Cross-cultural comparison of verbal and nonverbal strategies of apologizing. *Journal of International & Intercultural Communication*, *2*(1), 66–87. doi:10.1080/17513050802603471

Park, J. R. (2007). Interpersonal and affective communication in synchronous online discourse. *The Library Quarterly*, *77*(2), 133–155. doi:10.1086/517841

Park, N., Lee, K. M., & Cheong, P. H. (2008). University instructors' acceptance of electronic courseware: An application of the Technology Acceptance Model. *Journal of Computer-Mediated Communication*, *13*, 163–186. doi:10.1111/j.1083-6101.2007.00391.x

Park, Y. (2004). *Cultural difference and cognitive style affecting information search behaviors: A proposal for a new study.* Paper presented at the World Conference on Educational Multimedia, Hypermedia and Telecommunications 2004, Chesapeake, VA.

Paswan, A. K., & Ganesh, G. (2009). Higher education institutions: Satisfaction and loyalty among international students. *Journal of Marketing for Higher Education*, *19*, 65–84. doi:10.1080/08841240902904869

Patchin, J. W., & Hinduja, S. (2006). Bullies move beyond the schoolyard: A preliminary look at cyberbullying. *Youth Violence and Juvenile Justice*, *4*, 148–169. doi:10.1177/1541204006286288

Pauleen, D., & Yoong, P. (2001). Facilitating virtual team relationships via Internet and conventional communication channels. *Journal of Internet Research: Electronic Networking Applications and Policy*, *11*(3), 190–202. doi:10.1108/10662240110396450

Pauleen, D. J., & Yoong, P. (2001). Relationship building and the use of ICT in boundary-crossing virtual teams: A facilitator's perspective. *Journal of Information Technology*, *16*, 205–220. doi:10.1080/02683960110100391

Pearson, J. (1999). Electronic networking in initial teacher education: Is a virtual faculty of education possible? *Computers & Education*, *32*, 221–238. doi:10.1016/S0360-1315(99)00005-6

Pearson, K. (2010). *New neighbors: A human resource introduction to Latino employees in Georgia's green industry.* Retrieved August 8, 2010, from http://www.uvm.edu/~farmlabr/?Page=multicultural/differences.html&SM=multicultural/submenu_multicultural.html

Pedersen, P. (2010). Assessing intercultural effectiveness outcomes in a year-long study abroad program. *International Journal of Intercultural Relations*, *34*(1), 70–80. doi:10.1016/j.ijintrel.2009.09.003

Pelling, E. L., & White, K. M. (2009). The theory of planned behavior applied to young people's use of social networking websites. *Cyberpsychology & Behavior*, *12*(6), 755–759. doi:10.1089/cpb.2009.0109

Peña-Purcell, N. (2008). Hispanics' use of Internet health information: An exploratory study. *Journal of the Medical Library Association*, *96*(2), 101–107. doi:10.3163/1536-5050.96.2.101

People.com.cn. (2009). 2009网络新词出炉: "杯具"流行"不差钱"第一 [2009 New online lexicons: "glassware" is popular while "not a penny less" ranks first]. (2009, December). Retrieved October 10, 2010, from http://politics.people.com.cn/GB/1026/10576151.html

Pepper, D. (2007, March). Matchmaking Indian-style. *Fortune, 155*(5), 14.

Pepper, S. (2002). *The TAO of topic maps*. Retrieved January 12, 2006, from http://www.ontopia.net/topicmaps /materials/tao.html

Pepper, S., & Schwab, S. (2003). *Curing the Web's identity crisis*. Retrieved November 23, 2004, from http:// www.ontopia.net/topicmaps /materials/identitycrisis. html #Pepper2003

Perez, S. (2008). *Enterprise 2.0 to become a $4.6 billion industry by 2013*. Retrieved April 23, 2010, from www.readwriteweb.com/archives/ enterprise_20_to_ become_a_46_ billion_industry.php

Perkins, J. (1999). Communicating in a global, multicultural corporation: Other metaphors and strategies. In Lovitt, C., & Goswami, D. (Eds.), *Exploring the rhetoric of international professional communication: An agenda for teachers and researchers* (pp. 17–38). Amityville, NY: Baywood.

Perold, J. J., & Maree, D. J. F. (2003). Description of novelty, novelty of description: A dialectic analysis of a Web-based course. *Computers & Education, 41*(3), 225–249. doi:10.1016/S0360-1315(03)00047-2

Perrucci, R., & Hu, H. (1995). Satisfaction with social and educational experiences among international graduate students. *Research in Higher Education, 36*(4), 491–508. doi:10.1007/BF02207908

Peters, E. (2004). Maximize student time on task. *Science Scope, 28*(1), 38–39.

Peters, T. J. (1997). *The circle of innovation: You can't shrink your way to greatness* (1st ed.). New York, NY: Knopf.

Pew Internet & American Life Project. (2009). The shared search for health information on the Internet. Retrieved November 24, 2010, from http://pewresearch.org/ pubs/1248/americans-look-online-for-health-information

Pew Internet and American Life Project. (2010). *Hispanics and the Internet*. Retrieved March 25, 2010, from http:// www.pewInternet.org/Reports/2001/Hispanics-and-the-Internet

Pfeil, U., Arjan, R., & Zaphiris, P. (2009). Age differences in online social networking: a study of user profiles and the social capital divide among teenagers and older users in MySpace. *Computers in Human Behavior, 25*, 643–654. doi:10.1016/j.chb.2008.08.015

Pfeil, U., Zaphiris, P., & Ang, C. S. (2006). Cultural differences in collaborative authoring of Wikipedia. *Journal of Computer-Mediated Communication, 12*(1), 88–113. doi:10.1111/j.1083-6101.2006.00316.x

Phalet, K., & Schönpflug, U. (2001). Intergenerational transmission of collectivism and achievement values in two acculturation contexts: The case of Turkish families in Germany and Turkish and Moroccan families in the Netherlands. *Journal of Cross-Cultural Psychology, 3*(2), 186–201. doi:10.1177/0022022101032002006

Philip, A. (2005, October 17). *Getting married the snappy, global way*. Indian Express. Retrieved October 18, 2005, from http://www.expressindia.com/ fullstory. php?newsid= 56735&pn=0

Philipsen, G. (1990). Speaking "like a man" in Teamsterville. In D. Carbaugh (Ed.), *Cultural communication and intercultural contact* (pp. 11-26). Hillsdale, NJ: Lawrence Erlbaum.

Phillipson, R. (2009). *Linguistic imperialism continued*. New York, NY: Routledge.

Picciano, A. G. (2002). Beyond student perceptions: Issues of interaction, presence, and performance in an online course. *Journal of Asynchronous Learning Networks, 6*(1), 21–40.

Piecowye, J. (2003). Habitus in transition? CMC use and impacts among young women in the United Arab Emirates. *Journal of Computer-Mediated Communication, 8*(2). Retrieved December 10, 2010, from http://jcmc. indiana.edu/vol8/issue2 /piecowye.html

Pinker, S. (1994). *The language instinct: How the mind creates language*. New York, NY: William Morrow.

Polanyi, M. (1967). *The tacit dimension*. London, UK: Routledge.

Polhemus, L., Shih, L. F., & Swan, K. (2001). *Virtual interactivity: The representation of social presence in an online discussion*. Paper presented at the annual meeting of the American Educational Research Association, Seattle, WA.

Pollay, R., & Mittal, B. (1993). Here's the beef: Factors, determinants, and segments in consumer criticism of advertising. *Journal of Marketing, 57*(3), 99–114. doi:10.2307/1251857

Poster, M. (1999). National identities and communications technologies. *The Information Society, 15*, 235–240. doi:10.1080/019722499128394

Postle, G., Sturman, A., Mangubhai, F., Cronk, P., Carmichael, A., & McDonald, J. (2003). *Online teaching and learning in higher education: A case study.* Canberra, Australia: Department of Education, Science and Training.

Postmes, T., Spears, R., & Lea, M. (1998). Breaching or building the social boundaries? SIDE-Effects of computer-mediated communication. *Communication Research, 25*, 689–715. doi:10.1177/009365098025006006

Prahalad, C. K. (2010). *The fortune at the bottom of the pyramid. Eradicating poverty through profits.* Upper Saddle River, NJ: Pearson Education.

Prakasa, V. V., & Rao, V. N. (1979). Arranged marriages: An assessment of the attitudes of the college students in India. In Kurian, G. (Ed.), *Cross-cultural perspectives of mate-selection and marriage* (pp. 11–32). Connecticut: Greenwood Press.

Preece, J., & Maloney-Krichmar, D. (2005). Online communities: Design, theory, and practice. Journal of Computer-Mediated Communication, 10(4). Retrieved October 10, 2010, from http://jcmc.indiana.edu/vol10/issue4/preece.html

Prentice, C. M., & Kramer, M. W. (2006). Dialectical tensions in the classroom: Managing tension through communication. *The Southern Communication Journal, 71*(4), 339–361.

Price, S., & Oliver, M. (2007). A framework for conceptualizing the impact of technology on teaching and learning. *Journal of Educational Technology & Society, 10*(1), 16–27.

PricewaterhouseCoopers. (2008). *Managing the risks and rewards of collaboration.* Retrieved October 1, 2010, from http://www.pwc.com/ gx/ en/ technology/ technology-executive-connections/ index.jhtml

Putnam, R. D. (2000). *Bowling alone: The collapse and revival of American community.* New York, NY: Simon & Schuster.

Qiu, J. L. (2000). Virtual censorship in China: Keeping the gate between the cyberspaces. *International Journal of Communications Laws and Policy, 4*, 1–25.

Quartarola, B. (1984). *A research paper on time on task and the extended school day/year and their relationship to improving student achievement.* ERIC, ED245347.

Qureshi, S., & Zigurs, I. (2001). Paradoxes and prerogatives in global virtual collaboration. *Communications of the ACM, 44*(12), 85–88. doi:10.1145/501317.501354

Ragusa, A. T. (2009). Asynchronous communication forums: Improving learning & social engagement among distance education students. In Dumova, T. (Ed.), *Handbook of research on social interaction technologies and collaboration software* (pp. 181–193). Hershey, PA: IGI Global. doi:10.4018/978-1-60566-368-5.ch017

Ragusa, A. T. (2010b). Seeking trees or escaping traffic? Socio-cultural factors and tree change migration in Australia. In Luck, G., Black, R., & Race, D. (Eds.), *Demographic change in rural landscapes: What does it mean for society and the environment?* (pp. 71–99). New York, NY: Springer. doi:10.1007/978-90-481-9654-8_4

Ragusa, A. T. (2010a). Communication and social interactions in a technologically-mediated world. In Ragusa, A. T. (Ed.), *Interaction in communication technologies & virtual learning environments: Human factors* (pp. 1–6). Hershey, PA: IGI Global. doi:10.4018/978-1-60566-874-1.ch001

Ragusa, A. T. (2007). The impact of socio-cultural factors in multi-cultural virtual communication environments: A case example from an Australian university's provision of distance education in the global classroom. In St. Amant, K. (Ed.), *Linguistic and cultural online communication issues in the global age* (pp. 306–327). Hershey, PA: Idea Group Inc.doi:10.4018/978-1-59904-213-8.ch018

Rainie, L. (2010, January 5). *Pew Internet & American life project: Internet, broadband, and cell phone statistics.* Retrieved February 6, 2010 from http://www.pewinternet.org/ reports/ 2010/ Internet-broadband-and- cell-phone-statistics.aspx?r=1

Ramalingam, A., & Nair, S. (2005). Swayamvar in mouse mode: Matrimonials get an e-twist [Electronic version]. *The Financial Express*. Retrieved September 1, 2005, from http://www.financialexpress.com/ fe_full_story. php?content _id=82474

Ramanathan, V., & Atkinson, D. (2006). Individualism, academic writing, and ESL writers. In Matsuda, P., Cox, M., Jordan, C., & Ortmeier-Hooper, C. (Eds.), *Second language writing in the composition classroom: A critical sourcebook* (pp. 159–185). New York, NY: Bedford/ St. Martin's Press.

Ramirez, A., Palazolo, K. E., Savage, M. W., & Deiss, D. M. (2000). New directions in understanding cyberbullying. In Taiwo, R. (Ed.), *Handbook of research on discourse behavior and digital communication: Language structures and social interaction* (pp. 729–744). Hershey, PA: IGI Global.

Ramsay, S., Jones, E., & Barker, M. (2007). Relationship between adjustment and support types: Young and mature-aged local and international first-year university students. *Higher Education, 54*, 247–265. doi:10.1007/ s10734-006-9001-0

Ranganathan, S. R. (1987). *The colon classification* (7th ed.). Bangalore, India: Sarada Ranganathan Endowment for Library Science.

Rao, V. V. P., & Rao, V. N. (1982). *Marriage, the family, and women in India*. Columbia, MO: South Asia Books.

Ras, Z. W., & Dardzinska, A. (2004). Ontology-based distributed autonomous knowledge systems. *Information Systems, 29*(1), 47–58. doi:10.1016/S0306-4379(03)00033-4

Rayburn, J. M., & Conrad, C. (2004). China's Internet structure: Problems and control measures. *International Journal of Management, 21*(4), 471–480.

Realo, A. J. A., & Greenfield, B. (2008). Radius of trust: Social capital in relation to familism and institutional collectivism. *Journal of Cross-Cultural Psychology, 39*, 447–462. doi:10.1177/0022022108318096

Realo, A., & Allik, J. (1999). A cross-cultural study of collectivism: A comparison of American, Estonian, and Russian students. *The Journal of Social Psychology, 139*(2), 133–142. doi:10.1080/00224549909598367

Reeves, B., & Read, J. L. (2009). *Total engagement: Using games and virtual worlds to change the way people work and businesses compete*. Boston, MA: Harvard Business Press.

Reeves, T. C., & Reeves, P. (1997). Effective dimensions of interactive learning on the World Wide Web. In Khan, B. H. (Ed.), *Web-based instruction* (pp. 59–66). Englewood Cliffs, NJ: Educational Technology Publications.

Reichel, A., Uriely, N., & Shani, A. (2008). Ecotourism and simulated attractions: Tourists' attitudes towards integrated sites in a desert area. *Journal of Sustainable Tourism, 16*(1), 23–41. doi:10.2167/jost711.0

Reil, M., & Polin, L. (2004). Online learning communities: Common ground and critical differences in designing technical environments. In Barab, S. A., Kling, R., & Gray, J. H. (Eds.), *Designing for virtual communities in the service of learning* (pp. 16–50). Cambridge, UK: Cambridge University Press.

Reimers, F. (2010). Educating for global competency. In Coehn, J. E., & Malin, M. B. (Eds.), *International perspectives on the goals of universal basic and secondary education* (pp. 183–202). New York, NY: Routledge.

Retrieved January 3, 2010, from http://www.zeit. de/2008/21/ III-Gesellschaft-Japanhandys

Rettie, R. (2003). *Connectedness, awareness and social presence*. 6th International Presence Workshop. Aalborg, Denmark. Retrieved November 8, 2009 http://www. presence-research.org/ papers/ Rettie.pdf.

Rice, R. (1992). Task analyzability, use of new media, and effectiveness: A multi-site exploration of media richness. *Organization Science, 3*(4), 475–500. doi:10.1287/ orsc.3.4.475

Rice, R. E. (1993). Media appropriateness: Using social presence theory to compare traditional and new organizational media. *Human Communication Research, 19*, 451–484. doi:10.1111/j.1468-2958.1993.tb00309.x

Rice, R. E., & Aydin, C. (1991). Attitudes toward new organizational technology: Network proximity as a mechanism for social information processing. *Administrative Science Quarterly, 36*, 219–244. doi:10.2307/2393354

Rice, R. E., Grant, A., Schmitz, J., & Torobin, J. (1990). Individual and network influences on the adoption and perceived outcomes of electronic messaging. *Social Networks, 12*, 27–55. doi:10.1016/0378-8733(90)90021-Z

Rice, R. E., & Love, G. (1987). Electronic emotion: Socioemotional content in a computer-mediated network. *Communication Research, 14*, 85–108. doi:10.1177/009365087014001005

Richardson, W. (2009). *Blogs, wikis, podcasts, and other powerful Web tools for classrooms* (2nd ed.). Thousand Oaks, CA: Corwin Press.

Richardson, J., & Swan, K. (2003). Examining social presence in online courses in relation to students' perceived learning and satisfaction. *Journal of Asynchronous Learning Networks, 6*(1), 76–90.

Rickards, T. (2003). The future of innovation. In Shavinina, L. V. (Ed.), *The international handbook on innovation* (pp. 1094–1112). Boston, MA: Elsevier. doi:10.1016/B978-008044198-6/50071-1

Riegner, C. (2008). Wired China: The power of the world's largest Internet population. *Journal of Advertising Research, 48*(4), 496–505. doi:10.2501/S0021849908080574

Rimmington, G. M., & Alagic, M. (2008). *Third place learning: Reflective inquiry into intercultural and global cage painting.* Charlotte, NC: Information Age Publishing.

Riva, G., Davide, F., & Ijsselsteijn, W. A. (2003). *Being there: Concepts, effects and measurements of user presence in synthetic environments.* Washington, DC: IOS Press.

Rive, P. B. (2008). Knowledge transfer and marketing in Second Life. In Zemliansky, P., & St.Amant, K. (Eds.), *Handbook of research on virtual workplaces and the new nature of business practices* (pp. 424–438). Hershey, PA: Information Science Reference. doi:10.4018/978-1-59904-893-2.ch030

Rive, P. B., Thomassen, A., Lyons, M., & Billinghurst, M. (2008). *Face to face with the white rabbit: Sharing ideas in Second Life.* Paper presented at the IEEE International Professional Communications Conference.

Rivera, J. C., & Rice, M. L. (2002). A comparison of student outcomes & satisfaction between traditional and Web based course offerings. *Online Journal of Distance Learning Administration, 5*(3). Retrieved December 10, 2010, from http://www.westga.edu/ ~distance/ ojdla/ fall53/ rivera53.html

Robert, L. P., & Dennis, A. R. (2005). Paradox of richness: A cognitive model of media choice. *IEEE Transactions on Professional Communication, 48*(1), 10–21. doi:10.1109/TPC.2004.843292

Roberts, T., Lowry, P. B., & Sweeney, P. (2006). An evaluation of the impact of social presence through group size and the use of collaborative software on group member voice in face-to-face and computer-mediated task groups. *IEEE Transactions on Professional Communication, 49*(1), 28–43. doi:10.1109/TPC.2006.870460

Robey, D., Khoo, H. M., & Powers, C. (2000). Situated learning in cross-functional virtual teams. *Technical Communication, 47*(1), 51–66.

Robins, K., & Webster, F. (1999). *Times of the techno-culture.* New York, NY: Routledge.

Rockmann, K. W., & Northcraft, G. B. (2008). To be or not to be trusted: The influence of media richness on defection and deception. *Organizational Behavior and Human Decision Processes, 107*(2), 106–122. doi:10.1016/j.obhdp.2008.02.002

Roebuck, D. B., & Britt, A. C. (2002). Virtual teaming has come to stay: Guidelines and strategies for success. *Southern Business Review, 28*, 29–39.

Rogers, E. M. (2003). *Diffusion of innovations* (5th ed.). New York, NY: Free Press.

Rogers, P. C., Graham, C. R., & Mayes, C. T. (2007). Cultural competence and instructional design: Exploration research into the delivery of online instruction cross culturally (International Review). *Educational Technology Research and Development, 55*, 197–217. doi:10.1007/s11423-007-9033-x

Rohrbeck, C. A., Ginsburg-Block, M. D., Fantuzzo, J. W., & Miller, T. R. (2003). Peer-assisted learning interventions with elementary school students: A meta-analytic review. *Journal of Educational Psychology, 95*(2), 240–257. doi:10.1037/0022-0663.95.2.240

Rojas, V., Straubhaar, J., Roychowdhury, D., & Okur, O. (2004). Communities, cultural capital, and the digital divide. In Bucy, E. P., & Newhagen, J. E. (Eds.), *Media access: Social and psychological dimensions of new technology use* (pp. 107–130). Mahwah, NJ: Erlbaum.

Romano, D. (2002). Modern communications technology in ethnic nationalist hands: The case of Kurds. *Canadian Journal of Political Science, 35*(1), 127–149. doi:10.1017/S0008423902778207

Romero, E. (2004). Hispanic identity and acculturation: Implications for management. *Cross Cultural Management, 11*(1), 62–71. doi:10.1108/13527600410797756

Rooksby, E. (2002). *Email and ethics: Style and ethical relations in computer-mediated communication.* London, UK: Routledge. doi:10.4324/9780203217177

Rose, E. (2005, March-April). Cultural studies in instructional design: Building a bridge to practice. *Educational Technology, 45*, 5–10.

Ross, A. D. (1961). *The Hindu family in its urban setting.* Toronto, Canada: University of Toronto Press.

Ross, P. D. (1998). Interactive marketing and the law: The future rise of unfairness. *Journal of Interactive Marketing, 12*(3), 21–31. doi:10.1002/(SICI)1520-6653(199822)12:3<21::AID-DIR3>3.0.CO;2-4

Roth, K. (2001). Material culture and intercultural communication. *International Journal of Intercultural Relations, 25*(5), 563–580. doi:10.1016/S0147-1767(01)00023-2

Rourke, L., Anderson, T., Garrison, D. R., & Archer, W. (2001). Assessing social presence in asynchronous text-based computer conferencing. *Journal of Distance Education, 14*(2), 51–70.

Roy, M. H. (2001). Small group communication and performance: Do cognitive flexibility and context matter? *Management Decision, 39*(4), 323–330. doi:10.1108/00251740110391501

Rutkowski, A. F., Vogel, D. R., Genuchten, M. V., Bemelmans, T. M., & Favier, M. (2002). E-collaboration: The reality of virtuality. *IEEE Transactions on Professional Communication, 45*(4), 219–229. doi:10.1109/TPC.2002.805147

Rutkowski, A., Vogel, D., van Genuchten, M., & Saunders, C. (2001). Communication in virtual teams: Ten years of experience in education. *IEEE Transactions on Professional Communication, 51*(3), 302–312. doi:10.1109/TPC.2008.2001252

Saadé, R. G., He, X., & Kira, D. (2007). Exploring dimensions to online learning. *Computers in Human Behavior, 23*, 1721–1739. doi:10.1016/j.chb.2005.10.002

Sadri, H., & Flammia, M. (2009). Using technology to prepare students for the challenges of global citizenship. *Journal of Systemics, Cybernetics, and Informatics, 7*(5), 66–71.

Saeed, N., Yang, Y., & Sinnappan, S. (2009). Emerging Web technologies in higher education: A case of incorporating blogs, podcasts and social bookmarks in a Web programming course based on students' learning styles and technology preferences. *Journal of Educational Technology & Society, 12*(4), 98–109.

Sahin, Y. L., & Coklar, A. N. (2009). Social networking users' views on technology and the determination of technostress levels. *Procedia-Social and Behavioral Sciences, 1*, 1437–1442. doi:10.1016/j.sbspro.2009.01.253

Salbach, N. M., Guilcher, S. J. T., Jaglal, S. B., & Davis, D. A. (2009). Factors influencing information seeking by physical therapists providing stroke management. *Physical Therapy, 89*(10), 1039–1050. doi:10.2522/ptj.20090081

Salud.com (2010). Retrieved March 25, 2010, from http://www.salud.com

Salzman, M. L., & Matathia, I. (2007). *Next now: Trends for the future.* New York, NY: Palgrave Macmillan.

Sammons, M. (2007). Collaborative interaction. In Moore, M. G. (Ed.), *Handbook of distance education* (2nd ed., pp. 311–321). Mahwah, NJ: L. Erlbaum Associates.

Saphiere, D. H. (2000). Online cross-cultural collaboration. *Training & Development, 54*(10), 71–72.

Sapp, D. A. (2004). Global partnerships in business communication: An institutional collaboration between the United States and Cuba. *Business Communication Quarterly, 67*(3), 267–280. doi:10.1177/1080569904268051

Sarker, S., Sarker, S., & Schneider, C. (2009). Seeing remote team members as leaders: A study of U.S.-Scandinavian teams. *IEEE Transactions on Professional Communication*, *52*(1), 75–94. doi:10.1109/TPC.2008.2007871

Sawir, E., Marginson, S., Deumert, A., Nyland, C., & Ramia, G. (2008). Loneliness and international students: An Australian study. *Journal of Studies in International Education*, *12*(2), 181–203.

Scacci, W. (2010). Collaboration practices and affordances in free/open source software development. In Mistrik, I. (Eds.), *Collaborative software engineering* (pp. 307–328). Berlin, Germany: Springer-Verlag. doi:10.1007/978-3-642-10294-3_15

Scarcella, R. (2002). Some key factors affecting English learners' development of advanced literacy. In Schleppe-grell, M. J., & Colombi, M. C. (Eds.), *Developing advanced literacy in first and second languages: Meaning with power* (pp. 209–228). Mahwah, NJ: Lawrence Erlbaum.

Schafer, R. (2009). Introducing heuristics of cultural dimensions into the service-level technical communication classroom. *Journal of Technical Writing and Communication*, *39*(3), 305–319. doi:10.2190/TW.39.3.f

Schifter, C. (2004). Faculty participation in DE programs: Practices and plans. In Monolescu, D., Schifter, C. C., & Greenwood, L. (Eds.), *The distance education evolution: Issues and case studies* (pp. 1–21). Hershey, PA: Information Science Publishing. doi:10.4018/9781591401209.ch002

Schiller, H. I. (1996). *Information inequality: The deepening social crisis in America*. New York, NY: Routledge.

Schmidt, W. V., Conaway, R. N., Easton, S. S., & Wardrope, W. J. (2007). *Communicating globally: Intercultural communication and international business*. Thousand Oaks, CA: Sage.

Schmitz, J., & Fulk, J. (1991). Organizational colleagues, information richness, and electronic mail: A test of the social influence model of technology use. *Communication Research*, *18*, 487–523. doi:10.1177/009365091018004003

Schneider, S. M., & Foot, K. A. (2005). Web sphere analysis: An approach to studying online action. In Hine, C. (Ed.), *Virtual methods: Issues in social research on the Internet*. Basingstoke, UK: Berg Publishers.

Schoenmakers, Y. M. M., de Vries, R., & van Wijk, E. A. (2009). *Mountains of gold: An exploratory research on Nigerian 419-fraud*. Amsterdam, The Netherlands: SWP Publishing.

Schönberger, K. (2007). Technik als Querschnittsdimension. Kulturwissenschaftliche Technikforschung am Beispiel von Weblog-Nutzung in Frankreich und Deutschland. *Zeitschrift für Volkskunde*, *103*(2), 197–221.

Schwartzman, R. (2007). Refining the question: How can online instruction maximize opportunities for all students? *Communication Education*, *56*(1), 113–117. doi:10.1080/03634520601009728

Scott, J. B. (2003). *Risky rhetoric: AIDS and the cultural practices of HIV testing*. Carbondale, IL: Southern Illinois University Press.

Scott, G. (2005). *Promoting student retention and productive learning in universities: Research and action at UWS 2004-05*. Unpublished manuscript. Office of Planning and Quality. Penrith, NSW: University of Western Sydney.

Seale, J., & Cooper, M. (2010). E-learning and accessibility: An exploration of the potential role of generic pedagogical tools. *Computers & Education*, *54*(4), 1107–1116. doi:10.1016/j.compedu.2009.10.017

Sebell, M. H. (2008). *Stage gates: Good or bad for innovation*. Creative Realities. Retrieved October 29, 2008, from http://www.creativerealities.com/ knowledgeArticles.html

Secretariat, I. E. A. A. (2009). *Australian senate inquiry into international education*. Retrieved July 4, 2009, from www.ieaa.org.au/ NewsArticles/ NewsArticle.asp?articleNo=38

Seidenspinner, M., & Theuner, G. (2007). Intercultural aspects of online communication: A comparison of Mandarin-speaking, U.S., Egyptian, and German user preferences. *Journal of Business Economics & Management*, *8*(2), 101–109.

Selber, S. A. (2010). A rhetoric of electronic instruction sets. *Technical Communication Quarterly, 19*(2), 95–117. doi:10.1080/10572250903559340

Selfe, C. L. (1999). Lest we think the revolution is a revolution: Images of technology and the nature of change. In Hawisher, G. E., & Selfe, C. L. (Eds.), *Passions, pedagogies, and the 21ˢᵗ century technologies* (pp. 292–322). Logan, UT: Utah State University Press.

Selwyn, N. (2004). Reconsidering political and popular understandings of the Digital Divide. *New Media & Society, 6*(3), 341–362. doi:10.1177/1461444804042519

Sener, J. (2003). Improving access to online learning: Current issues, practices, and directions. In Bourne, J., & Moore, J. (Eds.), *Elements of quality online education: Practice and direction* (pp. 119–136). Needham, MA: Sloan Consortium.

Seper, C. (2008). *Untangling the web of medical advice.* Retrieved November 19, 2009, from http://blog.cleveland.com/health/2008/02/untangling_the_web_of_medical.html

Sev'er, A., & Yurdakul, G. (2001). Culture of honor, culture of change: A feminist analysis of honor killings in rural Turkey. *Violence Against Women, 7*(9), 964–998. doi:10.1177/10778010122182866

Shah, A. (2010a). *Poverty facts and stats: Global issues.* Retrieved May 2, 2010, from http://www.globalissues.org/article/26/poverty-facts-and-stats

Shah, A. (2010b). *Today, over 24,000 children died around the world: Global issues.* Retrieved May 2, 2010 from http://www.globalissues.org/article/715/today-over-24000-children-died-around-the-world

Sharma, A. (2006). *Girl seeks suitable boy: Indian marriage dot com.* Ph.D. dissertation, University of Toronto, Canada. Retrieved January 22, 2010, from Dissertations & Theses: Full Text.

Shaughnessy, J., Ross, P., & Jackson, A. (2008). Baptism by firewall? Computer-mediated collaborative projects as professional development opportunities for teachers. *Contemporary Issues in Technology & Teacher Education, 8*(4), 367–393.

Shavinina, L. V. (2003). *The international handbook on innovation.* Boston, MA: Elsevier.

Shavitt, S., Lalwani, A., Zhang, J., & Torelli, C. J. (2006). The horizontal/vertical distinction in cross-cultural consumer research. *Journal of Consumer Psychology, 16*, 325–342. doi:10.1207/s15327663jcp1604_3

Shavitt, S., Lowrey, P., & Haefner, J. (1998). Public attitudes toward advertising: More favorable than you might think. *Journal of Advertising Research, 38*(4), 7–22.

Shen, K. N., & Khalifa, M. (2007). Exploring multidimensional conceptualization of social presence in the context of online communities. In Jacko, J. (Ed.), *Human-computer interaction: HCI applications and services* (pp. 999–1008). New York, NY: Springer. doi:10.1007/978-3-540-73111-5_110

Sheyholislami, J. (2010). Identity, language, and new media: The Kurdish case. *Language Policy, 9*(4), 289–312. doi:10.1007/s10993-010-9179-y

Sheyholislami, J. (2011). *Kurdish identity, discourse, and new media.* New York, NY: Palgrave Macmillan.

Shields, R. (2003). *The virtual.* New York, NY: Routledge.

Shim, T. Y., Kim, M. S., & Martin, J. N. (2008). (Eds.). *Changing Korea: Understanding culture and communication.* New York, NY: Peter Lang.

Shirky, C. (2008). *Here comes everybody: The power of organizing without organizations.* New York, NY: Penguin Press.

Shome, R., & Hegde, R. S. (2002). Culture, communication, and the challenge of globalization. *Critical Studies in Media Communication, 19*(2), 172–189. doi:10.1080/07393180216560

Short, J., William, E., & Christie, B. (1976). *The social psychology of telecommunications.* Toronto, ON: Wiley.

Shuter, R. (1990). The centrality of culture. *Southern Journal of Communication, 55*, 237–249.

Shutter, R. (2008). The centrality of culture. In Asante, M. K., Miike, Y., & Yin, J. (Eds.), *The global intercultural communication reader* (pp. 11–26). New York, NY: Routledge.

Simon, S. J. (2001). The impact of culture and gender on websites: An empirical study. *The Data Base for Advances in Information Systems, 32*(1), 18–37.

Simpson, K., & Tan, W. S. (2009). A home away from home? Chinese student evaluations of an overseas study experience. *Journal of Studies in International Education, 13*(1), 5–21. doi:10.1177/1028315308317694

Singelis, T. M. (1994). The measurement of independent and interdependent self-construals. *Personality and Social Psychology Bulletin, 20*(5), 580–591. doi:10.1177/0146167294205014

Singelis, T. M., & Brown, W. J. (1995). Culture, self, and collectivist communication: Linking culture to individual behavior. *Human Communication Research, 21*(3), 354–389. doi:10.1111/j.1468-2958.1995.tb00351.x

Singh, N., Zhao, H., & Hu, X. (2005). Analyzing the cultural content of websites: A cross-national comparison of China, India, Japan, and US. *International Marketing Review, 22*(2), 129–146. doi:10.1108/02651330510593241

Singh, N., & Pereira, A. (2005). *The culturally customized website: Customizing websites for the global marketplace.* Burlington, MA: Elsevier Butterworth Heinemann.

Singh, N., & Baack, D. (2004). Web site adaptation: A cross-cultural comparison of U.S. and Mexican websites. *Journal of Computer-Mediated Communication, 4.* Retrieved October 10, 2010, from http://jcmc.indiana.edu/vol9/issue4/singh_baack.html

Singh, N., & Baack, D. W. (2004). Web site adaptation: A cross-cultural comparison of U.S. and Mexican websites. Journal of Computer-Mediated Communication, 9(4). Accessed May 4, 2007, from http://www.indiana.edu/vol.9/issue4/index.html

Singlis, T. M., Triandis, H. C., Bhawuk, D., & Gelfand, M. J. (1995). Horizontal and vertical dimensions of individualism and collectivism: A theoretical and measurement refinement. *Cross-Cultural Research, 29,* 240–275. doi:10.1177/106939719502900302

Síthigh, D. M. (2010). More than words: The introduction of internationalised domain names and the reform of generic top-level domains at ICANN. *International Journal of Law and Information Technology, 18*(3), 274–300. doi:10.1093/ijlit/eaq007

Sitkin, S. B., Sutcliffe, K. M., & Barrios-Choplin, J. R. (1992). A dual capacity model of communication media choice in organizations. *Human Communication Research, 18,* 563–598. doi:10.1111/j.1468-2958.1992.tb00572.x

Sivadas, E., Bruvold, N. T., & Nelson, M. R. (2008). A reduced version of the horizontal and vertical individualism and collectivism scale: A four-country assessment. *Journal of Business Research, 61,* 201–210. doi:10.1016/j.jbusres.2007.06.016

Sivunen, A., & Valo, M. (2006). Team leaders' technology choice in virtual teams. *IEEE Transactions on Professional Communication, 49,* 57–68. doi:10.1109/TPC.2006.870458

Sivunen, A., & Valo, M. (2006). Team leaders' technology choice in virtual teams. *IEEE Transactions on Professional Communication, 49*(1), 57–68. doi:10.1109/TPC.2006.870458

Skutnabb-Kangas, T. (2000). *Linguistic genocide in education - Or worldwide diversity and human rights?* Mahwah, NJ: Lawrence Erlbaum Associates.

Skutnabb-Kangas, T., & Fernandes, D. (2008). Kurds in Turkey and in (Iraqi) Kurdistan: A comparison of Kurdish educational language policy in two situations of occupation. *Genocide Studies and Prevention, 3*(1), 43–73. doi:10.3138/gsp.3.1.43

Slotnik, D. E. (2007, February 26). Too few friends? A website lets you buy some (and they're hot). *New York Times.* Retrieved November 19, 2010, from http://www.nytimes.com/2007/02/26/technology/26fake.html

Smith, P. J., Coldwell, J., Smith, S. N., & Murphy, K. L. (2005). Learning through computer-mediated communication: A comparison of Australian and Chinese heritage students. *Innovations in Education and Teaching International, 42*(2), 12–134. doi:10.1080/14703290500062441

Smith, A. (2009). Nigerian scam emails and the charms of capital. *Cultural Studies, 23*(1), 27–47. doi:10.1080/09502380802016162

Smith, A., Dunckley, L., French, T., Minoch, S., & Chang, Y. (2004). A process model for developing usable cross-cultural websites. *Interacting with Computers, 16*(1), 63–91. doi:10.1016/j.intcom.2003.11.005

Smith, A. (1998). *Nationalism and modernism.* London, UK: Routledge.

Smith, P. J., Coldwell, J., Smith, S. N., & Murphy, K. L. (2005). Learning through computer-mediated communication: A comparison of Australian and Chinese heritage students. *Innovations in Education and Teaching International, 42*(2), 12–134. doi:10.1080/14703290500062441

Smith, A. D. (2005). Exploring online dating and customer relationship management. *Online Information Review, 29*(1), 18-33. Emerald Group Publishing Limited. Retrieved September 18, 2005, from http://www.emeraldinsight.com/ Insight/viewContentItem.do? contentType=Article&contentId =1464923

Smith, H. (n.d.). *What is an ontology?* Retrieved December 16, 2004, from http://www.ontology.org/main / papers/faq.html

Smtih, D. J. (2007). *A culture of corruption: Everyday deception and popular discontent in Nigeria.* Princeton, NJ: Princeton University Press.

Sole, D., & Edmondson, A. (2002). Situated knowledge and learning in dispersed teams. *British Journal of Management, 13*, 517–534. doi:10.1111/1467-8551.13.s2.3

Solomon, C. M. (2001). Managing virtual teams. *Workforce, 80*(6), 60–65.

Sonnenwald, D. H., & Liewrouw, L. A. (1997). Collaboration during the design process: A case study of communication, information behavior, and project performance. In Vakkari, P., Savolainen, R., & Dervin, B. (Eds.), *Information seeking in context: Proceedings of an international conference on research in information needs, seeking and use in different contexts* (pp. 179–204). London, UK: Taylor Graham.

Soutar, G. N., & Turner, J. P. (2002). Students' preference for university: A conjoint analysis. *International Journal of Educational Management, 16*(1), 40–45. doi:10.1108/09513540210415523

SouthWest Walks. (2008, August 16). *Kerry Way self-guided 8-day holiday programme.* Retrieved November 1, 2010, from http://www.southwestwalks ireland.com/ walking-holiday-ireland-kerry-peninsula/ self-guided-walks.html

Southwick, K. (2004). Diagnosing WebMD. *CNET News.* Retrieved November 19, 2010, from http://news.cnet. com/Diagnosing-WebMD/2009-1017_3-5208510.html

Sovic, S. (2009). High-bye friends and the herd instinct: International and home students in the creative arts. *Higher Education, 58*, 747–761. doi:10.1007/s10734-009-9223-z

Spears, R., & Lea, M. (1992). Social influence and the influence of the "social" in computer-mediated communication. In M. Lea (Ed.), *Contexts of computer-mediated communication* (p. 30-65). Hemel Hempstead, UK: Harvester-Wheatsheaf.

Spinuzzi, C. (2003). *Tracing genres through organizations: A sociocultural approach to information design.* Cambridge, MA: The MIT Press.

Spinuzzi, C. (2008). *Network: Theorizing knowledge work in telecommunications.* New York, NY: Cambridge University Press. doi:10.1017/CBO9780511509605

Spitzberg, B. H., & Cupach, W. R. (1989). *Handbook of interpersonal competence research.* New York, NY: Springer-Verlag.

Spitzer, M. (1986). Writing styles in computer conferences. *IEEE Transactions on Professional Communication, 29*, 19–22.

SpotOnPR. (2009). *Middle East & North Africa Twitter demograhpics & user habits survey.* Retrieved December 10, 2010, from http://interactiveme.com/wp-content/ uploads/2009/09/twitter_survey_report_interactiveME.pdf

Springer, L., Stanne, M. E., & Donovan, S. S. (1999). Effects of small-group learning on undergraduates in science, mathematics, engineering, and technology: A meta-analysis. *Review of Educational Research, 69*(1), 21–51.

Sproull, L., & Kiesler, S. (1986). Reducing social context cues: Electronic mail in organizational communication. *Management Science, 32*, 1492–1512. doi:10.1287/mnsc.32.11.1492

Sprung, R. C. (Ed.). (2000). *Translating into success: Cutting-edge strategies for going multilingual in a global age.* Amsterdam, The Netherlands & Philadelphia, PA: John Benjamins.

Squires, S., & Byrne, B. (Eds.). (2002). *Creating breakthrough ideas: The collaboration of anthropologists and designers in the product development industry.* Westport, CT/London, UK: Bergin & Garvey.

St. Germaine-Madison, N. (2009). Localizing medical information for U.S. Spanish-speakers: The CDC campaign to increase public awareness about HPV. *Technical Communication, 47*(3), 235–247.

St.Amant, K. (2002). When cultures and computers collide: Rethinking computer-mediated communication according to international and intercultural communication expectations. *Journal of Business and Technical Communication, 16*(2), 196–214. doi:10.1177/1050651902016002003

St.Amant, K. (2001). Considering China: A perspective for technical communicators. *Technical Communication, 48*(4), 385–388.

St.Amant, K. (2002a). Integrating intercultural online learning experiences into the computer classroom. *Technical Communication Quarterly, 11*, 289–315. doi:10.1207/s15427625tcq1103_4

St.Amant, K. (2007). Online education in an age of globalization: Foundational perspectives and practices for technical communication instructors and trainers. *Technical Communication Quarterly, 16*(1), 13–30. doi:10.1207/s15427625tcq1601_2

Stacey, E. (2002). Social presence online: Networking learners at a distance, education and Information Technologies. *Education and Information Technologies, 7*(4), 287–294. doi:10.1023/A:1020901202588

Starke-Meyerring, D. (2008). Genre, knowledge and digital code in web-based communities: An integrated theoretical framework for shaping digital discursive spaces. *International Journal of Web-Based Communities, 4*, 398–417. doi:10.1504/IJWBC.2008.019547

Starke-Meyerring, D., & Andrews, D. (2006). Building a shared virtual learning culture: An international classroom partnership. *Business Communication Quarterly, 69*, 24–49. doi:10.1177/1080569905285543

Starke-Meyerring, D., Duin, A. H., & Palvetzian, T. (2007). Global partnerships: Positioning technical communication programs in the context of globalization. *Technical Communication Quarterly, 16*, 139–174. doi:10.1207/s15427625tcq1602_1

Starke-Meyerring, D., & Wilson, M. (2008). Globally networked learning environments: Shaping visionary futures. In Starke-Meyerring, D., & Wilson, M. (Eds.), *Designing global learning environments: Visionary partnerships, policies, and pedagogies* (pp. 218–230). Rotterdam, The Netherlands: Sense Publishers.

Stats, I. W. Usage and Population Statistics. (2009). *Home page*. Retrieved June 25, 2010, from: http://www.internetworldstats.com

Stein, D., & Wanstreet, C. (2003). *Role of social presence, choice of online or face-to-face group format, and satisfaction with perceived knowledge gained in a distance learning environment*. Paper Presented at the 2003 Midwest Research to Practice Conference in Adult Continuing and Community Education.

Stevens, C. R., & Campbell, P. J. (2006). Collaborating to connect global citizenship, information literacy, and lifelong learning in the global studies classroom. *References Services Review, 34*(4), 536–556. doi:10.1108/00907320610716431

Stevenson, C. (2007). Breaching the great firewall: China's Internet censorship and the quest for freedom of expression in a connected world. *Boston College International and Comparative Law Review, 30*, 531–558.

Stewart, T. A. (2001). *The wealth of knowledge: Intellectual capital and the twenty-first century organization* (1st ed.). New York, NY: Currency.

Stine, L. (2004). The best of both worlds: Teaching basic writers in class and online. *Journal of Basic Writing, 23*(2), 49–69.

Stoan, S. K. (1991). Research and information retrieval among academic researchers: Implications for library instruction. *Library Trends, 39*(3), 238–257.

Stojanovic, L., Stojanovic, N., & Handschuh, S. (2002). Evolution of the metadata in the ontology-based knowledge management systems. *Proceedings of the 1st German Workshop on on Experience Management: Sharing Experiences about the Sharing of Experience* (pp. 65-77). New York, NY: Association for Computing Machinery.

Street, B. (1984). *Literacy in theory and practice*. New York, NY: Cambridge University Press.

Su, X., Cao, N., Yang, Q., & Cui, J. (1996). *Hanziwenhua yinlun (An introduction to the culture of Chinese characters)*. Nanning, China: Guangxi Education Press.

Su, H.-Y. (2007). The multilingual and multiorthographic Taiwan-based Internet: Creative uses of writing systems on college-affiliated BBSs. In Danet, B., & Herring, S. C. (Eds.), *The multilingual Internet: Language, culture, and communication online* (pp. 46–86). New York, NY: Oxford University Press.

Suárez-Orozco, M. M., & Sattin, C. (2007). Wanted: Global citizens. *Educational Leadership, 64*(7), 58–62.

Sujo de Montes, L. E., Oran, S. M., & Willis, E. M. (2002). Power, language, and identity: Voices from an online course. *Computers and Composition, 19,* 251–271. doi:10.1016/S8755-4615(02)00127-5

Suler, J. (2004). The online disinhibition effect. *Cyberpsychology & Behavior, 7*(3), 321–326. doi:10.1089/1094931041291295

Sull, E. C. (2007, June). The #1 complaint of online students: Poor instructor feedback! *Online Classroom, 5.*

Sun, P. C., Tsai, R. J., Finger, G., Chen, Y. Y., & Yeh, D. (2007). What drives successful e-learning? An empirical investigation of the critical factors influencing learner satisfaction. *Computers & Education, 50*(4), 1183–1202. doi:10.1016/j.compedu.2006.11.007

Sunstein, C. R. (2006). *Infotopia: How many minds produce knowledge.* New York, NY: Oxford University Press.

Suri, J. F., & IDEO. (2005). *Thoughtless act: Observations on intuitive design* (1st ed.). San Francisco, CA: Chronicle Books.

Surowiecki, J. (2004). *The wisdom of crowds: Why the many are smarter than the few and how collective wisdom shapes business, economies, societies, and nations* (1st ed.). New York, NY: Doubleday.

Svenonius, E. (2000). *The intellectual foundation of information organization.* Cambridge, MA: The MIT Press.

Swan, K. (2002). Building communities in online courses: The importance of interaction. *Education Communication and Information, 2*(1), 23–49. doi:10.1080/1463631022000005016

Sweeney, A., Weaven, S., & Herington, C. (2008). Multicultural influences on group learning: A qualitative higher education study. *Assessment & Evaluation in Higher Education, 33*(2), 119–132. doi:10.1080/02602930601125665

Sykes, J., Oskoz, A., & Thorne, S. L. (2008). Web 2.0, synthetic immersive environments, and mobile resources for language education. *CALICO Journal, 25*(3), 528–546.

Synovate. (2008). *Global survey.* Retrieved December 10, 2010, from http://www.synovate.com/news /article/2008/09/global-survey- shows-58-of-people-don-t-know-what-social-networking-is-plus-over-one-third-of-social-networkers-are-losing-interest.html

Szurek, J. (1997). Resistance to technology-enhanced childbirth in Tuscany: The political economy of Italian birth. In Davis-Floyd, R. E., & Sargent, C. F. (Eds.), *Childbirth and authoritative knowledge* (pp. 287–314). Berkley, CA: University of California Press.

Tai, Z. (2006). *The Internet in China: Cyberspace and civil society.* New York, NY & London, UK: Routledge.

Taking, I. T. Global. (n.d.) *Guide to action: Simple steps toward change.* Retrieved November 20, 2010, from http://www.tigweb.org/ action/ guide/

Tallent-Runnels, M. K., Thomas, J. A., Lan, W. Y., Cooper, S., Ahern, T. C., Shaw, S. M., & Liu, X. (2006). Teaching courses online: A review of the research. *Review of Educational Research, 76*(1), 93–135. doi:10.3102/00346543076001093

Tan, B. C. Y., Wei, K. K., Huang, W. W., & Ng, G. N. (2000). A dialogue technique to enhance electronic communication in virtual teams. *IEEE Transactions on Professional Communication, 43,* 153–165. doi:10.1109/47.843643

Tan, B. C. Y., Wei, K., Watson, R. T., Clapper, D. L., & McLean, E. R. (1998). Computer-mediated communication and majority influence: Assessing the impact in an individualistic and collectivistic culture. *Management Science, 44*(9), 1263–1278. doi:10.1287/mnsc.44.9.1263

Tanfa, D. Y. (2006). *Advance fee fraud.* Unpublished doctoral dissertation, University of South Africa, Pretoria.

Tanis, M., & Postmes, T. (2003). Social cues and impression formation in CMC. *The Journal of Communication, 53*(4), 676–693. doi:10.1111/j.1460-2466.2003.tb02917.x

Tanis, M., & Postmes, T. (2005). Short communication. A social identity approach to trust: Interpersonal perception, group membership and trusting behaviour. *European Journal of Social Psychology*, *35*, 423–424. doi:10.1002/ejsp.256

Tanis, M., & Postmes, T. (2007). Two faces of anonymity: Paradoxical effects of cues to identity in CMC. *Computers in Human Behavior*, *23*(2), 955–970. doi:10.1016/j.chb.2005.08.004

Tapscott, D., & Williams, A. D. (2008). *Wikinomics: How mass collaboration changes everything*. New York, NY: Portfolio.

Taylor, T. L. (2006). *Play between worlds: Exploring online game culture*. Cambridge, MA: The MIT Press.

Taylor, A. (2004). *The organization of information* (2nd ed.). Westport, CT: Libraries Unlimited.

Technology companies in China. *Columbia Business Law Review, 2007*, 505-564.

Tee, R. (2005). Different directions in the mobile Internet: Analysing mobile Internet services in Japan and Europe. In Lasen, A., & Hamill, L. (Eds.), *Mobile world: Past, present and future (computer supported cooperative work)* (pp. 143–160). New York, NY: Springer.

Teece, D. J. (2000). *Managing intellectual capital: Organizational, strategic, and policy dimensions*. New York, NY: Oxford University Press.

Teece, D. J., & Nonaka, I. O. (2000). *Managing industrial knowledge*. London, UK: Sage.

Tenofsky, D. (2004). *Glossary of library terms*. Retrieved April 2, 2006, from http://www.lib.umich.edu/science / instruction/glossary.html

Tewar. (2002, July 4). *Blog entry*. Retrieved March 15, 2003, from http://wera.blogspot.com/2002/07/blog-post_04.html

The Rosetta Foundation. (2010). *Promoting equality through language and cultural diversity*. Retrieved May 12, 2010, from http://www.therosettafoundation.org/

Thelwall, M. (2008). Social networks, gender, and friending: An analysis of MySpace member profiles. *Journal of the American Society for Information Science and Technology*, *59*, 1321–1330. doi:10.1002/asi.20835

Thompson, L., & Ku, H.-Y. (2005). Chinese graduate students' experiences and attitudes toward online learning. *Educational Media International*, *42*(1), 33–47. doi:10.1080/09523980500116878

Thorne, S. L., & Black, R. (2007). Language and literacy development in computer-mediated contexts and communities. *Annual Review of Applied Linguistics*, *27*, 133–160. doi:10.1017/S0267190508070074

Thorne, S. L., & Payne, S. (Eds.). (2005). Computer-mediated communication and foreign language learning: Context, research and practice [Special issue]. *CALICO Journal*, *22*(3).

Thrush, E. A. (2001). Plain English? A study of plain English vocabulary and international audiences. *Technical Communication*, *48*(3), 289–296.

Thrush, E. A. (2001). High-context and low-context cultures: How much communication is too much? In Bosley, D. (Ed.), *Global contexts: Case studies in international communication* (pp. 27–41). Boston, MA: Allyn-Bacon.

Thurlow, C. (2003). Generatn txt? The sociolinguistics of young people's text-messaging. *Discourse Analysis Online*. Retrieved October 2, 2004, from http://extra.shu.ac.uk.daol/articles/vl/a3/thurlow2002003-paper.html

Thussu, D. K. (2000). *International communication: Continuity and change*. London, UK: Arnold.

Tickoo, U. (2006, August). *Yahoo! Inc. invests in Indian marriage portal*. Retrieved March 17, 2007, from http://www.thebizofcoding.com/ 2006/08/yahoo-inc-invests-in-indian-ma/

Tiffin, J., & Rajasingham, L. (2003). *The global virtual university*. New York, NY: Routledge Falmer. doi:10.4324/9780203464670

Tiffin, J., & Terashima, N. (2001). *HyperReality: Paradigm for the third millenium*. New York, NY: Routledge.

Ting-Toomey, S. (1999). *Communicating across cultures*. New York, NY: The Guilford Press.

Ting-Toomey, S., & Oetzel, J. G. (2002). Cross-cultural face concerns and conflict styles: Current status and future directions. In Gudykunst, W., & Mody, B. (Eds.), *Handbook of international and intercultural communication* (pp. 143–163). Thousand Oaks, CA: Sage.

Tive, C. (2006) *419 scam: Exploits of the Nigerian con man.* Bloomington, IN: iUniverse.

TNS-infratest. (2009). *Monitoring-Report Deutschland Digital.* Retrieved January 10, 2010, from http://www.tns-infratest.com/ monitoring-deutschland-digital

Togher, L., McDonald, S., & Code, C. (1999). Communication problems following traumatic brain injury. In McDonald, S., Togher, L., & Code, C. (Eds.), *Communication disorder following traumatic brain injury* (pp. 1–18). Hove, UK: Psychology Press Ltd.

Tolan, D. (2007, July). Making visible the invisible. *Online Classroom*, 7-8.

Triandis, H. C. (1995). *Individualism and collectivism.* Boulder, CO: Westview.

Triandis, H. C. (2001). Individualism-collectivism and personality. *Journal of Personality, 69*, 907–924. doi:10.1111/1467-6494.696169

Triandis, H. C., & Gelfand, M. J. (1998). Converging measurements of horizontal and vertical individualism and collectivism. *Journal of Personality and Social Psychology, 74*, 118–128. doi:10.1037/0022-3514.74.1.118

Triandis, H. C., & Suh, E. M. (2002). Cultural influences on personality. *Annual Review of Psychology, 53*, 133–160. doi:10.1146/annurev.psych.53.100901.135200

Triandis, H. C. (1989). The self and social behavior in differing cultural contexts. *Psychological Review, 96*, 506–520. doi:10.1037/0033-295X.96.3.506

Triandis, H. C., Bontempo, R., Villareal, M. J., Asai, M., & Lucca, N. (1988). Individualism and collectivism: Cross-cultural perspectives on self-ingroup relationships. *Journal of Personality and Social Psychology, 54*, 323–338. doi:10.1037/0022-3514.54.2.323

Triandis, H. C., McCusker, C., & Hui, C. H. (1990). Multimethod probes of individualism and collectivism. *Journal of Personality and Social Psychology, 59*, 1006–1020. doi:10.1037/0022-3514.59.5.1006

Trompenaars, F., & Hampden-Turner, C. (1998). *Riding the waves of culture: Understanding diversity in global business* (2nd ed.). New York, NY: McGraw-Hill.

Tsui, L. (2003). The panopticon as the antithesis of a space of freedom: Control and regulation of the Internet in China. *China Information, 17*(2), 65–82. doi:10.1177/0920203X0301700203

Tu, C. H. (2001). How Chinese perceive social presence: An examination of interaction in online learning environment. *Educational Media International, 38*(1), 45–60. doi:10.1080/09523980010021235

Tu, C. (2001). How Chinese perceive social presence: An examination inline learning environment. *Educational Media International, 38*(1), 45–60. doi:10.1080/09523980010021235

Tu, C. (2002). The measurement of social presence in an online learning environment. *International Journal on E-Learning, 1*(2), 34–45.

Tunc, T. E. (2009). Technologies of consumption: The social semiotics of Turkish shopping malls. In Vannini, P. (Ed.), *Material culture and technology in everyday life: Ethnographic approaches* (pp. 131–143). New York, NY: Peter Lang.

Turkle, S., & Papert, S. (1990). Epistemological pluralism: Styles and voices within the computer culture. *Signs, 16*, 128–157. doi:10.1086/494648

Tutty, J., & Klein, J. (2008). Computer-mediated instruction: A comparison of online and face-to-face collaboration. *Educational Technology Research and Development, 56*(2), 101–124. doi:10.1007/s11423-007-9050-9

Twenge, J. M. (2006). *Generation me: Why today's young Americans are more confident, assertive, entitled—And more miserable than ever before.* New York, NY: The Free Press.

Twenge, J. M., & Campbell, W. K. (2009). *The narcissism epidemic: Living in the age of entitlement.* New York, NY: The Free Press.

U. S. Bureau of the Census. (2006, July 1). Race chart. Retrieved October 14, 2006 from http://www.census.gov/ Press-Release/ www/ 2006/ cb06-123table1.xls

U. S. Department of Commerce. (2004). *A nation online: Entering the broadband age.* Retrieved June 15, 2009, from http://www.ntia.doc.gov/ reports/ anol/ NationOnlineBroadband04.htm

U.S. Bureau of the Census. (2001). *Statistical abstract of the United States*. Washington, DC: U.S. Census Bureau.

U.S. Department of Education, Office of Planning, Evaluation, and Policy Development. (2009). *Evaluation of evidence-based practices in online learning: A meta-analysis and review of online learning studies*. Washington, D.C., 2009. Retrieved April 6, 2010, from www.ed.gov/ about/ offices/ list/ opepd/ ppss/ reports.html

UAE Federal Government Portal. (2010). *E-commerce: Fact & figures*. Retrieved December 10, 2010, from http://www.government.ae/gov/ en/biz/ecommerce/facts.jsp

Uberoi, P. (Ed.). (2005). *Family, kinship and marriage in India*. Oxford University Press.

Ulijn, J., & St.Amant, K. (2000). Mutual intercultural perception: How does it affect technical communication? *Technical Communication, 47*(2), 220–237.

UNESCO. (2008). *Multilingualism in cyberspace*. Retrieved November 25, 2010, from http://portal.unesco.org/ci/en/ev.php-URL_ID=18147&URL_DO=DO_TOPIC&URL_SECTION=201.html

United States Census Bureau. (2000). Hispanic population of the United States. Retrieved August 8, 2010, from http://www.census.gov/population/www/socdemo/hispanic/census.html

United States Department of Justice. (2003). *Title VI of the Civil Rights Act of 1964. 42 U.S.C. § 2000d et seq. Civil Rights Division. Coordination and Review Section*. Retrieved May 5, 2010, from http://www.justice.gov/crt/cor/coord/titlevi.php

Universal McCann. (2009). *Power to the people: social media tracker wave 4*. Retrieved November 20, 2010, from http://universalmccann.bitecp.com /wave4/Wave4.pdf

Universities Australia. (2009). *Enhancing the student experience & student safety: A position paper*. Canberra, Australia: Universities Australia.

University of Missouri – St. Louis. (2010). *Student body profile fall 2009*. Retrieved September 2, 2010, from http://www.umsl.edu/ about/ studentprofile.html

Urban Institute. (2005). *High concentration of limited-English students challenges implementation of No Child Left Behind Act*. Retrieved June 11, 2009, from http://www.urban.org/url.cfm?ID=900884

Urtel, M. G. (2008). Assessing academic performance between traditional and distance education course formats. *Journal of Educational Technology & Society, 11*(1), 322–330.

Usunier, J. C., & Lee, J. A. (2009). *Marketing across cultures* (5th ed.). London, UK, New York, NY, Boston, MA: Prentice Hall.

Uzuner, S. (2009, June). Questions of culture in distance learning: A research review. *International Review of Research in Open and Distance Learning, 10*(3), 1–19.

Valenzuela, S., Park, N., & Kee, K. F. (2009). Is there social capital in a social network site? Facebook use and college students' life satisfaction, trust, and participation. *Journal of Computer-Mediated Communication, 14*, 875–901. doi:10.1111/j.1083-6101.2009.01474.x

van Bruinessen, M. (2000). *Kurdish ethno-nationalism versus nation-building states: Collected articles*. Istanbul, Turkey: The ISIS Press.

Van den Bos, M., & Nell, L. (2006). Territorial bounds to virtual space: Transnational online and offline networks of Iranian and Turkish-Kurdish immigrants in the Netherlands. *Global Networks, 6*(2), 201–220. doi:10.1111/j.1471-0374.2006.00141.x

Van der Meij, H. (2007). Goal-orientation, goal-setting, and goal-driven behavior in minimalist user instructions. *IEEE Transactions on Professional Communication, 50*(4), 295–305. doi:10.1109/TPC.2007.908728

van Dijk, J. (2004). Divides in succession: Possession, skills, and use of new media for societal participation. In Bucy, E. P., & Newhagen, J. E. (Eds.), *Media access: Social and psychological dimensions of new technology use* (pp. 233–254). Mahwah, NJ: Lawrence Erlbaum.

van Dijk, T. A. (1997). Discourse as interaction in society. In van Dijk, T. A. (Ed.), *Discourse as social interaction* (pp. 1–37). London, UK: Sage.

van Manen, M. (2003). *Researching lived experience: Human science for an action sensitive pedagogy* (2nd ed.). Ontario, Canada: The Althouse Press.

van Raaij, E. M., & Schepers, J. J. L. (2008). The acceptance and use of a virtual learning environment in China. *Computers & Education, 50*, 838–852. doi:10.1016/j.compedu.2006.09.001

Vesely, P., Bloom, L., & Sherlock, J. (2007). Key elements of building online community: Comparing faculty and student perceptions. *Journal of Online Learning and Teaching, 3*, 234–246.

Vida y Salud. (2010). *Home page*. Retrieved March 6, 2010, from http://www.vidaysalud.com

Vida y Salud. (2010). *Facebook Fan Page*. Retrieved March 22, 2010, from http://www.facebook.com/vidaysalud.

Villalva, K. E. (2006). Reforming high school writing: Opportunities and constraints for Generation 1.5 writers. In Matsuda, P., Ortmeier-Hooper, C., & You, X. (Eds.), *The politics of second language writing: In search of the promised land* (pp. 30–55). West Lafayette, IN: Parlor Press.

Virkus, S. (2008). Use of Web 2.0 technologies in LIS education: Experiences at Tallinn University, Estonia. *Program: Electronic Library and Information Systems, 42*(3), 262–274. doi:10.1108/00330330810892677

Vishwanath, A., & Chen, H. (2008, May). *Personal communication technologies as an extension of the self: A cross-cultural comparison of people's associations with technology and their symbolic proximity with others*. Paper presented at the annual meeting of the International Communication Association, Montreal, QC, Canada.

Vogel, D. R., van Genuchten, M., Lou, D., Verveen, S., van Eekout, M., & Adams, A. (2001). Exploratory research on the role of national and professional cultures in a distributed learning project. *IEEE Transactions on Professional Communication, 44*(2), 114–124. doi:10.1109/47.925514

Volet, S. E., & Ang, G. (1998). Culturally mixed groups on international campuses: An opportunity for inter-cultural learning. *Higher Education Research & Development, 17*(1), 5–23. doi:10.1080/0729436980170101

Volosinov, V. N. (1973). *Marxism and the philosophy of language* (Matejka, L., & Titunik, I. R., Trans.). Cambridge, MA: Harvard University Press.

Von Krogh, G., Nonaka, I., & Ichijo, K. (2000). *Enabling knowledge creation: How to unlock the mystery of tacit knowledge and release the power of innovation*. New York, NY: Oxford University Press.

Vroman, K., & Kovacich, J. (2002). Computer-mediated interdisciplinary teams: Theory and reality. *Journal of Interprofessional Care, 16*, 161–170. doi:10.1080/13561820220124175

Wacker, G. (2003). The Internet and censorship in China. In Hughes, C. R., & Wacker, G. (Eds.), *China and the Internet: Politics of the digital leap forward* (pp. 58–82). New York, NY: Routledge.

Wadsworth, B. C., Hecht, M. L., & Jung, E. (2008). The role of identity gaps, discrimination, and acculturation in international students' educational satisfaction in American classrooms. *Communication Education, 57*(1), 64–87. doi:10.1080/03634520701668407

Wagner, R. P. (2005). On software regulation. *Southern California Law Review, 78*, 457–516.

Wall, D. S. (2001). Cybercrimes and the Internet. In Wall, D. S. (Ed.), *Crime and the Internet* (pp. 1–17). New York, NY: Routledge.

Walther, J. B. (1992). Interpersonal effects in computer-mediated interaction: A relational perspective. *Communication Research, 19*, 52–90. doi:10.1177/009365092019001003

Walther, J. B. (1994). Anticipated ongoing interaction versus channel effects on relational communication in computer-mediated interaction. *Human Communication Research, 20*, 473–501. doi:10.1111/j.1468-2958.1994.tb00332.x

Walther, J. B. (1995). Relational aspects of computer-mediated communication: Experimental observations over time. *Organization Science, 6*(2), 186–203. doi:10.1287/orsc.6.2.186

Walther, J. B. (1997). Group and interpersonal effects in international computer-mediated collaboration. *Human Communication Research, 23*, 342–369. doi:10.1111/j.1468-2958.1997.tb00400.x

Walther, J. B., Anderson, J. E., & Park, D. (1994). Interpersonal effects in computer-mediated interaction: A meta analysis of social and antisocial communication. *Communication Research, 23*, 3–42. doi:10.1177/009365096023001001

Walther, J. B., & Burgoon, J. K. (1992). Relational communication in computer-mediated interaction. *Human Communication Research, 19,* 50–88. doi:10.1111/j.1468-2958.1992.tb00295.x

Walther, J. B. (1996). Computer-mediated communication: impersonal, interpersonal and hyperpersonal. *Communication Research, 23*(1), 3–43. doi:10.1177/009365096023001001

Walther, J. B. (2002). Time effects in computer-mediated groups: Past, present, and future. In Hinds, P., & Kiesler, S. (Eds.), *Distributed work* (pp. 235–257). Cambridge, MA: The MIT Press.

Wang, S. (2008). Changing models of China's policy agenda setting. *Modern China, 34*(1), 56–87. doi:10.1177/0097700407308169

Wang, M. (2007). Designing online courses that effectively engage learners from diverse cultural backgrounds. *British Journal of Educational Technology, 38*(2), 294–311. doi:10.1111/j.1467-8535.2006.00626.x

Wang, C. M., & Reeves, T. C. (2007). Synchronous online learning experiences: The perspectives of international students from Taiwan. *Educational Media International, 44*(4), 339–356. doi:10.1080/09523980701680821

Wang, C. M. (2004). Taking online courses in the United States: The perspectives of Asian students from China, Korea, Singapore, and Taiwan. In J. Nall & R. Robson (Eds.), *Proceedings of the E-Learn 2004 Conference: World Conference on e-learning in corporate, government, healthcare, & higher education* (pp. 2466-2468). Norfolk, VA: Association for the Advancement of Computing in Education (AACE).

Warden, C., Chen, J., & Caskey, D. (2005). Cultural values and communication online: Chinese and Southeast Asian students in a Taiwan international MBA class. *Business Communication Quarterly, 68*(2), 222–232. doi:10.1177/1080569905276669

Warschauer, M. (1998). Online learning in sociocultural context. *Anthropology & Education Quarterly, 29*(1), 68–88. doi:10.1525/aeq.1998.29.1.68

Warschauer, M. (2006). *Laptops and literacy: Learning in the wireless classroom.* New York, NY: Teachers College.

Warschauer, M. (1996). Computer assisted language learning: An introduction. In Fotos, S. (Ed.), *Multimedia language teaching* (pp. 3–20). Tokyo, Japan: Logos International.

Warschauer, M. (2000). Language, identity, and the Internet. In Kolko, B. E., Nakamura, L., & Rodman, G. B. (Eds.), *Race in cyberspace* (pp. 151–170). New York, NY: Routledge.

Wasserman, I. M., & Richmond-Abbott, M. (2005). Gender and the Internet: Causes of variation in access, level, and scope of use. *Social Science Quarterly, 86,* 252–270. doi:10.1111/j.0038-4941.2005.00301.x

Watson, R. T., Akselsen, S., & Pitt, L. (1998). Attractors: Building mountains in the flat landscape of the World Wide Web. *California Management Review, 40*(2), 36–56.

Watson-Manheim, M. B., & Belanger, F. (2002) Support for communication-based work processes in virtual work. *e-Service Journal, 1*(3), 61-82.

Web, M. D. (2010). *Website.* Retrieved March 17, 2010, from http://Webmd.com

Web, M. D. (2010). *WebMD in Spanish.* Retrieved March 17, 2010, from http://www.Webmd.com/news/spanish/default.htm

Webber, C., & Robertson, J. (2003). Developing an international partnership for tomorrow's educational leaders. *International Studies in Educational Administration, 31*(1), 15–32.

Weckert, J. (2000). What is so bad about Internet content regulation? *Ethics and Information Technology, 2*(2), 105–111. doi:10.1023/A:1010077520614

Wei, C. Y., & Kolko, B. E. (2005). Resistance to globalization: Language and Internet diffusion patterns in Uzbekistan. *New Review of Hypermedia and Multimedia, 11*(2), 205–220. doi:10.1080/13614560500402817

Weick, K. E. (1991). The nontraditional quality of organizational learning. *Organization Science, 2*(1), 116–124. doi:10.1287/orsc.2.1.116

Weiss, E. H. (1998). Technical communication across cultures: Five philosophical questions. *Journal of Business and Technical Communication, 12*(2), 253–269. doi:10.1177/1050651998012002005

Weiss, S., & Stripp, W. (1998). Negotiating with foreign business persons: An introduction for Americans with propositions for six cultures. In *S. Niemeier. C. P. Campbell, & R.*

Welker, J., & Berardino, L. (2005-2006). Blended learning: Understanding the middle ground between traditional classroom and fully online instruction. *Journal of Educational Technology Systems, 34*(1), 33–55. doi:10.2190/67FX-B7P8-PYUX-TDUP

Wellman, B., Haase, A. Q., Witte, J., & Hampton, K. (2001). Does the Internet increase, decrease, or supplement social capital? Social networks, participation, and community commitment. *The American Behavioral Scientist, 45*, 436–455. doi:10.1177/00027640121957286

Wellman, B. (2004). The three ages of Internet studies: Ten, five and zero years ago. *New Media & Society, 6*(1), 123–129. doi:10.1177/1461444804040633

Wellman, B. (1981). Applying network analysis to the study of support. In Gottlieb, B. H. (Ed.), *Social networks and social support* (pp. 171–200). London, UK: Sage.

Welty, C., & Guarino, N. (2001). Supporting ontological analysis of taxonomic relationships. *Data & Knowledge Engineering, 39*, 51–74. doi:10.1016/S0169-023X(01)00030-1

Wenger, E. (1998). *Communities of practice: Learning meaning and e-dentity*. Cambridge, UK: Cambridge University Press.

Wertheim, M. (1999). *The pearly gates of cyberspace: A history of space from Dante to the Internet*. New York, NY: W. W. Norton.

White, G. W., & Toms, L. (2009). Preparing college of business students for a global world. *The Delta Kappa Gamma Bulletin, 75*(4), 11-13, 26.

Whiteside, A. L. (2007). *Exploring social presence in communities of practice within a hybrid learning environment: A longitudinal examination of two case studies within the School Technology Leadership graduate-level certificate program*. Unpublished doctoral dissertation, University of Minnesota.

Whiteside, A. L., Hughes, J. E., & McLeod, S. (2005, September). *Opening the shades of isolationism: An examination of social presence in a hybrid-model certificate program*. Paper presented at the New Media Research @ UMN Conference, Minneapolis, MN.

Wiesenberg, F., & Stacey, E. (2005). Reflections on teaching and learning online: Quality program design, delivery and support issues from a cross-global perspective. *Distance Education, 26*(3), 385–404. doi:10.1080/01587910500291496

Wilcox, P., Winn, S., & Fyvie-Gauld, M. (2005). It was nothing to do with the university, it was just the people: The role of social support in the first-year experience of higher education. *Studies in Higher Education, 30*(6), 707–722. doi:10.1080/03075070500340036

Willard, N. E. (2005). *Cyberbullying and cyberthreats*. Paper presented at the U.S. Department of Education Office of Safe and Drug-free Schools National Conference, Washington, D.C.

Williams, D. (2007). The impact of time online: Social capital and cyberbalkanization. *Cyberpsychology & Behavior, 10*, 398–406. doi:10.1089/cpb.2006.9939

Williams, A., & Nussbaum, J. F. (2001). *Intergenerational communication across the lifespan*. Hillsdale, NJ: Lawrence Erlbaum.

Williams, W. (2008). *Tourism, landscape, and the Irish character: British travel writers in pre-famine Ireland*. Madison, WI: University of Wisconsin Press.

Williams, I. M., Warren, H. N., & Olaniran, B. A. (2009). Achieving cultural acquiescence through foreign language e-learning. In Chang, M., & Kuo, C. (Eds.), *Handbook of research on learning culture and language via ICTs: Methods for enhanced instruction*. Hershey, PA: IGI Global.

Wilson, M., Qayyum, A., & Boshier, R. (1998). World wide America? Think globally, click locally. *Distance Education, 19*(1), 109–123. doi:10.1080/0158791980190108

Wines, M. (2009a, June 17). Civic-minded Chinese find a voice online. *The New York Times*. Retrieved February 18, 2009, from http://www.nytimes.com/2009 /06/17/world/asia/17china.html

Wines, M. (2009b, March 12). A dirty pun tweaks China's online censors. *The New York Times*. Retrieved February 18, 2009, from http://www.nytimes.com/2009 /03/12/ world/asia/12beast.html?_r=1

Winner, L. (2000). Do artifacts have politics? In Teich, A. H. (Ed.), *Technology and the future* (8th ed., pp. 150–168). Boston, MA: Bedford/St Martin's.

Wise, A., Chang, J., Duffy, T., & Del Valle, R. (2004). The effects of teacher social presence on student satisfaction, engagement, and learning. *Journal of Educational Computing Research*, *31*(3), 247–271. doi:10.2190/V0LB-1M37-RNR8-Y2U1

Witkin, H. A., Moore, C. A., Goodenough, D. R., & Cox, P. W. (1977). Field-dependent and field-independent cognitive styles and their educational implications. *Review of Educational Research*, *47*(1), 1–64.

Wodak, R., de Cillia, R., Reisigl, M., & Liebhart, K. (2009). *The discursive construction of national identities* (2nd ed.). Edinburgh, UK: Edinburgh University Press.

Wolin, L., Korgaonkar, P., & Lund, D. (2002). Beliefs, attitudes and behavior towards Web advertising. *International Journal of Advertising*, *21*(1), 87–113.

Wong, K.-F., Xia, Y., & Li, W. (2006 June & Sept.). Linguistics and behavioural studies of Chinese chat language. *International Journal on Computer Processing of Oriental Languages, World Scientific, 19*(2&3), 133-152. doi:10.1142/S0219427906001475

Wood, A. F., & Fassett, D. (2003). Remote control: Identity, power and technology in the classroom. *Communication Education*, *32*(3/4), 286–296. doi:10.1080/0363452032000156253

Woods, R., & Ebersole, S. (2003). Becoming a communal architect in the online classroom—Integrating cognitive and affective learning for maximum effect in Web-based learning. *Online Journal of Distance Learning Administration*, *6*(1). Retrieved October 10, 2010, from www. westga.edu/ ~distance/ ojdla/ spring61/ woods61.htm

Wu, W. (1996). Great leap or long march: Some policy issues of the development of the Internet in China. *Telecommunications Policy*, *20*, 699–711. doi:10.1016/S0308-5961(96)00050-X

Wu, C. (2003). 中国网络语言研究概观 [A survey of China's cyber-language study]. *Journal of Social Science of Hunan Normal University*, *32*(6), 102–105.

Wurman, R. S. (1989). *Information anxiety*. New York, NY: Doubleday.

Würtz, E. (2005). A cross-cultural analysis of websites from high-context cultures and low-context cultures. *Journal of Computer-Mediated Communication, 11*(1). Retrieved October 10, 2010, from http://jcmc.indiana.edu/vol11/ issue1/wuertz.html

Wyatt, G. (2005). Satisfaction, academic rigor and interaction: Perceptions of online instruction. *Education*, *125*(3), 460–468.

Xiao, Q. (2008, June). *The rise of online public opinion and its political impact.* Paper presented at the Chinese Internet Research Conference, HK, China. Retrieved October 10, 2010, from http://jmsc.hku.hk/blogs/circ/files/2008/06/xiao_qiang.pdf

Xiaobo, L. (2006, February 20). Communist Internet censorship an internationally common practice? *The Epoch Times.* Retrieved October 15, 2006, from http://www.theepochtimes.com/ news/ 6-2-20/ 38388.html

Xin, D., Jia, J., & Yanhui, H. (2010). Research on distance education development in China. *British Journal of Educational Technology*, *41*(4), 582–592. doi:10.1111/j.1467-8535.2010.01093.x

Xinhuanet.com. (2009). 网络新词"另类表达"世情民心 [New online lexicons express public opinion]. (2009, December). Retrieved October 10, 2010, from http://news.xinhuanet.com/politics/2009-12/25/content_12701900.htm

Yamazaki, Y. (2005). Learning styles and typologies of cultural differences: A theoretical and empirical comparison. *International Journal of Intercultural Relations*, *29*, 521–548. doi:10.1016/j.ijintrel.2005.07.006

Yang, G. (2003). The Internet and the rise of a transnational Chinese cultural sphere. *Media Culture & Society*, *25*(4), 469–490. doi:10.1177/01634437030254003

Yang, G. (2009). *The power of the Internet in China: Citizen activism online*. New York, NY: Columbia University Press.

Yang, G. (2003). The Internet and civil society in China: A preliminary assessment. *Journal of Contemporary China*, *12*, 453–475. doi:10.1080/10670560305471

Yang, C. (2007). Chinese Internet language: A socio-linguistic analysis of adaptations of the Chinese writing system. *Language@Internet, 4*. Retrieved October 10, 2010, from http://www.languageatinternet.de/articles/2007/1142/index_html/

Yang, G. (2006). Activists beyond virtual borders: Internet-mediated networks and informational politics in China. *First Monday, 7*. Retrieved October 10, 2010, from http://firstmonday.org/issues/special11_9/yang

Yankelovich, N. (2007). *MPK20: Sun's virtual workplace*. Oracle. Retrieved October 1, 2010, from http://research.sun.com/ projects/ mc/ mpk20.html

Yao, Z. (2005). 略论网络?言中的词?变异现象 [A brief discussion of lexical deviations in internet language]. *Journal of Luoyang Normal University*, *6*, 99–103.

Ya'u, Y. Z. (2004). The new imperialism & Africa in the global electronic village. *Review of African Political Economy*, *99*, 11–29. doi:10.1080/0305624042000258397

Yee, N. (2006). The demographics, motivations, and derived experiences of users of massively multi-user online graphical environments. *Presence (Cambridge, Mass.)*, *15*(3), 309–329. doi:10.1162/pres.15.3.309

Yee, N., Bailenson, J. N., Urbanek, M., Chang, F., & Merget, D. (2007). The unbearable likeness of being digital: The persistence of nonverbal social norms in online virtual environments. *Cyberpsychology & Behavior*, *10*(1), 115–121. doi:10.1089/cpb.2006.9984

Yena, L., & Waggoner, Z. (2003). *One size fits all? Student perspectives on face-to-face and online writing pedagogies*. Computers & Composition Online. Retrieved June 13, 2009, from http://www.bgsu.edu/ cconline/ yena-waggoner/ index.html

Yi-Jokipii, H. (2001). The local and the global: An exploration into the Finnish and English websites of a Finnish company. *IEEE Transactions on Professional Communication*, *44*(2), 104–113. doi:10.1109/47.925512

Yildiz, S. (2009). Social presence in the Web-based classroom: Implications for intercultural communication. *Journal of Studies in International Education, 13*, 46–67. doi:10.1177/1028315308317654

Yoo, Y., & Alavi, M. (2001). Media and group cohesion: Relative influences on social presence, task participation, and group consensus. *Management Information Systems Quarterly*, *25*(3), 371–390. doi:10.2307/3250922

Young, J. R. (2005). Knowing when to log off. *The Chronicle of Higher Education*, A34.

Young, P. A. (2008). The culture based model: Constructing a model of culture. *Journal of Educational Technology & Society*, *11*(2), 107–118.

Younger, J. (1997). Resources description in the digital age. *Library Trends*, *45*(3).

Yu, Q., & Li, X. (2007). Hanzixieyin yu hanwenhua yanjiu zonglun (A review of studies concerning Chinese homophony and Chinese culture). [Philosophy and Social Sciences]. *Journal of Bohai University*, *6*, 125–129.

Yukselturk, E., & Bulut, S. (2007). Predictors for student success in an online course. *Journal of Educational Technology & Society*, *10*(2), 71–83.

Yum, Y. O., & Hara, K. (2005). Computer-mediated relationship development: A cross-cultural comparison. *Journal of Computer-Mediated Communication, 11*(1), article 7. Retrieved April 25, 2010, from http://jcmc.indiana.edu/ vol11/issue1/yum.html

Yunus, M. (2007). *Creating a world without poverty: Social business and the future of capitalism*. New York, NY: Public Affairs.

Zahedi, F. M., Van Pelt, W. V., & Song, J. A. (2001). Conceptual framework for international Web design. *IEEE Transactions on Professional Communication*, *44*(2), 83–103. doi:10.1109/47.925509

Zaidi, A. U., & Shuraydi, M. (2002). Perceptions of arranged marriages by young Pakistani Muslim women living in a western society. *Journal of Comparative Family Studies*, *33*(4), 495–514.

Zakaria, N., Amelinckz, A., & Wilemon, D. (2004). Working together apart? Building a knowledge-sharing culture for global virtual teams. *Creativity and Innovation Management, 13*, 15–29. doi:10.1111/j.1467-8691.2004.00290.x

Zembylas, M., & Vrasidas, C. (2005). Levinas and the "inter-face": The ethical challenge of online education. *Educational Theory, 55*(1), 61–78. doi:10.1111/j.1741-5446.2005.0005a.x

Zembylas, M., & Vrasidas, C. (2007). Listening for silence in text-based, online encounters. *Distance Education, 28*(1), 5–24. doi:10.1080/01587910701305285

Zemliansky, P., & St.Amant, K. (2008). Preface. In Zemliansky, P., & St.Amant, K. (Eds.), *Handbook of research on virtual workplaces and the new nature of business practices* (pp. xxvii–xxxii). Hershey, PA: Information Science Reference. doi:10.4018/978-1-59904-893-2

Zeng, M. L. (2005, August). Using software to teach thesaurus development and indexing in graduate programs of LIS and IAKM. *Bulletin of the American Society for Information Science and Technology*, (pp. 11-13).

Zhao, S., & Elesh, D. (2008). Copresence as "being with": Social contact in online public domains. *Information Communication and Society, 11*, 565–583. doi:10.1080/13691180801998995

Zhao, Y. (2008). *Communication in China: Political economy, power, and conflict*. New York, NY: Rowman & Littlefield Publishers, Inc.

Zhao, N., & McDougall, D. (2008). Cultural influences on Chinese students' asynchronous online learning in a Canadian university. *Journal of Distance Education, 22*(2), 59–80.

Zhao, C. M., Kuh, G. D., & Carini, R. M. (2005). A comparison of international student an American student engagement in effective educational practices. *The Journal of Higher Education, 76*(2), 209–231. doi:10.1353/jhe.2005.0018

Zheng, Y. (2008). *Technological empowerment: The Internet, state, and society in China*. Stanford, CA: Stanford University Press.

Zhou, Y. (2006). *Historicizing online politics: Telegraphy, the Internet, and political participation in China*. Stanford, CA: Stanford University Press.

Zhou, Y., & Moy, P. (2007). Parsing framing processes: The interplay between online public opinion and media coverage. *The Journal of Communication, 57*(1), 79–98.

Zhu, J. J. H., & Wang, E. (2005). Diffusion, use, and effect of the Internet in China. *Communications of the ACM, 48*, 49–53. doi:10.1145/1053291.1053317

Zhu, C., Valcke, M., & Schellens, T. (2009). Cultural differences in the perception of a social-constructivist e-learning environment. *British Journal of Educational Technology, 40*(1), 164–168. doi:10.1111/j.1467-8535.2008.00879.x

Zittrain, J., & Edelman, B. (2003). Internet filtering in China. *IEEE Internet Computing, 7*, 70–77. doi:10.1109/MIC.2003.1189191

Zittrain, J., & Palfrey, J. (2008). Internet filtering: The politics and mechanisms of control. In Deibert, R. (Eds.), *Access denied: The practice and policy of global Internet filtering* (pp. 29–56). Cambridge, MA: The MIT Press.

Zittrain, J., & Palfrey, J. (2008). Reluctant gatekeepers: Corporate ethics on a filtered Internet. In Deibert, R., Palfrey, J., Rohozinski, R., & Zittrain, J. (Eds.), *Access denied: The practice and policy of global Internet filtering* (pp. 103–122). Cambridge, MA: The MIT Press.

Zittrain, J., & Edelman, B. (2003). *Empirical analysis of Internet filtering in China*. Cambridge, MA: Berkman Center for Internet and Society, Harvard Law School. Retrieved October 10, 2010, from http://cyber.law.harvard.edu/filtering/china/

Zook, M. (2007). Your urgent assistance is requested: The intersection of 419 spam and new networks of imagination. *Ethics Place and Environment, 10*(1), 65–88. doi:10.1080/13668790601153713

Zywica, J., & Danowski, J. (2008). The faces of Facebookers: Investigating social enhancement and social compensation hypotheses: Predicting Facebook™ and offline popularity from sociability and self-esteem, and mapping the meanings of popularity with semantic networks. *Journal of Computer-Mediated Communication, 14*, 1–34. doi:10.1111/j.1083-6101.2008.01429.x

About the Contributors

Kirk St.Amant is an Associate Professor of Technical and Professional Communication and of International Studies at East Carolina University.

Sigrid Kelsey is a Full Librarian at Louisiana State University Libraries and General Editor of *Catholic Library World*. She is a 2010 recipient of the Association of College and Research Libraries (ACRL) College Library Section's ProQuest Innovation in College Librarianship Award, the Louisiana Library Association Anthony H. Benoit Mid-Career Award, and the *Baton Rouge Business Report* Forty under 40 award, and the 2009 recipient of the ACRL-Louisiana Scholar Librarian of the Year Award. Kelsey has written more than thirty articles that have appeared in books and journals, and has edited three books.

* * *

Pauline Hope Cheong (PhD, University of Southern California) is Associate Professor of Communication in the Hugh Downs School of Human Communication at Arizona State University. She is also graduate faculty member of the School of Justice and Social Inquiry, and Women and Gender Studies, and an affiliate faculty with the Department of Film and Media Studies, and the Center for the Study of Religion and Conflict. She is co-editing two books: (*Digital Religion, Social Media and Cultures; New Media and Intercultural Communication*) and co-authoring a book on mediated rumors in global strategic communication. She has presented more than 50 papers at international conferences and has publications in multiple key journals on new media, including *New Media and Society, The Information Society, Information, Communication and Society, Prometheus, Bulletin of Science and Society, M/C Journal: A Journal of Media and Culture, Journal of Computer-Mediated Communication, Journal of International and Intercultural Communication,* and *Journal of Communication.*

Sejung Marina Choi (PhD, Michigan State University) is Associate Professor of Advertising at the University of Texas at Austin. Her research interests include source credibility, consumer-brand relationships, social media, and cross-cultural consumer behavior. Dr. Choi's work has appeared or is forthcoming in the *Journal of Advertising, Psychology & Marketing, Journal of Cross-Cultural Psychology, Journal of Current Issues and Research in Advertising, International Journal of Advertising, Journal of Interactive Advertising, Journal of Marketing Communications, Journal of Computer-Mediated Communication, Computers in Human Behavior, Information, Communication, & Society, Journal of Consumer Affairs, Journal of American College Health,* and *Journal of Popular Culture*, among others, as well as in several book chapters and numerous conference proceedings.

Shu-Chuan Chu (PhD, The University of Texas at Austin) is an Assistant Professor of Advertising at the College of Communication at DePaul University. Her research interests include social media, user-generated content, electronic word-of-mouth (e-WOM), cross-cultural consumer behavior, and consumer-brand relationships. Her recent projects investigate how social relationship factors relate to e-WOM transmitted via online social websites. Her work has been published or forthcoming in the *International Journal of Advertising*, *Journal of Interactive Advertising*, *Journal of International Consumer Marketing*, *Journal of Marketing Communications*, and *Chinese Journal of Communication*, among others. Her work has also appeared in the *Handbook of Research on Digital Media and Advertising: User Generated Content Consumption* (1 volume) and various conferences including the American Marketing Association (AMA), American Academy of Advertising (AAA), Association for Education in Journalism and Mass Communication (AEJMC), and International Communication Association (ICA).

Madelyn Flammia is an Associate Professor in the Department of English at the University of Central Florida in Orlando, Florida. She teaches both graduate and undergraduate courses in Technical Communication. Her research interests include international technical communication, visual communication, and global virtual teams. Dr. Flammia has given presentations on intercultural communication at professional conferences and for corporate audiences. She is the co-author of *Intercultural Communication: A New Approach to International Relations and Global Challenges* and the editor of the Society for Technical Communication anthology, *Perspectives on the Profession of Technical Communication*.

Amy Garrett Dikkers, PhD, Assistant Professor, earned a PhD in Comparative and International Development Education at the University of Minnesota in 2006, a M.Ed. in Secondary English Education from Wake Forest University in 1996, and a BA in English from the University of North Carolina at Greensboro in 1995. Before her doctoral study, she taught secondary school English domestically and abroad. The focus of her doctoral study was international development education. She has taught face-to-face, hybrid, and online courses at the undergraduate and graduate levels in educational reform, school technology leadership, comparative education, human rights education, research design, and the educational foundations. Her professional interests include the preparation of educational leaders and the use of technology-enhanced and online learning in higher education. Current research centers on reflective practice, maximizing online learning, incorporating community professionals into courses through technology, and the use of video to provide authentic voice in the classroom.

Wengao Gong (PhD, National University of Singapore, 2009) is a Post-Doctoral Research Fellow at National Institute of Education, Nanyang Technological University, Singapore. His research interests include Internet-mediated communication, corpus linguistics, lexicography, English-Chinese biliteracy studies, and other SLA-related topics.

Indira Guzman is an Associate Professor at TUI University. Currently, she is the Director of the Computer Science and the Information Technology Management programs at TUI University. She received her PhD in Information Science and Technology from Syracuse University, USA; MS in Information Management also from Syracuse University; advanced graduate studies in Banking and Finance from the Bolivian Catholic University, Bolivia, and BS and MS in Computer Science Engineering from Polytechnic Institute of Donetsk, Ukraine. She joined TUI University in 2006. Her research interests include the impact of Information Technology in organizations, career orientations, gender and ethnic diversity, and occupational culture of IT professionals. Her work has been published in journals such as *The DATA BASE for Advances in Information Systems, Information Technology and People, Human Resource Management, Women's Studies,* and *the Journal of Digital Information.* She also published two books; the last one is *Information Nation: Education and Careers in the Emerging Information Professions,* co-authored with Jeffrey Stanton and Kathryn Stam, which came out in August of 2010 (http://books.infotoday.com/books/Information-Nation.shtml).

Anna M. Harrington received her MA in literature from Michigan State and is a doctoral candidate in the Composition & TESOL program at Indiana University of Pennsylvania. She is a Professor of English at Edison State College, currently completing her dissertation on modularized computer-assisted personalized system of instruction (CAPSI) developmental writing courses, and her specialty areas are developmental writing and program assessment. In addition to scholarly works, her creative writing has been published in the *GW Review, Yemassee, Fugue, Red Cedar Review,* and other nationally distributed journals. She has also studied abroad in London, Mexico, and Ecuador and has volunteered with school children in Thailand, Ecuador, and Peru.

Barbara Heifferon is Professor of English at Louisiana State University and Director of the University Writing Program; also, she's a former cardio-pulmonary technician. Her sixth book (in process) is a medical history of Cotton Mather's inoculation project in 1721. Her work has appeared in *Rhetoric Review, CCC, Nurse Practitioner, JAC, JBTC, TCQ,* and others. Her *Writing in the Health Professions* is used around the United States in undergraduate and graduate medical writing classes. Heifferon has also garnered grants with US Department of Agriculture (USDA) and the National Institutes of Health (NIH) doing technical writing projects with students and is currently a consultant with the State of Louisiana in online writing.

Marc Hermeking teaches and researches in international and cross-cultural marketing at the Institute for Intercultural Communications at the Ludwig-Maximilians University (LMU) in Munich, Germany. He studied Business Administration (diploma) and Marketing Psychology, European Ethnology and Intercultural Communications (doctor). During his study, he worked in the media industry. His doctoral thesis deals with influences of culture on the international transfer and usage of technology (Kulturen und Technik, published 2001). He established the "Seminar fuer Interkulturelles Marketing" at the Institute for Intercultural Communications in 2000. Since 2008, he has also been lecturer in cross-cultural website design for the Master's program "Leadership in Digital Communication" at the University of Arts (UdK) in Berlin, Germany. Additionally, he works as a trainer for diverse industrial corporations and has published several contributions for textbooks and journals.

John Humbley is a Professor in Applied Linguistics and Terminology at Université Paris 7–Denis-Diderot, France, in the Department for Intercultural Studies and Applied Languages (EILA), where he is in charge of the Master's degree. He has published in the field of terminology, lexicology, and translation studies, and participated in several dictionaries.

Melinda Jacobs holds a BA degree in Popular Culture from Bowling Green State University (US) and a research MA degree in Media Studies from Utrecht University (NL). She is the founder of Level Up Media, where she designs and produces games and game-inspired applications. Melinda's main research interests are exploring the effects of multiculturalism within cooperation in online communities and the use of cooperative game structures in nontraditional ways (such as her research on consumerism as gameplay). She has published and presented her research at a variety of international platforms including the *Journal for Cultural Research*, the Popular Culture Association, and the Digital Games Research Association. More information about Melinda and her research can be found at www.melindajacobs.org or you can find her on Twitter as @melindajacobs

Sara Kamal (PhD, The University of Texas at Austin) is an Assistant Professor of Marketing Communications at the American University in Dubai. Her research interests are economic effects of advertising, multicultural marketing and cross-cultural consumer behavior. Her research has appeared in the *International Journal of Advertising, Journal of Interactive Advertising* and various conferences including the American Advertising Academy (AAA) and Association for Education in Journalism and Mass Communication (AEJMC). E-mail: sarakamal@gmail.com

Yoojung Kim (MA, The University of Texas at Austin) is PhD candidate in the Department of Advertising at the University of Texas at Austin. Her research interests are in the areas of social media, corporate social responsibility, and cross-cultural consumer behavior. Her work has been published or is forthcoming in the *International Journal of Advertising, Computers in Human Behavior, Journal of Global Marketing,* and *Information, Communication & Society,* among others. Her work also has been presented at various conferences including the American Academy of Advertising (AAA), Association for Consumer Research (ACR), Association for Education in Journalism and Mass Communication (AEJMC), and International Communication Association (ICA). Prior to her graduate program, she worked for an advertising agency as a copywriter and a media planner. Her past clients include various multinational advertisers and local advertisers.

William Klein is a Teaching Professor of English at the University of Missouri – St. Louis where he has taught undergraduate and graduate courses in Writing, Composition Pedagogy, and Education Technology since 1985.

Archana Krishnan is a doctoral candidate in the Department of Communication Sciences at the University of Connecticut (UConn), Storrs. Her area of specialization is Computer-Mediated Communication (CMC) with a primary focus on the examination of new technology features and their effect on person perception. Her other areas of interest are scale development and validation, advertising effects, and visual communication. Ms. Krishnan has taught courses in Human Communication and Public Speaking at the University of Connecticut and is currently undergraduate advisor at the UConn Human Rights Institute. She has also co-authored and presented papers at national and international conferences on topics ranging from meta-analysis and sexual minorities to mass media and CMC effects.

Bernard E. La Berge (1943-2011) was Dean for Quality Assurance and program development at the Modern College of Business and Science in Muscat, Oman. He was associated with the college since

2001. Prior to this, he held administrative positions at Virginia Tech, the University of Tennessee, and the University of Northern Colorado.

Jyh-An Lee is an Assistant Professor of Law at National Chengchi University, Taipei, Taiwan, where he teaches Copyright, Trademark, Patent, International Intellectual Property, Entertainment Law, and Internet Law. He holds a J.S.D. from Stanford Law School and an LL.M from Harvard Law School. During his study at Stanford, he worked with Professor Lawrence Lessig and was appointed as the John M. Olin Fellow in Law and Economics. Lee's current research focuses on the interaction between law, human behavior, and digital technology. His academic honors include IP Thesis Scholarship, Asia-Pacific Intellectual Property Right Association (2001), First Place of Junior Legal Scholar Writing Competition (2001), Honorable Mention of *Harvard Journal of Law & Technology* Writing Competition (2005), Stanford Graduate Fellowship (2005), and Taiwan Merit Scholarship (2005-2009). Before starting his academic career, he was a practicing lawyer in Taiwan specializing in technology and business transactions.

Miriam O'Kane Mara studies Irish literature and culture, and medical rhetoric. Her early work investigates the trope of anorexia in Irish literature, while more recent work traces representation of disease in literature and medical texts. Publication venues include *Critique: Studies in Contemporary Literature, Dickens Studies Annual, Feminist Formations,* and *Innovative Higher Education.*

Andrew Mara specializes in responsive electracy. His research interests include posthumanism, the rhetoric of technology and scientific progress, university innovation, and corporate and organizational use of new media. His work has appeared in *Technical Communication Quarterly*, *IEEE Transactions on Professional Communication*, the *Journal of Business and Technical Communication, Innovative Higher Education*, and several essay collections.

Judith N. Martin (PhD, Pennsylvania State University) is Professor of Intercultural Communication in the Hugh Downs School of Human Communication at Arizona State University. Her principle research interests focus on the role of culture in online communication, interethnic and interracial communication, as well as sojourner adaptation and reentry. She has published numerous research articles in communication journals as well as other disciplinary journals and has co-authored three textbooks in intercultural communication with Thomas K. Nakayama: *Intercultural Communication in Contexts, Experiencing Intercultural Communication*, and *Readings in Intercultural Communication*. She is co-editing a book on *New Media and Intercultural Communication*. In 2001-2004 she was selected as the Jeanne Herberger Professor of Human Communication. She has developed and taught various communication courses (including intercultural communication) online for the past 10 years.

Bruce Maylath is a Professor of English at North Dakota State University, USA, where he teaches courses in technical communication and linguistics. His current research takes up translation issues in technical communication. Books he has co-edited include *Approaches to Teaching Non-Native English Speakers across the Curriculum, Language Awareness: A History and Implementations,* and *Revisiting the Past through Rhetorics of Memory and Amnesia*. His articles have appeared in *Research in the Teaching of English, Technical Communication Quarterly, Journal of Business and Technical Communication, IEEE-Transactions on Professional Communication*, and many others.

Birthe Mousten, MA Eng, PhD, is a lecturer of English at the Department of Language and Business Communication, Aarhus School of Business and Social Sciences, Aarhus University. She teaches Master's and Bachelor courses in technical communication and translation in and between the languages English and Danish as well as special language courses in business communication. She has published articles about cross-cultural technical communication, global and local communication, and offers courses for trade and industry in legal and technical communication, as well as in translation, revision, and reviewing texts.

Esin Sultan Oguz received her BSc (2001), MSc (2004) and PhD (2010) degrees from the Department of Information Management at Hacettepe University, located in Ankara, Turkey. Her areas of specialization include cultural policy and libraries, multicutural library and information services, Library Information Science education, and the internationalization of LIS higher education. During the Spring 2008 semester, Dr. Oguz was an Erasmus student at the Royal School of Information Science in Copenhagen, Denmark, where she studied knowledge organization. She served as the assistant editor of the national, peer-reviewed *Journal of Turkish Librarianship* (*Türk Kütüphaneciliği Dergisi*) between 2006 and 2009, and she is currently on the Executive Board of the Turkish Librarians' Association (Türk Kütüphaneciler Derneği).

Bolanle A. Olaniran is a Professor and interim Chair in the Department of Communication Studies at Texas Tech University, Lubbock, TX, USA. He is internationally known scholar. His research includes organization communication, cross-cultural communication, crisis communication, and communication technologies. He has authored several peer-reviewed articles in discipline focus and interdisciplinary journals (i.e., regional, national, and international) and authored several edited book chapters in each of these areas. He edited a book on e-learning. He also serves as consultant to organizations and universities at local, national, international, and government level. His works have gained recognition such as the American Communication Association's "Outstanding Scholarship in Communication field" among others.

Angela T. Ragusa is a Senior Lecturer in Sociology and Course Coordinator for the BA Honours program at Charles Sturt University in Australia. Born in New York City, Angela worked at investment banks, law firms, and the United Nations prior to completing a PhD and two Master's degrees at Virginia Tech. She has taught at universities since 1997, supervised honours and PhD students, and earned over $100K in grants. Editor-in-Chief of the journal *Rural Society* and board member for the *Information Resources Management, Open Sociology,* and *Open Communication* journals, she has also refereed manuscripts for Social Epistemology, textbooks for Pearson Education, Cengage Learning & Alexander Street Press, and is currently writing a textbook. With over 30 academic publications, recent achievements include an edited book, Interaction & Communication Technologies and Virtual Learning Environments: Human Factors, two research fellowships and judging the international Sakai teaching award.

Pete Rive, with over 25 years experience in screen production and post production as an editor, is a founding board member, and former Chair of Film Auckland, the current Chair of the CoLab Advisory Board, and a developer of the Screen Auckland social network. Pete is currently completing a PhD researching design innovation and collaboration in the virtual world, Second Life. He is also a futurist: founder and CEO of the innovation and collaboration consultancy, RainRaker. Pete is producing a co-production movie with China, and is an active member of the Asia Pacific Producer's Network, APN, that includes 100 of the region's most senior producers.

Natasha Rodriguez recently graduated from the Department of Communication Studies at Texas Tech University, Lubbock, TX. Her key interests and major areas of research include computer-mediated communication, e-learning in higher education and organizations, organizational communication, and domestic violence. Natasha continues to collaborate with Dr. Olaniran and Indi on journal articles and book chapters.

Nicole St. Germaine-McDaniel is the chair of Technical and Business Writing at Angelo State University. She is a senior member of STC, and was awarded the Society for Technical Communication's Frank R. Smith Outstanding Journal Article Award Distinguished Article *in Technical Communication* for her article "Localizing Medical Information for U.S. Spanish-Speakers: The CDC Campaign to Increase Public Awareness about HPV." Her research interests include technical communication in the health fields and international technical communication.

Reinhard Schäler has been involved in the localization industry in a variety of roles since 1987. He is the founder and editor of *Localisation Focus: The International Journal of Localisation*, a founding editor of the *Journal of Specialised Translation (JosTrans),* a former member of the editorial board of *Multilingual Computing*, a founder and CEO of The Institute of Localisation Professionals (TILP), and a member of OASIS. He is a Principal Investigator in the Centre for Next Generation Localisation (CNGL), a lecturer at the Department of Computer Science and Information Systems (CSIS), University of Limerick, and the founder and director of the Localisation Research Centre (LRC) at UL, established in 1995. In 2009, he established The Rosetta Foundation and the Dynamic Coalition for a Global Localization Platform: Localization4all, under the umbrella of the UN's Internet Governance Forum.

Jaffer Sheyholislami is Assistant Professor at the School of Linguistics and Language Studies, Carleton University, Canada. His PhD research in communication, completed in 2008, investigated the interface between national identity, language, and new media, focusing on the Kurds as case study. His current research concerns minority language media, blogging, critical multimodal analysis of Canadian identity discourse, and language policy and planning in Kurdistan.

Kathryn R. Stam, PhD is an Assistant Professor of Anthropology at SUNY Institute of Technology in Utica, New York. She is a faculty member in the Master's Program in Information Design and Technology (a fully online program), and contributes to the Sociology Dept. and the School of Arts and Sciences by teaching undergraduates in anthropology and sociology. Her specialties are cross-cultural communication, ethnography, and the social and ethical aspects of Information Technology. Her current research interests are related to virtual ethnography, the Information Technology profession, and distance learning. She has written two books and more than three dozen articles and conference papers. She was the recipient of the 2009 Chancellor's Award for Excellence in Teaching and received a Fulbright grant to study Thai cultural preservation at Mahasarakham University in 2010.

Emma Steinke is a Trans-National Education Program Manager at Charles Sturt University in Australia. Emma spent her childhood in NSW, Australia, and graduated from the University of Melbourne with a Bachelor of Commerce degree in 1991. She then worked for a number of years as a chartered accountant and spent time living in New Zealand before joining Charles Sturt University where she is currently completing a Master's degree and working in the University's Office of International Relations. This is Emma's first foray into research and academic publication. Her particular area of interest is the management of international education programs, with particular focus on the international student experience.

Rotimi Taiwo holds PhD in English Language, and he is a Senior Lecturer in the Department of English, Obafemi Awolowo University, Nigeria. For the last decade and a half, his research has focused on the application of discourse analytics, critical discourse analytics, and text-linguistic theories to a wide range of discourse contexts, such as those of the media, religion, students' compositions, the medical classroom, politics, popular culture, the Internet, and telecommunications. His publications have appeared as articles in several international journals and chapters in books. Some of the journals in which his articles have appeared include *The Internet TESL Journal, Issues in Political Discourse Analysis, Nordic Journal of African Linguistics, Linguistik Online, California Linguistic Notes, English Today,* and *International Journal of Language, Society and Culture.* He has also co-edited two books, one on media discourse and the other on discourse analysis. He was a post-doctoral fellow of the Alexander von Humboldt Foundation at Albert-Ludwigs University, Freiburg, Germany between September 2008 and August 2009. His most recent publication is an edited book is titled *Handbook of Research on Discourse Behavior and Digital Communication: Language Structures and Social Interaction* published by IGI Global, Pennsylvania, USA.

Gretchen Bourdeau Thomas is an instructor in the Learning, Design, and Technology program. She earned her Specialist Degree in Education in Instructional Technology at the University of Georgia in 2000. She teaches undergraduate courses in K-12 technology integration. While her work focuses on enhancing learning environments through technology, her real interest lies in the resources, people, and places that help people learn.

Aukje Thomassen is a Associate Professor and Research Director at Massey University's Institute for Communication Design in Wellington. Her research focuses on Social Innovation through Design Research (Philosophy, Didactics and Methodologies) and thereby studying Knowledge Creation in the Creative Industries (especially in the area of Digital Media/Game Design) within a theoretical framework of Cybernetics. She also supervises Master and PhD candidates in the area of innovation through design (such as serious games, virtual worlds, co-creation and creative leadership). Dr. Thomassen holds a PhD in Design on Technology Enhanced Learning and Interaction Design, funded through EU FP5-IST-LEDA.

Dennis Thoryk has held several positions at Onondaga Community College in Syracuse, NY since 2001. He is currently the Student Engagement Initiatives coordinator and an Adjunct Instructor in the Computer Studies department. As the Student Engagement Initiatives coordinator, he develops support programs for students in career and technical education degree programs and first-year students. He has a BS in Computer and Information Science from the SUNY Institute of Technology where he is currently completing his MS in the Information Design and Technology program.

Jinn-Wei Tsao is currently a fourth-year doctoral student in the department of Learning, Design, and Technology at the University of Georgia in USA. Jinn-Wei earned his Master's degree in Instructional Technology from the University of Georgia in 2007. His research interests include: intercultural competency in online environment, cross-cultural online communication, and collaboration.

Tanfer Emin Tunc is an Assistant Professor in the Department of American Culture and Literature at Hacettepe University, Ankara, Turkey. She received her BA, MA and PhD in American History, and an Advanced Graduate Certificate in Women's Studies, from the State University of New York at Stony Brook, and specializes in women's history/literature; gender, sexuality, and reproduction; feminist/cultural theory; American ethnic studies; and the American South. In addition to numerous book chapters, book reviews, and reference book entries, she has also published over twenty full-length articles on topics as diverse as reproductive health, women's history, consumer culture, and American literature, most of which have appeared in internationally-renowned journals such as *Rethinking History, Women's History Review*, and *Journal of Women's History*. Her books include *Technologies of Choice: A History of Abortion Techniques in the United States, 1850–1980* (VDM, 2008); *The Globetrotting Shopaholic: Consumer Spaces, Products, and their Cultural Places* (Cambridge Scholars Publishing, 2008); *The Theme of Cultural Adaptation in American History, Literature, and Film: Cases When the Discourse Changed* (The Edwin Mellen Press, 2009); and *Positioning the New: Chinese American Literature and the Changing Image of the American Literary Canon* (Cambridge Scholars Publishing, 2010).

Sonia Vandepitte is a lecturer of English. She teaches English grammar and translation from and into English, coaches student translation businesses, and co-ordinates research activities. She has published on intonation, causal expressions, knowledge retrieval, methodological issues in translation studies, translation competences, anticipation in interpreting, and international teaching projects. She supervises projects on parallel and comparable corpora, a Dutch clarity tool, and electronic feedback in ESL-learning.

Chun-Min Wang is currently an Assistant Professor in the department of Education at the National Hsinchu University of Education in Taiwan. Dr. Wang earned his doctoral degree in Instructional Technology from the University of Georgia in 2007. His research interests include: cultural considerations in online education, cross-cultural online collaboration, multimedia development and evaluation, integrating creativity into education, and the issues related to closing digital divide in rural areas. To know more about Dr. Wang, please feel free to visit his webpage at: http://www.nhcue.edu.tw/~cwang

Aimee L. Whiteside, PhD, is a Lecturer at the University of Wisconsin-Stout, which is Wisconsin's Polytechnic University. Aimee earned a PhD in Rhetoric and Scientific and Technical Communication at the University of Minnesota in August 2007, and she earned a graduate-level Certificate in Adult Learning Technology Integration. Her professional interests include the socio-cultural aspects of learning, blended and online learning, technology-enhanced learning, reflective practice, community partnerships in education, technical communication, and first-year writing. She has taught face-to-face, online, and blended courses at the undergraduate and graduate levels in technology-enhanced learning, Internet studies, leadership and small-group communication, oral communication, information design, technical communication, and first-year writing.

Indi Marie Williams is currently a doctoral student in Educational Technology at Arizona State University. Ms. Williams received her Master's in Communication Studies from Texas Technology University, Lubbock, Texas and a BA in Sociology from the University of Texas at Austin. Her research interests include social media, globalization, virtual learning communities, Web 2.0 & 3.0 e-learning, instructional communication in distance education, human-computer integration, Internet culture, and the anticipation of future interaction in online relationship development.

Ping Yang (PhD, Arizona State University, 2009) is Assistant Professor in the Department of Communication, Denison University, Ohio. She holds MA in Communication and Linguistics, a BA in English Language and Literature, and her Doctorate in Intercultural Communication. Her scholarship and teaching focus on the intersections of culture, communication, and technology. Her primary research interests include identity construction, cultural adaptation, media representation, heritage language education, and intercultural online communication. She has published various book chapters and journal articles in most of these and related areas. Dr. Yang teaches courses on theories of intercultural communication, language, culture, and communication, technology and communication, and new media and culture studies.

Myongho "Lee" Yi is an Assistant Professor at the School of Library and Information Studies, Texas Woman's University, where he teaches Information Storage and Retrieval Systems, Information and Communication Technology, and Web development for the information professions. Yi's research focuses on information organization and retrieval (evaluation and implementation of traditional and emerging information organizations approaches such as index, thesaurus, taxonomy, Semantic Web, and ontology) to enhance information retrieval. The goal is to evaluate and develop Information Systems that return "relevant resources," not merely "irrelevant/lengthy hits" and to mange unstructured digitally stored information. To ensure integrity of digital resources, Yi is also interested in information security.

Elaine J. Yuan, PhD Northwestern University, is an Assistant Professor in the Communication Department at the University of Illinois at Chicago. Her research interests have included social political implications of the new media in China and audience research. Currently she is researching issues of online community, online privacy, online journalism within cross-cultural and multiple modernist frameworks.

Index

Web 2.0 technologies 91-93, 95, 101-104, 106, 384, 393
Weblogs (Blogs) 75, 80, 83, 93, 95, 99, 101, 103-104, 110, 139, 153, 156, 171, 193, 196, 209, 241, 243-244, 252, 267, 280, 290, 307, 377-378, 392-393, 398, 421, 446
WebMD 252, 258, 264
WebQuests 386
Websphere 187-188, 190-194, 197, 199
World Health Organization (WHO) 11-12, 20-21, 23-25, 27-28, 30, 35, 37-39, 41-42, 49, 51, 53-56, 58, 71, 73, 75, 79-80, 85-86, 92-101, 107, 112, 114, 116-118, 122, 126-127, 131, 134, 136-137, 145-147, 149-150, 154, 157, 161, 163, 166, 169-170, 174-175, 177, 179-180, 182, 208-209, 218-219, 222-223, 229, 236, 238, 240, 242-243, 245, 256, 259-262, 269-276, 284, 287-289, 292-294, 296-299,

301, 309, 313, 319, 323, 328-329, 331-332, 334-335, 337-339, 342-343, 345, 349, 353, 355-358, 360-361, 363-364, 368, 370, 374-375, 377-378, 380-381, 389, 391, 398, 402, 404, 407, 415-423, 428, 430, 433-438, 440-441, 443, 449-452, 454-456, 458-459, 461, 464-466
World of Warcraft (WoW) 36, 43
World Wide Web Consortium (W3C) 208

X

Xinhua Dictionary 162
XML 206-207
XML Schema 206

Z

Zotero 188, 191-192, 197, 199